AF709251

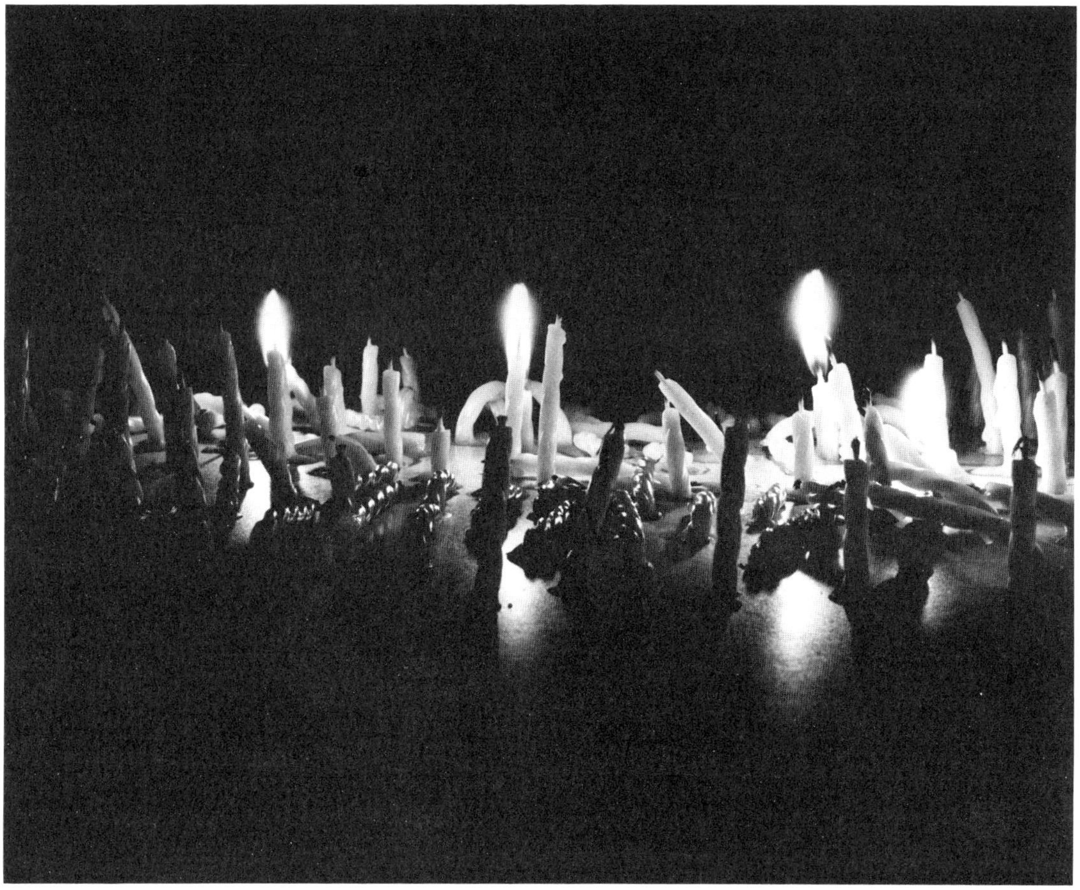

Discover your SELF through Photography

A Creative Workbook

Discover your SELF through Photography

for Amateur and Professional

by Ralph Hattersley

Association Press, New York

DISCOVER YOUR SELF THROUGH PHOTOGRAPHY

A Creative Workbook for Amateur and Professional

Copyright © 1971 by

Association Press

291 Broadway, New York, N.Y. 10007

All rights reserved. No part of this publication may be reprinted, reproduced, transmitted, stored in a retrieval system, or otherwise utilized, in any form or by any means, electronic or mechanical, including photocopying or recording, now existing or hereinafter invented, without the prior written permission of the publisher.

Standard Book Number: **8096-1784-6**

Library of Congress Catalog Card Number: **72-132396**

PRINTED IN THE UNITED STATES OF AMERICA

to Lisa

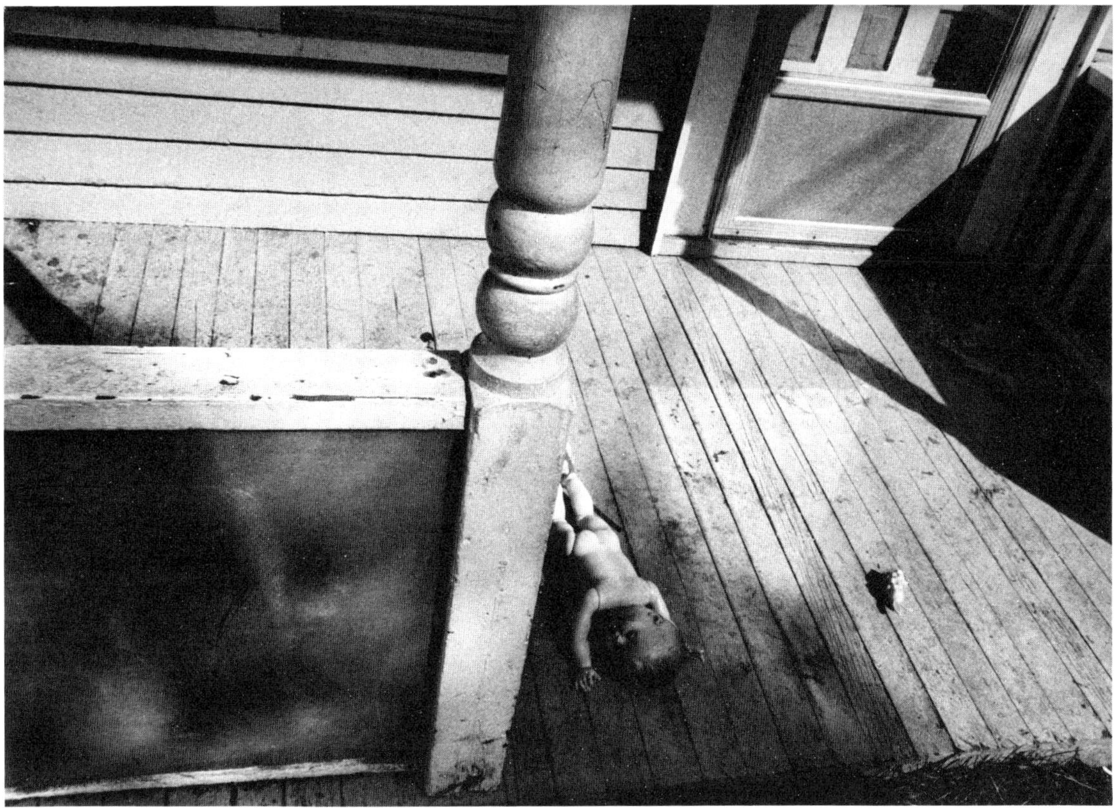

Acknowledgments

I wish to thank the Ziff-Davis Publishing Company for permission to reproduce materials which originally appeared in *Popular Photography, Introduction to Photography,* and the *Photography Annual.* My thanks to Karen Tweedy-Holmes for helping me with my manuscript. I thank my students for helping me to remember what it's like to be young. And my family, of course, for it is in family life that we learn the really important things.

Unless otherwise credited, the photographs in this book are by the author.

book designed by Simon Frankel

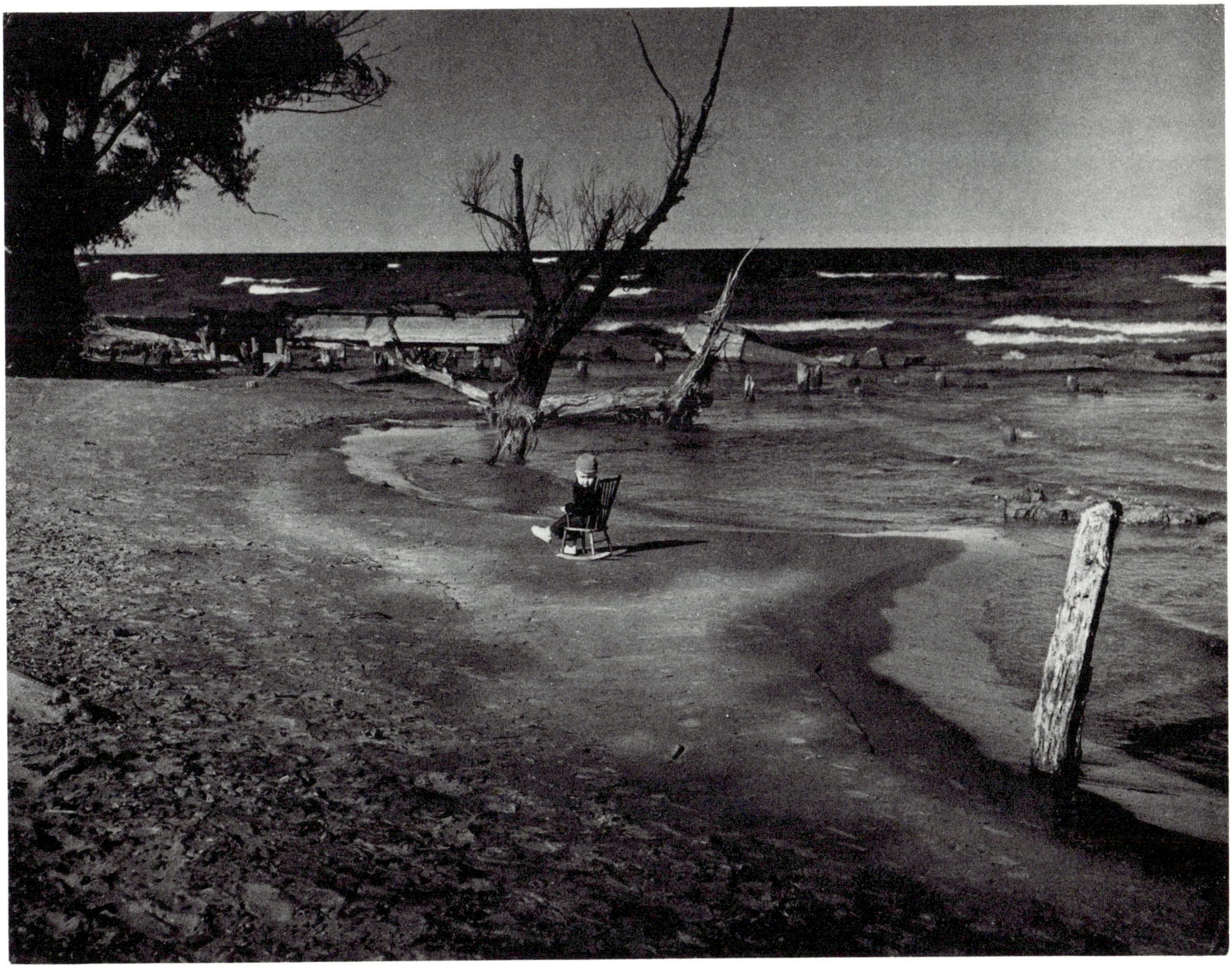

Contents

Introduction

In the introduction I'm supposed to tell you what my book is all about. Since I am one of photography's most notoriously sneaky characters, I'm not going to tell you everything. You must read it and find out for yourself. The book title will give you a clue, but don't jump to conclusions. To discover your Self may mean more than you think it does.

The book is multilevel. On one level you can hop through it and find lessons on photography which were formerly printed in *Popular Photography* magazine. They were designed for a wide readership among amateur photographers and are written in a rather chatty style. They assume that readers are intelligent and that they enjoy having their minds stimulated by ideas for things to do in photography. Most readers never get around to doing them, but they like to read about them anyway! Since the lessons were designed as much for entertainment as for doing, there is a fair amount of blarney in them —and what I hope will successfully pass for wit.

Some of the projects are easy enough for rank beginners. All of them are easy enough for almost-beginners. At the same time they are a challenge to advanced amateurs and even for some professionals. Most professionals, however, are more interested in the philosophy, psychology, and ethics of photography than in information on how to do various things. The how-to-do-it stuff they've mastered long ago.

If your main interest in photography is to have fun, the lessons will help. If you're just interested in experimenting with the medium, there are suggestions for this, too. If you enjoy being preached to and exhorted, help yourself—there are messages enough for all.

Since I've been unable to decide in my mind the age of my typical reader, the lessons are written for all ages. My stepson Jonathan and his friends do them in their high-school photography lab. My aunts say that they can understand them fairly well, though they are not interested in photography. And a lot of college-aged devotees of photography tell me that they read them.

Some of the lessons say, "Photography is for you. Dive in and enjoy a hearty swim." Though I often try to lure people into deep water, many people ignore my enticements and merely enjoy playing with the ideas I offer to them.

On another level, this book is a horse of an entirely different color. You will notice that some of the chapter and lesson introductions get rather weighty. In fact, a few of them may be a good deal too ponderous for your taste. This is because I've tried to get down to the central nut of what photography is really all about for those who take it seriously.

This plunge to more obscure depths came about because a certain man gave me some astute nudges. He said, in effect, "What are you *really* trying to say in all your writings?" This was Mr. Roland Burdick, Assistant Director of Association Press. He had already handed me a fine title: "Discover Your Self Through Photography." I got to thinking about his nudges and the title. I discovered that one of my main aims for my readers had always been Self-discovery. On thinking this over I asked myself, "Could a reader actually discover himself through using the information I've already published on the subject?" My conclusion after several days of thought was that he could not, for he still hadn't been given certain important pieces of information. The desire to discover your Self is not quite enough. You also have to know how to do it.

I've called Burdick's prodding astute because it happened to fit my nature very well. I myself have been consciously embarked on a journey of Self-discovery for many years. In the last five it has been the central motive in my life. Photography has been one of the several tools I've used for this purpose, though not the major one. Therefore, it seemed appropriate that I should try to share with other photographers what I had learned about the medium as a tool for Self-discovery.

I have not, of course, fully discovered my own Self. As I see it this may take me many more lifetimes. Nonetheless, I've managed to uncover a part of this Self and to see a path for additional Self-discovery laid out ahead of me. In learning this much I've also seen that everyone has to follow the same general path. I also made the encouraging discovery that man's Great Teachers have already trod this narrow path to its very end and have left us abundant information concerning how we can follow them. This meant that I didn't have to rely on my own fragile ideas but could depend entirely on theirs. All I would have to contribute would be concepts showing how the basic ideas fit in with the practice of photography. This was easy enough, for I've been working on the problem many years as a teacher, writer and photographer.

Several years ago I was brought up short by a question which I asked myself: "Can the blind lead the blind?" My conclusion then was a definite "No!" This naturally led to a very serious crisis in my writing and teaching, for I knew very well that I was one of the blind. My misery was almost complete for several years. In the midst of it, however, I made an amazing discovery—the blind *can* lead the blind, up to a point. Somehow, well-intentioned blind men have managed to keep the human race going after a fashion. I began to see that I myself fitted in this class and that there might be some virtue in my trying to provide people in photography some leadership, up to a point.

This book is therefore intended to provide you limited guidance toward Self-discovery. After that, you'll have to rely on wiser men than I. Fortunately, their wisdom has always been available to anyone who wanted it. Perhaps the things I write will make you want to seek it and help you to understand what it means.

As you read this book you should constantly remember that you are listening to advice from a blind man. Not to remember would be to do a terrible disservice to yourself. On the other hand, you should bear in mind that within certain limitations the blind can lead the blind. In fact, you've never had a teacher, except in certain books, who *wasn't* blind. The way to use a blind teacher safely is to listen to him with selective and suspicious openmindedness. Accept no idea whatsoever until you have thoroughly tested it for yourself. But do not let suspicion grind you to a halt. Where you are now with respect to Self-knowledge is not a very good place. If you don't move, you'll stay there. It is better to move and make mistakes than not to move at all.

This book is entirely autobiographical. It would be a good thing for you to keep this, too, in mind. The author has seen a few things correctly. On the other hand, he has made numerous mistakes. You will read about a good many foolish things you can do as a human being and photographer. Your author has done them all or is still entrapped in doing them. Reading won't help you avoid making similar mistakes, but it will help you understand them after you have made them.

I must now dwell for a moment on some of the problems you'll have in reading my book. If you are reading it just for fun you won't have any, but if you're reading it seriously you will. The chief problem is that the central term, Self, shifts meaning all the time. Here it means one thing. There it means something else. This is something a writer cannot avoid. His most important terms have many meanings and he can't always tell you specifically when he is shifting from one to another. Thus, the reader has to carry part of the burden of deciding which meaning is intended.

I've tried to clarify my meanings by the use of capital and lower case letters. Thus the term 'Self' means something entirely different than 'self.' I follow the same procedure with compound terms, e.g. 'Self-discovery' and 'self-pity.' The first term refers to a noble event, purpose or type of action. The second refers to something decidedly ignoble, of course.

The variations in meaning are often a good deal more complex than this, however. Sometimes I've even had to use terms which were incorrect because they gave a part of my meaning, though not all of it. An example is 'Self-destruction' or 'Self-destructive.' In the sense that I use the term, a 'Self' isn't actually destructible at all, for it persists forever. However, there are things which go against the welfare of a Self and can thus loosely be described as Self-destructive. Some of these things are so deleterious that if we persist in doing them, we might as well not have a Self at all, for all the good it will do us.

We come now to an even more difficult point: What I mean by a Self is distinctly different than what almost everyone else means by the same term. Thus, if the reader sticks to his own meaning of the term he can't possibly understand what I mean by it. To help him provisionally abandon his meaning in favor of mine, I've defined mine time and again in various contexts. If he is open-minded enough this will help him to see what I am talking about.

Another difficulty is that numerous people see no point whatsoever in trying to discover their Selves. Many erroneously think they've already done so. Others see the very concept of Self as meaningless and limit themselves to exploring the dimensions of ego, or personality. Furthermore, their ignorance in this matter is something to which they are very strongly attached. Rather than surrender their delusion of Self-knowledge they will deliberately avoid or sabotage any effort to help them really discover their Selves.

One of the problems is that few people begin to suspect that they ever have Selves until they've allowed egotism to completely mess up their lives. In their suffering they discover that they have egos, that egos are responsible for their suffering and that their psyches may possibly contain something besides egos—real Selves, in fact. Even then, the existence of a Self as distinct from an ego is a fact seen but dimly.

For people who don't believe in the actual existence of Selves as I define them, this book will have to serve as a workbook for Self-expression, not Self-discovery. There is no harm in this. In fact, there's much to gain. Even if a person doesn't believe in his Self he can use photography as a means for giving it expression. At the same time he will probably make substantial progress in giving his Self its freedom.

For those people who are curious and would like to know more about the nature of human Selves I recommend two books: *Bhagavad-Gita,* the Prabhavananda and Isherwood translation, and *The Perennial Philosophy,* by Aldous Huxley. Though there are a good many other suitable texts, these are good for both beginning and advanced searchers for the Self. As you will see, they develop the concept of Self a good deal further than I was able to in the context of a book on photography.

For quite different purposes I recommend another book: *The Screwtape Letters,* by C. S. Lewis. If you are a reader who takes himself and photography too seriously you could easily take my book the same way. C. S. Lewis will help you jar yourself loose from this and at the same time give you another angle of view on some of the things I'm trying to tell you. I suggest that you treat his book and mine as companion volumes, with his considered as the more authoritative. Read them together or alternately.

If you are curious concerning the rather strange philosophy which runs through this book I suggest you dip into even more books: *The Sufis* by Idries Shah; *All and Everything* and *Meetings with Remarkable Men* by G. I. Gurdjieff; *The Teachers of Gurdjieff* by Rafael Lefort; *In Search of the Miraculous* by P. D. Ouspensky; *Ascent to Mount Carmel* and *Dark Night of the Soul* by St. John of the Cross; *There is a River* by Thomas Sugrue; and *The New Man* by Maurice Nicoll.

As you read along you will find that each chapter, indeed each lesson within a chapter, is an entity complete within itself. At the same time you will find that there has been little effort made to connect them. That is, there are very few cross-references from chapter to chapter and from lesson to lesson. I make no apologies for this, nor do I think I ought to. This organization—or, in some lights, lack of it—stems from my concept of the reader to whom I'm addressing myself. He likes and can cope with things in discrete bits, but doesn't care for and can't cope with major themes carefully strung out through an entire book. There is one continuing theme, however: This book is exclusively about Self-discovery through photography, even when it seems to go off in completely unrelated directions.

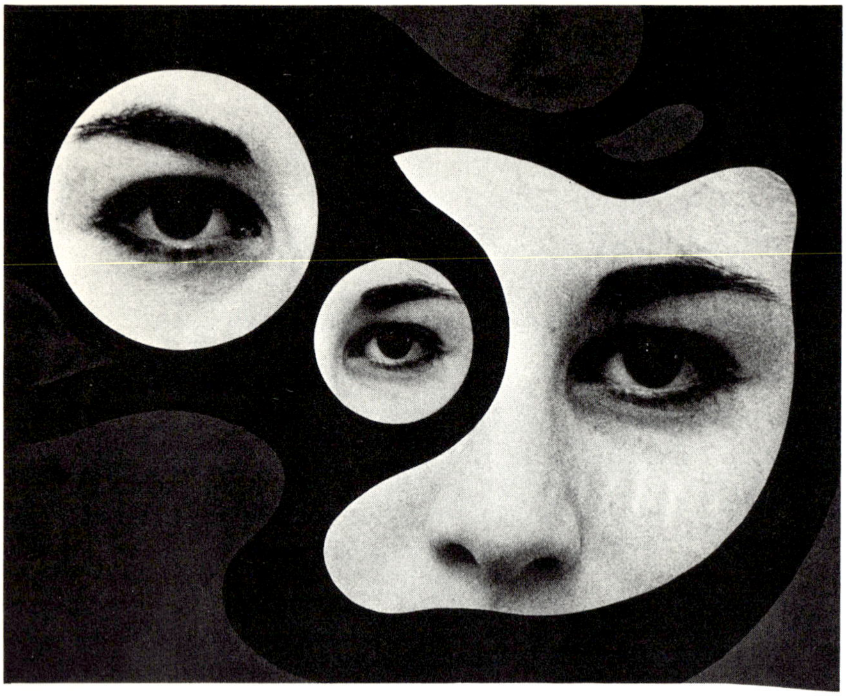

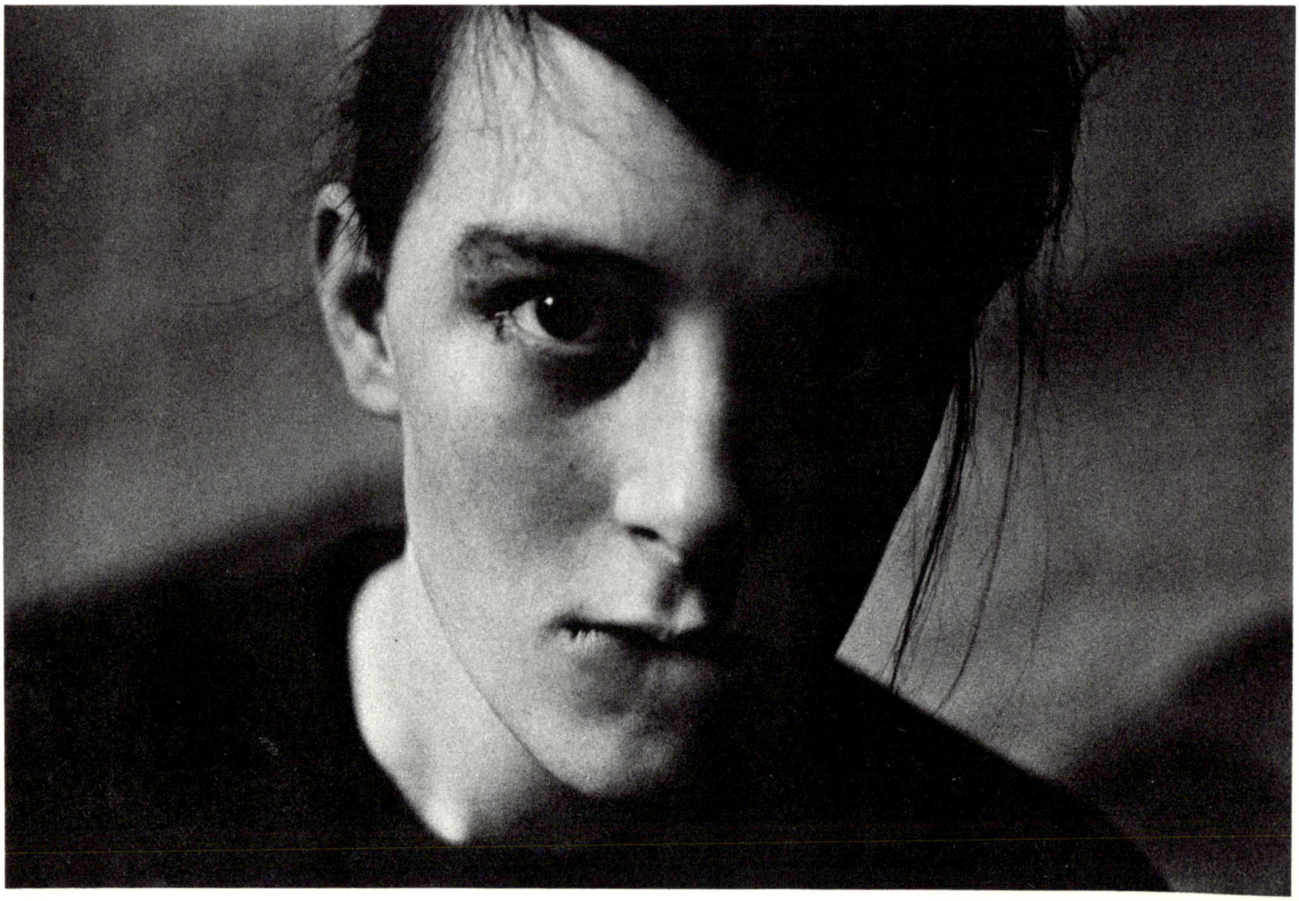

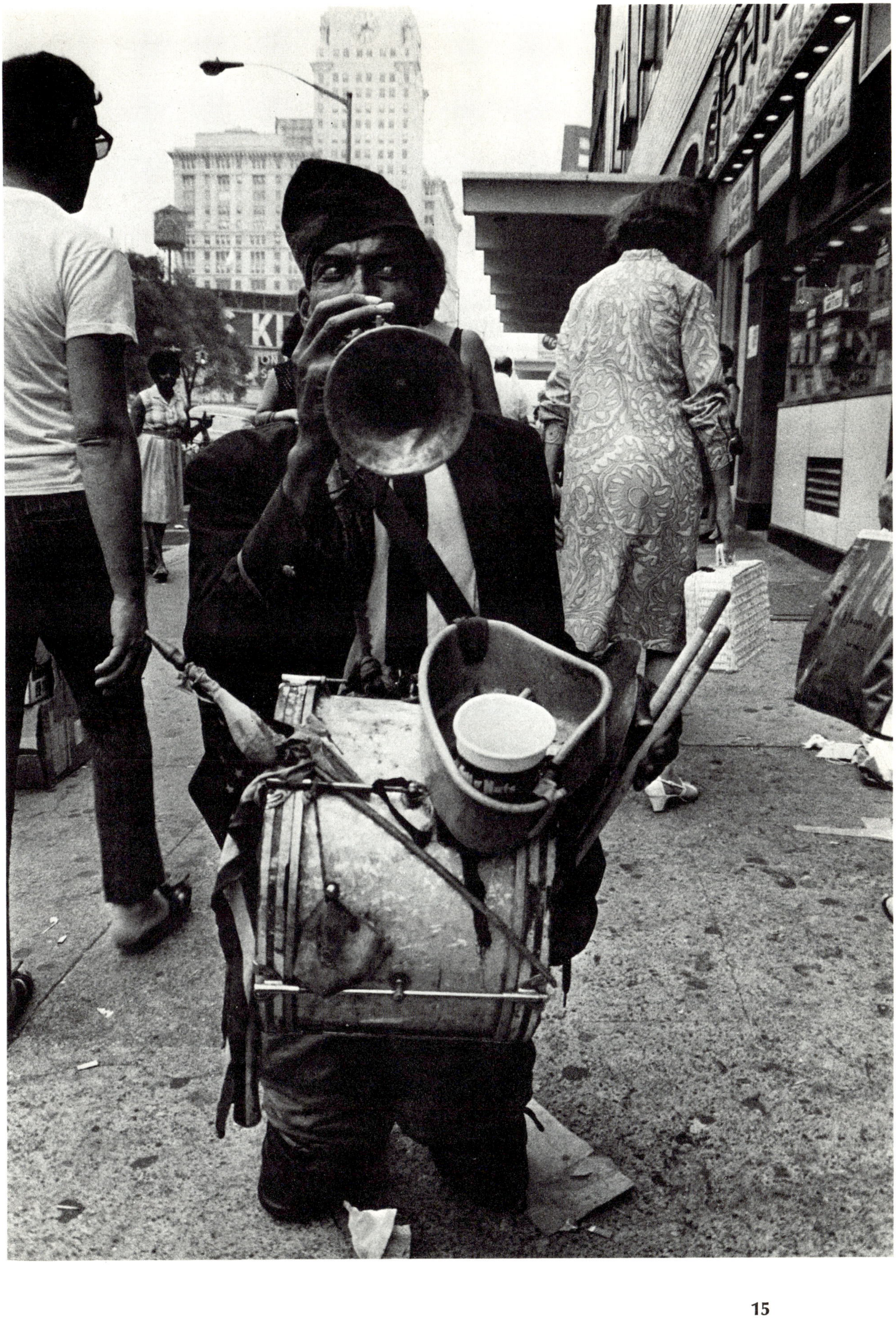
FISH CHIPS

FREE your creative mind

Getting ideas for photographs by using methods which are in attunement with the creativity patterns of your mind. Conventional and unconventional approaches to picture ideas.

When people become really involved in photography they find themselves completely at a loss for ideas at first. That is, they do if they realize there is such a thing as a photographic idea. Some people don't, of course, so they don't worry about it. This chapter is for those who do.

We'll take two approaches: one, by reviewing ideas already popular among photographers; two, by seeing how a person can create his own ideas. Each approach is useful, and each has its own special place in photographic thinking. We'll start with popular ideas.

1

Some people are afraid that they may use photography to do things which aren't already being done. If such a person has a teacher his first and oft-repeated question is, "What am I supposed to do?" He is certain that he is "supposed to do" things for very definite reasons. It is not enough to tell him, "Go out and enjoy yourself with your camera" or "Try to be creative." In a sense, an amateur who is involved in photography for his own amusement and illumination isn't "supposed to do" anything. That is, there are no rules which say, "Do this and don't do that." In this light, what he wants to do is enough. His thought should be, "I'm supposed to use photography for any purpose I desire." He can shoot pictures of songbirds or garbage cans, communicate or not communicate with photography, have fun with his camera or create useful suffering for himself, make pretty pictures or ugly ones, and so forth. The point is that no emperor is saying to him: "Thou art supposed to do this." Nonetheless, our poor beginner still wants to know what he's "supposed to do."

It's customary to call such people creeps or squares and to accuse them of low intelligence and even less imagination. However, making such accusations isn't very intelligent. It happens that there are, indeed, a good many things which you're "supposed to do" in photography—if you want certain results. It's like cooking: After you've poured cake batter into a baking tin, you're "supposed to" put it in the oven—if you want a cake.

In this context it is sensible to have a certain reluctance to use photography in ways which haven't already been mapped out. If you try to, certain things may happen. Possibly no one will understand what you're trying to say with your pictures, if you use photography in an entirely original way. An important thing in using any language (photography can be a visual language) is to follow certain conventions. If a person is using the word "butter" he does it with the conventional understanding that it refers to a yellow, oily something which comes indirectly from cows. He may use "butter" as a synonym for "head" or as a verb meaning "to commit rape." He might then write such things as "Since catching cold my butter has been all stuffed up" or "He was apprehended by police while attempting butter." This kind of thing may be fun but he'd be terrified if it were the best he could do to communicate clearly. In various ways this can happen in photography if one doesn't know the conventions.

The person who asks what he's supposed to do may actually wish to know how to use the medium in order to communicate well. At the same time, he may wish to avoid appearing foolish in public. From long experience he knows that not knowing the conventions can lead to public ridicule. He learned this long ago from the children at kindergarten when he tried drinking chicken soup from his overshoe experimentally. It was reaffirmed in middle life when he was considered a bit crazy for wearing a ring on his thumb. Anyone who has been long in photography knows that there are all kinds of "Thou shalt nots." Though most of them are stupid, there's no getting around the fact that you risk being ridiculed if you violate them.

Many people want to know what to do because they have very little basis for knowing what they should get out of the experience of being a photographer. They assume that there must be some worthwhile things, but they don't know what or how many they are. They assume, furthermore, that those who have been in photography for a long while must know something about its uses and pleasures and how to learn about them as a beginner. The tendency of experienced photographers is to think that the benefits one can derive from photography are self-evident. This is very strange, considering how long it took *them* to develop insight into the benefits and how they are earned.

Another thing people have in mind when they ask for guidance is to save themselves time. This is certainly reasonable. There is not much point in approaching photography as if you had to re-invent the whole art yourself, starting way back in 1839. It makes better sense to ask people to help you use the machines, processes, materials and ideas which have already been accumulated over the years.

The material in this chapter should help the reader decide what he can do without having to feel foolish. It will tell him about ideas which photographers have for many years found interesting, sensible and stimulating. It won't always say why they've found them this way, but other chapters in the book will illuminate this question. Some of the material has to do with creating ideas for oneself. I'll say more about this later.

Sixty Picture Ideas

Illustrations by Paul Coker

When this article was printed in the 1966 *Invitation to Photography,* I was congratulated on all the "new" ideas I had thought up. This is odd, because there is not even *one* new idea in it; nor was there even supposed to be. My central notion was to pick ideas which had been proved time and again.

In my way of thinking, an idea has been proved if hundreds of photographers have deeply enjoyed working with it, if it has helped them make pictures they liked and found meaningful, and if it was relatively easy to carry out. Added to this, an idea ought to be adaptable, so that slight variations on it produce pictures with elements of uniqueness and surprise. It ought to offer the photographer opportunities for Self-exploration and Self-understanding.

I picked these ideas because I knew that the rankest beginners in photography would be able to carry them out. At the same time, any that I accepted had to also be of a nature that would make them both interesting and challenging to a professional. In short, I wanted the beginner to feel challenged within his present capability; but I also wanted him to feel he could go all the way to the moon with a bit of luck and photographic insight. I wanted him to know he wasn't being talked down to because of his lack of experience.

I'm going to pause for a moment to defend old ideas. In the American culture we've been carefully and systematically led to the lunatic notion that only new ideas are worth bothering with. This queer notion prompts us to buy huge quantities of second-rate detergents, toothpaste and electrical gadgets. It is the motivating principle in the publications world, especially in advertising. We hear it in classrooms, have it blared at us from our TV sets and are forced to look at it on outdoor signboards in letters ten feet high. Everywhere we hear "new, new, new." If something isn't new it's supposed to be dull, outmoded and useless.

Contrary to this mad concept, it happens that in many ways ideas are like barrels. When they are brand new they are empty. The exhorters want us all to buy empty barrels just because they're new. Wiser hands prefer to collect them after they've been filled and their contents properly aged or ripened.

Like barrels, ideas must be filled. They are filled by being used, by having thought and emotion and experience poured into them. Through usage they are shaped, the rough edges are smoothed down and the useless parts discarded. Through time and usage, meaning slowly attaches itself to them. A brand new idea often doesn't fit the pattern of the human psyche. But after a time it actually begins to adjust to the mental and emotional patterns of the people who work with it. In this sense, any idea which hasn't ripened for at least a thousand years isn't really worth bothering with.

New ideas which haven't yet been forced to run the very tough obstacle course of long testing and usage are as apt to be mad as they are sane. This has not yet been understood. Though we've come into an age when many of our mad new ideas are coming home to roost in the form of hydrogen bombs and a seriously threatened ecology, people still haven't learned to question the axiom "If it's new it must be good." We'd better learn to question it before it's too late.

As for the ideas in this particular article, you don't have to worry about them. They've circulated through the veins of so many photographers that they've lost all their virulence, if indeed they ever had any. With respect to this book as a whole, I have this to say: Unless I've made a serious mistake somewhere, there is not a single new idea in it.

The sixty time-tested ideas are given in a very condensed form, so that all of them could be stuffed into a few pages. Being so compressed, they need a little imaginative expansion from the reader. He might think them over until his own mind has put meat and fat on their bones. It is even better just to jump right into a project and find out all the other things it can mean after you're actually engaged in doing it.

For example, instead of thinking a long time about, say, the "Where Fire Has Been" project, just find such a place and begin photographing it. If you've found a fairly good one, certain things you wanted to know will practically force themselves into your mind without your even asking. Say you wanted to know what you'd personally get from the experience, aside from pictures. For one thing, you'll probably feel very primitive emotions welling up within you. They're interesting to experience and worthwhile speculating about: Where do they come from? What do they mean? What can they tell you about a side of yourself you don't know very well?

Something may strike you subliminally and thrust your memory back into a forgotten corner of childhood. Smells of wet, burned wood tend to do this. You may even experience the feeling of having lived before, of knowing all about this particular smouldering house from having seen it a thousand years ago.

Perhaps this charred wreck will help you remember fire as a great and dangerous force, not just some little thing you ignite under a panful of lamb chops. It's good to remember life's great forces, especially in an age when they're so easily covered over with enameled steel and forgotten.

Maybe you'll learn that nostalgia is like a bittersweet taste in the mouth. Or maybe you'll feel it as a door opening to a room long sealed off in your brain. Perhaps you'll feel guilt: "I did this thing. I burned this house." Maybe you've forgotten what such feelings are like and need to remember them again.

What about pictures? We can't be certain of pretty ones, can we? How about sad pictures? There may be interesting chances to use photography to describe despair and gloom or, on the contrary, hope for something new arising from the ashes. Nightmare pictures: There ought to be opportunities for these, the unreality of night translated into an equally unreal day time. Perhaps wakefulness and sleep are more interchangeable than we realize. Here's a chance to find out.

What if people think you're weird for hopping about in a charred ruin with a camera? Well, that's really their problem, not yours. If they don't know the possibilities of ruins, they're the losers. If you like, you could use your camera to tell them what they're missing, what they're failing to understand concerning the imaginative nature of man's brain and emotions. As I've said, you can fatten out these lean projects with your mind. Better yet, do it through direct experience.

The chapter title promises to help you free your creative mind. One way of doing this is to give it permission to let it get itself involved in certain things. With sixty projects, each with at least sixty variations, you give your creative mind a broad spectrum of things to explore without having to feel foolish about it. Remember, this permission comes from at least ten thousand photographers, not just the author of one book.

The lesson:

When someone first gets involved in photography, he generally has no difficulty in deciding what to photograph. He shoots anything and everything, then awaits the results eagerly. At this point, he is not so much interested in making terrific pictures as in witnessing how photography works as a very magical process. If he does his own developing and printing, he is deeply involved in the challenge of understanding and mastering procedures. This can occupy his attention for a long while. Eventually, however, he begins to turn his attention to the pictures themselves. He sees they aren't all that they could be and wonders what to do about it. He has reached a crisis.

Though a few people can decide for themselves how to improve their pictures, some find it useful to turn to others for guidance. Photographic books and magazines are loaded with good advice. You can pick up ideas from studying the movies and TV. There are photographic exhibits by expert picture-makers. By joining a camera club, you can get free advice from people quite experienced in photography. Camera salesmen are often very helpful to beginners. Indeed, there are many places to find help. They should all be explored, for in photography those who know something about it generally delight in passing along their information to others.

One good source of help is a formal class in photography led by a competent photographer-teacher, but such classes aren't available everywhere. To substitute for a class, or perhaps even improve on it, here's a group of assignments or challenges especially chosen for those who wish to rise above the snapshot level. They are like those you might get in a formal class.

These projects can be done in either black-and-white or color. Most of them can be done almost anywhere at any time. They call for subject matter that is readily available to anyone who is willing to put himself out even a little bit. Most could be done with the simplest, least expensive camera equipment, though some would benefit by the use of such accessories as close-up attachments or color filters. Available light will suffice for all of them, but it would be good to have a clamp-on photoflood or two so you can explore additional lighting possibilities. Some of the problems have very wide possibilities; others are carefully, deliberately restricted. Though they are especially selected for beginners, they have for years excited advanced amateurs and professionals, too.

There are enough ideas here to make up two or three formal courses in photography. They are all tried and true. Use them to stimulate your thinking or, better, do some of them. Pick up your camera and have fun. You'll learn to see better and will thrill yourself because of it.

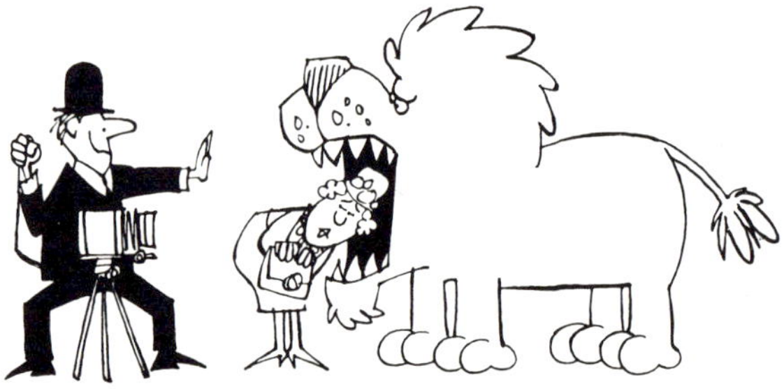

Object in Unusual Environment

One of the easiest ways to give a familiar object new and exciting interest is to put it in an unlikely place. In fact, professionals do this all the time. Imagine a rocking chair up in a tree, an egg on a busy sidewalk and people's reactions to it, a puppy sitting in a pot on the stove, a hamburger studded with nails, a white mouse inside a wine glass, a tin soldier in a graveyard at sunset, three beer bottles sticking out of a snowbank, a statuette in a mud puddle, or nine tooth brushes stuck in a birthday cake. But you don't have to be this far out to get interest. Try it your way.

Facial Contortions

For ten thousand years, people have amused others by making faces at them—funny faces, ugly, and whatever. Get your friends or your family to make faces for your camera. It's a great lark that with good backgrounds and interesting lighting can yield fascinating pictures. Some interesting contortions can be made by pushing or pulling at the face with fingers, pressing it against a window, wrapping plastic or nylon tightly around it, and from putting things in the mouth to puff out the cheeks. Eating a lemon does things; so does smelling a rotten odor. Use your imagination here, and don't underestimate the possibilities.

Victorian House

Photographers have always adored Victorian houses. Try one for yourself and see why. Find one in a slum, on a shady street, or on a lonely hill. Listen for the romantic whispers from the past at sunset. Explore up close for exciting bric-a-brac. Make mournful pictures of decay. If you look hard and long enough, you'll find just the house for you. Interpret it carefully; don't just snapshoot. And wait until the time of day and the weather (it can be either good or bad) are just right for what you want to say.

Exploring the Baby

If you have a baby, make snapshots—lots of 'em—but try other things, too. Come in close with your camera for details: a tiny foot being washed or held, a clutching hand, a head from the back, a beautiful back and tender bottom, a nose in profile, ears, face close up. Photograph the child in all details and from every angle. You'll be glad you did.

Statues on Car Dashboards

If you look through enough car windshields, you'll see that the little arrangements of things people make on dashboards range from the religious to the profane, the ridiculous to the pathetic. They make good photographs, very revealing of people, but you have to move around a bit to find good angles. Try shooting them at night silhouetted against street or car lights, or shoot through rain- or snow-spattered windshields. You could try for a gentle, religious feeling. If you're a cynic, you might, for laughs, make your own dashboard still life (the more improbable the better).

Hands

They're surprisingly photographic, once you really look at them. Hands at prayer or on a sacred text, nervous hands twisting and sweating, ancient hands, young ones, hands talking, wrenching, thrusting, striking. Holding hands—in how many ways can it be done? You can go ape, too; a stack of fists two feet high, silhouetted picket fence made of fingers, five clutching hands and a face, a hairy hand painted white, hands as dancers, hands posed like flowers or entwined like snakes. Once you learn to see them, hands are terrific.

Child or Children on a Swing

Let's restrict ourselves here: make the swing seem as if it were a hundred miles up in the air (by lying on the ground and shooting it against the sky). But variations can come from who is swinging and how. Small children may howl with glee, hang on terrified, look totally unimpressed, etc. Father might take son up in a swing between his legs. Teenagers try to go "over the top" or in pairs perform dangerous high jinks for any willing photographer. Oldsters sit in swings to remember how it was. Pretty maidens bare lithe legs and toss their heads coyly as their lovers push them.

Policeman

Cops are always around as subjects for pictures. Try these: a cop seemingly smothered in traffic, a young one trying to look tough and unimpressed, close-up showing the magnificent array of miscellany hung on belts or stuffed in pockets, artistic swinging of a nightstick, bored cops, tired ones, beautiful or ugly. If you're bold, follow one around on his beat, walk into a station and get permission to take pictures, or get to know a policeman and photograph his behind-the-scenes and off-duty life.

Loneliness

This is a favorite theme of photographers, for everybody feels loneliness and is deeply moved by it. Here is a new type of problem for you: taking an abstract verbal idea and translating it into pictorial reality. Furthermore, you're completely on your own this time concerning how to solve the problem.

Patterns in Structural Steel

The steel skeletons of new buildings fascinate people, especially men. They have great abstract design possibilities. Try silhouettes, multiple exposures, printing with two or more negatives sandwiched together, high-contrast prints. For color: steel against colorful sunset, or use color filters for interesting monochromes. A black-and-white print from a color slide could be great. How about the sun or moon framed in steel, or maybe birds or workmen?

Roll-at-a-Time Double Exposures

Some of our pros are very fond of this trick. You shoot a roll of film, re-roll it, then shoot it again, thus getting double images on each frame. The number of things you can combine is endless; for example, dancers and trees, faces and patterns, clouds and buildings, rooftops and street scenes, old houses and eyes, silhouettes and non-silhouettes, stoplights and landscapes. Perhaps the nicest thing about this idea is that you may truly surprise yourself with what you get. It requires a venturous spirit, however, and you will waste a bit of film getting something interesting.

Patterns on Faces

Strangely, the idea of changing human skin texture or of superimposing patterns on it has always interested people. Through

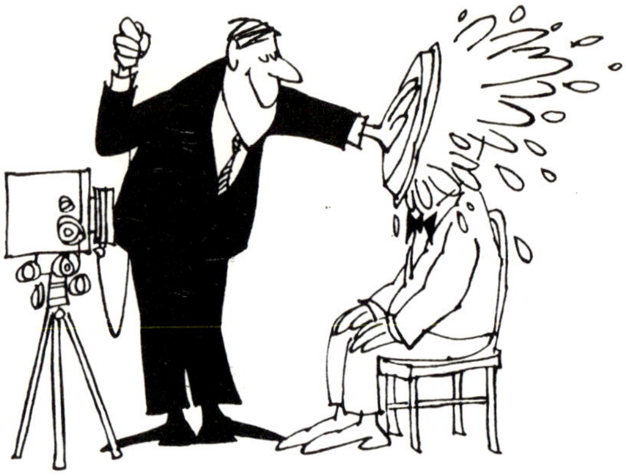

photography, this is easy. While the results are often rather weird, they can be delicate and beautiful, too. You can print a face negative sandwiched together with a texture or pattern negative, or put two color transparencies in the same mount. Shadow patterns on faces can be very interesting and extremely varied. You can photograph faces through various fabrics, patterned plastics, patterned glass, window screens, rain- or dirt-spattered windows, frost patterns on windows. Patterns can be put directly on faces with make-up, tempera, soapsuds, mud packs, and other harmless substances.

A Very Special Tree

At one time or another, practically everybody photographs a tree, but the pictures usually don't amount to much. They're not selective enough. You must look for very special ones—lacework trees, fantastically gnarled ones, ghost-story trees, trees silver-coated in ice, lonely trees, trees shining against a dark mountain or sky, trees that are fantastic roosts for birds or small boys. Always be on the lookout for *your* special tree, and when you find it, work on it until your photographs express what you mean.

Steichen's Project

Many years ago the master photographer Edward Steichen challenged himself to make as many photographs as he could of a single cup and saucer—each one interesting, handsome, and different from all the others. This is still a great challenge for everyone, beginner or professional. For our special purposes, let us set twenty-five pictures as our goal. You might consider this as a mastery project: If you really do it well, your photographic vision and sensitivity have arrived somewhere. Warning: The first three or four pictures may be fairly easy, but after that you'll have to sweat some to make the others different and handsome, too. Take your time—a year if necessary. As you study photography, apply *everything* you learn to this project.

Handsome Picture of Glassware

Though you've probably been unimpressed by the hundreds of advertising pictures of glassware you've seen, you will still get enormous pleasure from making a fine one yourself, and learn surprising things about photography, too. There is a very basic trick you should know: Let no direct light whatsoever strike the glassware you are photographing, but let it be on the background instead. Surprisingly, glassware thus seen has brilliant, clean black lines and tones in it. You might try arranging your background light so that the tone is graded, varying smoothly from white to medium gray. Though you've just heard what to do, you won't really understand this visually until you've tried it yourself. For comparison, photograph your glassware with light striking it directly.

Where Fire Has Been

Fire often leaves interesting residues. Consider: fire-eaten trees rising out of the mist, jagged ruins silhouetted against dramatic sky, close-up of charred wood glistening like metal in the rain, sad owner poking through the ruins, fantastic fire-melted glass shapes, sad remembrances of what was before the fire came, fire shapes like modern sculpture, fire shapes reflected in puddles of water, abstract patterns in partially charred draperies, the pathetic remains of a child's toy. Enough! The rest you must discover for yourself. Mere words won't do the job, not in this or any other project.

Bert Stern's Project

Several years ago Stern set himself a problem that has become famous in photography. His solutions to it propelled him, then a newcomer in photography, to the top of the advertising photography profession, where he has been ever since. The problem was to make some fascinating pictures of a martini. This is still a terrific project for anyone. Since Stern was trying to sell vodka, he was limited; but you're not. You can try to make a martini seem weird, dangerous to health, evil-tasting, ridiculous, funny, or improbable. You can combine your martini with other things which were out of bounds for Stern; e.g., a martini and a dead bird, mud puddle, baby, burned out building, cat, tombstone, stop sign, bare foot, wrecked automobile, chocolate syrup. You have opinions on liquor. Illustrate them.

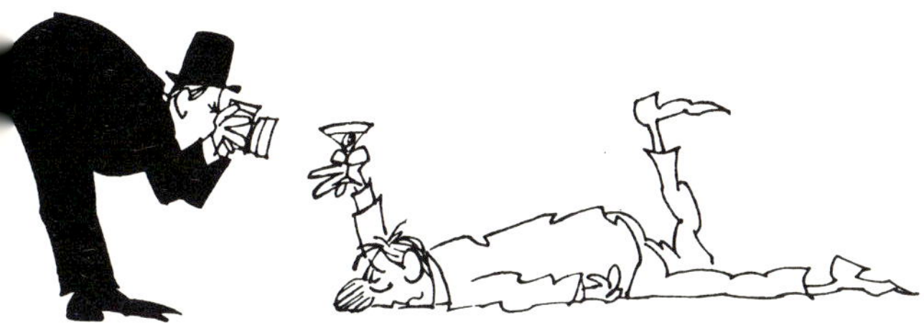

White on White

One would think that if a white object were photographed on a white background, the whole picture would come out white, but it isn't so. Light itself creates a variety of tones, from white through various grays to black. Seeing clearly, perhaps for the first time, what light really does is fascinating, and it is most easily done in this kind of project. Create as many different lighting situations as possible, either with floodlamps or by moving your subject matter into as many different kinds of natural light as you can find. Since there may not be available as many white objects as you'd like, paint some things. For fun, spray-paint a plant, a bunch of grapes, a lobster, a hand, a doll, a pair of old shoes. Changing things this way makes them more interesting.

Long-Format Picture

Playing with format (picture proportion) can lead to interesting photographs and interesting problems which must be solved in order to get them. Try this: make a horizontal picture in a 4x8 inch (or length 2 times greater than height) format. You will find yourself doing a lot of looking and thinking in your search for things which will both fit the format and make sense. Once you've solved this problem to your satisfaction, try the same proportion for a vertical shot.

Triple Portrait, Long Format

Make a horizontal picture of three people using the above format, then make a vertical. Pose and light your people with imagination. Try using a different pose for each person. One could be in the light, the others silhouetted. You could group two on one side, isolate the other. And so on. Play around with this. Anything goes.

Framing a Face

Though beginners usually put the people they photograph right in the middle of their pictures, there are other places that may be much more interesting. To learn how to frame (or crop) better, try this: With one subject and a plain background make a series of close-up pictures with the head in as many locations as you can think of. Though little more than the head should be included, you can still vary the camera distance considerably from picture to picture, even coming in close enough to crop right into the head. In addition, study magazine photographs to see how the pros solve this everyday but very important problem. Later, try cropping variations against different kinds of backgrounds.

Opposites

In life or in pictures, opposites can make for interest. Common pictorial opposites are: large and small, dark and light, sharp and soft, warm color and cool color, bright color and muted color, complex and simple, far and near. Add to this list as many other opposites as you can think of, then make a picture which emphasizes one pair of them more than the other pairs which may be present. Also, try to figure out how the opposites are affecting the way you feel about the picture. For example, a cool color may either emphasize or neutralize a warm color, a dark tone make a light tone seem brighter to you, or a large thing make a smaller one seem really tiny. The number of possible effects is enormous.

Flowers and Backgrounds

Carefully arrange a bunch of flowers in your handsomest bowl, then carry them around, indoors and out, to see how many interesting backgrounds you can find for them, photographing each one for later comparison. Study each background carefully before shooting. You may find it appropriate to vary the flower arrangement from background to background.

White on White in Color

If you're shooting color, the white-on-white project can be shot as already given, but it can also be modified for some delightful effects. Try putting colored filters or layers of colored cellophane over your lens for handsome monochromes. To determine exposures, put the filters in front of your exposure meter when making your readings. For very beautiful multi-color effects, put different colored cellophane (or theatrical gelatins) over two or more photoflood reflectors. The more layers of cellophane, the stronger the colors. They show up beautifully on white. Don't leave the lights on long, or the cellophane will melt. Or you can use regular light bulbs, which are not as hot as photoflood lamps.

Love for a Pet

One of the really beautiful things in life is the love people show for their pets. It is, of course, expressed in many, many ways. In a carefully thought out, well composed picture, illustrate this love, making your picture say as clearly as possible that it is about love.

Family Ham

Members of your family probably tend consciously or unconsciously to ham it up when you photograph them. Instead of getting upset about this, why not carry it to the logical extreme: try deliberately to make the world's hammiest family snapshot. It could be fun with the family's cooperation, perhaps more fun if they were unaware of what you were up to. It could also make a fascinating picture.

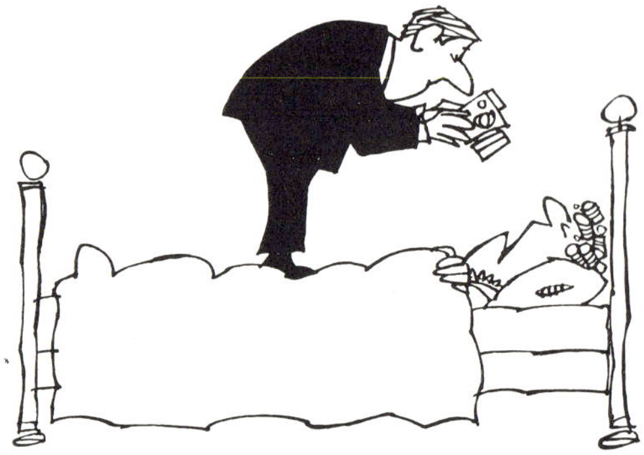

Family Asleep

There is a most wonderful peace in a sleeping face: tender, innocent, quietly free of care. Why not photograph each member of your family this way? It will make your heart swell with tenderness. Perhaps the best time for this is early on a spring or summer morning, when there is plenty of light for photography coming in from outdoors, and the amount of it isn't disturbing to the sleeper.

Weathered Sculpture

Weather does fascinating things to sculpture, ranging from the pathos of crumbling or erosion to the surrealism of staining. Pigeons often make interesting contributions. Occasionally, weather makes statues more realistic. Sometimes weathering is even humorous. Statues covered with mud, snow, or rain are fine. So be a statue-hunter.

Dog's-Eye View

One reason we become bored with the world is that we always see it from either a standing or sitting position. To see it once again as exciting, spend a week or two taking pictures (or at least looking through your camera viewfinder) from the ground or floor level. You will be delightfully surprised many, many times at what you see.

Bird's-Eye View

For the same reasons, try the bird's-eye view. In any city or town, there are many high places that a photographer can reach if he puts his mind to it. But sometimes, just standing on a chair or stepladder will make enough difference to put fresh excitement into a picture. Live with the birds for a while.

Close-Up View

A somewhat similar technique is to set your camera at its closest focusing distance and determinedly leave it there for several days while cruising around places that interest you and looking for pictures. To make this idea really pay off, however, you have to force yourself to stick with it for a while. The same is true for the dog's-eye- and bird's-eye-view problems. The longer you force yourself, the better your chances of getting exciting pictures.

Harvey Lloyd's Project

A problem which magazine photographer Harvey Lloyd set himself recently is an interesting example of how rigorous self-limitation and self-forcing can pay off. He decided to make close-ups of various types of flowers with the evening sun behind them. By sticking to it, he got a fascinating set of pictures. This is a project with which beginners as well as pros could have great fun.

Stake-Out

A favorite approach of a great many fine photographers is the stake-out. The idea is to find a place that interests you for some reason and then to hang around waiting for things to happen, going back day after day if necessary. The better the photographer, the longer he'll wait. Only by doing this kind of shooting now and then can you learn to see all the possibilities of a given place. If you always skip about like a butterfly, you never learn to see anything really well.

Beauty in Ugliness

It is immensely rewarding to use your camera to re-examine things you've always thought of as ugly to see if they might also have a certain beauty. The beauty might be brought out by lighting, camera angle or distance, atmospheric conditions, background or environment, color, focus. An even greater excitement is to find something you can photograph once as really ugly and again as truly beautiful. There are also many opportunities for beauty and ugliness to coexist in pictures in very interesting ways. This has always been one of the great themes in almost any art form.

Exciting Egg

One of nature's great artistic triumphs is the hen's egg, a sculpturally perfect form. But we see it so often we don't really see it at all and find great difficulty thinking of mere food as art. So here's a tough assignment for you: a photograph which shows an egg as beautiful and exciting, even to jaded artistic tastes. Try this approach: Carefully re-study all the other picture ideas in search of those that might conceivably apply to your egg picture, then pick one or more and put them to use.

Symbolic Bread

One of man's most ancient and revered symbols is bread, the staff of life. But in this over-fed culture, it is often seen as the least remarkable of foodstuffs. Your problem: Photograph bread in such a way that it becomes visually impressive and gives a feeling of its symbolic meaning and importance. Tip: Be selective in the type of bread you choose and in what you have happening to it.

Cracks

Cracks in concrete, paint, mirrors, glass, facial packs, wood, dried mudpuddles, and plastic can be very interesting if you look hard enough to find the really good ones. In fact, certain fine photographers have gone so far as to do picture essays on them. They're easy to photograph and easy to find.

Unexpected Traces of Man

In a city, practically everything that exists

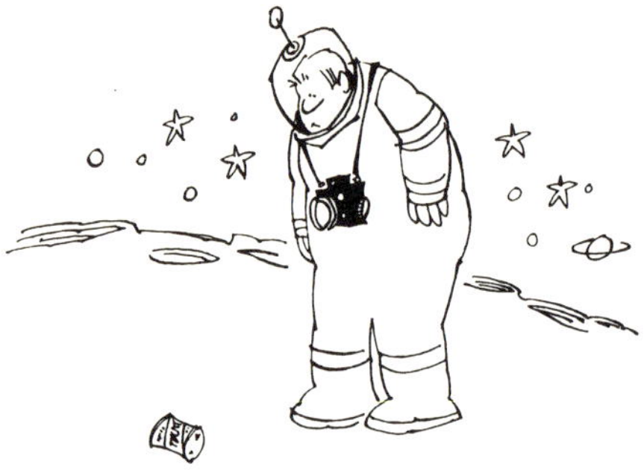

is a trace of man and not very interesting as such. But many of these same things become interesting if they're found in the wilderness. So, on your next romp in the great outdoors be on the lookout for them. If they happen to be ancient or weather-beaten, all the better. Romance and nostalgia, you see.

Live Tin Soldier

If you have a close-up attachment for your camera, try making a tin soldier come to life by finding the right lighting and background environment for him. This will take a lot of looking around, but it works. The secret is to obscure him somewhat by backlighting, silhouetting, cutting off part of him with some object, putting him and his surroundings a little out-of-focus, etc. Some small backgrounds out-of-focus tend to look large. For example, a clump of wild grass can look like a canebrake, a bit of parsley can look like a tree, a small rock can look like a large one.

Bad Weather Beauty

If you can overcome your discomfort at being out in it, bad weather—rain, sleet, snow, dust, smoke, and fog—can be seen as beautiful. In fact, it has always been a very favorite subject for pictorial photographers. Many a beginner thinks he can photograph only in full sunshine and that he doesn't have enough experience for bad weather. Not so. If he has an exposure meter, it will tell him what to do as long as there is enough light to register on the dial. So try bad weather for yourself. It's the very heart's blood of pictorial photography.

Minor White's Project

A famous teacher of photography, Minor White, has one project that is especially interesting: to photograph something for what it is and (again) for what else it is. It happens that under certain conditions of lighting, camera angle, camera distance, focus, environmental surroundings, etc., a thing looks like only what it is; but under other circumstances of the same type, it can look more like something else altogether. A twig becomes a tree, a nude back a hill, a puddle an aerial view of a lake, cracks in old paint a moonscape, a coke bottle a tower of glass, a human hand a monument in bronze. A great many things can be transformed this way photographically, if you play around with them long enough. It's great sport either to half transform something or to go all the way.

By Its Own Light

A great many things can be photographed by their own light—light bulbs, neon signs, fireworks, candles, bonfires, molten metal, etc.—and you should certainly try them all as time goes by. However, you may find it more fun to set your own little fires. If things aren't combustible, pour lighter fluid or alcohol on them. Imagine the following glowing or flaming brightly: bowl of eggs, doll or statuette, handsome glass with brandy in it, piece of paper twisting and fraying in the heat, old shoe, ship model, doorknob, pile of quarters and dimes, abstract sculpture made of marshmallows. With imagination, you can find many things never before seen in their own light. You could even light your own ear if you were a wee bit mad. For additional fun, try finding interesting environments in which to set your little conflagrations.

Long Hair with a Difference

Long hair has always attracted photographers. They've photographed it blowing in the wind, draping across eyes or faces, put up on curlers, dripping water, getting combed or brushed. These ideas are still worth trying. But doesn't long hair have other possibilities, too? Did you ever see the horrendous pile it makes when back-combed, before the top layer is smoothed down? Hair pulling (faked, of course) could be interesting. What about the numberless things that could be braided into hair, from flowers to fish? Hair and water clay (harmless) sculptures? Medusa snakes of hair and stiff soapsuds? Hair standing straight up in the air (subject hangs upside down, then the picture is reversed)? With all this hair around there must be something we can do with it. Don't forget the boys, who are getting hairier every minute! Intricate patterns could be woven across faces with hair dampened with one of the stickier (ugh!) hair sprays. How about grandma back-combed?

Strange Sunset

Eventually, everyone photographs sunsets. They are easy to do and always pretty; but they can be much more in addition to being handsome: weird, puzzling, exciting, thought-provoking. What could you combine with a sunset to make it strange and interesting? A stuffed owl? A creepy old, run-down house? A screaming seagull? An empty rocking chair? A cut-out of Batman? Use the mad part of your mind on this one.

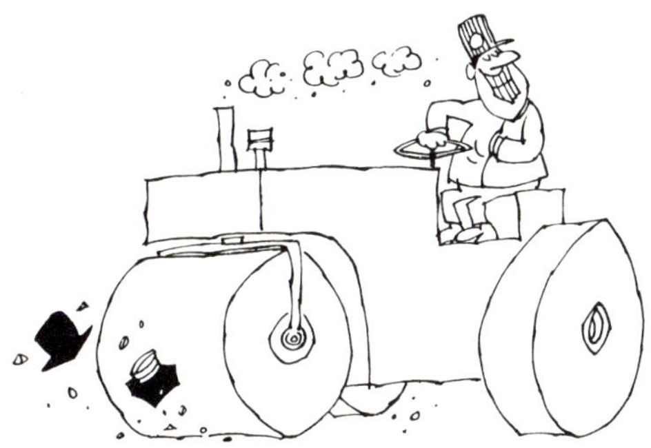

Men at Work

Those who've never tried it before nearly always get a big kick out of photographing a man or men at work—there are so many, many possibilities. All you have to do is look around. And they generally love to be photographed, because it makes what they are doing seem important to them. Try it.

Blowing Soap Bubbles

A classical photographic project that is always fun is a child blowing soap bubbles. Since one problem is to find lighting and background that will make the bubbles show up well, you should move your little model around a bit until you do. Choose your camera distance and camera angle carefully, too.

The Great Cliché

Perhaps the greatest and longest-lived idea in all photography is the "whole lot of nothing and a little bit of something" cliché, and anyone who is anyone in the field has had to master it. Furthermore, it's fun. It goes like this: tiny skier—large mountainside, little bird—huge sky, small man—great empty plaza, little spot of red —big mass of green, etc. Since it seems destined to go on forever, you really ought to jump into the swim and give it a try.

Deadly Looking Weapon

Men generally like weapons and enjoy creating situations to make them look deadly in a photograph. There is a lot of room for ingenuity here, too. If you're a woman, this project probably won't interest you much. Tip: A feeling of night and obscurity might be just the thing, as well as a hint of possible violence to come.

Blurred Bird

Nearly everyone seems to be blurring birds with slow shutter speeds these days. The pleasure is in seeing how much blur you can get and still have a bird, or in making him look like something else altogether. The slower the shutter speed, the greater the blur. Have you blurred yours today?

Jugscape

Carry a clear glass, one-gallon jug around with you for a while to take pictures through. The glass distorts the image somewhat, but with some subject matter this can be very exciting. This is an easy one.

Non-Accidental Hand

When you accidentally get your hand in

front of the lens while taking a picture, you curse yourself. But this same accident can be modified for very interesting pictures, especially if you use single-lens reflex cameras. Try shooting different subjects and vary the distance of the hand (your own, perhaps) from the lens between six inches and two feet. The hand will make out-of-focus, abstract shapes, which can be mysterious or intriguing, depending on the subjects you photograph them with. Though it's easy to do, a lot of pros use this trick nowadays.

Neon Bubbles

If you photograph neon signs at night and put them out-of-focus, they change delightfully into brightly colored bubbles floating mysteriously in the air. A nice project for color film, but not much good for black-and-white.

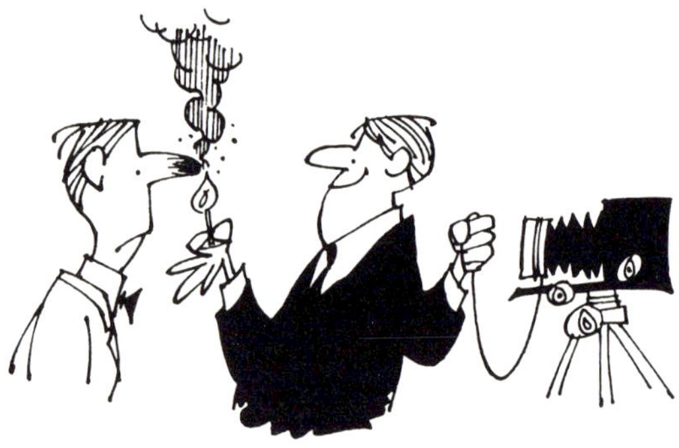

Drama with a Match

A person lighting a cigarette or holding a match up to his face in a darkened room makes an interesting, dramatic picture. If you have an exposure meter it's very easy; but be careful to take your reading from the light that reaches the face, not the match itself.

Soft and Sharp

Pictures of certain romantic subjects—lovely girls, angelic children, lovers, evening landscapes—often look even more romantic if their centers are sharp but their edges soft. To get this effect, smear petroleum jelly on the edges of a plate of glass, leaving a clean circle in the middle, then hold it in front of your lens. Somewhat the

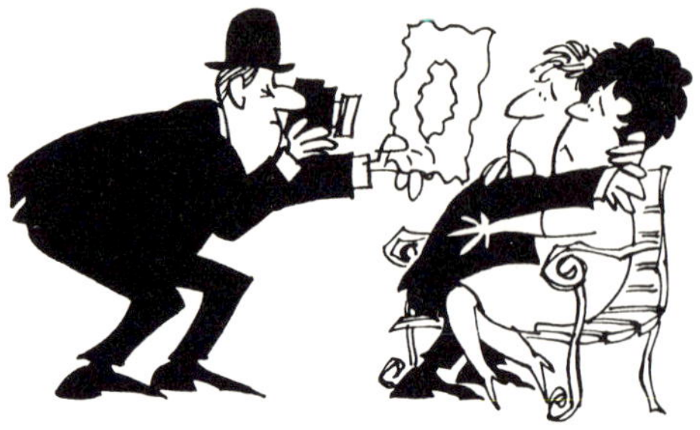

same effect can be obtained by rumpling a sheet of cellophane, re-straightening it, then cutting the center out. To see the effect you're getting and to find the right distance from smeared glass to lens, you need either a view camera or a single-lens reflex.

Out-of-Focus

On rare occasions, a subject looks more interesting out-of-focus than sharp. Still, it happens often enough to make it worth your while at least to look at each subject out-of-focus (if you have a single- or twin-lens reflex camera). If one looks interesting, photograph it. Many of our best creative photographers do this constant looking and occasional photographing all the time. This is much better for color than for black-and-white. Though you can do this out-of-focus shooting for itself, it would probably be better just to tack it onto the other assignments as good subjects present themselves.

Star Bursts

Magazine photographer Joe Baker discovered that a light petroleum jelly "X" smeared on the lens of his SLR would make a light source into a four-pointed star, an extra line making it six points, etc. Though it may not work on your particular camera, it's worth a try, as star-making is all the rage. Remove the jelly carefully with lens tissue. It's harmless to the lens.

Romantic Softness

If you scratch irregular patterns in a piece of clear plastic with a pin and then tape the plastic in front of your lens, it will diffuse or soften the image. The more scratches, the greater the diffusion. It's often useful for rather romantic landscapes and portraits. For portraits, it tends to soften wrinkles and diminish minor facial blemishes. It doesn't improve all images, however, so experiment to find what looks best.

Studies of a Bridge

A bridge is one of those interesting objects we pay little attention to until we set out to photograph it. Taking just one picture won't do much for you, but doing a series gets many beginners very involved and deeply enchanted. Examine it from all angles and distances, in different kinds of weather and at various times of day, evening or night. If there are several bridges you can get to, pick the one for you carefully. And spend a little time on this idea. You'll be repaid.

Backlighting

There is an old adage that you should never take a picture unless the light is coming over your shoulder. Not true. Many pictures are terrific because the light was coming from behind the subject. Backlighting doesn't always work, so you have to play around with it a bit to discover what you like. However, if you didn't have to work, where would the challenge be?

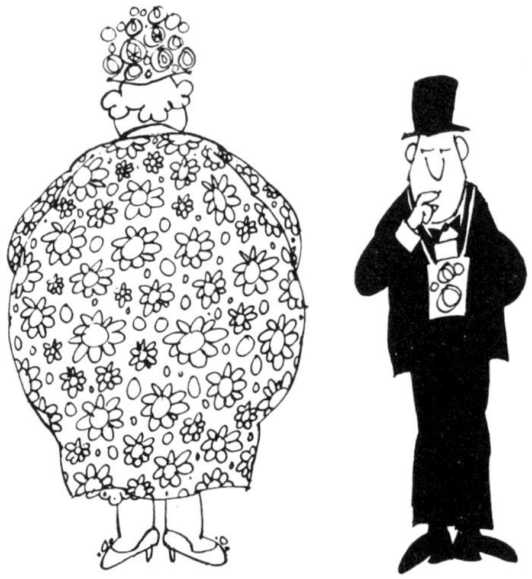

From Behind

There are many subjects, people especially, that we normally photograph only from the front. However, the view from behind is sometimes just as interesting or more so. Most beginners have to force themselves even to think of this possibility. Try this: For a set period of time (a month at least) force yourself to look at and think about the back of everything you've found photographically interesting from the front, when this is possible. There will be at least a few things you like. Sticking with it will make for success; doing it for just one afternoon will get you nowhere at all.

Beg, Borrow, and Steal

A photographer can get all uptight at the thought of using ideas already in existence. He feels that unless he creates an idea entirely by himself he shouldn't permit himself to use it. I've seen his like many a time and can assure you he never gets anywhere. He always ends up in a tight bag with several thousand others who've had the same notion. Put their pictures together and they all look alike. This points to one of photography's few absolutes: Try too hard to be unique and you'll end up as a mirror for everyone else who tried.

The person who tries too hard usually has few ideas to start with. After laboriously giving birth to one, he values it too highly. Truly creative people eventually come to understand that an idea per se has no value whatsoever, nor does it matter a whit whether it's old or new. All that counts is that it means something or that it guides the photographer truly in his pursuit of meaning.

The picture ideas in "Beg, Borrow and Steal" are all at least as old as the moon. That the pictures are all lively and fresh suggests that age hasn't harmed them a bit. It also suggests that the person who borrows from them can come up with interesting pictures, which is most certainly the truth.

As you read the list, you'll see that there are certain definite techniques for borrowing and adapting ideas. These, too, are as old as Time. The builders of the Great Pyramid probably used them freely. Though they require a certain clarity of thinking, this can be developed through practice. And like playing a well-conceived game, it's an interesting way to pass the time.

There are more techniques in the article than one might suppose, so look for them carefully. They are not introduced with the words "Hereafter follows a technique." Some are introduced by the turn of a phrase, others by a single word. If your mind is generally barren of ideas, get out your shovel and dig.

Some of the techniques have to do with using your mind in the way it naturally works best; for example, the one which tells you to do things backwards. Since the mind is a very maverick thing, there are times when it should be turned loose to have its own way. Not permanently, I must add, for that leads to the mental hospital, no matter how much fun one has along the way. Temporarily. Let the good dog loose, then command him back after he's had his run. Unless you're a genius, don't worry about letting him loose for too long; you won't be able to figure out how to do it. Your problem is more likely to be getting him to run loose at all.

After you've developed a reasonable mastery of basic techniques, you'll find ideas popping into mind rather easily. At this point it is good to let your mind range freely. It takes a while to learn for sure what an idea really is, as differentiated from pieces of ideas and emotions. At first you may think that a fragment of an idea is a whole one or that feelings like anger and joy are ideas, which they're not. If you can learn to be patient with it your mind will eventually learn to distinguish between real and pseudo-ideas.

You may wonder where your creativity emerges in borrowing time-tested ideas. It comes in your juxtaposition or adaptation or melding of those ideas. While you're mastering the basic concepts, you'll discover that you are beginning to apply your own creative touch, that uniqueness that is your Self. In fact, your ideas will become so much your own that you'll hardly be able to remember the borrowed ideas you started with. Don't let pride prevent you from borrowing. Creative people through all the ages have done it and it has never inhibited even slightly their natural creativity. Scientists have a sensible notion concerning borrowing. They say that any young scientist in his right mind will always try to take his first steps off the shoulders of all the world's scientists who have preceded him.

The Lesson:

Some people have no trouble getting photographic ideas. They go for years taking successful pictures by the score without giving the matter of ideas a thought. Though their pictures may be literally loaded with visual concepts, they may be entirely unaware of it. Such people are a very small minority. There are others, however, who are painfully aware both that pictorial ideas are important and that they have great difficulty in thinking them up. There are many ways in which they can be helped in learning to generate or develop ideas.

One of the best ways for getting ideas is not to think them up but to discover and harvest those that are already lying around more or less unnoticed. They can be harvested or mined from paintings, books, conversations, museums, television, motion pictures, and so on. In fact, any area in which humanity has expressed itself is potentially a mine or harvest field. One of the most fruitful areas to explore is other people's photographs. In existing pictures can be found ideas by the hundreds already cast in a form that is ideal for photography. Ideas from books or conversations may require considerable recasting.

On the surface this would appear to be plagiarism, but it doesn't have to be. Plagiarism is trying to steal all the ideas in a picture at once by making an exact copy, then claiming credit for it. What I'm suggesting is minor idea-borrowing followed by adaptation and development. These are time-honored processes in the arts. From one picture we take a secondary idea and turn it into a major one in photographs of our own. From another we take one that is merely latent or vaguely hinted

From this picture let us borrow certain ideas and deliberately ignore others. We'll borrow: (1) a man and woman, (2) they can relate or not relate, (3) one person close to the camera, and (4) faces in the picture may be hard to make out. Let us now extend or adapt the borrowed ideas. We could modify the first one (man and woman) by contrast: young with old, pretty with homely, dark-skinned with light, fat with thin, angry with happy, relaxed with tense, etc. With the second idea (relationship) we might try other combinations: two people in love, one in love while the other is doubtful, a provoker and victim, one person pleading while the other holds out, people physically near but spiritually far apart, etc. For the third (near and far) let's try separating them farther, introducing soft focus to either the near or far person, have each in an entirely different light. With the fourth (relative obscurity) consider one person obscure and the other clearly seen, obscure in front and clear in back, reverse the two, etc. You should now see there are enough ideas here to keep anyone who is interested in male-female relationships busy for months. On your own you should add to these ideas as many more as you can.

photo by JO-ANN REDDING

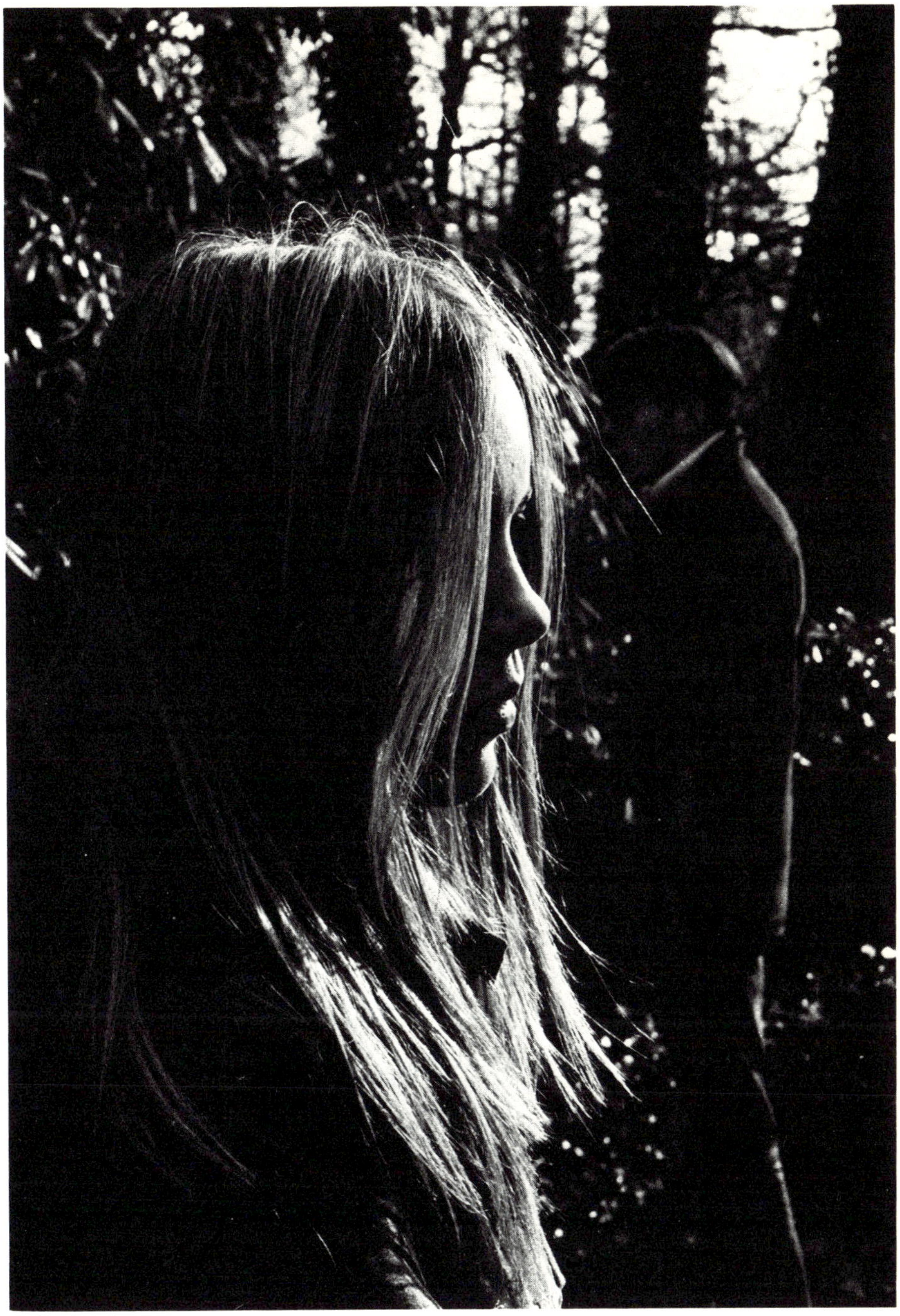

at, then develop it. From a third we take two ideas and combine them with three that we've already thought up. And from still another we borrow ideas used in one context and adapt them to a completely different one. Through such procedures we make the borrowed ideas our own.

If you find that deliberately mining photographs for ideas doesn't unduly disturb your ego, there remain only the problems of learning to recognize pictorial ideas when you see them and adapting them for pictures of your own. Neither process is easy—but does it really matter

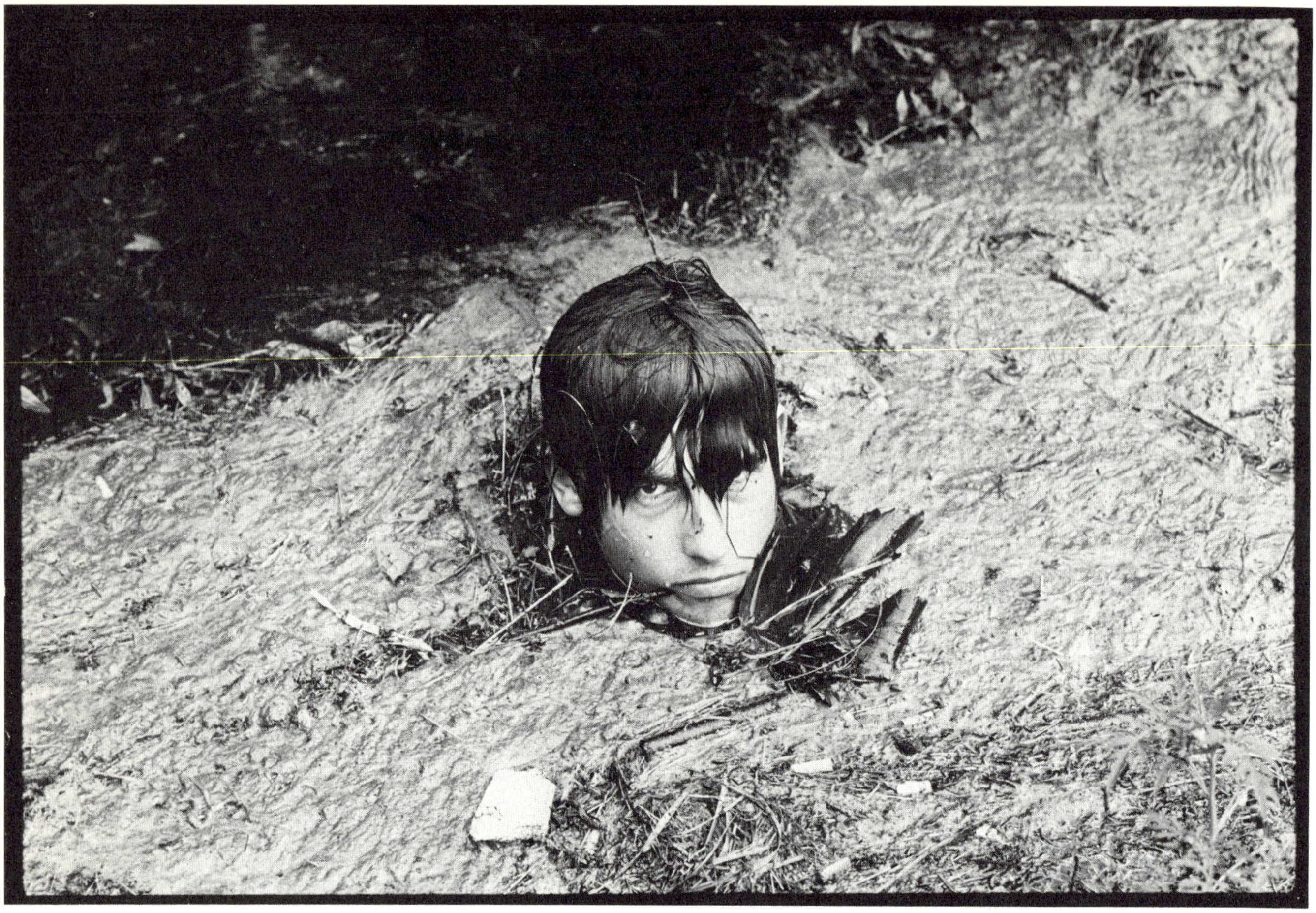

This is a self-portrait but it also shows a severed head with a certain antagonism toward people who react to it. It suggests two directions: decapitation portraits and kooky self-portraits. Start with the latter, but call it a messy self-portrait. Write a list of the messes you wouldn't mind dumping on yourself. Don't worry about the illogic of your behavior, for you can later make it seem logical when people admire your fascinating pictures. Now for decapitations: The commonest method is to put someone up to his neck in water or mud, but it can also be done with spotlights, montage, paste-up, etc.

photo by RON TUNISON

to you? Haven't you found that the tricky problems in photography make it more interesting?

For an initial experience in seeing how ideas can be dug out of pictures, try reading the captions accompanying the illustrations. These photographs are all by students in the three-year photography course at New York's School of Visual Arts. They were not done to illustrate this article but to solve problems set by various teachers or problems they thought up themselves. After reading the captions you might return to the text for some advice on idea-harvesting methods.

Harvesting and developing ideas can be either hard work or fun. Since the creative mind tends to grind to a halt when it is made to work, it is better to approach ideation as a game. Following are some mind-tickling games in common use among creative people.

Backwards: To a much greater degree than any of us realize we've been conditioned (like Pavlov's dogs) by education and experience. Thus when we try to think new thoughts we only come up with conditioned responses, that is, ideas already planted in our heads long ago by cultural influences. One way to break part-way

We seem to be looking at a man with a very long torso, with a weird twist in the part that is behind the panel. To borrow and adapt this idea easily, let's rephrase it: Parts of several things can be used in such a way they look as if they are of the same object. In a wild way, they can even look normal. You've noticed I left things out; they are the specifics and I used generalizations. Leaving out often opens up wider possibilities for an idea, such as two-headed people, six-legged ones, etc. Interesting ideas with inanimate things. Combinations of various species. Leave out or you'll merely copy.

photo by SHELDON LEVI

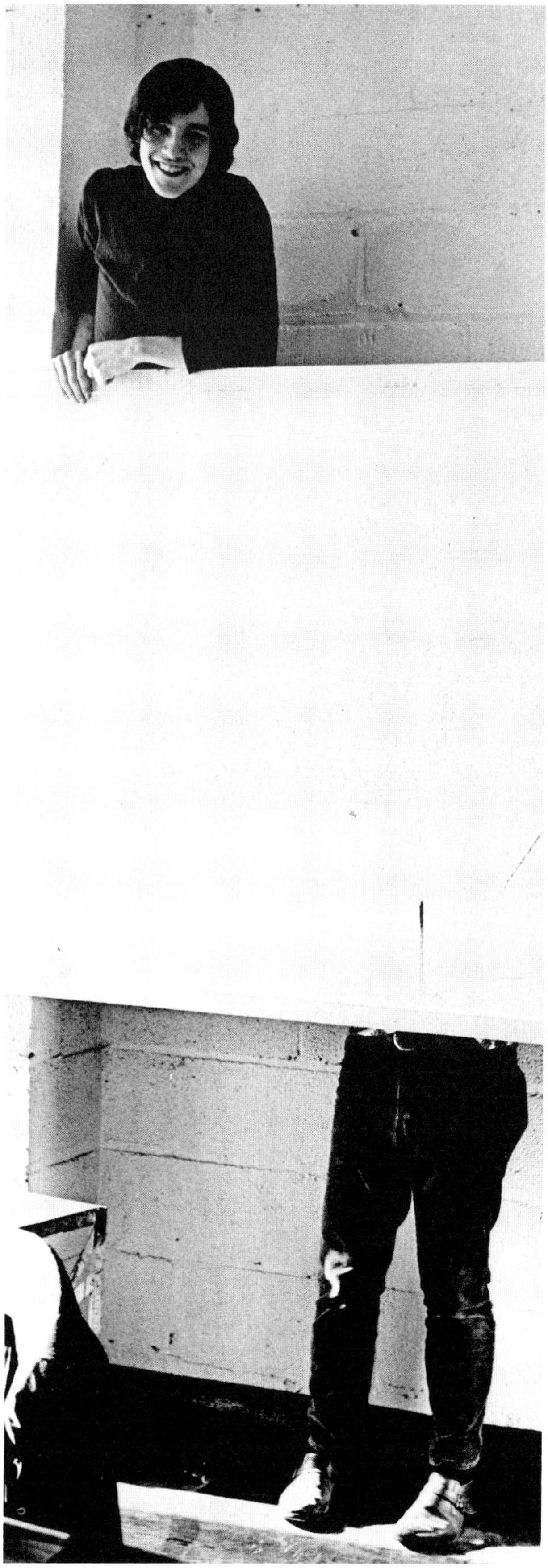

through this conditioning is to think backwards, or in as irrational a way as possible. For example, in trying to find a good use for an idea, start out by thinking of all the things it isn't good for. Push this to a point where your thinking seems completely preposterous. Be as silly about this as you can. This kind of behavior frees and excites the mind long enough so that it generates all kinds of ideas, both preposterous and entirely reasonable. Later, one can discard all the intentionally projected garbage and develop the good, new ideas that have slipped past the conditioning patterns in which the mind is usually imprisoned.

Dissection and discard: It can be said that any picture has one main idea and a lot of subordinate ones. For most people it's best to throw away the main ideas—they're often too abstract and philosophical—and play with the secondary ones. But first you have to dissect the picture thoroughly, making mental note of anything that happens to strike your eye, no matter how unimportant it may seem to you. Throw out the big ideas and play with the little ones. For example, the main idea of a picture might be that there is majesty in man, but majesty is terribly hard to grasp in a pictorial sense—unless it is phony majesty. So forget about it. Concentrate your attention on interesting details of lighting, expression, environment, pose, and so on. From what is happening in these areas you can get very specific ideas of things to try when photographing someone. If the only thought in your mind were "majesty" your creative thinking might very well stall. When you play with subordinate ideas, you often find they grow into major ideas in your own pictures, which is exactly what you want.

Opposites: Immediately after you've dug an idea out of a picture, try to think of its opposite. It may provide even better picture material than the original idea. For example, if you see a picture in which a mountain seems very solid and real you might ponder the means of making it look soft and ethereal. If a portrait technique makes a certain type of person look tender and sweet you might try to think of ways to make her appear bitchy. Frequently, you find that thinking about an idea in terms of its supposed opposites enables you to understand it better. If this happens you could then deliberately forget the notion of opposites and work with the original idea itself. Those who wish to increase their creativity should understand this very important thing: You do not have to carry out an idea just because you thought it up. In this case we've worked to think of opposites, then deliberately thrown them away. The principle is that the more ideas you throw away the more you'll get. But this can only happen if you don't permit yourself to feel guilty about discarding good concepts. On the other hand, if you think you should do something about every good idea you get, you'll soon dry yourself up.

Word lists: Many people have great difficulty in translating what they see in pictures into whole thoughts. All they get are disconnected fragments—feelings, words, impressions. There may be little or no mental coherence, which can be quite disturbing. Since a lot of terrific photographers have this problem it should not be seen as the great block to photographic creativity that it seems to be. These inchoate fragments that pop into mind can even be put to use for stimulating the gray cells. One way is to expend some effort trying to translate these feelings and impressions into words, then to write them down. It

Hippies asking for a handout, a common practice. Since most are middle class and intelligent, we assume they could get money in other ways. Begging may mean something else to them, like deliberately humbling oneself for spiritual development. Often it is aggressive role-playing to put on square people, sorely testing their patience and charity. Let's see what new ideas come up now. Imagine a picture story called "The Roles Beggars Play." They play them, of course, to get money through people's sympathy, guilt and fear. If you read Charles Dickens, you'll know that some people give a lot of thought to beggarly roles. For another source of ideas, consider self-humbling, some religions teach that it is good for the soul. You could photograph people who are trying this. Perhaps you could parody or illustrate the methods. The hippy's humility isn't believable, is it?

photo by MEHDI KHONSARI

If the feather picture merely turns you on to feathers, fine. They're photogenic. Analyzing the picture can help us go beyond feathers. An object is being dramatized through association with a favorite subject, the setting sun. Sunsets are popular dramatizers; try them. Try going far out with small, very small or minute objects. Try indoor objects outdoors, ugly things with sunset beauty, things never before seen in a sunset, your aunt's goldfish, for example. Don't light your subjects with the sunset but with special lights, such as candles, flashlights, matches, auto headlights, or a regular bare lightbulb. Stage a dawn-type tableau or a police court scene. Make a heroic picture of your dog or a haunting one of your cat seen as a tiger. Shoot a silver wedding picture of your great aunt Emma.

photo by MARTIN H. SCHREIBER

You can mine a picture for ideas by merely making a list of all the things you see in it. Then you can recombine them in new environments for your own pictures. In the picture of the girl (far right) we see a face, part of a plant, large dark areas, smaller areas of mid-tone and minute light areas. Now list what is happening to them: the girl's eye obscured by the leaf, parts of her body by shadow. What are the expressions? The plant is serious and sedate but the girl's expression is strange; she seems ambivalent about being photographed. How do you feel about things? Hot for the girl? Jealous of the plant? Curious about the photographer who made the picture? Gather a bunch of observations and impressions and see if they help you make a picture which adapts and uses some of them.

photo by DAVID McNEIL

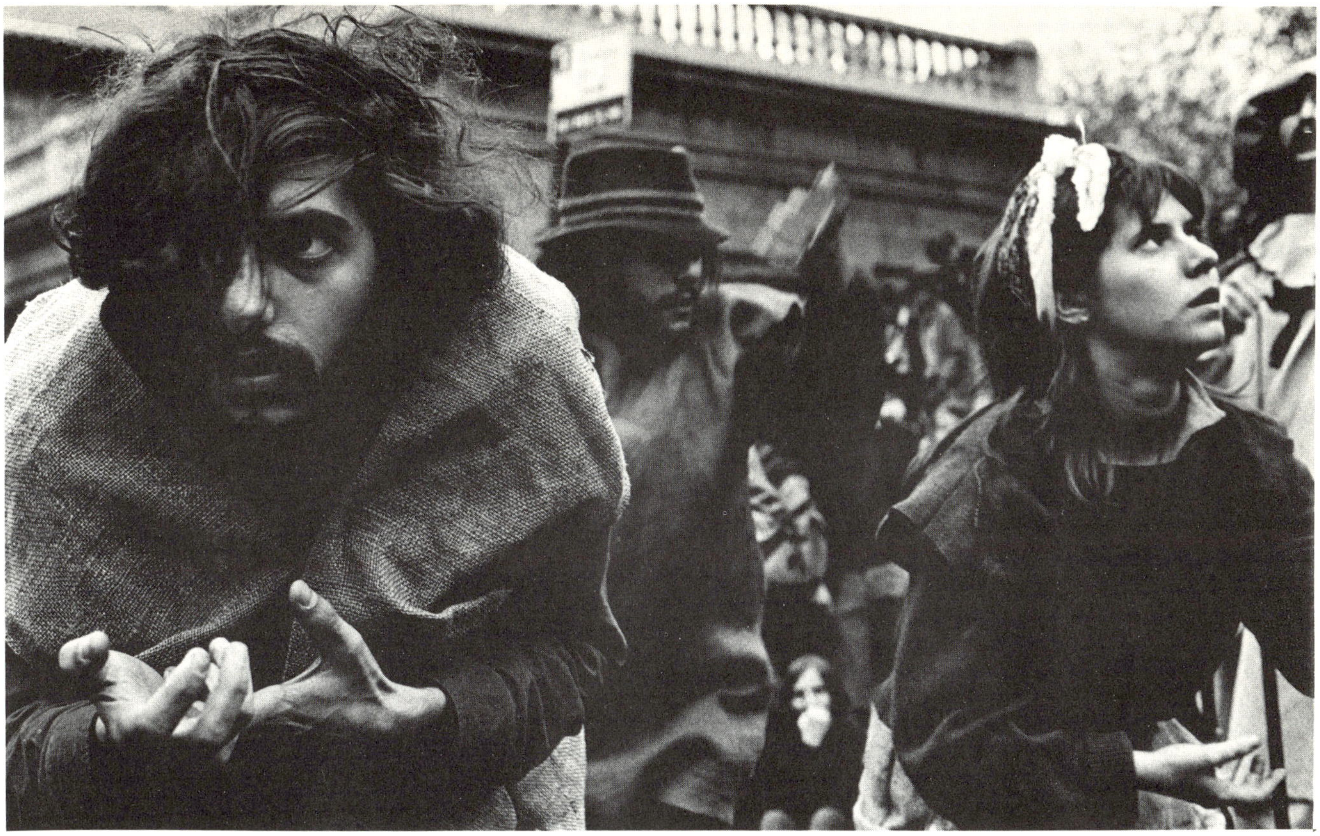

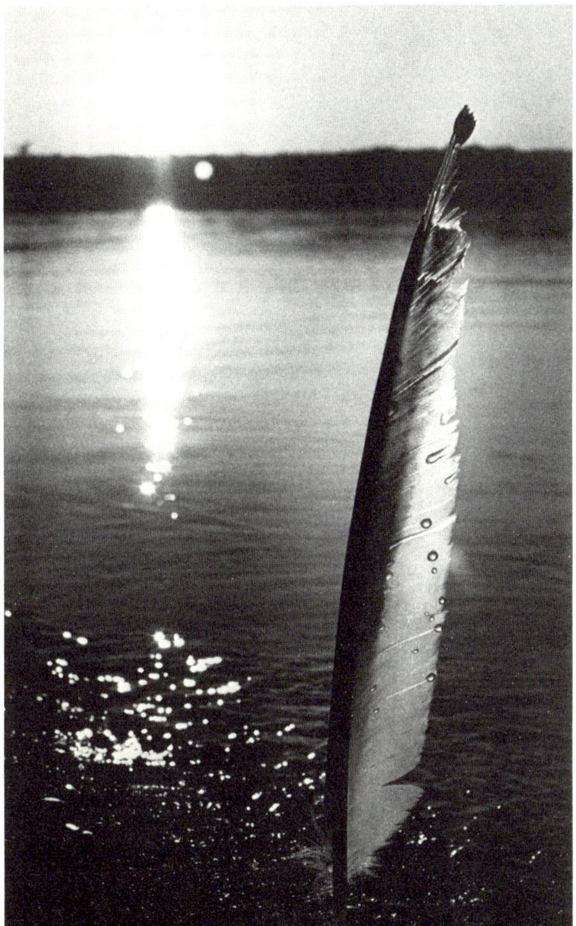

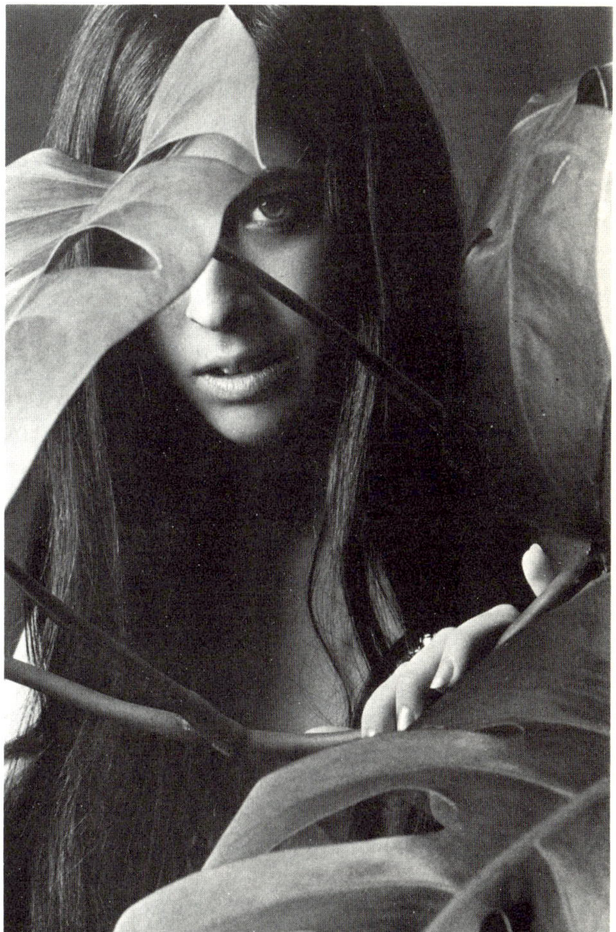

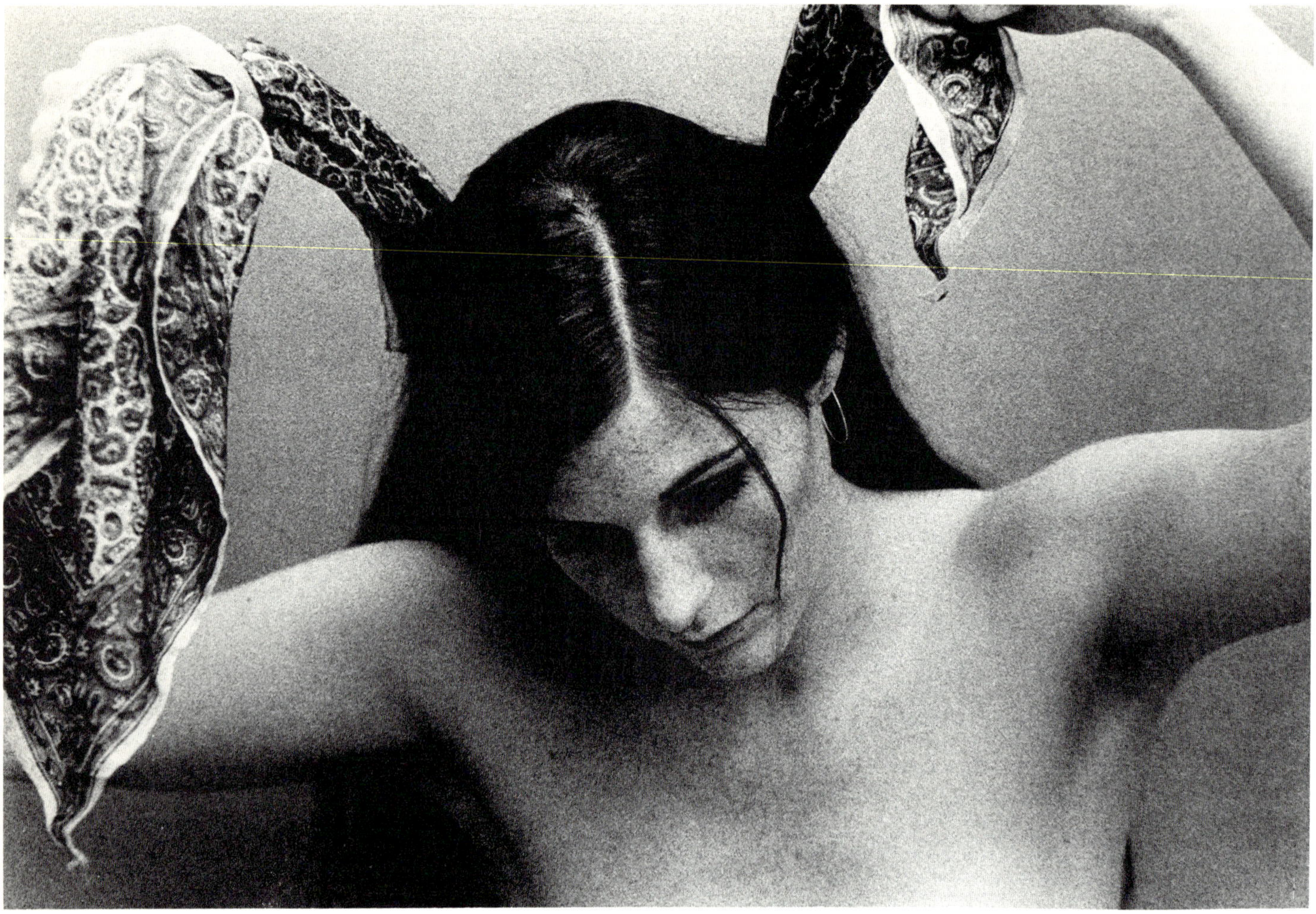

is not at all important if the words are misspelled, sloppily written down, meaningless to people other than oneself, even relatively meaningless to the person who writes them down. Nor does it matter whether they're nouns, adjectives, or verbs, or even if the photographer doesn't know one part of speech from the other. The point is just to jot them down any old way, then to look at the list to let it stimulate the mind.

Permission: Strange as it seems, people may have few ideas because they won't permit themselves to have more. Their problem is that they've had little respect for the few ideas they've had and they've unconsciously denied themselves permission to have any more, lest they be embarrassed by them. It would help them if they knew that the very best idea people come up with whole truckloads of ideas that are literally terrible. They've learned to overcome their pain at seeing corny, dumb, meaningless ideas pop out of their own heads. They've learned through experience that if they just let all this trash spill out unchecked something good will eventually come up. In other words, they've given their minds permission to work the way minds like to work, which is mainly illogically and irresponsibly. They've granted themselves permission, as it were, to be only human.

One of the easiest ways to begin to give yourself permission to function freely and creatively as a photographer is to do it formally as a proclamation to yourself. Make a list of things you think you should let yourself do, then read it aloud to yourself. Do this again and again and again. The

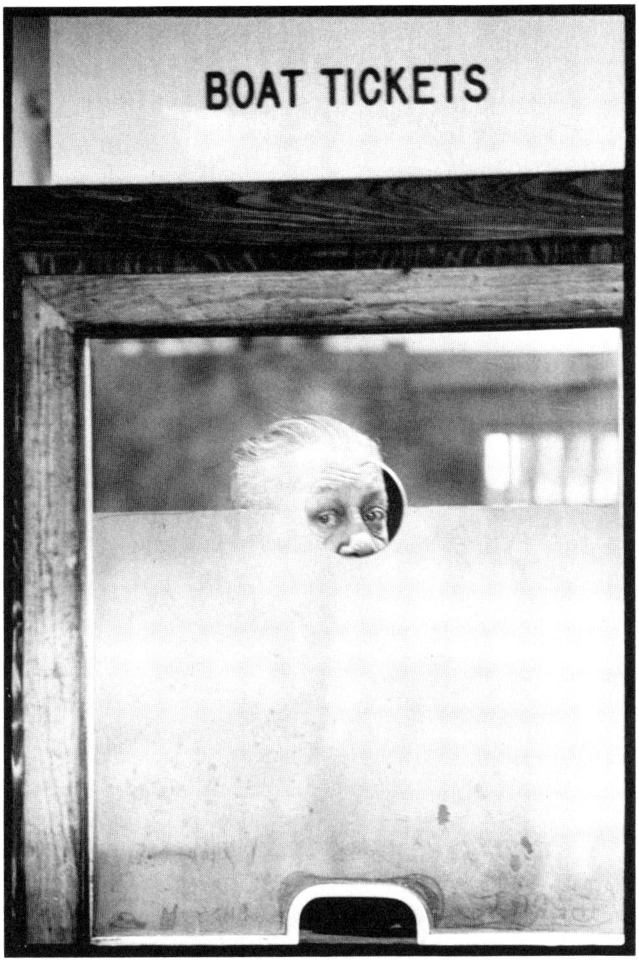

A pretty girl tying her hair (far left) is an old theme in photography. How can you make it fresh again for yourself? The best answer: Don't try too hard. Just photograph as if you'd never seen it before; your pictures will be vital enough. Look for new viewpoints. Try making yourself aware of your young lady's constantly shifting emotional states. Ask her to think thoughts romantic to her and see what they do to her. Think such thoughts yourself and see how they change your pictures. Then think critically of her awhile, see how your vision changes. Try imagining how she was ten years ago and how she'll be forty years from now. As you change your thoughts your vision will change. Try gimmicks such as far, medium, close and super-close-up shots. Try talking too much when close to her to see the effect. Stand back silent with a telephoto lens and be as much like wallpaper as you can: invisible, non-threatening, silent.

photo by CAROLYN BRAUN

Apprehensive peeping from a place of safe concealment (left). We all find peeping an attractive idea, so it has many picture possibilities. Safely hidden ourselves, we'd like to peep on others, a primitive survival instinct, no doubt. The seer has the advantage over the seen. Now think of some of the types of seeing from hidey-holes. There are frightened peeping, lascivious, cute (as in baby animals or children), the contemplative peeping of the hungry carnivore. Men adore the flirtatious peeping of pretty girls.

photo by DENNIS McGUIRE

unconscious part of the mind, which is the mother of creativity and endlessly amenable to suggestion, will respond gladly to this and start throwing out new ideas by the carload. Oddly enough, this repetitious permission-giving will work fairly well even if you are consciously aware that you may not *really* be giving it. It works better, of course, if you truly mean it.

What should appear on a given list will vary with the individual. My own list would read more or less as follows: I hereby give myself permission to have ideas (or make pictures) that are (1) half-baked, (2) juvenile, (3) imitative, (4) cliché, (5) illogical, (6) just plain dumb, (7) corny, (8) gooily sentimental, (9) incomprehensible to others, (10) incomprehensible to myself, (11) ambivalent, (12) basically pointless, etc. I furthermore permit myself to make half-baked imitations of Ansel Adams, Edward Weston, Cartier-Bresson, Wingate Paine, Bruce Davidson, Elliott Erwitt, John Smith, Mamie Snorkel, my stepson Jonathan, or anyone else who ever pushed a camera shutter button. I permit myself to make pictures I alone like, snapshots, record shots, pictures of things I like, others of things I hate, and still others of things I don't really know whether I like or dislike. Though this personal list goes on to much greater length, I think we can arbitrarily end it here. The point is that people can give themselves permission to do specific kinds of things, deliberately impress it on their unconscious minds, and end up having more of their natural creativity liberated.

I hope you enjoy playing some of these games. They are tried and true creativity stimulators that have been in use for hundreds of years. With a little ingenuity

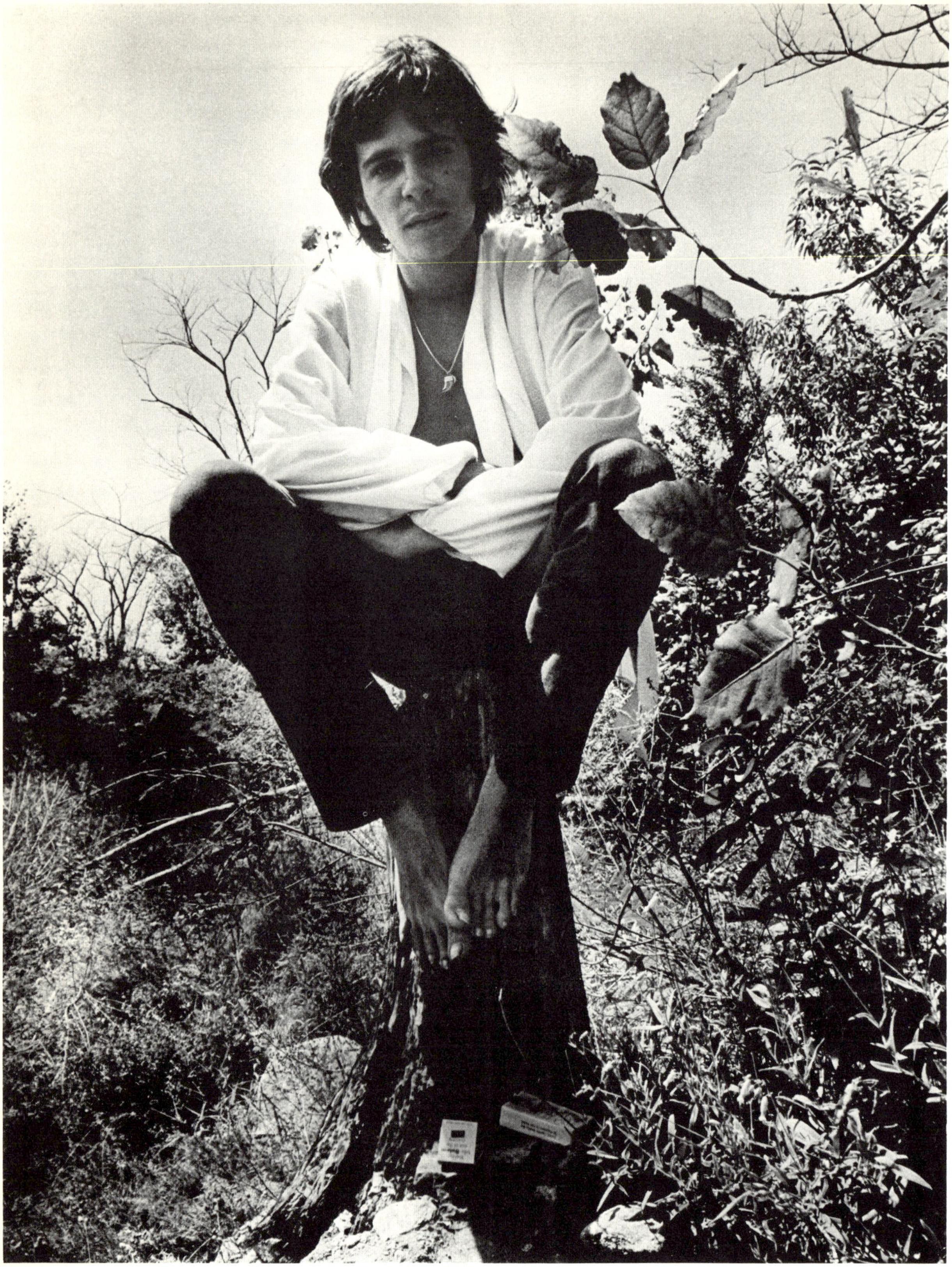

What can we steal from this pic of a young man on a most uncomfortable roost? Why not roosting as a characteristic of the young? They're like tigers roosting, aren't they? So graceful and poised in such absurd places. How many places are there for youngsters to roost in? Think of things for them to do on their perches: drink sodas, hang by their tails, gather in coveys, carry on histrionics, talk about Siddhartha, gab on telephones. Try spending a day looking for especially improbable roosts, then see if you can get anyone to occupy them. Tired of kids? See if you can get older folk to hang by their heels from a banister or recline on bookcases with martinis or mandolins.

photo by MARK W. CHIN

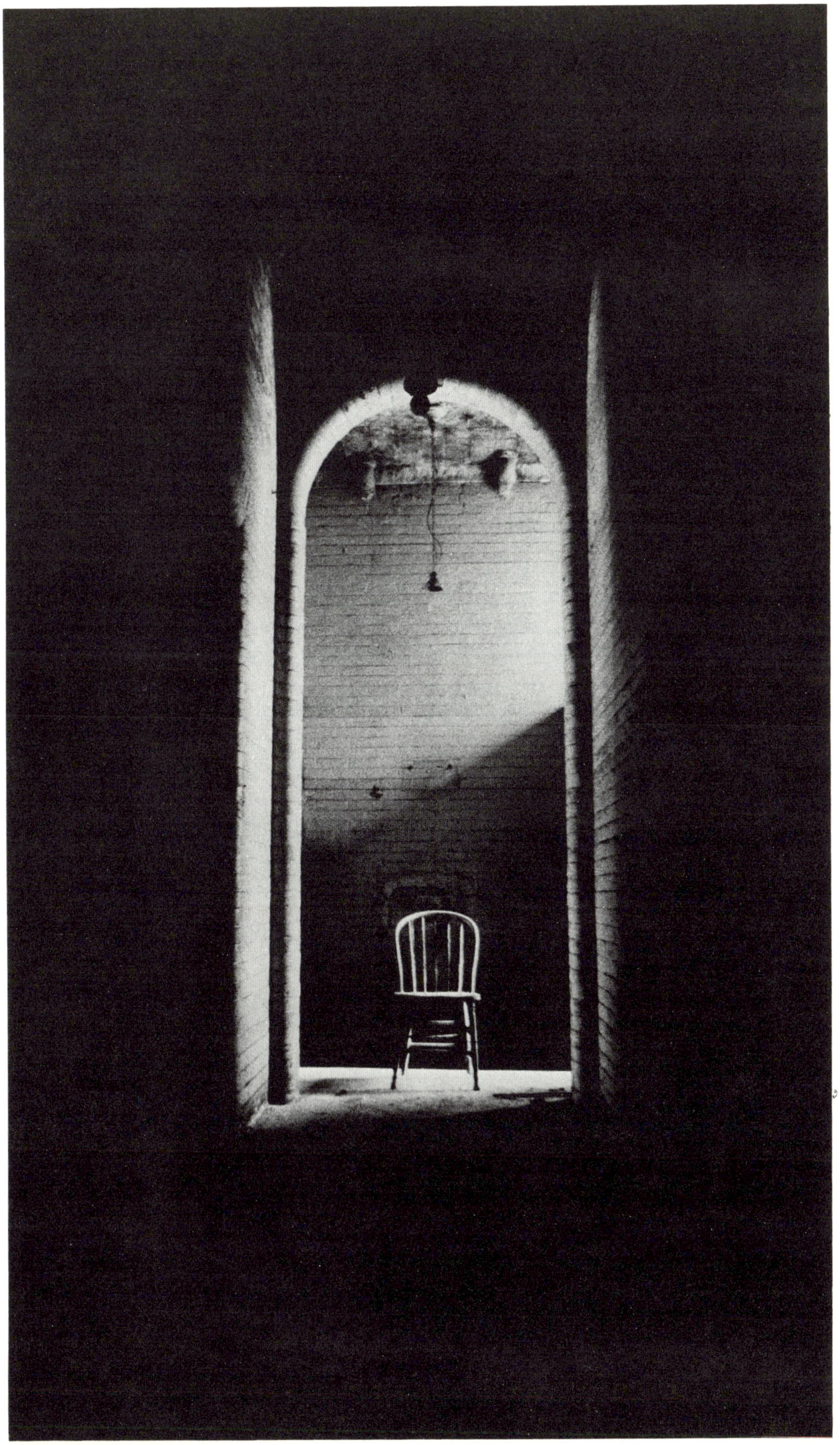

In the School of Visual Arts in New York this picture caused much creative borrowing. A whole class asked their teacher to let them use it as a basis of an assignment. As the theme is here it's an old chair in a darkened hallway. We needn't stop here, however, but might expand our thinking by attaching adjective to chair—lonely chair, ghostly chair, broken, old, evil, sweet, insane. Try the same thing with hallway—dark, light, soft-focus, sharp-focus, clean, weird. Try starting with the kind of picture you want, then fitting a chair into it somehow. Don't be afraid of goofy ideas unrelated to chairs; they may prove very interesting after you've thought them over.

photo by VALERIE ADAMI

Let's catalogue the obvious, then jump into something unique. The picture below has a nude man, rooftop, skyline, sunset. With these elements alone you could make many exciting pictures. Let's now stretch out in a stranger direction: Consider the buildings as phallic symbols. Not softly organic, of course, but at least longish and erect. Let's now redefine the project: nude man with phallic symbols; nude woman with vaginal symbols; nude of one sex with the symbols of the opposite. Oddly, people really enjoy working with symbols of their own sex.

photo by VALERIE ADAMI

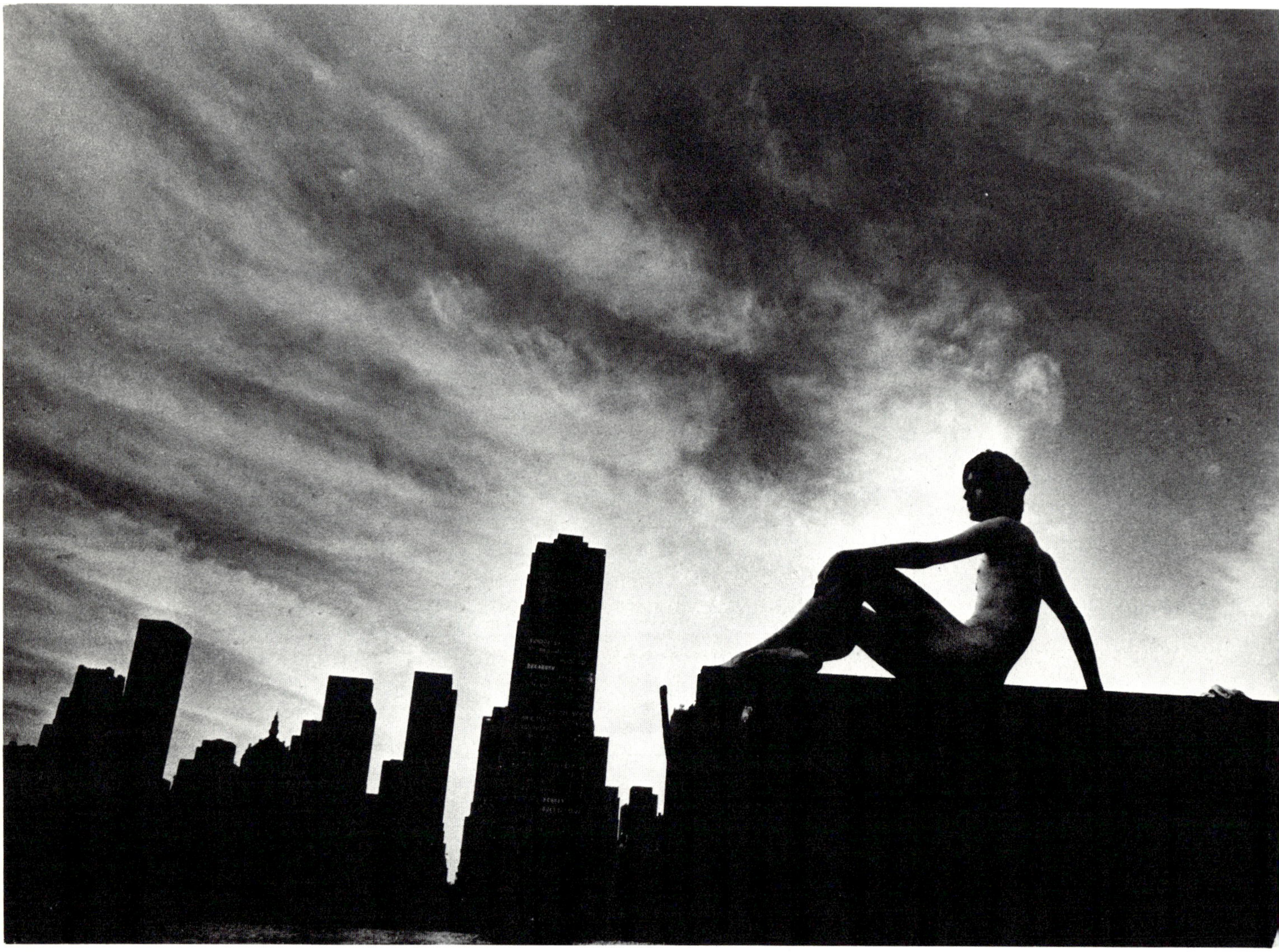

you can think up others for yourself.

How to Make a Left Turn off the Beaten Path

In this lesson we have some more techniques for generating original ideas. It also gets into some techniques you can use to learn if you're programmed or conditioned. If you know or suspect that you are, you may find my advice useful. For people who are heavily conditioned it will be useful only on the level of thinking up new ideas. Such people invariably think they're not conditioned at all. Naturally, they see no point in struggling to overcome an affliction they're sure they haven't got.

My point of view is that all of us are conditioned to a terrifying degree and that the situation is rapidly getting worse. The more we develop our so-called civilization the faster it turns us into automata. My views in this respect have been strengthened and greatly amplified by the teachings of Gurdjieff, Ouspensky, Idries Shah, Maurice Nicoll and others. My investigations of Zen, Sufism, Vedanta and esoteric Christianity have similarly strengthened my opinion. At the same time, I've learned that it is nearly futile to talk about or protest the conditioning, though it greatly lessens our humanity. People refuse to believe the bitter truth about themselves.

People who suspect they're conditioned will find some starting places for unwinding the nets in which they've entrapped themselves. Those who do not suspect will enjoy the techniques for idea creation.

The Lesson:

Nearly all photographers follow well-beaten paths, though they generally are not very aware that they are doing so. They get on these paths by unconsciously imitating what other photographers are doing, or they gradually build up paths of their own, also more or less unconsciously. Following a path gives one a great sense of security and a feeling that he really knows what he is doing and where he is going. However, it also leads to dull pictures. For this reason it makes good sense for a person to try to get off the track now and then.

Most people have a great deal of difficulty in turning off the path. For one thing, they don't realize they are actually on one in the first place. They have little idea of what makes up the path. And they lack the courage to be nonconformists. Furthermore, they see no virtue in nonconformity.

The objective of this lesson is to try to persuade you to try a little nonconformity—this has a very salubrious effect on the soul—and to give you some idea how this can be done, once you've made up your mind to it.

The first thing to do is realize that you are on a path, whether you are a beginner, advanced amateur, or pro. This may be very difficult for you to accept, so you have to do a lot of thinking about yourself and your photographs in order to see it. Then you have to discover what constitutes your personal path. This, again, is not at all easy. Were I to tell you that it is, I would do you a great disservice. However, once you've discovered what your path is, getting off it is the easiest thing in the world—if you have the courage. Make no mistake about the need for courage. I suppose it's very easy to kill dragons, too—if you have the courage.

To discover what your path is, you have to learn to observe yourself as you photograph. You will find that certain types of shooting come easily, logically, automatically, and comfortably. This indicates that you are squarely centered in the safety of your path. However, the outlines of your track may still be obscure to you. To see them better you have to learn to frighten or upset yourself deliberately by going against what is easy, logical, automatic, and comfortable. Here is where the courage comes in. Our best photographers have always been the most courageous (though no writer has ever thought to mention this) and that is why their pictures are interesting. They have the nerve to step off the beaten path and risk being laughed at. They also have learned to accept the fact that when a person is being his most creative, he often feels as if he might be a fool or a madman. Creativity has its price, which is one reason there is so little of it in the world of photography or elsewhere.

When you are observing yourself while photographing something (in order to discover what comes easily, logically, automatically, and comfortably) and noting what specific things you do all the while, the next thing to do is try to think of other ways of going about making your picture. Look for ideas that upset you. If such ideas don't come naturally, you

Tiny figures in a large surrounding, far from everyday picture thinking. Isn't one supposed to get close to people he's photographing? Nuts! Play the game imaginatively, get as far away as you'd like. See if you can work out tricks for making people visible when they're blocks away. They'd be visible on snow, too.

photo by STEVE WILSON

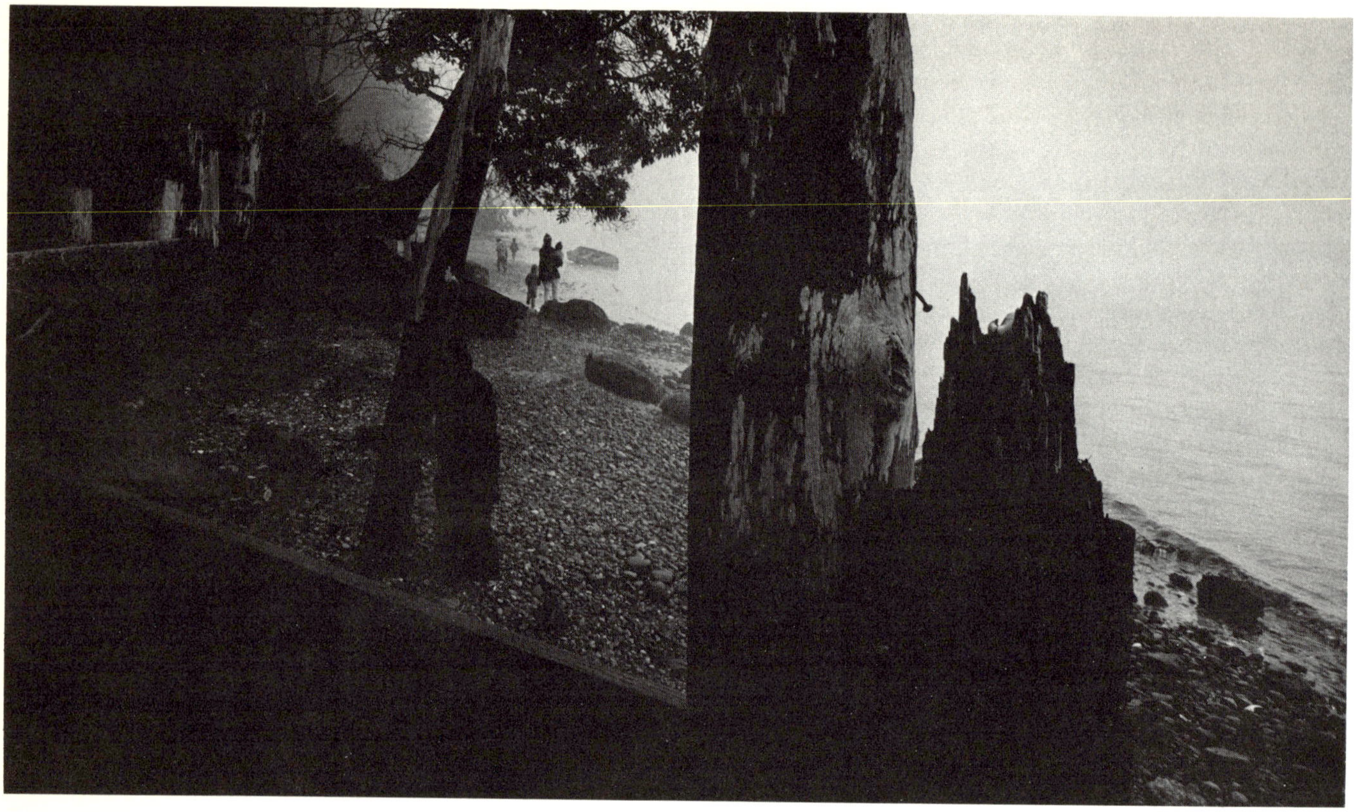

should deliberately set out to make them come. You may have to practice this quite a bit. These upsetting ideas define the boundaries of your personal beaten path. They upset you because they are off the path. You should force yourself to try some of these ideas. This is where the payoff is.

Let us see how this might work in practice. A photographer discovers during self-observation that in making pictures of people he invariably has them at least six feet from his camera. In trying to think of other things he might do, he notices that the thought of coming up close to them with his camera gives him a twinge. So this is precisely what he does, thus expanding his scope of people photography and making possible certain insights into himself and his relations with people. The price he pays in discomfort is eventually repaid by more self-understanding. Let us say he carries this further. He observes that when a girl looks at him at a short camera distance he is acutely uncomfortable, so he deliberately asks her to do it, thus once more expanding his range as a photographer and getting pictures that are, for him, very original and creative. Of course, this takes courage on the part of a person so affected by the proximity and glances of a girl. And he might have to work close to people with his camera for months before he makes a significant breakthrough in his personal and photographic limitations. But it's worth it—really and truly worth it to achieve this victory.

Another photographer observes that he seems overconcerned with holding his camera level, so he deliberately goes against his grain by tilting it now and then. Though his tilted pictures upset him considerably at first, in part because the tilting as such makes no particular sense, he eventually learns to make tilt an effective

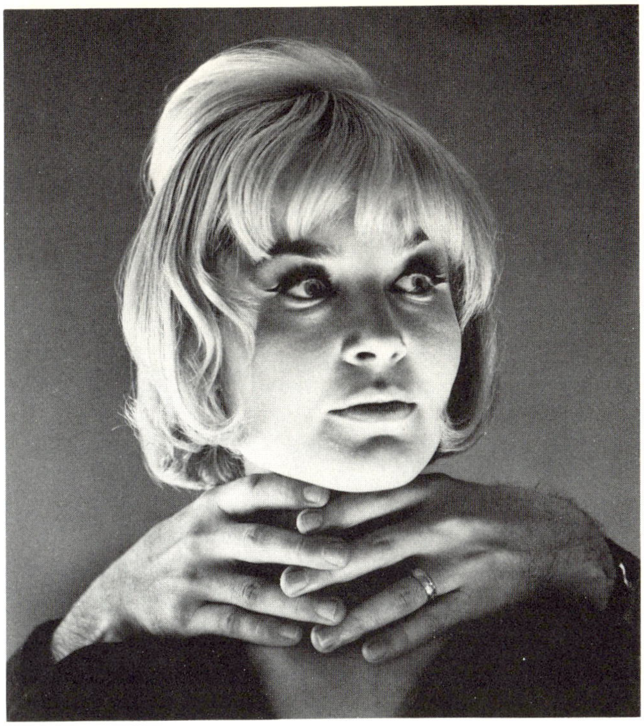

Right face, wrong hands—is it madness or creativity? Do you really know the difference? The idea of mismatching parts goes back to ancient times and is still very popular. It kind of stirs up the ghoul in each of us. Could you mismatch grandpa with his cow somehow?

Serious picture of a make-believe devil (below). Does it follow the beaten path? Of course not. Why not try doing a few serious things lightly with your camera, and some funny or silly things with deadly seriousness? Actually, this is an old trick that is still effective.

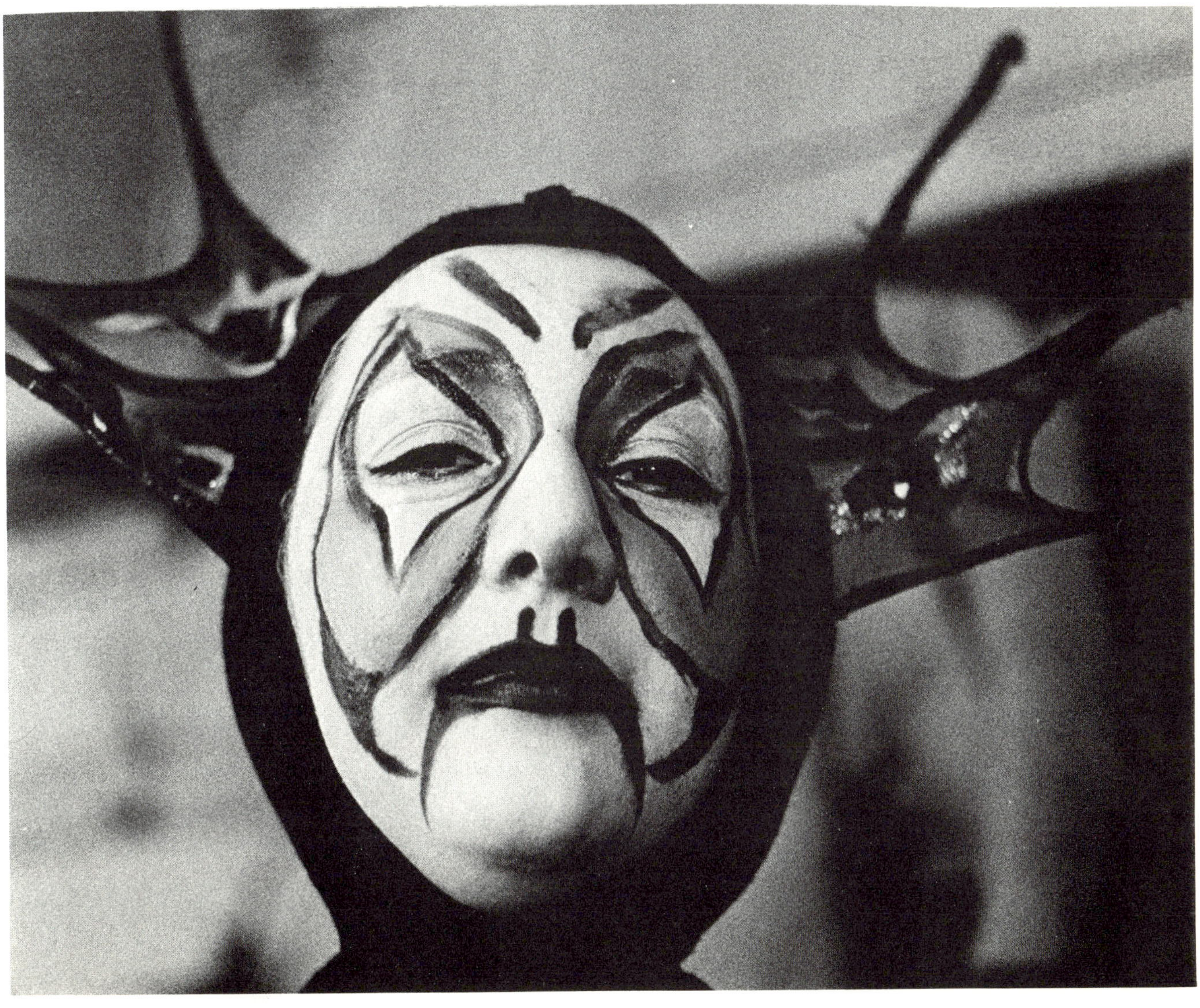

A heterosexual in drag is enough to pull any photographer off the beaten path, provided he's alert enough to see that there is something slightly unusual happening. Or is it really so unusual?

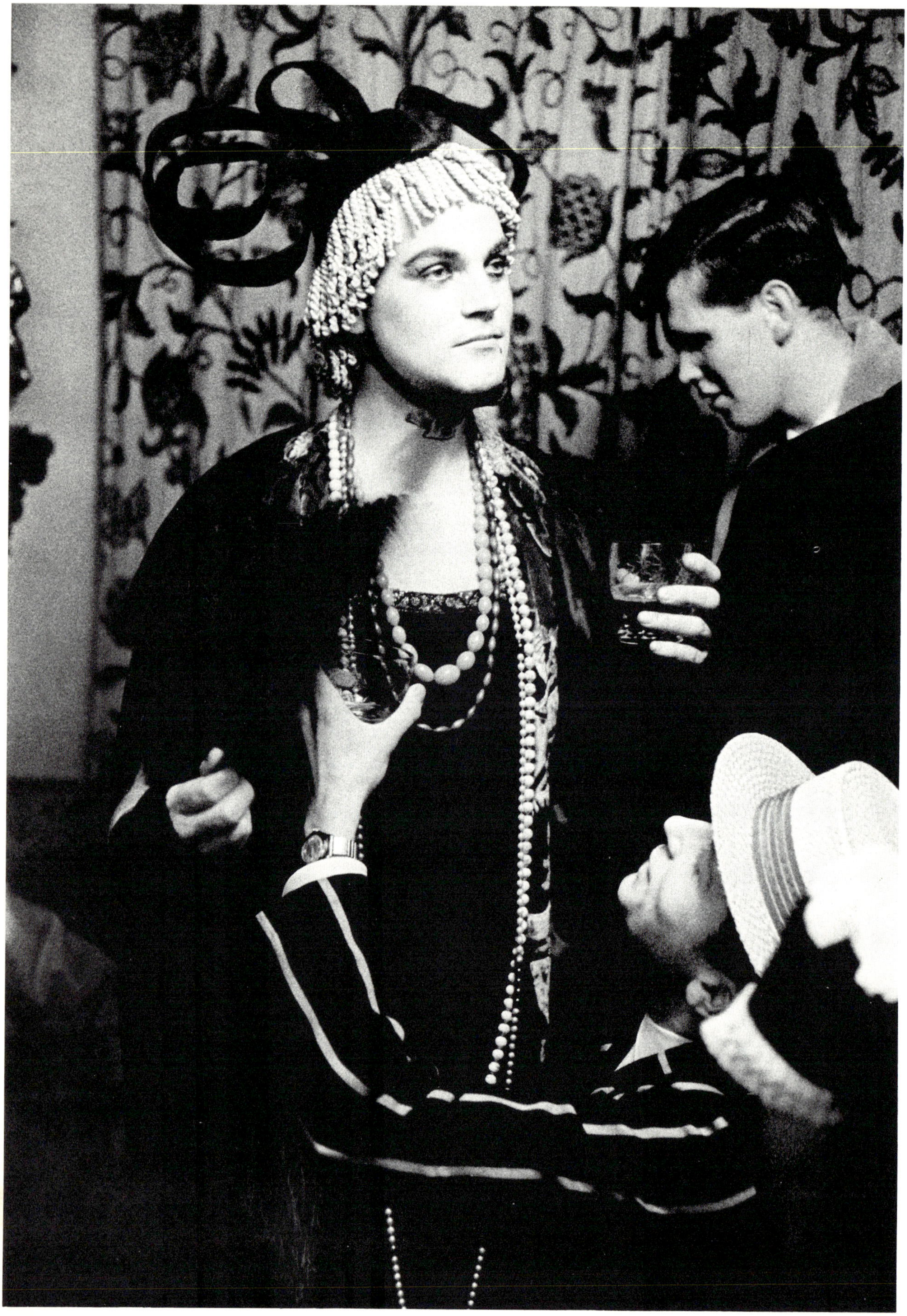

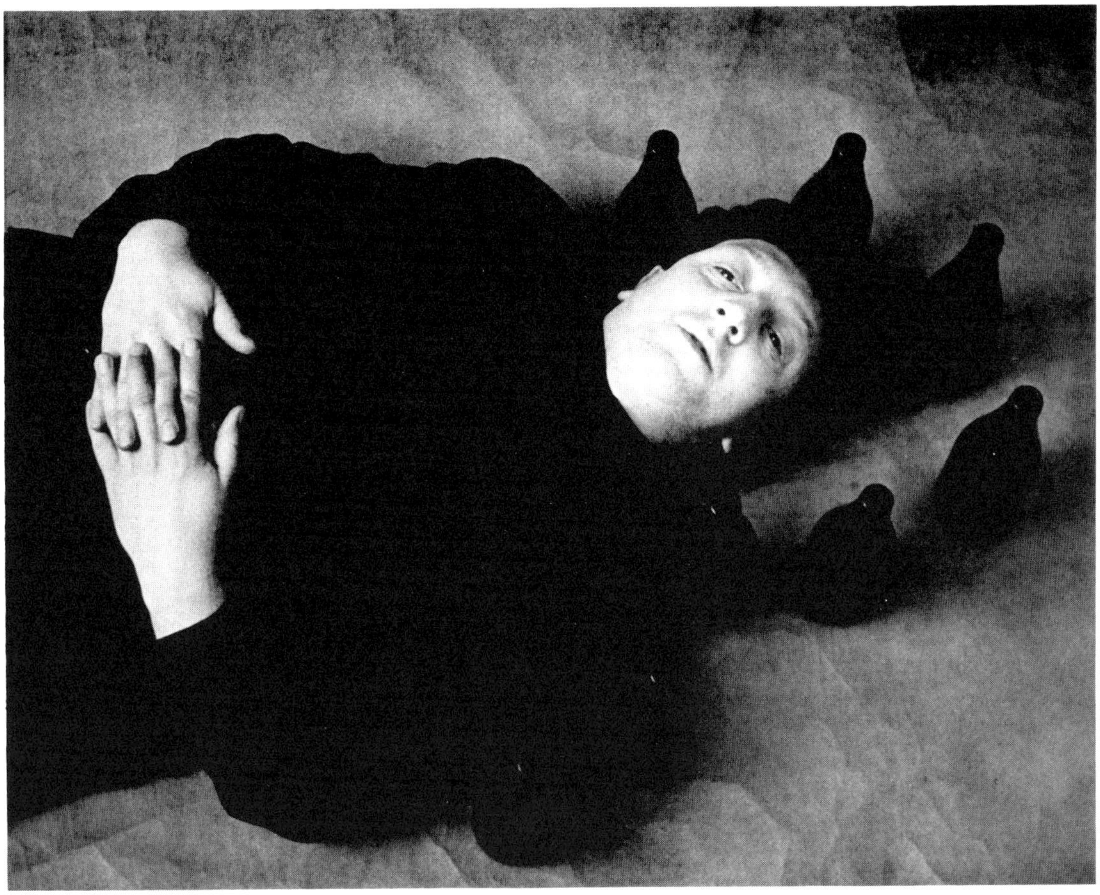

How not to take a portrait (left). I'll admit I felt quite odd in asking Tony Morton to lie on his back while I did a portrait of him and quite out of my mind when I added the beer bottles, though beer is his favorite food. But Tony didn't think this strange at all. Later he told me that something deeply representative of his real self had entered into the picture. Thus my 'insanity' had resulted in honest character interpretation.

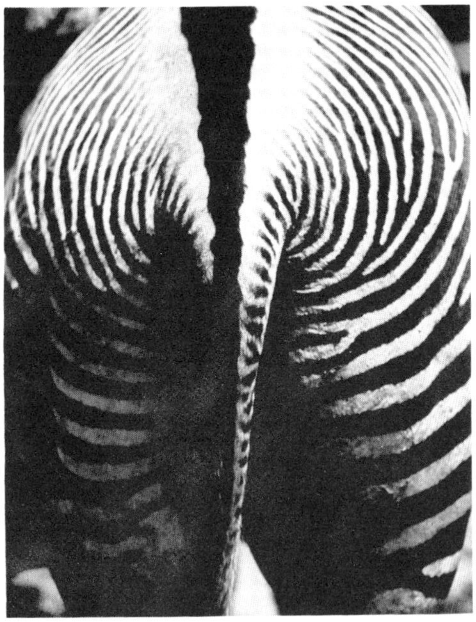

Zebra bottom got my attention, but I don't remember why. Perhaps it was the only part close to me. Or maybe I had an Oriental death wish of some kind. Ridiculous, isn't it? The real reason was that zebra bottoms are like moving Rorschach tests, good for psyching oneself.

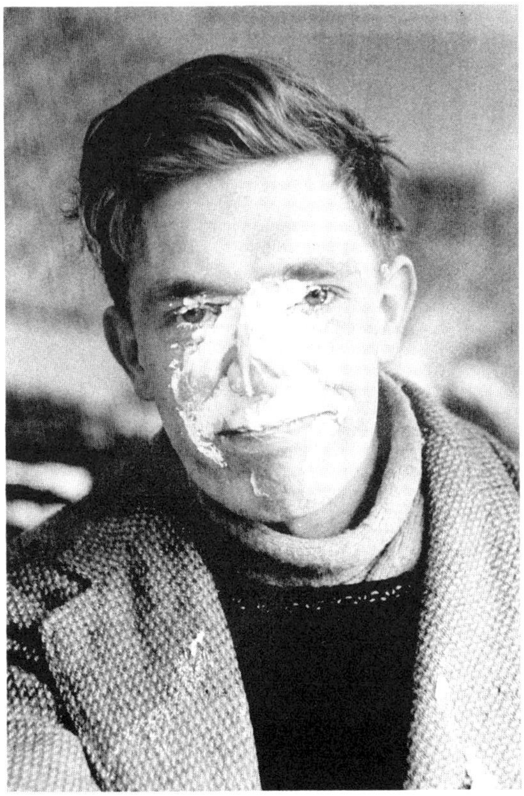

When one friend shoves a pie in another friend's face (left) it gets the photographer off the beaten path in a hurry. The victim spoiled the joke by not blowing his cool. The joker got me with a pie too.

and reasonable factor in certain kinds of pictures. Thus, by jousting with himself he has expanded his photographic world.

I hope you've grasped the general idea by now—that you've got to fight against your natural inclinations to get off your beaten path or even to discover what it is. Please do not accuse me of recommending senseless masochism or of trying to take the joy out of photography. If you don't compete with yourself, the joy will soon leave you anyway; your photography will become an empty, idiot game. And you will completely miss a much greater joy—that of discovering and defeating the limitations to your creativity and personal growth. If in other writings I've given the impression that photographic creativity is merely a fun thing, I'm sorry. It is obviously much more than that. However, photographic writers tend to discuss photography as if it didn't really mean anything deep to people. I think it does—or can, if the people are perceptive.

Creative Destruction

Here are more techniques for generating original ideas and more information on conditioning, which is herein called attachment or identification. To a limited degree, the mind can outwit the mind. That is, the tiny part of the mind which is still relatively free can occasionally outwit the mass of the mind, which is thoroughly mechanized. Learning to play this game is a very good thing, for it can eventually lead you to see what a sorry pickle you've gotten yourself into and that there is still a faint hope you can get out again.

The lesson ends with the exhortation: Be creative. I will now formally amend it: Use the tiny remainder of your creativity to penetrate the fog of your conditioning and free your mind to do its duty in serving your Higher Self. This may sound like I'm offering you a very sour apple. I am, but your system deeply craves it.

If you're interested in following up on the idea of conditioning you might start by reading the *Bhagavad-Gita,* in which it is called attachment. From this classic text you'll certainly get the idea that conditioning is not a very good thing. For writing closer to the Western mind, try the works of Idries Shah. The subject is taken up again in Chapter Six of this book, but not in great detail.

The Lesson:

One of the fascinations of photography is the discovery that it can be a subtle and demanding craft. No matter how much sensitivity and technique you pour into a photograph, it can still absorb more. This is a great challenge, of course. But it can lead to the hang-up of being overimpressed with craftsmanship at the expense of everything else. People who fall in this trap generally turn themselves into unhappy, nit-picking old maids who are terrified of making technical mistakes. To avoid them, they conduct endless experiments with technical trivialities or ceaselessly repeat past technical triumphs.

The cure for this morbid craftsmanship hang-up is simple, inspired anticraftsmanship. Or call it creative destruction. Though this may seem like a weird notion, it really isn't, for destruction is often just another form of creation. Destruction per se can clear the way for more creation. You knock down an old building to put up a new one. Or you can destroy restrictive notions in your mind and thus make way for ideas with greater scope. In expanding your creativity, destruction is necessary.

Those who are relatively new to photography may not know that creative destruction has a time-honored place in it. But the old hands realize that creative photography today is what it is largely because of the destructive-constructive play of creative rebels. In this lesson we'll adopt the approaches they've used successfully.

The creators have always been eager to discover things they weren't supposed to do. For example, they study Kodak bulletins and booklets avidly, looking for instructions such as: Never do this to film or you'll ruin your picture. This is the very first thing they try. Not just once, but again and again—until they know all the graphic variations of the ruin they are being warned against.

Somewhere along the line they hope to find a variation with interesting visual possibilities. Then they experiment with it industriously until they learn to control it. You might say they're searching for *controllable* ruin. An example would be a technique that loosens gelatin from film base. One would want it loosened in a particular way and to a certain degree, but not so much that it would slide down the drain.

The creatively inclined student should start keeping a personal Thou Shalt Not list. From time to time he should select one item and experiment extensively with it, inventing every variation he can on how to do what he isn't supposed to do. Helpful hint: If you'd like to try to get a jump on the pros, pick things you think no one in his right mind would try. They've already tried most of them, but you might find something they've missed. And don't be upset to learn you're not the first to try printing a negative through a slice of Swiss cheese. Even if you don't try any of your ideas, just methodically keeping a list will tend to stir up your creative gray cells.

My experience is that many photographers have an almost insurmountable resistance to trying creative destruction. Unconsciously, they feel like mothers being asked to destroy their children. There's more to it than that, but it's a hang-up psychologically described as being "attached to" or "identified with" one's work. It's a bad bag. Doing creative destruction many times in a straightforward way is one way of eventually getting out of it. It can be painful and discouraging, however. I recommend the Wise Man's Formula: When confronted by an impenetrable wall, don't try to ram through it with your head. Find a path around it. Beat your head on lesser walls until it gets hard enough for heavy-duty work. Since you yourself create the walls, the trick is to outwit yourself and find your way around them.

Defeat the 'mother chicken' hang-up:

1. On a given subject, create so many extra children (negatives, transparencies, prints, etc.) that you don't mind bumping off a few. The more they're alike, the less you'll miss them. For example, shoot a scene or still life exactly the way you want it. Then, being sure not to change anything, shoot an extra roll or half-roll to get negatives to play with. Be sure to have *lots* of extras, or the mother chicken syndrome will continue to exert a powerful effect.

2. Create *exact* duplicate children (copy negatives, copy transparencies, etc.) in such abundance that you'd feel foolish not to get rid of at least *some* of them.

3. Create idiot children and practice creative euthanasia. Relax your technical discipline in printing, making wild guesses at exposure. Snapshoot things you don't give much of a damn about one way or another. Shoot pictures for the wrong reasons, or no reason at all.

4. Stop lying to yourself about the idiot children you already have and subject them to creative destruction. Remember that this is a magical process that might even transform the ugly little trolls into fairy queens. But if you continue to try to convince yourself that your failures are successes, you'll evenutally strip your own gears.

I'm sometimes accused of exaggerating the psychology bit, but the fact is I've had hundreds of students hung up in the mother chicken role. In its various disguises, it's one of the biggest hang-ups in photography. So I don't feel a bit embarrassed about suggesting workable techniques for getting you out of this dead end. If the techniques help you as a person, too —fine!

The editors picked my most conservative destructions: out-of-focus, double exposure, trick printing—old stuff. Okay. You can be conservative too, if you like. But you should have seen my print from a negative sandwiched with chipped beef. My experiments with Drano solution were great. And I had ten ways for using heat in creative destruction. Ah, well . . . the point is, be creative.

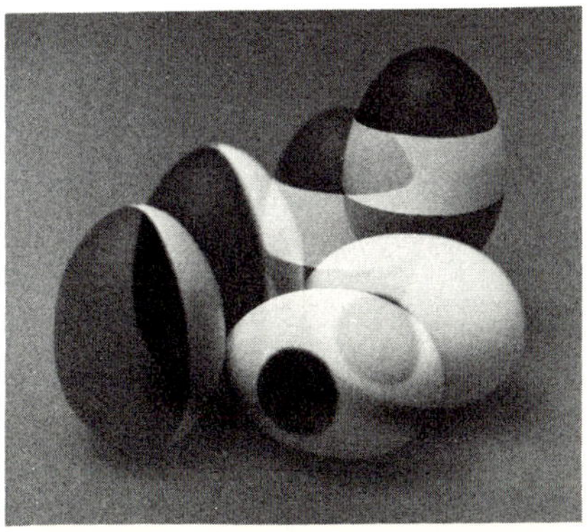

Multiple exposures flip you out in a hurry, especially if you don't keep track of what is on each frame of film. Two or three people can multiple expose the same roll of film and have a whee of a time printing it.

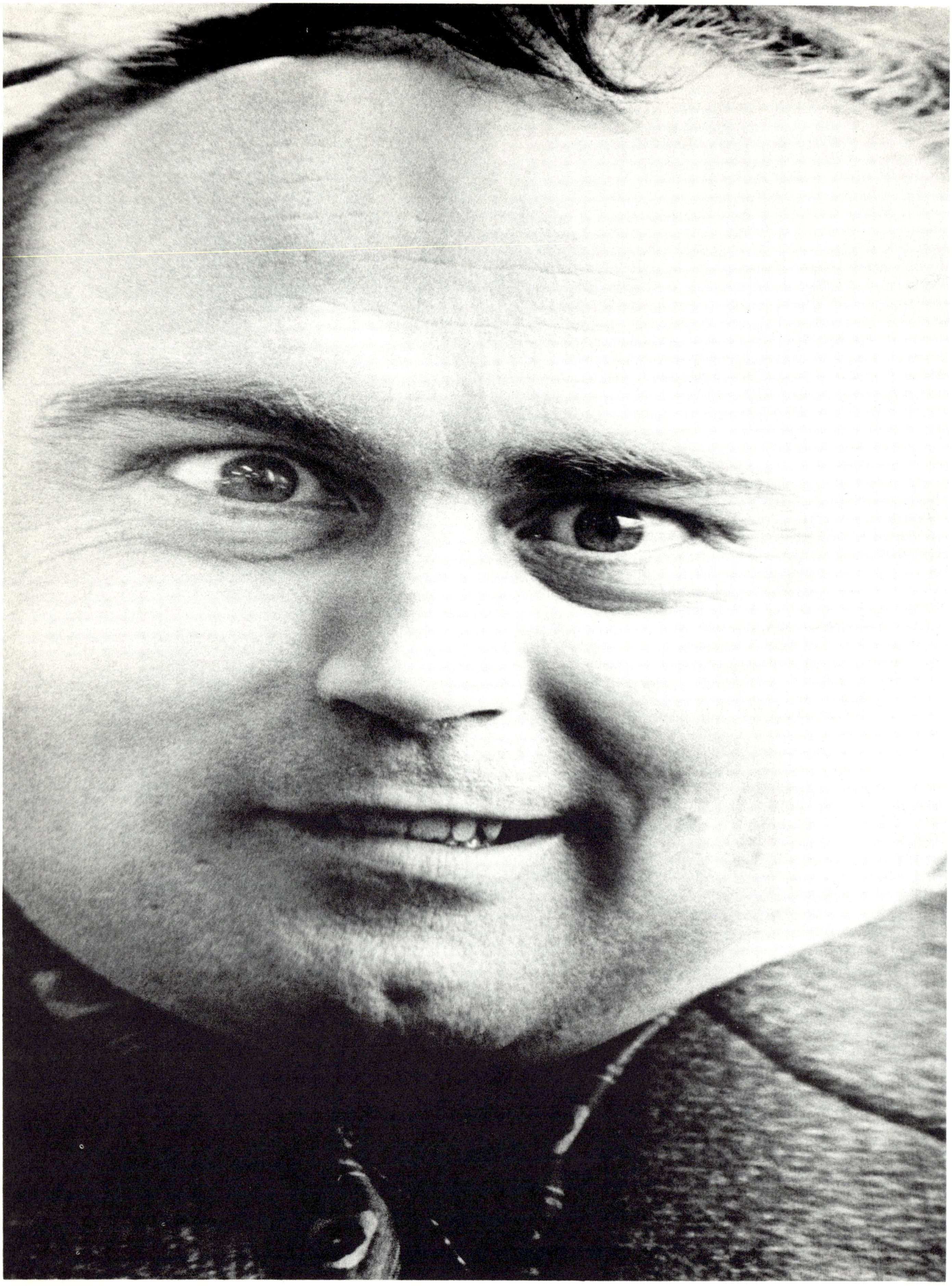

I curled the printing paper and taped the edges down. The more you curl the more you distort. You have to stop way down to get it sharp.

These dark figures against a bright wall were photographed with the lens way out of focus. In black and white fuzzy pictures the contrast between figures and background is very important. It doesn't matter much for fuzzy color photographs. Too little contrast in black and white pictures turns everything into a morbid grayness.

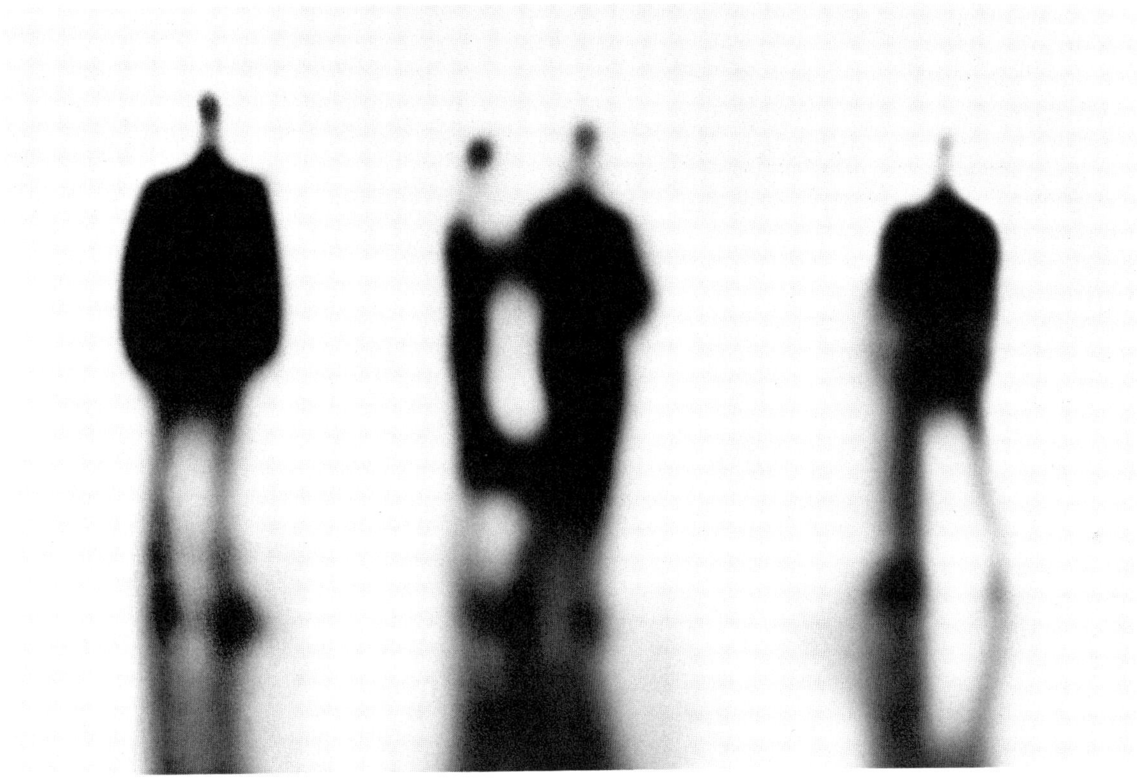

The fractured face (below) was made by clamping a copy negative between two pieces of slide glass, then holding it over a gas stove burner until it started to melt.

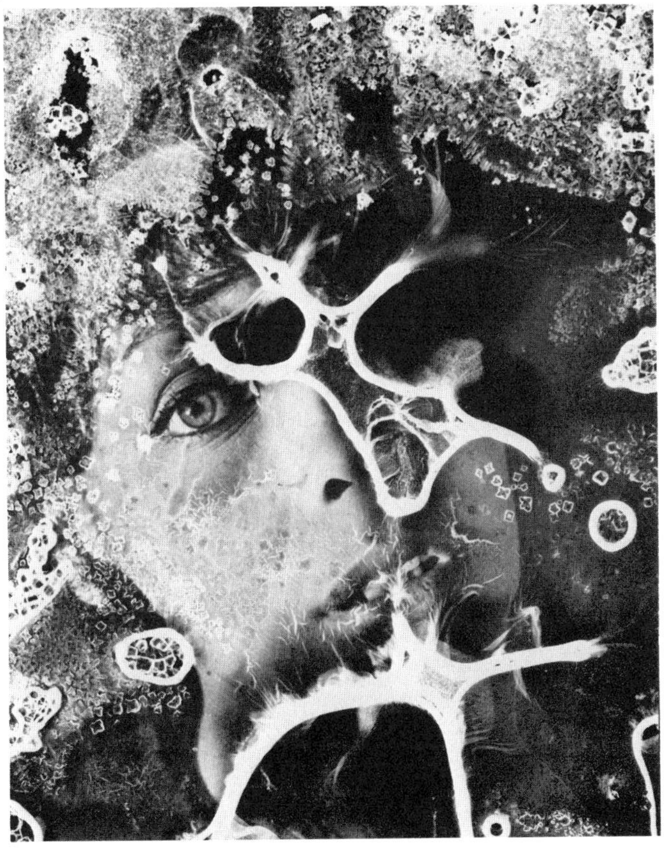

This dancer in Hell was put there by burning the edges of the negative with a match.

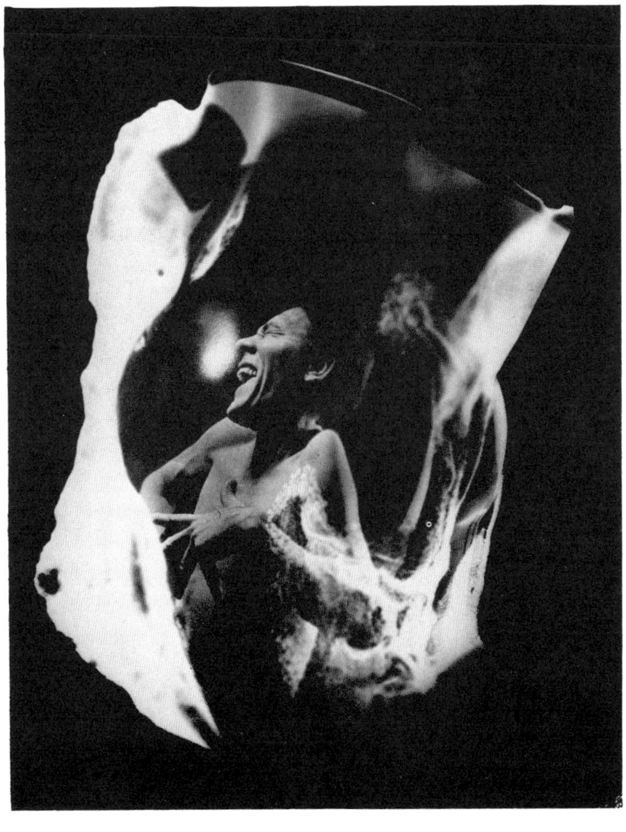

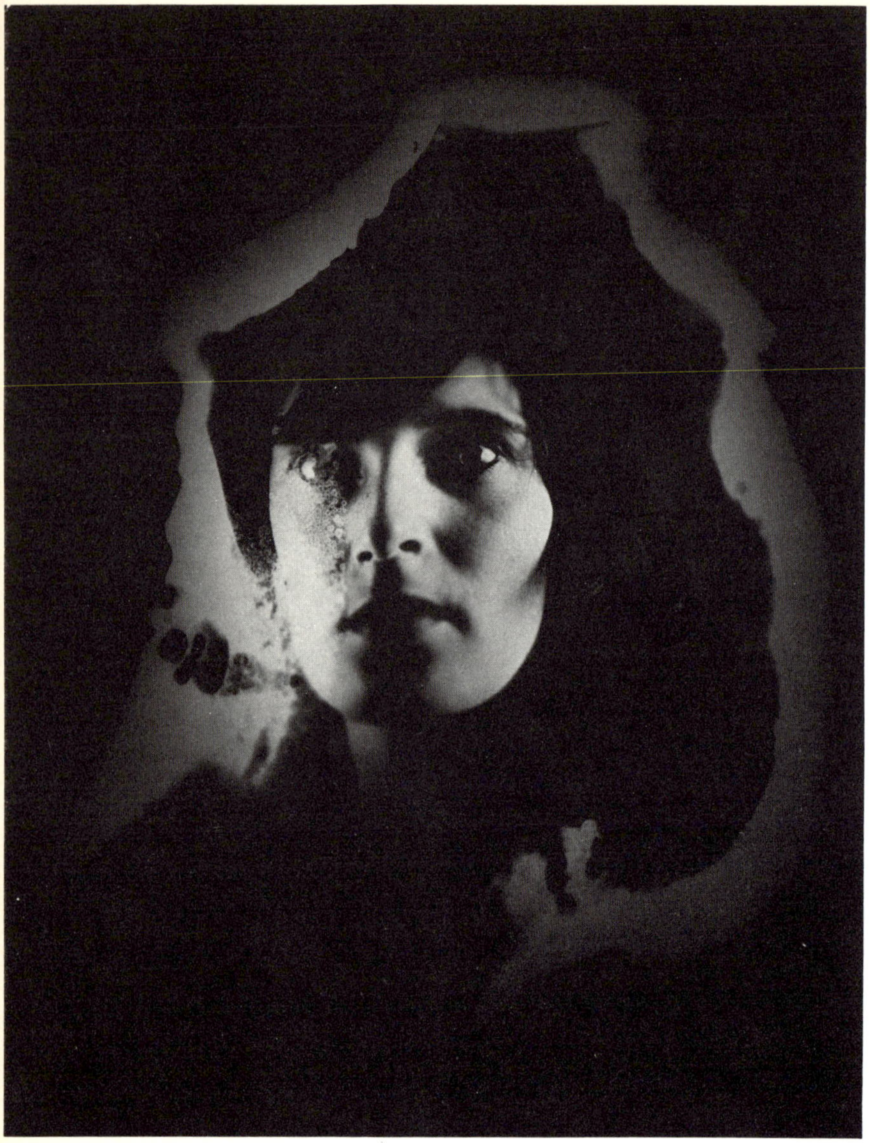

A burned-up negative of a way-out girl (left). I held it over a gas burner until its edges curled up. The gray shape around her head is the curled part of the negative, heavily burned in. Because of the curl I had to use a piece of glass instead of a negative carrier.

I put the enlarger far out of focus to print a sharp negative of this girl (below). There is supposed to be quite a difference between pictures shot fuzzy and those merely printed that way. I've never discovered exactly what it is, but you might like to experiment to learn the answer.

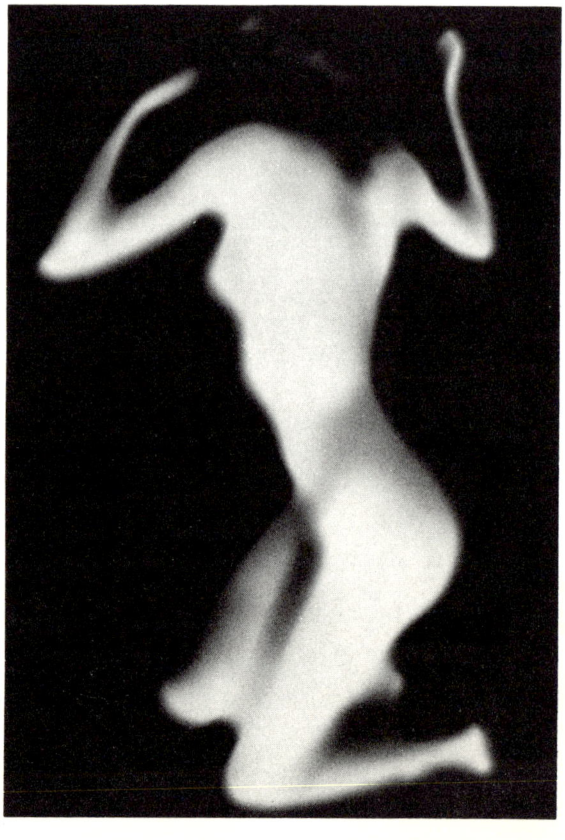

RELATE to your friends and neighbors better

Using your camera to help you understand your friends and neighbors better and to relate to them on a deeper level.

If you use it correctly your camera can be a passport to friendship and understanding. Because it is controlled by a consciousness and records things in the visible world, the photographs it makes represent a way of looking at things. There can be right ways of looking at things and wrong ways. People have a good deal of trouble with this. They wish to look at things in the right ways but they're not sure how. Right and wrong ways get all mixed up, appearing to be very much alike a lot of the time. With your camera, you can help them solve this problem for themselves. You can help them see themselves, their neighbors and you. You can help them do it in the right way, which is with patience, humility and compassion.

2

But where does one start doing this? There are many starting places and it's not so hard to find them. Start with a friend for example. Take some pictures of him, ordinary snapshots if you wish. Already you are starting him in the right way of seeing himself. By snapping half a dozen pictures you've already hinted at something very important: that he is worth looking at. You've shown this by the fact that you're bothering to do it—through your camera viewfinder. Many people think they're not worth the bother, which is a very wrong way of seeing oneself. You can help them correct it.

There are ways of pushing your point home to him, if merely snapping the pictures doesn't do it. After they're developed you can give him prints and say, "I like these pictures and want to share them with you." He may very well say, "I don't see why. Whatever is there in a picture of me that you find even remotely likeable?" You can answer, "I like them because they say something about you. I'm not sure what, but something. And it's a something I find good to look it. Please don't protest. I know it's there and that I like it."

You can go a step farther. You can make enlargements of the pictures and put them up around your room to look at. This makes your argument even more powerful. You like him enough to live with him, as it were, for his pictures are a constant presence. You're saying to him, "There are some intelligent people in this world who find admirable things in you. Perhaps it would be intelligent for you to learn to see these same things."

There are things you can do you shouldn't tell him about, for they have more to do with your problems than his. You might, for example, put pictures of him around because you *don't* like him very much or because you *don't* find anything admirable in him. Though this sounds like a silly thing to do it really isn't. It is one of the most reasonable things you can possibly do with pictures.

The objective of this strange procedure is to learn why you don't have as many friends as you'd like or why you don't care enough for the ones you do have. You put up pictures of your friend to help you focus your attention on him and to make him more real than he'd be if you depended entirely on your imagination and memory in thinking about him. Without pictorial guidelines your mind might turn him into almost anyone, ranging from Attila the Hun to Percy Simpwhistle. Though your mind is your salvation you must learn not to trust it.

As you see, I've suggested a procedure which even in the beginning starts to shift your attention from your friend to yourself. In a moment I'll ask you to concentrate even more heavily on yourself. You may ask, "But what has this got to do with my problem of attracting friends? Doesn't the answer relate more to the fact that people as a whole aren't much good?" I can only insist that the locus of the problem is in you yourself and is related only indirectly to the fact that people in general aren't all that they ought to be. To help you understand this I'll give you some facts about people.

The first important fact is that things which distress or anger you in other people are also characteristic of yourself. If they weren't, you wouldn't be upset by them. If they were not also in you, you would see them only with puzzlement, indifference or understanding tolerance. Negative characteristics in others can't upset you unless you also have them. This is not a fact which one likes to accept. Nonetheless, it is irrefutably true.

Another important fact is that one of the greatest contributions a friend can make to your life is to help you discover and eventually eliminate these negative things in yourself. He helps by causing you anger and distress. If you realize that they stem from negative attitudes which you share in common, you can then use your friend as a mirror of things in yourself which you need to overcome. These are the very things which make it impossible for a person to have as many friends as he'd like. They repel potential friends like angry rattlesnakes.

It is useful to know that the anger and distress caused by a friend can burn up your negative attitudes in time, so that they are gone from you forever. However, if you wish this to happen in yourself you must do certain things. You should not avoid the situations in which your friend has this effect on you. On the contrary, you should welcome them for what they can contribute to your life. You should not permit yourself to blame your friend for your negative feelings, nor should you permit yourself any other negative attitudes with respect to him. If you can't rid yourself of negative attitudes brought on by your interaction with him, under no circumstance should you give expression to them, in speech, writing or in any other form of behavior. You must maintain this rule not only when you're with him but when you're apart. If you don't, the thing you've partly cleansed yourself of will creep right back in. And you'll continue to be a person who hasn't as many friends as he'd like.

There are some things which you should know about your photographs of your friends. One of them is that in one of two forms they almost invariably record the things you dislike about them. One form is parody, the other avoidance. When you use your camera to parody something in a friend, you're not usually conscious that you're doing it. There's a good clue, however, and that is in feeling a sense of satisfaction which is accompanied by a twinge of guilt. You try to tell yourself you're being a good guy when you press the camera shutter release; but something inside you says you're not. You may feel this satisfaction-guilt combination when you shoot the picture, when you print it or any time later when you look at it. It's always a truthful sign that you're up to no good with your mind. With it may come the gloating feeling, "Aha, Jack me boy, I've caught you out this time. I've captured your self-delusion on film." If you realized you shared the same delusions you mightn't be so happy.

Offhand, one might think it's impossible to parody a person by taking a picture of him, unless you ask him to parody himself. The notion is that a person is in control of his own face and that all you can capture in a portrait is what he permits you to. This is true only to a degree. In the first place, he's not fully aware of the expressions flitting across his face, and his degree of awareness varies from time to time. At one moment he might be acutely aware of a slight expression of self-satisfaction on his face. At another time he might be grinning like an egotistical Cheshire cat and not have a clue he's doing it. The photographer who wants to parody merely waits for such an expression, then he shoots it. We can say that he parodies his subject by the process of selection. The important thing here is his intention, not the specific way in which he carries it out. Another way of putting it is that people unconsciously parody themselves very frequently. The photographic parodist merely has to select from the expressions which his subject inadvertently offers him. The particular expression he snaps reveals his intention as a parodist. That is, it tells which of his model's weaknesses he wishes to emphasize.

It is possible to use photography to parody a person's egotistical weaknesses even if he's clever enough to not let them be revealed in his face. There are lighting patterns, camera angles, poses, and so forth which make it look as if the weaknesses are showing, even if they aren't. However, one must be a rather experienced photographer to know how to use them well. Among more experienced photographers, parodying friends and family is a commonplace thing. Though the photographers are not usually aware they're doing it, their victims often know it for a certainty.

The point in telling you about parody is to help you look for it in your own pictures. In doing this to your friends you're not treating them well. And the things which you parody in them because you dislike them are also characteristic of yourself. As I've said, if you can discover what they are you can help yourself get rid of them and make of yourself a person to whom people will come for friendship.

The other way in which you photographically record something you dislike in a person is by avoidance. You see this thing in him either consciously or intuitively. It may be written in his facial expression, his gestures, the way he combs his hair, his choice of clothing, the way he sits or stands, etc. Since you don't like certain of these things because of what they symbolize, you try not to get them in your pictures. In looking at your photographs later you can usually remember the things you tried to obscure, eliminate or diminish. They furnish clues to things in the other person (and in yourself, remember) which you dislike or find distressing.

Some common methods of avoidance are picture cropping, camera angle, camera distance, photographing gestures you like and refusing to snap those you don't. We can also avoid things by being directors. When a person does certain things we don't like, we direct him to do something else instead. We avoid by creating selective obscurity, that is, things we like we show clearly; things we don't like we obscure by putting them in dark shadows, throwing them out of focus, putting them behind other things, cropping part of them off, and so on. To many advanced photographers these avoidance tricks are very important, but they think of them only as ways for making better pictures. They would learn a lot if they could come to see that they're also tricks for hiding unpleasant things from themselves.

I started off this introduction by describing simple-hearted means for improving other people's well-being with your camera. But then I got into a more sinister thing, the use of photography in the struggle against negative aspects of oneself. Which kind of thing should *you* do? That depends. Some people can use photography to do both. A few kindly souls no longer need the struggle. The majority, however, ought to put their primary emphasis on Self-discovery and Self-improvement through learning to put up with other people. In the self is the crux of their problem of having a friend and being one.

I should say a little more about studying pictures which you make of your friends. It's not at all easy to figure out what you've done to them or why. You have to keep after a problem like this, sometimes for many years. The point is that when you use a camera to subtly mistreat friends, you don't want to let yourself know you've done it. Blindness to such a thing can be extreme. The closer you are to a person, the more apt you are to be blind to the fact you've used your camera to malign him. For example, I've seen numerous fond husbands who have figuratively ripped their wives to shreds in photographs and been sublimely unaware of it. It's nearly as likely to happen with close friends. Since we're desperately afraid of discovering that we do such things, don't expect to learn immediately all your pictures have to tell you about yourself.

There is another interesting and peculiar thing about Self-discovery through one's own photographs. It is that for nearly every negative thing you put into a picture there seems to be an equal and opposite positive one. This positive thing is usually just as difficult to discover as the negative one. For example, you may with some difficulty discover you've used a picture to parody a certain weakness in a friend. Its opposite may be evidence that you're really very fond of him, anyway. But you'll have to work just as hard to find it as to find the parody.

A friend of mine suggested bringing the philosopher Hegel into my book at this point. He said that if Hegel could have played with a camera he might well have called this photographic dialectics: the apposition of opposites which synthesize into a total-personality portrait. This positive thing (Hegel's thesis) is usually just as difficult to discover as the negative one (his 'antithesis').

Not having read Hegel, I was unaware of his concepts of thesis and antithesis. The difficulty in discovering the two I found out for myself. However, I was helped in this by a period of study with the contemporary poet-philosopher Eli Siegel, who makes a great deal out of man's problems with opposites in himself and the world. The notions in the following paragraph are strongly influenced by Siegel's teaching. The ethical notions scattered throughout this book are also influenced by Siegel's philosophy, which he calls Aesthetic Realism. One of his notions is that discovering the Self is an ethical problem. Another is that one should not devote his entire time looking for things for which to condemn himself. In fact, he has no use for Self-condemnation.

Agreeing with Siegel, I think it's important that you know that in your struggle to understand yourself you will find things in yourself you can respect very deeply. You'll find anger and contempt, to be sure, but you'll also find love and compassion. But don't make the mistake so many do; don't discard the good things in cynical disbelief. Don't fall into Self-condemnation, which is a disguised form of egotism. Instead of this, get rid of your cynicism, for it is also egotism in disguise. Anyone who wishes to make a serious effort to discover his Self must commit himself to a lifelong struggle against egotism in all its forms, for egotism is the chief culprit in driving the Self into hiding in the first place.

After this heavy-footed introduction you'll feel relieved to move along to the first lesson, "The Girl Next Door." Here you'll find good advice served up with a little more sugar and lightheartedness.

The Girl Next Door

Photographers Bill Barley and Gary Ludwick are old friends and former students of mine. When I asked them to shoot some pictures they were pleased to help me out. I said, "Why don't you two guys make some pictures which will show my readers how to photograph the pretty girl next door?" They correctly assumed that I wanted some old-fashioned corn tricked out in currently fashionable photographic clichés. They were supposed to give me Pretty Miss Average America, the dream girl of every red-blooded Boy Scout.

Fortunately, their model, Pat Clyburn, didn't go along with this. Though the lads did their damndest to fulfill their assignment by squeezing her into a preconceived mold, Pat proved to be very unsqueezable in this context. Her reaction to their efforts shows up in her angry facial expressions in many of the photographs. They make the pictures interesting and lead us to a useful fact: Women don't like to be prejudged by men.

However, prejudging women is the mode in photography and has been for years. The idea is not to carefully explore the true nature of women, then sensitively interpret what you find. On the contrary, it is vigorously to avoid seeing their natures and to use women merely as raw material for creating illusions which satisfy the male ego. Naturally, women don't much dig this idea. Its prevalence in American photography does much to undermine the female sense of identity.

Responding to Pat Clyburn's angry frustration, I suggested in the lesson you should let your model help select the role she will play for the camera. However, I didn't go nearly far enough in this direction. And I made another mistake even more serious. I wrote what almost adds up to a manual on how to manipulate people without their being aware of it. Though the camera magazines have been filled with such insidious nonsense for years, that doesn't make it right.

It is true that these tricks in handling people actually work. Advanced amateurs and professionals use them all the time. However, one must not permit himself to use them for the wrong reasons, for if he does he's defeating the very meaning of friendship. Use them as a means of relieving tension and uncertainty so that friendship will have a peaceful environment in which to grow and flourish. Do not use them merely to get 'good' photographs. Photography is not all that important, and don't you ever forget this.

If you must, use the tension-relieving tricks in order to make your presence welcome. This will give you time to learn what kind of a person your model is. Then with her help you can try to express in pictures what you've learned. If your objective is only to use a pretty neighbor as raw material for illustrating your illusions with respect to women, consider yourself a person not worthy of her friendship.

The Lesson:

Last Spring in South Carolina I visited two old friends, Gary Ludwick and Bill Barley, a pair of very sharp young photographers. Working out of the little town of Cayce, they service national photographic accounts that want coverage in the southland by capable photographers thoroughly familiar with the region. I saw their work and liked it very much. Later, they introduced me to a close friend, a pretty girl named Pat Clyburn, very sweet and charming.

A light popped on in my head as my con-man instincts were aroused. I said, "Look, you guys—I need more regional flavor in my column. Why don't you take pretty Pat here and show my readers how to photograph the pretty girl next door? In return, I'll tell people where they can find you (Photo-Graphics, Inc., P.O. Box 447, 829 Knox Abbott Drive, Cayce, S.C. 29033)."

Well, things didn't quite work out as we thought they would. Gary and Bill wanted to stick with the theme, "The Girl Next Door," while Pat, with a career in mind, wanted to portray the sophisticated advertising model. Being friends, they found it easy to disagree rather violently. So, the theme became, at least in part,

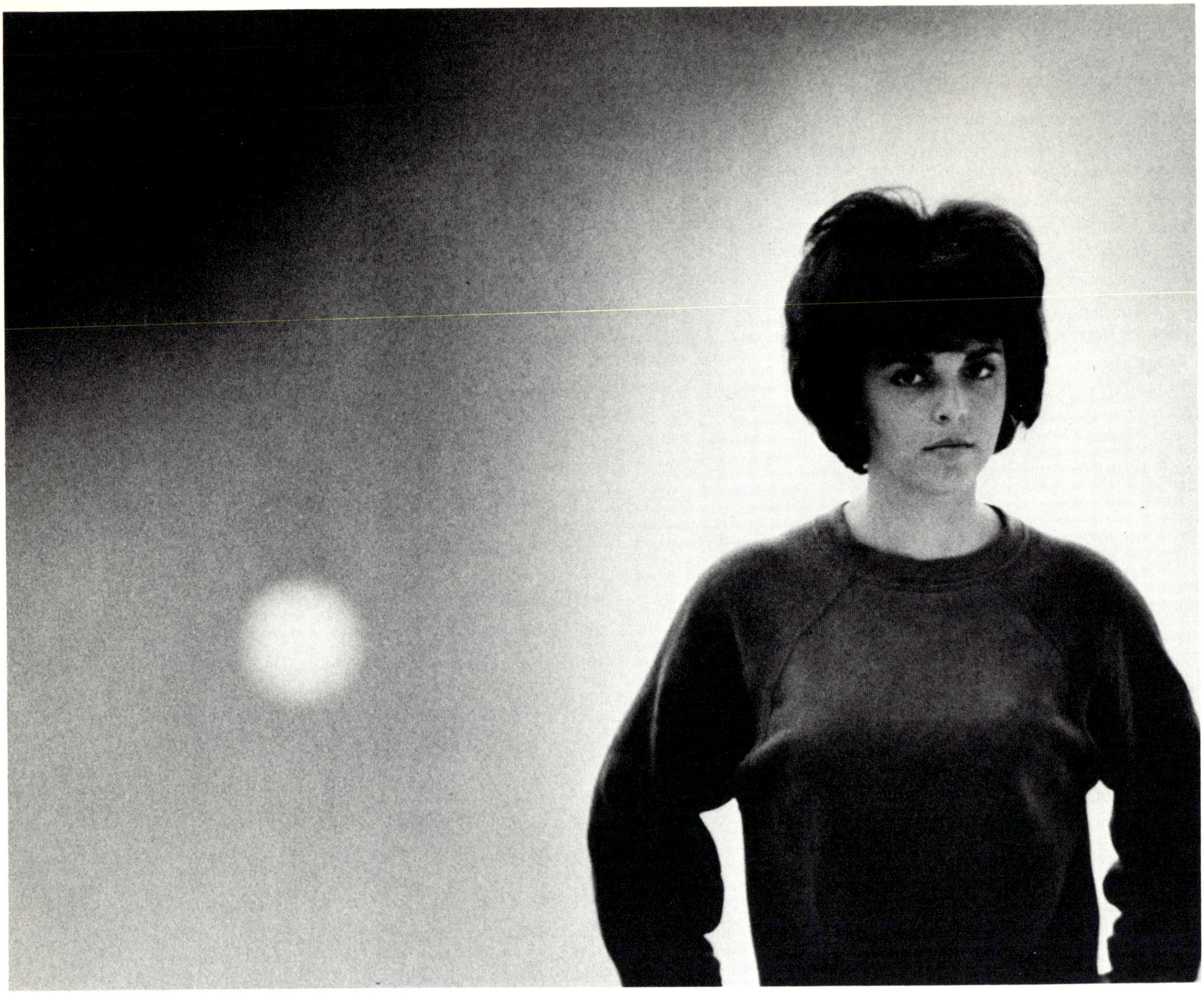

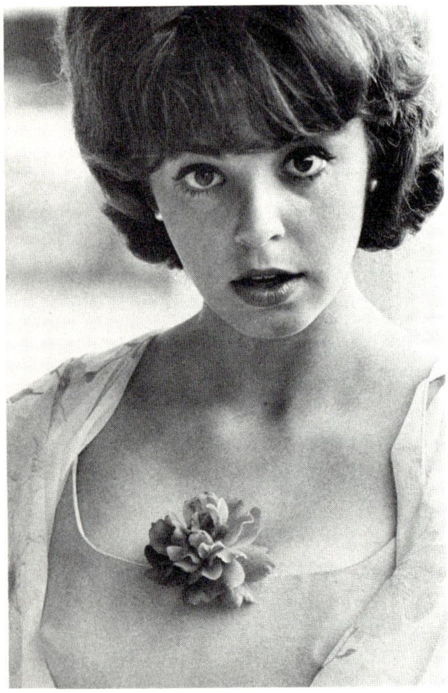

If pretty neighbors can be tigers, more power to them (above). The threatening sun and her expression create female ferocity. Does this depict part of the true nature of women? Perhaps it is Pat Clyburn wishing the photographers would crawl back under a rock. Is she miffed at them or acting on direction? We don't know but see that Ludwick and Barley have turned an unlikely idea or situation into an interesting picture; but stirring up women is trouble.

photo by PHOTO-GRAPHICS

Charming and beautiful, Pat Clyburn has a mind of her own. She says she wants to be a TV and advertising model and has won such important beauty contests as Miss High School of America.

photo by PHOTO-GRAPHICS

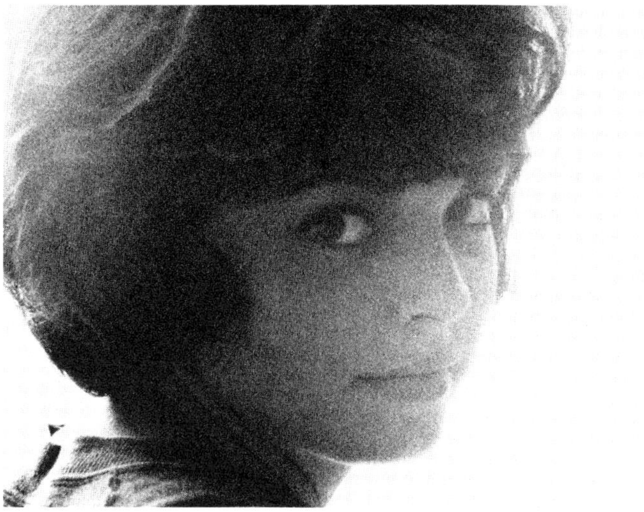

Quiet beauty and subtle sweetness (above). By shooting against a very bright background the photographers have gotten lens flare, which flattens the tones and adds an element of mystery. Professionals use flare for a variety of expressive purposes.

photo by PHOTO-GRAPHICS

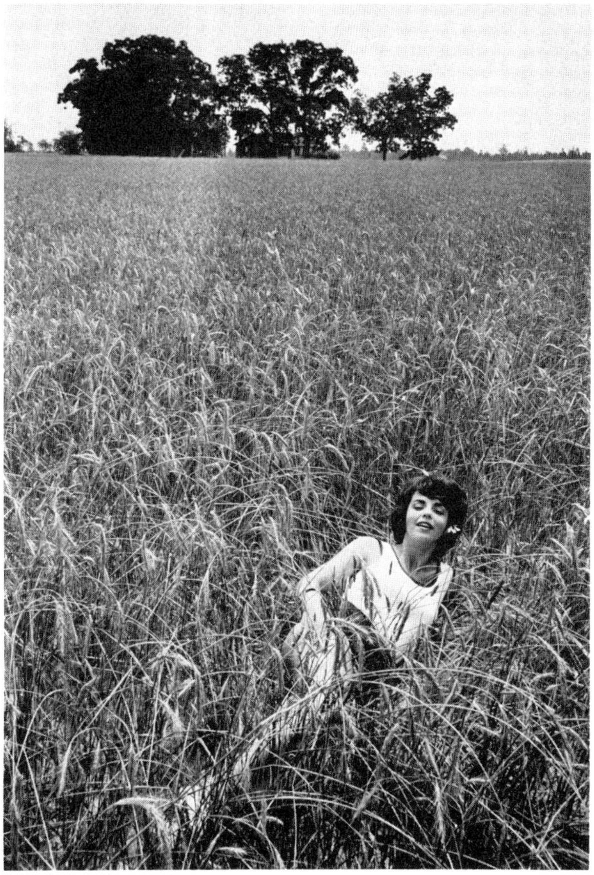

Corny picture (right). Or is it wheat or rye or barley? Too many photographers don't realize that corny pictures like this are a lot of fun. I hereby elect Pat Miss Wheat Fields, U.S.A., since she's so obviously enjoying what she's doing.

photo by PHOTO-GRAPHICS

"How to Photograph an Angry Young Woman." Since angry women can be interesting and since amateurs are even more likely to find themselves working at cross purposes with their models than experienced pros like Bill and Gary, I thought we still had an interesting and useful lesson here.

The first piece of advice they have for us is: "If you happen to stir up the tiger in a girl you are photographing, go ahead and make pictorial use of it. Pretty tigers are fun."

Then, "Don't make the mistake of thinking the girl next door wants to be photographed as 'The Girl Next Door.' In her secret heart she may see herself as the Queen of Sheba or Cleopatra. You can either go along with her or prepare for a pitched battle.

"Watch how she reacts to the clothes she's wearing. A girl changes roles when she changes clothes. Fashion clothes, fashion girl; hip clothes, hip girl; sultry clothes, sultry girl. Your only chance of photographing the 'girl next door' is to catch her when she's dressed for the part. Even then she's likely to turn into a South Seas siren or a haughty queen.

"Don't try to act too professional, too knowing, too sharp. You might frighten her into a role completely unsuited to her. So, relax; take it easy and slow.

"Get her involved in doing things she delights in; then she'll forget you're there and let her real self come out."

I have some advice, too. Don't try to photograph your pretty neighbor until you know deep inside that your motives are right. If you'd really rather be chasing her

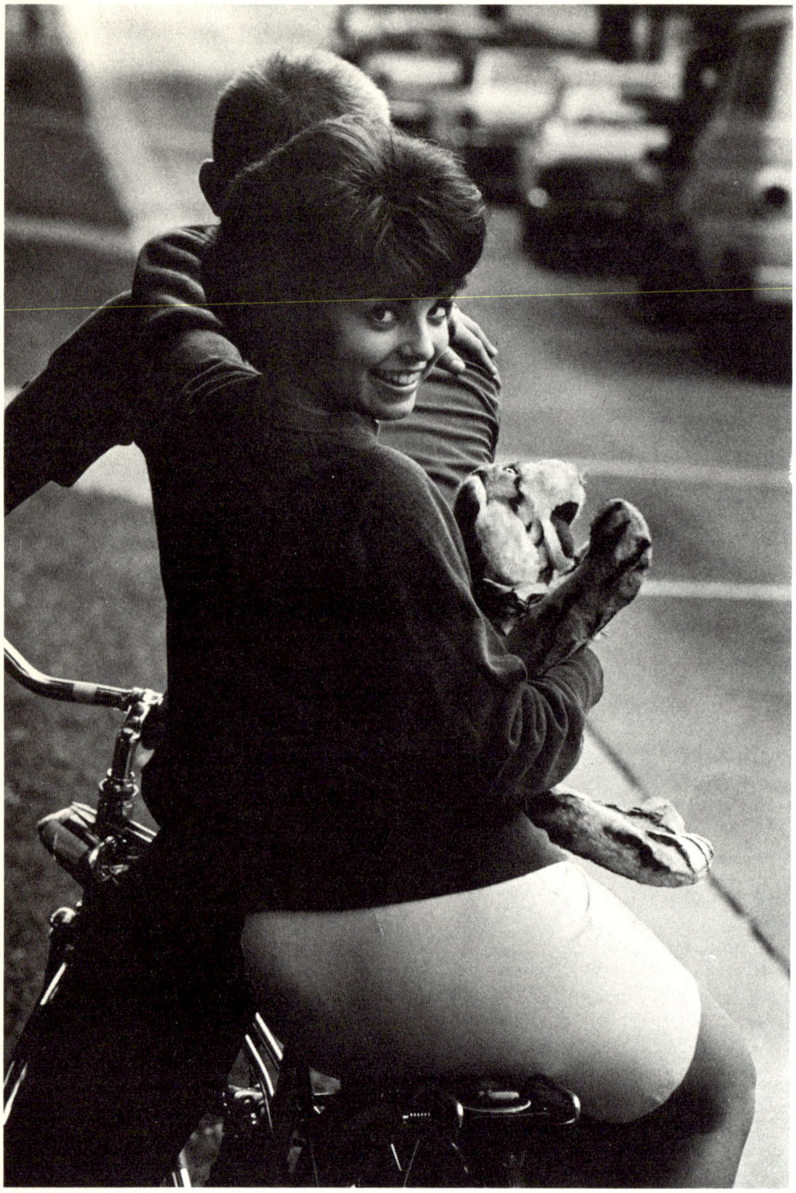

Her pet tiger, a new bicycle and an arm around a young man's neck bring out the imp in our South Carolina belle (left). If your pretty neighbor looks too sad, put her on a bicycle, swing, teeter-totter, row-boat, carousel, or hobby horse. Gay young props will bring out the youth in most of us.

photo by PHOTO-GRAPHICS

Pretty speedy neighbor (below). This swift picture was made by using a slow shutter speed (1/30 sec.?) and panning the camera to blur the background. It's a big change of pace from the close-up photographs. This picture doesn't do much for me.

photo by PHOTO-GRAPHICS

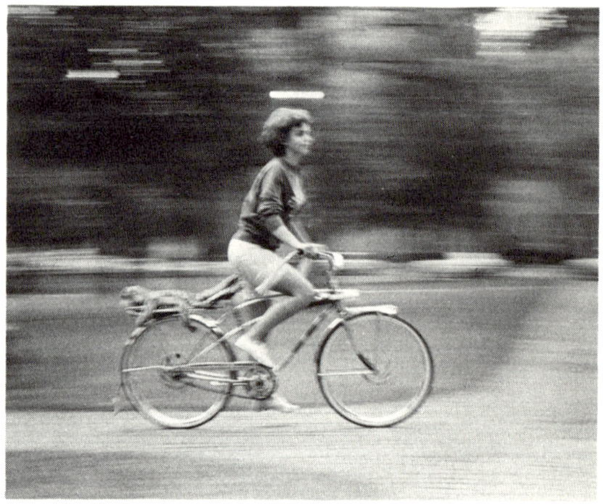

around the room, or you feel like putting her down because she is so pretty and inaccessible to you, she'll know it immediately; and you certainly won't get the pictures you want. Photograph when you are comfortable with her and when you feel delighted by everything she is and everything she does. Gentle laughter and general good humor are wonderful working tools for the photographer.

It's a good idea to try to think and see like a pro but to act outwardly like a snapshooter. Even take obvious snapshots now and then; this takes the pressure off your model.

Be like a mother hen; make gentle, assuring, clucking sounds from time to time. The girl who feels sure in your good opinion of her will bloom like a rose. Soft clucks mean approval. Or a nod of the head or an "Ummm, that's nice" will work as well. Your approval is perhaps most important when your model thinks she least merits it.

If possible, scout your backgrounds and lighting conditions in advance. Let your pretty neighbor know you are using them because they do terrific things for her looks.

The clicks of your shutter tell your

model how you want her to behave. If they come when she is at ease with herself and not too aware of you, this is good. But if they come when she is trying to play a role unsuited to her, she'll try to push herself even further into it.

Don't zero in too strongly on her. If you take a few pictures of her cat or the back yard she will get the impression you're one of those delightful people who find the whole world charming. Thus she knows she herself doesn't have to jump through hoops in order to please you. You might even encourage her to fiddle with your camera a little bit. This will help her overcome her tendency to see it as a fiendish device designed to strip the very meat from her bones.

Put your camera down from time to time and forget it. Don't keep it in your hands every instant like a weapon. Handle it like a snapshot machine, not like a precious idol.

If your model wants to come up with pictorial ideas of her own, encourage her by photographing every one, getting what

Woman and water—who would have thought of this? As part of your assignment why don't you see how many ideas you can think up involving the two elements? Shoot for twenty-five good ideas, all written down on paper. Being in the water brought out something very different in Pat.

photo by PHOTO-GRAPHICS

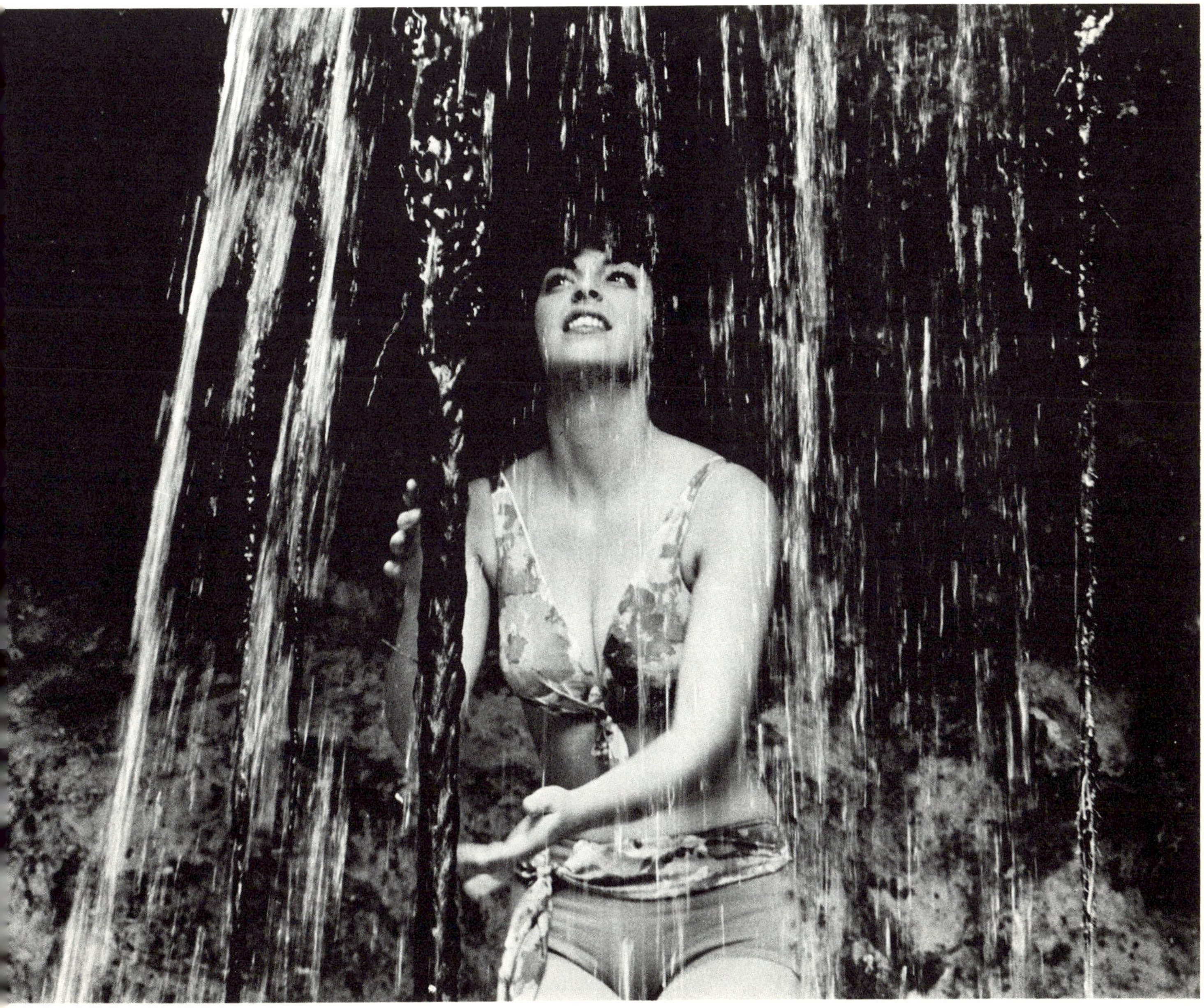

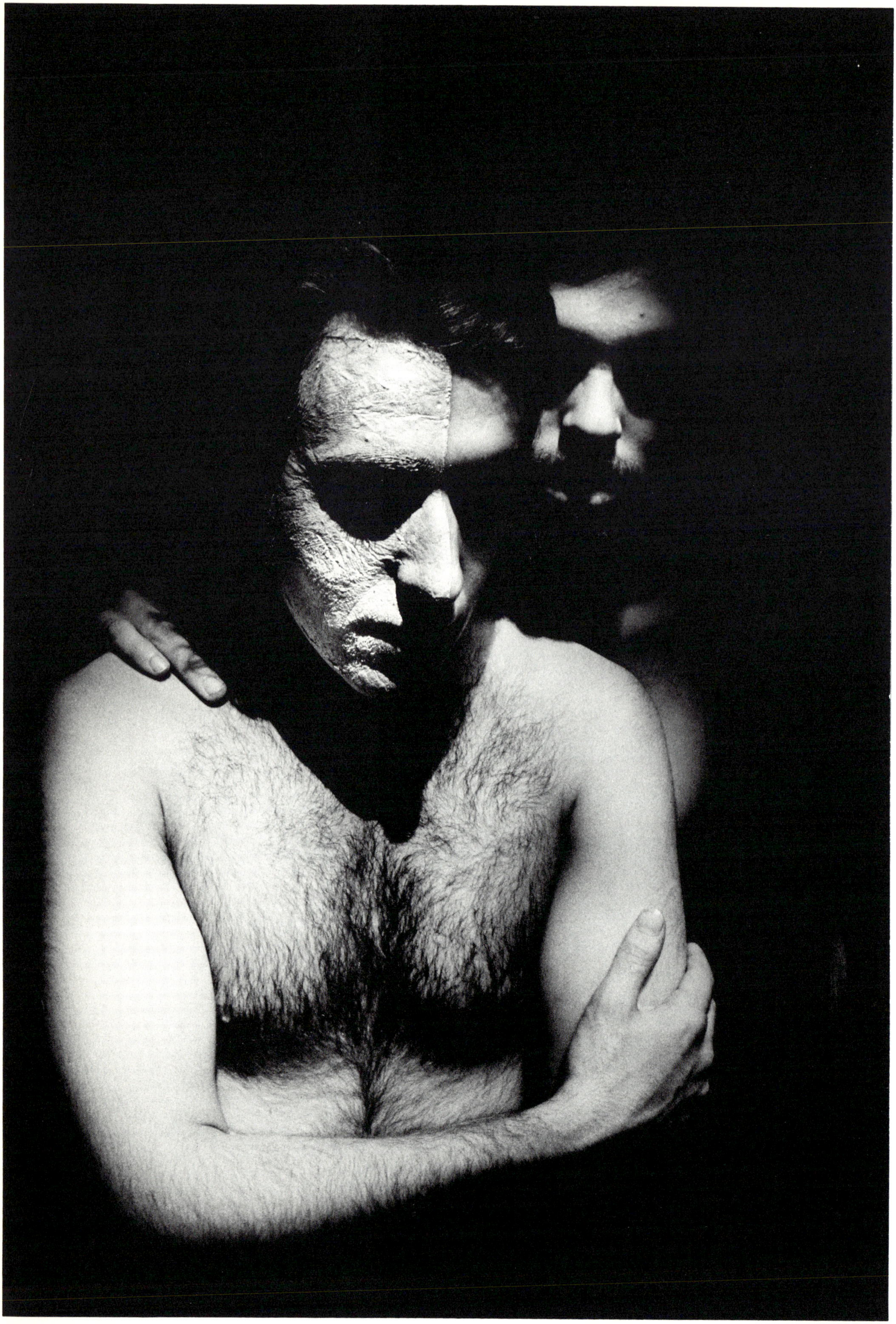

When Eugene Ginsberg saw this picture of himself he was really shaken up. He felt it said things about him that were too true.

photo by JOHN SHEARER

you yourself want in between. If she starts getting painfully corny, photograph her anyway. It may be just a prelude to her completely relaxing in your presence. In fact, she may be testing your willingness to let her be herself. And if it isn't herself you're interested in you have no business trying to photograph her in the first place.

You should be aware that everyone has certain expressions he knows to be unflattering. When you see them, don't click the shutter, or you'll label yourself as an aggressor.

On the other hand she may have delightful expressions which she thinks are terrible. In this case you should tell her. And she certainly won't mind learning she's beautiful more often than she thought.

Most important, try making a friend of your pretty neighbor before you decide that she's the girl you want as your photographic model.

One Man, Many Portraits

This lesson gets closer to the nitty-gritty than "The Girl Next Door," which is mainly directed toward young men who are really uptight around girls. It gets into the kinds of things which are being explored in "confrontation groups." These groups are made up of people who wish to get rid of their fear of others and to learn how to stop lying to themselves about their real feelings with respect to other people and themselves. It takes a strong person to join such a group and stick with it. One must be equally strong to do a lesson like this in the right way. If it's done in the wrong way, there's no point to it at all.

The Lesson:

One of the most useful learning tools in photography is the group project in which everyone shoots the same subject. This is usually done with some inanimate object or at an assigned location. It's much more interesting with a person.

First, select the person. This can be someone not a member of your group, camera club, or class. What will result is a series of pictures that tend to emphasize technical gimmicks or embody a standardized photographic romanticism. Mostly, they will show a person looking as if he wishes he'd dropped dead instead of agreeing to be the model. If you have a beautiful girl, the results may be prettier, perhaps, but still devoid of real human content. And some photographers are scared to death of beautiful girls and will avoid taking their share of photographs. The best thing is to choose someone from the class.

Of course, you should pick someone with a non-threatening personality. If you don't, three-fourths of the group will cop out of the project and the others will snapshoot it so fast their film catches fire. Even if you choose a gentle soul, the group should agree that it is accepting a challenge of a high order: to personally confront, really look at, and sensitively interpret one of its own members.

Each person should work alone with the subject. Group sessions will turn the project into a cop-out. If the project is done honestly—courageously and with a real attempt at communion between subject and photographer—it is worthwhile for everyone in the group. If all can't agree to this purpose, don't do the project.

In addition to formal teaching, I've had long experience with casual groups and camera clubs. They don't do nearly as much as they should to work together on the problem of confronting other people. It takes a lot of courage, naturally, but I see it as one of the most important things a group can do. The first step is for all to admit that face-to-face confrontation makes them uneasy. It may even terrify some of the people. Once this is admitted, they can work to help one another. If camera clubs were formed with this idea as a basis, they'd be much more meaning-

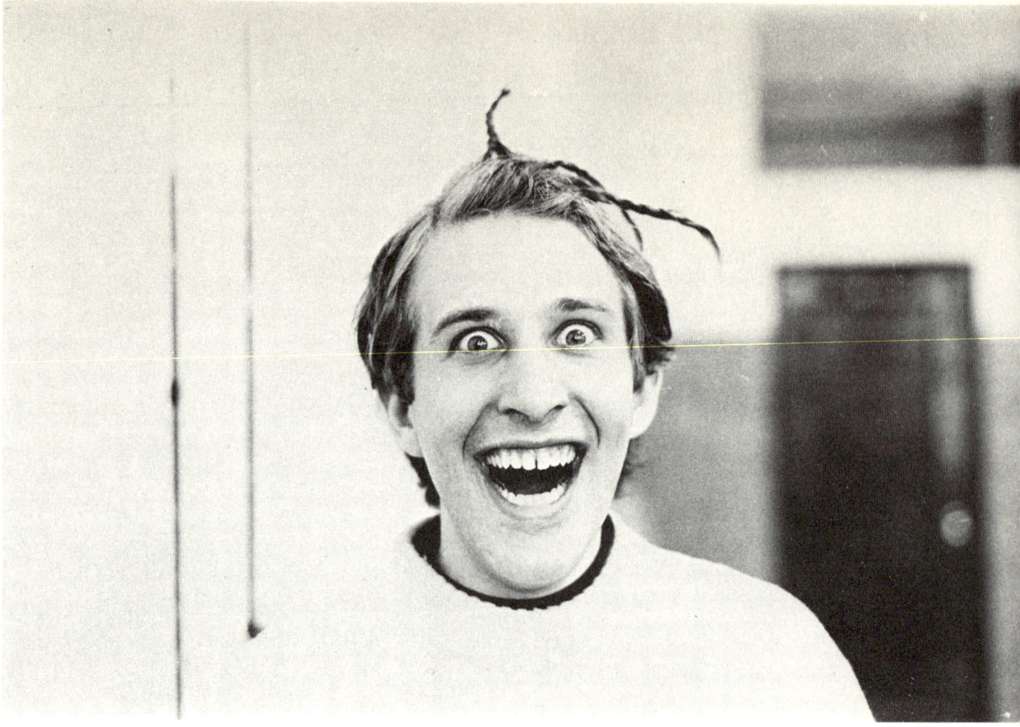

Laughing Boy (right). Mama sends him off to school with a smile and a big apple for his teacher.

photo by MIKE LICHTENSTEIN

A reflection and the real Eugene Ginsberg (below). Which is which? Gene is at the top the reflection below.

photo by FRANK JAMES

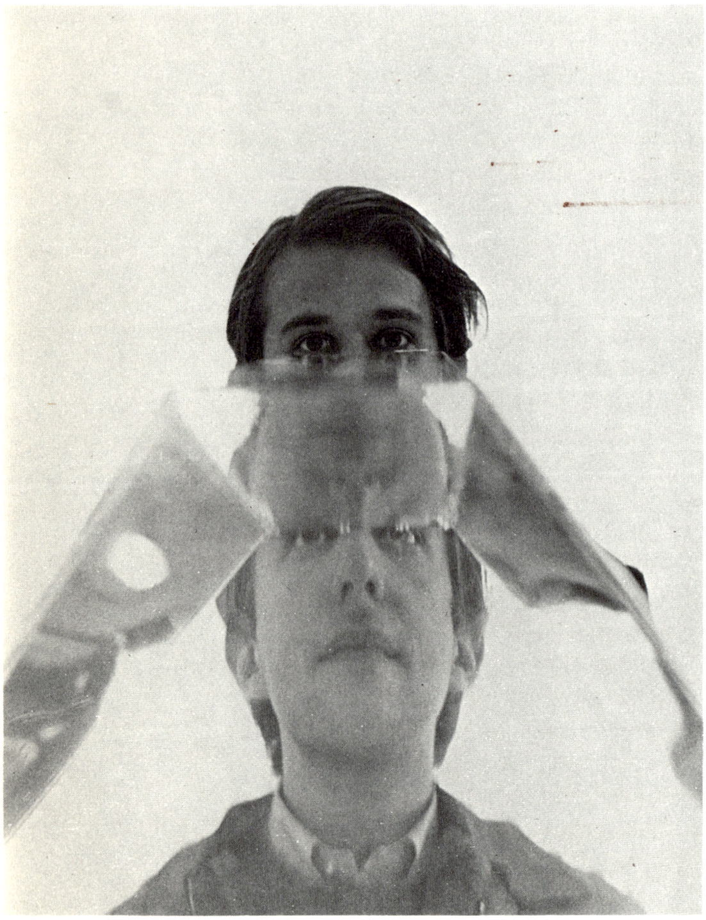

ful. And they would produce good photographers. Such a club could produce a Brotherhood of the Meek.

This notion will probably be frightening to many camera clubs. But I believe that the idea might appeal to young people, who could start their own club. It seems that the young are beginning to realize that unless they can *confront* their fear of people, they will be permanent slaves of terror. So this lesson is aimed primarily at them.

Young rebels, hear me out! This lesson is a problem in confrontation and freedom. If you can't look another person in the eye, you're a slave to every Tom, Dick, and Harry you'll ever meet. You know what the problem is. I don't have to say another word. Let us—as you do when you're together—examine the cop-outs and see what can be done.

Your camera can be a cop-out. If you zoom in on somebody with your camera in front of your face, you're hiding. If you let your camera dangle and zoom in with your bare eyeballs, then you're getting down to the nitty-gritty. But this is tough, very tough. You want to photograph somebody. You want to do it fairly. But it's hard. You need a little know-how, a starting

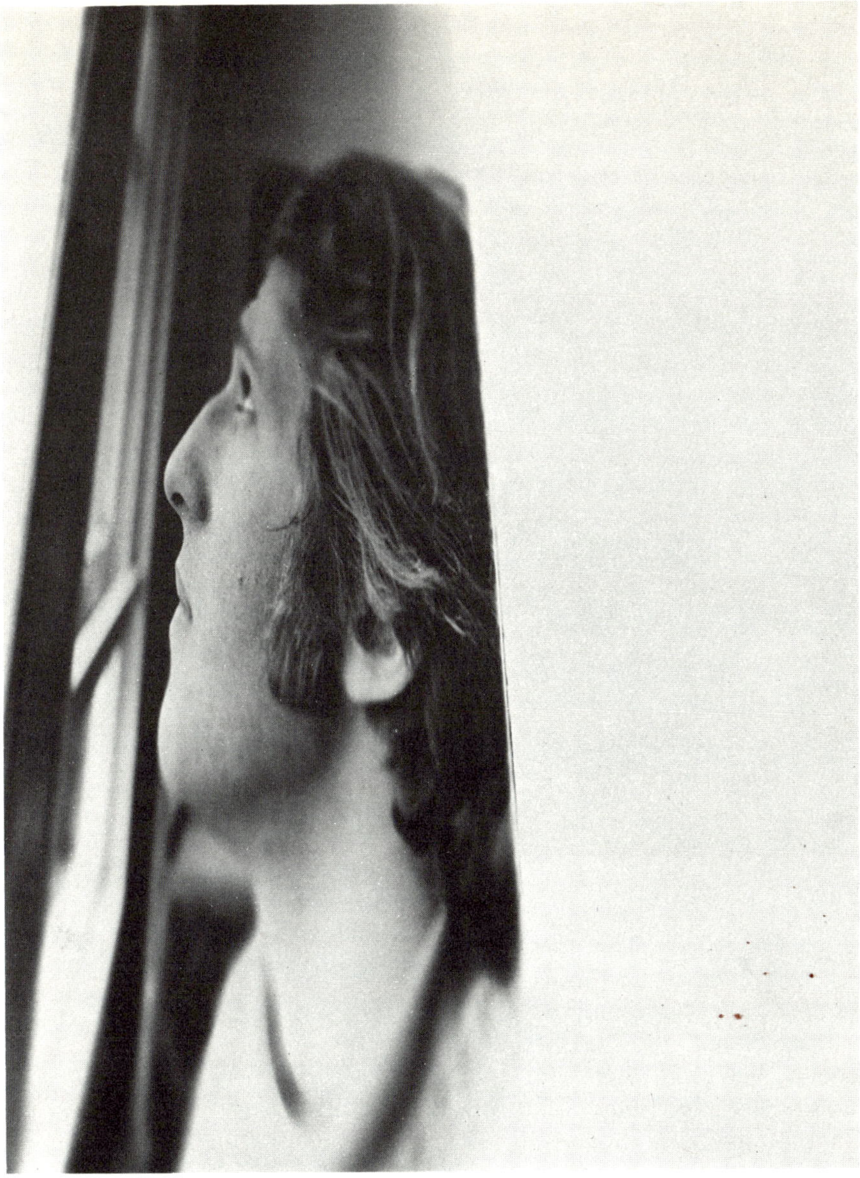

In a serious mood, Eugene somberly contemplates the universe. A tilted printing easel made his face appear very long.

photo by JOHN MULVANY

place. You might say, "I want to photograph you and treat you fairly, but I'm afraid. Help me overcome my fear of seeing you as you really are." But this approach takes lots of guts.

A contemptuous attitude can be a cop-out. Subconsciously, you say to yourself, "This person isn't much. I'll manipulate him; he's not smart enough to know the difference." This is a sad mistake, holding another person in contempt and creating fake courage in yourself in order to photograph him. Contempt is a cop-out that conceals your fear of other people. Stick to your contempt and you'll get punched in the nose—I've seen it happen dozens of times. Wrestle with your contempt and eventually you'll be able to photograph people honestly.

Role playing can be a cop out. For each upsetting kind of situation a person faces, he has a special role to slip into. It is like an actor going into character as he walks on stage. Each role is you imitating someone in your past life, or some creature of your imagination, who you think is capable of coping with the problem. In short, instead of being yourself, you're try-

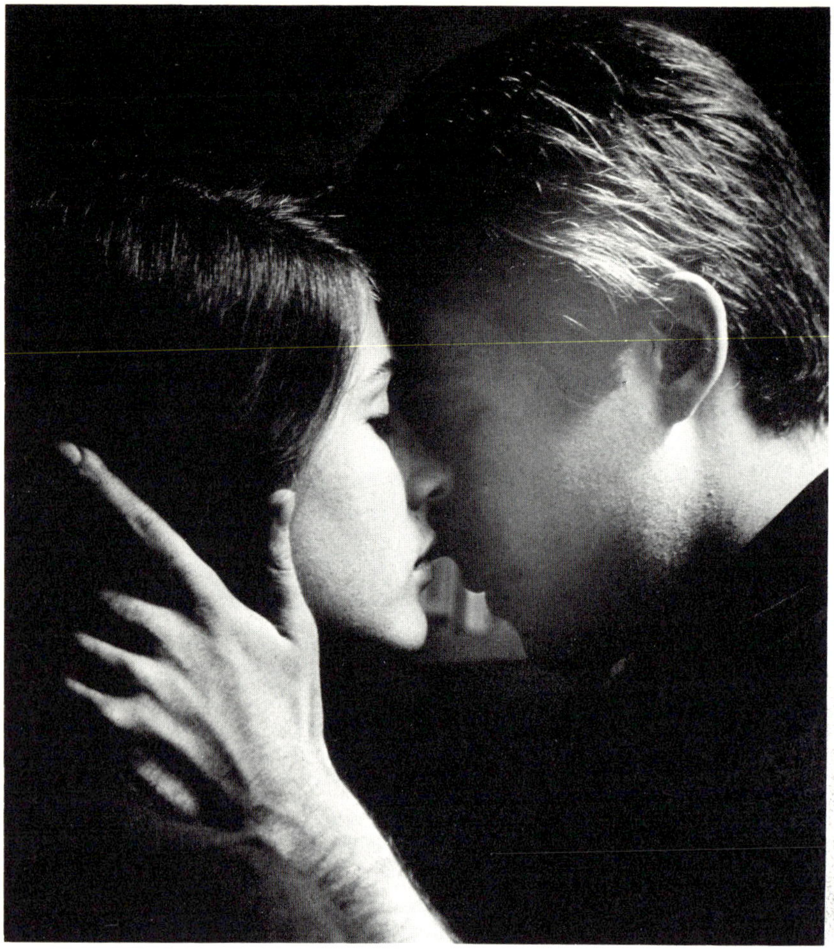

Tender contemplation, two souls reaching out to each other through the sense of touch and the sound of muted breaths. In silence, Eugene seeks the meaning of love and tenderness.

photo by DAVID ROSEN

ing to be someone you're not. This will introduce a note of phoniness into a shooting situation and throw the photographer-model relationship off balance. This is just as likely to happen with someone you know as with a stranger. The only way around this is to try courageously and honestly to go through the session as no one but yourself. By working in this way, you steadily grow in strength.

Your photographic gimmicks may be a cop-out. Though tricks per se are valid, one tends to use them as a smokescreen that blinds both the photographer and his model to the realities of a confrontation. The idea is that you come into a shooting session with well-formed ideas about gimmicks you want to try on your subject. With your mind completely absorbed by them, you are spared from really thinking about the model or even looking at him at all. This reduces your anxiety. However, he is likely to feel like an inanimate object or a castaway. He'll feel this all the more if he sees that your gimmicks aren't efforts to interpret him creatively as he is, but ways of avoiding contacting him as an individual.

If you want to use gimmicks correctly, first confront your model as a person. Then enter into communication with him and decide what your mutual purpose is in having a shooting session. From this you will get some real idea of *whom* you are shooting. You are now in a position to use gimmicks that can accurately portray some aspect of him. He will feel this and respond warmly.

There are many other cop-outs. You can be aware of your own if you watch out for them. The main idea is that instead of copping-out, you should confront another person, look right at him. When two people do this they are really helping each other to confront their fears. Portraits approached in this manner tend to be much more sensitive and meaningful than those produced during shooting sessions in which photographer and subject are not attuned to each other's individual personity.

There are some additional reasons for having a whole group photographing one person. The most obvious is that you see a lot of different ways of using the medium. One tends to think with a given subject that there are only one or two reasonable ways to photograph him. When the work of a group is seen as a whole, you discover that there may be 20 or 30 ways —all of them valid.

Another advantage is that your ideas concerning a particular person undergo revision and expansion, and this can carry over to your concepts of other people, too. We tend to sum up each person we know, stick him into a cubbyhole. A portrait can be such a cubbyhole. In his portrait of a person, one tries to say: "This is the entire sum of Jack Johnson, as I see him." What happens next is that we see in the work of our fellow photographers 20 or 30 other "accurate sums" of the real Johnson. Naturally, this forces us to expand our concept of him, to see him as having many facets. This is good, for a photographer should see each of his subjects as a universe—not some piddling thing to stuff into a cubbyhole. Insofar as we make other people small we shrink our own world. It could be put this way: If you want to possess the universe, see just one other person as being as large as he really is. This sounds crazy, but it works.

Another interesting thing happens. As the group's pictures are displayed, we see that each one is a mirror reflecting what was happening between the photographer and subject. In one we see anger, in another, frustration, and in a third, delight. The responses often run the gamut of emotions. In a well-knit group, this kind of thing can be talked about. By questioning the model and his photographers, we can try to discover what happened in each session to give rise to the various emotions.

The pictures for this lesson were done by students in one of my classes at The School of Visual Arts in New York. I got the idea after noticing that quite a few of them had already photographed Eugene Ginsberg and that all of them seemed to like him. In addition to being a nonthreatening and gentle soul, he has other virtues: being curious about his subconscious nature and having the courage to face up to whatever he might discover. This courage came in handy, for he was really shaken up more than once. Of the pictures printed here (out of about twenty), the picture by John Shearer rattled him the most. Perhaps you can guess the reasons.

I think it taught him some important things about himself. Maybe he wasn't quite ready for them, but I'm certain he's glad he learned about them. The mysterious figure whispering in his ear suggests that he may be prone to listening to advice, from his inner self or from others. The blank eye sockets hint that perhaps he's hiding his eyes (the doors into himself) from others. The overall quality of the picture says rather strongly that Gene has a morbid vein in his character. Eugene wasn't particularly happy to discover these things. To see the Self isn't always comfortable—but it's enlightening.

The Psychology of People Pictures

This is an essay which applies basic psychology to an understanding of what happens when people make pictures of people. It is very definitely not for people who are uptight. Even those who are fairly loose will find that it rattles their cages a bit. And this is exactly what it's supposed to do: rattle cages.

My motive for writing it is the knowledge that we are all prisoners of our own egos (see Chapter Six). The only way out of this prison is to batter down the walls. The essay is intentionally designed for use as a battering ram. The reader can use it to batter down the walls in which his egotism has imprisoned him. He does this by reading, then thinking about what he's read to see if it applies to himself. I've tried to phrase my ideas in such a way that he can't escape the fact it *does* apply. If

I've been successful in this, it will take a very artful dodger to read the whole thing through without getting his ears pinned back.

Sensitive readers will see that the writing is psychologically aggressive in the nth degree. My notion is that if you're going to help someone batter down a prison cage you might just as well do a thorough job of it. Years ago I used to worry that writing so aggressive might stack people up in mental hospitals by showing them too much about themselves too soon. In time I learned that people have such cleverly constructed and powerfully defended ego-defense systems (lie systems) that the chance of this is extremely remote. As I see it now, "The Psychology of People Pictures" has as little chance of breaching the prison wall as a dried-up creampuff. Nonetheless, people can use it as a bludgeon if they really wish to.

In addition to trying to help egotistical readers give themselves a thorough boxing around the ears, I've offered them what I've learned to see as helpful information. One of the reasons we suffer distress when we're around people, photographing them or not, is that we don't know what's going through their minds. That we should even worry about such a thing is a sign of well-advanced egotism. The right kind of information serves both to relieve the distress and the egotism which gives rise to it. I think there's an abundance of it in the essay.

People may object that it doesn't look like an essay. I, for one, don't care what it looks like, as long as it does the job for which it was designed. I call it an essay because years of experience and thought, and nearly two months of hard writing, went into it. This is not to say I think it's a great piece of work. After all, by my definition an orang-utan could write an essay as easily as I. But it is offered with seriousness and good will. Some people have told me they benefited from it.

The psychology in it is of a very basic sort. In fact, one might call it merely advanced common sense. Since I've never felt comfortable writing about egos, ids, abreactions, cathexis, and so on, I couldn't ethically use these terms here. The only term I do use is 'ego', which I don't define in the same way as most psychologists do (Chapters Eight and Nine).

The essay was not written to make anyone happy. On the contrary, I hoped to make people suffer in a useful way. It may be fun to tear down someone else's prison walls, but I've never heard anyone laugh joyously while tearing down his own. However, it does give one a great sense of accomplishment when he realizes he's pried even one brick loose.

The Essay:

Photography apparently means people to most of America's fifty-three million amateur photographers. Of the two-and-one-quarter billion photographs they make each year, more than half are of people, mostly their families or close friends—the people they love. Since photography records people wonderfully well, people are more interested in people than in anything else, and love is the greatest human need and highest human virtue, there is nothing surprising about this. Reasonably well aware of what people wanted to use photography for, the photographic press has devoted years to teaching its readers how *to take portraits of people. Is there anything else that needs to be said about the subject?*

There is plenty of 'how to' information available these days, and it's easy to take photographs. However, long years of experience in teaching photography to people who have had great difficulty in approaching other human beings with cameras, and my own twenty-five years of intermittent trauma caused by the "simple" act of trying to make satisfactory pictures of people I care about have convinced me that not only is there a lot to say but that it is time someone said it. Taking pictures of people is one of the world's most upsetting hobbies—enchanting, inspiring, challenging, rewarding, and all that, but damned upsetting too. It is so very upsetting that those of us fascinated

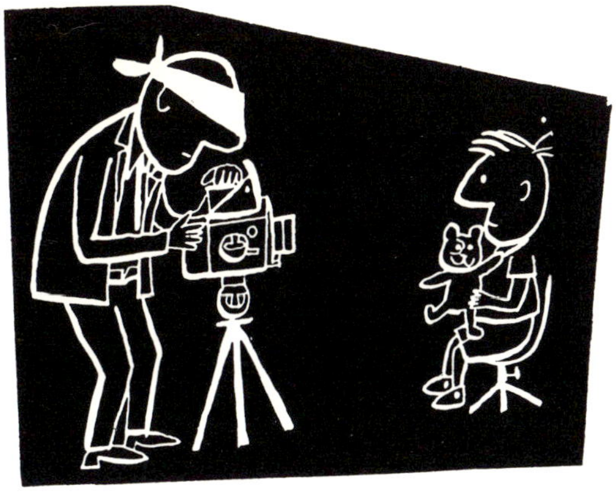

by it give it up for good, every month or so.

There are two ways of taking pictures of people. One is not to think about what you are doing or about the person you are photographing, allow your emotions any chance for expression, nor really look at the human being you're pointing your camera at. The other is to think, feel and look. The first approach is that of the snapshooter. Since it involves less possibility of psychological suffering, it is the most frequently used by far. But the latter approach is the most meaningful and the only one worth writing about.

Since the reason people avoid really looking at, reacting to, or thinking about one another is that they are afraid to, we must discuss many of the reasons for this. The idea will be to open the doors for a type of photographic approach to people which could enrich your life. You don't have to settle for the type of picture which captures only a minute part of what makes your family and friends important to you, nor must they always be strangers to you.

The camera can be a means of learning to understand people and of recording what you have understood in its fullest dimension. Those whom you understand are not strangers. This is a distant and difficult goal, however, and it means you must delve deeply into yourself. Since it is a kind of digging that modern man likes, you shouldn't find it dull and unrewarding. You have probably already done much of this kind of searching in areas other than photography. Perhaps seeing your search-for-yourself in this new context will not only make photography more significant to you but also give you new insights into your everyday search for Self.

You may ask, and rightly so, "Who is this man who thinks he can tell me something?" The answer is: "He is a middle-aged man who has spent his life in the common search of all men. He has perhaps as much to tell you as you would have to tell him about *your* search."

To be completely honest with you—and at the risk of being labeled a colossal egotist or just plain stupid—I cannot bring myself to believe that the material presented by most writers on the problems of photographic interpretation of people ever really gets to the heart of the matter. I will avoid, therefore, the ground over which they so commonly plod. Despite what anyone says, the secret of making good portraits is not in lighting, posing, make-up, retouching, printing, choice of color film, use of close-up attachments on cameras, control of graininess on film, and choice of camera; nor can it be found in all these things together.

The secret is not to be learned in a darkroom, camera store, or photographic salon. It is not a matter of gimmicks, creativity, or pursuit of the esoteric. You will not learn it by buying new equipment or by fitting adapters to the old. The secret—if there is one—is not for sale. Of these things I am very positive. I repeat: Photographic books and magazines have failed to get to the heart of the matter.

Out of very sincere conviction and a considerable personal experience in making people-pictures, I must present ideas that some of you will find extremely odd. At worst, though they do fail in their intent, they will be newly minted, perhaps original. At best these ideas will lead intelligent people to comprehend fully what I have so dimly seen and, discarding my errors, to strike out for themselves to find the secret.

People mean something to people. This is the place to begin our study. You and I photograph people for no other reason, unless we've been misled into attacking our own spiritual values or into deifying the worthless. You or I photograph a wife or lover, son or daughter, or friend

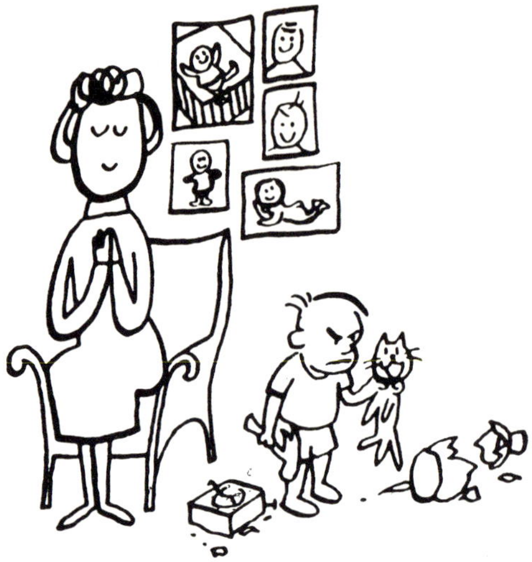

because of what they mean to us and despite the fact that we may not understand this meaning very well. Despite the fact? Yes.

I am a human being, and I cannot be comfortable doing what I don't understand (*if* I'm aware that I don't, and that the lack of understanding is significant). When photographing people, I fumble blindly for what it is that they mean to me, what it is they mean in the total scheme of things. It is difficult to continue, of course; but can I as a human being afford to leave off the search? One look at a zombie who has given up is enough to put me back on the trail—or one day of feeling completely isolated from my fellow men. I must use any means at my command in my search for the meaning of man—photography is such a means.

But not all is desperation. There are the very real, positive things, too. I can look at an old picture of my infant son, now a grown man, and there is a light: "Now I know why I couldn't love him then! And why I do now!" A picture of my wife: "I can see that she's afraid of me. Afraid of me! How can this be, how could I have not understood before?" A picture of a friend: "Why, I do believe, he loves me. Can there be such a thing in this world, a friend who loves *me*?" A picture of another friend: "No one could make a picture like this unless he disliked the subject. Does this mean that I really don't like John at all? Can I fool myself that well?" Though such understanding is painful sometimes, it is the sweet pain of an organism assured of continued growth and virility. It hurts to understand, but not to understand at all is for me a living death.

Your personal values are deeply involved in your portraiture. What do you value, what do you believe in? Do you know or seek to know? Either you know, and knowing for sure what it is that you hold dear is very important to you, or you seek to know. Or both. Your sense of values makes its mark on everything you do. When you make a photograph, just as when you write a serious letter to a friend to whom you are trying to explain yourself, this sense of values, or the search for values, is indelibly written. Once written, it will not leave you alone for it insists on projecting itself into your consciousness. If you are satisfied with what you have written in the letter or photograph, you can continue writing or photographing. If not, you are stymied—discouraged, frustrated, frightened, despairing, perhaps immobilized. This is true whether or not you realize that your problem is one of values.

When you make a portrait, you absolutely cannot help projecting into it your personal values concerning people, the particular person photographed, and yourself. Even your choice of person is a reflection of values. Though you inevitably make this statement of belief in some subtle way in every picture, it is very difficult for you, unless you are philosophically sophisticated, to translate it into words. Thus, its meaning is obscure, difficult to cope with.

But obscure or not, it often hits you with great emotional impact, sometimes leaving you confused and depressed. Though you have somehow revealed yourself, you are never quite sure how and to what extent. That you may have been in the past totally unaware of expressing personal values in each picture doesn't change the fact: Your beliefs have been inscribed for all to see ('sense' is probably a more accurate word, because we are dealing with a phenomenon which is for most of us beyond verbal description).

The fact of stating values in your pictures has many consequences to you, some readily perceived, others not. Let me invent some people to explain this:

John Brown doesn't like to photograph his wife, for every time he does he is overwhelmed with the ugliness of her nose—not that it is really that monstrous. Ordinarily, he likes it well enough; but when he points a camera at her, its homeliness grows in his mind until she turns into a gigantic nose. Almost invariably, his pictures of her accentuate this unfortunate feature, though that is not at all what he consciously wishes to do. His ashamed feelings about the nose and his vague but persistent awareness that he caricatures it in photographs bring him into the fierce crossfire of his conscience.

He is intelligent enough to know that his cosmetic prejudices have been unduly influenced by pernicious Hollywood influences in our culture. Though he hates these influences for what they do to the minds and emotions of people, they've also penetrated his always inadequate defenses and molded his taste. He has warped prejudices which he can't get rid of, no matter how hard he tries.

Also, many of his petty animosities toward his wife find their outlet in his silent condemnation of her looks. He knows that in this area she feels herself completely inadequate and defenseless against any slur or disapproving glance. Thus, when John photographs her he knows—and she knows—he obliquely attacks her. This makes him a true sewer rat. And when he uses his camera to put her on a cross he painfully bruises his own values. His photographs of her shout at him, "You don't really believe what you tell yourself you do! You turn an act of love into an act of hate!" Though he bought his camera to photograph the people he loves, love seldom shows itself in his pictures. Not understanding the nature of marriage, he naturally hadn't expected this to happen.

Even in this age of constant self-examination the anger which exists in the average marriage is seldom talked about. It is as if only men and women who get divorces ever get angry at one another, and Lord knows there are enough of them. But anger is nearly always there in a marriage, whether it be a good one or bad. The reasons for it are many. One of the most basic ones is that when people marry they are forced to see how badly they do at living according to their own ideals. This gives rise to much anger, though it may be mainly unconscious.

It happens in this way: I marry a woman, determined to love and honor her the rest of my life. Furthermore, my basic concept of myself is that I'm a loving person. After I live with her for awhile, however, I frequently have hostile thoughts toward her running through my mind. I see all her faults, blame her for everything that goes awry in our home and in our relationship. But I also, unavoidably, see something concerning the true nature of these hostile thoughts of mine. To my great dismay, I see that most of them are entirely irrational. What I call her faults are not necessarily faults at all, unless I insist on seeing them that way. Furthermore, I may even make the self-shaking discovery that such real faults as she has are only mirror-images of my own and that this is really why I find them so upsetting. There is a true saying that nothing in another person can upset you unless it is also to be found in you.

But why should all this make me angry at my wife? A simple answer: Merely living with her has forced me to begin to see things in myself I absolutely do not want to know. She has 'caused' this; therefore I'm angry at her. Though I also know that seeing her as the cause of my suffering through self-discovery is irrational thinking, I'm angry anyway.

Anger as such is entirely irrational, so why should it be surprising that people get angry for the wrong reasons? There are, in fact, no right reasons for it, unless one is angered on grounds which are truly and deeply spiritual. In this case, one is never angry at another person, but only at something in him that isn't as it should be. These two types of anger are entirely different. One of my basic reasons for being angry at my wife is that her mere presence within the threshold of my consciousness forces me to see that my anger is nearly always of the wrong kind and that as a lover (in the spiritual sense) I'm almost a total washout.

There are very good reasons why the Church has called marriage a sacrament. The idea is not that two people come together and automatically start living in heavenly bliss. It is that as partners they can learn through mutual suffering to eventually destroy in themselves such things as non-spiritual anger. The marriage sacrament is a trial by fire. The bliss is a very real possibility, but it must be earned.

Sarah Jones, a young mother, can't stand screaming children, but values above all else the idealized love of a mother for her child. This afternoon she is certain she is a monster, because the hate welling up in her during her baby's two days and nights of constant screaming can no longer be denied her conscious awareness. Later, when the little one is finally asleep, beautiful in his helpless fatigue and surrender to slumber, Sarah will drag out her well-thumbed snapshots of him and feel herself reaffirmed. Somehow, she always manages to project her values positively when she photographs her baby, as most mothers do. When she sees the pictures she knows them for what they truly are: messages of love, her love for the most precious being in all the world.

Her husband's numerous photographs of her loved one she seldom looks at. They are larger, sharper, and more technically brilliant than hers; but they show only how much he values his conquest of the photographic process. In them, his feelings for the baby seem to be stated as questions or he doesn't see the child at all except as an object in a composition. Yet Sarah's own poor snapshots reaffirm her to herself as a true woman with a right to at least a little self-respect.

Bill Smith wanders the streets of town shooting many pictures, but seldom photographs people. One might think this is because he doesn't value them. Actually, he values them very highly, but being extremely shy he approaches them awkwardly. As a result, in his pictures they appear ill at ease, slightly hostile, or frightened. This compounds his isolation from people, his inability to associate graciously with them. More than anything else, he would like to make strong, rich, and meaningful pictures of people. Since he makes so few people-pictures, he expresses certain of his values by omission.

Homely **Mary Jenkins,** who ordinarily takes dozens of snaps of people close to her, has never taken a picture of her boyfriend. He is young, handsome, and, understandably, a trifle vain. Unconsciously, Mary feels very hostile at being outshone. If she photographed him, she would not only flatter a vanity she finds aggravating but stand in danger of accidentally discovering how bitchy she feels toward someone she loves. Capturing his youthful vanity in a photograph (any simple snap of him would show it, too) would irritate her. If she looked for the reasons for her irritation, she would inevitably learn that she doesn't measure up to her own youthful puritanical standards of saintliness, tolerance, and understanding. Naturally, she doesn't want to learn that she violates her own code of values.

Since I am as interested in why people *don't* take photographs (when they have cameras) as in why they do, I wish to re-emphasize the fact that, as in the lives of John Brown, Sarah Jones, Bill Smith, and Mary Jenkins, values have a lot to do with non-performance. If taking photographs will violate our values, lead us to see that they are shallow or contradictory, tell us that we don't really have any, lead us to question those inherited from our parents or culture, or force us into the painful process of developing values where we have none, we will usually take a less painful way out and stop trying to make photographs.

Paul James takes pictures of his wife at a distance of ten feet or more, though he has an expensive camera which would let him come quite close to her and still get sharp pictures if he chose to. He likes her best when he doesn't see her too well, i.e., when he doesn't have to question himself as to how much, or how little, he values her, and why. I suspect this is one of the main reasons that snapshots are so frequently taken at this distance—or not at all.

Though **Ted Johnson** expresses great love in his pictures of his son, he seldom takes his camera off the shelf. When he looks at his few pictures of his beloved boy, he is always overcome with remorse, thinking, "How little I have to give this wonderful child, how often I put him entirely out of my mind, how little I've tried to understand him as a person." Even more upsetting, he sometimes thinks, "He's too fat and clumsy." In Johnson's case, taking photographs doesn't offend his code of values. His trouble is that they serve as persistent reminders that he seldom lives up to his own expectations for himself. Certainly, this is another of the main reasons why so few people-pictures are taken (though more than a billion a year is a lot of pictures, it's not very many for fifty-three million people to take—around twenty a year per picture-shooter).

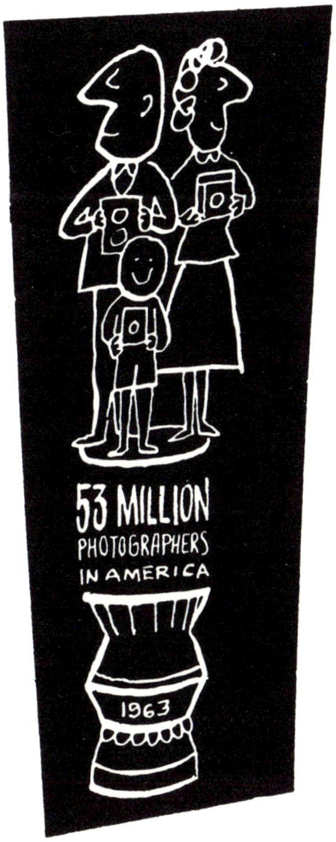

Our values have everything to do with whether we do or do not take people-pictures, how we take them, whether we feel rewarded while doing it or afterwards, and the degree to which making such pictures and looking at them contributes to our making sense of our relationships with people. In light of this, it is very odd that those who write about photographing people have little or nothing to say on the subject of values. No matter how much a reader may learn about solving the technical problems of making portraits (you may have noticed that the terms "portrait," "people-picture," and "picture of a person" are being used interchangeably here), he will never be happy making them, nor will he even try, if he finds himself embroiled in painful inner conflicts and self-accusation. The central problem in amateur portraiture is man's understanding of man.

Just as values have a great influence on what photography means to us, so do our purposes in making photographs. Values and conscious purposes are related in that the former give birth to the latter. Or, we can say that our day-to-day conscious purpose in using an expressive medium is to give voice to our values. Our values are in the very fabric of our being; they are broad, unvoiced generalizations which give our lives direction. Our conscious purposes are the everyday signposts we select to help us live hour by hour in a meaningful way. For everything we do we have a little group of selected purposes. Our values stand in the background and direct our lives as a whole.

The commonly stated, easily understood conscious purposes for making pictures of people might be categorized as follows:

An aid to memory. We all have pictures which recall half-forgotten vacation trips, faraway members of our family or friends, our sons and daughters in their childhood, and so on. Our purpose in snapping the pictures was to remember.

Time-freezing. An event flying through time must be frozen in a photograph to be fully enjoyed, understood, studied leisurely, or even seen clearly at all—Marcia's quizzical look, Larry's nervous peek at his bride, the children vigorously showing

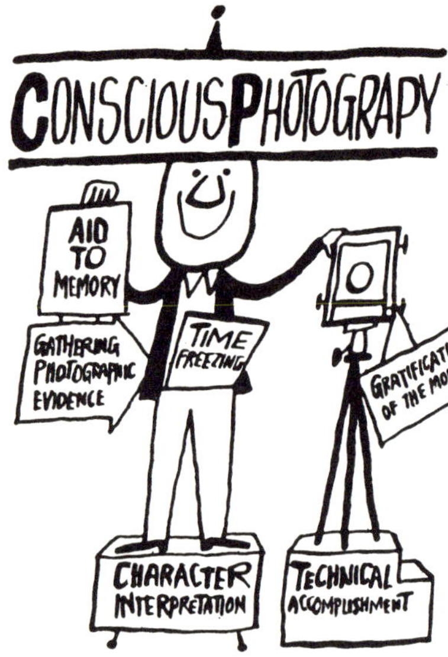

off for Uncle George, the exact moment when Ellen hits her high note, Bob winning the 100-yard dash in the high-school track meet.

Gathering photographic evidence. "Mary stood right in front of Old Faithful when it erupted, as you can plainly see. It is obvious that my mother was a beautiful girl. This picture shows how much Mona hates to be seen with her hair in curlers. My wife and I had a truly grand wedding. Jimmy licked the neighbor's boy in a wrestling match. I can handle water skis." The evidence can be used for bragging, winning arguments, convincing people that an improbability is true, sharing interesting experiences, conveying simple information. For most people, photographic evidence is irrefutable, which is one reason why gathering it is such a popular pastime.

Gratification of the model. When you make portraits for other people, not because you yourself want the pictures, you try to please *them,* generally by leaning as far as your skill will allow toward romanticized, commercial, cosmetic portraiture, for that is the kind of picture most people want of themselves. Gratification of your subject usually means skillful flattery by means of special photographic techniques —posing, cosmetic lighting, retouching, expert printing, and so on. Since few amateurs have any real skill here, gratification of the model is a purpose in which they are generally frustrated.

Technical accomplishment. From reading camera magazines and books an amateur photographer picks up some notions as to what technically constitutes a good picture—fine and sharp grain, long tonal range, rich blacks and sparkling whites, or, in color slides and prints, pleasing color harmonies, well-saturated colors, clean whites, rich and neutral blacks. He may get so interested in these qualities that producing them is his only purpose in making a portrait (or any other kind of photograph), and things like personality, naturalness, and character are ignored. On the other hand, he may strive for technical accomplishment but keep it subordinate to expressive and interpretive purposes.

Character interpretation. As I understand it, character is an elusive something that some people have and others do not. It is interesting to try to figure out what it is that gives a person character and then to try making photographs in which these hard-to-understand qualities are explained. Since each of us is in some degree concerned with his own character and must study character in other people to get a perspective on himself, using photography for this purpose has a great fascination.

Though the average, so-called character study is so superficial that it reveals only the photographer's lack of character, there are many studies made which communicate deep and remarkable intuitions. There is one thing which can be very disturbing to one who studies character through portraiture: discovering in his own pictures how naive, shallow, ill-considered, and banal are his own notions with respect to character. I suppose that all of us who experiment in character interpretation have made such disheartening discoveries many, many times.

These are some of the most commonly mentioned reasons for taking pictures of people. They are frequently hashed and rehashed in the photographic press. Nearly every photographer finds them acceptable, but few of them ask if these are the real reasons why people take pictures of one another. It so happens that they're not. To find the real ones we must move to another realm: unconscious purpose. Here we find that not everything is goodness and light. Values and purposes are in misalignment.

If our conscious purposes and our codes of value go hand-in-hand, our unconscious purposes and our values are involved in civil war. It is a war fought in the jungle at night among blind combatants.

You Have An Unconscious Mind

The 'unconscious mind' means precisely what the term sounds as if it ought to mean, though few people will believe it. Let's monkey around with it for a while. Now, if you're unconscious—as if you've been slammed on the head with a sledge hammer—you're really out like a busted Mazda. As far as you can possibly tell when you are in this condition, you are nobody doing nothing, nowhere.

When awake your mind is like an iceberg, with a small part (the 'you,' or conscious part) above the surface and a larger part (the unknown, unconscious self) below the surface. You (*as you*) are always completely above the surface. What is down below, only the sharks know. As far as the familiar 'you' can tell (except by inductive reasoning following long and astute self-observation), the underneath part doesn't even exist. Can you imagine the ridiculous situation of a very intelligent iceberg thinking it is sitting on *top* of the water? That is precisely the human situation.

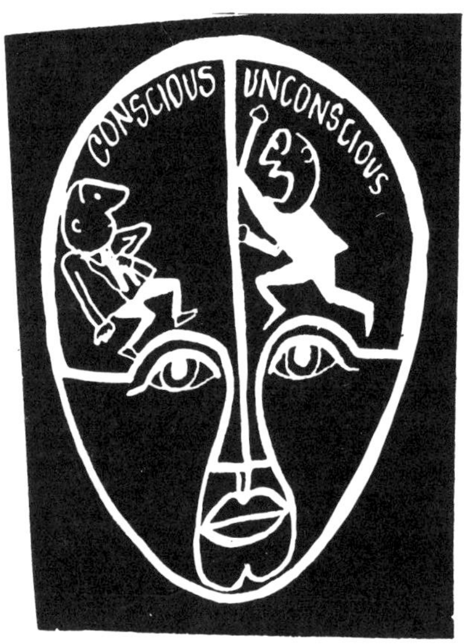

It's as if ninety percent of you had been clubbed on the head while the other ten percent is not only awake but bright and cheery as a button. At least, that's the way in which the bright (conscious) part of your mind comprehends it (it obviously doesn't comprehend the *real* truth at all). However, not only is the knocked-out part of your mind not really knocked-out at all but instead it is busy as a beaver colony when the dam blows out. Furthermore, it is doing its damndest to run the whole circus: that's *you*.

One of the hardest things to understand about the unconscious mind is that there is one—in every human being. I don't know about you, but I'm unhappy about the whole situation. I can never completely accept: first, that I have an unconscious; second, that I can't browse around in it at will; and third, that I can't tell it what to do. Fourth, it gives me a rough time every waking minute. The largest part of 'me' is outside my awareness and impervious to direct inquiry. Even more exasperating to accept is the fact that this part of my mind is responsible for much of my behavior—it's sort of like being run by an alien bug from Mars who has set up housekeeping in my brain.

Enough of Freud. At this point, it is plain that if you are psychologically sophisticated you will accept some of what follows, and that if you are not you will throw his whole essay in the trash barrel. You either believe there is such a thing as an unconscious—and that you've got one, too—or you don't. The same goes for unconscious purposes. Since any attempt to explain the meaning of people-photography involves the notion of the unconscious mind (that is, if the explanation is supposed to really explain anything), I have no alternative but to proceed as planned.

One of the reasons that unconscious purposes *are* unconscious is that they are too uncomfortable to live with. For example, if I were to become aware of an impulse which I immediately recognized as irrefutably sadistic, I would have to jump off a cliff. As a self-acknowledged sadist I couldn't bear to live with myself. It doesn't make me happy to know that the reason I like women with large breasts is that I was weaned too soon, either.

My 'for-example people' who will be used to illustrate the unconscious purposes in people-photography do not and cannot know their motives. If the same motives happen to fit you, indications of it to you may be: rage, complete inability to understand what is being said, compulsive sleepiness, your mind going blank, a powerful urge to call the author a flaming idiot, dryness of the mouth, profuse sweating, giving your Leica to your son-in-law or father-in-law, headache, nausea, memories intruding between you and the text, cramps, a tightening of the stomach, a smug feeling of superiority, or some other symptom. Whatever may happen, they may very well be some of the same things you feel when you try to persuade yourself to take your camera off the shelf to take a picture of someone.

The Unconscious Purposes of Portraiture

If you are going to make sense out of this section you must bear in mind the fact that the unconscious is actually unconscious. The people I'm going to talk about are totally unaware, therefore, of the unconscious aspects of their involvement in taking pictures of people. Furthermore, it is not my intention to say that their hidden purposes are *bad*. They are hidden only because the people in whom they occur cannot, for a number of reasons which depend entirely on the individual, accept them into consciousness. The *badness* or *goodness* of purposes is in the domain of ethics, which is out of the mainstream of this discussion. The purposes which follow are human and extremely commonplace.

Playing God. Most of us, I suppose, are not really very satisfied with people, ourselves included. There is little indication in literature that anyone who has really thought about it ever has been satisfied. One of the main functions of the arts, photography included, has always been to give man the viable materials with which he can remake the human race according to his standards.

In photography, it is much easier than one might suppose to remake or modify people. In fact, it is possible for a picture snapper to do it quite unawares. People are constantly presenting different visual versions of themselves to the world: Any experienced visual person (painter, sculptor or photographer) will tell you that they never look quite the same twice in a lifetime. In short, there are numberless versions of every single human being.

If a picture-shooter wishes to 'change' John Jones, all he has to do is watch Jones until that version of him he wants flits into existence, then freeze it forever with a camera. While Jones then becomes something else, the picture remains. If it happened to be an atypical expression on his face, the picture is 'not really' Jones. Thus, the photographer has 'changed' Jones. That is, he is saying that something which is Jones-like on rare occasions—or only once in a lifetime—is the real, everyday Jones: Jones himself.

Though it is very difficult to prove, it is nonetheless true that every one of us who photographs someone captures a very photographer-opinionated version of him, so much so, sometimes, that a friend of the subject won't even recognize him from the photograph. People who know very little about photography do this much of the time. Those who know a lot about photography do it all the time (knowing the photographic process makes it possible to introduce changes in a subject in various ways: exposure, composition, printing, symbol manipulation, color selection, and so on).

It should be obvious that one of the main attractions of portraiture is the opportunity to remold people. Let's take you, for example: How many people have you seen recently whom you felt could not have been improved? If you have at least a modicum of skill with photography, enough to know some of the changes which can be made in people, wouldn't you enjoy trying it on some of these 'defectives'? Sure you would. It would make you feel like a god, which is how every human being most likes to feel.

Some picture-makers are obsessed with 'improving' people. They fiddle for years with lighting, posing, make-up, trick printing, diffusion, distortion, color filters, cropping, grain and texture effects, all put to use to change people from what they are into something else. A tiny bit of success in modifying human beings is enough to sustain them for months. On the other hand, one of the main reasons that others drop photography as a hobby is that in their pictures they find they're catching things too much the way they really are and don't know enough about photography to do anything about it. Though they can't help making petty changes, that isn't enough. They want to make total changes.

So far, it would be difficult to guess why I say that the desire to remold people is an unconscious objective. It is more accurate to say that there are many aspects of this desire, some of which we are aware of, others not. For example, those who are religiously devout would not like to think that their desire to change people is a rejection of God's work, and that they may be trying to do God one better. It's fine to accept his work in the abstract (and only when in church), but reject the everyday exemplifications of it. Is it, really? There is, too, in this will to change other people the implication that the changer is superior and everyone else inferior. There is the implication of rejection; do I wish to change my wife in a photograph because I don't really accept her the way she is? This thought shocks me to the core as being arrogant and unloving.

Intimidation and domination. Let's return to my vignettes of hypothetical people. They are crudely done, oversimplified, and each offers only one instance of something that occurs in many people and is expressed in many different ways. Draw on your own life experience to fill out the dimensions of my characters and bring more of them onto the stage.

Sam senses the circumstances that cause people to be terribly afraid of cameras and he greatly enjoys using his for this purpose. Though he makes a play of kindliness and of interest in his subjects, he always 'accidentally' does things which are ordinarily interpreted as meaningless or ambiguous but which his subjects are certain to interpret in such a way as to make them completely miserable. Instead of hitting good old Sam on the nose, however, they fall for his fictitious good will and take the blame on themselves.

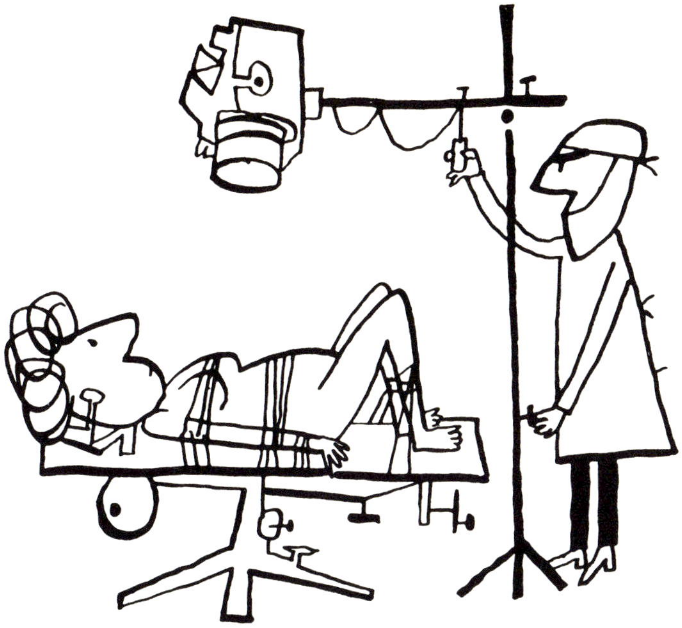

After Sam passes their way with his camera people are always aware of their pimples, double chins, ill-fitting clothes, wrinkles, bald heads, how they walk, and how they stand. Sam likes to run things, and when he drags out his camera his friends always squirm into line. Of course, Sam, being Sam, thinks of himself as a humanitarian. He doesn't realize that the gifts which keep his victims coming around are more like chains than roses.

Possessing another person. Allow me to don a disguise and play a role, too. I, **Richard,** am a young blunderer—two left feet and ten thumbs. I am fascinated by Lisa —beautiful, intelligent, voluptuous, and two years older than I. But I am frightened and on extremely rare occasions admit it to myself. Also, I am homely, somber, stupid, and undramatically soggy-doggish. When I talk to the flaming Lisa I'm tongue-tied and desperate. At a party I snap her picture while pretending to be clicking someone else (I'm probably the best photographer in our high-school camera club).

Now, she's mine, all mine! I talk to her as she sparkles down at me from my bedroom wall. How welcoming she is as I stand flexing imaginary muscles and baring my teeth in a specially provocative way. The bubble shatters when my mother calls me down to dinner. I'm flooded with shame (Mother will know, she'll read my mind!) and vow I'll never take a picture again. Tomorrow, however, there will be a new bubble—thank God—and Lisa once again mine.

I've also possessed my father, who never lets me close enough to know him and love him; my sister, who aggravates me too much in the life outside of her pictures for me to even want to possess her then; my hero, the first-string fullback; and many, many others. Some of the kids seem to be able to talk to people. Not me. I catch friends with my camera.

There's nothing really frightening so far in Richard's story, is there? Let me add a few bits which he would rather no one knew. He happens to be one of the town's leading 'peeping toms,' is known by close friends to have a very violent temper when provoked, and has mistreated his only sweetheart with sadistic delight. Everything he does he uses as a means of escape from reality—photography too, no doubt. When disturbed, he has a barely detectible stutter. His coordination is bad. He is a constant daydreamer, his fantasies concerned mainly with power and being adulated by others. Are these things and his interest in photography related? If so, perhaps we have some reason to be disturbed.

To belittle people. Let us now talk about a young woman for a while. **Carol** is a slum shooter, poet of the 'winos.' She says, "I guess I'm a sociologist at heart. I want to show people what horrible things go on in their precious city so that they'll get off their tails and do something about it." Oh yes, she feels this way all right, and her pictures may help to improve things. Still, the *prime* force which drives her into the slums is more closely related to hate than to love. She doesn't like the slum dwellers; despises them, if anything. How, then, can we explain her spending so much time photographing them and the fact that she has taken one of them, whom she derogatingly regards as 'typical,' as a lover? You know, picking up a camera doesn't change people into something else. If your life wasn't Candy Land before you bought your camera, it won't be afterward. And 'real photographers' are not superanimals, despite what the camera magazines say about them.

As the writers have it, this is what photography is all about: "Then the photographer picked up his camera and, smiling sweetly at his wife, made a gorgeous picture without getting in the least personally involved. Next, he made a swell picture of his wonderful baby in her sparkling clean diapers. Finally, he went into his impeccable rose garden and, using Kodachrome II, a skylight filter, and a Super Hoptoflex made a picture which he knew everyone at the camera club would pat him on the back for."

Ridiculous! Carol has a lover, twenty-six years older than herself, and who has a cast in one eye. They despise each other for entirely different reasons and get along wonderfully well, all things considered. I repeat, how can we explain Carol?

It's fairly obvious that she must hold herself in extremely low regard. From an upper-middle-class family, she has never in four years of her interest in photography photographed anyone in that social stratum. Pointing a camera at such a person would mean thinking about them and, more important, being analyzed in return. Since she completely rejects herself, she is certain that anyone who took a good look at her through the same kind of rose-colored glasses she was brought up with will do likewise. Why ask for misery? Naturally, she stays away from them. She can photograph slum folk because she feels superior to them. They are the only people in the world she feels comfortable with.

However, because they speak English with a heavy accent or not at all, she is so isolated from them she doesn't realize they have the same problems—money lenders, not enough love, general confusion with respect to the meaning of life—that she does. She hates them for having freedom she doesn't have, so all her pictures turn them into slop. Not knowing what she is up to, they all accept her. For the same reason, she accepts herself.

Maybe you can't identify with Carol, so I'll try another person. I remember a young man highly skilled in photography who made a picture of a girl that made her look as if her face had been eaten by roaches. Gruesome? You bet! As long as I live I'll never forget the shock which burned his face when a hip friend suggested that he had symbolically mutilated the girl. He was really floored, for once the fact had been presented to him, he absolutely could not evade it. That he could have spent weeks fiddling with this picture without discovering what he had done may surprise you, unless you've had a lot of experience with amateur and professional photographers. But it's really commonplace.

It's not at all unusual for young men to make pictures like this of girls. Unconsciously, most of them are afraid of girls, and this is one way of getting back at them for the suffering they feel the girls have caused. There's hardly a male photographer in the world who doesn't at one time or another take revenge on women for being women.

How come people don't see that they're doing such things? Well, in photography there are wonderful distractions to hide under—concern with printing technique, worry about whether the color is right, cropping, focus, ad infinitum. Perhaps one of photography's main attractions to some people is that there are so many ways for them to prevent themselves from learning what they are doing.

I'll hazard the guess that in 25 percent of all amateur people-pictures, unconscious belittlement is a factor. Since putting people down is considered an ignoble purpose except by the very ignorant or the extremely sophisticated, and since a person who unconsciously does it always stands in danger of looking at his photographs and learning what he has done, this unconscious purpose must account for at least three billion of the people-pictures that should have been taken but weren't.

Writing one's own life on the faces of others. Most of us didn't come into life with the equipment we thought we deserved. Let us now talk about a young man whom God shortchanged. **Johnny** has the wrong face (as have most of us)—plump, freckle-dusted, open, short-sighted, and sort of lost—to go along with his inner rages and Machiavellian dream-schemes for revenge against the brute world. On Saturdays he wanders the streets of town with a camera and telephoto lens, carefully collecting the faces he should have had and living the life he should be leading through the fantasies he builds around his collection of strangers. He doesn't understand exactly that this is what he is doing, however. For knowing it would bring him face to face with his shocking self-rejection. John absolutely cannot afford to know fully how little he really cares for and respects John.

Though most of us picture-takers do this to some degree, practically none of us can admit it to him or herself. One of the most shocking things that ever happened to me personally was comprehending that I had written my life on the face of a man I neither knew very well nor liked. To top it off, I called the damned thing "Oedipus." When I realized that the despair and agony I had written there were mine, I was shaken beyond belief. Though the times happened to have been bad for me, had I fully realized my misery I would inevitably have jumped in front of a train. Perhaps expressing the pain through photography made survival possible. I want you to know that I write from the middle of the muddle, not from the safe shore. I'll return now to another acquaintance.

Peter photographs Karen again and again. Through her beauty, he expresses his deepest yearning and highest hopes for beauty in man. He tells his frustration in his manliness, his emptiness, his loneliness. He doesn't seek to know her as a woman, to sleep in her arms, to offer his manhood to her and be told "You are a man." He's too afraid. Karen—real, live Karen—must forever remain his dream, an empty symbol. This is beautiful Karen's tragedy, of course. How many frightened young men have I seen with their poor Karens in tow!

How can this be? How can a man write his story on a woman? Why that is just the place where he is most likely to write it! Practically every picture of a woman you've seen in magazines, movies, or on television has been some man's version of himself, his dreams, or his troubles.

Making sense out of one's life. Because the photographs which we take of people are in a way records of our successes or failures in our relationships with them, and because making sense out of our lives involves examining such relationships, you would think we could allow this purpose full, conscious recognition. We should be able to say, "We are making photographs to understand what our lives mean to us."

We don't, however. Why? Well, we would have to make certain extremely painful admissions to ourselves first. We would have to admit before seeking something that there is something missing, something very worth seeking. We would have to admit that our lives, as they stand, don't make sense to us by any 'rules of sense' we have ever heard of. Such an admission is extremely disheartening. To those brought up in the belief of a sensible, logical universe, it is almost impossible to make. None of us ever make it willingly; we are forced into it by the relative meaninglessness of our experiences—the meaninglessness to *us,* that is.

When we are young, God gives our lives sense. If not God, some primitive juju of our childhood. Then doubt comes—doubt in God, doubt in selves, doubt in magic and immortality, doubt in a sensible universe. Even with God, doubt comes; in youth we understand His will full well, in adulthood we're not so sure. Capacity to tolerate doubt is a measure of maturity. The decision to deliberately use an art form to find sense in one's life—or put it there—implies a very considerable maturity. It is much more probable that we will use it this way many years before discovering its true function.

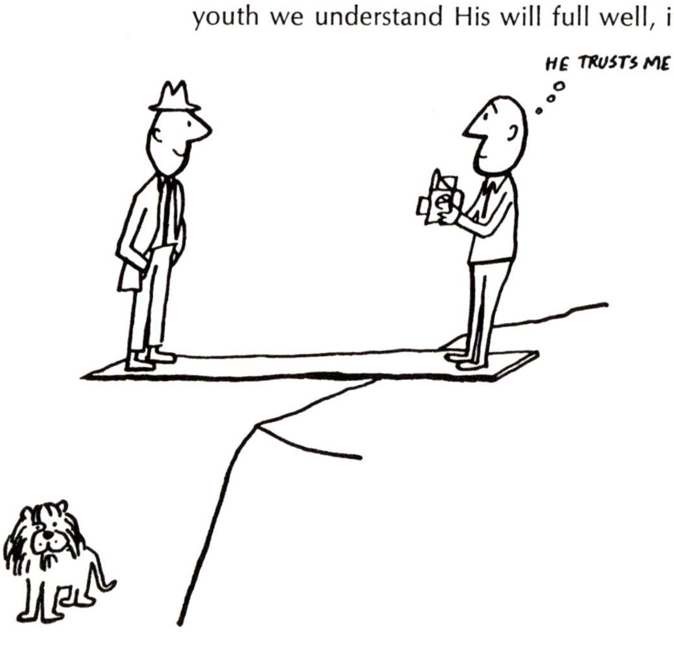

In maturity, I learn that whatever meaning my life has, I, aided by my friends, have put there. How would making a photograph contribute to this meaning? Let's see what happens when I photograph a friend. I point my camera at him, and he looks back at me with trusting eye. This means something to me: My behavior has been such, recently and over the long haul, that Fred trusts me, despite the fearsome presence of the camera.

Over the next few months, as I look at the resulting picture, I ask, "Why *did* he trust me?" (That he did so is written indelibably in the photograph.) The answer I eventually arrive at is part of what I would call 'making sense out of life.' Discovering how very much Fred means to me is another part of it, and that life without such friends would be terrible to me, another bit.

The sense of one's life doesn't come instantly with a great crash of cymbals. It dribbles in, piece by piece. One learns to welcome each tiny mote with great joy. Life is long, and many pieces make a pile. Should anyone be irritated by what he might call my 'air of superiority,' I will admit that my personal pile isn't as yet very large. But give me another two hundred years—wow!

In this section we've talked about people's unconscious purposes for making portraits. A good many more of them are discussed in Chapter Six in the section entitled "Games Photographers Play." Since reading material like this can make people terribly uncomfortable, I think I ought to explain myself a little bit.

First of all, I'm deliberately making you as uncomfortable as I can. It is only through experiencing pain that you can rid yourself of the kind of psychic garbage I'm talking about. By deliberately facing up to it you gradually eliminate it from

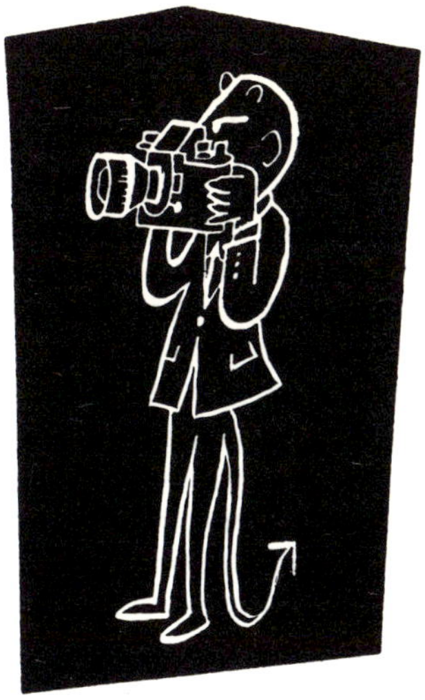

yourself. If you don't consciously do this you'll forever be ruled by unconscious drives you see as being less than admirable. So, in your own behalf you need to be hurt. And I'm just the ornery cuss who will help you.

There is something else which ought to be explained, too. I've talked as if only ugly things arise from the unconscious. From this, one might suppose there's no point in digging into himself, for everything he finds will smell like a dead cow. Who wants smelling dead cows as a way of life? There's more to the story, however. The human unconscious is very much more than a foul mess of abominations. In fact, that part of it which originates the drives we're ashamed of is but a tiny bit of the whole. We might call it the 'superficial unconscious.' This is that part of the hidden self with which Freudian psychology—and much of modern literature—concerns itself exclusively. However, there is much more to mankind than Freud ever learned.

There is a vast part of the unconscious mind which is marvelous beyond words. To bring that part into conscious awareness is to experience Divinity Itself. There is no greater thing that a human being can strive to do. However, there is a high barrier around this marvelous part of the Self. It is the garbage-ridden superficial unconscious.

Until this wall is breached and destroyed the higher Self must forever remain a prisoner. The way to do this is to deliberately dredge up all the foul muck, bring it into the light of consciousness. It's a terribly painful process, naturally, for it means we must surrender all our dearly beloved illusions with respect to ourselves. But once we know, in all their dimensions, these negative depths of our beings, things get better. Once in the light, our negative drives gradually wither and die. We are rid of them once and for all and can look forward to a life of meaning and joy.

It is not enough for a person to create something. He also has to understand what it is he has made. If he doesn't he's unhappy with himself and his creation. This is especially true if it didn't come out the way he intended. Though he knows what his problem is, he doesn't know how to solve it. He needs some basis for forming judgements about his creation.

When a picture-shooter makes a portrait it is seldom what he expected it to be. He doesn't understand it as well as he would like to. Even if it comes out exactly as planned, there are elements in it which baffle him. This is a very serious problem to both amateur and pro. Whenever we make something, whether it be a cake or a picture, we need some basis for interpreting it. We must find some way of deciding whether it is good or bad, beautiful or ugly, significant or not, understandable or puzzling. Otherwise, we will find ourselves confused and begin to doubt the logic of our behavior.

I have seen dozens, hundreds of people-pictures made by people who couldn't figure out what their own pictures meant. Though most of these photographs were perfectly fine and sensible, the people who made them were terribly frustrated and upset. Many of them gave up photography of people altogether, unable to stand the confusion their own pictures caused them to feel. Obviously, it is not enough to know how to do something. One must also know how to think about the finished product.

Unfortunately, the literature of photography has done little so far in establishing bases for photographic interpretation, or criticism. Perhaps it cannot develop far in this direction until readers admit to themselves that they have very large and aggravated problems stemming from their inability to understand their own photographs. Is this a difficult admission for a person to make? I think that it may be.

There are a few teachers and writers in photography who attack directly the problem of finding the real meaning of photographs. Most of them, however, devote themselves to becoming agile dodgers who can sidestep meaning altogether without other people's becoming aware of it. There are few, therefore, to whom the confused photographer can turn for help on problems outside the realm of photographic technique.

In attempting to make my small contribution to the problem of interpretation of people-pictures, I will ask a few questions, then proceed to examine what people do about interpretation in everyday life. Have you ever attempted to make an intelligible, handsome, and revealing picture of someone and been frustrated by the inability to measure the degree to which you succeeded? When you look at your pictures, do you often whisper to yourself, "Why in hell did I do this?" Are you satisfied with the usual standards for measuring your photographs, with knowing that they are accurately exposed, sharp, pleasantly colored, neatly composed, and so on?

Have you ever looked at your own work and been overwhelmed with the suspicion that you were looking at nonsense? Are you willing to spend time creating nonsense or creating that which you may possibly discover to be nonsense after you've done it? On the other hand, would you be interested to know that with an expanded interpretative capacity you will be able to find sense in all your pictures, no matter how nonsensical they may have appeared to you at one time? If these questions intrigue you, the chances are that you would benefit by giving some thought to interpretation, or criticism.

Semi-Unconscious Interpretations of Portraits

Everyone, whether interested in photography per se or not, sees many a photograph of people each day (magazines, newspapers, television, etc.), and he interprets each one. It is his nature as a human being to do so. If he is an untrained critic, he makes his interpretations of these pictures semiconsciously or unconsciously, at great speed and superficially.

He uses no conscious and rational standards of judgment and gives free play to his personal prejudices, unaware that they are operating. All measurements and decisions are made in terms of himself—his feelings, needs, experiences, life goals. He derives certain personal benefits from looking at the pictures, or otherwise, he wouldn't bother. His judgments are always biased in such a way as to give him the maximum feeling of benefit.

Now, it makes considerable difference in his interpretation whether he himself has made a given picture or someone else has. It makes a difference if he knows the person in the photograph. If he is looking at a reproduction in a magazine or newspaper, or watching something on television, the chances are very great that he is looking at a picture of a stranger made by another stranger, of whose influence he is entirely unaware. What does he think about? Let us frame his interpretation in terms of the questions he might ask himself:

Interpretation of pictures of strangers made by strange photographers:

1. Is this person in the photograph sexually attractive to me?
2. How strong is my desire for him (her)?
3. If I met him (her), what would be my chances of 'making it'?
4. What strategy would work best on this kind of person?
5. What are his (her) morals?
6. What kind of person is he (she)?
7. Would I want him (her) for a brother (sister, mother, father, friend, playmate, lover, uncle, aunt, boss, employee, etc.)?
8. How is he (she) like or unlike me?
9. Were I to know him (her) which of us would be the dominant personality?
10. Would he (she) be likely to uncover my weaknesses and my shame?

11. Would he (she) use these weaknesses against me?
12. How would I benefit from knowing him (her)?
13. Why does someone (an editor perhaps) think I should be interested in this person?
14. Why is he (she) doing what he (she) is doing?
15. What sense for me is there in it?
16. Am I jealous that he (she) is doing it?
17. Would this person like and respect me?
18. How would I have to behave to earn this liking and respect?
19. What is his (her) social status compared with mine?
20. How would I, therefore, react in his (her) company?
21. How do we compare in age and vitality?
22. What is his (her) opinion of self as shown in this picture?
23. In *my* opinion, is this other person's estimate of self justified?
24. How would I measure up to him (her) as a personality?
25. Would I feel self-conscious in his (her) company?
26. What has his (her) life done to or for him (her) that my life has or hasn't done to or for me?
27. How would my friends react if this person were to come into our midst with me as his (her) sponsor?
28. Is this an important person? If so, why?
29. How and why am I impressed by his (her) importance?
30. Is his (her) personality or life attractive enough to me that I can enter into it in fantasy for my pleasure?
31. Is he (she) as good a person as I, or worse?
32. Do I accept or reject him (her) as a person?

If a person is looking at a portrait he himself has made, he will ask himself many of the above questions and the following ones too. Here is the possible interpretation of a picture of a person by the one who made it:

33. What was he (she) thinking when I took his (her) picture?
34. Why is he (she) looking at me that way?
35. What did I do to make him (her) so unnatural, so unlike his (her) usual self?
36. How much do I really care for this person?
37. Why don't I like this picture very much?
38. Why do I feel vaguely ashamed or guilty when I look at it?
39. Did I do something to upset him (her)?
40. Were my purposes in making the photograph noble or ignoble?
41. Does he (she) love me, like me, feel indifferent toward me, or dislike me?
42. How will he (she) react to this picture of him (her)?
43. What can I do or say to this person to defend my picture and make him (her) accept and like it?
44. How well do I really know this person?
45. Am I willing to take the time and trouble to know him (her) better?
46. What in hell prompted me to take the picture at all?
47. Why did I take it in this particular way?
48. What can I do with this picture now that I have it?
49. What will other people think of it?
50. Do I, as of now, wish to move closer to this person or to retreat?
51. If I attempted to move closer, what emotional commitments would I have to make to him (her)?
52. What would I get in return for making these commitments?
53. Why do I have a vague feeling that I was defeated in my purposes for making this picture?
54. Just what were my purposes, anyway?

In the second group of questions, the element of puzzlement and self-doubt that is nearly always present when one is making pictures of people is clearly evident. It should by now be apparent that taking a picture of someone is by no means as simple a problem as is commonly thought. The writers and teachers of photography mistakenly assume—at least, they do in print—that it is the easiest thing in the world to make a studied picture of someone close to you, though they themselves have as much trouble doing it as you perhaps do.

When a professional photographer writes on portraiture, he tends to forget that his own problem is to photograph strangers, while the interest of the amateur is in photographing people he knows. All things considered, it is much easier to photograph strangers. The farther they are from the photographer's social and cultural group, the easier it is.

Though the list of questions is too long to cope with in casual reading, it should serve as a starting point for those who wish to investigate seriously the problems of interpretation of pictures of people. For each question, there is a large number of possible answers. To attempt presenting the answers here would be far beyond our scope and impossible within the space available.

The dedicated advanced amateur tends to ignore the foregoing questions and to ask himself things which generally take him far from the central concerns of photography of people. I'm inclined to think it is neurotic to forget the questions listed, for they are, after all, the normal thoughts of people when they are thinking about their relationships with others. If you have ever listened to a criticism of portraits at a camera club print clinic, you can't help understanding what I mean.

One of the most frightening things about taking a picture of someone is having to look closely at him. As anyone knows, people don't like to be minutely examined, or even examined at all unless in admiration. All of us have had very upsetting experiences in looking and being looked at. After the age of six, the average human being spends much of his time figuring out how to avoid them. Unfortunately, they tend to become more and more painful the older one gets, unless one can develop a philosophy for seeing them in an acceptable perspective.

Do you remember when you were a child and had told a lie to your father, and he said, "Look me in the eye and say that again!"? Your legs turned to water and your stomach to stone.

Do you remember the grade-school bully who was always forcing you into a contest of trying to stare him down? He always won, didn't he, calling you a coward or milk-sop as he did?

Have you ever said, "I love you," and had the other person look you in the eyes and see your lie?

When "listening intently" have you ever missed a cue and looked up when you were supposed to have looked down and heard the words, "You haven't heard a single thing I've said"?

Have you ever offered your true love, the love of eyes looking into eyes, and heard your loved one say, "Of course, I love you too . . . ," while desperately trying to return your look, then failing to?

Of course you have experienced such things, time and again. It is part of the normal fabric of human existence.

There is a special 'language of eyes' which all of us learn, but none of us ever talks about. Talking about it is an unspoken taboo. The protocol in this language is extremely rigid, and breaches of etiquette unforgivable. It is a language whose use we do our best to avoid. It is not surprising, therefore, that a would-be photographer is shocked when he discovers that taking portraits involves looking directly at people.

A young photographer (pro) friend of mine was talking to me some time ago: "So, you're writing something on portraiture, are you? You poor bastard! What people don't know! A lot of them think it's merely a matter of sticking a 90-mm lens on a 35-mm camera and banging away. What a laugh. You've got to *look* at them!"

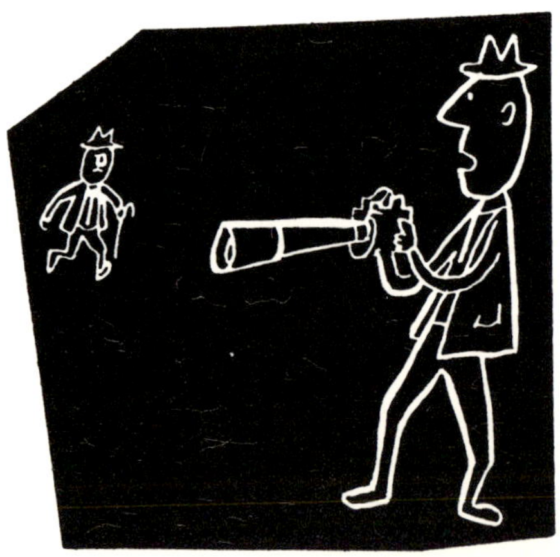

Sure, you put a 90-mm lens on, then a 120-, then a 180-, then a 300-, then, by God, you're so far away from whomever you're photographing you don't have to look at him at all, and he can't see you for haze. If he even tries, you can turn around and run like hell!

Another friend explained, "Looking right at someone, taking his picture, is having a rusty shovel stuck in your guts, with a brawny devil on the other end twisting like mad on the handle."

Maybe you don't know what I'm talking about yet, though I find this very hard to believe. In case you really don't, I will sketch some little scenes which show how the 'language of eyes,' or 'the eye game,' operates.

Bob and **George,** newly acquainted, are talking together and silently trying to gauge their relationship:

(George looks at Bob) Bob: "I wonder if he thinks I'm queer."

(Bob looks at George) George: "I think he's trying to dominate me. I wonder if I should look away or try to stare him down. *Could* I stare him down?"

(George looks away from Bob in exactly the right manner) Bob: "No, he doesn't think I am. He has read my look as an accusation. I will look away first next time in order to express my apology."

(They look at each other, then away simultaneously) Both: "He really understands the language of eyes and our mutual fright of male confronting male. Perhaps there is, after all, a chance for us to become friends."

Natural **Jane** and shy **Fred** are getting acquainted:

(Jane looks directly at Fred) Fred: "That look is a prelude to a proposition; but she'll read in my eyes that I'm impotent. A man should kill a woman for knowing that about him!"

(Fred steals a glance at Jane) Jane: "He seems very upset. What have I done wrong? I'll try making contact again."

(She looks directly at him again) Fred: "I knew it! The dirty slut!"

Mr. Brown is trying to develop a friendly man-to-man talk with his teen-aged son **Larry:**

(Mr. Brown gives Larry what is meant to be a kindly glance) Larry: "Oh, God! What has he found out about me now!"

(Larry looks away) Mr. Brown: "He's seen me again for the incompetent I am, and rejected me, as usual. When will he learn to forgive me for being merely human?"

Are these sketches exaggerated? You know very well they aren't! You know as well as I that a whole encyclopedia filled with them would hardly begin to tell the story—the story of what so often happens when two people try to reach one another. Are my examples unnecessarily dramatic? I think not. They are very average, everyday situations. Average and explosive.

Over the years I've come to believe that this language of the eyes is the 'emotional primary' language, and that all other forms of human communication, outside of sex and body-contact sports, are emotionally emasculated in comparison. Yet it is the language that everyone knows but that no one talks about. It is, furthermore, *the language in which people invariably misinterpret one another,* unless they are fortunate enough to be true lovers. Then the message received is sometimes the one that was actually sent.

I feel very defensive in writing this, for I can just hear some great portrait photographer saying, "This man is mad, quite mad!" In response, I argue that if I'm mad, so is everyone else. I say, further, that anyone who makes such great claim to being able to interpret accurately human beings through photography has never actually looked at one and seen him *as a human being.* He has seen only beautiful lighting, poses, compositions, retouching marks, and 'photographic quality.'

Why should I think a famous portraitist would call me mad? Because not a one of them has ever hinted, in writings or interviews, that the primary problem in making a picture of someone is to really look at him or to find some way of not really seeing him as a person and still be able to photograph him. But perhaps this is only tilting at windmills. Famous portraitists are probably acutely aware of the problem.

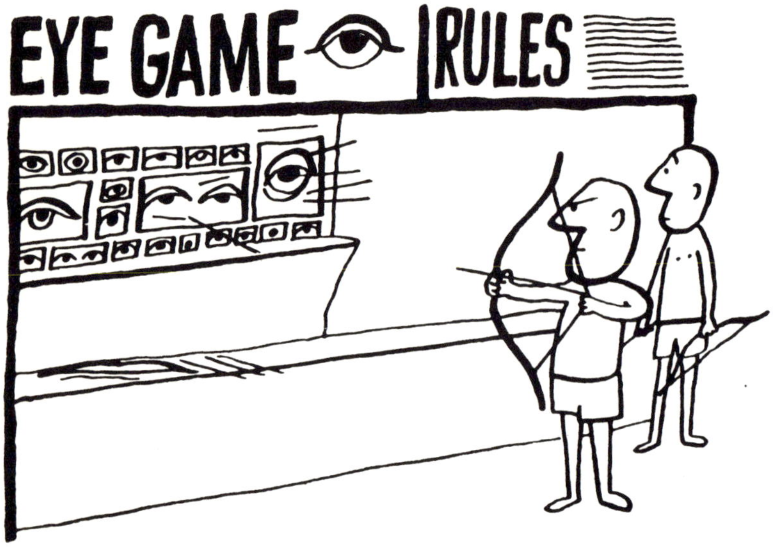

The Unspoken Rules of the 'Eye Game'

There are general rules applying to both sexes, masculine rules, feminine rules, rules applying to eye-to-eye communication between friends, rules applying to relationships between strangers, and so on. Almost every type of interpersonal experience gives rise to its own special rules.

Let no one underestimate how important it is to learn these rules. Because I was twice in my youth brutally beaten for not following them, both times by gangs of complete strangers, I was impelled to ask many people their experiences. The answer I invariably got: "You *must* know the rules for your own safety!" Obviously, one must also know them as one of the social graces.

General rules:

1. Never look at anyone more than absolutely necessary.

2. Be particularly careful to avoid looking at strangers.

3. When you are actually looking at someone, avoid thinking about it. Otherwise, he will become aware that he is being looked at by someone aware of doing it; and the relationship will become very strained.

4. When someone is telling you a lie, be very careful not to let your eyes inform him he is detected.

5. When two people are looking directly into each other's eyes, the more courteous one always breaks eye contact first.

6. If you have been looking at someone while listening to him, and suddenly find yourself looking *through* him, either bring your attention back to him or, if he has noticed, apologize for momentarily being distracted from his conversation.

7. When you are looking at someone and he does something you think he would prefer were invisible—rubs his nose, blinks away a tear, twitches, etc.—allow the 'blind look' to come into your eyes as an indication that you respect his feelings by not seeing what he has done.

8. If you are telling someone a lie, and you know that he is aware it is a lie, do not look him directly in the eye, for that would make you a *monstrous* liar rather than an *ordinary* liar.

9. When looking at someone, take great care to omit the 'you are being judged' expression from your eyes. That is, always keep your expression neutral.

10. If you look into someone's eyes and discover that he is suffering from some kind of acute emotional distress, do not allow your eyes to reveal your discovery to him.

There are, to be sure, other general rules. I suggest that the reader try completing this list for himself.

Since I don't know much about women, I will make no real attempt to write a comprehensive list of rules for them. The woman reader should revise my list in the light of her own experience and extend it to a reasonable length.

Rules for women:

1. Looking too long at a strange man will make him think you are sizing him up sexually or laughing inwardly at him.

2. Never stare a man down unless you wish him to feel impotent or to believe you are trying to prove yourself a better man than he.

3. Looking too long at another woman means you've found fault with her make-up or attire.

4. Since women are, as a general rule, more sensitive to their own emotional states than men, they are often able to excel men in the 'eye game.' It is courteous to keep this secret from men.

So much for woman. If I said more, I would only prove my colossal ignorance.
Rules for men:
1. Never stare at a strange man, especially a drunk, unless you are looking for a fist fight.
2. Staring another man down may suggest to him that you are a bully, a psychopath, or an aggressive homosexual.
3. If against considerable inner resistance you stare a woman down, she will comprehend your fear of her, but think your fear may be overcompensated for by sadistic tendencies.
4. Never stare down one of your children unless you wish him to fear you.
5. Do not try to prove your masculinity and power by aggression of the eyes. It will only make you feared and hated.
6. If you wish to prove to your employer that you are worthy of advancement, play the 'eye game' stalwartly, but don't beat him at it.
7. Remember when you are looking directly at another man that this may lead him to question his own masculinity. Putting pressure on him through the eyes may lead to results which are extremely uncomfortable for both of you.

Again, this list is only fragmentary. The reader must complete it for himself. My contribution is to suggest that the language of the eyes can be considered objectively. Of course, I'm also suggesting that this particular kind of visual language should be taken into consideration when one starts to make pictures of people.

The general meanings of glances or looks. To help you extend the above lists of rules I offer you a highly generalized list of possible interpretations which can be given a look or glance. Because this is a very large subject, far beyond our scope here, I am compelled to oversimplify drastically. Looking is:
1. Asking for love or affection.
2. An attempt to dominate.
3. Judging and measuring.
4. Telling another person that your heart is open to him (her).
5. Attacking and ridiculing.
6. Finding another person inadequate.
7. Hating.
8. Repelling an assault.
9. Bragging about one's ego strength.
10. A way of strengthening the Self.
11. Sexual possession or invitation.
12. Accepting.
13. Knowing and understanding.
14. Discovering someone else's secrets.
15. Sharing a secret.
16. Throwing up a barrier while creating the illusion of letting one down.
17. Innocence.
18. Stupidity.
19. Madness.
20. A risk of giving away personal secrets.
21. Challenging to a contest.
22. A search for the odd or unusual.
23. An effort to comprehend the order of a world or of a human relationship.
24. Lying.
25. Crying for help.
26. Curiosity.

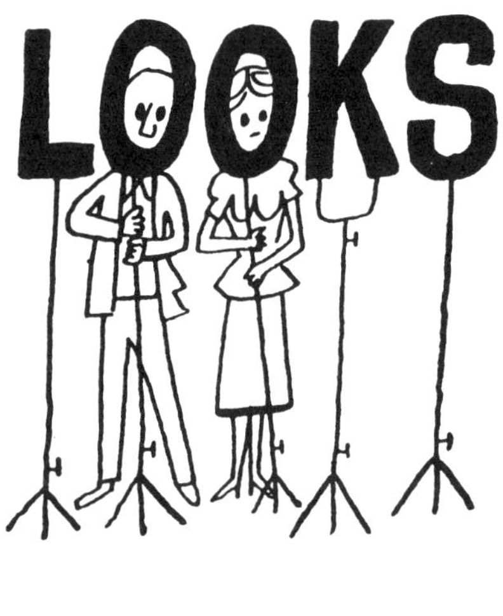

The general meanings of looking away. The language of eyes includes both looking at and looking away from. In addition, both are supplemented by words, gestures, the physical location with respect to one another of two people within an environment, background 'noises' (visual and auditory), cultural factors, the circumstances which brought the two people together, and many other factors. Here, briefly, are some of the possible meanings of looking away.
Looking away is:
1. Rejecting another person.
2. Indicating one feels rejected by the other person.
3. An admission of ego weakness.
4. Admitting to having just told a lie.

5. An indication of having been hurt.
6. Loss of interest in another person.
7. An acknowledgement of one's awareness that the uncomfortable 'eye game' has accidentally been started.
8. An admission of the hopelessness of a visual interchange.
9. Escape from a painful encounter.
10. Escape into the safety of one's self.
11. Hiding one's secrets.
12. Tenderness in relieving another person's dismay at being looked at.

Experimentation Going On

One would think that people would try to clarify what happens in a type of communication which is not only very important to them but frightening and confusing, too. It is not surprising, therefore, that there is considerable experimentation going on today. Lead by psychologists, much of it occurs in the therapy groups which specialize in interpersonal confrontation. In most of them, visual confrontation seems to be of paramount importance.

Realizing that the fear of looking at people has made many people abjectly miserable, group leaders encourage members to force themselves to overcome this fear by staring right into each other's eyes. Those who've been most frightened of doing it sometimes experience a relief of great magnitude. It is as if for the first time in years they've actually started to live again. They also feel very close to other people, whereas before they felt almost entirely shut off. These experiments prove how terribly concerned people are to have good eye-to-eye communication. They also show what profound changes can be made by very simple techniques. Some people feel that their entire lives have been changed.

Interesting though it is, this kind of experimentation should not be carried on as a party game. It's like playing games with nitroglycerine. The effect of prolonged eye contact on some people is so profound that it projects them into what is called 'manic euphoria.' This is often followed by a suicidal depression. People who wish to experiment should only do it in groups led by qualified psychologists. They should also be extremely careful in choosing the psychologist they wish to work with.

Imprecise Intuition Only Aid

Though people are fully aware that they are reading other people's glances and having theirs read in turn, the eye language lacks the systematic grammar which would make precise communication possible. The entire burden of deciphering meaning is thrown on individual intuition, a most imprecise instrument. A result is that people seldom know what is being expressed and much pain is involved in visual interchange. This is not to suggest that a grammar should be developed, for when two people do manage to communicate well and visually the circumstance is filled with tremendous emotional significance for both. Tampering with the system might block off all possibilities of very deep emotional interchange through the eyes—a most terrifying possibility.

The rarity of good person-to-person visual communication emphasizes man's isolation from man, which leads to desperation in eye-to-eye interchanges. This only complicates things further and fills human relationships with pain.

When two people are talking to each other, they are also looking, which means that two types (at least) of communication are involved. Generally, what is being communicated by one means is quite different in meaning and emotional content than what is communicated by the other means. Frequently, there is a complete contradiction. The people who are thus involved seldom have more than a vague idea of what is going on.

If any proof is needed that making pictures of people is a complex thing, what I've written so far should provide it. When we think that photography itself is a means of communication, it is easy to understand the uncertainties of picture-snappers. Though photography involves the usual forms of eye language, it also requires special variations on these forms which can be learned only through experience in making pictures. Since people seldom have the occasion to think through

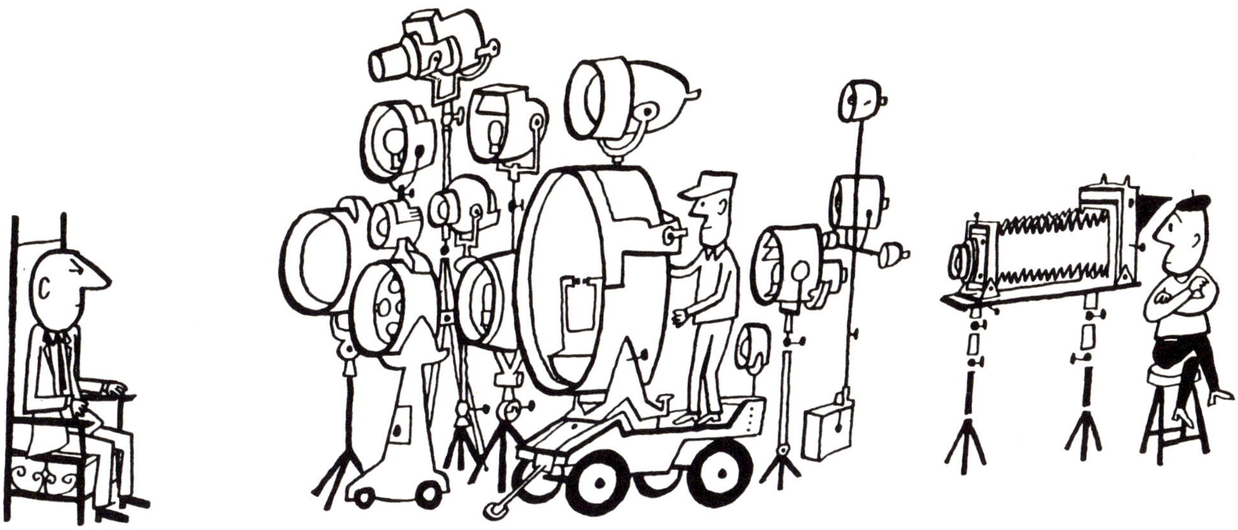

the things presented here, it is small wonder they don't comprehend their reluctance to make more than a very few pictures of people.

Long Lens—Less Involvement

The 'eye game' is a historical problem in photography. The history of photography is loaded with instances in which photographers have worked out clever, often elaborate tricks and invented special gadgets in order to avoid painful involvement in the 'eye game.' Some examples are spy cameras, the use of telephoto lenses in portraiture, and the recent development of 'sneak-shot' candid photography.

Though the commonly given excuse for using long lenses in portraiture is that they eliminate facial distortion (which really isn't much of a problem at all with normal focal-length lenses, the real reason that a photographer likes them is that they lessen his personal involvement with his subjects:
(a) He doesn't have to stand close to a person, therefore (b) he doesn't appear to be examining his model closely, nor (c) must he submit to examination in return. (d) A possible clash of wills or battle for dominance is avoided; (e) the distance separating them allows both photographer and subject to find strength and comfort by retreating into themselves. (f) The subject, sensing his relative isolation and safety, drops his 'worn only in public' expression in favor of one which is more natural to his inner personality, and (g) at this safe distance the photographer is relieved of 'worries of the flesh,' and can concentrate on seeing his subject as shape, three-dimensional form and a complex of colors.

He can manipulate these factors objectively now to create beauty, to interpret, or to communicate. I am not, incidentally, condemning the use of the long focal-length or the telephoto lens. For many people, this is the only means by which they can approach other people to photograph them.

In 'how-to-do-it' books written by portrait photographers you usually find another device for skirting around the 'eye contest,' though it is never identified as such. It is an overconcern with the nuances of portrait lighting. My experience in visiting a class in professional photographic portraiture will show how this overconcern helps a photographer not to look at his model as a person but as a 'light modulator,' which is a much more comfortable thing to do. Since I was a stranger, I assume that the teacher and his students were doing their best to show me what a clinic in portraiture should ideally be.

They spent more than a half-hour talking about a portrait which one of the students had made of a young woman. They discussed the main light (position, distance from subject, feathering, relative diffusion, actinic quality); fill light (same considerations as with the main light, plus the brightness range on the subject's face, tonal reproduction of photographic films and paper, 'modeling' in the tone-change areas between highlights and shadows, the 'brightness-range' method of using an exposure meter in portraiture, whether or not both main light and fill were striking the model's left ear, and the relative inadvisability of such an occurrence, the horror of 'double shadows' under the nose, etc.); background light (same stuff and new additions); hair light (long debate here); supplementary fill lights; skin-texture pick-up lights; supplementary main lights; the 'roundness' or 'flatness' of the lighting in the picture; the tonal relationships between various parts of the background and model; and on and on.

I sat on the edge of my chair and waited for it to happen, but it never did. No one, including the teacher, ever stumbled onto the very obvious fact that the girl in the picture looked so acutely uncomfortable that she must have been on the verge of either screaming or weeping when the shutter was clicked. My suspicion is that this is the one thing they did *not* want to discover. I'm still proud of myself for having kept my mouth shut, too.

Again, I don't wish to decry an interest in lighting, for it is important in making handsome portraits, and a very fascinating preoccupation, too. Furthermore, without such a powerful distraction many a beginning portrait maker would be unable to force himself to confront another human being with a camera. From what I've said, however, you can easily see how an overconcern with lighting—or posing, composition, color, technical quality, etc.—prevents many people-picture makers from ever in their lifetimes discovering that the main subject of portraits is *people*. Considering how frightened people are of one another, this may be all for the best.

Here very briefly are a few more of the common avoidance devices:

Focusing cloth: The photographer hides himself safely under it while submitting his subject to critical examination on the groundglass.

Focusing hood on a reflex camera: same as above.

Lighting 'screen': By pointing photofloods at his subject the photographer builds up the illumination difference between the area in which the subject sits and the area in which he stands with his camera, so that the model perceives both photographer and camera as black emptiness (in short, the subject can't see the photographer).

A distraction for the model: The model is distracted from him or herself, the photographer, and the fact that he or she is being photographed by the presence of other people in the room, music being played, the photographer pretending to fiddle with his equipment, or by his astute comments.

Sneak shot: The photographer shoots the picture either before or after he seems to be shooting it.

Decoy: While apparently shooting one person, the picture-snapper is really shooting another.

Camera testing: The picture maker uses a person as a 'test object,' usually claiming he is getting ready to photograph someone else.

Remote shutter release: After sighting his camera on his subject, the photographer wanders casually off somewhere, releases the shutter electronically when his subject is relaxed.

One more avoidance technique should be described at greater length. This is the use of the modern miniature or subminiature camera. If one uses a small camera with an air of casualness, he seems to be saying to his subject, "Don't worry. This is just a funny little game I'm playing with

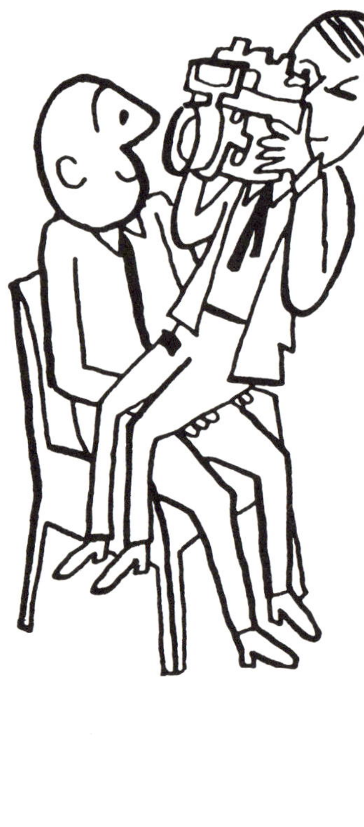

my cute little camera. Bang, bang, bang. See how rapidly and uncaringly I shoot. I'm not really looking at you at all. Honestly I'm not."

He doesn't have to tell his model (who doesn't quite understand that he *is* a model, or subject of study) that a people-picture maker learns to make very rapid and explicit photographic judgments, many of them long before he even begins to shoot. Although the subject may be under very critical examination, he need not ever know it. Another advantage of the small camera is its very fast lens: The photographer doesn't have to upset his subject with the frightening paraphernalia of the studio portraitist—light stands, tripod, backgrounds, head screens, posing benches, and other gear.

I would think that the Polaroid Land cameras would have the same advantages and more. Since they are so obviously associated with the person who is completely unable to cope with the complicated techniques of photography, they should be very fine instruments for seriously studying people without appearing to do so.

Playing the 'Eye Game' Instead of Circumventing It

It is actually possible to confront a person with a camera without having kittens or flying into a nervous fit. Even a great coward can do it, as I know from personal experience. Some time ago, I spent a whole year shooting literally hundreds of portraits, of friends of mine and family, using the close-up attachment on a two-stage Summicron lens (Leica M-3), which meant that my subjects and I were practically sitting in one another's laps. For the first time in a long and varied career as a dedicated amateur portraitist, I really looked at the people I was photographing. Before being able to work so close to people, however, I had to figure a few things out for myself.

If one suggests to a photographic subject that, for reasons unclear to himself, he has trouble really looking at people (people in general, not the subject), tacitly accepting the fact that the subject also may have this trouble (but carefully avoiding forcing a similar admission from him), this person is put in the comfortable position of offering help to a friend, the photographer. This is a very good thing for him to think, especially since it is true.

Both people now know that the 'eye game' is not meant by either of them to be a clash of wills, battle for dominance, visual aggression, a sexual pass, judging and rejecting, or a plea for affection. It is very easy at this point for the picture-snapper to tell his subject that the reason he wishes to photograph him is that he likes him and values the friendship. Though one would hope that such maneuvering between friends should not be necessary, my experience indicates that it often is.

Some photographers tend to stare ferociously or accusingly when they look at people through cameras (I do). They are greatly relieved when they learn that the 'ferocity' can be explained as a peculiarity of picture-snappers caused by some difficulty in concentrating through viewfinders, not as condemning judgments directed at innocent subjects.

When a photographer makes direct visual contact with a subject, he should always break contact first. This relieves the person's incipient fear. While concentrating on photographing, it is difficult sometimes to remember to do this. The thing to do then is to put the camera aside momentarily and break visual contact during casual conversation. When the subject seems reassured, photography can be resumed.

A photographer should be aware that an average person does things which are not supposed to be noticed by polite folks. Certain expressions (hostility, fear, egotism) flit over his face, he rubs his nose or grimaces, he makes awkward gestures. One should pointedly *not* photograph these things, no matter how interesting they are. I have found, however, that I can photograph such things without fouling up the works, *if I tell my subjects in advance what my intentions are and give plausible reasons.* Some people can be approached this way, others not (they would be too upset). Don't ever make the mistake of thinking that people are unaware of their slips.

For maneuvers such as these to be effective, the photographer must allow himself to be aware of his own fear of people. If he forces these fears completely aside, he becomes a person to be feared by others. There is nothing as fearsome as a frightened man unaware of his fear.

If a man is photographing a woman, and is afraid of women in general, he should talk about it with his subject. Not only is this a topic with which all people are fascinated (with little opportunity to learn anything about it directly from a person thus troubled), but talking about it is a marvelous tension reliever.

A man who is consciously forcing himself to look into a woman's eyes often feels compelled to make a pass at her, as if failing to do so would condemn his masculinity in her eyes. This will, of course, louse up any picture session and lead to nothing more than mutual embarrassment and acute despair. Since women frequently encounter this disturbing behavior in men (that is, if they are attractive to men), they are more than glad to talk about it with them. A few minutes' talk is enough to relieve the male compulsion.

Women prefer propositions backed up by real love. If a man refuses to even look at a woman he is photographing (a common enough occurrence) she is both upset and hurt. It is better to talk about the problem. Obviously, any hint of evasion, deceit, or cynicism is completely inappropriate. Also, women very seldom bite men for admitting to them that they are only human.

In the American culture it is a waste of time for two heterosexual males to try to learn to look at each other if they don't already know how. The American male, especially if he is very literate, is so uncertain of his masculinity that the homosexuality question is almost always evoked by a prolonged exchange of glances. Since the self-doubt is often on the unconscious level, it does no good to try talking about it. Needless to say, the great fear of homosexuality makes it difficult for man to photograph man unless he employs tricks for avoiding emotional communication. Fortunately, some of those which are in common everyday use work very well in portraiture.

The common device by which two American males test one another as possible friends (if they are not at least potential friends, circumstances permitting, they are doomed forever to being mutually uncomfortable when together) might be accurately called "the lowest common denominator trick." All the trick consists of is each man doing his damndest to convince the other that he himself is the more stupid, immoral, greedy, hopeless, and unattractive person. The term "common denominator" comes from the fact that they learn the same "horrible" things about each other.

The object is to use a special brand of inverse bragging and self-torturing humor to bring out personal secrets that could put both men in jail, estrange them from their families, or generally ruin their lives. Only when two men 'have the goods' on each other can they be completely comfortable together. Thereafter, each one knows it would be an unnecessary waste of time to lie about himself to the other. Thus, he can relax and be himself—an average, no-good slob.

If carried far enough, the trick will lead men to discuss honestly the things which really bother them—their fear of impotence and homosexuality, the truth of their problems with women, their contempt for themselves, etc. Men who cannot enter into this game must turn to female confidantes to learn what other men are really like. Men who don't play the game invariably lie to one another on all questions really important to them as men.

I have frequently found it necessary to use variations on this trick to clear the air when photographing men, though every time I've done it, I've felt very sad about the human race and its lack of understanding of itself. After hearing other people's black secrets for many years they all begin to sound alike, all of them pitifully, naively human.

There are undoubtedly other ways in which two men can establish the feeling that they are true rogues working out some nefarious scheme together. They should be useful when they are photographing one another. Perhaps it's asking too much to expect a man to tell a friend that he wants to photograph him simply because he loves and respects him.

It takes very little experience in making pictures of people to learn that being approached as a possible subject and then being photographed is upsetting to many people. If not upsetting on a particular occasion, it is always potentially so, and most people know this. Thus, the picture-snapper begins to have his doubts with respect to whether his intrusion into other people's lives is justifiable. As nearly as I can discern, people insensitive to other people are not thus troubled. Sensitive people are often nearly paralyzed with doubt. If self-justification is one of your troubles, perhaps some of the following comments will help solve your problem.

Asking someone to pose for you, or merely pointing your camera in his direction, is a way of telling him that for some reason (which you should probably explain to him, lest your motives be misinterpreted) he is an exceptional person, worthy of being studied via the camera or recorded for posterity. If you dig around in your motives for awhile you'll generally find that you have such a reason; otherwise, why would you want to photograph him? Once he knows you feel this way about him, the act of being photographed is changed from a situation charged with doubt and unconscious fear to one in which he feels honestly praised. It seems to me that there is something in nearly everyone for which he deserves to be thus commended.

If you doubt yourself deeply, saying, "Why should a fool like me have the temerity to intrude into the life of another?", you really ought to try liking yourself more. Also, you can look at this intrusion notion in another way. If a person knows he would be doing you a favor to let you intrude a little bit, he would do it joyfully. There is nothing a person gets more personal reward from than doing someone else a favor, especially if he isn't seriously deprived by doing so. Back to you again: It is a shabby kind of pride which prevents you from asking a favor of another person when you know he will feel better for granting it, isn't it? This kind of destructive pride has given me personally a great deal of misery. You have my sympathies if you also are afflicted with it.

Look at the problem on an impersonal level. Everyone who is honestly trying to interpret another person with a camera is making a contribution to society. The resulting picture, whether it be a masterpiece or just a middling snapshot, has something of value for anyone who will take the trouble to study it.

Look at yourself on the societal level, too. If you are trying to learn something worthwhile, you as a learner are society's bright hope. No matter how insignificant you may think yourself, this is true. The very survival of man may be determined by 'little people' who are quite sure they are making no significant contribution to the world. Are people-pictures important? They certainly are. They take us directly to the center of man's problem of comprehending man.

If you are a perpetual self-doubter, think of this: It is the self-doubter who makes the largest contribution of all to society—if he can force himself to be productive in spite of doubt. Most truly civilized social inventions have sprung from self-doubters. People without doubt seldom have anything important to say.

Because the problem of self-justification is a very large human concern, I feel incapable of doing justice to it. I can only draw attention to the fact that it is as much a problem in photography as anywhere else. I may contribute something by suggesting that a person who applies himself industriously to the problem can improve his lot somewhat, even though when viewed on the cosmic scale, his solutions may seem unsophisticated.

While you are approaching a person directly to ask him if you can take his picture, or sidling about in his vicinity to photograph him without verbally asking

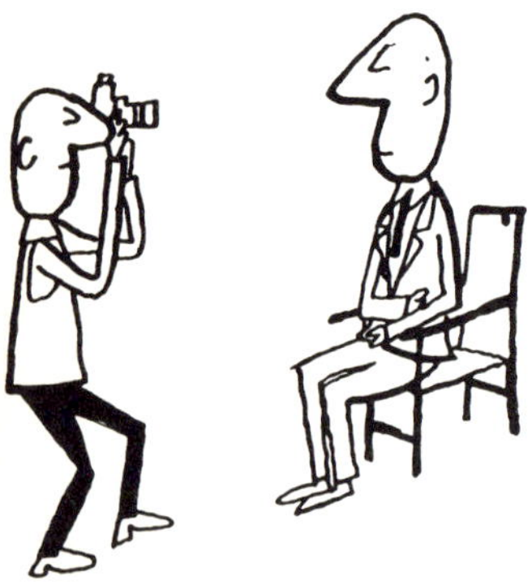

him, you and he are working out a kind of contractual agreement, whether or not either of you fully realizes it. There are always two sides to a contract. Each person agrees to give something in exchange for something he holds to be of equal value. Since an understanding of how such contracts work and how they are arrived at helps the picture-maker justify his intrusion into another person's life, I will explain.

If you are a professional photographic portraitist, the lines of the contract are clearly drawn between your subject and yourself. In exchange for a picture of himself he gives you money. He wants the picture for the satisfactions it will give him. You want money for its satisfactions. You do not want the picture for yourself, nor will you even keep a copy of it except for filing purposes or display (if it happens to be one of the rare and very unusual pictures that you feel are worth displaying). This is not at all the situation in amateur people-photography. It is the photographer who wants the picture, not the subject. Furthermore, though the amateur may promise his model a print (a promise which he usually breaks), the chances are that the model doesn't want the picture at the time the promise is made and has even less desire for it when, if ever, he finally sees the finished print. What, then, is the basis for exchange? What has the photographer to offer his subject?

Surprising as it may seem, the picture-snapper has a great deal to offer, whether or not his picture comes out well. In fact, for every satisfaction he himself derives, there is a parallel one for his subject (that is, there can be if the photographer informs his model of what he is trying to accomplish). These satisfactions can be paired somewhat as follows:

FOR THE PHOTOGRAPHER	FOR THE SUBJECT
Attempting to understand another person	Knowing that someone cares enough about him to try to understand
Keeping a person alive in his memory by means of a photograph	Knowing that someone finds him interesting enough, or cares enough, to cherish his memory
Communicating to the world what he has discovered of value in a specific individual	Knowing that a person who is concerned with the problems of value has found something of value in him
Recording the visible aspects, or signs, of how a person evaluates or judges himself	Knowing that someone is acceptant enough of his self-evaluation, and interested enough, to want to record it for himself
Capturing the beauty of another person	Knowing that someone finds beauty in him
Discovering some meaning in his life by discovering meaning in the person and activities of another	Knowing that his person and actions are of use to other people
Capturing an interesting moment in another person's life	Knowing that another person shares his opinion as to what is interesting, being able to share joy and experiences, feeling pride in being a person whose activities are of interest to others
Trying to strengthen a friendship or love by trying to see the other person better	Strengthening a friendship or love by trying to allow himself to be seen clearly
Making a general statement on the general meaning of human existence by interpreting a specific individual	Apprehending that his own small existence can cast at least a little light on the cosmos as a whole

If the photographer wishes to be at all comfortable while making people-pictures he should do everything possible to clarify to his subjects the meaning of both sides of the contract. When it remains an unspoken contract, there are often great misunderstandings. Once clarified it creates a warm area of mutual appreciation in which photographer and subject can work toward a common goal, man understanding man.

If he does not try to explain what he is attempting to do, he runs the danger of having his subjects jump to conclusions such as the following:

"He thinks I'm ridiculous and is trying to get a picture which will make me a laughing stock."

"He thinks me physically peculiar and is attempting to add me to his photographic zoo."

"He dislikes my behavior and will use his photograph to shame me in the eyes of others."

"He probably intends to use his photograph for selfish ends which will do my reputation harm."

Shoot with a Smile

So, it would seem plain that when a picture-taker is talking to a potential subject (family, friend, or stranger), or maneuvering about in his vicinity, his talk or his behavior should be such as to convince the person he has good in his heart rather than evil, and that he knows the difference between the two. Also, it is a good thing to remember that many people have such low opinions of themselves that even cool and neutral behavior on the part of the photographer will make them think they are being maligned or ridiculed. His behavior must be positively friendly. A smile is his most effective working tool.

To negotiate successfully his informal contract, there are certain other things the photographer should keep in mind:

1. American women over the age of 39 are certain that they look like hell. One cannot explain to them that there is a special and wonderful kind of beauty in the mature woman. Thus, there is no assurance a photographer can give a woman that he will be able to complete his side of the contract: To make her like and respect her physical self.

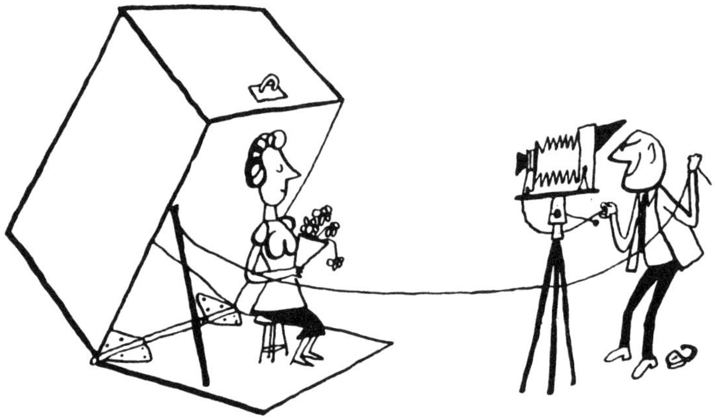

2. There are places where people consider themselves fair game for being looked at and photographed. There are other places which, though they may be public, are generally considered "off limits." For example, only a lunatic believes that women like to be photographed in beauty parlors. At places where people are consciously and conspicuously at their best (theaters, night clubs, openings, fancy dress balls, cocktail parties) photography is all right. Vacation resorts are places one goes especially for people—looking and being looked at; cameras are a normal part of the decor.

Certain beaches are all right. Others should be thought of as extensions of the family bathroom: nix on photography. Since bars and saloons are still secretly frowned on in this puritanical society, one doesn't casually photograph people there, not even old soaks who haven't seen genuine daylight in years. Observation backed up by a little thought will generally tell a person whether his camera is welcome.

However, some people behave in such a way as to be welcomed as photographers almost anywhere; whereas, the behavior of others makes them always unwelcome, often even subject to physical attack by resentful targets. I even knew a young man who was constantly being thrown in jail in various cities for walking down main streets with a camera around his neck. The charge was usually 'on suspicion'—suspicion of what, nobody ever found out.

3. The more carefully a woman does her make-up, selects clothing, walks and sits, enunciates her words, holds a cocktail glass, and so on, the more carefully must she be approached by a picture-snapper, whether friend or stranger. These things are all too frequently clues that, holding herself in low esteem, she makes her big play for acceptance on her looks. If she's not photogenic, she knows it; stay away. You can only cause her misery.

4. Men as a rule can't conceive of any reason why another person might wish to photograph them, especially if they are at work or engaged in some sport. The picture-shooter should approach them casually, making no effort to disprove their notion that he must be a real oddball for wanting pictures of them. If an issue is made of the 'unspoken contract,' a man will often smell a rat and refuse to be photographed on general principles. The contractual arrangements must be subtly made, so to speak. Women, on the other hand, sometimes practically force the photographer to tell them how terrific they are before they can be persuaded to pose or allow candid shots.

5. If a person carrying a camera gives a strong impression that he belongs whereever he happens to be, people will believe him. Shy and evasive behavior invariably evokes suspicion with respect to motives. A snapper's best friend will turn his back on him if he suspects his rights (the friend hasn't the vaguest notion of what his rights actually consist of) are about to be violated. Since people frequently ridicule others via photography, this reaction shouldn't be surprising.

6. The closer one gets to a person with a camera, the more uncertain this person is as to whether he likes it or not, or should tolerate it. This is the reason why standard snapshot procedure—subject ten feet away standing in front of a lilac bush —is the only one which can be used on many people, especially self-conscious elderly aunts. Anyone who wants to get *all* the people he cares for on film had better learn to value the snapshot—or get a long telephoto lens.

7. The better one knows a person the greater the necessity that he tell him specifically why he wants to take his picture. Unless he is told he will think: "This person knows my weaknesses. He's lost his fear of me so that he can now let me know in his pictures what he *really* thinks of me. I cannot play a role to deceive him and save face, as I might with a stranger. Since he knows me well enough to realize that I don't amount to much, he must have some ulterior motive for wanting to take my picture." This explains in part why husbands and wives have such difficulty photographing one another. This kind of thinking doesn't so much illustrate how little regard a person has for his friends and loved ones as it shows his lack of love and respect for himself.

One more comment: A picture-maker should remember that a photograph may be the *least* thing he can give to a person he has snapped. This is certainly true if while photographing he has expressed even a hint of love, honor and respect. There are no finer gifts. After all, people don't expect amateur photographers to make great portraits. All they ask of them, as friends, is their affection.

In conclusion. I have tried to explain, insofar as my personal experience allows me to, some of the things that happen in photographing people. I hope I've helped you find your way to people via photography or to understand your reasons for preferring not to follow this route.

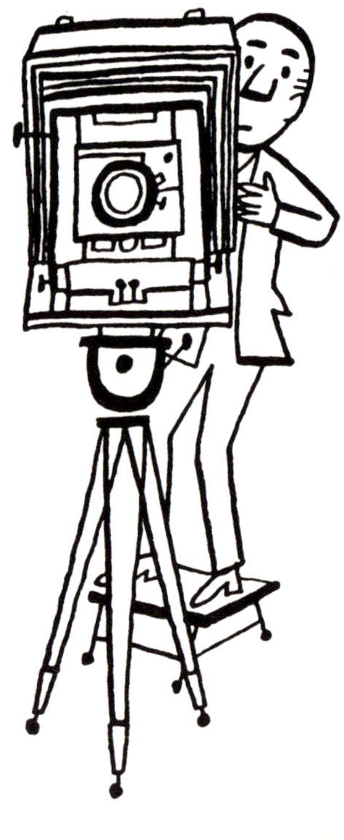

UNDERSTAND your aesthetic sense

Photographing the nude to help you improve your perceptivity and to understand and feel the relation between aesthetics and sensuality. Uncovering hidden facets of yourself.

Photographing the nude can have a profound positive effect on a photographer's life. If he does it often enough it can contribute greatly to his photographic skills. Some of the reasons for these photographic benefits are fairly easy to explain; others lie well beyond my understanding and must ultimately be fathomed by each individual within himself or herself. One of the reasons for the profound effect is the strength of the sex drive. So powerful is it that it gives people the strength to do things they just couldn't do without it. One of them is to overcome visual laziness.

3

If you've been a photographer for long you know that learning to see is a very hard task. Indeed, it is so difficult that it can cause the beginner acute nausea, again and again. In the face of such an overwhelming task, vision naturally lets itself become lazy, or should we say reluctant to let itself suffer? Because of the suffering, people avoid trying to see things well. It's easier to go along half blind. But people in the visual arts must go through the suffering and overcome the blindness if they wish to master their media. Fortunately, there are some subjects we're so interested in that we'll pay the price in suffering in order to learn to see them well. One of them is the naked human body. Once we've learned to see human bodies well it becomes relatively easy to see everything else. Thus the sex drive can be harnessed to create an overall improvement in vision. This is one of the main reasons why art schools almost invariably insist that their students should have considerable experience in figure drawing. For the same reason figure photography should be included in photographic education.

To see how sexual curiosity overcomes visual laziness (or fear of suffering), let us examine a typical man's first attempt to photograph a nude woman. Since he has certain other pressing problems we'll talk about them too. He can learn nearly as much about himself by solving them as by making photographs. For example, before he confronts his naked subject he is worried that he'll be carried away by lust. When she is far away he enjoys his lust immensely, but as the time for the posing session draws nigh, he's afraid it will lead him to make a fool of himself. Here he has some very good opportunities for self-observation. If he has sufficient insight his observations will reveal a wide range of facts concerning the way he relates, or fails to relate, to women. He can also learn much with respect to how he reacts to a powerful drive within himself: sex.

His first look at his casually disrobed model hits him a hard jolt in the stomach. If he has sufficient insight he realizes he's frightened! But he's also relieved to discover the lust he feared so much is entirely gone. "I may be nervous," he thinks, "but at least I won't make a fool of myself." He discovers at this point that it's very handy to have a camera. He can cover his confusion by fiddling with it and get his mind off his anxiety. It also draws a sharp line which defines the objective of the photographer-model relationship: It is to make pictures, not indulge in sex play. This also helps quiet his fear. In a few minutes it's entirely gone and he starts to pay close attention to what he's seeing through the camera viewfinder.

In his first session he doesn't make any good pictures, though he doesn't discover this until later. The thing he's most aware of is that it's great to be around a woman who has dropped her camouflage and that healthy female bodies are very nice. He pushes his photographic lights around quite a bit, but doesn't really see what his various lightings do to the girl's figure. He shoots many pictures from many camera angles and doesn't see what they do, either. He begins to learn when he makes his prints.

When he starts to make prints he's full of enthusiasm well-laced with sexual expectancy. After he's made a few, however, he begins to suspect that his pictures aren't as beautiful as he thought they'd be. In another two hours he's finally managed to admit to himself that they are nearly gruesome. This is no exaggeration, I assure you. I've seen it happen with literally hundreds of young men. If our poor photographer's pictures were of a magnolia bush he'd throw them in the wastebasket and let it go at that. However, they're of something he's really interested in, an unclothed woman. We must add to this the fact that lust is once again a factor to be considered.

At the end of the posing session he'd become quite indifferent to his model's nudity. Lust was nowhere in sight. However, when the photographer makes his prints, it is hours or days after he last saw the girl. His imagination has had plenty of time to work overtime and he finds that he is sexually excited once more. Sexual excitement drives him to look at his miserable, disheartening pictures until he can figure out what went wrong with them. I wish to make it very clear to the reader that this is *terribly* hard work. He looks very hard at them, continuing to study them critically long after visual nausea has set in. His aroused sexuality ameliorates the suffering caused by straining his perceptual capacities. Slowly, very slowly, he begins to see some of the things he didn't see when he was using his camera.

Before continuing with my story I wish to make a few side remarks about 'visual nausea.' If you haven't personally experienced it this suggests two things: that you have a natural 'artistic eye' (very rare) or that you haven't even an inkling of the labor and suffering involved in learning how to see. For most people the price of artistic vision is very high and it is paid almost entirely in suffering up to and far beyond visual nausea. More than anything else this explains the ubiquitous presence of the nude figure in art schools. If it weren't for sex's ameliorating force, few people could bear to pay the price of good seeing.

Psychologists have long known about sex as the great ameliorating or healing force. They've time and again pointed out that when people are afflicted by conflicts which would drive them to suicide or total despair, the sexual forces save them. When this happens the psychologists say that these negative forces (anger, fear, jealousy, despair, etc.) have been 'sexualized.' Though we call such people 'perverts' (e.g., a person whose anger is sexualized is a sadist), they are, at least, surviving perverts. What is sometimes overlooked is that things like anger, fear and jealousy are terribly painful and destructive to the human organism. When they are sexualized they become bearable; and the organism survives.

Though many psychologists have seen that the sex forces ameliorate negative drives, they haven't been so quick to see that they can also be deliberately used for necessary suffering. I would call learning to see better a human necessity. That is, it is necessary if man wishes to improve himself spiritually. There are a good many things which fall in the category of necessary suffering, that is, things which men ought to do for their spiritual evolution but which are very painful. There are very ancient and still surviving schools of thought (Sufism, for example) which have developed methods for deliberately using the sexual forces to make necessary suffering bearable. The use of nude models in art and photography schools is a crude but workable example of such a method.

The foregoing paragraphs explain why I've introduced our photographer's lust in so blunt a manner, though such a thing has never before (to my knowledge) been mentioned in the context of photography of the nude. The point is that you have to suffer in order to learn to see. Seeing well is a very high art and worth any price. The sexual forces can be intentionally used in an ethical way in order to make the necessary suffering bearable. Though there are undoubtedly much more sophisticated (thus more acceptable) ways of using these forces, each person must find his own personal starting point. With most people the beginning is closer to lust than it is to sainthood. We will now return to our typical beginner in photography of the nude.

In his next model session, and all others that follow, he discovers more and more things as they are actually happening, and makes fewer disheartening discoveries while printing. He sees that some poses are better than others. Even more, he begins to understand *why* they are—in terms of line, contour, mass, color, background, lighting, etc. These are things he's never really been aware of before with *any* subject. Once he's learned to see them, it becomes relatively easy, easy in working with nude models, easy in photographing anything else.

With his models he learns what light does. No longer does he think of it as merely something necessary for exposing film. Light *does* things to figures. Light makes figures seem hard or soft, pretty or ugly, round or flat, real or unreal, unhealthy or healthy, rhythmic or graceless, alive or dead, radiant or dull. All these things that he's beginning to see were formerly beyond his perception. Once he's learned how to see them he can use his vitalized vision to help him solve every kind of visual problem. Though it may not seem much to some readers, the last two paragraphs adequately summarize the objectives of a four-year, college course in photography. Learn these things and you've got a wonderful start in photography, either as an art or as a profession.

Some people may take a dim view of my idea that sexuality should be used to sharpen vision. Their notion may be that anything of this sort is only a way of giving freedom to lust and that it is better to grab lust around the neck and throttle it. In the first place, making nude photographs works against lust, not for it. In the second, lust can't be throttled. Pushed out of consciousness, it pops up again in various fiendish disguises. In these forms it raises havoc in the human race. In some of them it preaches abstinence, asceticism, or the fear and horror of sin, hell, the torments of sinners, and eternal fire. In others it foments revolutions, robs, burns and kills. It creates gooey sentimentality or, on the contrary, jealousy and cruelty. In whatever form it appears it is useless and Self-destructive. For a general picture of man's almost infinite capacity to fool himself in this way, try reading Aldous Huxley's book *The Devils of Loudun*. Though it deals specifically with an age long past, it has a good deal to say about America today. It is also a terrifying look at the effects of conditioning, a thing which all contemporary Americans should be deeply concerned with.

Sexual Fantasy

I have suggested that the sex drive helps one bear the suffering which accompanies the effort of learning to see better. In the print lab this takes the form of sexual fantasy. As he prints, the photographer fantasizes a woman who is the ideal sex object and at the same time tries to make his picture measure up to the quality of his dreams. This leads him to work very hard at his printing. And it also helps him bear the pain of seeing how far he's missed the mark in his lighting, posing, cropping and so on. Sexual fantasy has other positive uses too, though they're not usually talked about.

I don't wish to defend sexual fantasy as such. It is, after all, a product of man's lower carnal nature and he's better off without it. However, there's no getting around the fact that people do fantasize and that figure photography tends to promote this. Since this is the case we'd be better off putting fantasy to good use than in trying hopelessly to ignore it. The way to use fantasy is to observe it analytically and to see what it implies about oneself. This limits our enjoyment of it considerably but it does direct it toward higher and more useful goals.

In searching for the Self it is productive to examine *all* of one's daydreams in order to uncover their hidden implications. As a specialized form of daydreaming, sexual fantasy has certain attributes which make it extremely useful for Self-analytical purposes. One of them is its limited range. Daydreams as a whole are so flitting and expansive that it is hard to grasp them analytically. But sexual fantasies are limited and repetitious. We belabor the same themes over and over again. Furthermore, we remember old fantasies well, whereas most daydreams are here today and gone tomorrow. Taken together, these characteristics of sexual fantasies constitute a highway which can lead us far into the secrets of the inner Self.

Each person must determine for himself how he should go about analyzing his fantasies. A general background in Freudian psychology helps a good deal. For those without it some general questions may be useful. Why do I fantasize these particular types of people and erotic situations instead of other possible ones? In what ways do I lie to myself about sex? About myself? About members of the opposite sex? About workable relations, erotic or otherwise, between men and women? What am I really trying to get from my involvement in figure photography?

You may find it helpful to review "The Psychology of People Pictures" in Chapter Two and to skip ahead to "Games Photographers Play" in Chapter Six.

I suppose some photographers will be indignant because I've extended photography of the nude to include sexual fantasy. They might feel that the sole object of figure photography is to make fine pictures. However, in the context of photography as a means of Self-discovery, anything that happens to one while making pictures can legitimately be included. If a photographer invariably develops a tic in his eye when photographing trees he should look into it. If he concentrates his attention entirely on his pictures he misses nine-tenths of the psychological side of the photographic process. Though photographers seldom indulge in sexual fantasy when they're actually photographing nudes, fantasy almost invariably precedes modeling sessions and follows them later. Therefore, it should be investigated, especially since it's such a fine highway leading to the hidden Self.

Unfair Criticism of Women

When examined in its broader aspects, figure photography can lead to an improvement in the relations between the sexes. One of the reasons men find it so difficult to get along with women is that they're criticizing them unfairly, either in words or thoughts. Women are upset and angered by this, of course, so they repay men by psychologically castrating them, avoiding them or undermining them in other ways. Photographing nude women gives men a very good opportunity to discover in themselves one of the more obvious and destructive forms of unfair criticism. It may even lead them to see it's a bad thing and that they should give it up.

I've already said that through figure photography men sharpen their perception of many things. One of the things they become extremely sensitive to is perfection and imperfection in the female body. They learn to love perfection dearly and at the same time develop a strong distaste for imperfection. Though this sounds like a good thing, it actually isn't. It leads men to be very negative and critical concerning women whose bodies are less than perfect. One should learn to recognize both beauty and imperfection in human beings, of course, but the proper attitude toward both is loving indifference.

This loving indifference is not what develops first in the male photographer. As he becomes more and more sensitive to imperfections in his female photographic subjects he becomes more and more critical in an extremely negative sense. In fact he soon gets to the point—if he hasn't already been there for years—where he can accept nothing less than perfection in a female body. This is terribly unfair to women and can have disastrous consequences for men who make such demands on them.

However, photography of the nude can have positive consequences for the man, despite his rejection of female imperfection. Unless he's a complete noodlehead, he'll eventually come to question his impossibly high standards and to ask himself what right he has to judge women by them. He might even find himself overcome with well-earned remorse for holding such narrow and destructive attitudes toward women who are less than perfect. If he's really intelligent, he may discover that his negative criticism extends far beyond mere physique to a woman's mind and spirit. Since most men are this way, it is very good for one if he can discover it in himself. Appalled by the unfairness of it, he might even try to change himself. In so doing he could even transform himself into a creature women couldn't help loving.

Men with little insight will settle for the *Playboy* pull-out as the ideal for figure photography, not realizing that it is an insult to women and an indication of very unfair attitudes in themselves. If they follow such a retouched, pneumatic ideal they use their photography only in order to 'improve' women. Women detest this, of course, for they realize that the men who are trying to improve them don't understand them in the least. They see it as ignorant, egotistical meddling and resent it deeply. In the very deepest sense this so-called improvement represents rejection of, or contempt for, women.

Men with more insight use their photography not to improve women but to see their imperfections with tenderness and grace. They learn they can make beautiful photographs of women who are not very well built. If they push their discoveries far enough they eventually come to the point where they never see physical ugliness when they look at other human beings. When this happens they are really using the photographic medium well—for themselves and everyone else in the world.

Fear of Women

There's a pretty fair chance that through figure photography men will learn they're afraid of women. Though this is almost a universal characteristic of men, few of them are aware of it. This is actually a fear of an aspect of themselves (see Chapter Four). Men are afraid of the feminine component of manhood. This fear of self is displaced to fear of women and leads men to unconsciously reject and maltreat them. It is perhaps the main cause of the wide gulf between the sexes. To show how the fear is discovered we must return to sexual fantasy.

In contemplating a modeling session already arranged for, a male photographer thinks of some of the photographic problems involved—with about a one-fiftieth part of his mind. With the rest he's fantasizing means for getting the woman to have sex with him in the improbable ways which will give him maximum pleasure. Though he greatly enjoys fantasy far removed from probability, his joy is not complete. There's a part of him which wants to translate fantasy into reality. This part of his mind forces him to bring his fantasy out of the clouds into the realm of probabilities. As his fantasy nears reality the fly in the ointment becomes visible. Even in his imagination he can see he's afraid to proposition her for fear of being turned down. This can be interpreted as being essentially a fear that she will do to him precisely what he has already done to her in his unconscious mind: He has rejected her. More accurately, he has rejected the feminine side of himself, for which she is an obvious symbol. His reason and sense of justice tell him that like should beget like. Even more inescapable is his intuition that like invariably *does* beget like. He will get the rejection he has coming to him.

Fear of women and fear of the feminine aspect of the self are, for practical purposes, the same thing. However, a man has a much better chance of discovering he fears women than learning it is actually something in himself he fears. Discovering the latter requires long experience and considerable insight.

Let us say that a man does *not* discover his fear of women as he tries to bring his fantasies closer to probability. There is still a good chance that he will after the modeling session begins. Before his model's arrival he has worked out a definite plan of seduction. But when he confronts

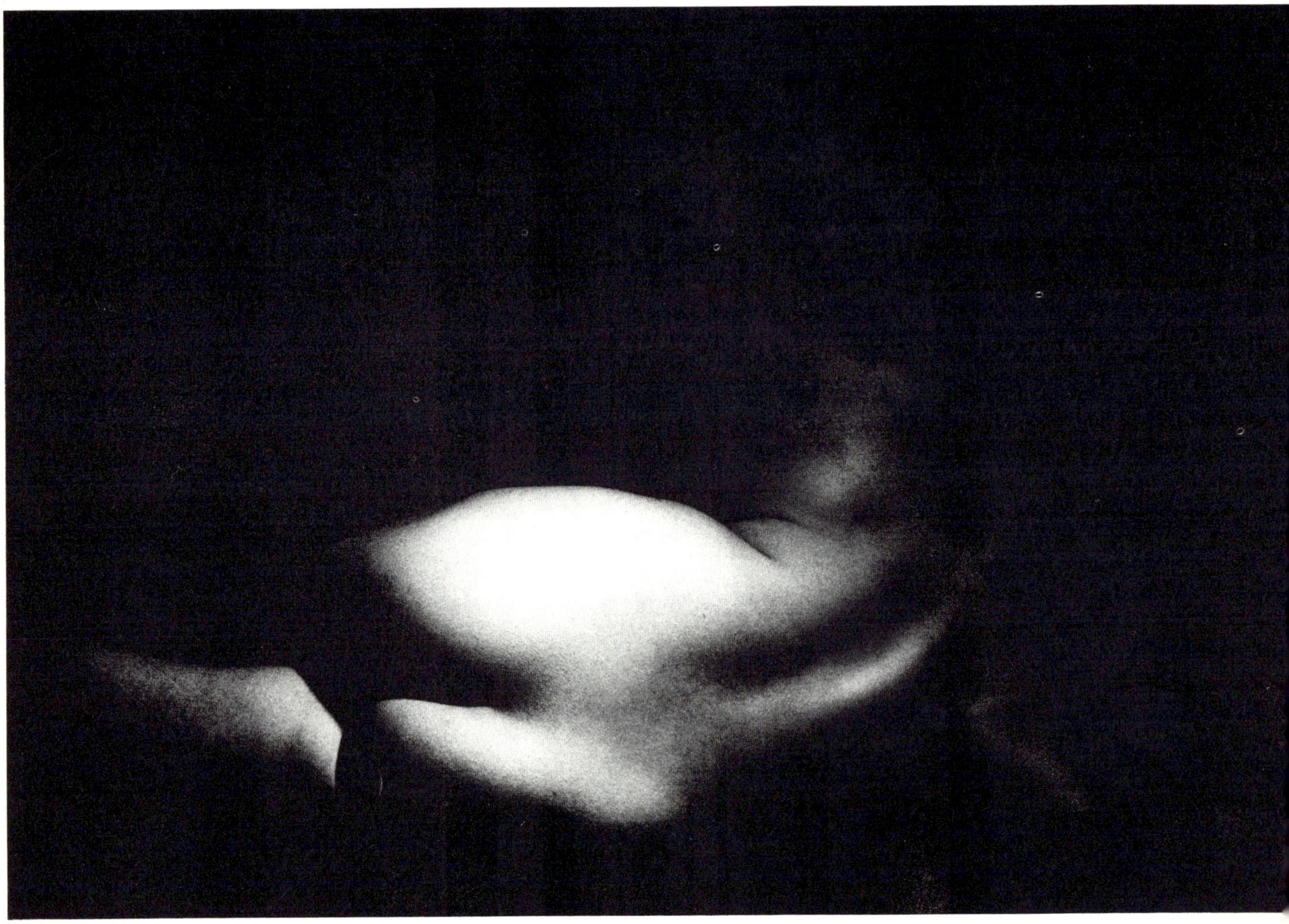

This lovely nude is both mathematically abstract and intensely, romantically feminine. It relates woman to beautiful natural forms (hills, fruits, sand dunes) and abstract modern sculpture. Obscurity is very important here; things lost in the shadows take on special importance. Light touches this body reverently.

photo by JOSEPH H. S. LEPAGE

her he finds that there is something which stops him: his fear. Or if he's so blinded by his fear he doesn't discover it even then, there's still another chance. He may actually proposition her and in blurting out his words learn how terrified he is.

One might say that the above description doesn't apply to all men. That's true, it doesn't. But it certainly applies to the majority of those who do figure photography. If the fear weren't there they'd spend their time making love, not photographs. I don't think I exaggerate when I say that figure photography is generally a displacement of the sexual act, nor do I see any reason why anyone should find it surprising. There is certainly no reason to condemn it because it is, for fear makes people do many strange things.

I'm certain that some photographers will be dismayed or disgusted at what I've written so far. "Good grief," they'll mutter, "can't this poor fool see that the only object of figure photography is to make great pictures?" I'm sorry I must disagree with them. Very often the least important thing that happens in making a photograph is the picture itself. For a man to discover that he's afraid of women is more valuable to him in the long run than making the world's hundred best photographs. It is a large step along the road to Self-discovery. Discovering just one Self is worth more than all the great pictures that have ever been made.

Women Photographers in Figure Photography

Though not many of them try it, women enjoy photographing both male and female nudes. Their fantasies are undoubtedly different before and after the modeling sessions, but in what ways I couldn't say.

In photographing nude women, female photographers seem to identify strongly with them. That is, they see themselves as the women who are being photographed. Thus they indirectly experience what the models do. To them this is an opportunity for an interesting and useful kind of self-observation.

For most men, photographing nude members of their own sex is an unpleasant experience giving rise to emotions ranging from distaste to acute anxiety. They are terrified that they will find their male models physically attractive. The basis of this is actually their fear of their femininity, which they unconsciously interpret as repressed homosexuality.

Since women aren't generally afraid of their own masculinity they don't have a parallel problem in photographing nude members of their own sex. If they find their models attractive they're not frightened, though jealousy and cattiness are often aroused.

Though women are interested in men's physiques they're not much inclined toward being negatively critical of them. They're more likely to judge a man by his character, intelligence and temperament than by how he looks on the outside. It's not that women can't get turned on by a man's looks, but that they don't get as carried away by looks as men do.

Women very much enjoy figure photography but don't get as hung up on it as men do. I doubt, therefore, if the sex drive is for them such a useful force for overcoming visual laziness. In this area, a man will force himself to see better, even if the effort should half kill him. I think that this very thought would rather amuse women.

Self, World, and Sex

I've suggested that the motive force for learning to see the subtleties of the female form is sex and that this is not such a bad thing. The sex forces can be used in all efforts to learn to see better, no matter what subject matter we're looking at. Without our sex drives—sublimated, to be sure—we would find it impossible to make ourselves struggle hard enough to develop really fine perceptual sensitivity. We should not forget that very real suffering accompanies this struggle and that sex makes it bearable.

Sex should be understood in a broader context than mere lust. It is the procreative force, creating all things. It is the dynamo in man from which his creative energies flow. Though it is often diverted from its proper channels, thus causing most of man's problems, it is also the energy source which gives him his greatest opportunities. Understood and used well, it is a most wondrous thing.

Struggle and suffering boost sex energies to a higher level of vibration, if one is working for the right things. Trying to see better is a right thing. So is trying to outwit the carnal ego in order to see the Self. Figure photography gives you a good field for both of these battles, if you're willing to use it this way. You can use your sexuality to help you accept the painful burden of learning to see better. Use your sexual fantasies to help you uncover many of your own lies to yourself. These are not merely mundane matters. If you follow courses like these persistently and courageously you can boost the level of the sex vibrations and develop the so-called spiritual body within yourself. If you use your sexual forces for the wrong things they will be your undoing, but I'm sure you don't need to be told this. For further information on vibrations you might read P. D. Ouspensky's book *In Search of the Miraculous.* Though this is not the definitive text on such matters it is a very good beginning. Young folk talk a lot about vibrations these days. I wonder how many actually take the trouble to learn what they are all about.

The things which your sensuality can help you see are the tendons and ligaments of the universe, for the principles which make the human body function are the very same ones which make functional creation as a whole. This is true in all dimensions, including the visual. A line well-seen on a woman's hip can also be seen on a blackboard in an advanced physics classroom at M.I.T. Formulas which describe the complex curve of a woman's belly are written in the log of the astronaut returning through space from a visit to the moon. As the very ancient saying goes: As above, so below. This means simply that anything we learn which is true about the Self is also true of all creation, for every man is a miniature model of the universe.

What is this aesthetic sense mentioned in the title of this chapter? It is man accurately sensing himself and the world at the same time. It is a thing which you feel simultaneously in your mind, your eyes and all your internal organs. It is sensuality reaching for the right goals. It's what you're trying to attune yourself to as you do photography of the nude.

Nudes

This is a lesson containing lots of useful how-to-do-it information. By following it carefully you can help yourself avoid what usually happens to people in their first attempt at figure photography: terrible pictures. If you carefully follow the advice given here the chances are that some of your pictures will be quite good, even if you haven't yet learned to see the nuances of pose, lighting, camera angle, camera distance, etc.

The information is packed in rather tightly, so read carefully. You would be wise to assume that every word has an important bearing on your problem of learning how to make handsome figure pictures rather than ugly ones.

The Lesson:

There is no area of photography more interesting than the nude. Our vast interest in and yearning for the opposite sex probably accounts for this. Nude photography is a great challenge to the pictorial vision of the advanced photographer, yet a wonderful starting place for the serious beginner, whom I address here.

However, shooting a really good full-figure nude is an extremely difficult—if not impossible—task for the beginner (he will try it, of course, but fail). His best starting place is with abstractions. Once he has mastered them he is ready for the full figure.

The chief difficulty is to see the figure in terms of beauty (or ugliness) of line, contour, texture, tone, form, and composition. Sex and personality insistently interfere with seeing, so that a beginning photographer can shoot a picture that is visually abominable without being at all aware of it. And if it is visually bad, it tends to look degraded or pornographic. However, by fixing attention on abstract areas of the body you can with deliberate effort overcome the influence of sex and personality, thus giving your sensitivity to beauty and ugliness a chance to ripen. On this sensitivity good photography is founded.

My illustrations have both beauty and ugliness in them in a balance making for interest. They are strong, not delicate. The beginner should try to follow his or her own special interests, not imitate me.

If you pose a girl (or a man) on an Edward Weston sand dune, you're likely to get art. If you pose your model dramatically on a torn settee you get pornography—automatically. That is the background situation. The first is unreal, the latter altogether too real. Unreality is the secret. Against an unreal background a nude is art, against a real one, mere flesh —the realer, the fleshier. Flesh can equal pornography.

Professional photographers have pretty well outlined the *acceptable* outdoor backgrounds—sand dunes, water, and sylvan glades. The Empire State building is *out*. So is Waukegan, Illinois. Snow banks would be nice if they weren't so cold. Indoors, the no-seam paper background is best, as it tends to remove the idea of *place* altogether. If you must have place, make the surroundings attractive. Or else try sticking up a no-seam background (with two-inch adhesive tape). I recommend the medium gray for beginners.

If you must have place, the more improbable the better—a temple in Tibet, a steel mill, or the U.N. Better forget it. Fortunately, with abstract close-ups of the figure, place is easily diminished by cropping it out altogether or by being out of focus. If a normal-length lens won't clobber place thoroughly enough, try a telephoto. That will change the kitchen stove into a supernatural blob.

Indoors, try patternless carpeting, the ceiling, empty wall space, a dark blanket, a plain window, or the floor.

With a beautiful model almost any lighting will work. In other cases, the secret is obscurity—dark or out-of-focus areas into which it is difficult to see. Intentional use of obscurity is one of the great secrets of photography. The thing to do is highlight good points of the figure and obscure bad ones.

Some lightings only reveal. Others simultaneously reveal *and* conceal. If a light (floodlamp or sun) strikes a less-than-perfect model from the front or evenly from all sides at once, his or her inadequacies are totally revealed, crudely naked. The only thing which can be beautiful in almost anyone—sculptural form—is completely flattened out and lost. However, if a diffuse light strikes gently from one side, that side is richly highlighted, imperfections sink into dark obscurity toward the other side, and sculptural form grows magically.

An easy way to create this magic lighting is to shine a floodlamp on a wall to the side or slightly behind the model. Diffused in bouncing, it creates soft shadows without edges. The same light turned directly on the model causes sharp-edged, ugly, harsh, form-mutilating shadows unless the photographer is extremely skilled with lights. For this reason I recommend only side diffuse (side bounce) light for beginners.

In side bounce, obscurity (and contrast) are highest close to the lighted wall, diminishing on the other side of the room. There the other wall reflects light into the shadows, nearly eliminating them. The beginner should move the model around the room to see these changes.

In full-figure photography, good posing calls for an extremely sophisticated photographer. The beginner, with a naive idea of glamor, usually comes up with results that are merely pathetic. However, even a bad pose can result in a good abstract picture or two if the model is examined from all angles. Perhaps the best thing to do in terms of this lesson is to get your model into as many positions as you can just to see the abstract visual possibilities. If the overall poses are bad, don't worry.

Some beginners when first confronted with a model make only two or three pictures in a session because they fuss over minor details. Though I don't recommend unrestrained shooting, I do say the beginner should view each pose from as many angles as possible, shooting both the good

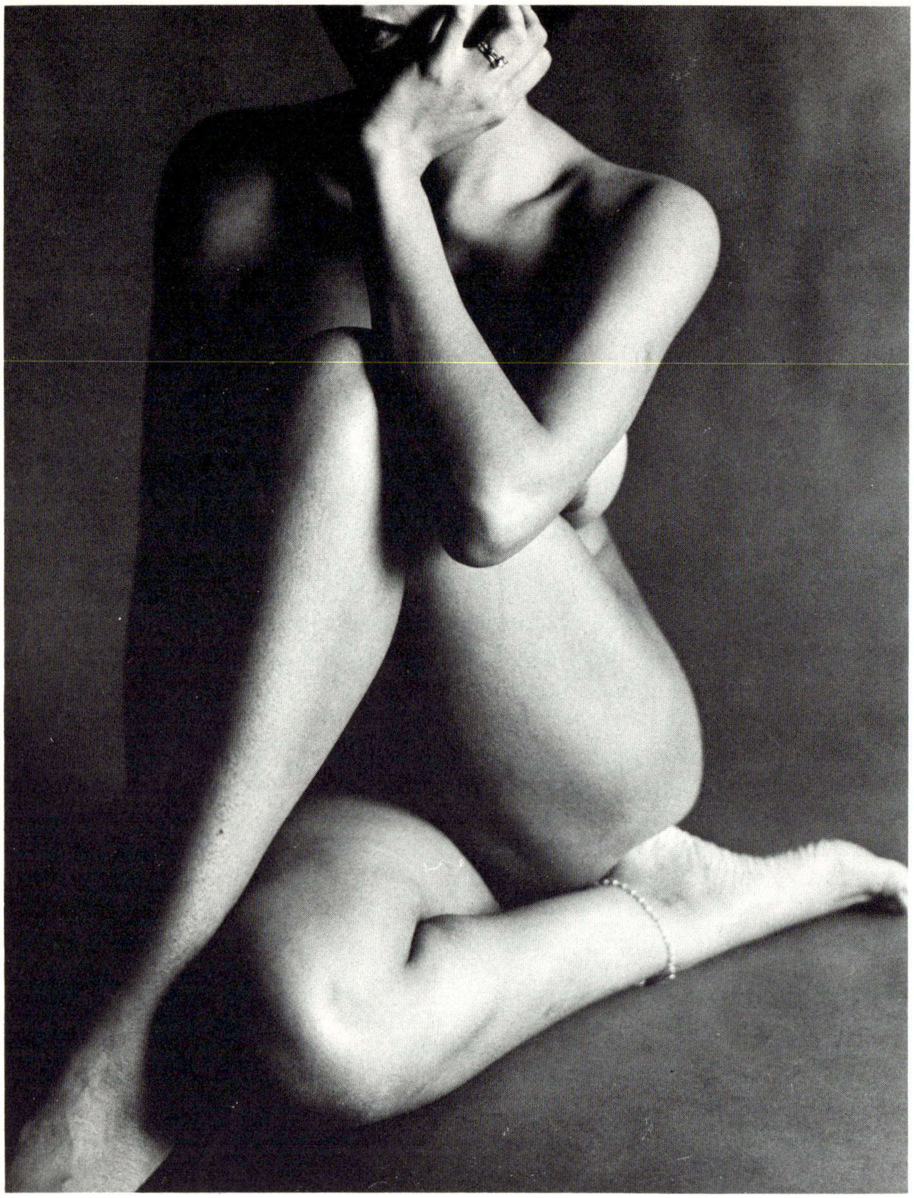

This angle of view and cropping makes it seem that the arms and legs don't quite belong to the body but are separate parts stacked in a heap. This is disturbing, yet interesting. The background is gray, no-seam paper. It is very simple and completely unobtrusive. Together with the figure it creates the feeling of space, but not very much of it. Though the body looks like piled-up parts, the picture has a strong feeling of organization. The lighting is very sculptural. A light was bounced off a wall near the right side of the picture. That is, it was pointed at the wall and reflected from it onto the figure. This bounce light creates shadows with soft edges rather than sharp ones. Nothing is more flattering to the nude human figure, male or female. If a light is pointed directly at the figure it causes sharp-edged shadows, which make the body look mutilated or slashed.

Here the body resembles a stone bridge carved by wind and water in the Arizona desert. It also reminds one of man-made sculptures and buildings. It is easy to find many forms like these in the world of nature around us, for they are universal.

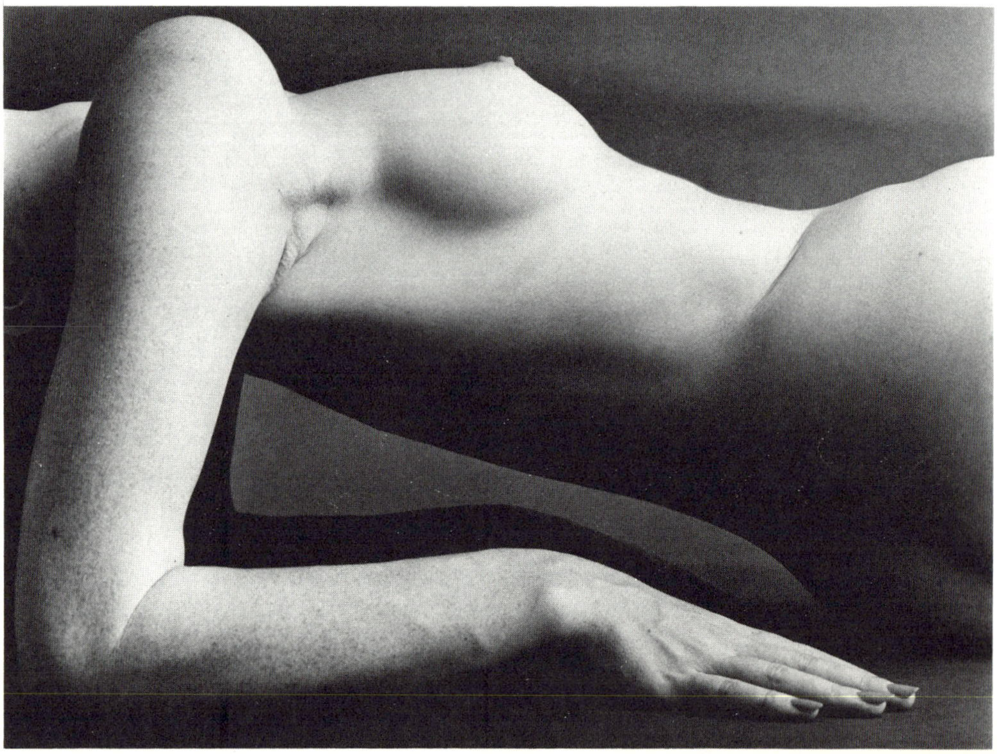

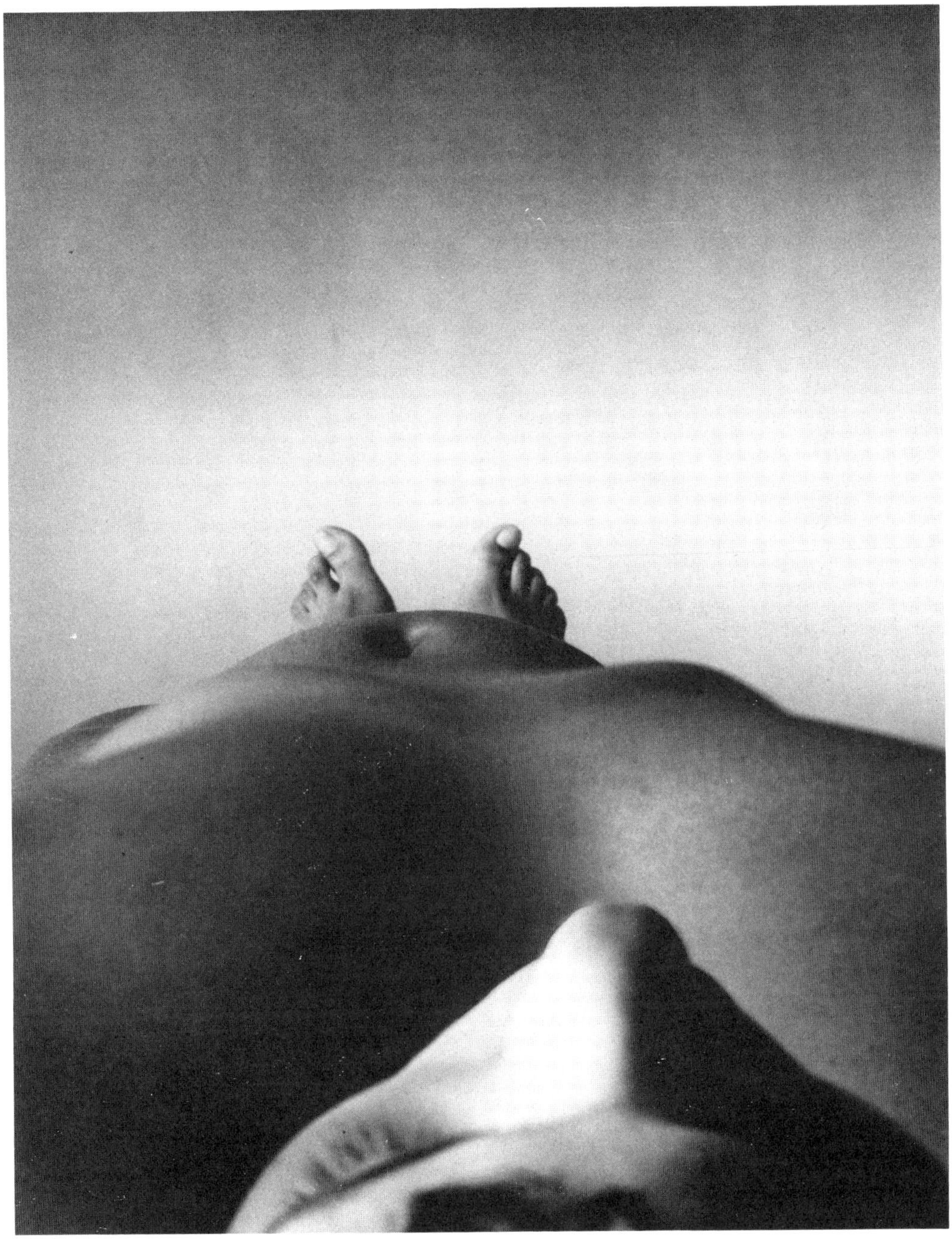

This picture is a deliberate attempt to equate the female figure to Western hill and rock forms. The light was bounced at a very low angle from the left side. To give the effect of sky, the area above the feet was dodged somewhat and the top of the picture burned in quite a bit. Since a picture like this requires great depth of field, I stopped down to f/32.

and the bad for future comparison. Use up film. Try not to worry about technique too much.

With sidelighted figures there is a tendency to read only the brightest areas, causing underexposure. Either include some dark in your meter reading or read the highlights and double the suggested

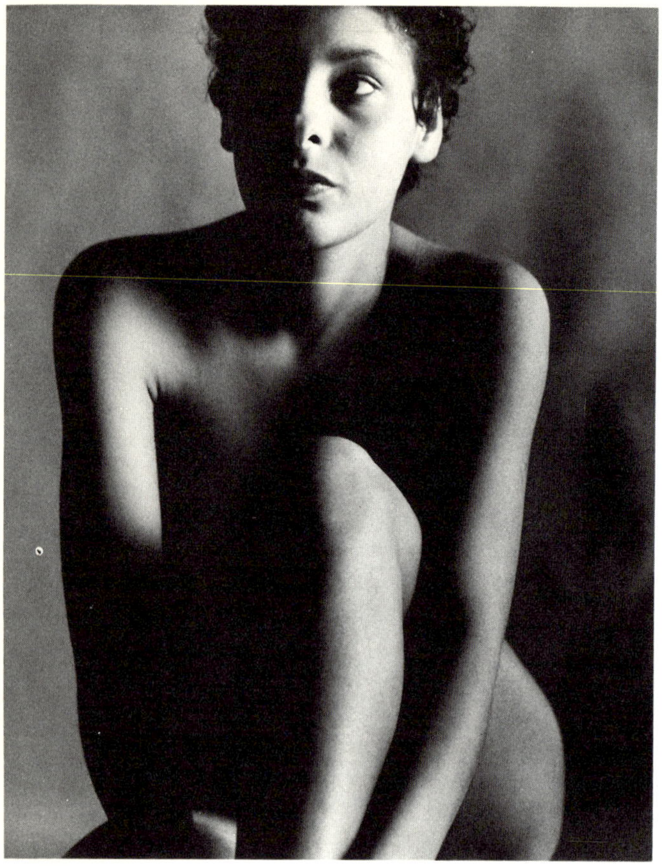

The strong contrast between dark and light (left) was created by having a bounce light very close to the model. In addition, the wall at the left side of the picture was far away, so that little light reflected from it to lighten the darks. Having a model near to or far away from a reflecting wall is a very good way of making contrast either high or low.

There is something about knees (below) that bothers me. Perhaps it is that they are so bony and hard, like rocks. But that's the way things are, isn't it? Some parts of the figure are hard, others soft. One can't have his choice all the time.

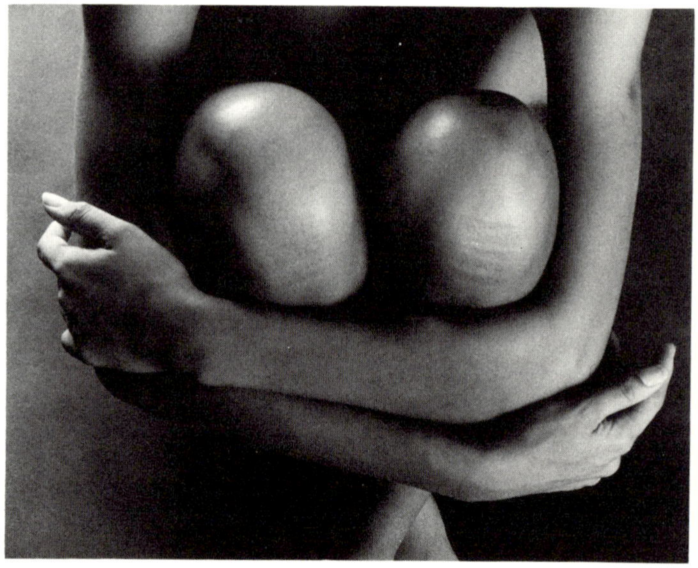

exposure. By taking careful readings with your exposure meter, you'll get the best possible gradation of middle tones in the photograph.

With bouncelighting (floodlights; with flash you can't see what your light is doing) you get fairly long exposures, making it difficult to hand-hold a camera. I suggest a tripod, preferably one easy to adjust, and a variety of boxes and stacks of books on which to prop your camera for the low angles. For hand-holding, use these things to lean against or sit on.

Non-Nude Nudes

Nudes can look like people and a lot of other things, too. We tend to like the things resembling people, or parts of them; it's a way of celebrating our humanity. Our liking for such things also shapes our aesthetic sense, which is the theme of this chapter.

There is a problem in seeing how non-human things relate to human beings, for it is not always obvious. One way of solving it is to make abstracts of nudes that are both human and something else, too.

In time this will help us see the interrelatedness of all things. I hope my nude abstracts will help you believe it is possible. I suggest you study them, clip more from photography annuals, and try the same thing in your figure photography. You'll find it exciting and expansive of your aesthetic awareness.

Another solution is to work the other way around. Instead of making people look like nature, reverse the procedure. Look for people forms in plants, rocks, snow banks and sand dunes.

Karen Tweedy-Holmes disagrees. Her work makes this point: "Look for human personality in nudes, for that is the important thing." She's right, of course, but she overestimates the ability of most photographers to confront nudes as human beings. For many photographers this would put things on a much too personal basis. To help overcome their nervousness they'd prefer to approach the human form as an object and to work on more abstract problems such as I suggest.

Another difficulty for the beginner is separating the forest from the trees. Whole people, including personalities and numerous complex flesh forms and bones, are a veritable jungle of things to keep track of and handle well photographically. It is much easier to cope with single trees or hills: arms, legs, thighs, breasts, buttocks. Having seen how light, tone, line and form function in simple things, you'll find it's easier to see how they work in the complexity of the figure as a whole.

When the process is reversed and one looks for human things in nature, another problem arises. Unless you know a lot about figures you won't recognize resemblances when you see them. Intellect won't work here. It's not enough to surmise that a fire hydrant must look like a phallus; the question is, does it really? Numerous students have shown me pictures of hydrants, extolling their phallic virtues. A person really aware of anatomy wouldn't make this mistake. If the designers of fire hydrants had also been more knowledgeable, we'd be living in more aesthetic environments.

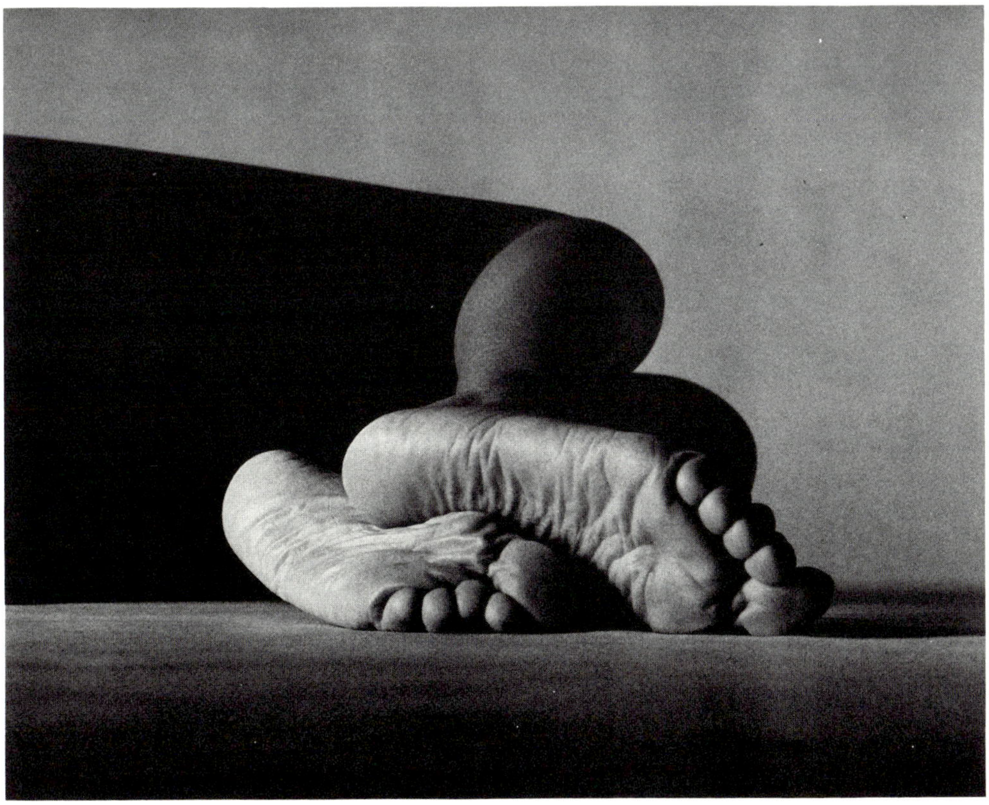

Ordinarily, I find feet slightly revolting. They're ugly and they smell. But these feet were clean, waxy and luminous. I didn't capture these things in the picture, but thought it interesting anyway. It seems to me that the feet look like creatures from another planet, not like human appendages.

The figure below looks something like a hill and equally like a piece of water-worn driftwood. Shapes like this are often found in rocks, snow-banks and sand.

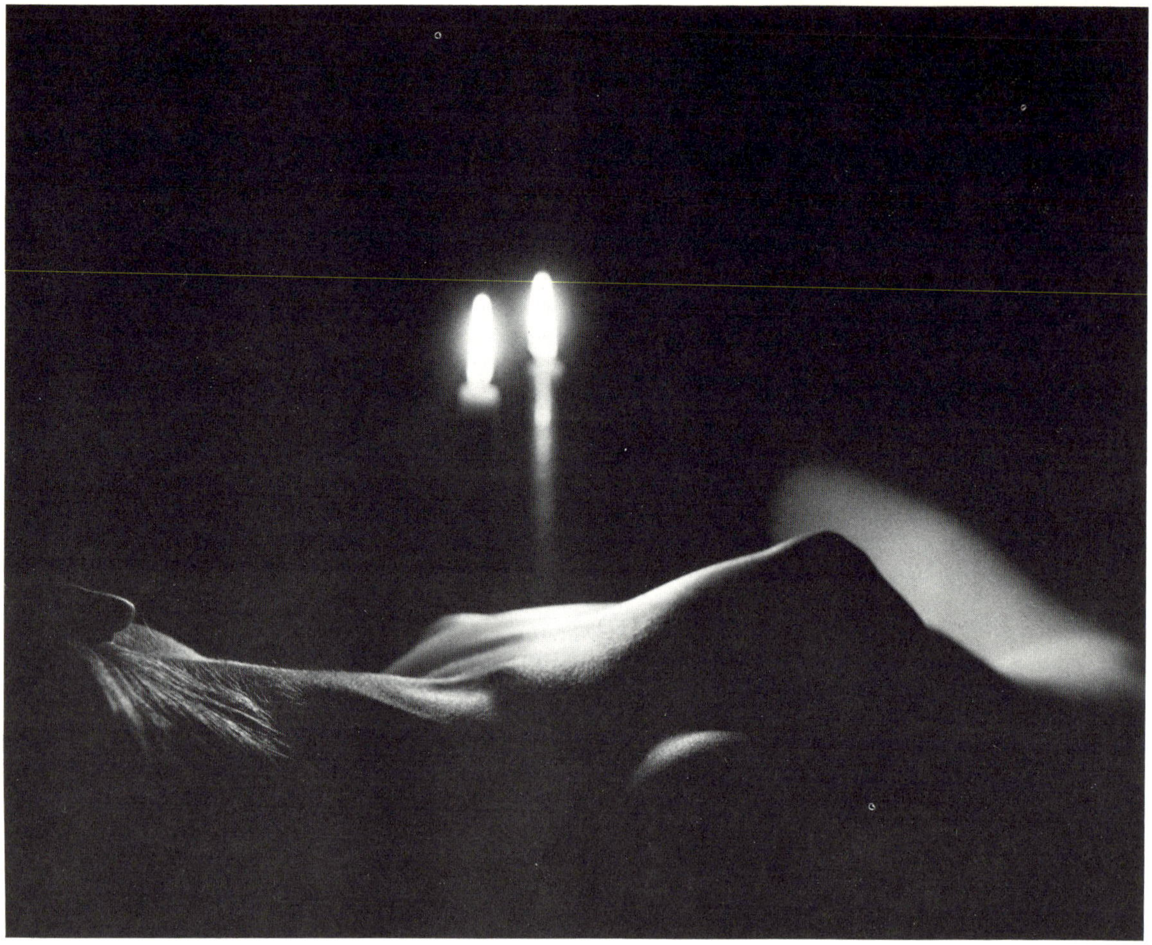

When a person is ignorant of how things really look he can only keep on staring at them until he learns. Fortunately, the sexual drive makes it enjoyable when he uses it to motivate his labor. It can also be used in communing with nature. For example, a person indifferent to the beauties of water-worn stone might learn to dig it through seeing its resemblance to things he's sexually interested in. I've seen art students spend hours mastering lines of a plant because these reminded them so much of lines on nude figures in drawing classes. I think this must also help, say, automobile designers as they sweat to master the lines of radiators and headlights. The idea is to be sensually turned on in solving problems which relate quite indirectly to sex. Where else can one find the energy to master the art of seeing?

I've given hundreds of students the task of converting human into nature forms, and vice versa. For many it was an illuminating experience. A few quickened their awareness of beauty in only a week or two, but they were already strongly visual people. As a student I wasn't visual, so it took a long time. Fortunately, I was so interested in sex I could drive myself hard months on end. I'm personal proof the aesthetically blind can learn to see if they work hard enough. In fact, this whole book reflects my struggles.

A Woman's Approach to the Male Nude

Male nudes nonplus males, myself included. We really don't know what to think of them. So I've decided to introduce someone who does know: Karen Tweedy-Holmes. She's an expert at figure photography and has the intelligence to discover what motivates her so she can tell us. But more: She's a woman. Who could tell us

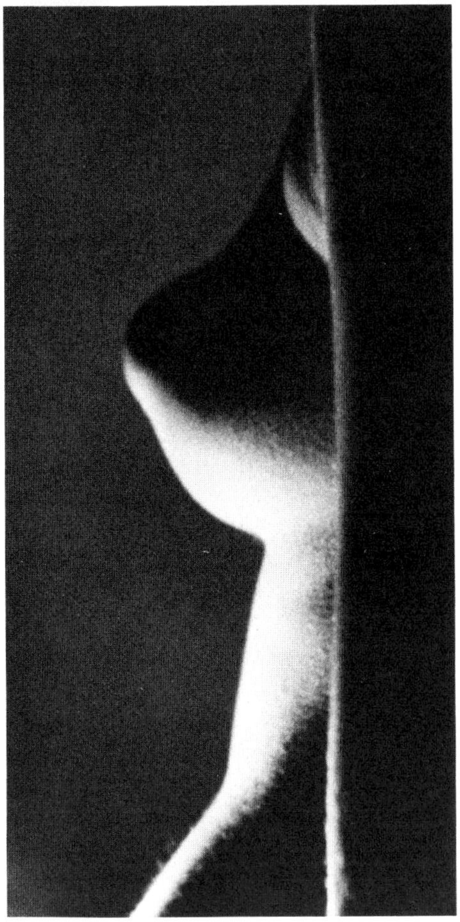

I'm not sure what this looks like, but I wouldn't want to meet it in a dark alley. It looks ferocious.

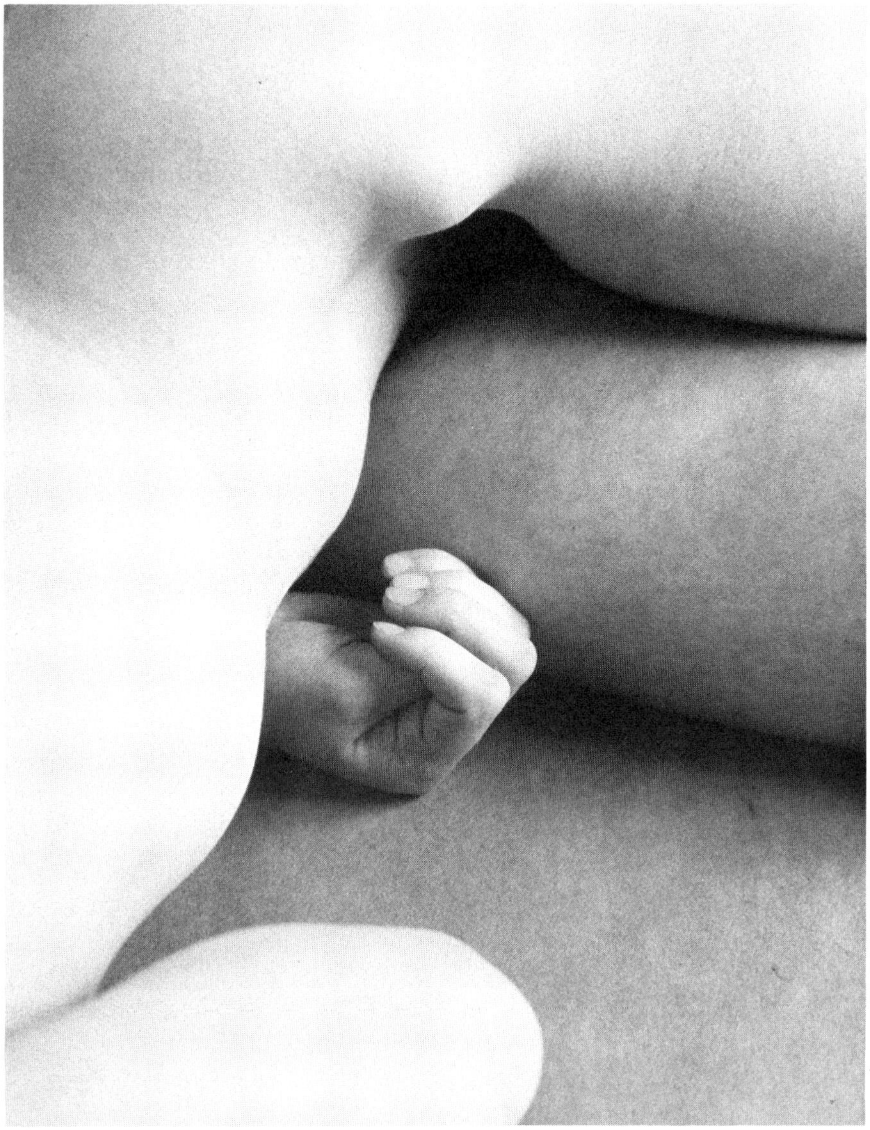

The hips and torso (right) look like light, water-worn rock. The hand is like a small bird's claw.

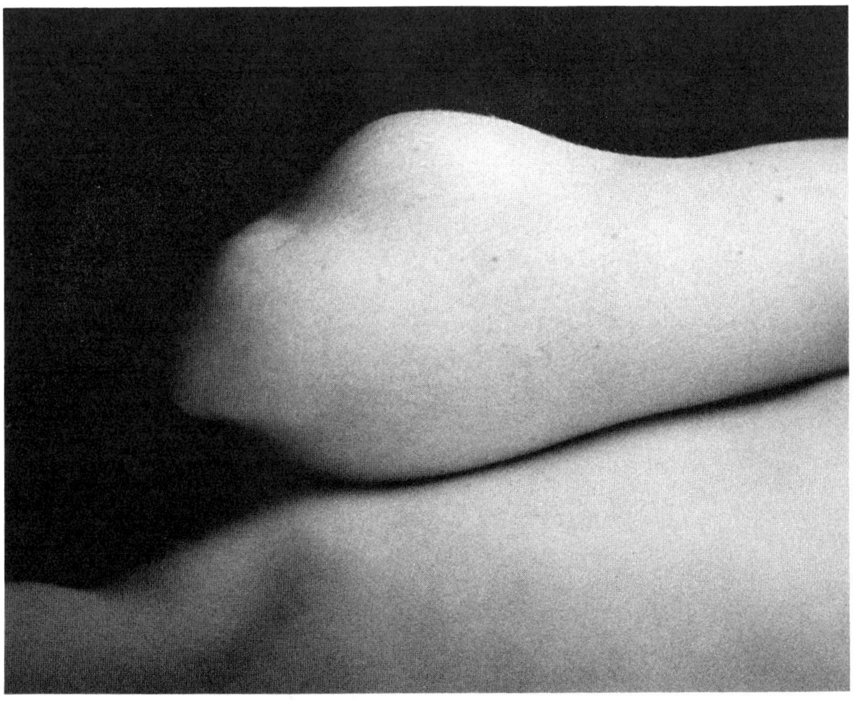

This arm looks like a gourd or the nose end of a fish. It is so streamlined and simple that it resembles many man-made and nature forms. Oddly, it doesn't look much like an arm, for the picture was taken from an unusual point of view.

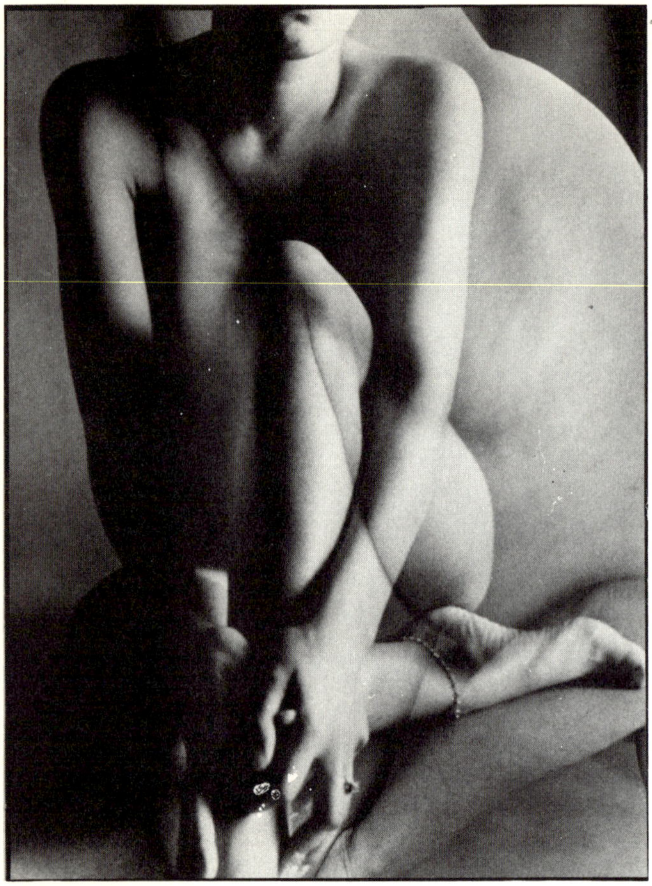

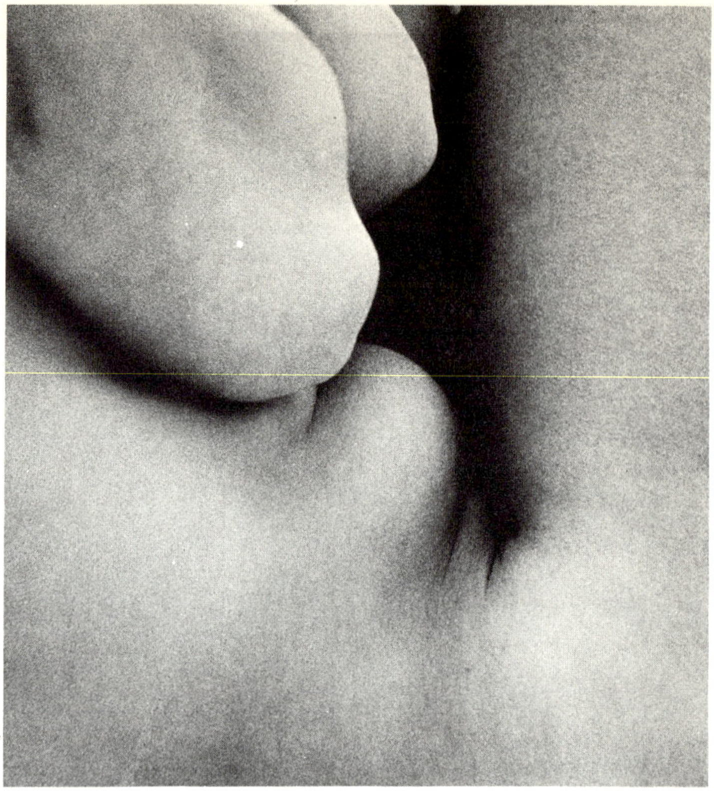

Trees with smooth bark have bulges and knotholes that look a lot like this picture.

High contrast print (right) of a bottom in a bathtub. Like rocks in the tide.

Sandwiching two negatives together created a form which resembles water-worn rock or an aerial view of an alluvial plain. It also looks like a tangle of plant roots.

better about the pleasures of photographing men sans clothing?

I used to be disturbed by her pictures of naked men, fearing that to enjoy them might question my maleness. Through Karen I've learned to really let myself get turned on and I want others to also.

Why on earth the *male* nude? Until recently a woman couldn't come right out and admit that she likes looking at naked men. In our culture men have always been too busy fulfilling their function as workhorses to stand around and be admired at length as merely beautiful. Men do, women are. The conventions, those in photography included, imply that a woman had better concentrate on a man's ability to get a living when she begins to consider her choice of mate; she'll probably be dependent on him, at least economically, for a long while. She oughtn't to waste time just looking at men.

In any case, since Kinsey we've been certain that women aren't much aroused by the sight of the male figure. Women have long been asked to repress their sensual responses to visual stimuli to conform with some pretty far-fetched theories. And advertisers and publishers still subscribe to those theories. So men's bare bods are not used for selling jockstraps or jewelry; their eyes don't smile suggestively from hundreds of magazine covers per week; their sexuality is not defined in terms of the expanse of skin revealed by the necklines of their shirts. Their bodies are not turned to profit and, outside of Times Square where the subject and the product are only sex, photographs of unclad men do not abound. (Can you imagine a photographic annual called *MAN—1970?*)

For several years I have been photographing both men and women without their clothes. The most satisfactory result of this work, to my eye, is the portrait rather than the academic exercise in form

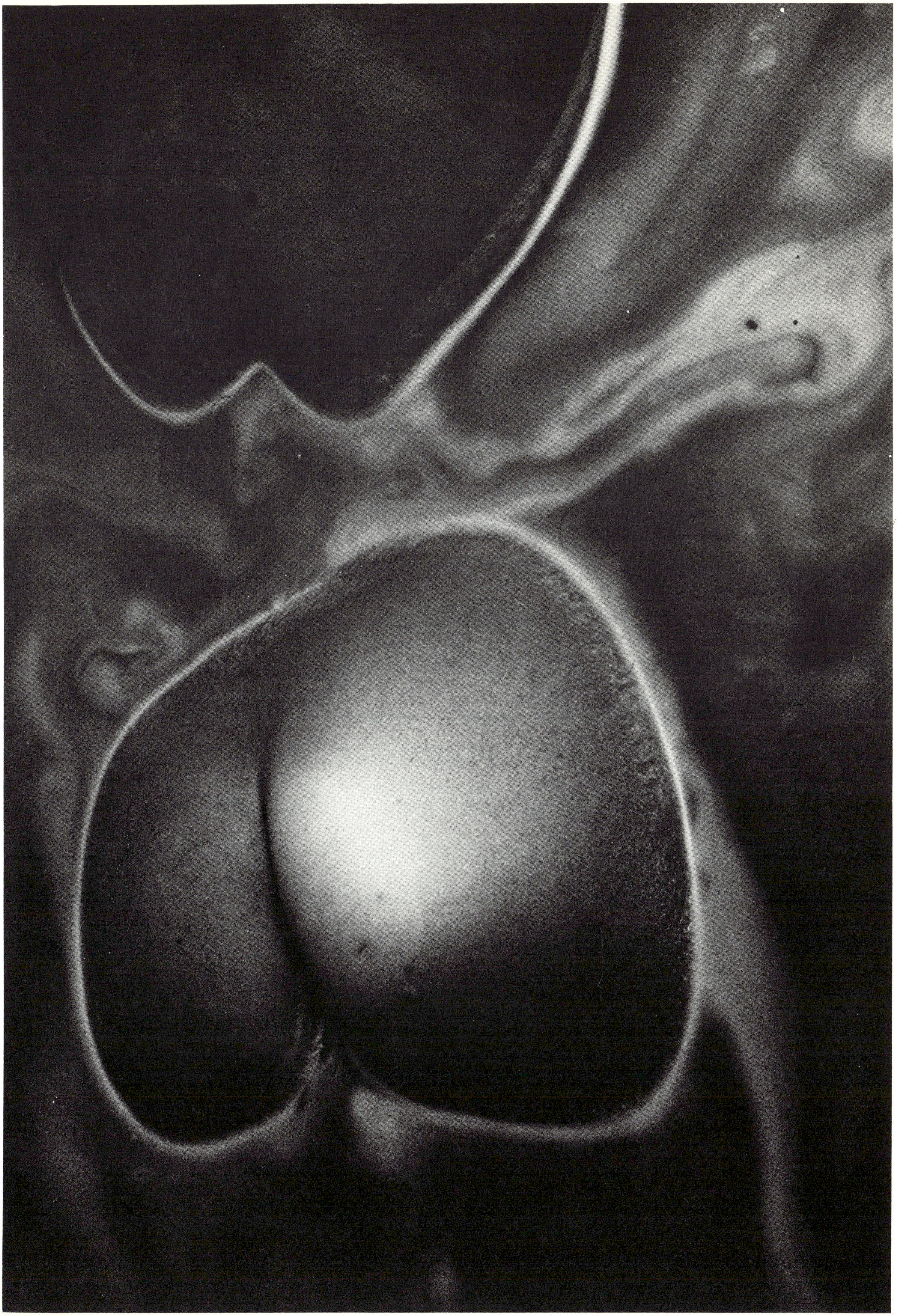

or the poetic metaphor. Although the human body is one of the most elegant designs around, it is the body plus face expressing *persona* that excites me.

The nude woman is used too often to represent all womankind. She's a lovely, soft, round bore, a sensual abstract, a nauseating centerfold. By equating her with Nature or Mother Earth or some less lofty intellectual conceit, the photographer denies her uniqueness; he forgoes the delight of confronting a real woman's nature, and demeans his own individuality in the process. His elaborate fantasies become the subject of his pictures, while the reality in front of him is ignored. Women who are photographers, accustomed to the same tired depiction of their gender, too frequently repeat it.

Since photography became popular, men have rarely made figure studies of men (again except for the hard-core trade). Wondering why, I've questioned male photographers only to be dismissed with "It has never even entered my head," or "Who'd look at them if I did?" (I submit that at least half the species would look with pleasure, given the chance.)

The more introspective of these men have added something about not wanting to risk being thought homosexual. Even the one most in tune with his motives gloomily admitted he is afraid that, faced with an undressed like-made creature, he might reveal carefully suppressed homosexual tendencies. Somehow all these reasons seem awfully speculative, and fine opportunities for insight are thereby wasted. Fortunately the artists of Ancient and Renaissance times felt otherwise.

(A digression on the subject of museums: Isn't it amazing that the selfsame souls who stand rapt before a classical sculpture of a naked man are horrified by a photograph of the same subject? Museums almost never hang photographs of the male nude. Why is a photographic print so very much more real, so much more threatening, if you will, than oil on canvas or a hunk of stone? It's just a piece of paper, a medium—not an actual presence of palpitating flesh.)

To cases: My particular choice of photographic options undoubtedly implies something about me. What choices do I consciously make? I shoot only my friends

A charred tree root (below) with the black worn off the outer parts through the action of water and sand. Or maybe it's an animal skeleton.

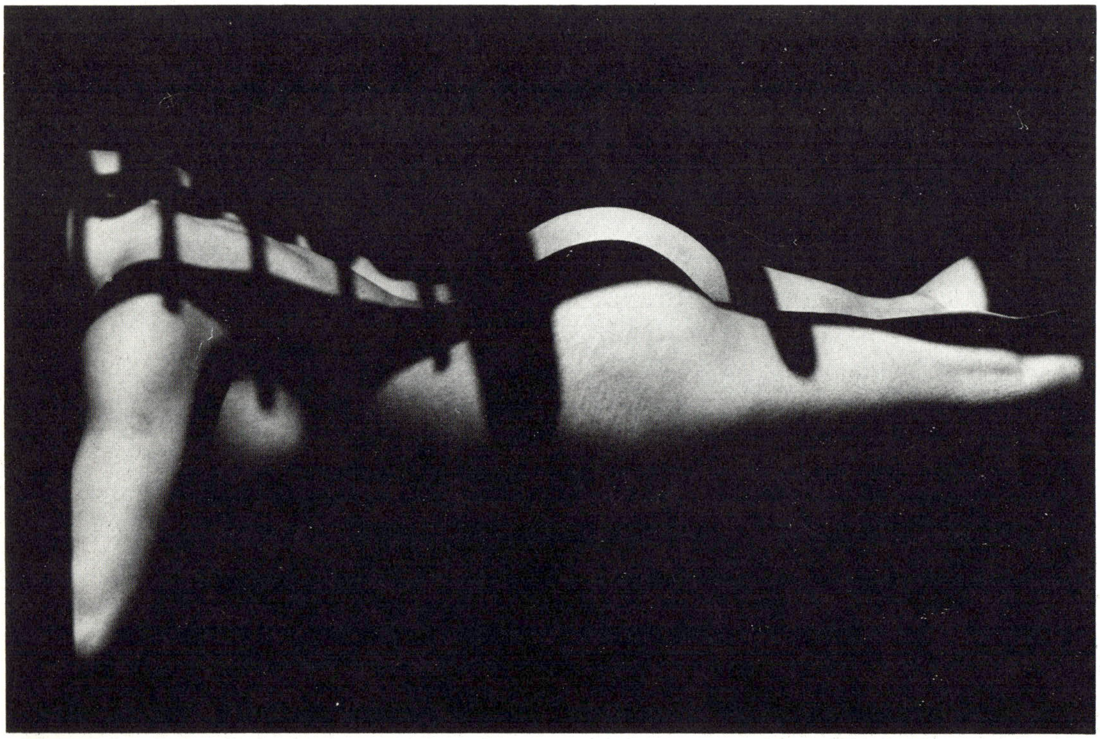

undressed, never professionals. My friends are readily available, they model for free, and they are not as likely to impel me to art-class clichés. But by far the most important reason is that I am, in fact, photographing a relationship, not just a body. Whether or not my subject approaches some nebulous physical ideal isn't relevant to what I'm doing. As a result nobody feels intimidated; so far our sessions have been relaxed, sometimes verging on the hilarious.

I've come to love specific environments. The thrill of seamless paper has palled somewhat over the years. A real, live background says something about my model, if only an allegorical something. I try hard not to objectify him. Infrequently do I rob him of that which makes him unique, cropping his head to produce a generalization.

I think men are fantastically beautiful beings. I want to show each how very beautiful he is to me, just being himself, not symbolizing anything greater than himself. Stripped to the skin, sans the thousand defenses of clothing, it's his Self, in the Hattersley sense, I attempt to see.

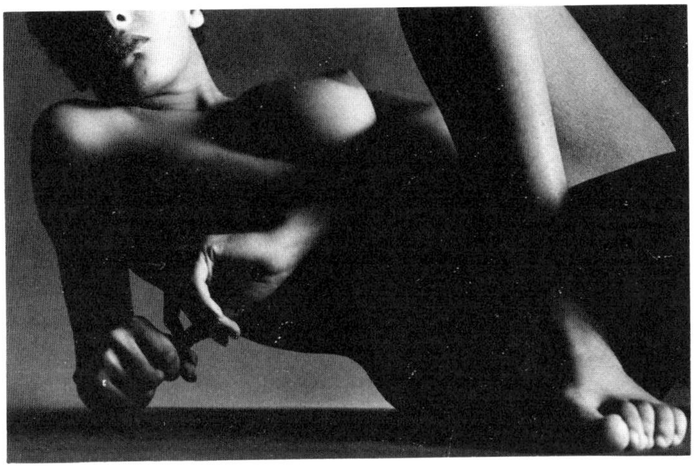

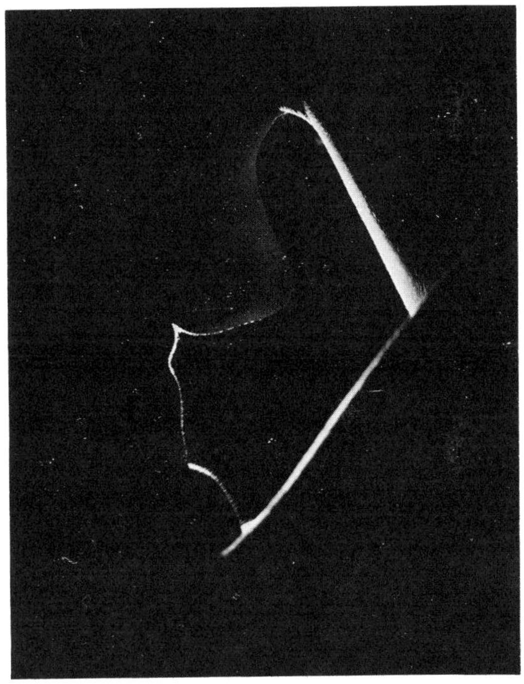

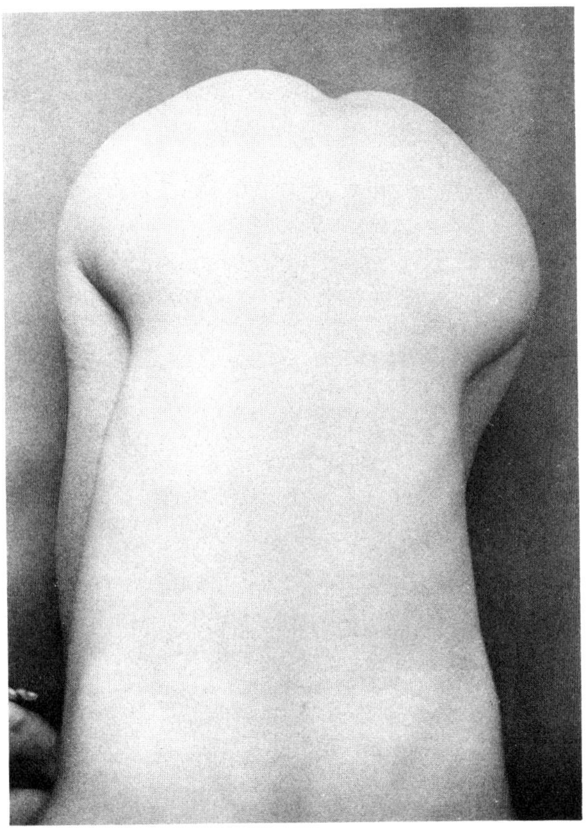

A heap of spare parts (above left) with an underlying feeling of organization. Chinese brush calligraphy (above)? Or a note from an automobile designer's sketchbook? It looks like some kind of nature form, but I'm not sure what. The phallic back (left) shows my male preoccupation with masculinity. It also looks like the end of a bone.

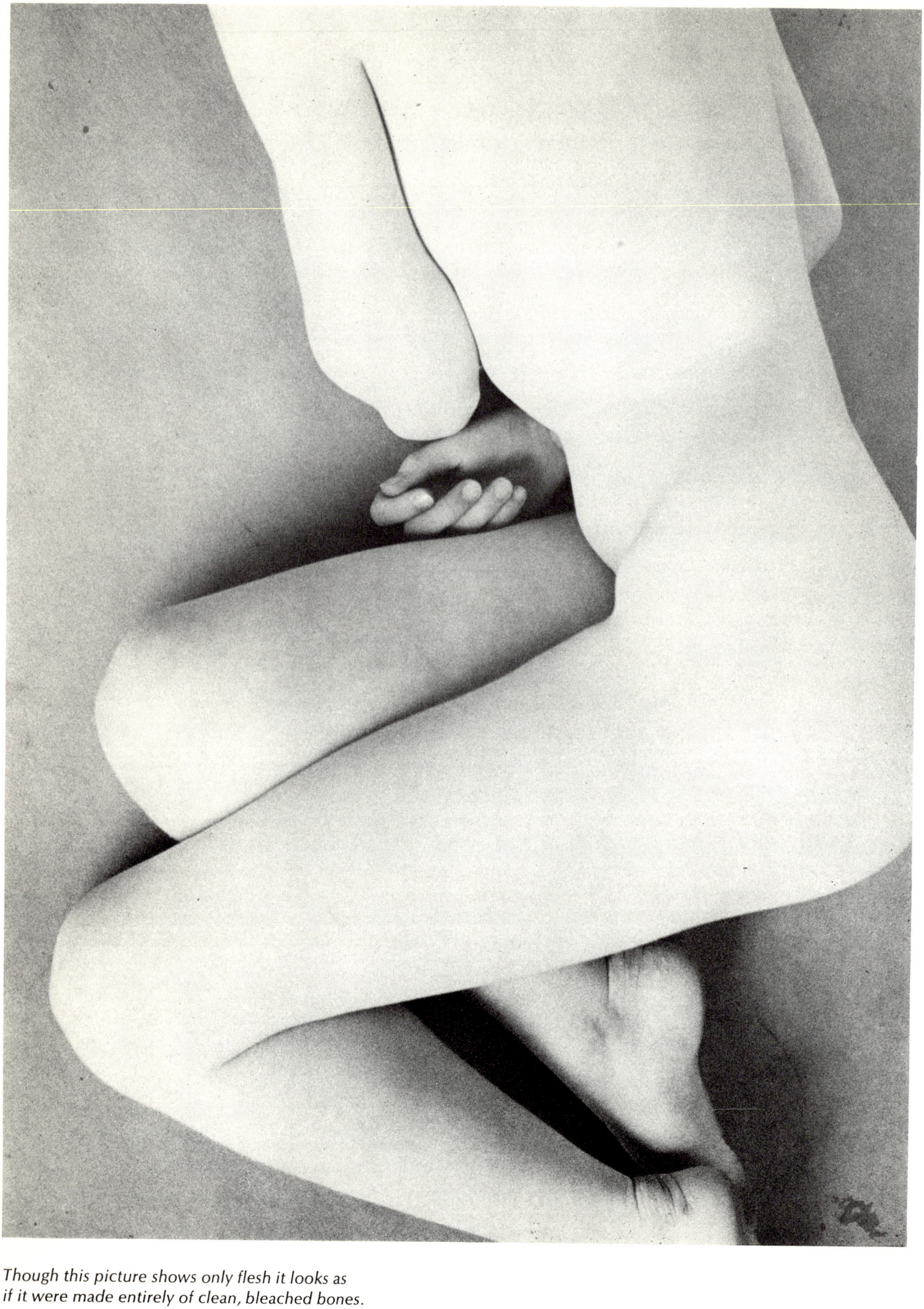

Though this picture shows only flesh it looks as if it were made entirely of clean, bleached bones.

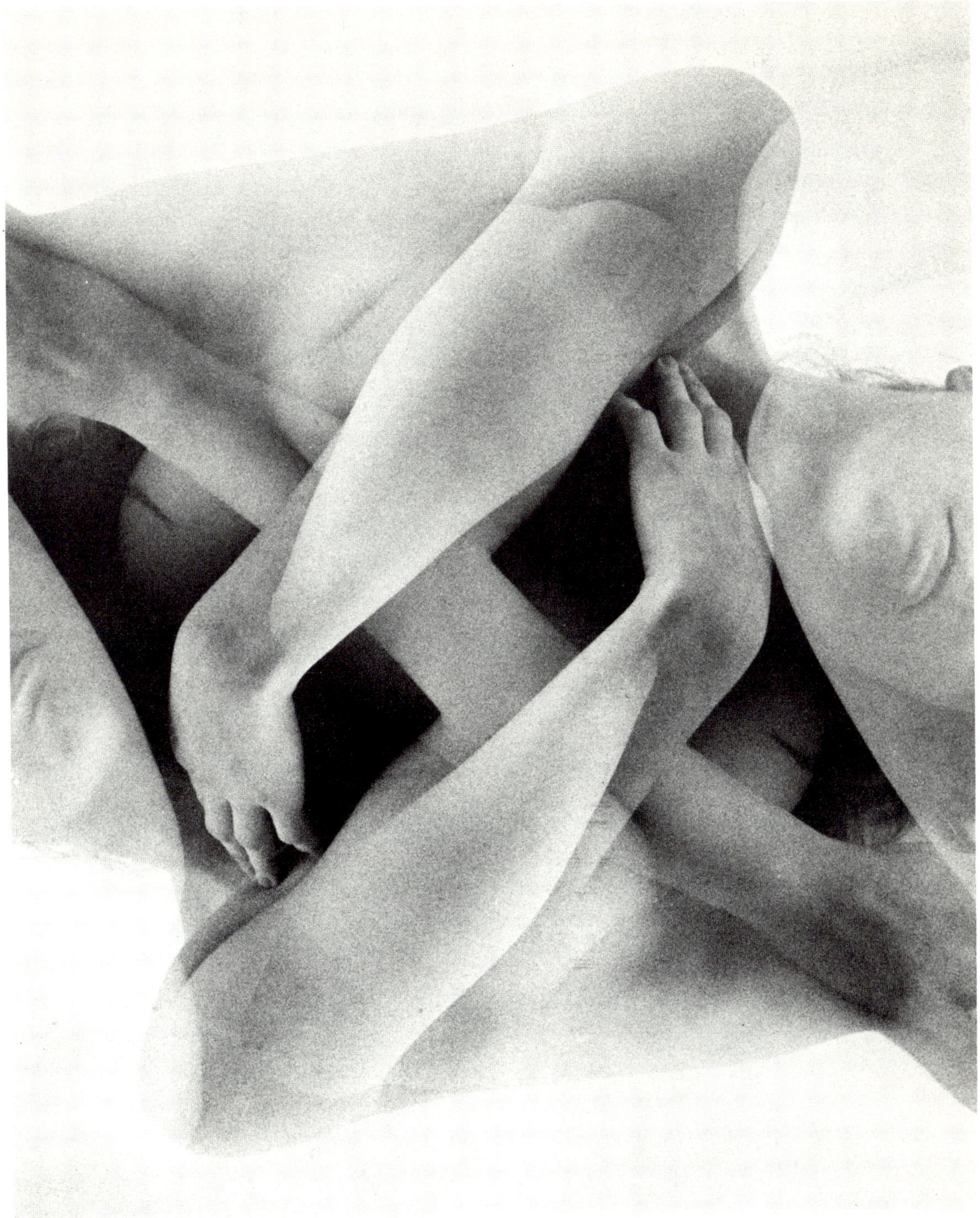

Double exposure created this tangle of arms which looks so much like roots woven together. Linear rhythms give the picture an organic quality, making it look like an interior view of man.

This man is a desirable, erotically stimulating corporeal entity. If my photograph says that I think so, it works. If that is all it says about him, it very definitely fails.

Kinsey-brainwashed public opinion may raise its three eyebrows if it likes, but no woman I know has ever turned away from these images, has ever done other than look long and hard at them. She is not simply curious to see what's been hidden under a fig leaf for so long. She has quite discernible reactions to the individual described by the portrait. I think the fact that he's nude somehow intensifies her perception of his personality, though I'm not sure why.

I'm sorry to report that a fair percentage of the men who've been shown my male nudes have felt obliged to remark: "They don't do anything for *me,*" as they pass them back with the briefest of glances. Dredging up all the good humor at my command, I still find this attitude frustrating, entrenched as it is in rock-hard traditionalist thinking.

The general public in this country still finds the nether regions of a man's body totally objectionable in photographs. In fact, the penis is clearly so unacceptable a sight that I am prohibited from reproducing for this chapter any picture of mine which includes so much as a few pubic hairs. Artistic freedoms apart, the attitude this reflects is harmful to the human spirit of self-understanding. In portraying a man naked I seek to draw attention to the mystery of man as well as his beauty. What is so terrible about his sex that it cannot be investigated in a photograph along with the rest of him, that it cannot be seen as an essential part of his mystery and beauty? I have sought to draw attention to the mystery of a man's body and mind as well as his beauty. Since I was a child, I've been hearing how terribly mysterious and unknowable are women. I'm convinced that the same is true of men. Seen here as a function of sensuality, mystery could as easily describe a man's head.

Verbiage aside, a photograph must speak for itself. No amount of chatter about the picture can qualify it to the extent of making it work if it does not. Soon, I fervently hope, the shock effect inherent still in this subject will fade altogether as more people work with the male nude to discover new worlds within their friends and within themselves.

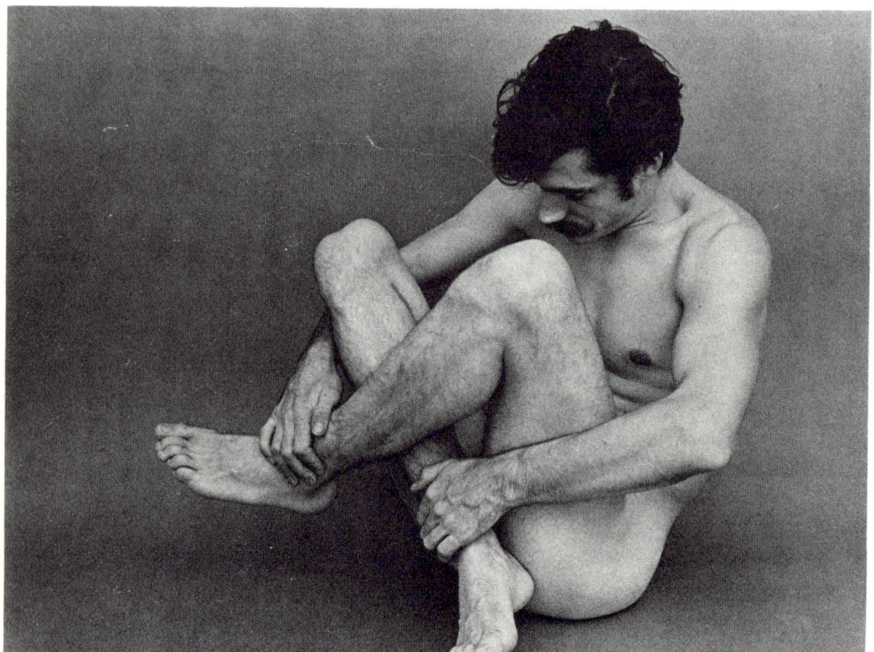

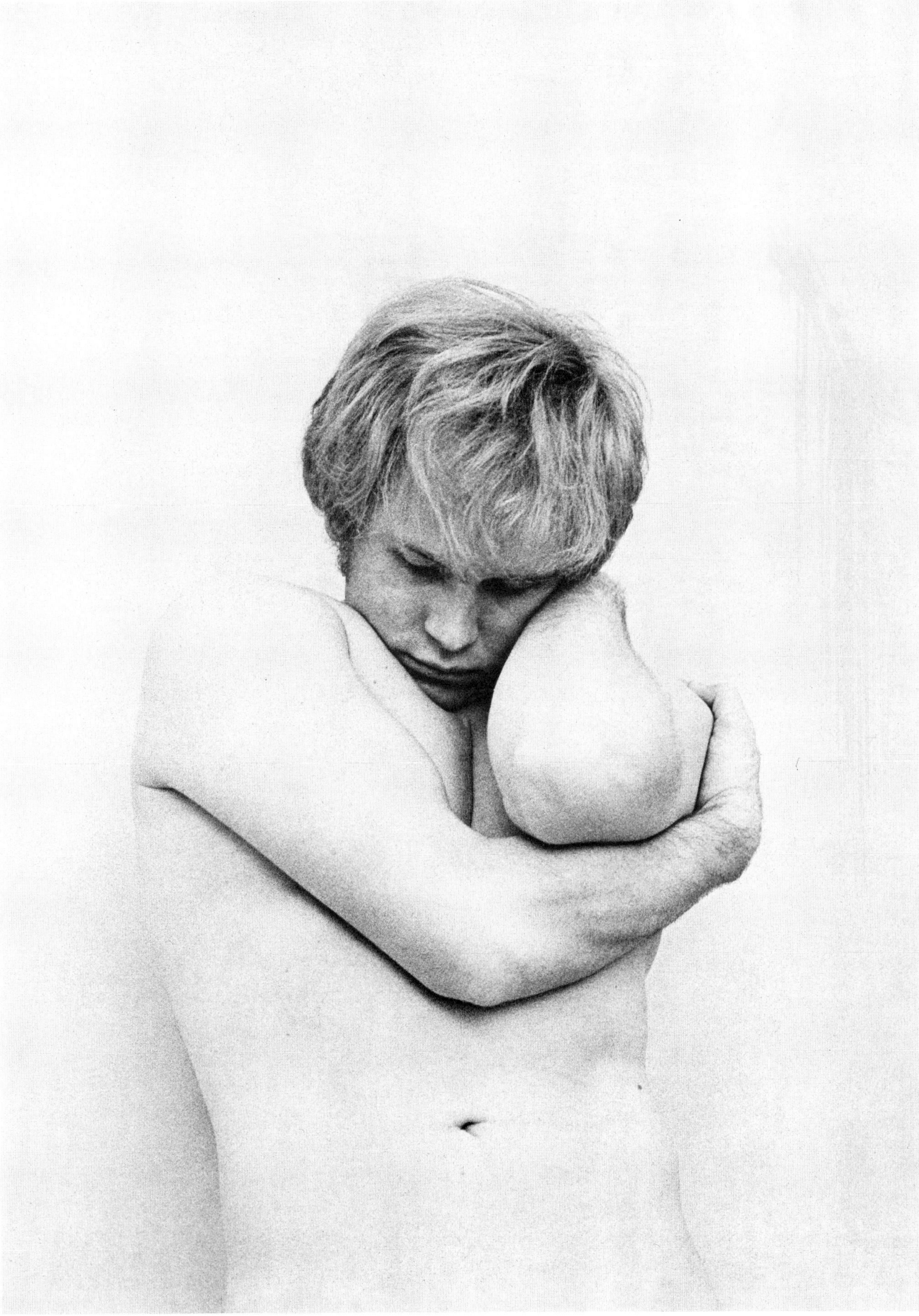

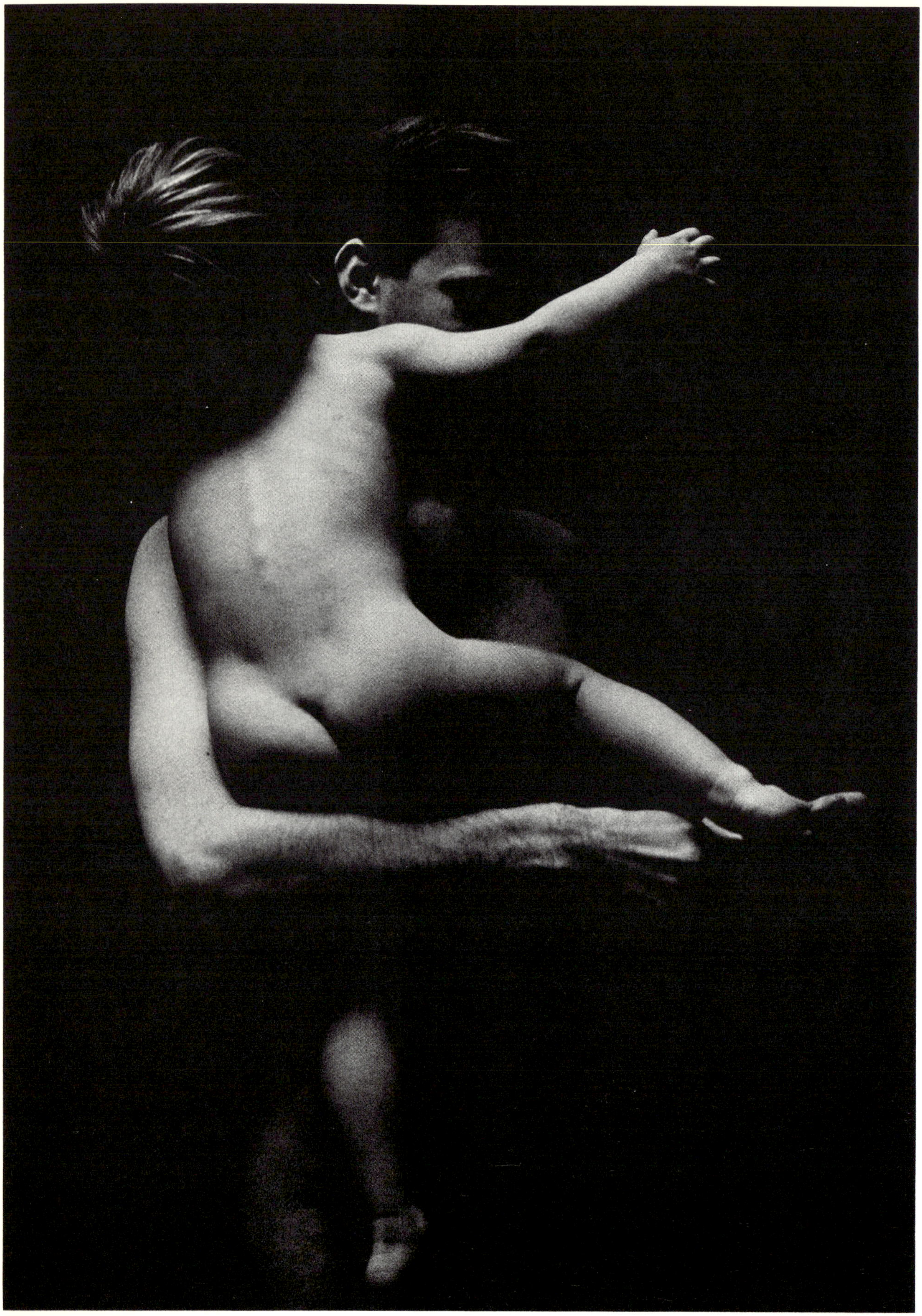

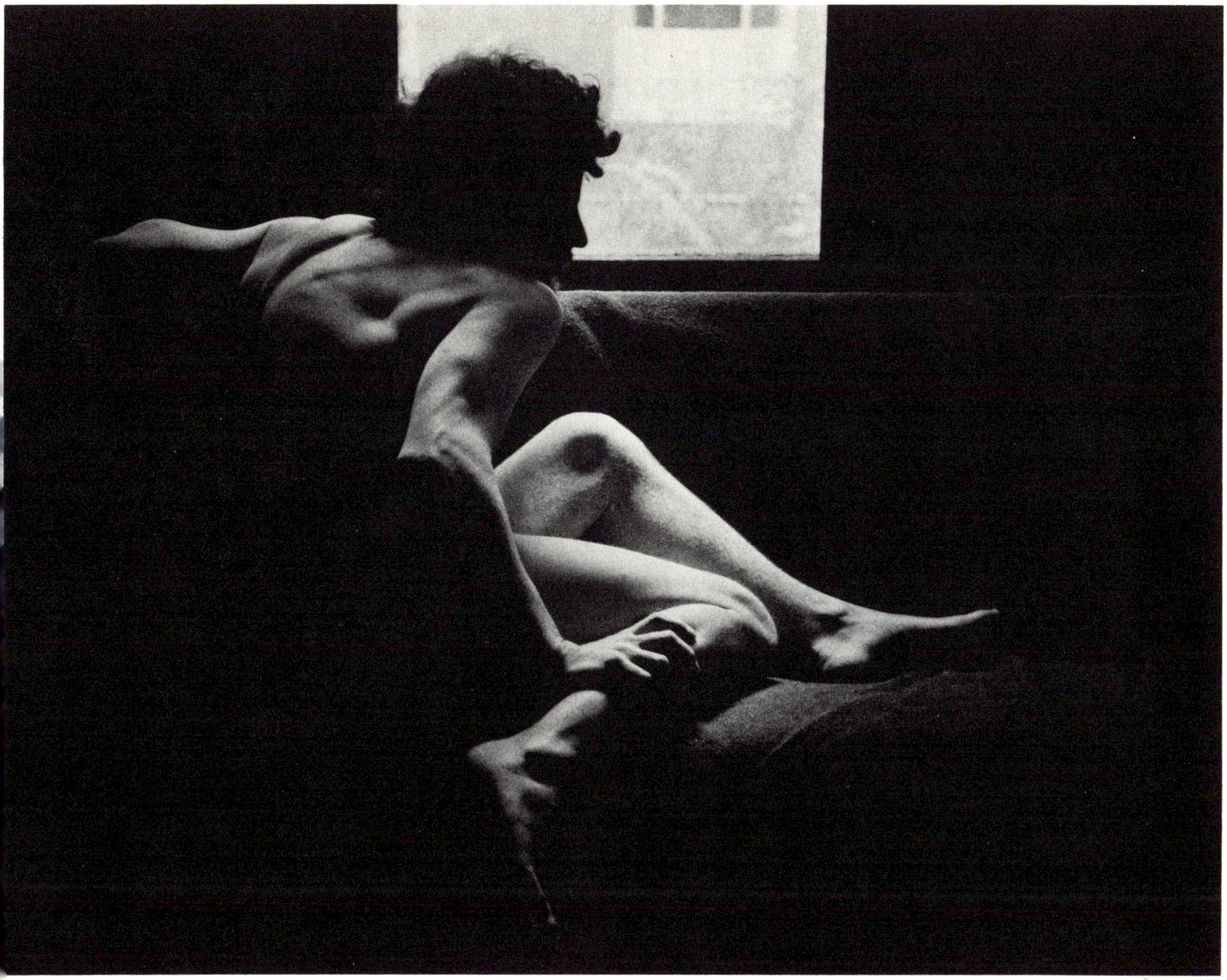

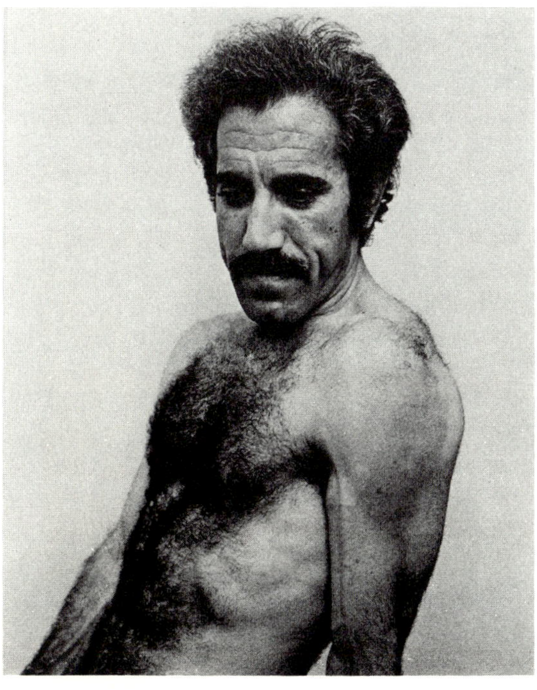

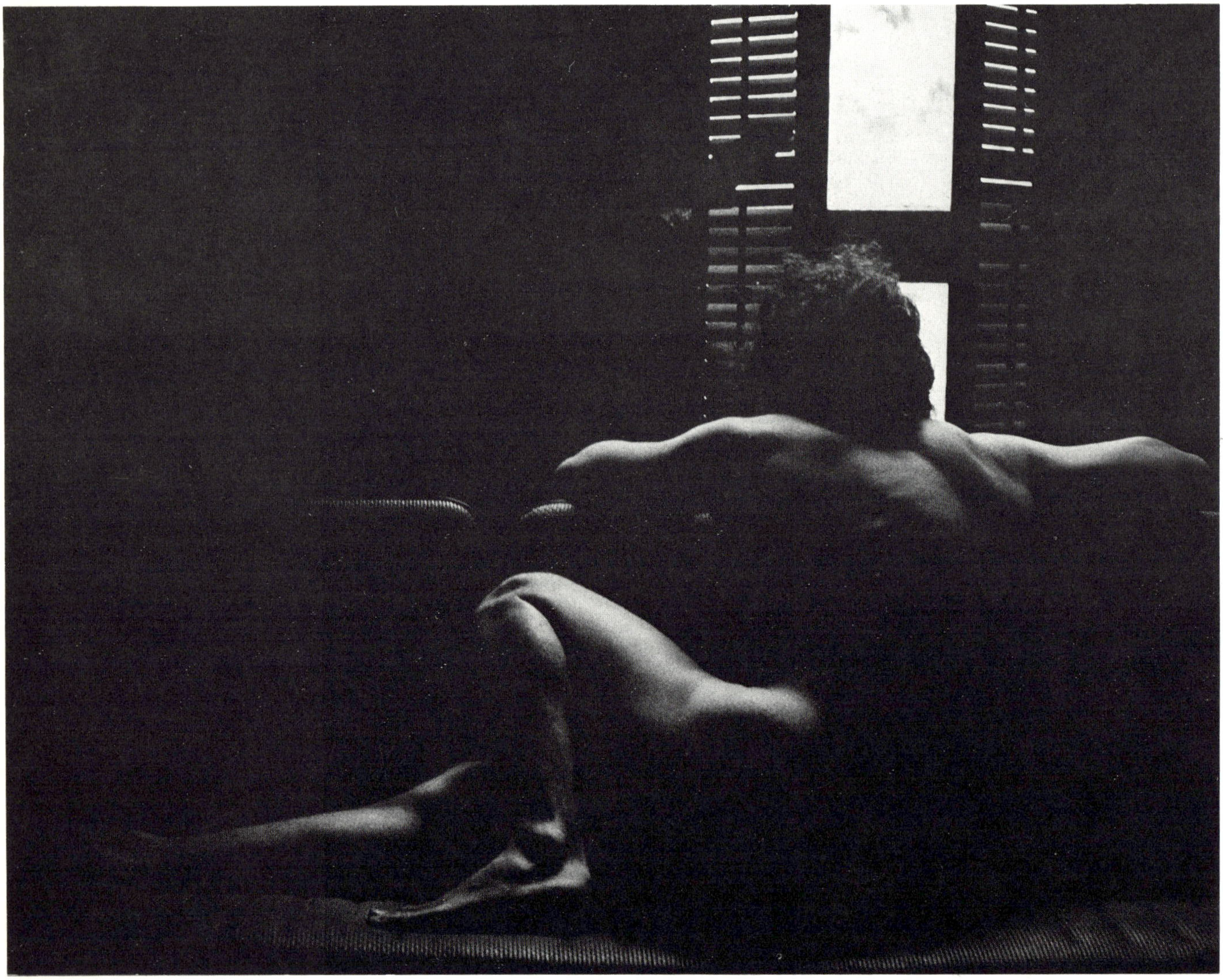

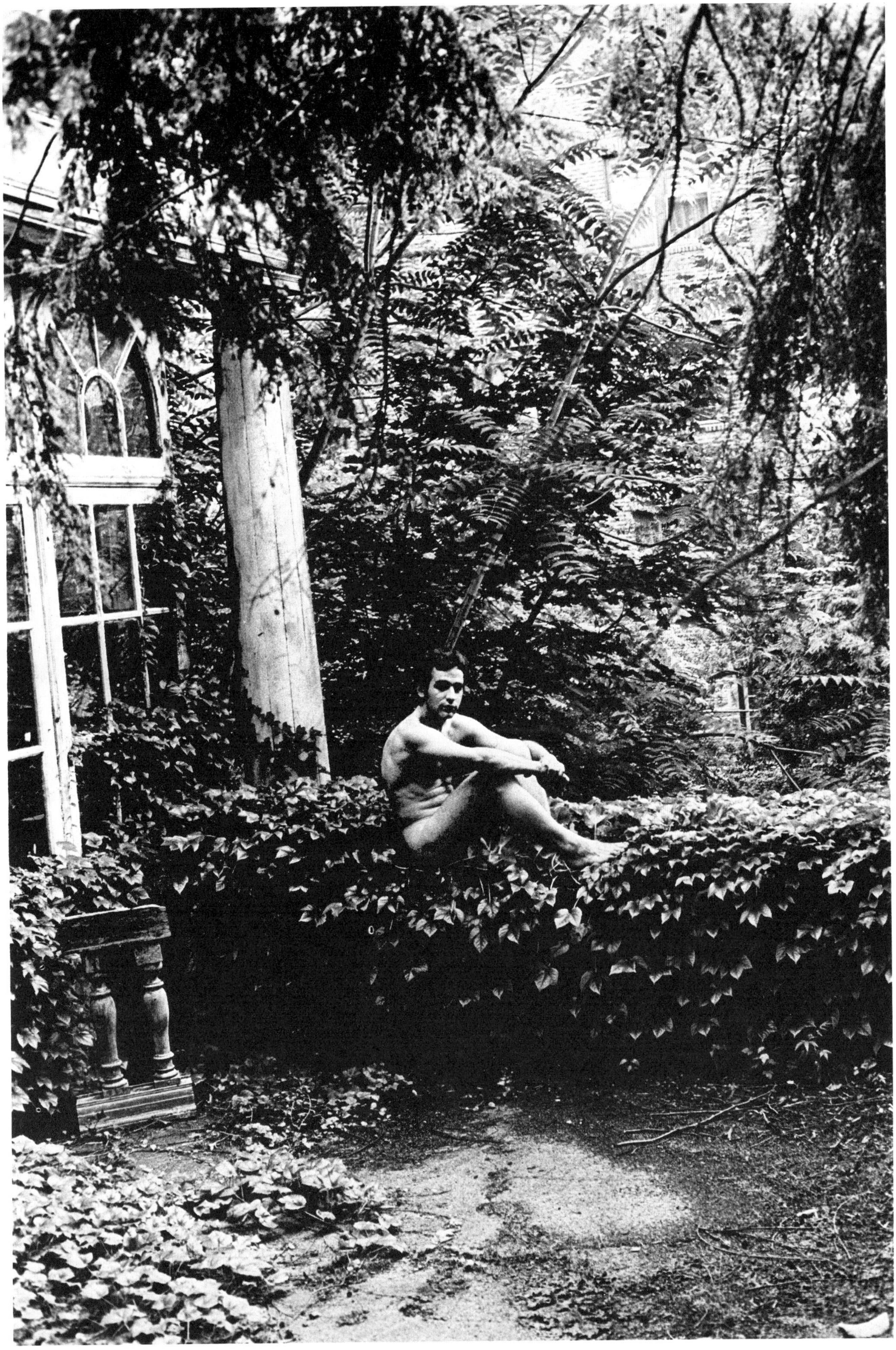

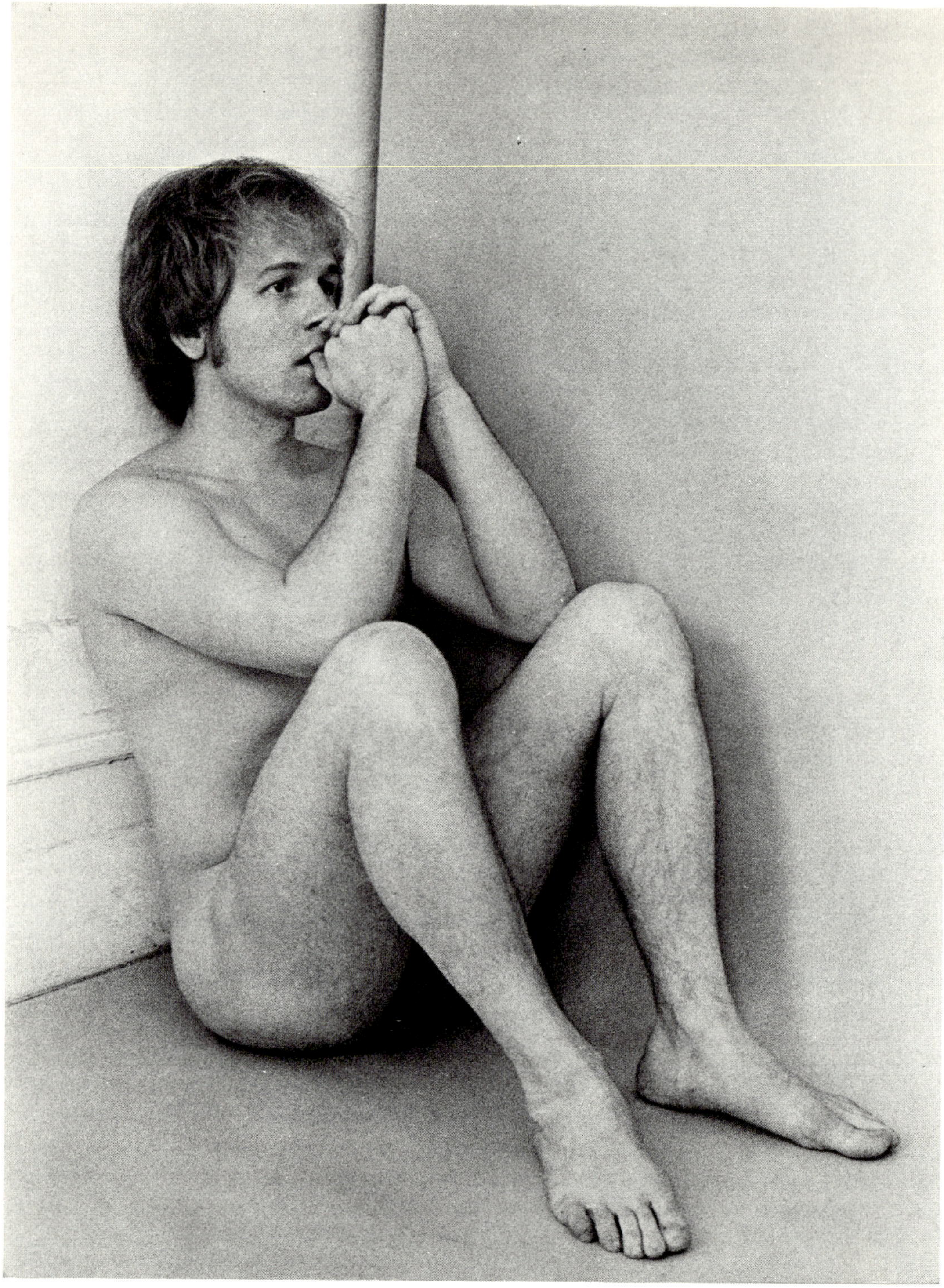

DISCOVER both sides of yourself

Using photography to discover, analyze and express visually the two sides of yourself: the masculine and the feminine.

An important but poorly understood truth about human beings is that each person has two large and very different sides: the masculine and the feminine. Because we don't understand this we experience no end of suffering and confusion in our lives. Information has always been available, but we've ignored it. The Great Teachers have tried to tell us that only when we understand both sides and bring them into harmony will we be physically, mentally and spiritually whole.

In a limited sense we've known for many years about this fundamental division in man, though we've by no means unraveled all its complexity. Scientists in many disciplines are studying it. Biologists have approached it by analyzing the organs, glands and secretions. They've shown that each person has all the organs of the opposite sex in vestigial form, mammaries, penises, testes, hormone-producing glands, and so forth. Not only are they there but they exert a profound effect on us. Studies of the male-female hormonal balance have shown this. Taken as a whole, the evidence strongly indicates that biologically we are all male-female beings. To say that a man is 'all man' or a woman 'all woman' just doesn't make biological sense.

4

Psychologists have also seen our essential male-female natures. As some put it, we're psychosexual hermaphrodites. This sounds frightening, but it shouldn't. All it means is that our psychic natures parallel the physical. Psychologically, we are all male-female. In some cultures this idea is easily accepted. In our own, however, it is greeted with unconscious terror. So great is their fear of bisexuality (male-femaleness) that many people have become deeply neurotic. Men who are afraid of their femaleness repress it and become neurotically over-masculine. Women become neurotically over-feminine. Instead of seeing this psychic imbalance as a kind of sickness, we pride ourselves on it and make ourselves sicker. Over-masculine men strive to become more masculine. Over-feminine women strive to become even more feminine.

Though over-masculine men and over-feminine women have always been in the majority, there have been a few people who intuitively knew that this psychosexual imbalance is a sickness of mind and emotion. Today, the best examples of this way of thinking are our long-haired young men and the girls they associate with. We could all benefit by observing them closely.

Young Men With Long Hair

It's impossible to escape the fact that some of our young men are growing long hair like women. Oddly, many of them do it in order to look more like men! Their reasoning seems to be that this is the way they were intended to look, so they let Nature take her course and come out with long hair and beards. There are others, however, who grow long hair in order to look as much like women as possible. Some are even pleased when you tell them, "My, you certainly look like a girl." Not only do they let their hair grow but they dress to look more like girls.

For people who object to this behavior, it is comforting to think that these young men are homosexuals. Thinking thus, they can avoid the fact that they themselves might be entirely wrong in their notions concerning healthy male and femaleness. It is much easier for them to think, "These kids are just fags, and growing long hair is what a young fag would do." There are a lot of people whose thoughts on the subject are even more perverse. They call young long-hairs communists and think that in thus labeling them they've summed up the problem. They have no inkling that long hair for men is very much in disfavor in communist countries.

Not all of the long-haired boys are trying to look like girls or encourage the development of female traits in themselves. From many talks with those who *are* trying to be more feminine I've reached the conclusion that most of them are far from being homosexuals. They wouldn't even fit into the psychological classification of effeminate men. Though they are criticized from all sides, most of them seem to be aware that what they're doing is entirely normal. They are trying to give expression to a normal part of themselves: the female. At the same time, they have no wish to diminish their masculine side. All they want to do is let their two halves come into proper balance and harmony. To do this they must for awhile put special emphasis on expressing the half they had heretofore repressed. Later, when balance is established, they can express both halves equally.

A few of these lads have even higher goals. They are using their long hair and the reactions it causes in other people for distinctly spiritual purposes. Here I'm not speaking of those who fancy themselves as looking like Jesus and who tend to assume that because they're like him in one respect they are like him in all. Their thinking is naive and egotistical but it is at least pointed toward a being from whom they have much to gain.

I'm speaking of those who make conscious spiritual use of the fact that their long hair has made them social outcasts. They use the taunts hurled at them to strengthen themselves. Some of them have intuitively seen that if they don't respond to taunts and slurs by having negative attitudes, they will build spirituality within themselves.

This method for developing one's spirituality has a long history. In the East it is sometimes called 'Taking the path of blame.' The idea is to put oneself deliberately in a position constantly being criticized, blamed, taunted or thought ill of. By resisting the temptation to react aggressively, in action or thought, a person develops humility and patience. Furthermore, his inner struggle not to permit himself negative attitudes burns up certain psychic impurities which he would find it difficult to be rid of otherwise. Some of these impurities are anger, pride, egotism and selfishness.

Using long hair to follow the path of blame and using it in order to help unite the two halves of the Self are closely related ideas. Both will lead people to psychological Self-evolution. Both will lead to higher spirituality. I don't believe that all long-haired young men have such high purposes in mind; the majority of them obviously do not. However, there are enough who consciously have such purposes for it to be well worthwhile to examine carefully what they're doing. As I've said, we have something to learn from them.

Quite a few of these young folk are deeply interested in photography, but this doesn't imply that they are using it to unite the two halves of the Self. My primary reason for mentioning them at all was to point out that there *are* some young men who are intuitively aware that they have a feminine half and that it needs to be developed and given an opportunity to express itself.

Photography and Self-unification

Having taken a brief look at the problem it is now time to ask what photography can do to help us unite our two halves. It would be nice if we could do it merely by making pictures, but it just doesn't work that way. Thousands of men have gone on for years expressing nothing but their masculinity through photography. Thousands of women have expressed nothing but their femininity. Photography is only a tool. There is no built-in factor which makes it an automatic repair mechanism for the damaged or incomplete psyche.

In order to use photography as a means of Self-completion you must do more than just snap pictures. You must learn to be an acute observer of yourself while you are thinking about pictures, making them and analyzing them afterwards. You must deliberately use the medium to help promote a struggle against that part of yourself which hates and strongly resists Self-investigation. You must use it to help uncover the lies you tell yourself. Also you should use it to become an astute observer of other people's behavior. Though it is fairly obvious that Self-investigation is necessary, it is less apparent why we should investigate the behavior of others.

It seems to be a psychic law that if you want to see yourself clearly you must also learn to see others. In fact, the two types of perception, inner and outer, should develop at the same time. Observing only oneself can lead to very strong self-centeredness, which is a powerful barrier against Self-discovery. Or it can leave one entirely without reference points. You may make discoveries but have no basis of human experience from which to determine their meaning. However, self-centeredness appears to be the primary barrier. It is a basic human truth that a person can discover himself only through his fellow human beings. This is an inconvenient truth, to be sure, for it would be much simpler to leave the rest of the human race behind when embarked on the journey of Self-discovery.

We need other people for more than just study purposes. We must interact with them in hundreds of different ways. Each type of interaction can give us clues concerning some aspect of the Self. When we're looking for some special thing in the Self, we can direct our attention to the types of human relations which will help reveal it to us. For example, when a man is trying to discover what constitutes femininity he can best see this through observing and interacting with women and vice versa. Though men and women ordinarily do this without being told to, few of them are aware that they should be looking for something in the opposite sex which should also be strongly represented in themselves.

Photography can be used with great success in this kind of study. Men should examine the photographs of women and listen to what they say about their work. Women should analyze men's work and their comments concerning it. Since people are not naturally prone to listen carefully to one another, this type of thing is not easy to do. With time and patience one can learn.

The Photography of Karen Tweedy-Holmes

For seven years I've thought about Karen Tweedy-Holmes' photographs, wondering how they express her female nature. She expresses it wonderfully in everything she does, so I assumed she must also do it in her photography.

Karen's femaleness is most easily seen in the way she relates to the people she portrays. Her passivity is obvious. Her subjects don't feel her as an outgoing, hostile force. She has comfortable vibrations and is a refuge for her subjects as she works with them.

Female passivity should be considered in the metaphysical sense. It is not something just sitting still and doing nothing. It is truly a force and can be the motive power for prodigious amounts of work. I think this is true in Karen, for she is monumentally productive in her photography and many other interests.

The passive force in Karen makes her a sponge for humanity. She can soak up people by the truckload. She has many friends and absorbs impressions of them in huge quantities. I would guess she could talk for six hours about any of them without even stopping to gather her thoughts.

When the passive force absorbs life it leaves it undisturbed, while the active male force disrupts it. When Karen strips impressions and information from her friends, she leaves them intact. But more: She replenishes them. You see, Karen is a very female female.

She replenishes them by her wholehearted interest in them. With her photographs she invariably tries to show them things in themselves they can honestly admire. She recently made some fine portraits of me, for example. I look at them and think "Gee, I'm not such a bad guy after all."

Karen's femaleness shows in her infinite interest in the emotions glimmering in faces she's photographing. She doesn't record emotion as an end in itself but to create a meaningful memory file of her friends. She can ponder over her prints for hours, seeing in each image important nuances of feeling. Though she has stacks of contacts of some of her friends, this doesn't satisfy her. As time passes friends change in subtle ways; her goal is a complete, up-to-date composite of everyone she loves.

Karen and I agree people should develop psyches which are both male and female but disagree on definitions of male and female. She admits her photographs often bring out the masculine aspects of women and the female qualities in men. In looking at her portraits and the male nudes in the last chapter, you can see her women are sometimes tough and her men tender. She sees hardness in men when she wishes, but feels the tender side is so culturally neglected that it badly needs expression. Similarly, she finds the male attributes of women overlooked. In some photographs she brings them out, yet grants her women friends all their femaleness, too.

When I talk at length on the Soul as androgynous, Karen listens patiently. She doesn't share my passion for metaphysics. Yet she frequently shows people as androgynes and thinks it's past time for people to give up their fear of homosexuality. We're bisexual by nature so let's stop worrying about it, says she. Her friends are proof she means it; she couldn't care less if they're heterosexual, homosexual, bisexual, trisexual or omni. She thinks it splendid that people are merely people and have widely assorted sexual natures. She doesn't need metaphysics to feel this way.

The male and female forces seem well balanced in Karen's photography. When logic (male) is appropriate she has it in abundance and intuition (female) when she needs it instead. She can organize as well as any man I know and intuit with the best of women. She makes pictures strong or delicate. She composes with admirable logic and depth of feeling.

Some of her images are so powerful you'd swear a man made them, others as delicate as lace. She seems to turn power on and off at will, yet uses it with detachment. I can't imagine her hung up on it. Nor is she interested in controlling her subjects; she'd rather they be themselves while she empathizes with them with heart and camera. When her pictures capture their trouble and anxiety, she may worry about them for weeks.

I am writing a chapter on the two

sides of the self and fit Karen Tweedy-Holmes into it. I don't think of her that way, however, not as a nest of cubbyholes with a collection of male and female attributes. I see her as a whole creature, female because of her plumbing but complete as a person. Her photographs impress me as unities. Unified artistic and personal statements on the inner nature of Man.

She's a fine photographer and uses her medium for worthwhile purposes. She cares deeply about the world and will help preserve all the good in it with her pictures. She loves animals, Man included, and shows others why they are lovely.

If she meets enough famous people she will likely be the Julia Margaret Cameron of our age. Or with animals she might show where Ylla could have gone had she lived longer. Though she photographs only her friends, that means almost anyone. She's so open to people she's New York's instant friend, available to all who will let her into their lives. I don't mean she's unselectively gregarious; far from it. It's that she's a sucker for creatures in need.

I can't predict which way her career will turn. As a portraitist of women she's masterful in showing dimensions seldom seen, their strength for example. With men it is primarily lovable sweetness, for she sees them that way. Her pictures show it even in men she met for the first time on the day of the shooting session. She has such acceptant and non-hostile vibrations, a captain of industry would feel safe in coming on as a boy merely playing tycoon. Perhaps she'll make her mark here, showing that even the driving personalities in our land are still boys inside. She wouldn't search for them, as their fame doesn't interest her. Coming to her, they would be treated with warmth despite the aura of power surrounding them.

Though she disagrees with me in much of it, Karen helped me greatly in making sense in my essay at the end of the chapter.

photo by KAREN TWEEDY-HOLMES

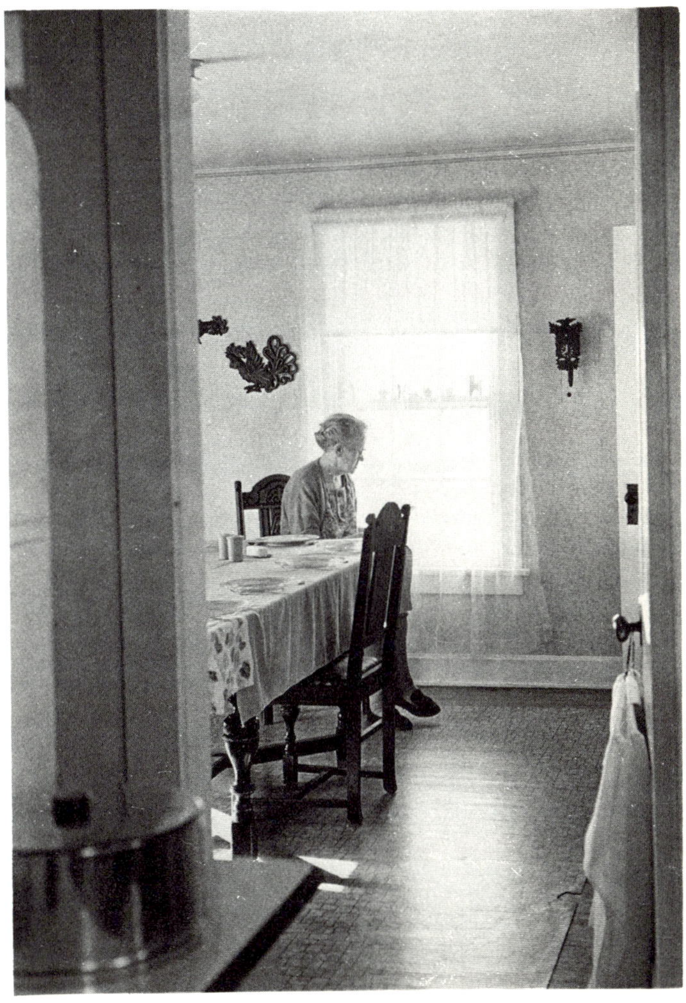

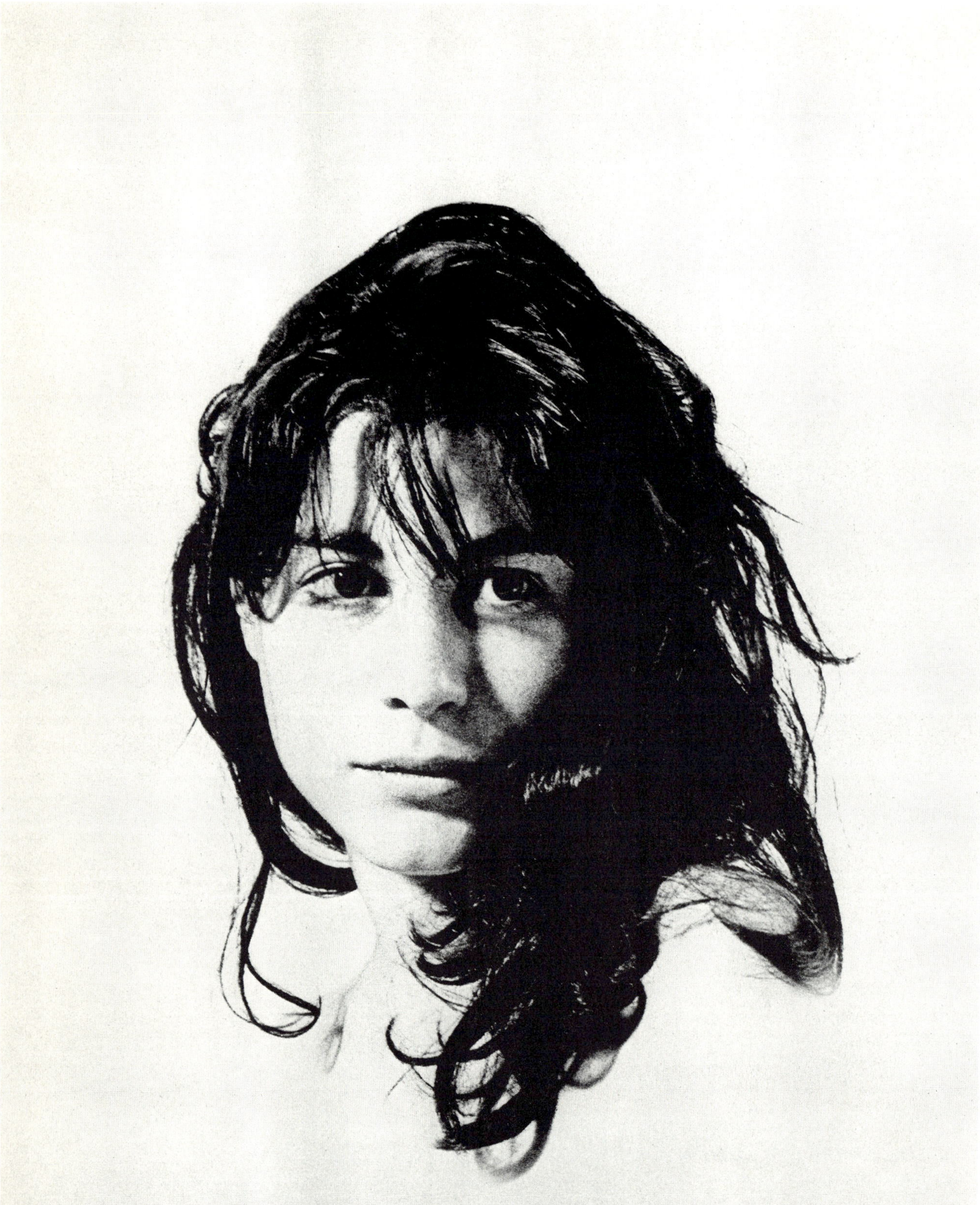

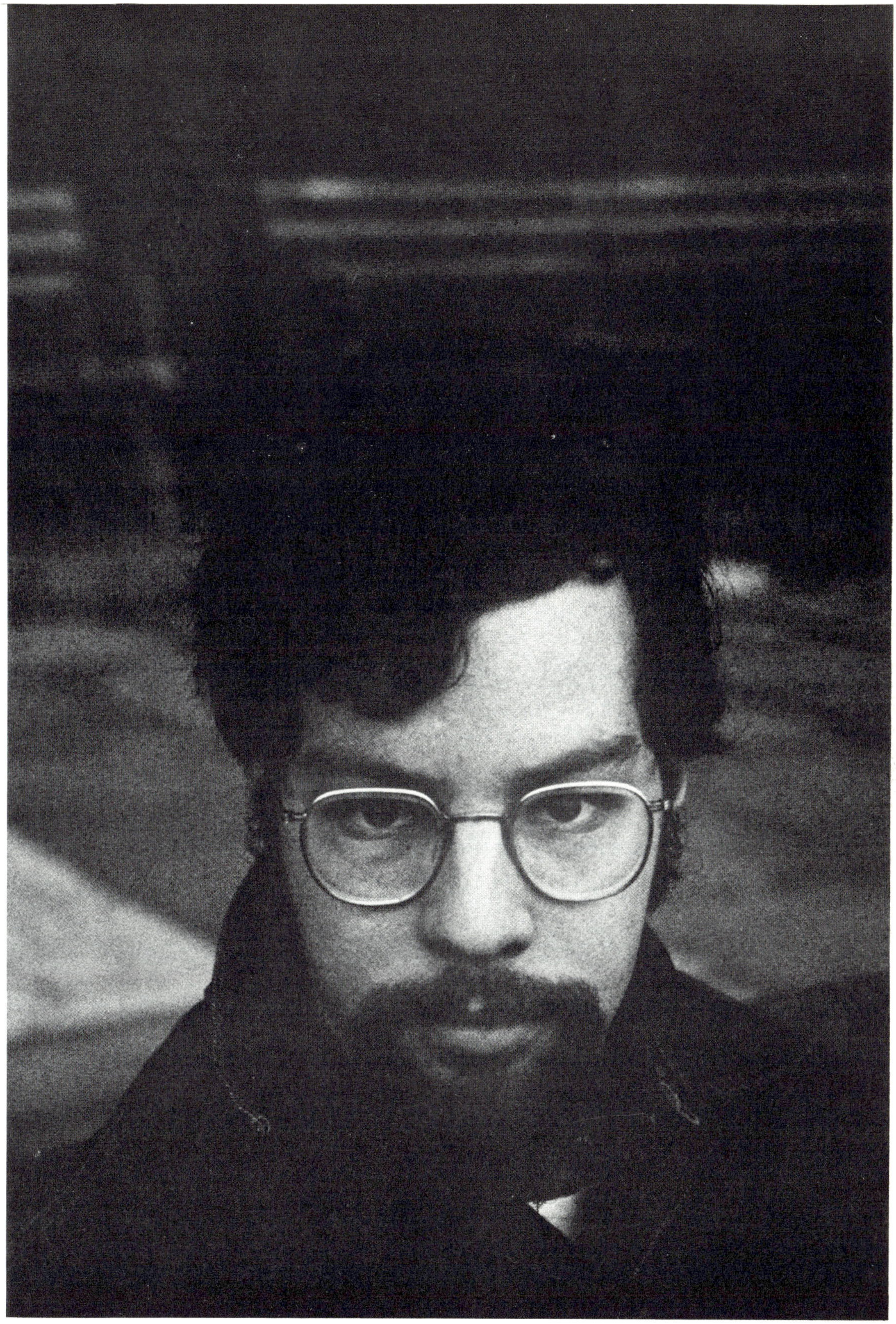

photos by KAREN TWEEDY-HOLMES

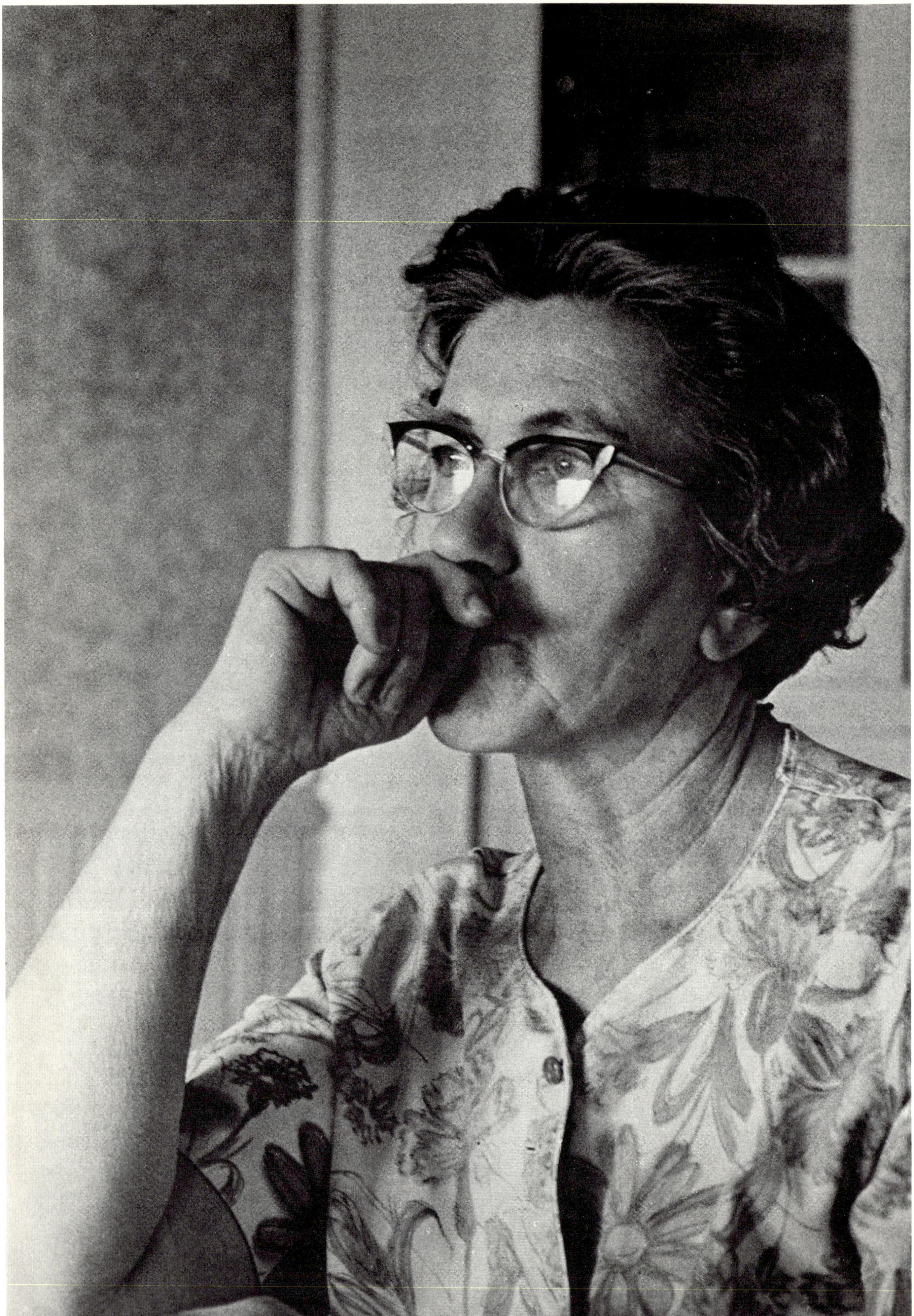

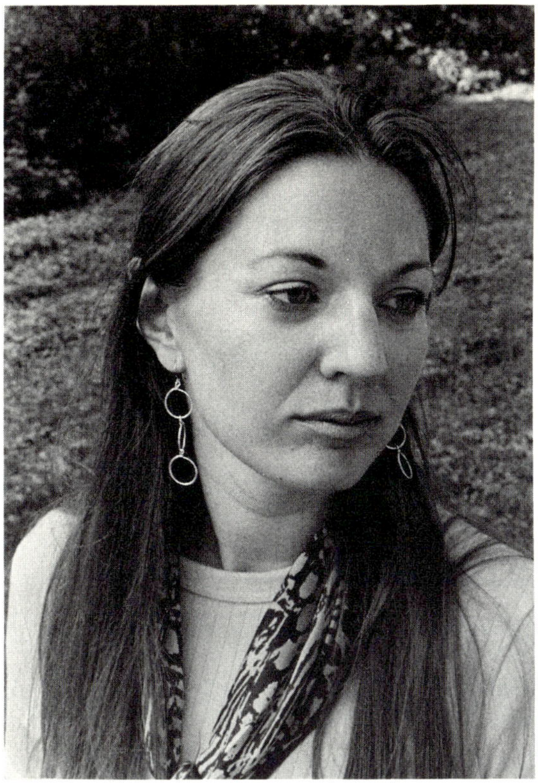

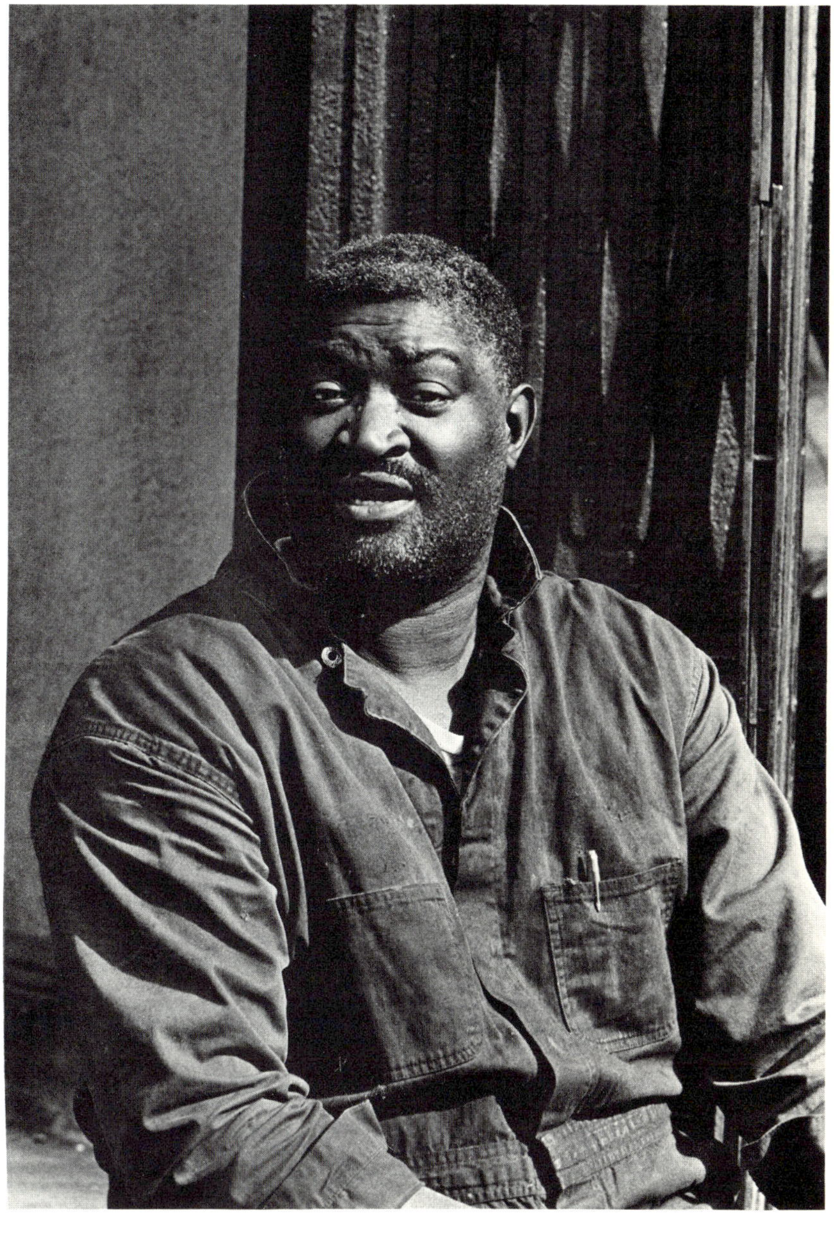

photos by KAREN TWEEDY-HOLMES

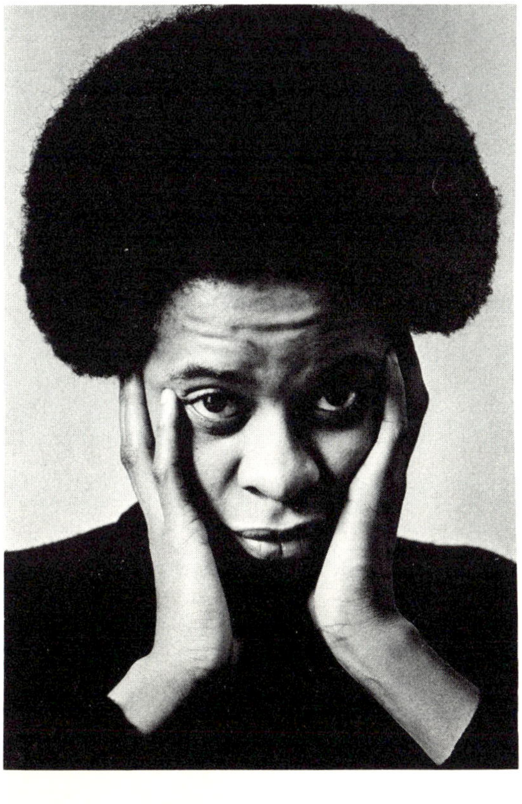

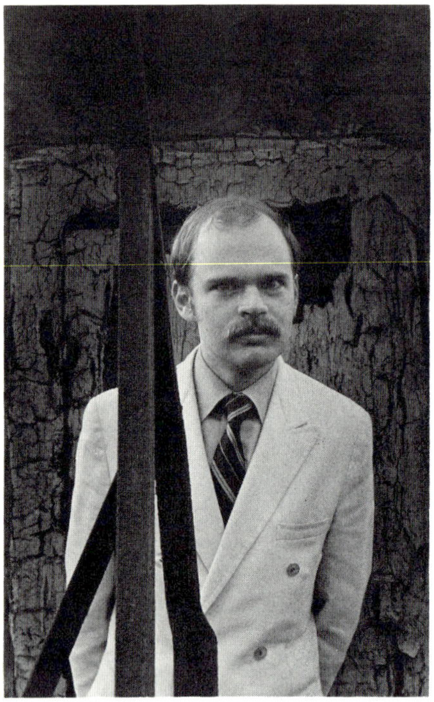

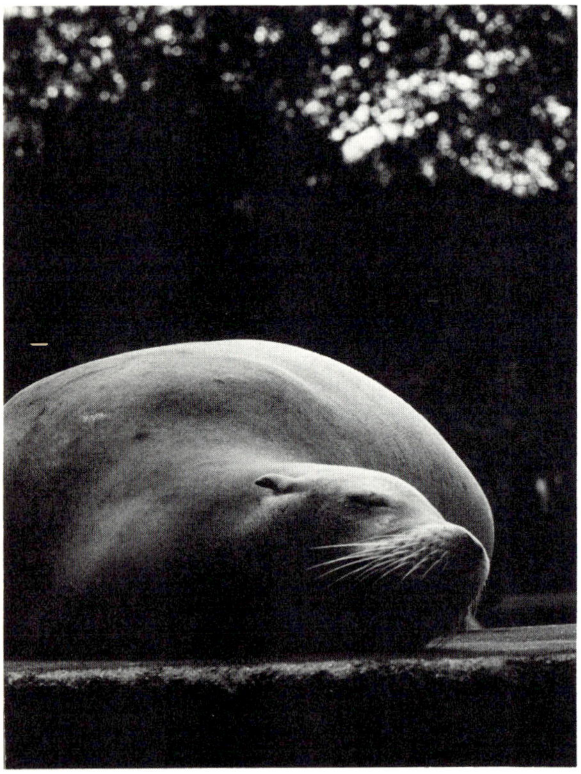

photos by KAREN TWEEDY-HOLMES

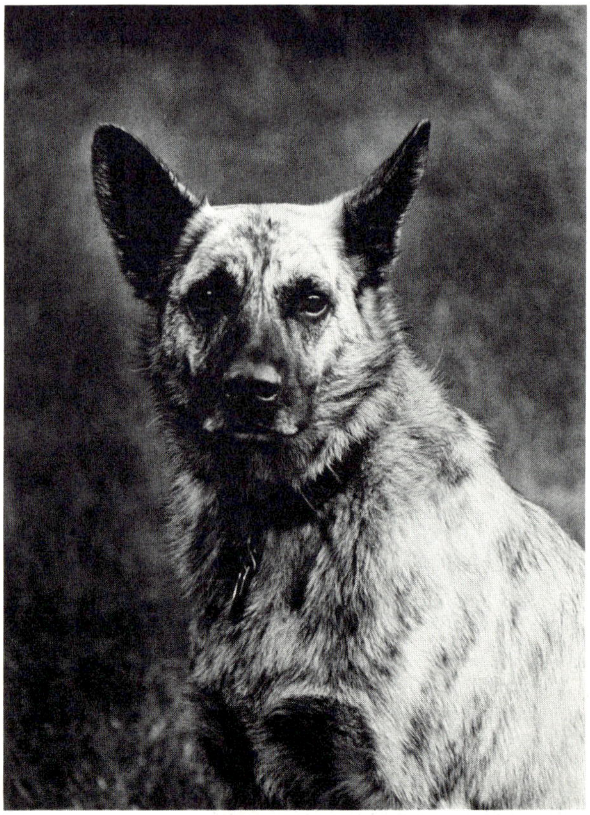

photo by RYSZARD HOROWITZ

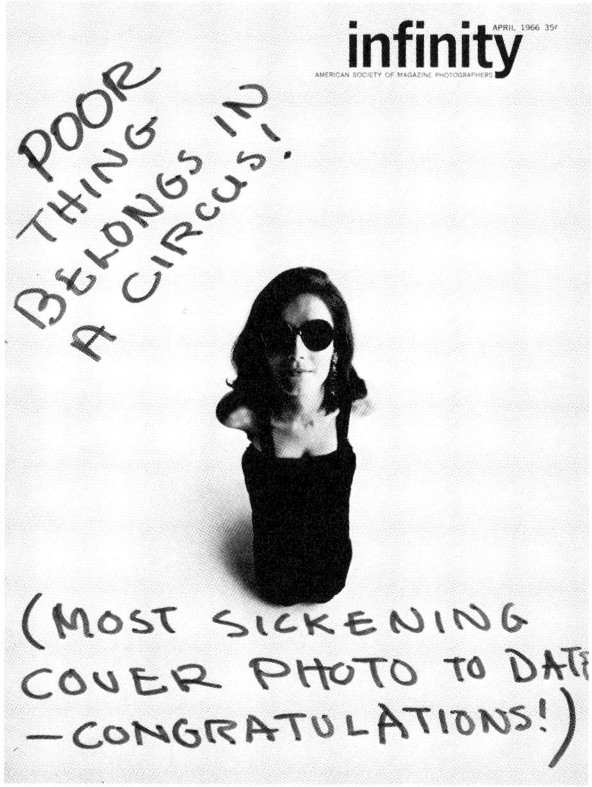

Reflections on Reactions to a 'Sick' Picture

The short essay with this title appeared several years ago in *Infinity* magazine. The editor, Charles Reynolds, had asked me to write it as a response to adverse reader reactions to an *Infinity* cover picture. Many readers were very upset and wrote Reynolds to tell him they thought the picture terribly sick.

Instead of trying to make these readers feel better I thought it would be more therapeutic if I tried to make them feel worse. Since they were already irate I tried to drive them further into a howling fury. My idea was to force them to examine their own anger.

I snipe at people for two reasons, one of them spiritual in intent, the other decidedly carnal. A part of me likes to try to help people. Another part likes giving them a hard time just for sport. However, the two purposes can sometimes work together, like a wolf lying down in peace with a lamb. My approach is somewhat similar to a surgeon's: He sublimates his desire to cut people to the more spiritual purpose of making them well. He cuts them, to be sure, but for good reasons.

My feeling is that people who become angry at the *Infinity* picture are lying to themselves about something. My notion in trying to make them even more angry is to lead them to become suspicious of the validity of their anger. Should they get started on this path they might learn about some things in themselves decidedly in need of improvement. I'm fairly sure I know exactly what these things are, for I myself have had trouble with the same ones for many years. This is one of the sources of my joy in launching attacks. When I'm shafting other people's devils I know I'm also giving my own a hard time.

Some readers will look at the picture and my comments about it and wonder what the fuss was all about. They'll find it impossible to believe anyone could be driven to a fury by them. Nonetheless, the world is full of people who can be easily enraged in this manner. The particular ones I was singling out for my karate-chop therapy are what I call 'over-masculine' men.

Men of this type (I include myself) are unconsciously terrified of the female side of themselves. I attempted to prod them vigorously toward a style of thinking

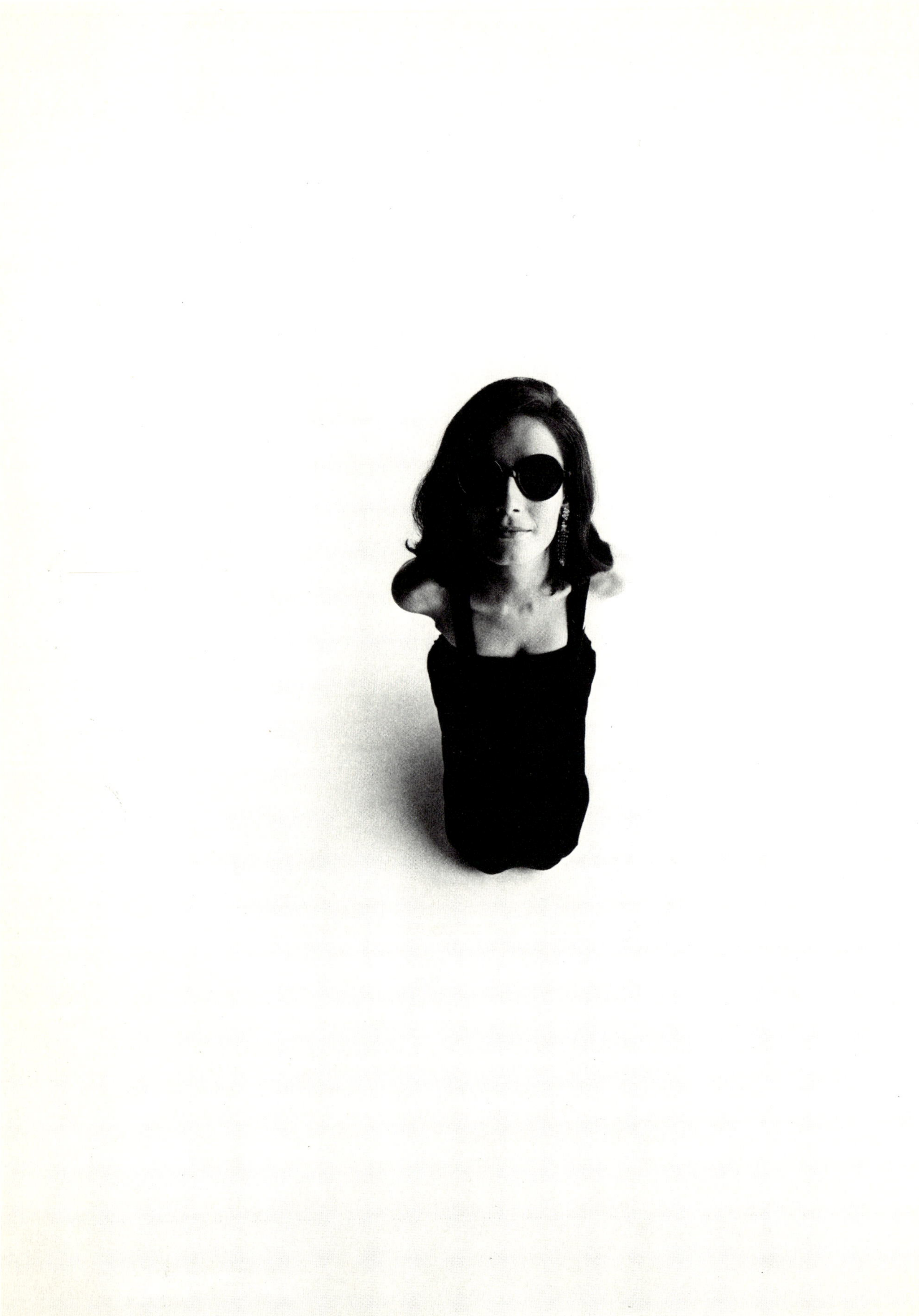

which might lead them to discover their terror and to see how irrational it is. Having discovered the irrational terror, they would then be in a fairly good position to begin to do something about it. For them, the ideal objective would eventually be to establish a harmonious equilibrium between masculine and feminine forces in themselves.

If you're sensitive to such things you'll see that the *Infinity* essay is very aggressive. Wouldn't gentle reasoning have been better? Perhaps so, but I have little talent for it. Furthermore, the types of devils I was trying to spear are well-protected by heavy walls they've erected around themselves. They can only be pierced by the most aggressive attacks.

In terms of still another kind of reader, aggressive writing has its good points. I'm thinking here of people who think they've already solved the problems being discussed. Sly, aggressive reasoning makes them take another look at their so-called solutions. In terms of good masculine-feminine balance within the Self, I have yet to meet a person who has fully achieved it. I've seen quite a few who had made good progress but had stopped far short of the goal they should have been aiming for. I hope by my onslaughts to arouse such people to further efforts.

Perhaps I'm not wise to reveal myself as an aggressive, even hostile, writer. I uncover myself at this time in order to make the point that a teacher or writer doesn't always tell his students what he has in mind for them and his methods for helping them achieve it. People get bored with talk of educational methodology and discussions of higher goals. So teachers soon learn not to talk too much about such things.

Let us return to the over-masculine man whom I chose to assault in the *Infinity* essay. Remember that his over-masculinity stems from fear of his female Self. This unconscious fear leads directly to his fear of women, for they are powerful symbols for this aspect of himself. His fear of women leads to his unconsciously being angry at them practically all of the time, for anger follows fear as sure as night follows day.

Thus, over-masculine men are the world's natural woman-haters. Oddly, the majority of them are certain they are woman-*lovers*. They are so certain that there's little chance of making them see that the truth is otherwise. They may even act all the time as if they were genuine woman-lovers. They tend to treat women courteously in the extreme, literally burying them in flowers, buying them large engagement rings, carrying perfumed tokens of them next to their hearts. Nonetheless, they are natural woman-haters and will continue to be until they overcome their fear of their feminine selves. For all that they are treated well by them, women see through woman-haters, intuitively if not consciously. These are the men whom women cut to ribbons, for there is nothing more insulting to a woman than to be assiduously pursued by a woman-hater.

Woman-haters will react predictably to pictures like the one which provoked such a controversy as an *Infinity* cover. They will be deeply offended, even outraged. They will accuse the photographer of being sick, a mentally diseased polluter of all that is good in women.

The truth is that it is not woman who is being undermined. It is the woman-hater's stereotyped image of her. His mental stereotype is his main defense against her. As such, it is also his defense against awareness of his fear of his female Self. It also helps him to remain unaware of his constant unconscious anger both at women and a large part of himself. Naturally, if anything tends to erode his all-important, self-defensive stereotype he will fly against it in a fury. Consciously, he thinks he's defending women against attack by men who actually wish them ill. Actually, these so-called attackers (e.g. Mr. Horowitz, author of the *Infinity* picture) usually like women a good deal more than the irate woman-hater. The woman-hater himself, acting in his self-deceptive disguise of courtesy and fond good will, is the real destroyer of women.

Another predictable response of the

to by RYSZARD HOROWITZ

over-masculine woman-hater is that he will call a picture like *Infinity*'s sick. He thinks it really is and for his very life can't see anything but sickness and perversion in it. It would never occur to him to question his *own* preferences in pictures of women. And it is quite beyond his powers of imagination to see that the pictures he likes best are sometimes immensely more sick than the *Infinity* cover.

The natural woman-hater almost invariably goes for commonplace, rigidly standardized, peaches-and-cream pictures of pretty girls. There are only a few poses and camera angles which he'll accept. All others he sees as ugly, distorted or perverted. The girls themselves must be pretty in ways which fit current American movie-star standards for good looks. They must also conform to standards with their figures, smiles, hair styles, clothing and make-up. What he's looking for, you see, is a blueprint he doesn't really have to think about. If he thought too much about real women he might make uncomfortable discoveries about a dreaded part of himself.

To continue drawing the blueprint, the over-masculine man limits the number of things he thinks a picture of a woman should express: motherly love, wifely love, playful camaraderie, shyness, innocence and so on. In all these things, the picture must conform to arbitrary standards current in American photography. When it comes to sexy pictures of women his choice is even more odd; he generally goes for a female version of himself, a man-hater or castrator. In choosing her he runs little danger of premature discoveries concerning the essential nature of femininity, either in himself or in women.

The pictures which please the woman-hater are nearly always made by photographers who are also woman-haters, many of whom specialize in taking pictures of women. They invariably use their photography to thrust their female subjects into cubbyholes, thus depriving womanhood of its immense complexity and variety. Always, these cubbyholes are familiar and safe; one doesn't have to think about them too much. In seeing a picture of a woman who has been stuffed into one, the woman-hater thinks he's seen her for what she truly is. Unfortunately, he has a great many notions concerning what a woman should be and almost none relating to what she really is. He doesn't want to know, for if he did he'd run the risk of discovering too much about his female nature. Unconsciously, he sees this as a great danger to himself. In a sense it is, for seeing his feminine aspect would force him to surrender many of his illusions concerning himself. He would find this very painful.

I don't think I've dwelt too long on the woman-hater. All of my male readers have some of his blood in their veins. If they wish to bring their psyches into proper balance they must come to realize it is there. As for women readers, I think they can profit by understanding that men are actually afraid of them and that this fear accounts for some of the things women wonder about in men.

The Essay:

The cover picture of the April issue of Infinity *has caused considerable comment both pro and con. The cover reproduced on page 133 is an example of one of the passionate reactions to Ryszard Horowitz's photograph. Ralph Hattersley, teacher, critic and past editor of* Infinity, *discusses the photograph and offers his interpretation of some of the responses to it.*

The picture by Ryszard Horowitz on the cover of the April 1966 *Infinity* has stirred people up. Though a good many may not have been affected by it at all, some have been deeply angered by it and others highly delighted. I am very interested in the possible reasons for either delight or anger because they have a considerable bearing on what photography means to people, which is something about which we know very little.

I've heard some photographers call it a very sick picture. Though I don't agree with them I think I can see some of their reasons for saying it. It doesn't take much imagination to see that for some people it represents an expression of unmitigated hostility toward women, motivated entirely by the photographer's resentment and anger. Horowitz has used a wide-angle lens to turn his subject into a basket case, a grown up thalidomide baby. She is no longer a woman at all but a thing. Not only has he deprived her of her female form but he's deprived her of her personality as well by hiding her eyes, the outward symbols of selfhood. He has further depersonalized her by removing her from environments associated usually with people, putting her instead in the midst of a no-seam paper nowhere. Her small size in relation to that no-seam nowhere diminishes her even more. For a man to change a woman in such manner and in such degree can also indicate his desire to have power over her.

Now, it is not at all unusual for men to have hostile feelings toward women. In fact, psychologists tell us that all men have, or have had, these feelings in some degree, though they are frequently unaware of having them. Though having such feelings is undoubtedly a kind of sickness, it is common to all men, not just to those few who happen to give artistic expression to it. This is why I don't approve of people calling Horowitz and those like him sick photographers. People in glass houses shouldn't throw stones.

Though feeling hostility toward women is a general sickness in men, giving expression to it through an art form is not a sickness at all but a means of reaching health. When a photographer makes a picture such as this one of Horowitz's he is often driven and guided by unconscious motives he either understands but vaguely or not at all. However, once the motives have been embodied visibly in an art form he stands a chance of consciously discovering what his unconscious mind led him to say. Then he can begin to deal with the motives rationally, eventually ridding himself of them altogether. In other words, the underlying reason for expressing something such as hostility is to destroy it in oneself. If it is not expressed and gotten rid of it may very well destroy the person who unconsciously harbors it. One of the main humane functions of an art form is to allow the artist to express symbolically (and evenutally come to understand) that which he cannot allow himself to express through direct action, for example beating up women.

The question now arises as to whether photographers should be encouraged to, as it were, wash their souls in public. My answer to this is that it is one of the few things a photographer can do which are really worth doing, letting himself be seen for what he really, deeply is. The photographer who constantly hides himself, as most do, is a very dangerous liar. In the picture by Horowitz we can sense the true outlines of a real human being, not the dangerous fictionalized versions of men with whom we are usually confronted. In sensing a real human being embodied in the picture we find another person with whom we can safely compare ourselves. This is by no means a comfortable process but a very important one, nonetheless.

I have no doubt that some men will sense the Horowitz picture as a personal assault against themselves. I have no way of knowing if he intended it this way, but if he did I'm all for him. I think it's a very good, healthful thing. My reason for saying this is that by deeply offending certain men, Horowitz may be leading them toward eventually seeing something very sick which is buried in their unconscious minds. It is hostility toward women, the very thing of which they accuse Horowitz. Horowitz deeply angers them because he brings them closer than they wish to come toward seeing a buried sickness in themselves. I'll put this very bluntly: Those photographers who call Horowitz a sicknik have things backwards. They themselves are the sickniks, which alone can account for their great anger at Horowitz. A normal person doesn't become incensed at a person he believes to be ill. Horowitz is doing a very good job in dealing with the anger in himself and has the courage to share his inner feelings with others, while those who call him sick are stewing in their own juices and through their own ignorance are damning themselves to perdition, particularly in their relationships with women. A man who doesn't recognize and understand his hostility toward women has very little chance of ever entering into a successful love relationship with one. If this isn't perdition, what is?

I'm not trying to say that Horowitz doesn't have his hang-ups. He's got his normal share, no doubt. But I do wish to make it very damned plain that those who are screaming aloud at him and others of his sort should root around in their own cellars a bit before continuing with the noise. I also wish to make it very clear that in dissecting Horowitz in public this way I am paying him a very high compliment. I don't in the least suppose he'll like what I'm saying, but I do think he has the guts to stand up to this treatment and the intelligence to realize that through him I'm doing my honest best to make a contribution to the understanding of photography.

I am, incidentally, under no illusion that this critique of mine will be popular. I've been called a maniac often enough to realize that those who do their very best to bring an understanding to photography deeply anger all those who have a vested interest in seeing that it is not understood. If photography should be understood a lot of photographers who use it as a means of hiding from themselves would find themselves very uncomfortable.

To return to the Horowitz picture—passing it off as nothing more than an expression of hostility toward women would be a grave injustice to Horowitz, the picture itself and the reader. It is many more things than that. For example, it is a way of saying that there are more ways of looking at women than the ones we are accustomed to and therefore accept. It is also a way of saying that it is a good thing for men to see women in as many ways as possible, rather than limiting themselves to the stereotyped ways of seeing them that wreak so much havoc in the relationships between the sexes. Women can't bear being seen through rose-colored glasses. They want to be seen as what they are in all their possible dimensions. In this they are very much like men.

The Horowitz picture is also a way of seeing woman as related to other things in the world, also a very good thing. To deprive a woman of relatedness is to consign her to mediocrity and meaninglessness. If a man does this to a woman who is close to him, she'll spend her life making him regret it. In the picture I see a woman as related to an amoeba, an abstract sculpture shape, a cork for a champagne bottle, a wind-worn rock, a seal, and a baby wrapped in a dark blanket. I can see that a woman is a lot more than I had thought and that, perhaps, I can never know her well enough to say to her positively, "I know precisely who and what you are." No woman can stand this; and any man who says it will be made to pay.

Horowitz helps us find the strength to look at death and deformity, which we all must do if we are to ever become masters of ourselves. This is a fear that must be overcome. Since deformity in Horowitz's model is not real, but a product of lens distortion, angle of view and posing—and we very well know it—we can bear to look at it. Looking at simulated deformities gradually helps us find the strength to look at real ones and eventually to understand the basis for our fears.

One of my students told me that the picture evoked his pity and that it was a wonderful feeling. I couldn't understand his attempts to explain the reasons for it but accepted the fact that it had really happened to him and that it was a good thing. I also felt it showed a possibility of the picture which might be easily overlooked by someone unduly hung up on the idea of hostility toward women.

No professional photographer could miss the fact that the picture was made with an extreme wide-angle lens. However, some may have been hiding from themselves the real basis for our interest in the effects of these lenses. Basically, our fascination is with deformity, of people or the world in general. Though there are very probably other factors, this one seems to be central and the picture makes this very plain. Undoubtedly, many photographers would rather not know what they are really doing. However, it is my opinion that it is better for their emotional health if they do, even though it be painful for them to learn the truth.

Another thing that the picture points up is the photographer's preoccupation with power over and control of reality.

Here it is hard to miss that something has been radically changed from what it is (as we ordinarily think of it) into something else. Many photographers would prefer not to know of this preoccupation of theirs, swearing loudly to the world that the camera merely records reality, not shaping it into what the photographer wants it to be. This is a most unhealthy blindness to the photographer's motives, both for the photographer himself and the public he reaches. Until the photographer accepts his manipulation of reality for what it really is he will never arrive at full responsibility for his behavior as a photographer.

Those people who feel aggressed against by Horowitz's picture may be in part reacting to the fact that in a way Horowitz has told them that they don't really know how to see. Here, after all, is a very normal-looking woman; but the camera has forcefully shown a way of looking at her most people have never even thought of. The fact is, a lot of people have seen one this way without being in the least aware of it. One doesn't need a wide-angle lens to see this effect, for this is precisely how a woman really looks in a certain pose, at a particular angle of view and at a particular distance. Though in terms of the total possibilities of human vision people, even photographers, don't see well at all, they don't like to have it brought to their consciousness. In fact, few things will make them more angry.

The picture is also an attack on our narrowness of view of what women actually look like. Though it is much to their detriment, men insist on seeing very little of what is there when they look at or think of women. And photographers who persist in popping up with new ways of seeing them are cordially hated. Actually, they should be greatly honored and thanked, for they do a great service to us all.

Though what Horowitz has done with his subject is not at all uncommon in the other arts, the fact that he used photography seems to have a special significance. I think this may be because he has unequivocally shown that there is a relationship between what is in the inner mind of men and exterior reality. I can't honestly say I know what this means; but I sense that it is of some importance.

I suspect that some people are somewhat upset because Horowitz has 'used' a woman, perhaps without her knowledge of what he was really up to. That is, he has used a woman to create something, a creature of his own mind, which is not quite a woman but something else. Though this has been going on in the arts for thousands of years it seems to be particularly disturbing when it happens in photography. The trouble may be that the photograph shows us that we know a good deal less about what is real than we think we do, which of course is very upsetting. Though we may accept such a notion as a philosophical point, it is quite another thing to be badly confronted with the inescapable truth of it. This 'something else' that Horowitz has come up with is actually not something else at all but another true facet of what women actually are; and our belief in the reality of photographs won't let us escape from this fact. In truth, he has only used a woman to show us what a woman is (from one point of view), not to create something that is not woman at all.

In my opinion the picture is one of the most significant ones *Infinity* has ever published, mainly because it could lead the viewer closer to understanding things like those I've discussed here. However, in a year or two the manipulations of the wide-angle lens will have become so commonplace that we'll all be as blind as bats to them. In photography, as elsewhere, familiarity leads to blindness. In a few years those who've been upset by the picture will be wondering what in the world they were so upset about. For their own good they should think about it now, while their anger is hot. If I, too, have made them angry they should give this another thought. It is possible that Ralph Hattersley has managed to grasp a small fragment of the truth.

I mentioned in the beginning that certain people have been delighted by the picture and that their delight should be accounted for. Since I've rambled on at great length already I won't attempt this now beyond saying that some of the delight may have come from sensing some of the things I've seen.

The Female Aspect of Vision

This previously unpublished essay is an attempt to penetrate the female nature to a greater depth than most men have reached. Since I am a man we can be sure it has built-in bias and embodies my unconscious prejudices concerning masculinity and femininity. Like everyone else, authors find it dreadfully difficult to discover these hidden things in themselves.

I think that most of my male readers haven't discovered their prejudices either. They are incorporated in what we might call the male world view, or masculine way of looking at things. It is mainly unconscious and mostly constructed of unstated and untested assumptions. Being unconscious, it is impervious to easy discovery and analysis. It is something men accept without thinking and use to regulate their lives.

Women readers may see the prejudices standing out in bold relief. Since the female world view is substantially different than the male, it should be easier for women to detect men's biases. Then what can women get from an essay written with a male warp? Well, they can learn more about men and their difficulties in understanding women. And there may be enough truth in it to make it worthwhile.

One of the great undiscovered facts of the age is that there is a female aspect of vision which can be differentiated from the male aspect. Also undiscovered is the fact that it is a normal part of vision for both men and women. This female vision is not new; it has always existed. It is very, very different from the male vision and always has been. It is a thing all men will wish to have once they know of its existence and come to understand some of the things it can do to improve their lives. However, not one man in a thousand is remotely aware of its existence. This is not so strange, for many extremely important facts about people remain to be discovered. If it took us millennia to discover our dependency on oxygen in the air, why should we suppose that important truths are easily discovered and that we've found them all?

Women, too, are often unaware of having a specifically female vision, though a few of them have figured it out for themselves. Having lived with it all their lives it has never occurred to the majority to examine its nature or to compare it with the male aspect of vision. For women, it's a fact of existence, just as water must be a fact for a fish. How many fish spend their days pondering the nature of water?

There is another explanation. Like men, women tend to think the opposite sex is more like theirs than it actually is. Men have been trying to sell them on this notion for aeons with a certain degree of success. Though women don't go nearly as far in this absurd direction, many of them are inclined to think men see in approximately the same way they do.

Men are also unaware of having a type of vision which is specifically an attribute of their sex. With the exception of certain male homosexuals, I've seldom found a man aware of the two types of vision. Hardheaded, over-masculine men usually haven't a clue. Women as a whole seem much closer to the truth.

I think that the perception of women is considerably more sophisticated than that of men, especially in matters that really count in life. I also think that the next major revolution in photography will come when men learn to develop female vision in addition to their own. We will then learn what great photography really is. And women photographers will finally come into their own for the first time. In my opinion this revolution is already well under way.

Men Won't Listen to Women

One of the basic problems is that few men ever listen to women carefully. If they had, they would have long ago learned of the existence of the female vision. Furthermore, they would have learned approximately what it is and have had some basis for starting its development in themselves. Like men, women talk about what they've seen. The content of their conversation draws heavily on that kind of vision which is specifically and uniquely theirs. When we analyze their talk, we find that it clearly defines the nature of the vision on which it is based. It couldn't be otherwise. Nonetheless, the vast majority of men are sublimely unaware of what and how women see. They haven't an inkling that their own seeing will be crippled and incomplete, until it incorporates the female within itself. Women are in roughly the same predicament with respect to developing the male vision, but they don't fear its existence as much. Therefore, I would say they have a lesser problem in this respect.

To say merely that men could learn about the vital female view by listening to women is not enough. The trouble is that listening is a very difficult and sophisticated art. Listening carefully to members of the opposite sex is doubly difficult, for men and women are creatures totally alien to one another. Neither sex sees any good reason for trying to listen to the other, unless flirtation, sex play or some other carnal objective is the motive. The problem is compounded beyond all reason when we see that many people find the idea abhorrent that they should listen to their sexual opposites to discover characteristics worth developing in themselves.

The Larger Problem

Vision is only a small part of the problem, however. What each of us really needs is to develop in him or herself the psychological characteristics of the opposite sex as well as that of his or her own. My study of metaphysics and my experience in life have led me to this point of view. Both have also led me to the belief that human beings have souls. Certain religious teachers, whose testimony I accept as truthful, say that the human soul is androgynous, that is, both male and female and, in a sense, neither. They say, further, that as man evolves, his earthly personality will have to take on the androgynous nature of his soul, for the split is artificial and must eventually be healed. This notion is imparted through the Chinese notion of yin and yang and in many other teachings. In the West, the best approach to the subject in my estimation is in the Edgar Cayce readings. I accept them as valid testimony concerning the spiritual nature of man and think they support my assertions concerning the soul. I'm not suggesting that readers accept testimony because I believe it; this would be spiritually injurious. They deserve to know who has influenced me and, if they wish, can evaluate my teachers for themselves. Each man should learn from his own experiences, not from mere hearsay.

On this metaphysical basis I will clarify what I mean by male and female. I define a male characteristic as one which a good many more men have than women today. Similarly, a female characteristic relates more, at the present time, to women than to men. Thus, female vision relates to how women see now, male vision to men's current way of seeing things. As the race develops the distinction between the two types will disappear. We will then have only one kind in which the opposites are united. Herein I hope to promote the joining process which is part of the larger problem of bringing the entire Self into harmony.

Though many people think that unity of vision already exists, I maintain that for thousands of years there has been a very deep split. It is difficult to see, but the polarity is definitely there. Thinking it does not exist won't make it go away. On the contrary, we can make it disappear only by discovering it, understanding its nature and taking positive steps to heal it.

I write here specifically about female vision because it is the half of normal human vision that we haven't as yet discovered. Information concerning the male half is splattered all over the universe and we don't have to look hard to find it.

Comparison Between the Male and Female Aspects of Vision

The following chart contrasts the two kinds of vision, showing them as opposites. The split is abnormal and may disappear when (and if) the human species evolves. It is possible that in rare instances it has already healed.

Female Vision	Male Vision
Passive: quiescent, waiting. It consciously searches for nothing yet sees everything.	*Active:* restless, moving. It consciously looks for particular things and excludes all else.
Non-logical: not filtered through a structure of concepts. Not logically motivated. Not bothered by what males see as the chaos in the universe.	*Logical:* filtered through, and directed by, logical systems. Tries to shut out the chaos of the universe. Motivated by the desire to see the sense of things.
Non-aggressive: content to see things as they are and leave them that way. Content not to have a strong effect on them. Interested in things for themselves.	*Aggressive:* tends to see things as it would like them to be. Motivated by the desire to change or powerfully influence them. More interested in what things could be than what they are.
Receptive: open to incorporate the visual world within itself.	*Projective:* closed; projects its inner male world onto the visual world outside.
Compassionate: empathizes with the world it has incorporated within itself.	*Coldly rational:* assesses the world in terms of how it has affected it or will in the future.
Synthetical: sees in unities, combines things into gestalts. Understands in gestalts. Tends to see all opposites as one. Doesn't like to dismantle.	*Analytical:* sees things as sums of their parts, not unities. Dismantles things in order to understand them through the inferred relation of their parts.
Emotional: filtered through, directed, and limited by emotion. Its values, which tell one what is worth looking at, are built on emotional bases. Non-intellectual.	*Intellectual:* filtered through, directed and limited by intellect. Its values are built on intellectual bases. Non-emotional. Offended by emotion.
Subtle: interested in the infinitudes of life's subtleties, welcoming them all, allowing itself to be affected by all.	*Gross:* sees life in terms of its gross, rather than fine, differences. Irritated by, or indifferent to, subtleties, not affected by them.
Now-centered: interested mainly in what is happening right now.	*Future-centered:* Interested mainly in what will happen in the future.
Here-centered: concerned mainly with what surrounds it: the family, home, friends, place of work.	*Elsewhere centered:* concerned mainly with what is elsewhere. Uninterested in, and mainly blind to, that which surrounds it.
Non-competitive: except with other women, non-competitive. Doesn't have to excel other people in everything. Doesn't have to see better than others.	*Competitive:* always trying to penetrate more deeply, widely and creatively than others. Never content to lose.

As I see it, these are the main points of comparison between the two sorts of vision. If you find your own sometimes described best on one side of the list, sometimes on the other, don't be dismayed. The duality of vision is latent in us all, awaiting development. Most of us have developed it irregularly. If your kind of seeing is listed altogether under the opposite sex, that too is no cause for alarm.

The type of seeing specific to your sex may have temporarily been developed far enough, so that your psyche is concentrating on its opposite to create harmony within itself. We must remember, furthermore, that we're not discussing things which are intrinsically either male or female. The properly balanced psyche is both. So if a man finds a female trait developing in himself he should shout, "Hurrah! It's about time." And vice versa.

If you will think awhile about the two sides of the list, you will understand better why men and women have such a hard time communicating with one another. Consider the fact that woman is a synthesizer, and man an analyzer. What happens when a man and woman observe the same event? The woman sees it in big chunks (gestalts). She makes no attempt to dissect and analyze it. Her unconscious automatically fits together the minor parts for her. Though she may miss seeing the logical relationships between parts of the happening, she doesn't care in the least. She has no faith that logic would help her understand what happened.

For his part, the man dissects the event, breaking it down into discrete pieces. Then he examines each piece to determine its relationship to all the others. He ends by trying to put all the pieces back together again and to see them as a whole. He seldom manages to re-unite them perfectly. Though he may learn a good deal concerning the interrelation of parts, he may arrive at few or no large gestalts. Still he has seen quite a bit.

What happens when a couple discuss an experience they've shared? The woman describes what she thinks went on. He replies, "Why do you say that?" By this he actually means, "How did you dissect it and what are the relationships between arbitrarily selected parts?"

She answers, "I have no reasons. I just know that's the way it was."

"But you can't be right," says he, "not without reasons."

"I can be right; I do have reasons for thinking that I am."

"Well, let me hear them," says he, "if you're so sure you've got some."

"I can't list them. I just know they're there. You have to accept this fact if you really want to know what I've seen."

This conversation highlights some of the difficulties in communication between the sexes. It shows the man playing a typically aggressive male role. The woman despairs of ever getting across to him what she feels, thinks, and sees, for his pushing is almost too much for her to cope with. Instead of examining his own thinking, he attacks hers. He doesn't comprehend that what she says results from a valid and effective way of thinking. As far as he's concerned, she doesn't really think at all. He just can't believe that a person can come to accurate conclusions without reasons of which she is consciously aware—his kind of dissective reasons. But the truth is she can; and well she knows it.

What happens when the woman listens to the man's analysis of what they've observed? She senses strongly that in breaking it up into pieces he has somehow missed much of what she saw as both obvious and significant. Furthermore, she knows (without knowing how and why she knows) that after taking the event apart, he didn't see the whole correctly.

The Feminization of Photography

Having discussed some of the preliminaries, it is time for me to give the reader another reason for this essay. I've said that for psychic reasons people need to develop both kinds of perception within themselves. They also need to do it for another, lesser motive: to keep up with what is going on in photography.

One of the most significant things happening is a feminization process. The medium is beginning to make room for the female type of vision to express itself and photographers are being profoundly affected. This means that in many photographers male and female opposites of vision are slowly being made into one. When (and if) the unification is completed it will be proper to describe it as normally evolved human vision.

An evidence of this change is that the over-masculine type of vision which has dominated photography from the beginning is slowly being relegated to the sidelines. Photographers who were considered great thirty years ago because they expressed this vision so well are now considered as primitive as survivors of the Stone Age. One way of assessing the current disinterest in their work is to look at old camera annuals. Though most of the pictures were once thought masterful, modern photographers find them empty and boring.

In the world of photographic education, especially on the college level, the female vision has made large inroads. As evidence of this we see the willingness of students and teachers to look seriously at pictures in terms of fine differences. Formerly, the emphasis was on the aggressive male spirit: The only important thing was to make great (i.e. unique) pictures. But it was not considered necessary to examine them closely after they were made. Older teachers who have promoted this change toward subtlety are men like Minor White, Harry Callahan, Henry Holmes Smith. Among the younger generation are Arthur Freed, Jerry Uelsmann, Phil Perkas and Carl Chiarenza.

In amateur photography female vision is making itself felt, too. No longer is the camera emphasized as a means of conquest. It is now being seen more and more as an instrument for recording subtleties. There was a time when a photographer could capture a hundred people on film and not have an inkling of how even one of them was feeling, though there was evidence of emotion written all over the pictures. That day seems to be passing. Photographers are finally learning to see nuances of emotional expression in photographs.

The Insufficiency of Male Vision

I've suggested that male vision alone is incomplete, crippled in fact. To clarify what I mean I'll tell you of my experience involving a certain picture and two editors of a photography magazine who are also good photographers. Since I've had similar experiences hundreds of times, I call it typical.

I showed these editors a close-up photograph of a middle-aged woman and her twenty-year-old daughter. Both faces showed great, though stifled, anger. Anger was heavily carved in the lines of the mother's face. The daughter's was a minor essay on how to irritate a parent beyond endurance by hostile withdrawal into oneself. So great was the hostility in both faces that I assumed everyone would see it immediately. Imagine my surprise when my two friends saw no anger at all in the picture.

One of them even said, "You tell me they are mother and daughter. I see this picture expressing a warm and loving relationship between them." The other agreed and said I was entirely wrong in seeing anger in the women. At first I was upset by what I considered gross and faulty vision, but then I thought they might be right. So I decided to run an objective test of the picture by showing it to twenty people and asking for their comments.

Almost invariably the women said, "My God! They're so angry at each other!" With two exceptions, the men saw no anger at all. What was really happening between the two women? Within two weeks the daughter left home forever. The mother went to the hospital with a complete nervous breakdown. They were both torn apart by anger.

Female perception takes in certain things that male perception ignores or overlooks. The reader may object that he knows men who would have seen the anger and women who wouldn't have. This is quite true. Dividing vision into male and female types is arbitrary; both should be found in a normal person of either sex. However, at our present level of psychological evolution, the male way of seeing still predominates in men, the female in women. That the predominance is reversed in a few people doesn't change the fact.

We still have to try to understand why most men saw no anger in the picture, while women usually did. The men didn't see anger because they didn't want to. There are numerous reasons for this. For one, men so deeply distrust emotion that they tend to exclude it from their perceptual field. Only when it is blatant in a picture, or referred to in a caption, are they likely to see it. Women spot signs of emotion easily. What they would call blatant emotion is for men subtle, or even non-existent. Women admit emotion as part of the very fabric of life, men as something they'd rather not think about or see, so they don't see it much of the time. For a woman, not to see the emotion in a face is not to see the face at all.

Remember also that the anger in the picture was in women's faces. This above all a man doesn't want to see, for when women are angry, logic is useless against them. Since men depend on logic to keep women safely in their places, they must run like hell when it becomes irrelevant.

To a man, female anger (or any other strong emotion) is highly irrational. A woman doesn't feel it necessary to explain her anger in logical terms. She may have good reasons for it, but, to her, logistical thinking (a male phenomenon) has nothing to do with them. Pushed hard enough by a man, she'll fish desperately for reasons he'll accept as logical. Issuing from a mind unaccustomed to juggling with logic, they sound to him like sheer madness. For the male the equation is: A woman angry is a woman insane. There are few things he fears more than a raging (or even silently fuming) female. One way of running from anger, even in a picture, is not to see it at all.

Women saw anger in the picture because their vision is open to emotions, even unpleasant ones. Since the culture permits them to express their emotions fully, they're not so uptight about them as men are. Men are deprived of this and, as a consequence, are often emotionally strung out. The editors who saw the mother and daughter as a loving pair were culturally forced to. Their thinking was strongly affected by certain intellectual assumptions, most of them undoubtedly unconscious. They must have thought somewhat as follows:

1. Anger in general is bad. Female anger is worse. Therefore, I won't permit it to exist in this photograph.

2. The subjects of the picture are mother and daughter. The proper feeling between mother and daughter is love. Therefore their relationship is loving.

3. A male photographer wouldn't pose a mother and daughter together unless he meant to say something nice about their relationship. He has posed these two together. Therefore he means to say their relationship is good. Because he is a very good photographer (a marvelous craftsman) he must have communicated their lovingness clearly. I'm obliged to insist it's there, even if I don't see it.

4. I'm afraid of my own anger and what it might make me do. If I even admit that anger exists I may open the way for getting angry now and then. Therefore, anger doesn't exist—in this picture or anywhere else.

I've called this kind of seeing intellectual and in the chart shown that women don't see this way. In this context, intellectual doesn't mean intelligent, for there's sometimes a wide difference. One who sees intellectually strains perception through a conceptual apparatus and tries to exclude from awareness how he is affected emotionally by what he sees. One who sees intelligently, on the other hand, perceives with *both* mind and emotion.

The Insufficiency of Female Vision

We will stick with the mother and daughter anger picture for a while yet and use it to talk about the insufficiency of female vision when unaccompanied by its opposite. Talking about the picture is also useful for the purpose of telling us what kind of data we should analyze in determining the differences and similarities between the two types of vision.

The women who saw the picture spotted the anger immediately because their vision is emotion-oriented. This doesn't mean, however, that they saw more intelligently than the men who looked at it and missed the anger altogether. We can say that the women saw the anger emotionally—on account of, by means of their emotional systems. Seeing anger in this way is merely to see it and feel it in oneself. This doesn't do much good, for the anger still exists and nothing has been done about it. Intelligent seeing, by comparison, is first perceiving emotionally that there is anger in people, then arriving intellectually at something useful to do about it.

In the case of seeing anger in a picture, the intellectual male view might concern itself with looking for visual clues to its cause and to what might be done about it. Or it could lead a man to review in his mind what he knows about anger, then to speculate on what he might do to overcome its hold on others and himself.

Though I'm greatly impressed by women's way of seeing things, I must insist that merely perceiving emotionally that something is happening doesn't solve the problem. Of course, the emotion-blind, over-masculine person who misses it altogether isn't getting anywhere either. To solve human problems one needs both natures.

The photographer who made our mother-daughter picture is one of the few people I know who consciously uses his photography as a means of Self-discovery. Here he was trying to develop the female side of his vision. A very masculine man, he's often thrown into a state of puzzled uncertainty when he sees emotions in others. He's not sure what emotions are, what causes them, and what they mean.

He knows the women in the mother-daughter picture well. (I can't publish it without endangering the friendship.) One day he developed a strong suspicion there was something very wrong in their relationship, though their overt behavior seemed to indicate they were getting along famously. So he took the photograph in order to amplify his perception. He was fairly sure he was seeing repressed or deliberately camouflaged anger. When many of the people who looked at the picture also saw it, his suspicion was confirmed.

Strangely, he could clearly see the anger in the picture, though he had been uncertain of his perception of it as it was expressed in real life. This greater awareness made possible by the photograph didn't come to him immediately; he had to think about it a lot before he was sure of what he saw. Later, when the daughter left home and the mother entered a hospital, his intuition was proved accurate.

It seems strange to a woman that a man would go to so much trouble to prove the obvious—to them. However, in the world of men it's not strange at all. To ten different men, the anger was invisible. They would have been equally blind had they stood by the photographer's shoulder and carefully observed the two women talking.

Men Attempt to Expand Their Vision

For at least fifteen years there has been ample evidence that men are trying to expand their vision to permit the perception of emotion. The outstanding indications of this are the thousands of pictures we've seen in the illustrated press which show faces expressing strong emotion. So commonplace are they that one supposes the central aim of some photographers is to lock emotion onto film. It seems that unless they see it clearly marked on a face, they are unwilling to press the shutter release. They are unconsciously trying to develop the female vision in themselves, to really see the emotion in other human beings. It doesn't matter that they haven't a name for it and aren't conscious they're striving for it. They haven't gone very far with it yet. Most of their emotion pictures shout their messages so loudly and crudely that they become caricatures. Even a bedbug could look at one and tell whether it was supposed to communicate joy or fear.

But there are a few photographers like Bruce Davidson who can express emotion subtly. Bruce doesn't have to wait until his subjects experience an emotional crisis in order to see it in their faces. All faces are reflecting emotion all the time, but it takes an enlightened male eye to see this.

I'm inclined to think that Davidson may be our best example of a photographer who has forced in himself the development of the female kind of vision. If so, he also represents best the degree to which contemporary photographers have been able to bring their psyches into balance. I suspect it hasn't been easy for him. A man must smash down tremendous inner resistance before he can liberate the female side of himself. He must deliberately experience the suffering caused by ripping to shreds his lopsided illusions. This suffering is a heavy price to pay for Self-evolution, but there is no other way to achieve balanced vision in oneself.

That some male photographers are intuitively trying to develop the female part of their vision, isn't proof they're going about it right. The truth that so few have gone far suggests that most lack the proper approach. So I will note a few details of method.

Learning to Listen

It is not enough for a man to know that women are his greatest potential source of information on something he needs to develop in himself. He has a very difficult problem in learning how to get from them the information, and in disciplining himself to pay close attention to what they're saying. All over the world women have become so accustomed to being treated as inferior beings by men that they've become extremely reticent about talking honestly in front of them. Rather than tell men what they see and how they see it, they try to talk about the things they think men are interested in. They've learned that this is the only way they can hold their attention. All women know that as soon as they start to talk 'woman talk' men rapidly lose interest. There are, indeed, many women who can't remember a single instance in their lives when a man paid close attention to them while they were discussing their own interests. The typical man is not in the least interested in what a woman says unless she is flirting or talking about him and his interests. The predictable consequence is that early in life women learn to clam up concerning what they see.

Say that a man manages to convince himself he would benefit by listening to women. Would this solve his problem? Far from it! He still has the tremendous task of learning how to do it. Considering how men feel about women's conversation, his basic task can be seen as one of learning to put up with endless boredom. At the same time he must hide all evidence of being bored, which is even harder. This is necessary, for conversation dries up as soon as boredom shows itself.

The Metaphysics of Listening

Learning to listen is such a difficult problem that I'm going to turn to metaphysics to explain why it is worthwhile. Metaphysics deals with the things man has to do in order to realize his highest potentials. It promises much and asks much in labor and suffering. It is also called higher psychology. It differs in many ways from ordinary psychology, for example in seeing suffering as a necessary tool for man's Self-evolution.

I've said that the chief problem in learning how to listen is boredom. This is obviously a form of suffering. One can gradually learn to listen skillfully by merely tolerating it. However, this learning may take several lifetimes. A man can learn faster if he deliberately invites the boredom and holds the correct attitudes toward the people who are the cause of it.

To ask people deliberately to invite suffering sounds like the height of madness. Nonetheless, the great metaphysical systems have insisted for centuries that it is a good thing to do. They also say it is an essential part of intentional Self-evolution. When I speak of an evolved human being I'm thinking of a person who has done much more than become an expert photographer. I've said that listening is the way for a man to develop his female vision. It is also a road to immensely more important goals. The reader should bear this in mind while debating my invitation to invite boredom on himself.

Boredom from listening is a disguised fear reaction. We are afraid but don't know it. One root of this fear is the semi-conscious feeling that we're opening our minds to attack by a strong alien force: another person's head. Not only do we feel attacked, but our sanity is questioned. Sometimes we're conscious of this, feeling that either we are crazy or the people we're listening to are. If the talkers make sense, according to culturally established modes of conversion, we are unconsciously overwhelmed by the thought that we are the insane ones. Then we pull down mental shutters to block the assault, which results in a stifled feeling. We call it boredom.

Considering its nature, it's not surprising that we see boredom as something we should avoid if possible. We see the idea of deliberately inviting it as ridiculous. Before we can see the sense of this idea we must learn what it leads to. Happily, it eventually destroys the hang-ups that make boredom possible. Strange as it seems, there are people on earth who can't be bored anymore.

Even higher rewards can be earned by inviting boredom. As a person's basic capacity to be bored is gradually worn away, his unconscious feeling that other people are alien also disappears. He can now feel deep in his being that all men are brothers. In a tangible sense, this one man has become all men. It is as if he has incorporated them into himself. Comfortable with people now, he no longer has to struggle fearfully to shut them out. Instead of sensing other human beings as forces he must defend himself against, he now knows them as willing sources of renewed energy.

There is more to the method than inviting boredom on oneself. It must be done for the right reasons. The person submitting himself to boredom caused by another person's conversation must also force himself to have the right attitudes with respect to that person. Done for the wrong reasons and with the wrong attitudes, self-invited boredom is worthless as a means of Self-evolution.

The right reasons for submitting oneself to boredom are ethical ones. Non-ethical reasons are always wrong ones. Trying to evolve oneself is highly ethical, for the evolved Self is entirely unselfish. Such a Self is devoted to serving others. Because of his nature, the ordinary, unevolved person must listen to others for primarily selfish reasons. Yet his long-term goal can be to make himself unselfish; even the effort will help him get there. He will also help the people he listens to, even if his reasons for doing it are sometimes bad. In their own ego-involvement they will overlook much of his; his efforts will give them hope and a feeling of being appreciated.

Wrong reasons for listening are ego reasons; one listens to inflate his self-esteem. He says to himself, "My, what a saint I am for paying attention to another human being." Or in talking to others he tells things he's learned through listening, indirectly bragging about his compassion and trustworthiness. Ego reasons for listening make a very long list, but the reader can write it for himself from his experience with his own egotism.

It is encouraging to know that some of the people who distress us the most have the most to offer us if we listen to them for the right reasons and with the right attitudes. Listening in the right way burns out impurities in our psyches and opens channels through which we can incorporate all mankind into ourselves. The more they distress us the more rapidly our psyches are purified. Moreover, the kind of suffering created is necessary for our Self-evolution. Without it we would have little reason for hope.

Those interested in metaphysics will find that there is an extensive literature on intentional suffering as a means of Self-evolution. What I've written is the gist of it and sufficient to get the reader started on improving himself as a listener.

Men Listening to Women

The main reason a man will listen to a woman is sexual. Listening becomes a form of flirtation. In terms of listening for Self-evolution, however, his sexual interests are likely to be a disadvantage. He has too great an inclination to use the sexual forces entirely for mental and physical self-gratification. Listening for such egotistical purposes is very unlike listening to evolve the Self.

A man who really wishes to learn to listen to women should practice listening to those who don't attract him much sexually. They might be women much older or younger than himself, friends from childhood, members of his own family, or long-time neighbors. Married men should try listening to their wives after they've been married long enough for their passions to cool a bit. Daughters from the ages of seven to seventy are also very fine.

One difficulty men have in listening to women is that they are deeply afraid of them and don't know it. This makes them turn listening into an attack used for diminishing women as threatening forces. It is helpful to look into the nature of this fear and its causes. It is not a fear of women as such. Instead, it is a fear of them for the things they unconsciously symbolize to men, one of which is the female half of the male Self. Men have unconsciously been terrified of this for thousands of years. During all this time their fear has been displaced, so that they've become fearful of women too.

A consequence of this fear is that men have been angry at women, for anger at something normally follows a fear of it. In fact, anger and fear may be the same thing. Anger has made it very difficult for men to learn anything about the female nature from women themselves. When women feel anger it makes them reluctant to talk about the things most apt to provoke it. One of the things most apt to arouse male hostility is anything women say about specifically female ways of seeing things. Fearing the female in themselves, men are angry at (or afraid of) such things.

Another consequence of men's fear is that they have mistreated women for millenia. This has had a karmic effect on men. Because we have made women suffer for so long, we are now paying the price for it in karmic suffering. Our fear itself can be a form of karmic suffering. And so can our anger, for that matter.

Most men think that the idea of men fearing women is preposterous. They don't realize that many of their fears are unconscious. Perhaps they could learn the truth by looking into the nature of their own boredom at listening to female conversation.

The man who seriously wishes to discover an important part of himself by listening to women should first of all welcome his boredom instead of trying to escape it. As his fear of women (and himself) disappears, so will the boredom. Secondly, he should not let his fear become sexualized if he can help it. This is a cop-out which prevents him from experiencing the kind of suffering which will eventually purge his psyche.

I have already mentioned some of the benefits which result from deliberately inviting boredom for the right reasons and from holding carefully to the right attitudes while experiencing it. I haven't before mentioned one direct result which can be very important to photographers. Intentional suffering frees certain channels within the Self. Clearing them permits a man's female vision to operate.

Listening and Photography

In this essay I've concentrated on the problem of developing the female aspect of vision within men. Though women should also develop male vision, I see this as a less difficult problem. I think the way is already open for them, whereas the way for men has not really opened up yet.

I have suggested skilled and disciplined listening as the method which will promote the growth of balanced vision in both men and women. Listening will do the job and we don't need photography or any other visual art form to help do it.

For photographers, therefore, I suggest little discussion groups composed of both men and women. In addition, it is good for couples to make pictures and talk about them. Groups function best on one level, pairs on another. In either case it is important for participants to be as honest as possible with one another. Boredom as an important factor should be acknowledged and dealt with forthrightly. So should the notion that suffering is necessary and that it has a therapeutic function which makes possible the extension of vision for both men and women. With this in mind, people may be able to remember that photographic discussion groups work most effectively for Self-evolution when the initial excitement of meeting and conversing with new people has worn off and boredom has crept in. Boredom is a useful tool. Use it for extending your vision—and for escaping forever from boredom.

DISCOVER your own secret symbols

Using photography to unearth your unconscious psychic symbols and to discover what they really mean to you.

Though you may not be especially aware of it, one of your main motives for making photographs is to project your Self onto photographic paper so that you can get a better look at it. There is a problem, however, because the Self expresses itself in symbols which may appear meaningless to you until you've studied them for a long time. Sometimes even years of study won't reveal their meanings. Even so it is good to get them exteriorized, i.e. out of yourself and into prints. Though you may never consciously see their meaning they will still do very useful work in your behalf. There is a part of you that knows full well what they are all about and which allows itself to be affected by them in a good way.

5

Another problem is that the symbols come from many levels of one's being. The deepest one we might call the 'Self proper' or 'Essence.' It might be best to call the shallowest one the 'unconscious ego.' They have been called many things in the course of history, but these names will serve our purposes well. In the metaphysical sense ego, conscious or unconscious, is not Self at all, though we commonly confuse the two terms. In fact, ego and Self are in direct conflict in most matters; ego would like to destroy Self altogether. And Self would like to deprive ego of dominion over the psyche.

We are unaware of both the Self and the unconscious ego. Nonetheless, they try to get our conscious attention through symbols they project into our photographs. In dividing the unconscious into just 'Self' or 'Essence' and 'unconscious ego,' I am greatly oversimplifying things. In addition to these two divisions we could postulate reasonably almost as many others as we'd like. All are engaged in the communication business. Some are doing their best to talk to the conscious mind via symbols. Messages come from several sources and for a variety of purposes which makes it difficult to interpret the symbols.

An equally forbidding problem for most people is that they can't bring themselves to believe that any symbols at all are getting into their photographs. They see the contents of their pictures only as trees, buildings, or people and as nothing more. That these things might also be functioning as symbols is peculiar and alien and many people are distressed to hear about it. Something in all of us dreads hearing from mysterious and unconscious sources.

These problems are solvable, and every intelligent person can work out partial solutions which will help him learn many important things about himself. On the positive side of the ledger, the puzzles he runs into may be so intriguing that they will keep him interested for many years in using photography as a tool of Self-discovery.

The Message Originators

A human being can be accurately described as an immense communication network compressed into a very small space. If all the computers in the world were hooked up together, they wouldn't even begin to equal the complexity of one human brain. But the head brain is only a small part of a person's intercom system; in a significant sense the entire body is a brain.

There are systems and subsystems all the way down to the cellular level which both send and receive messages. To isolate and name a few of them I will turn to Eastern science and psychology. I will have to introduce here the notion of levels. On one we have three separate but interrelated brain systems—the head brain, the spinal brain and the solar brain (part of the latter located in the solar plexus, the rest distributed elsewhere around the body). On another level we have a seven-brain system composed of the endocrine glands, which the Hindus call *chakras*. Each of them is able to send and receive communication and has its own memory system, not only for events in this life but for earlier lives.

Contrary to popular belief, the mind itself is not a function of these systems. It is actually an independent entity which merely operates through them. On its own level it is tied in with every other human mind and the Overmind as well. Operating outside of time and space, it connects to them now, in the past and in the future. Its higher memory system, called the akashic record, has in its memory banks every thought that has ever been thought since time began.

You can call the foregoing a gross exaggeration if you wish. However, in fairness to yourself you should tentatively concede the point that the human intercom system is a good deal more complex than generally supposed. In addition, you should tentatively accept the idea that there is more than one source from which an unconscious, symbolic message can originate. For simplicity's sake we can pare the number down to two: the Essence and the unconscious ego. Any statement concerning them must necessarily be a little vague and should be given a poetic interpretation.

The Essence

We can say that the Essence is the Self and that it includes the Soul, the Spirit and the Superconscious Mind. It won't serve our present purposes to try to describe them or differentiate between them. It will help us understand the types of symbols they project into our photographs if we ascribe to them certain fundamental purposes. These purposes are ethical and spiritual and aimed toward the eventual unification of the individual human entity with the Higher Forces.

From our great religious leaders we have a pretty good idea of what these ethical-spiritual purposes are and the type of behavior which exemplifies them. On the earthly level their highest expression is: "Love one another." Thus, in digging into our photographs to discover Essence symbols we should look for things which attempt to push us toward this goal or which encourage attempts we're already making in this direction.

In addition we should look for symbolic messages whose purpose is to defeat egotism, or selfishness, for self-centeredness of any sort thwarts the Essence and its purposes. As a rule messages of this type try to show us that we are indeed selfish, tell us how we disguise our selfishness from ourselves and try to lead us toward the type of behavior through which we can eventually overcome it.

When we are looking at photographs there is a very good clue which tells us if they contain symbols of the first type. It is a wonderful feeling of warmth toward beings or things outside of ourselves. We sense this feeling as being separate from ego somehow and greatly enjoy its presence. With it may come a feeling of hope which relieves inner anxiety and counteracts everyday feelings of Self-negation.

We can tell if we're encountering symbols of the second type when we experience suffering while looking at photographs. We feel like cringing, hiding from other people, condemning ourselves, striking back at the world and so on. Here it is the ego which is suffering, not the real Self, or Essence. Furthermore, each bit of suffering indicates that energy is being taken away from the ego and released for service to the Essence. The relief and pleasure we sometimes experience after ego-suffering tells us that the energy is indeed there. If there is no relief it means that the battle to subordinate the ego is still going on.

The Unconscious Ego

We can say that the unconscious ego is the repressed part of the conscious ego. It is a system made up of forbidden thoughts held in bondage by energy in the form of constantly reiterated lies which deny the nature of the thoughts or that they even exist at all. This all takes place at the unconscious level and we are, therefore, unaware that it is happening. The thoughts are those which the ego, in the course of its development from childhood, has found both enchanting and frightening. In general, we can say that they are ideas concerning what the ego thinks it would like to do (or would have liked to have done earlier in the life of the entity) if there were no chance whatsoever of being found out, either by other people or the Conscience. The Conscience is, of course, a representative of the Essence.

Many of the thoughts, pushed into the unconscious early in life, are relatively harmless, e.g. the childish desire to taste horse manure or play in a place dangerous to children. Some were pushed there because they violated, or appeared to the youthful mind to violate, various taboos. Others are of a type that openly celebrates selfishness, at the expense of other beings, the world in general and the Essence. Taken together they represent all the things that the conscious part of the ego doesn't want to know about its unconscious part.

There are powerful unconscious forces which want the ego to be fully informed concerning the contents of its unconscious part. If all this material were conscious, the ego could be persuaded to relinquish its dominion of the psyche to its rightful master, the Essence. However, the ego is terrified of the repressed material and will do its best to keep it entirely unconscious. The ego is a very clever energy thief. It steals as much as it can of the organism's available energy and uses a large part of it to hold its forbidden thoughts in bondage in the unconscious.

As long as there is some energy which is still accessible to it, the Essence uses as much as it can get to combat the ego's purposes. One way in which it does this is by projecting symbols into dreams, reveries, photographs, slips of tongue, and so forth to help the ego see that it can safely permit certain repressed material to come into consciousness. The Essence communicates in symbols because they are multidimensional, fitting to its own nature, and because symbols can be slipped through the ego's defenses against hearing anything it doesn't want to hear. There are other reasons, but we don't need to go into them here.

In some people the ego eventually manages to block off entirely the Essence's access to energy, thus totally defeating its purposes. When this happens the Essence may leave the body altogether, though the body may live on for years without its owner's noticing anything particularly strange in its behavior or appearance. Certain psychics can detect a wrongness, though they may not know how to explain it.

The unconscious ego is always projecting symbols into our photographs in order to support the morale of its conscious part and to encourage its looting of the resources of the psyche. One way in which we can tell if our pictures contain this kind of symbol is through feeling a type of satisfaction we have no desire to examine or have a positive resistance to examining. It may be accompanied by feelings of self-righteousness, admiration for essentially negative ideas, inner pomposity, inflated vanity and so on. Unconscious ego symbols support us in holding to selfish ideas; they lessen our feelings of responsibility for things outside ourselves and requite our egotistical desire to have power over things.

The Wolf

Anyone who wishes success in discovering and decoding his own secret symbols ought to take a very close look at his ego as a whole, both its conscious and unconscious aspects. Looking at the ego objectively is difficult, mainly because it thinks it is the Self. It helps if we give the ego a name, a device which has been used by a great many people in their search for the Self. One very useful name comes to us from antiquity: the wolf. If we think of the supposed characteristics of wolves we can use them to describe the ego with considerable accuracy. For example, wolves are said to be thieves (I've already described the ego as an energy thief). And while we're doing this we can also hold onto the idea that ego and Self are not the same thing.

Wolves (wolves mythically anthropomorphized) are fiendishly clever, but only in the carnal realm. They are very difficult to defeat in anything they're trying to do. They are terribly self-centered. They will devour anything they can catch or turn it to their advantage in some other way. They are pathological liars. Though they are superficially very strong and imposing they are cowards underneath. Because their ability to function at all depends largely on conceit they will do anything in their power to conceal from themselves how frightened and cowardly they actually are. Though they love to inflict pain (often disguising their hostility as friendship) they are terribly afraid of receiving it. And so on.

In the average human being the wolf rules both the conscious and unconscious aspects of the psyche, but old lupus is so gullible concerning his own lies to himself that he often thinks he's a veritable lamb. He is such a constant and confirmed liar that he sees reality, most of all himself, upside down. Furthermore, he spends most of his time desperately stealing energy from the organism and converting it into lies with which to hold unconscious ideas in bondage so that he can't become aware of them. If they were all to escape suddenly he would go insane; if gradually, he would slowly but surely learn he isn't at all what he thinks he is and that he's illegally ruling the house of a Master immensely greater than he.

Let us get to your photography. Your wolf doesn't want you to discover your secret symbols which are in your photographs, for the process of discovering them would make him suffer and would lessen his dominion over your psyche. When you discover your Essence symbols they encourage you toward ethical behavior at a deeper and deeper level. Essentially, ethical behavior means devoting your energies to something other than your wolf, or ego. He doesn't like this and will do his best to prevent it. Though your photographs may be literally loaded with Essence symbols, he may be clever enough to prevent your finding even one of them.

Your wolf will try to keep Essence symbols out of your pictures altogether if he can, not only because your recognition of them might make him suffer, but because they are a nourishing spiritual food for your Essence itself. Above all, the wolf wishes to withhold nourishment from the Essence. To help in this he will try hard to convince you that what you're now reading is sheer gibberish.

The Essence feeds from its own symbols in several ways. To explain this I ask you to think of the Essence as being multilevel. At the top level is Spirit (or God in man). At a much lower one is Soul. Though Soul knows a good deal more than ego, its knowledge is still very finite compared with Spirit. In fact, man's purpose in life is to get an education for his Soul and thus permit it to rejoin the Higher Forces. Not only does the Soul need experience and information; it also needs encouragement. The higher part of the Essence, or Self, can provide the Soul nourishment through the symbols it projects. This could be in the form of information and encouragement. Since this goes on at the unconscious level, we are entirely unaware of it. The fact that it happens may explain why so many artists make no attempt to delve into the meaning of their work. Whether or not they consciously understand it, it gives them spiritual nourishment from the symbols they've projected into it.

Essence symbols are also food in an entirely different way. Let us say that there is a type of symbol designed specifically to communicate with the unconscious ego. Its purpose is to educate the unconscious ego concerning the type of material it is keeping locked up in itself, at the cost of a great expenditure of energy. It tells the ego that many of the forbidden thoughts it is holding in bondage are really very harmless and that it can safely release them. When the unconscious ego frees them, energy is released. The Essence will get some of it before the ego captures it again and uses it for its own purposes. For the Essence, energy is food, as it is indeed for all the rest of the organism. This is again an entirely unconscious process in which we are nourished by our art without being aware of it.

Your wolf also gets a good deal of nourishment from the symbols in your photographs. These are the ones projected by the unconscious ego; call them ego symbols if you wish. They feed your wolf by saying that he is really a god incarnate, right in every self-centered thing he thinks, lovable no matter how badly he neglects or maltreats others and so on. Many of the messages expressed in unconscious ego symbols are so terribly farfetched that if your wolf became conscious of them he would have to give them up out of sheer embarrassment. Though he's not bright in comparison to the Self, he's not entirely stupid either. Naturally, your wolf tries to keep the meaning of his ego symbols unconscious so that he can continue to use them for purposes of self-inflation. Essence, on the other hand, tries to make you aware of what these ego symbols are and what they mean.

The Wolf Must Suffer

It should now be obvious why so many serious photographers experience more suffering than joy from their photography. They are intuitively using it to thwart the wolf, or selfishness. Every twinge they suffer when making photographs, looking at them or thinking about them represents energy stolen back from the wolf and diverted to Essence purposes.

You have probably already discovered that in spite of yourself you sometimes make yourself miserable with your photography. I hope you can now see that this may be a good thing and that you might be wise to backtrack to the particular things which made your ego suffer. Once you are firmly embarked on this path, the wolf will no longer be able to consistently outwit you, no matter how hard he tries. He will be very clever, you may be sure, but you will eventually find many of your symbols and the keys to their meanings.

Only the wolf stands between you and your Self. To discover the Self you must make the wolf suffer through giving up his carefully guarded lie systems. People do this all the time anyway, intuitively realizing that only through ego-suffering can freedom be won.

I have sometimes been accused of being a killjoy and a polluter of photography. My critics accuse me of being entirely nihilistic. I think I'm not so much pessimistic as realistic. If a person experiences pure joy through his photography, fine; more power to him. If it makes him suffer, however, he can look at his suffering in a positive way. By putting up with the suffering —even inviting it—he has something wonderful to gain: a Self.

And the suffering doesn't last forever. After a while, many things which were the cause of much misery no longer bring it on. Some, indeed, now become sources of immense delight. Real joy is experienced, not the paltry substitutes for it which our egos try to talk us into accepting as real. For suffering photographers the medium slowly but surely turns into a source of pleasure and an endlessly adaptable tool for use in further Self-discovery.

We will now turn again to the lessons formerly printed in *Popular Photography*. Since here they appear in a book whose central aim is to help readers toward Self-discovery, the pictures need re-examination in this new context.

The Real Me?

This is a project which can lead you to express things about yourself you haven't known before. You do it by approaching self-portraiture in a rather strange way. If you were to take a more traditional approach, you'd probably end up with a portrait stereotype. All that a stereotype can tell you is that you've been thoroughly conditioned by the American culture, by writings on photography, and by yourself. Though it's important to know this about yourself, there are other things you need to know, too. The project helps you learn some of these things, for the very oddness of the approach helps you outwit your own conditioning.

In the lesson itself, very little was said about what the self-portraits mean. Since this is what we're really interested in here, I will extend the interpretations of several of them.

When Ron Tunison made his self-portrait, his only conscious thought was that by shooting himself underwater in the bathtub he would get a very interesting photograph. I'm fairly sure he was unaware of deeper unconscious intentions and hidden meanings. Since he's made a good many other pictures with approximately the same meaning, it is fairly obvious he's trying to tell himself something.

We know that when the picture was taken Ron was perfectly safe under the water in his own bathtub. If we cling to this thought it will lead us away from what the picture is actually trying to tell Ron. However, if we ask ourself what the picture looks like, rather than what it actually records, we are directly on the track of the hidden meaning.

First of all, it appears that we're looking at someone who is dead, specifically Ron Tunison. Death is a very common theme in Ron's pictures. Young men in general are very prone to find it attractive. The question is, why? Do young men yearn for death? In some ways they do, in fact. But it is important to understand what it is they'd like to have killed. There is no doubt whatsoever that Ron wants to destroy something.

To discover what it is we can discuss young men in general, for many share Ron's inner problem. After years of yearning to break away from parental control a young man manages to do it; but he doesn't find the freedom he expected. He does only what he wants when he wants to —and finds the cherished freedom moving ever farther away from him. There is some inner thing which is defeating his purposes. This is what he would like to see dead.

The inner thing which is the destroyer

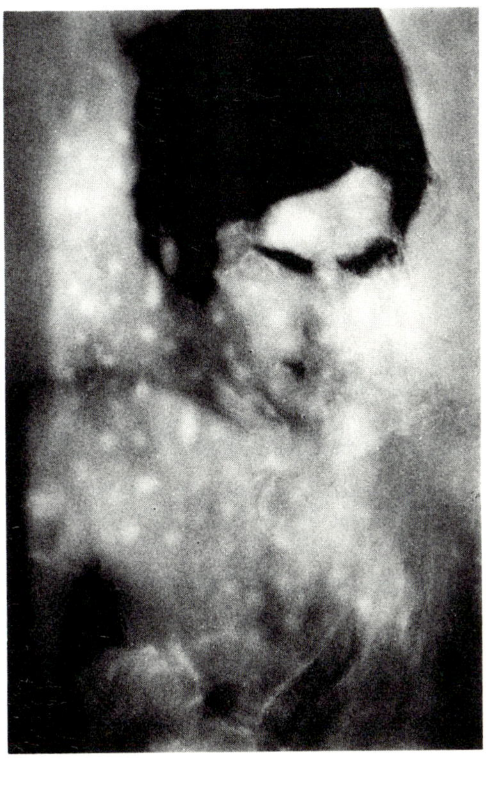

Self-portrait of Ron Tunison in a bathtub. Because he looks dead here, we can assume there is something in himself he would like to see die. The question is, what?

photo by RON TUNISON

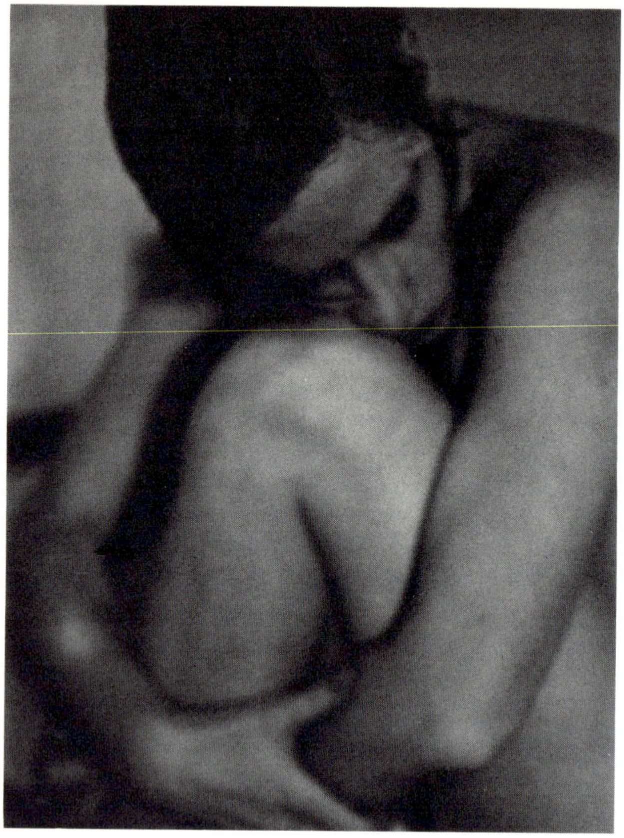

Bill Kaye's mother loves his self-portrait, but it makes his father uneasy. Bill's generation is more given to self-revelation than his father's. Young folk seek freedom through self-revelation.

photo by BILL KAYE

of happiness and cheerful expectations is personality, or ego. The more one strives for freedom through indulging personality's wishes, the tighter becomes the bondage. The chances are that both personality and Essence are speaking through Ron's picture. Personality says: "By giving me a free reign you've permitted me to bring myself so much suffering that I want to die." Essence says: "In letting personality usurp the energies of the psyche you are cutting yourself off from me, your real Self. To live cut off from one's inner Self is a state equivalent to death."

Do you wonder what my young friend Ron will think when he reads this interpretation? I'll bet ten dollars he'll think it's unadulterated hogwash. Though I've seen the suffering build up in him for three years, he has yet to discover it. Until he does, he'll find it impossible to believe how strongly he yearns for the death of egotism. We all share Ron's problem: Until we discover our suffering, there's little chance we'll learn how to use it in freeing our Selves, our Essences. Knowing how to suffer correctly is a spiritual art of the highest order. The death we deeply yearn for, the death of egotism, is bought only through the suffering which comes with Self-discovery.

Nowadays, quite a few young men make self-portraits of themselves in the nude. Though it's a good way of shocking parents and friends, there's a good deal more to it than that. It's important that we see such pictures in a proper light and eliminate interpretations which only lead us around the barn. For example, in this self-portrait by Bill Kaye we should eliminate the notion that it has anything whatsoever to do with sexual license. And it has nothing to do with public exhibitionism. Bill made the picture entirely for himself. It is only in a book because I asked his permission to print it and Bill feels he can trust the ways in which I try to use photographs.

One of Bill's problems is that, like most people, he doesn't like himself enough. In this picture he's liking himself in a physical way. Skin feels good against skin. How many of us have forgotten this? Through liking himself for a moment in a physical way, Bill is probably telling himself how deeply he yearns to like himself in other ways, too. It couldn't be otherwise, for all people have this selfsame yearning.

Not only is an inner something telling Bill how much he craves his own approval but it is also telling him how to go about getting it. The pathway to self-approval is symbolized by nudity. One of the new generation, Bill isn't enthralled with the idea of nudity as such. I find it impossible to imagine that he would, say, fantasize the thrills he might get by romping around naked in a nudist camp. It is far more likely that Bill sees nudity as a symbol for, and a step toward, something else.

In the picture, Bill's Essence is confirming what he has already more or less figured out for himself. It is telling him, "Be nude in all things, not just in body." Put in other terms it says, "Stand before the world naked in truth if you want your happiness back. Don't lie to yourself. Don't lie to others except to save them suffering. Give up all the roles you play in life, stripping yourself down to nude Essence. If you do this you'll be given the keys to the Kingdom: your Self."

Bill's picture is also about respect. He's been given a temple in which to live but hasn't taken very good care of it. Here he's paying it respect by letting himself feel it in a warm, sensual, friendly way.

Jay Winans has consciously been searching for his Self for quite a long time. He knows from personal experience that finding it is terribly difficult. His picture seems to show Self as a mystery; the obscured eyes (which often symbolize the Self) express this. The fact that we can't see them symbolizes the degree to which Jay's true Self is hidden.

Since Jay is a very complex person we can expect that his picture is telling him many things, some of them contradictory. Though the Self is lost, he seems to be getting a certain self-defeating enjoyment from it. The picture seems to be talking about some kind of implacable inner anger, too. Jay may be prone to respect it too much, whereas he'd be better off fighting against it. Anger can be a symbol of a man, for mankind is by nature aggressive. But anger also separates him from his inner Self. In fact, it is one of the greatest barriers to Self-discovery.

In a sense, blacking out one's own eyes in a portrait is equivalent to wearing dark glasses. Through the dark you can see what other people are doing but they can't see the essential you, which is reflected in your eyes. Being obscure in the understanding and perception of others is a way of having power over them. Though power is a very dangerous thing, men are prone to strive for it. Jay's picture seems to be saying something about this.

The picture also seems to talk about naked force. Whether it's Essence force or ego force is hard to tell. Man is a much greater force than he realizes and it's good that he should know this fact. Perhaps Jay was feeling vitiated when he made the picture and his Essence was trying to tell him there were still unknown forces within himself upon which he could draw at a time of need and despair.

The picture may be saying that Jay is both strong and weak at the same time. The strength is in the pose, lighting and facial expression. The weakness is in the necessity to hide. If this is part of the true meaning of the picture, Jay's self-portrait speaks of a problem common to all human beings.

In her self-portrait picture, Paula Peltz has dramatized eyes and seashells. What she's done with her eyes probably has several meanings. By retouching, she has removed the pupils. It happens that she has very dramatic and beautiful eyes. They could give her great power over men. In turning them into empty, plaster orbs she may be symbolically giving up this power and any other misuse of beautiful eyes. Or her inner Self may be telling her that this is what she *ought* to do. Since Paula is quite shy, it would naturally be difficult for her to surrender such a splendid defensive and aggressive weapon.

There may be other reasons why she blocked out her eyes, however. Eyes can symbolize curiosity. Undisciplined curiosity can lead one far away from the Self. Her picture may be telling her, "Imprison (or blind) your curiosity so that you can turn your attention inward and discover what is happening to your Self." Though we tend to rate curiosity as a virtue, it is more often than not merely a toy which the ego uses in finding gratification for itself.

Blocking out the eyes can also symbolize giving in to the desire to shut out the rest of the world and set up a private world within the ego. Though this is a very bad thing, most of us have felt the temptation to do it. We suffer so much pain from what we see that we want to shut our eyes to it and become safe little islands unto ourselves.

Gary Modick may be saying that the essential Gary is unknown to anyone, including himself. This unknown person combines strangeness with quiet glee. The inner self is always strange.

photo by GARY MODICK

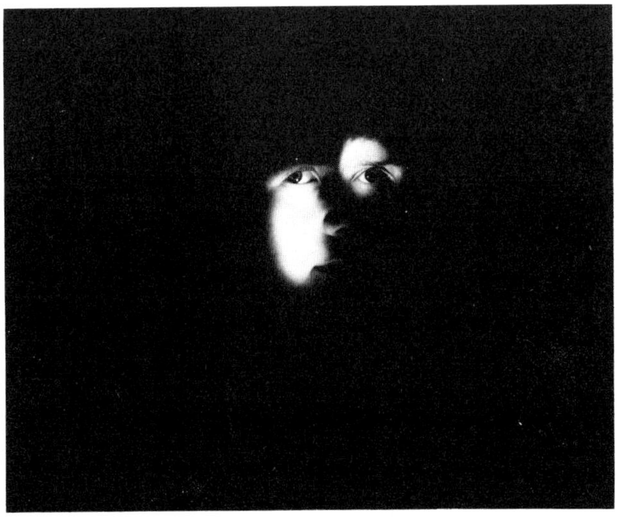

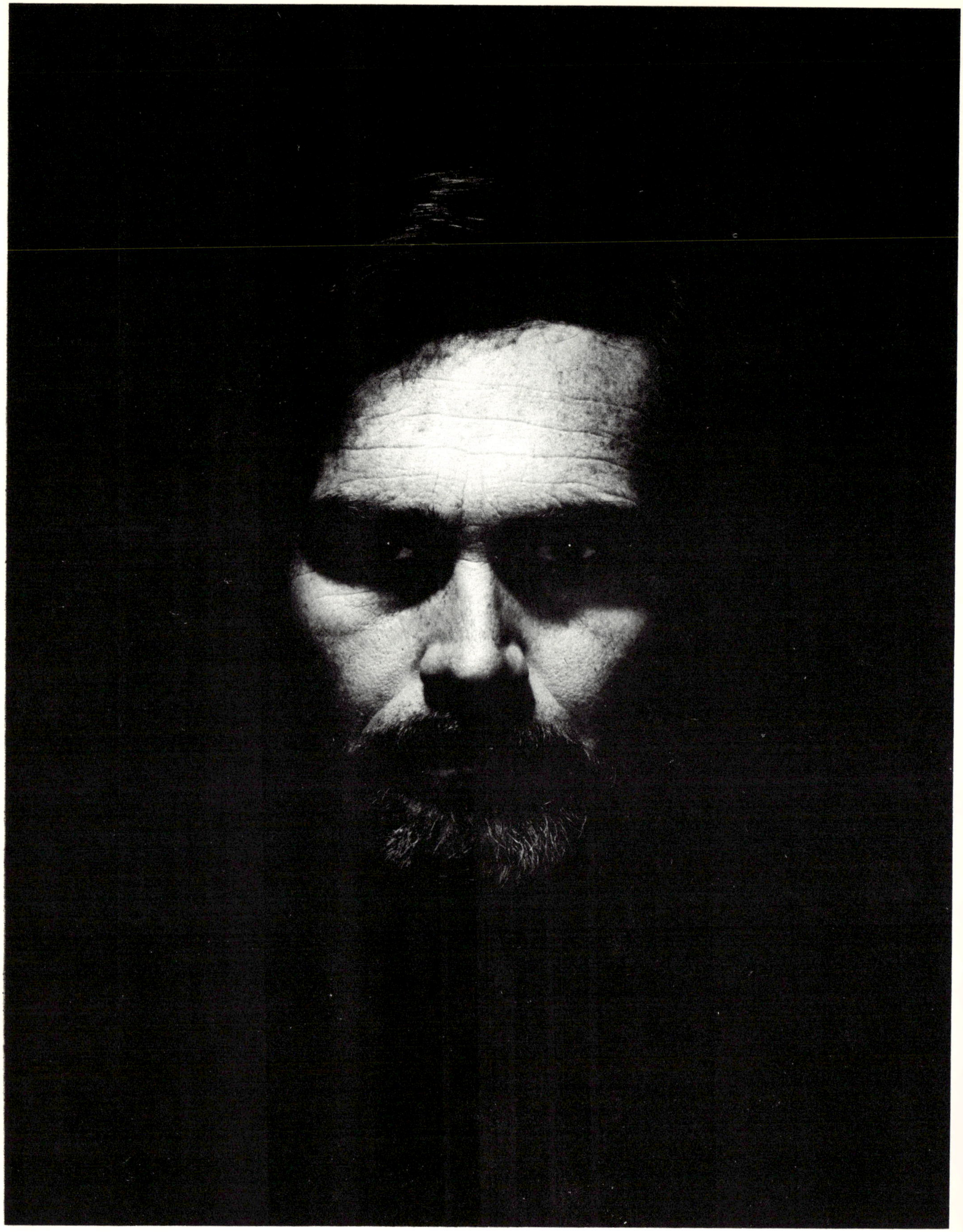

Jay Winans thought possibly there is evil in himself and symbolized it as a force lurking behind half-shaded eyes. He may be fascinated with power, too.

photo by JAY WINANS

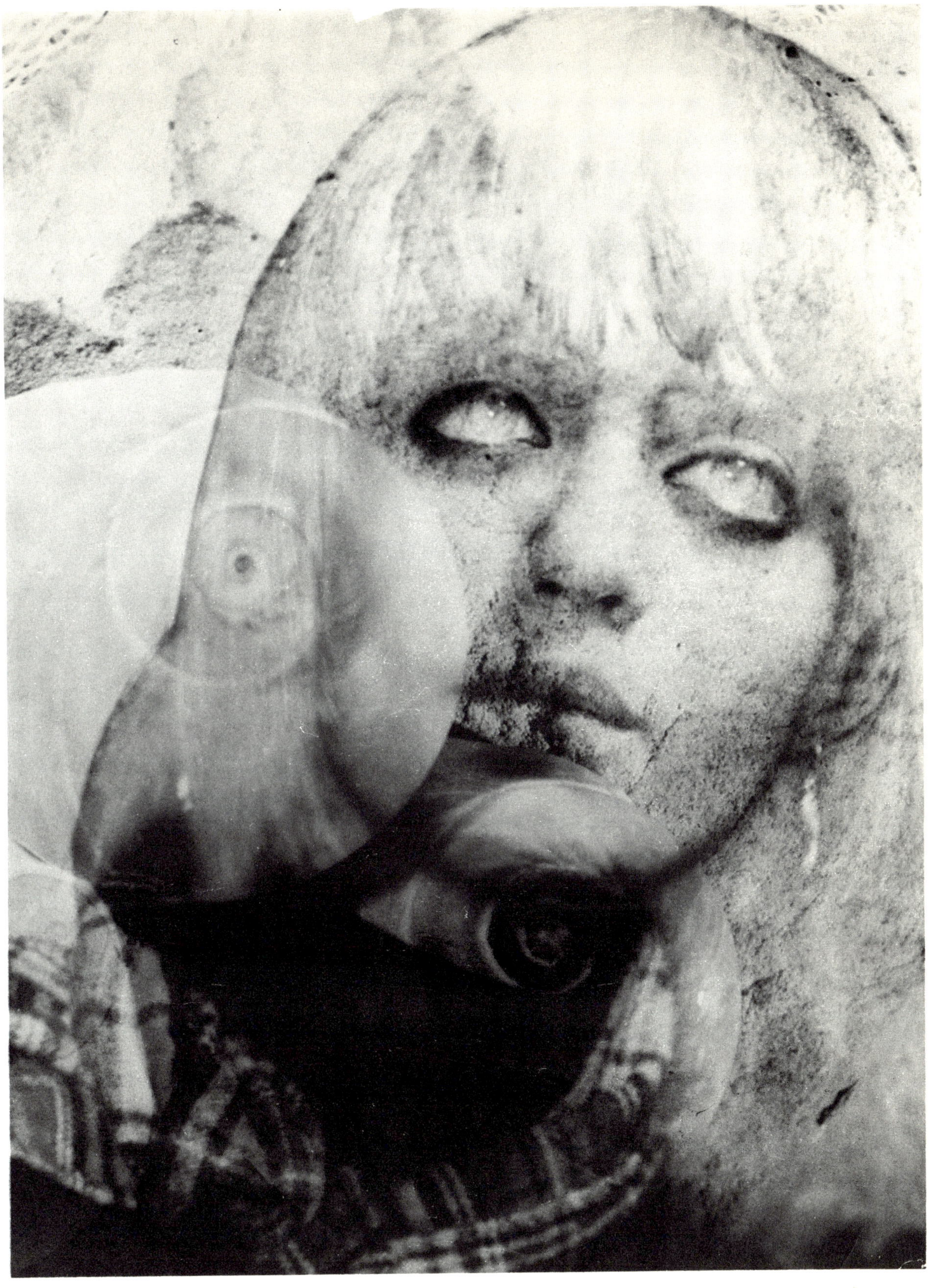

Paula Peltz uses symbols of a return to the sea, then shows herself as blind. The sea: a symbol of spirituality. Symbolic blindness: a way to tell yourself to turn your vision inward and away from material things.

photo by PAULA PELTZ

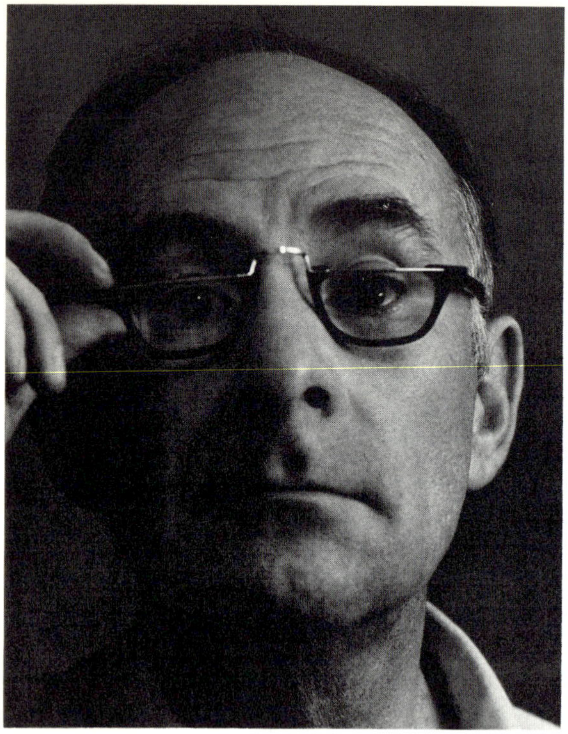

Ed Fine (above) intended to spoof himself, yet made a photograph in which he is treated gently. It reflects the way he treats others and may indicate that in forgiving his neighbors he is also learning to forgive himself.

photo by ED FINE

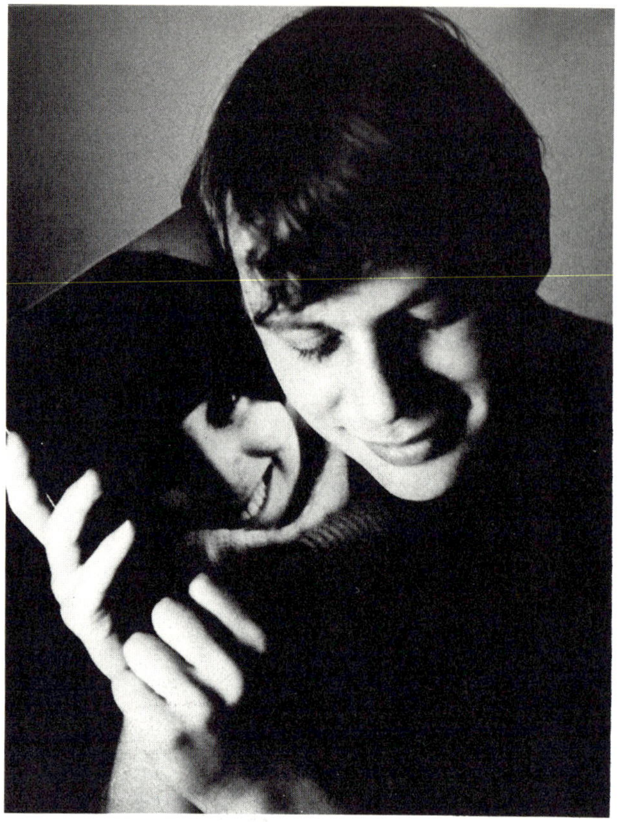

Lenny Myerson (above) intended to satirize his feelings for his sweetheart, but gave us a picture of a genuinely tender young man responding truly to the dictates of his heart.

photo by LENNY MYERSON

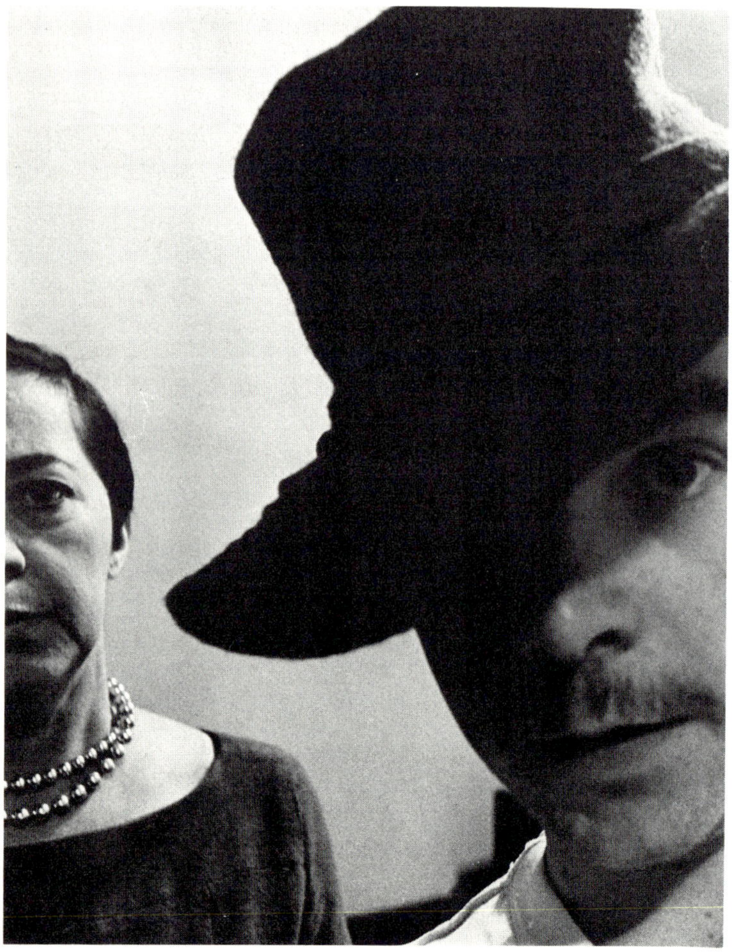

Jim Nicol (left) felt that his mother belonged in his self-portrait. The lostness in his face and the quiet concern in hers move me deeply. For how many thousands of years have mothers looked at their sons in exactly this way?

photo by JIM NICOL

I'm strongly inclined to think that the central message of the picture is that something within Paula wishes her to explore her own spiritual possibilities. In getting the sea into her photograph, she may be talking about spirituality. In many, many people this is what the sea symbolizes: the spirit, which is the mother of human life. The shell, a Many-chambered Nautilus, has a fascinating growth spiral which could very well symbolize spiritual growth.

In blocking off her eyes, Paula has told herself, "Turn your vision inward." Her Essence may be telling her that other types of self-change may be necessary. Her natural brunette hair has been made blond in the picture, a rather radical change in a physical sense. It may symbolize radical spiritual change as well. Physically, she has changed dark into light. Spiritually she must do the same thing. Though blinded, her eyes are turning up-

On the surface, Kim Smith is self-contained and successful. Her self-portrait shows that within her are wide realms of yearning and quiet sadness.

photo by KIM SMITH

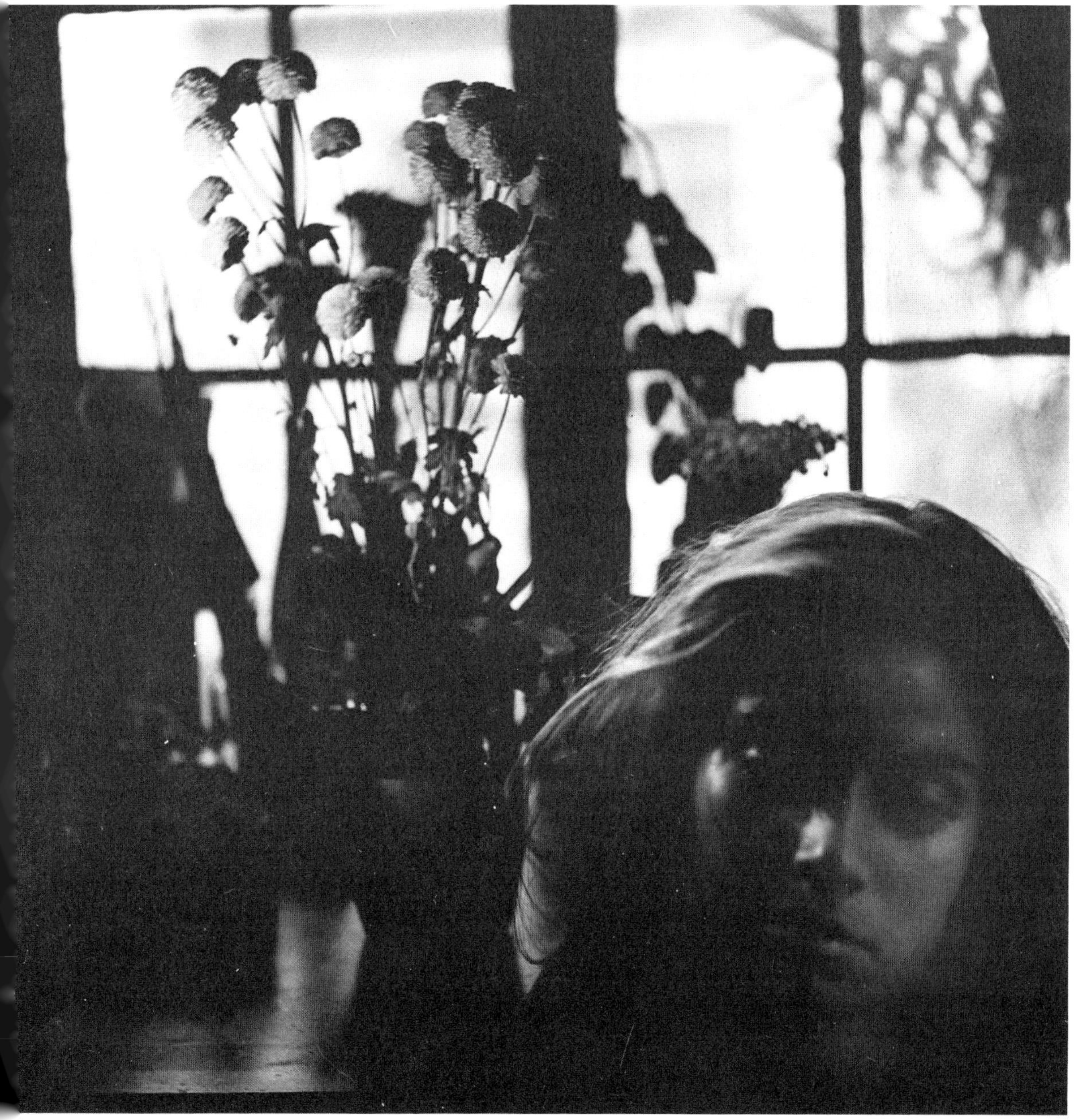

ward toward the light. Spiritually, upward and inward mean the same thing.

The interpretations I've given are incomplete. However, I'm fairly sure that they are accurate as far as they go. Even if I hadn't personally known the people who made these self-portraits I would be willing to bet on the accuracy. The reason is that the problems the photographs have talked about are common to all people.

The Lesson:
Many of us spend much of our lives trying to discover who and what we are. We soon learn to our dismay that the real Self, the essential spirit, is obscured by every kind of camouflage that the perverse and uncontrolled human imagination has been able to invent throughout aeons of time. Though we yearn for this primal Self with all our hearts, the yearning is largely unrequited.

Darkly veiled behind the multitudes of lies we tell ourselves, our real selves are constantly trying to communicate with our consciousness. They speak through our dreams, our slips of tongue, our rare moments of self-transcendence. They can also communicate to us through our photographs, if we give them half a chance.

All this was brought home to me with rare poignancy when I saw the series of pictures Ron Tunison was making of himself. If ever there was a case of a self trying to communicate with itself, this was it. On the surface, he'd merely gotten the idea of taking a series of pictures of himself arranged in various ways in the bathtub under water. But surfaces be damned, there was very much more than that going on—real soul stuff.

Borrowing and adapting Ron's idea, I asked other students in my classes at the School of Visual Arts and at the Germain School of Photography in New York to photograph themselves, but in a very special way. This same assignment I'll also give to you.

Ron's approach had something different. How to give other students this opportunity for Self-discovery? Pondering the problem, I found a solution that seemed to work: Photograph yourself in two ways, (1) treat yourself with great kindness, even if you think you don't deserve it; (2) treat yourself with contempt. If the word 'contempt' doesn't ring a bell for you, try these terms: satire, put-down, put-on, self-excoriation, self-criticism, self-stripping and so on. Oddly, they'll give you unsuspected opportunities for Self-discovery. Every one of the beautifully expressive pictures in this lesson came from the "contempt" category.

The Hattersley Museum of Fine Art

This is a project which will help you outwit your conditioning in order to create or discover your personal symbols. It will work especially well if you take the risk which is mentioned in the text.

When this lesson was originally printed, multiple exposure was presented as just a way to make groovy pictures. Now we can talk about more important things. The title was not my idea, incidentally, but since it has already been published we might just as well stick to it.

When you do this project you put into your pictures symbols which represent you. This comes about in several ways. One is that you pick them up from other artists. Modern art is largely concerned with unconscious symbols, so you'll naturally find a lot of them when you're looking at paintings and sculptures, as the lesson asks you to. It happens that one person's symbols will often represent another person almost as well. In making your pictures of paintings and sculptures, or pieces of them, you naturally select for your camera the things which interest you the most. This is the same as saying you naturally pick the things which symbolize yourself. That is, they are the symbols which your Essence thinks you're ready to discover. Ones which would lead you to premature insight won't attract your attention or interest you. When you are ready for them they will attract you.

Another reason why your symbols come to the surface is that a multiple-image process breaks up reality as you've conditioned yourself to see it. Conditioning yourself to something is the same as blinding yourself to it. Breaking up a familiar reality leads you around previous conditioning to another type of reality to which you're not yet conditioned yourself. When you see this new reality (your multiple-image pictures), you see its substance in two ways: by fitting it in with your previous visual habits (or self-conditioning), or by giving it a symbolic interpretation.

Fortunately, your multiple-image pictures are so unlike reality as you've experienced it all your life that they don't fit in with your old visual habits very well. This gives your Self the freedom to impose a symbolic meaning on whatever is created by the multiple-image process.

If you take the risk approach mentioned in the lesson you give your unconscious an even freer range and outwit previous conditioning to an even greater degree. In consciousness, you deliberately let yourself forget what you've previously photographed on a roll of film, so that what gets superimposed on what is not fully a conscious choice. This gives your unconscious the opportunity to be the chooser, though it won't necessarily take advantage of it. To understand how it actually has a choice concerning how images are overlapped, you have to understand some of its characteristics.

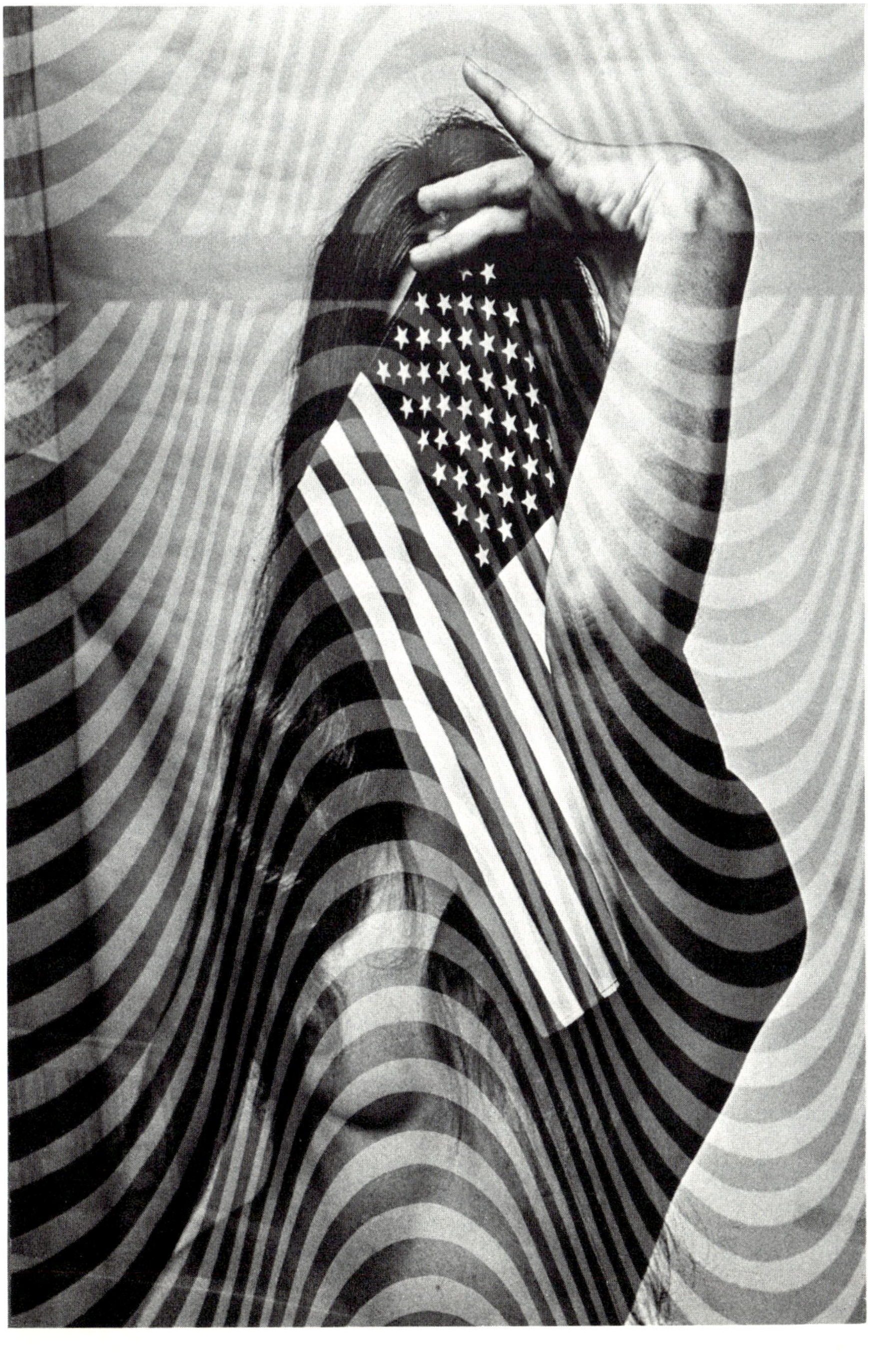

Does this picture desecrate the flag? Probably. There are good reasons for doing it, and they don't involve being a bad citizen.

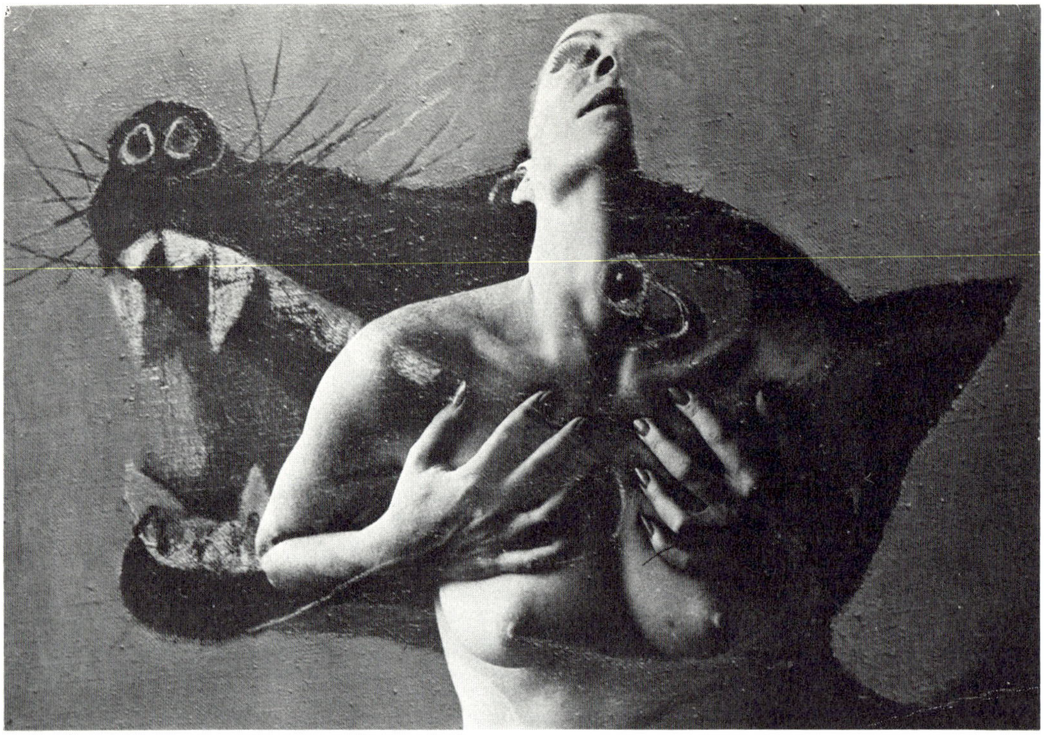

What does this picture say about the photographer who made it? More than he'd really like to admit in public.

The unconscious doesn't forget things. Everything that you've ever perceived through any of your senses during many lifetimes is clearly recorded there. When you see the scope of unconscious memory it's not too hard to believe that your unconscious remembers everything you've got on your film, even if your conscious mind doesn't. For the unconscious mind, remembering is a relatively piddling problem. Though the unconscious is not entirely free to get all the combinations it wants into your pictures, it is free enough to get in quite a few of them. Whether you recognize the symbols it has collected or created for you is another proposition. Your pictures could be literally loaded with personal symbols without your recognizing even one of them.

There is another aspect to this project which I'll mention but not go into in very great detail. The risk approach is a very good way of giving the ego a therapeutic rough time, especially for photographers who are strongly hung up on the idea of exerting strong control over the photographic medium. The approach will make them feel extremely uncomfortable, but it's good for them.

Since the pictures in this section are my own, I don't have to worry about getting sued for libel for what I say about them. Among other things, this picture is a strong put-down of women. Since thinking negatively about women has been one of my chief proclivities for many years, I'm not surprised. Though I'd like to get over this extremely Self-destructive habit, it appears that I've still got a long way to go.

As a deliberate desecration of the American flag, the first picture is also an attack against the early years of conditioning which turned me into a pious, self-satisfied nationalist. The fact that I'm rather indifferent to the desecration indicates that most of the conditioning has already been overcome. How one reacts to the desecration of a symbol is a very good indicator. Neither a feeling of triumph nor one of revulsion is good, though the first is the better. Revulsion at seeing a sacred symbol violated means that you're imprisoned in a conditioning system and don't even know it. Hostile triumph means that you either know or suspect and that you're pleased to be going after the conditioning with an axe. When the system is entirely wiped out, the desecration is seen with complete indifference.

An attack against jingoistic conditioning symbolizes a desire to attack all kinds of conditioning. If this were understood, youngsters wouldn't be so reviled for making free with the American flag. They are right in what they are attempting to do for themselves. And they are choosing a way of going about it which actually helps them a lot.

Since I already know that the flag represents nationalistic conditioning, I may be using the picture to tell myself that there is other conditioning in me which is equally destructive. The suggestion, obviously, is that I ought to look more deeply into my attitudes toward women to find ways in which I've conditioned myself and which I've not yet discovered.

I can't honestly say that I understand the picture of the woman and the wolf very well, but I'll make a try at interpretation. Things like the howling, self-pitying wolf have appeared in my pictures often enough for me to recognize them as ego-symbols. My name, Ralph, even *means* wolf. The wolf is probably ego, suffering the consequences of its self-centered domination of the psyche. It seems singularly appropriate that I've chosen to call ego 'the wolf' in this book. The wolf is feeling pretty rotten, as you can see. I've experienced this suffering for years and know it well. And all the while I've known that my self-centeredness was the source of it.

The woman is apparently suffering terribly and the wolf Hattersley is paying her no attention. Man, that's a shaft which *really* hits home! For years it has galled me almost to desperation that when my wife is hurt or sick the first thing I think of is myself. "How will this affect me?" One could hardly call this "loving." Egotism is a rotten thing, and when a thought like this flits through your mind you pay its bitter price in acutely painful guilt.

On the positive side, the picture may be trying to evoke my sympathy for wom-

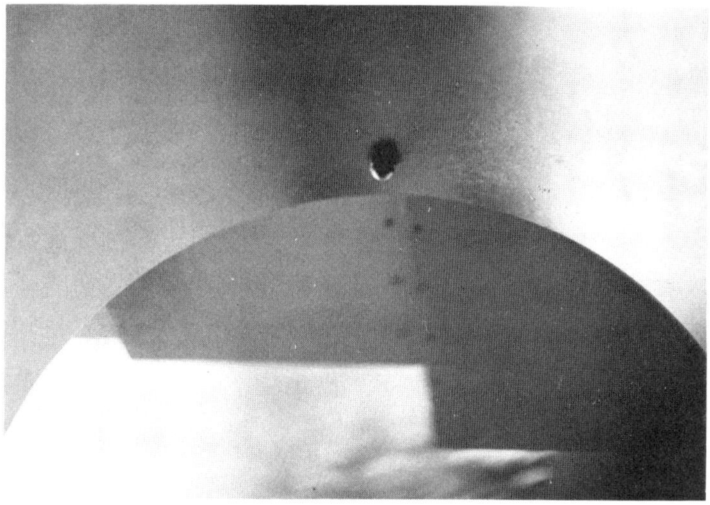

Not a double exposure (above) but a closeup of a modern sculpture in a museum.

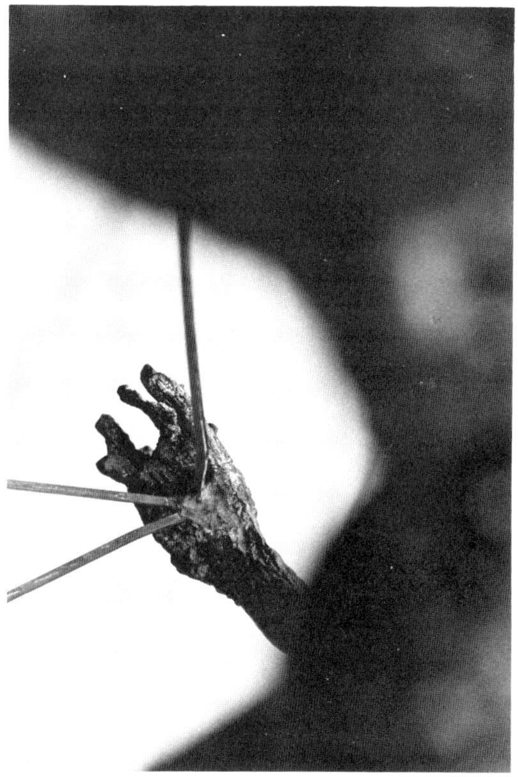

Closeup of a figure in the sculpture garden at the Museum of Modern Art in New York City. Though a simple picture, it has strong emotion.

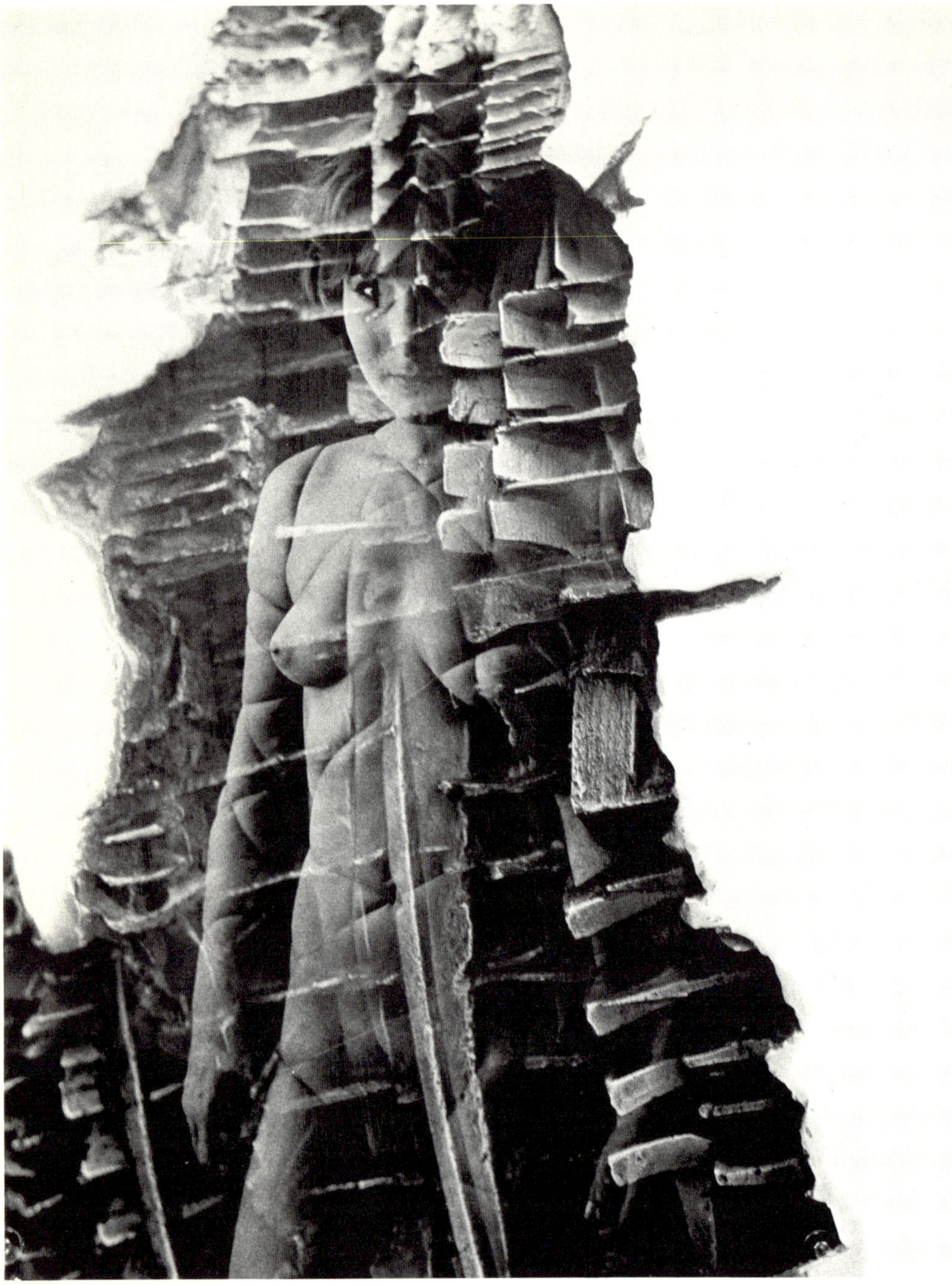

I once titled the picture "I Understand Her Well." From what I've written, do you think I actually do?

en by showing that they suffer and have some of the same problems as I. The wolf could represent the woman's ego as well as mine. It could also represent non-ego forces in which the woman is hopelessly entoiled. Some kind of Devil maybe? Or possession by discarnate entities?

Since I look at the woman in the picture and feel fondness toward her, the chances are there are more positive symbols here than I've been able to figure out. It's important to look for the positive as well as the negative since looking only for the negative can be egotism working in disguise, leading to Self-condemnation and the glory of wallowing in one's own supposed rottenness.

Something not so positive symbolized

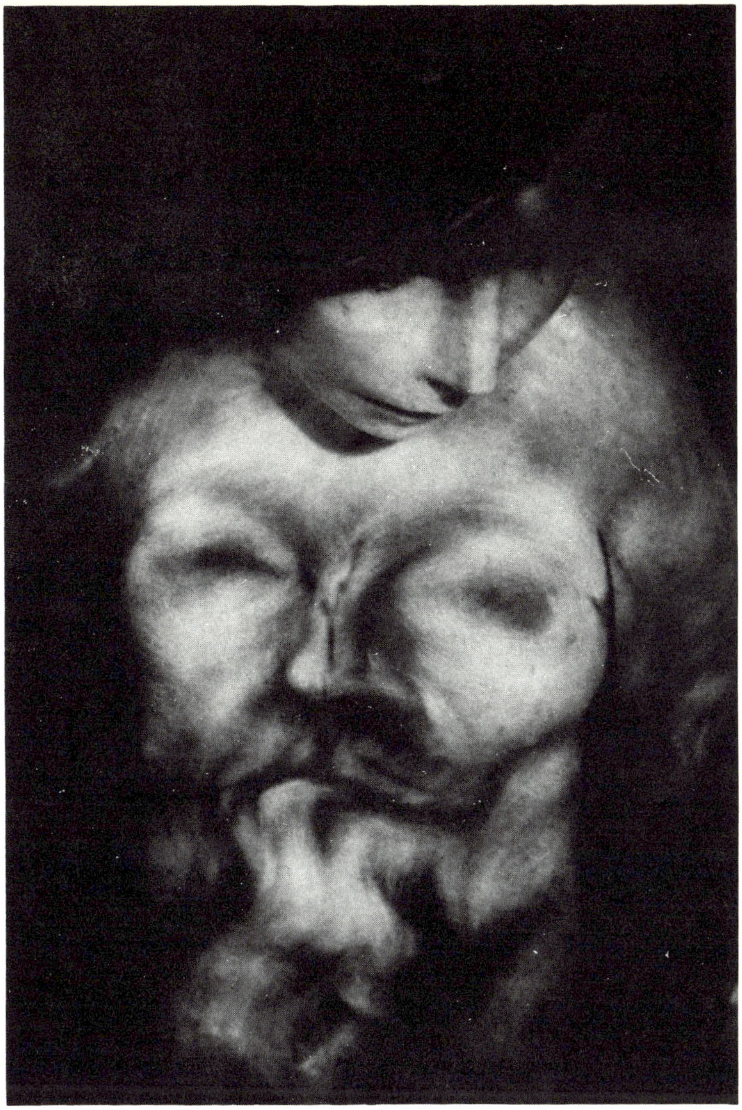

"She Remembers Him." The picture and title stir my middle-agèd soul.

My son's left eye superimposed on a detail of a painting by Rousseau. I haven't figured out why I like this picture a lot.

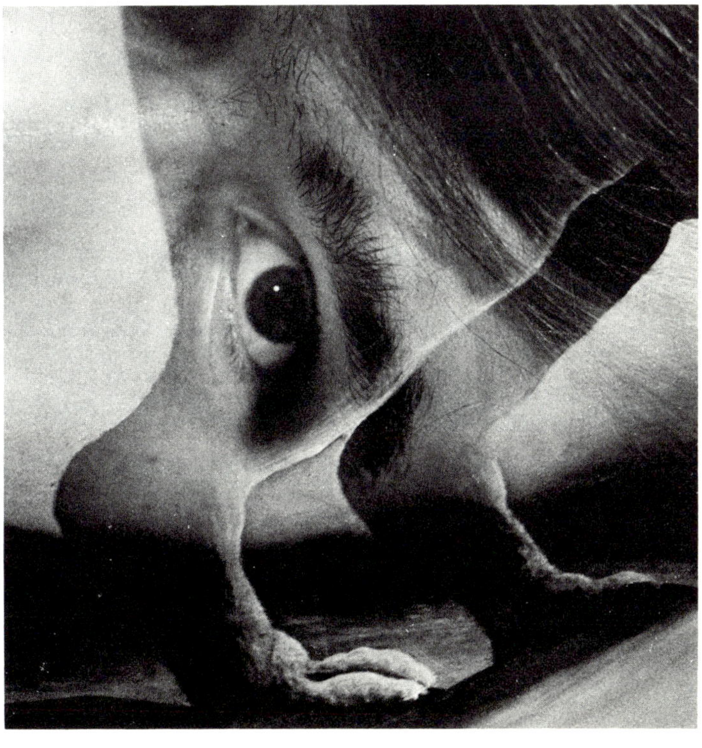

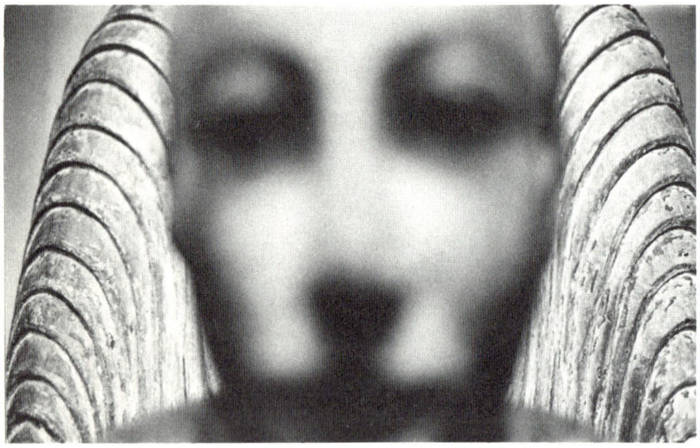

Out of focus, the stone priestess looks alive. The eyes make it hard to tell what the second image is unless you turn them upside-down.

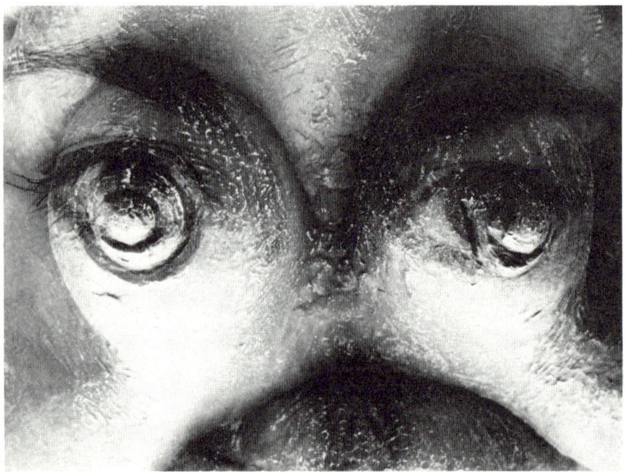

here is my delight in controlling women. I've really controlled this one, as you can see, turned her into a picture and a symbol, made her appear to be suffering when she really wasn't, and stripped her naked in public. Though this is all standard male behavior it still isn't good.

From what I've said elsewhere in this chapter you ought to be able to interpret the rest of the pictures in this lesson for yourself. Doing this might have the salutary affect of destroying some of the illusions you have concerning the author. Nowhere in the book have I written about problems which are foreign to me. They are mine as they are yours. For you to think otherwise would be a grave injustice to yourself.

The Lesson:

Most people like to take pictures in art museums. They strive valiantly to take great pictures of this or that work of art. After that, they go to the museum curio

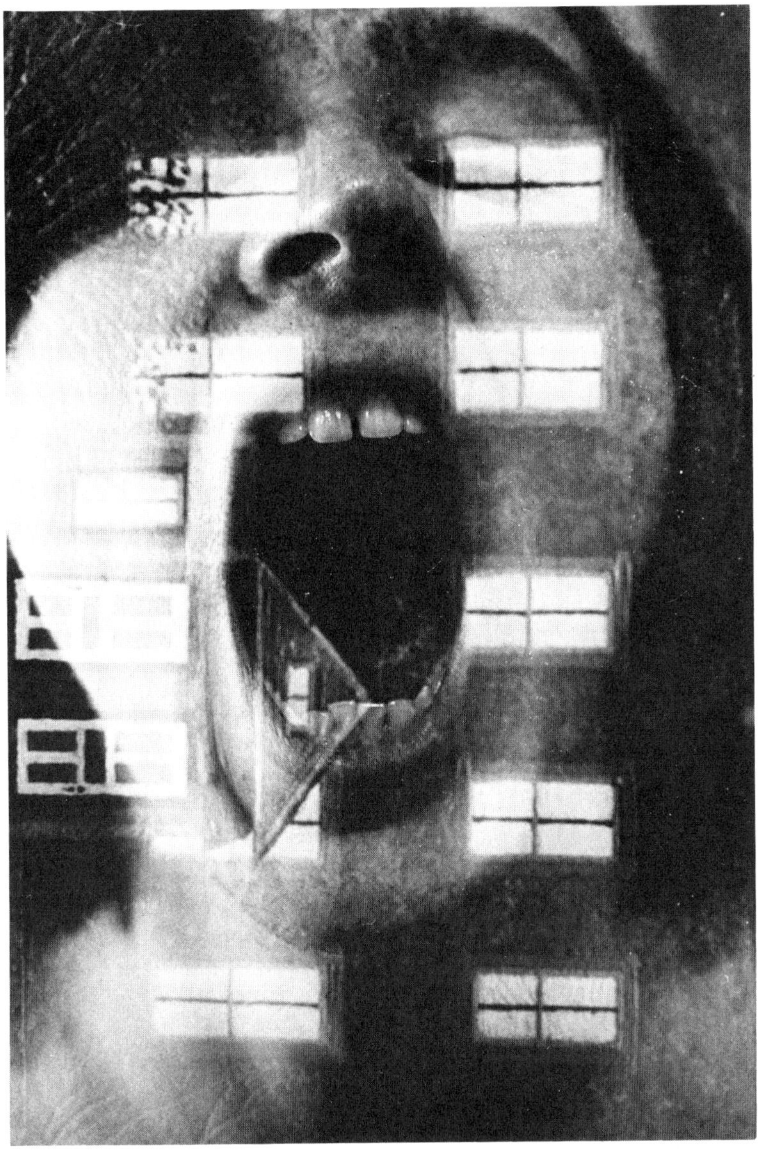

For reasons unclear to me I called this picture of my son "Too Many Windows." What psychology would explain this title?

shop to look at postcards. To their chagrin, they discover that the museum staff photographer has done a much better job than they because he had portable lights and could arrange the art as he pleased.

But there are other things to do aside from photographing works of art as a whole. One can select interesting little pieces, as it were. Use close-up lenses. Play with selective focus. Create blurred movement effects. Change positive pictures to negative. Invent interesting contrast effects. This lesson is concerned mainly with just one technique: double exposure. As you can see from the examples, it can lead to very unusual effects. You can also raise havoc by adding titles, if you have a flair for stirring people up.

The technique is very simple. Expose a roll of film. Rewind. Make exposures on the same roll again. With 35-mm film, you can make a mark on the film leader across from a certain part of the camera mechanism—say a certain sprocket. If you line up this mark both times in loading, the picture frames will be in register. With 120-mm film, there is no problem as long as you line up the numbers or dots on the back of the paper leader as you're supposed to. The only problem is that you have to re-roll in a darkroom or use a changing bag.

Since each frame is exposed twice, you will overexpose it if you set your exposure meter on the film's rated ASA speed. The answer is simple: double the film's ASA speed and set the new number on your meter. No other exposure compensation is necessary. For example, using Tri-X, normal ASA 400: Change the ASA rating to 800. Shooting it twice at 800 is the same as exposing it once at 400. I'll leave it to the technical hotshots to figure out what ASA conversion factors to use for running the film through four or five times.

At the risk of confusing you, I'll mention a special case in which one uses the normal ASA speed for both runs of the film. Say I'm photographing black knotholes in trees (which I did) with the notion of later photographing faces to fit into the knotholes. Well, the black knotholes do nothing to the film at all: no light reflected from them, no exposure. If I photograph heads at 800 onto a part of the film that has no exposure at all, they will be one stop underexposed. So I photograph them at ASA 400, giving them normal exposure.

The same reasoning applies to the tree bark surrounding the black holes. If I photograph the heads against a black background, the bark will be one stop underexposed if I've been using ASA 800. You see, the black background is like the black knotholes in that no light comes from them.

Regarding exposure, do the same thing with color film that you do with black-and-white. Some fairly sophisticated

Calling this "The Armpit Inspector" amuses me greatly. It bares my psyche, I suppose, or encourages unconscious bad habits.

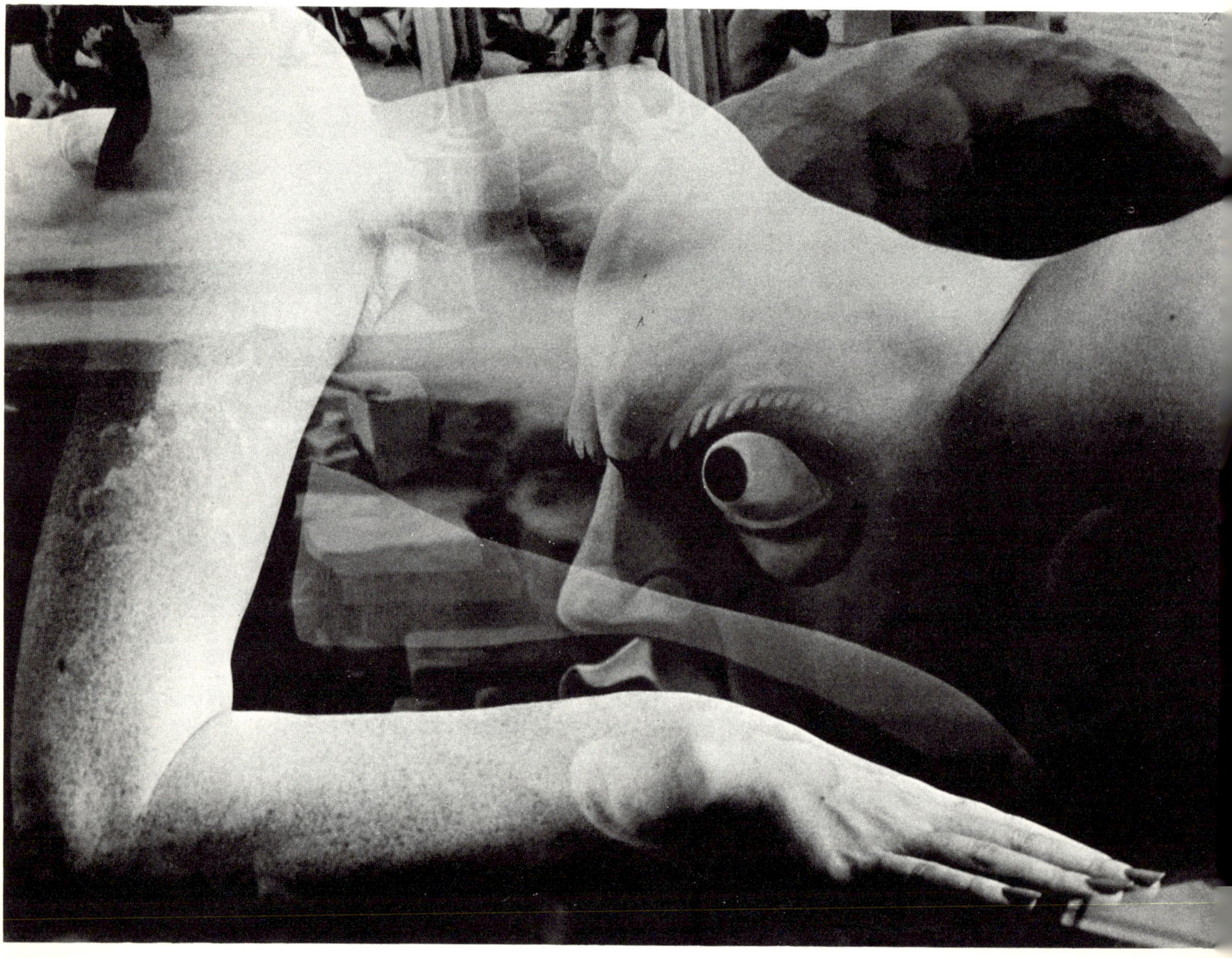

people may get their brains twisted out of joint by this information, but it is true, nonetheless. Beginners can just take my word for it, and go out and get great pictures.

There are several ways to approach this project. One is to make crude little sketches of each thing you shoot the first time you run the roll through. Number each frame as you shoot. Then, the second time you run the roll you'll know just what is being double-exposed onto what.

A more exciting and risky way is to make no effort at all to remember and just see what comes out. The fascinating thing here is that you'll discover that you can often get better pictures almost by accident than on purpose. Also, things you couldn't possibly discover with your head alone will pop up. I recommend this ap-

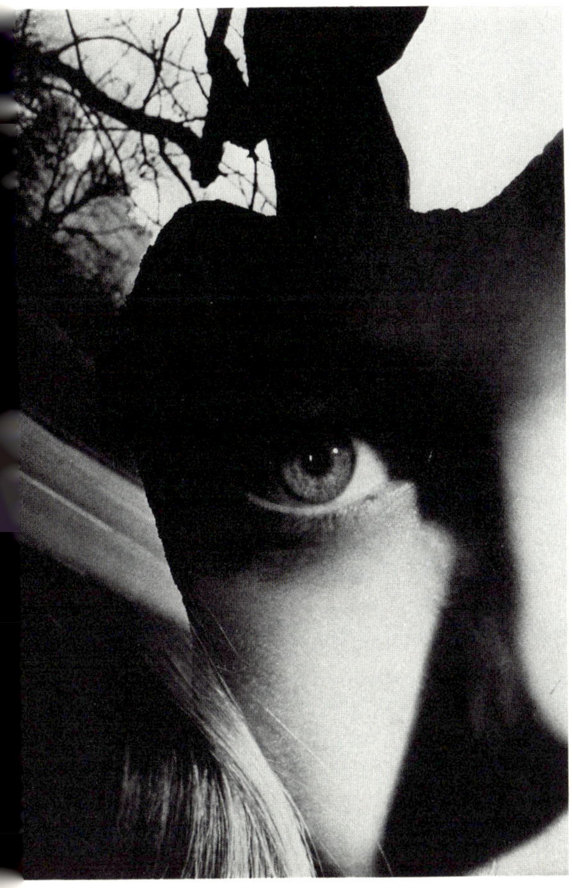

Since I made no effort to keep track of what I was shooting, I didn't expect to find an eye in a tree. To me, it implies that trees have intelligence and emotion of a sort.

Unconsciously, men like the notion of innocent nymphs, provided they can be the first to deprive them of their virginity. An idea typical of men.

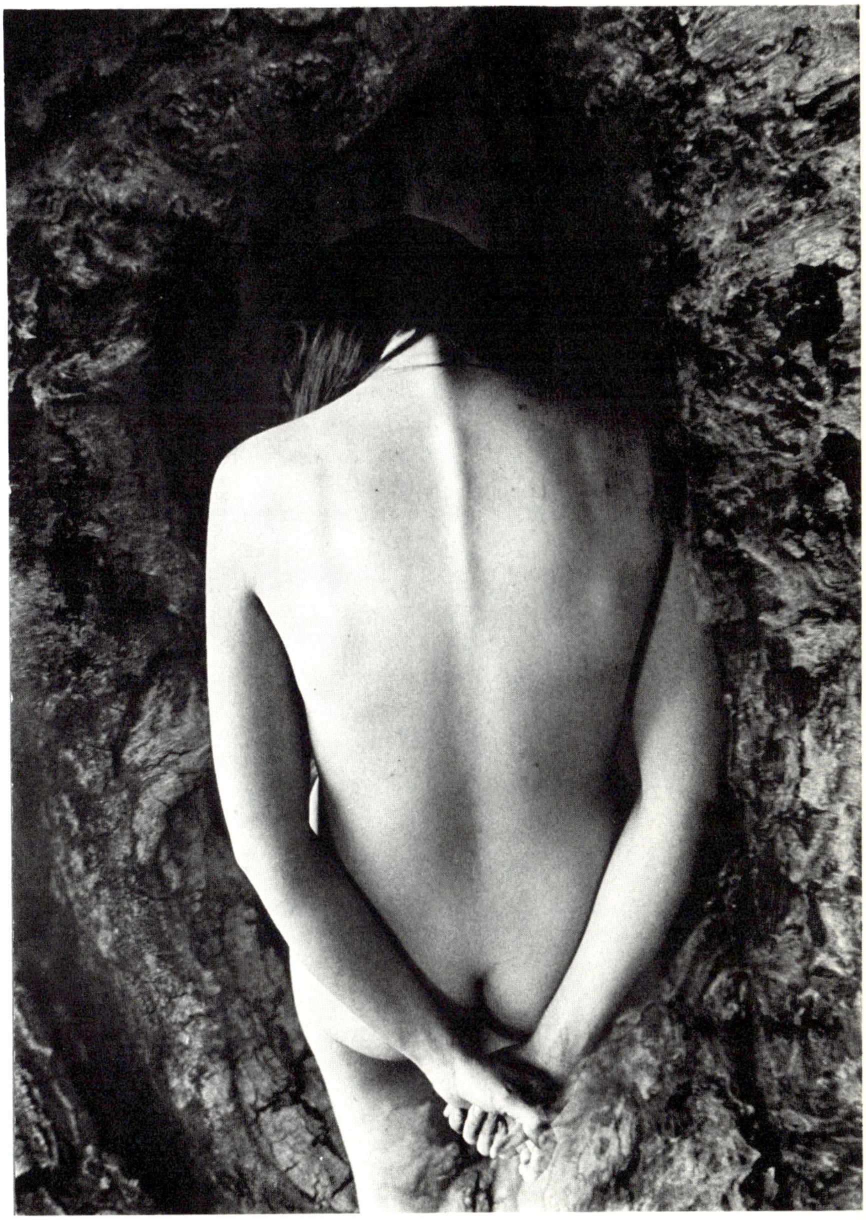

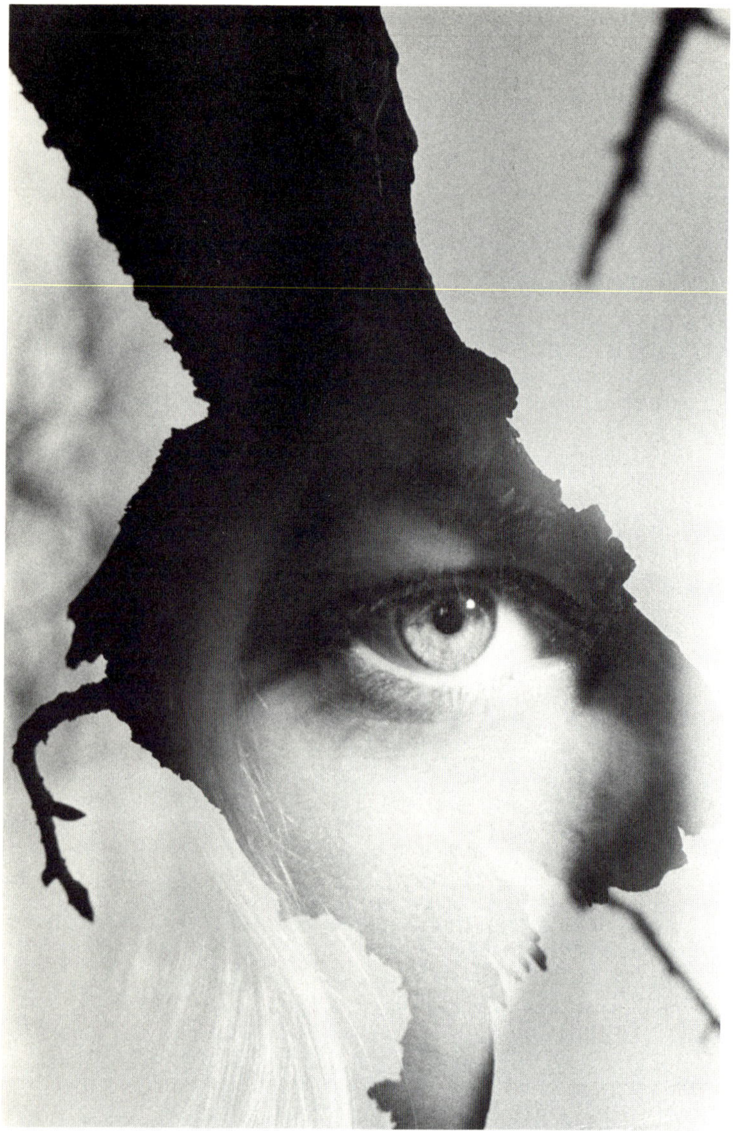

Another eye accidentally superimposed on a tree. The tree also looks like a crack in the sky, and a powerful female divinity is looking out.

proach to old-timers who've developed such control over the photographic medium that they are no longer able to surprise themselves. Such a person should shoot at least five rolls. With accident naturally being a large factor, shoot for the percentage. Two percent success is good, five percent exceptional. The note-takers will, of course, have a higher percentage, but not necessarily better pictures.

When you have a roll or three exposed once with bits and pieces of things at the art gallery, it's a fun thing to leave the gallery and see what you can find elsewhere to combine with them. In this case, the sky's the limit. Street scenes, members of your family, scenic views, store windows—you name it. I personally got the biggest kick out of rephotographing prints I'd already made or shooting pictures of friends and family. In the museum, I had my best luck with paintings, especially those with about equal amounts of light and dark. With sculptures I had indifferent luck, though some of my students have done well with them. Many of them found that with a little ingenuity in cropping, they could turn rather unlikely pictures into surprisingly good ones.

Nature Montages

In terms of photographic technique, this lesson is an extension of the Hattersley Museum one. It gives you more information on how to do roll-at-a-time double exposures without getting into technical difficulties.

In terms of what it will help you do in Self-discovery, it is a very different kind of thing. It gets you into the realm of your relationship to nature and natural forces. Since modern man has severed himself from his source, re-establishing the connection is very important for him. What his normal relation to nature is he can learn through the symbols he creates or discovers in his photographs.

The project also can get you into the important symbolic realm of anthropomorphism: man seeing things in nature as extensions of himself. If seen in the right way, anthropomorphism is a useful thing, for all created beings are truly our fellows

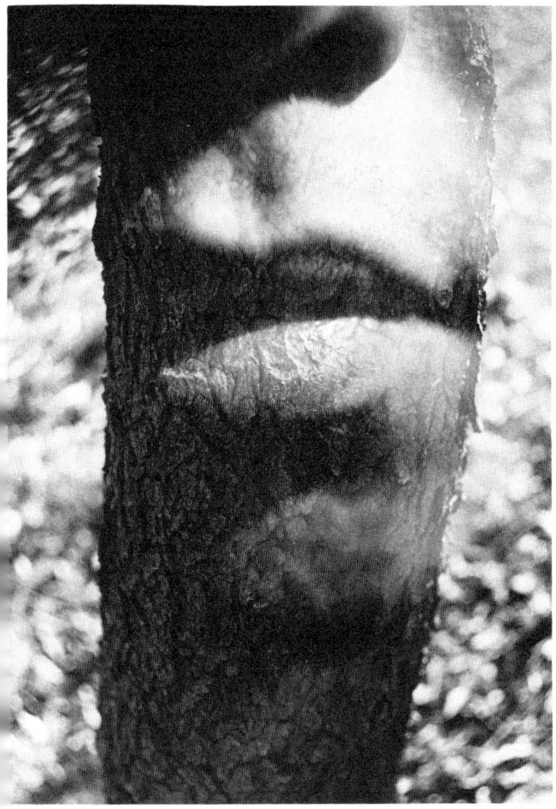

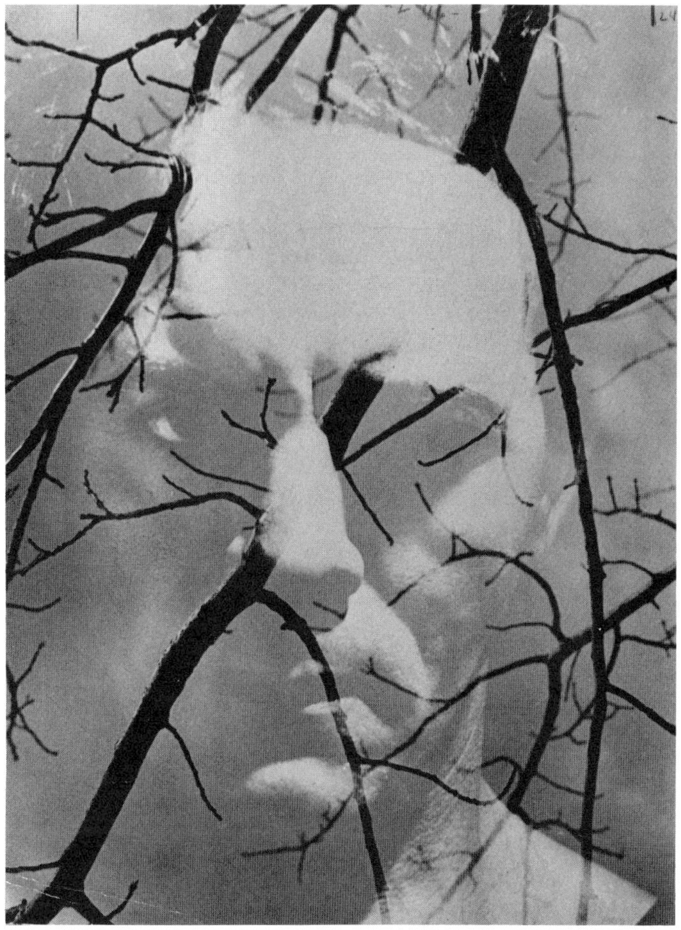

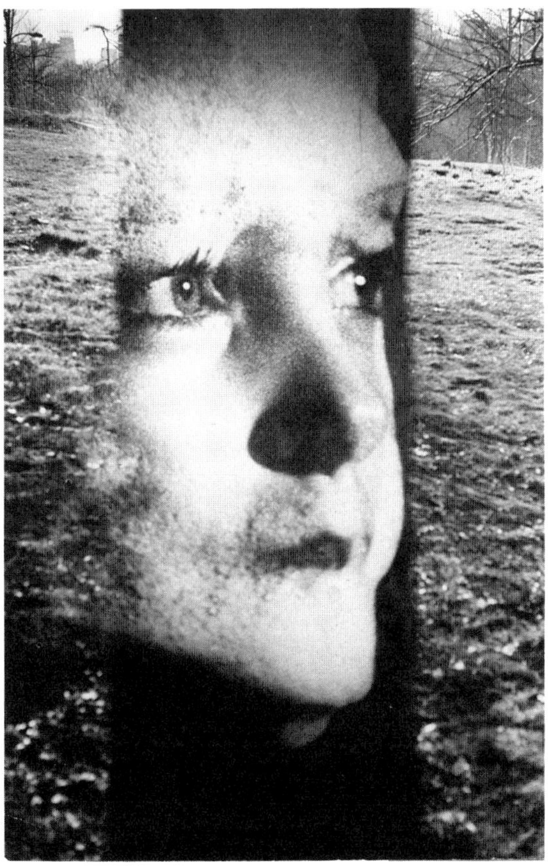

A tree with a mouth (top left) might tell secrets never heard before by Man. Perhaps their present silence is to protect us from the shock of knowing too much too soon. Is there a powerful malevolence (above) in some kinds of trees? If so, I'll take my vanishing powder on my camping trips. However, a tree may be like a serious child (left) who listens quietly and very thoughtfully to me.

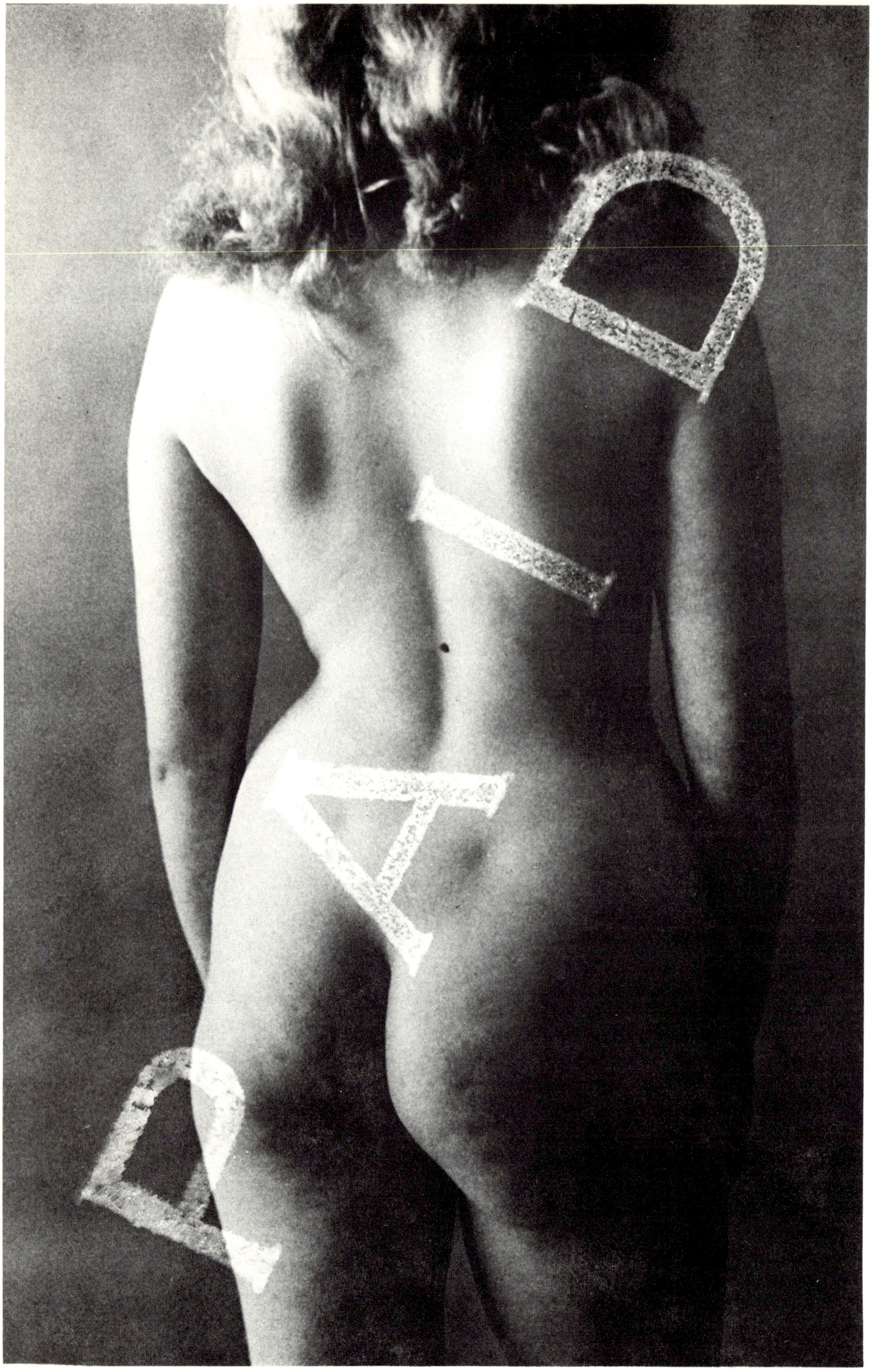

My "paid nude" always reminds me of a certain cosmic joke—that if you want a woman's love you have to pay for it by loving her in return. Few men will pay such an enormous price.

in one sense or another. It can be destructive, however, especially when it becomes an unconscious ego game whose object is to inflate man's self-importance. Since the anthropomorphizing tendency is undoubtedly in your blood, it would be a good thing for you to take its measure and see if you're using it well or badly.

Another useful thing about this approach is that when you see eyes and mouths speaking to you from rocks and trees it is easier to think that you may be getting communications from your Essence. Essence and nature are still one, while ego and nature are split far apart. Working with natural things will help you make a mystical attunement to yourself which might be very difficult to bring about in any other way. Some of the symbols which you'll uncover may be very close to your deepest Self.

The Lesson:

One of the grooviest things in photography is artificially combining natural forms and human forms in the same picture. Photographers have taken great glee in this for years. Something about it really turns them on—so let's find out what it is.

The traditional ways of doing this have been to sandwich together two or more negatives, then print them. Or to print first one negative on a sheet of printing paper, then print another on the same paper. These techniques—montage—work well and provide much excitement for the experimental photographer. However, there is a modern technique that is much faster and more adventurous.

The modern system involves re-exposing film that has already been through the camera. It works especially well with the 35-mm format. Photographers such as Pete Turner will often run one roll through as many as five times, each time superimposing different images on the previous ones, all this on Kodachrome II. My suggestion to the less skilled photographer is that he settle in the beginning for shooting each roll only twice. Pete Turner is, after all, one of the top color craftsmen in the business. Few can duplicate his artistry and technical competence.

The path of adventure is to make no effort whatsoever to keep track of what image is getting superimposed on what. Of course, one does miss a few shots that way. But the answer is to shoot a few more pictures than you ordinarily would and to bank on the percentages being on your side. You'll come up with graphic ideas that you wouldn't be able to think up without the random factor.

This random factor is, incidentally, something that many of the experiment-minded pros lean on heavily, since it is difficult for them to avoid repeating themselves. Thus, they'll go to no end of trouble to invent ways to introduce factors whose results they can't predict. This method becomes one of their main sources of ideas.

There are several parts to the solution of the "on-frame problem," the problem of negative overlap. One is to cock and fire the shutter of the empty camera immediately before loading. This insures that the take-up mechanism is not partly wound. If it is, you'll certainly get overlap when you run the film the next time.

Another step is to make sure that in loading the film you don't move the gears on the film take-up mechanism. This, too, would throw you off-frame.

Next is to cock the shutter and advance the film one frame while the camera back is still open. While doing this make sure that the gears on the take-up mechanism don't skip a sprocket hole. If they do, start again. Repeat this until you've seen for certain that a sprocket hole hasn't been skipped. Remember: Each time you reload, be sure that the camera has been fully cocked and make certain that the shutter has been released.

Now, close the camera back and take up two more frames. Here you may also have a problem with the take-up gears skipping a sprocket hole. If you hold your camera back to your ear while flipping the film take-up lever, you can hear if it skips. It makes a distinctive clicking sound, just what you'd expect from a gear picking at film but not engaging it neatly. If this happens, rewind the film until it is disengaged from the take-up mechanism, and start over again.

The photographer often can superimpose his own feelings on the subject. Such was the case here: the model was a gentle soul whom I made appear like Svengali. He didn't like the picture because it had nothing to do with his real personality. This untrue portrait resulted because I unknowingly projected my distress on him by the way I lighted his face.

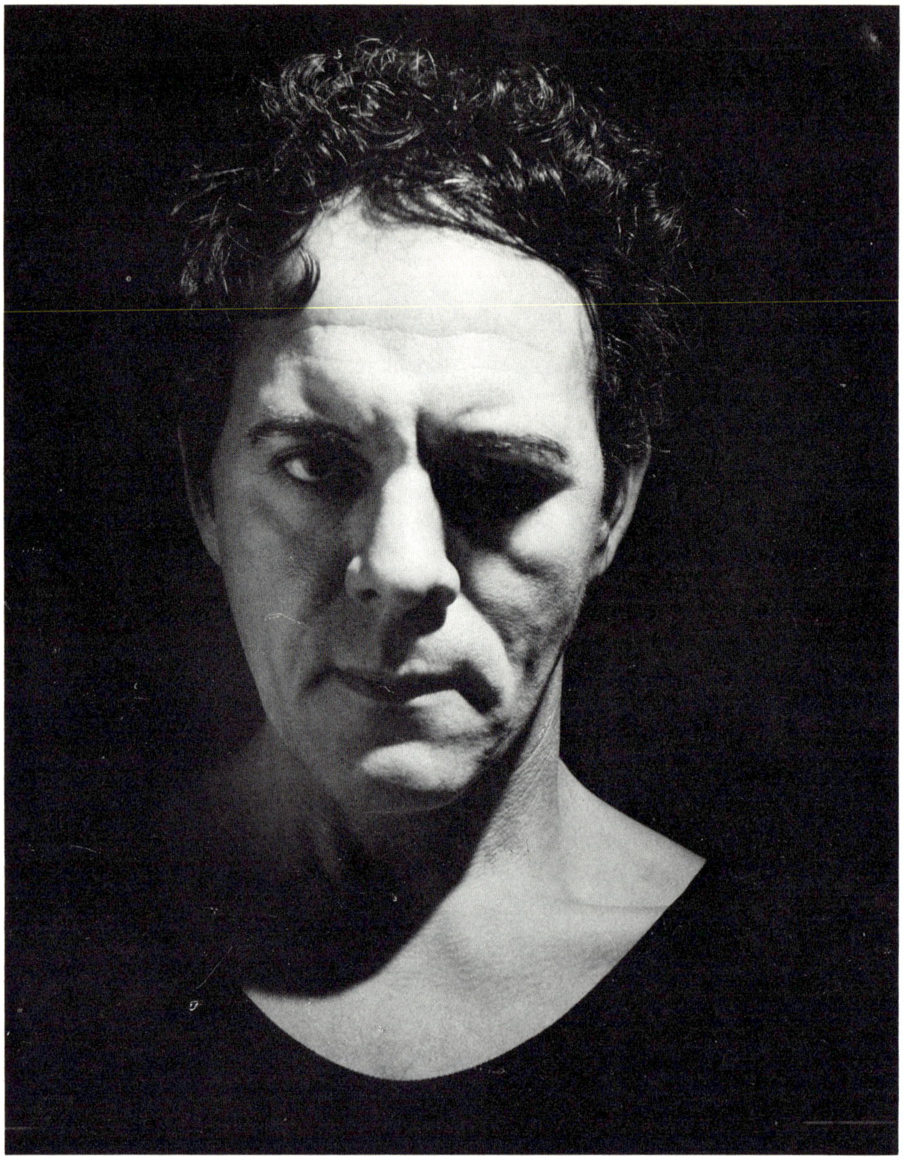

This sounds complicated, I know, but it really isn't. Once you get to know the quirks of the particular camera you use, it becomes easy.

A next crucial step will assure being on-frame each time the film is run through —if you do everything else as described. When the film is loaded the first time, but the film advance has not yet been wound even once, make a mark on the leader next to something in your camera back that easily strikes the eye.

This could be the edge of the rectangular orifice the film moves across in the camera back, a stud, etc. Better not make the mark of alignment across from a gear tooth, for, since it's a moving part, it may not be in the same place next time. For your marker, use one of the *indelible* type nylon tip pens. Marks from the non-indelible type rub off when the film is wound.

The next time you load the same roll, line the mark on the leader up with the stud, or whatever you've chosen as your guide. Then, when you've done the other things mentioned, you can be *certain* you're on-frame. You can run the roll through a hundred times and always have a correct alignment. (The fine points of this technique, by the way, come from Pete Turner.)

I suggest that the professional thing is to always load your film exactly this way if you think you may want to shift to

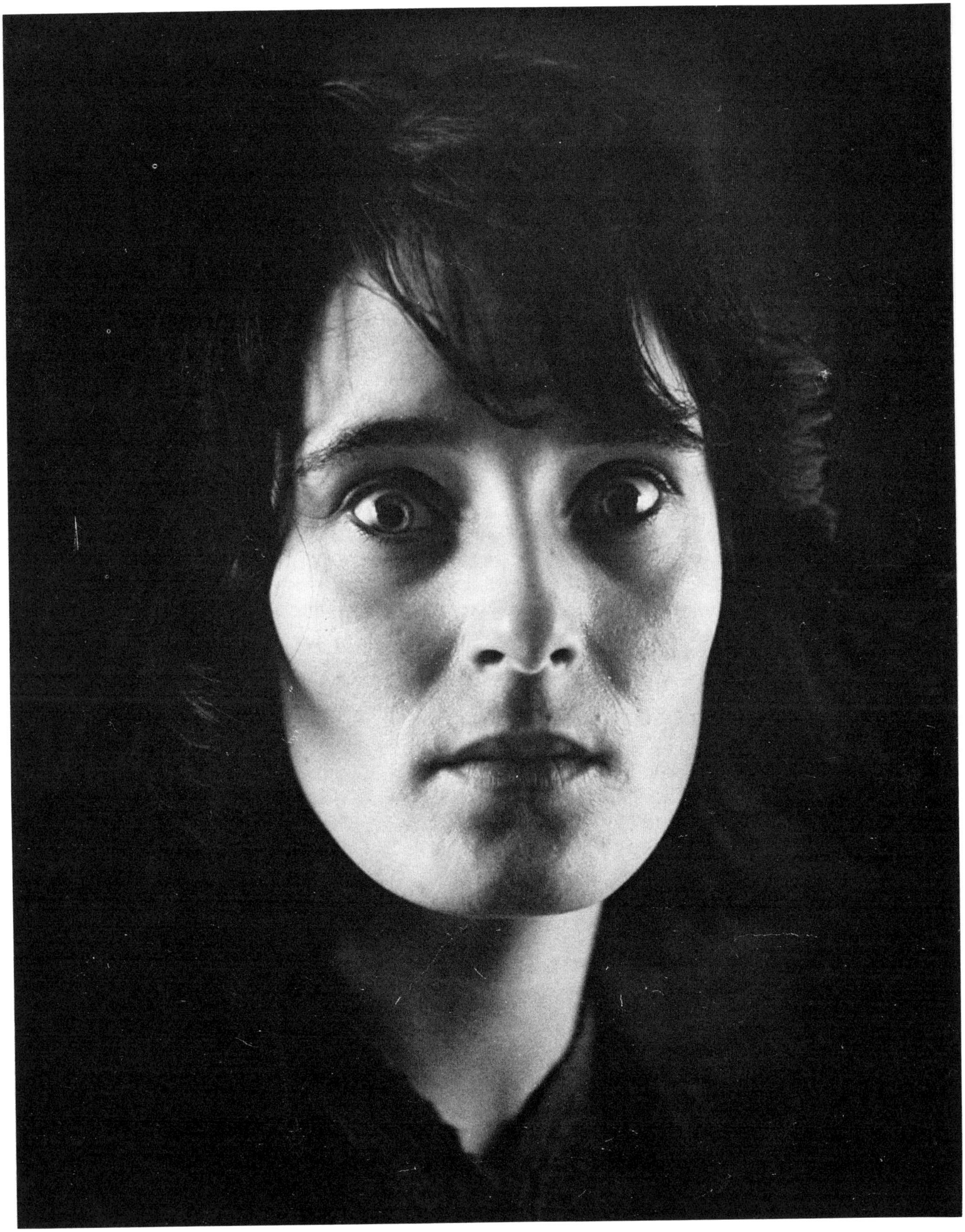

I created the despair in this picture by asking the model to stare with her eyes as wide open as possible. Then I contrived a lighting which would give the effect you see here. Looking back, I would say I had a power hang-up, wishing in my imagination to dominate a woman with terror and to tell clever lies with my picture.

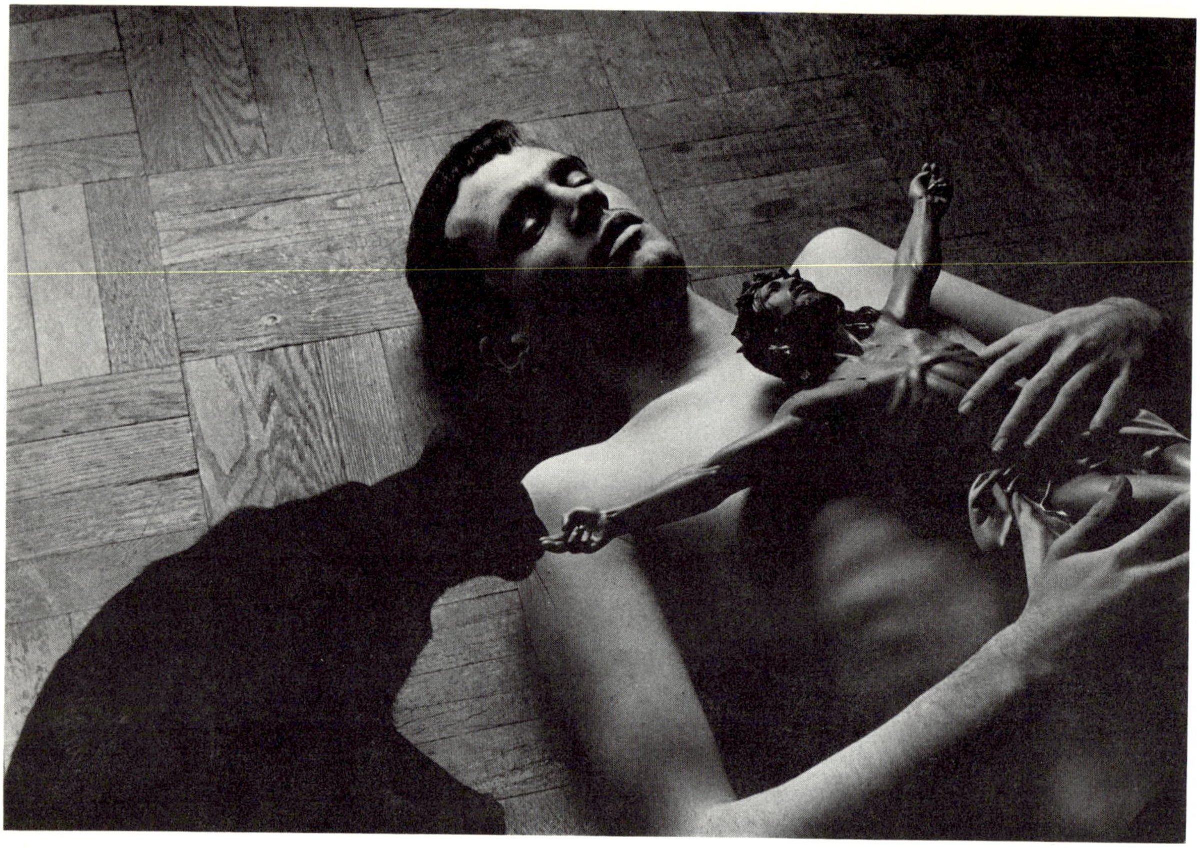

Several years ago, a monthly magazine of considerable prestige assigned me to photograph a Christmas theme in a controversial way. The editor's intention was to really shake up his readers. Tradition-bound religionists will find this picture disturbing, and I (then an agnostic) found it disturbing, too.

another type of film. Later, you can run the first roll through again and finish it off. All you have to do is wind it to the next unexposed frame.

To keep a record, stick a bunch of one-inch pieces of tan masking tape onto your camera case. When you remove a partly exposed roll, mark the next frame number on the tape, then stick it onto the roll. This easy recording device is very useful.

Some people have difficulty in rewinding only until the film leader just sticks out of the cassette. They rewind too far and lose it. And if they're using Kodak film, with the burglar-proof staked cartridge, their only recourse is to go into a darkroom, blast the cartridge apart, and reroll the film into a self-load cartridge.

Generally, you can tell when the rewound film has disengaged itself from the take-up mechanism by a distinct lessening of the tension it exerts against the rewind handle. This works most of the time, but not always, unfortunately.

Sometimes the film rerolls so limply and freely that you can't detect the relaxed tension. Here again, the answer is to listen. As the film pulls free from the take-up mechanism, it makes a distinctive little sound. (Of course, this wouldn't work if you're photographing folk rock in action.) I suggest that this is a project that can really turn you on—provided you like nature and people.

Find Yourself in Your Pictures

In this lesson I've taken some of my own pictures and told the readers of *Popular Photography* a few of the things I've learned from them. In a way, this lesson is a condensed version of this entire chapter. You'll be interested in how I interpreted the pictures. You'll also get some more information on the person who is writing this book. If you see him accurately the book will be a good deal more useful to you than it would be otherwise.

The Lesson:

The great cry of the contemporary artist is, "Express yourself!" It rings loudly throughout the land and nearly everyone agrees that it's important. However noble it sounds to modern ears, it's only half a formula. The vital missing part should read, "and do your best to decipher the meaning of what you've expressed." The object is Self-understanding.

For an artist to project himself into his art doesn't guarantee he'll understand in the least what he's said about himself. Truly, a substantial understanding is the rare exception rather than the rule. The majority of people don't seem to care. All over the country, people are making pictures and not paying the slightest attention to what the photographs could tell them about themselves.

Self-expression for its own sake has its place in photography. When people first get involved in making pictures, they find that for a year or two they can express their feelings and at the same time avoid understanding what they are. Some, indeed, can do it for years. More power to them! May they long enjoy their fictional happiness!

Serious photographers, however, find that a preoccupation with photography is more often a kind of suffering, rather than fun. The reason may be that, intentionally or not, they're using it in searching for themselves—a process that takes years!

It is a bitter fact that what we initially discover about ourselves on the long journey toward self-completion is very upsetting. We just don't measure up the way we think we ought to. Often, we suspect we're even horrible as human beings. Naturally, we are strongly inclined to turn away, which means giving up photography if we've inadvertently used it for Self-discovery and analyzing our motivation.

But turning away from the Self is the saddest mistake that man can make. It can change a person into a zombie by his mid-thirties. He must run away from himself now and then—no doubt of that. But he should return to the attack as soon as he has the strength. The alternative, zombie-ism, is terrifying to contemplate.

The pictures with this lesson are mine. I don't know if they're good or bad and don't really care. I like them for what they tell me about myself. Nothing flattering, I assure you, but useful. Some of the things I discovered might help you in your own search for Self. It is sometimes said that Self-discovery is the foundation on which all virtue is built.

I wouldn't say that my experience in photography has made me gloriously happy. As far as I could see in the beginning, it was only an intermittent compulsion, one among many. I think I've given it up for good as often as anyone in the U.S. Every now and then I'd get really interested in it, enjoy it for awhile, then automatically use it to punch myself squarely on the jaw. Somehow, I would always make pictures that would tell me something about myself—usually much more than I actually wanted to know.

Oh, I wanted to know—everybody does—but I also wanted to bury it safely six feet under. Through the years I've gradually and painfully come to understand why they inscribed on the temple of the famous Delphic Oracle the words, "Know Thyself." It was the greatest and most worthwhile challenge the brilliant Greek mind could conceive.

But it's such a *rotten* row to hoe! What one discovers is so *crude!* Unconsciously, I was using photography to know my Self. Can you wonder it didn't make me particularly happy? In looking back, however, I'm grateful for every bit of Self-informative misery it brought me.

In describing it now, I'm unable to communicate the original emotional impact of my pictures on me, for I'm writing about water long ago gone over the dam. If you assume that everything I mention really jarred me, you'll get the general feeling. It should give you faith in your own pursuit of Self to realize that the things that shatter a person are really very mundane, after all. What one sees as monstrous in the beginning, he later comprehends as childish or merely human, on reaching maturity.

The other day I met a young woman who said, "Gee, you're not really a monster after all!" She'd seen my picture, "Paid," and then decided its maker must be the prime male creep of the universe. No wonder. It's as rotten as a picture can be and an insult to all womankind.

I see it as a friendly warning, reminding me of my youthful, unconscious contempt for women and the heavy price I paid for it. I suspect that my liking it might indicate that the inclination to be contemptuous is still there. It's good to remember things, for if a man can't recall his mistakes, he's doomed to repeat them.

On the other hand, I deeply enjoy paying women back for "all they've done to me"—making me spend half my life thinking only of sex, refusing to let me understand them without making an effort, being unwilling to give me undying love without my earning it, dragging their heels when I tried to turn them into mother substitutes, outshining my male logic with female intuition. Most of all by merely existing they've confronted me with a side of myself—the female—that I feared for many years.

Women haven't done these things to me, of course; they were all in my head. Nonetheless, I enjoy getting revenge for crimes not really committed against me. This is usually the nature of vengeance, isn't it?

But stamping 'paid' across a woman is also very realistic, for even the best one has her price. It is love. Since I've had very little love to give, I've had to compensate by endlessly and often hopelessly struggling against what stands in love's way: my boundless self-centeredness. And that's a heavy price to pay for a woman's regard! I've spent most of my life's energy fighting my own ego without making perceptible progress. But a woman is worth it, I've finally learned.

When I made "Despair" (the portrait of a girl) 10 years ago, I was very concerned with proving that photography is a powerful medium for telling lies. I still think it's important for everyone to understand this. Unless we do, we become the victims of every clever, lying photographer—and there are plenty of them around.

When the picture was made, the model (a good friend of mine) was horsing around, making funny faces for my camera. I adjusted the lighting and asked her to take this pose. Then I told her to hold her facial muscles still and at the same time pop her eyes wide open. I expected to get the effect of a woman staring into the abyss. I believe the picture proves my contention that a photograph can tell a powerful lie. Even my model hadn't the slightest idea of the effect I was trying to get and its purpose.

But is it *really* a lie? Nowadays, I very much doubt it. I suspect that circumstances combined in such a way that Ann Lawrence was able to let something from her deepest self come through and show itself to the world. Her face shows the plight of all lost souls. And the rest of us are her spiritually lost sisters and brothers.

If this picture is indeed a truth, it shows that a deliberate liar will sometimes tell the truth in spite of himself.

Occasionally I've used photography to attack things I don't respect in people. A kind of strong-arm, amateur psychotherapy. I've naively assumed it might accomplish something, though it probably doesn't. The idea in my picture, "Christ and Friends," is to needle the kind of narrow pietism that insists that Christ be jailed in a church and kept well out of human reach. For a pietist to see Christ on a young man's bare chest being sniffed by a cat—a black one at that—ought to bring on convulsions.

My idea is that the drama of experiencing an apoplectic attack might possibly help him see there is something irrational about his anger. Christ, after all, said "Love one another," and he certainly didn't exclude beasts and bare-chested men. The irrational anger that is under attack is one of love's greatest enemies.

When I shot this picture, one of a series, I was more concerned (I thought) with saying something sensible about the

Christ than with actually trying to learn something about Him. This is a common failing of the spiritually ignorant. Later events in my life have indicated that in shooting the pictures, I was probably trying to tell myself my life would improve greatly if I would try to understand and practice Christ's way, as shown in His teachings.

Eventually, I got the message. For several years now, religion has been my main field of study. And my life *has* improved tremendously. This shows that one can sometimes learn things from his own pictures that give him hope rather than merely shake him up without subsequent benefit.

When I first saw the man whose portrait I titled, "Oedipus," his face really turned me on, though I didn't discover why for years. When I did, it shook me to the core. To my amazement, I learned he has *my* face, the one I should have had instead of the one I got.

Furthermore, I discovered I'd used the photographic art to draw a lethally accurate self-portrait on it. Though the notion of a photographer using other men's faces to make self-portraits is now old stuff to me, in earlier days it had never even crossed my mind. I just can't describe how rudely I was shaken by my awakening.

Then there was the title I'd given it: Oedipus. That, too, was autobiographical. As a poet friend of mine once expressed the idea:

Do not think I'm overjoyed
To learn I'm something out of Freud.

To read about the Oedipal conflict in textbooks on psychoanalysis is one thing, but to learn you're living it is something else. It ain't fun.

The way I handled my subject gave him an intense appearance of self-centeredness and highly romanticized agony. I assure you it was my treatment, not the man himself. He himself was very gentle and sweet. That I should use photography to manhandle him so terribly is indicative of something else: my total unwillingness to make pictures for anything but my own selfish purposes.

I could have made a picture he would like and knew fairly well what it would be —certainly not this one. However, I completely overrode his reasonable desires and used him mercilessly as a canvas on which to paint my own sad story.

When the picture was finished, I really dug it, which is a sign of its great accuracy concerning my inward state. The fact that I still like it very much could indicate I haven't changed much. Unhappy thought, but here it is for all to see and consider.

I've shown you some of the kinds of things a person can learn about himself through his pictures. From each of the ones discussed, I've learned much more than I had space to write about. In this lesson, I won't try to give you an easy, ready-made formula for pictorial Self-analysis.

The first and most important step is to accept the fact that it is possible. Once you've convinced yourself that your own photographs may be symbolic mirrors of yourself, you can probably work out a method of approach to the idea on your own.

FIGHT your way out of the bag

Using photography to help you overcome cultural and self-conditioning. Using it to discover and confront your fears.

In common with humor and folk wisdom, slang has a way of illuminating unpleasant truths in such a way that we can both understand them better and learn to accept them. Such is the case with the slang expression 'my bag.' The various ways in which it is used point to the fact that people have become robots. Let us therefore start this chapter by listening to how the term is used by two youths, Pete and Phil:

"Hi, Pete, what's your bag today? You're sure uptight about something!"

"Dunno, Phil. Who knows his own bag? Last week I was sure I'd got out of the bag, but now I find I'm in another."

It is fairly obvious here that to be 'in a bag' means to be imprisoned in some way and that the person thus imprisoned is in the dark concerning what kind of prison it is and how he got there. All he knows is that he has lost his freedom and that his desperate efforts to escape don't lead to the outside but to some other part of the prison compound, another 'bag.'

6

Though the terminology is new, the phenomenon it attempts to describe is as old as the history of mankind. In various ages there have been different names for it. The terms which make the most sense to literate, modern Americans are: to be identified, attached, conditioned, or programmed. The same idea is expressed in the slang term 'being hung up on' something and in the old saw that "Men are creatures of habit." In this chapter we will use mainly the terms 'conditioning' and 'conditioning systems.'

Though this choice of terms seems to lean toward Pavlovian, or behaviorist, psychology I don't want it to imply also that I accept Pavlovian psychology as it stands. It has its points but has also made grievous errors, among which is the suggestion that the forces which condition a person work only from outside him. There are many such forces in any culture, of course, but the most destructive force is self-conditioning, which can be talked about best in Freudian terms. In Freudian psychology a conditioning system is an ego defense system and the various mechanisms which make it operable are called ego defense mechanisms. Neither of these psychologies sees the seriousness of the problem, however, and that the ego is the chief culprit. To talk about it at what I think is a reasonable level I will use notions which are primarily Sufistic. In a sense, Sufism is a higher psychology, though Sufis don't ordinarily use this term to describe it.

As the Sufis see it, our problem is that we've all become machines, or robots. They mean this in a very literal sense. We've split our minds into two parts, conscious and unconscious, so that by far the greatest part of our mental force is no longer accessible to us. We're no longer awake, even when we're sure we are. What we call consciousness is merely a form of sleep, waking sleep. In terms of true awareness of reality it is inferior to what we ordinarily refer to as sleep.

We now have another synonym: sleep. To be conditioned means to be asleep, and fighting our conditioning means trying to wake up. Thus this chapter is concerned with the use of photography as a means for awakening oneself. If you would like still another term for this, try Enlightenment, for it means the very same thing. If you are Enlightened you are Awake. Buddha, the great exemplar of Enlightenment, was thus the Awakened, De-conditioned, Non-attached, Non-identified one. He had fought his way out of all of his bags.

Discovering That You Are Conditioned, or Asleep

One of man's most difficult problems related to escaping successfully the prison of conditioning is to convince himself he is actually in prison. If he doesn't believe that he is, he will make no effort to escape. Stated in another way, if he doesn't know he's asleep, he'll not try to wake up. The fact that all the people around him are also asleep makes his problem even more difficult. In his eyes they seem to be quite awake, and he's awake in theirs. Therefore, he and the people around him support one another in believing in the illusion of consciousness.

For various reasons, people sometimes escape their conditioning and wake up for a short time. The change is often so dramatic that they know they are awake for the first time; and the people around them even look like sleepwalkers to them. Though they once again fall captive to their conditioning they may remember enough about the state of real Consciousness to dimly comprehend that there is something wrong with them. Some of the things which may cause temporary Consciousness (or a very good imitation of it) are extreme fatigue, near starvation, psychosis, certain drugs and severe emotional or physical trauma.

The only psychosis I can discuss with any authority is manic-depression. In the state called euphoric mania a person may escape his conditioning, sometimes for weeks or even months at a time. However, this escape is not always complete nor is it a necessary concomitant of mania. After experiencing Consciousness for quite a while the manic begins to realize he's awake and everyone else asleep. However, this state is followed by others so distressing that he is terrified and blocks out all memory of the wakened state because he associates it with madness.

People who experience extreme fatigue fairly often find that at a point far beyond what they've conceived to be their limit of endurance they cut into another source of energy they didn't even know they had. If they push themselves even further, they may wake up for a while, perhaps for a few minutes or hours. Since they don't stay de-conditioned for long they usually forget what they've experienced after returning to 'normal' waking sleep.

People who momentarily escape their conditioning due to severe trauma may be genuinely awake for awhile. However, when they return to 'normal' they associate their Consciousness with their distress and usually convince themselves, with the help of friends, that what they experienced while de-conditioned was some form of insanity. Naturally, they will either block out memory of the state or become extremely reluctant to make any attempts to return to it, for who wants to deliberately drive himself crazy?

Certain drugs such as LSD, peyote, hallucinogenic mushrooms and even hashish will sometimes temporarily cancel out or sidetrack conditioning systems and induce the Conscious state or, more likely, a close simulacrum of it. Again, the state is temporary and memory of it either flees entirely or rapidly becomes hazy.

In addition to their temporary nature another characteristic of these means of outwitting conditioning is that they all involve severe deprivation of some kind. That is, certain neural channels or systems are blocked off or temporarily put out of commission by being drugged, starved or incapacitated with psychic poisons (terror, implacable anger, psychotic certainty, and such). The awakening they induce is, therefore, much more likely to be a simulacrum (though perhaps a very good one) than the real thing. However, they do give people hope that there may be such a thing as awakening and that it is at least a possibility for them if they can manage to remember, however vaguely, what they experience in such states.

Since the majority of people don't permit themselves to go through such experiences, they have no notion either that they are normally in the state of wakened sleep or that such a thing as real Consciousness is even possible. In fact they think they are already Conscious. Other ways to a truer form of Consciousness, e.g. Yoga or Zen, invariably involve so many long years of extremely rigorous self-discipline that most people can't find the strength to get properly started in them. The result of all this is that few people even suspect they are asleep, though almost all of them are. Unaware they're asleep, they ignore or ridicule efforts to help them awaken.

A Chapter For Fools and Maniacs

For the reasons just given there is no chance whatsoever that so-called 'normal' people will really understand what this chapter is basically all about. As they see it, asking them to awaken is the height of absurdity, for they are already awake. Telling them to escape the prison of conditioning is equally absurd, for they're certain they're not in one. In these circumstances the natural question is why include such a chapter at all? My answer: for the people the 'normals' call fools and maniacs.

These are the very people for whom sanity (another synonym for Consciousness) is actually a possibility, while for the normals it is not, in this lifetime. These potentially sane beings need people to help them understand what they are experiencing in life. In this group we find a few people of all ages. Today we're finding more and more of our youth in it, e.g. hippies and members of the rapidly expanding drug sub-culture. Though many of them should be classified as the potentially sane they should also be seen as those who could just as easily lose themselves beyond redemption. The things that they are experimenting with can be dangerous beyond imagination, and not just in areas involving genetics. Because they have experienced partial awakening, or good imitations of it, they need guidance lest they throw their opportunities away and create for themselves long years of needless suffering.

Conditioning Systems

To be conditioned is somewhat like being a computer which has been programmed. Once programmed, the computer can only do what its program permits it to when the activating button has been pushed. A human being is like an immensely complex computer, or a complex system of interrelated computers. Unlike a computer, he can be programmed in literally hundreds of different ways. It can happen accidentally and without his knowledge it is happening. He can be programmed, or program himself, for hundreds of different programs.

We can call a given program a conditioning system. Unless man consciously and constantly fights programming, or conditioning, it goes on all the time throughout his being, even in his sleep. That is, programs are constantly being fed into him. Even worse, he is constantly programming himself; one of the chief culprits in this is his ego. However, there are others, including his body itself, which is prone to develop habits. Habits are conditioning. Everything that enters man's system through his five senses can contribute to programming unless he takes steps to prevent or counteract it. Unless he's aware it is happening it will not even occur to him to do anything about it.

It is not quite accurate to say that everything affecting the five senses will contribute to conditioning. Two necessary factors are pattern and the duration of sensory stimuli. If a stimulus has a definite pattern which endures, repeats itself over and over again for a considerable period of time, it will cause some degree of conditioning. We must also consider the strength of the stimulus and the human organism's relative susceptibility to it. To explain what happens, it is best to turn to music, a powerful conditioning force. Though visual conditioning may be even more powerful, it is very difficult to explain.

Young folk nowadays are doing a very effective job of conditioning themselves through their own music. It's hard to tell what the consequences will be. They will certainly be bad, perhaps disastrous, for conditioning of any kind is imprisonment which lessens a human being's possibilities for psychic growth.

We'll examine how the youngsters program themselves by using, say, a Beatles album. In each song and in the album as a whole we have the pattern element. The fact that the kids play it over and over again furnishes the duration component. The human organism is strongly susceptible both to music as such and to musical conditioning. We must note the fact that the Beatles are a very powerful stimulus for young folk. They and their musical cousins have provided the material which an entire generation has used to condition itself. Another important factor in this is that the youngsters welcome conditioned behavior in themselves and interpret it as being 'with it.'

When a conditioning system builds up in a human being, his responses to outward and inward stimuli are automated. When he perceives a sensory pattern analogous to the one responsible for his conditioning his response to it is conditioned, or automated. Described in this way the situation seems relatively harmless. But the response pattern frequently develops an independent life of its own, which is not so good. If a person receives just a small fragment of a familiar stimulus pattern an entire response sequence may be activated.

The dedicated (thoroughly programmed) Beatles fan hears just four bars of "Lucy in the Sky With Diamonds." It may set off in him a conditioned response pattern which goes on for hours or even days. The 'victim' can do nothing about it for it is now beyond both his control and his conscious awareness. He is only a programmed computer that has had one of its buttons pushed. Another way of saying it is that he has gotten himself into a bag, or partially robotized himself.

If stimulus and response systems had a simple, one-to-one relationship, things wouldn't be so terribly bad. However, the human organism has the habit of cross-connecting stimulus-response systems. Learning 'who is doing what to whom' within oneself gets to be a problem of majestic proportions. This is part of the meaning of jumping out of one bag into another. A person intuits that he's imprisoned in a conditioning system and tries to fight his way out. For a while he thinks he has made it, only to soon discover he's face-to-face with another wall of his prison. He often interprets this as being in an altogether different prison, or bag. Due to cross-connections, all bags are one bag.

Conditioning systems originate from both outside a person and inside him. Consider for a moment those originating on the outside. It is a well-known fact that a large number of people and organizations have a vested interest in trying to condition others. Governments, for example, condition people to be nationalists. Teachers condition pupils to what is mis-labeled education. Parents condition children to fit them into the form of group insanity which is called society. Manufacturers condition people to desire things they neither want nor need. These are some of the more obvious conditioning forces, but there are others much more subtle and sinister. I've already mentioned music. Language is an immensely powerful conditioning force. Visual languages, especially photography, are in some ways even more powerful. Culture as such is a conditioning force.

When we take it all apart, we discover to our dismay that nearly every artifact created by the hand of man is in one sense or another a force for human conditioning. Even more disheartening is that much of this is intentional, though sometimes well meant, and that it is deeply injurious to the Self.

Self-conditioning

Though conditioning by forces outside oneself is a very serious problem, self-conditioning is worse by a large order of magnitude. It is also done by a force outside of the Self proper: the ego. In the last chapter I talked about the ego and suggested calling it the wolf. I said that it steals most of the accessible energy of the human organism and converts it into constantly reiterated unconscious lies which are used to hold forbidden thoughts in bondage in the unconscious ego. These are not isolated thoughts, however, nor are the lies isolated. There are whole systems of thoughts paired with the lies which imprison them, and systems within systems within systems. Furthermore, they are in constant flux as the thoughts and lies undergo modification.

Using Freudian terminology we could call each lie-thought system an ego defense system and the entire contents of the unconscious ego (all the systems taken together) as *the* ego defense system. The ego defends itself against its own unconscious thoughts. My concept of the unconscious ego is not Freudian, incidentally, for it fixes responsibility for man's problems on himself and doesn't see the mind as merely a *tabula rasa* on which a mindless and directionless universe programs its accidental perversities.

Shifting to Pavlovian terminology (but not Pavlovian psychology and materialism) we can call each thought-lie system a conditioned (or conditional) response system, a stimulus-response system or just a conditioning system. Thus we could call the contents of the unconscious ego as a whole a complex of conditioning systems. Perhaps modern Americans can make more sense out of what I'm trying to say if I call the unconscious ego a vast, unconscious repository of computer programs which the ego has fed into the psyche in order to maintain its domination over it. In other words, our egos rule us by turning us into machines. If we can free our Selves we become human again.

We've now come to the point where I can give a brief description of some of the things which happen in the real conscious (awakened, enlightened, de-programmed, de-conditioned, non-identified, non-attached) state, or in other states which resemble it but which are not genuine. Since I'm writing this chapter especially for the fools and maniacs who have experienced these real or surrogate states of true Consciousness, I will use a kind of verbal shorthand. However, I will do my best to sound coherent to suspicious normals too, though my prospects for this aren't very hopeful.

Some Characteristics of Consciousness

In this section I will discuss characteristics of partial consciousness, not the real thing. I'm in no sense qualified to talk about the latter. Those who are say that language is entirely inadequate for describing what it is really like. I will also mention only very commonplace experiences, those which my fools and maniacs have probably had.

When one enters the partially conscious state or a good imitation of it the following things are very likely to happen:
1. The ego releases energy bound up in unconscious lie systems. There is a tremendous flow of energy, which may cause a feeling of divine peace or euphoria. This is usually apprehended as a non-ego state.
2. Habits (conditioning) entirely disap-

pear. When they leave we apprehend for the first time how many thousands of habits we have and how we've desperately clung to them.

3. There is a blessed relief from ego-suffering (experienced usually in the solar plexus or one of the endocrine glands). For the first time we are fully aware of how much we've been suffering all along.

4. The various brain systems in the body come into perfect coordination. With this comes perfect bodily grace and the delightful apprehension that one has it.

5. Our perception of time is radically altered. We sense that our minds are working more leisurely than usual yet know that they are immensely speeded up. The faster the mind goes the more leisurely it seems to become. With its increased speed time slows down, until it comes to a halt altogether. While the minute hand on the clock stands still the mind races slowly through an eternity.

6. The nature of sleep changes entirely. If our awakened hours are true Consciousness of a sort, sleep is an even higher form of it. It is no longer automatic but in control of the will and is devoted to a kind of thinking and experiencing eons beyond our normal capacity. Awakeness and sleep are a continuity; and one passes back and forth between the two states without losing threads of thought.

7. Fear entirely disappears. When this happens the spinal brain relinquishes control over our reflex nervous system and all formerly automatic responses to outside stimuli come under the control of the will. Whether we react to a stimulus, however abrupt, strong or unexpected, becomes a matter of Conscious choice.

8. Released from the control of conditioning systems, our perceptual systems begin to operate in radically new ways, usually moving into the ESP realm. For example, we may develop vision which permits us to greatly magnify or shrink things at will, smell emotions or sickness in other people, hear what they are thinking and so on.

I'm going to stop here. As any of my fools and maniacs can tell you, this is not the half of it. However, this section has served its purpose, which is to let some people know that I realize where their heads are at, and to give them some basis for deciding whether to take the advice which follows. For normals my purpose is to implant the suggestion that things are not necessarily what they seem to be and that the drug sub-culture children are reaching for things their parents may not understand. They will not easily be persuaded to stop.

For all readers, the section is a very brief sketch of what it is like to discover one's Self. To say that one is Conscious, or deconditioned, is the same thing as saying he has discovered his Self. Since this book is about Self-discovery, the reader may wonder why I don't expand on my sketch. The reason is simple: no one would believe me.

The Opportunities and Burdens of Temporary Consciousness

Temporary Consciousness, whatever be its cause, is a gift from Above of the highest order. It also saddles one with a terrible burden which can as easily lead him to total ruin as to permanent Consciousness. The spiritual law involved can be expressed thus: The higher the opportunity the greater the danger.

The experience of Consciousness, or a close imitation, gives a person the following spiritual opportunities: It helps him see his ego objectively (see it as an object which is distinct from the Self). It awakens him to the severity of his everyday suffering and the fact it is nearly constant except when he's asleep. It helps him see that it is his ego which suffers, not his Self. It makes him aware of the intensity of his fear and the fact that his whole being is literally riddled with it. And it helps him comprehend that selfishness, or egotism, is the sole source of this fear.

A person ordinarily learns about these things in their full dimension only when they temporarily disappear altogether, as happens during temporary deconditioned, or awakened, states. If he's lucky he doesn't forget them again when he slips back into ordinary consciousness, or waking sleep. However, he seldom sees this as an opportunity but as one of the worst things which could possibly happen to him. He therefore does everything he can think of to get back into ecstatic states to escape his fear, suffering and inescapable selfishness. This terrible desire to escape, usually by means of drugs, is the great danger. If he succumbs to it he may waste his life and squander opportunities that even saints pray to have.

To take advantage of these spiritual opportunities a person must be aware of the fact that his suffering is caused by selfishness. Very often he doesn't have to be told, because events in his own life lead him to this conclusion. For records of how various people have figured this out for themselves you might try reading several books: *Varieties of Religious Experience,* by William James; *Mysticism,* by Evelyn Underhill; *Ascent to Mount Carmel* and *The Dark Night of the Soul,* by St. John of the Cross. These are profound books by people who know what they're talking about.

If you understand the relation between egotism, or selfishness, and suffering you can construct very accurate guidelines which will help you detect all your spiritual mistakes and help you decide how to overcome them. It helps if you know that every bit of ego suffering indicates certain very important things: Your Self-imprisoning conditioning systems are being attacked; energy is being taken away from the ego and made available to the Self; you are putting yourself on the Way which leads to permanent Consciousness.

We will now turn to the lessons and lesson introductions. There I will try to show you how to act on this information in a safe and effective way.

Hate It? Shoot It!

For many years amateur photographers have been conditioned to think they should only take pictures of things they like and that the only reason they should like things, as photographers, is that they are pretty. This notion is a very severe restriction on Self-expression. If followed religiously it turns the photographer into a mindless Gertie Good-Girl, a Self-blinded patron of sentimentality and second-rate art. The universe, after all, contains much more than things which are likeable and pretty. To deny this fact in one's photography is to turn oneself intentionally into an ostrich with his head in the sand. I'm not saying that beauty should be denied but that other things should be given some attention, too.

When this lesson originally appeared in *Popular Photography,* it evoked a very large and favorable response, though a few people complained bitterly because their conditioning was under attack. Most people apparently interpreted it as official permission from an authoritative source to step out of the Gertie Good-Girl bag and expand their photographic expression to include more of the things in life which actually interest and concern them. They did this with obvious gusto and sent us hundreds of pictures to prove that we had struck a responsive chord in them.

Though the lesson can be interpreted as a method for counteracting cultural conditioning in oneself, it can have other equally useful interpretations. For example, it can be seen as a method for expanding the photographer's opportunities for Self-observation. To explain here I must make a brief attack on another shibboleth of photography, the strange notion that the only object of being a photographer is to make good pictures. This is, again, a very severe and Self-limiting restriction which can lead a person to blind himself to some of the most important things which happen to him through his involvement with the medium.

One of them is that as he looks around for pictures he is also looking at himself looking for pictures. While he is doing this he is examining in a very personal way the meaning of certain adjectives which are commonly attached to the word photograph: good, bad, pretty, ugly, interesting, uninteresting, effective, ineffective and so on. This is a very important aspect of the search for the Self, for it is a questioning of language itself and helps one to see how he is conditioned to think and perceive in certain restricted patterns by the very language he uses.

Being taught a language is a form of conditioning, or programming. Examining this language piece by piece, and its effect on oneself, is a way of escaping the conditioning, so that language becomes the servant rather than the master. Though language limits vision, it also can be used to expand vision.

Another important thing a person can observe in himself as he makes photographs is a constant parade of individual and often contradictory 'I's' parading through his head. He can feel a number of others without being able to identify them clearly. What one 'I' likes another may dislike, a third find interesting and a fourth see as something to which the terms like and dislike, or interesting and uninteresting, do not apply. For example, one 'I' dominates the psyche for a while and takes a picture of something because it likes it and finds it pretty. Another 'I' dominates when the contact print is being examined and thinks that the subject of the picture is both uninteresting and homely. A week later a third 'I' looks at the contact and finds it interesting, but not because it is either likeable or pretty. And the next week a fourth 'I' looks at the picture again and is totally indifferent to it.

Watching a long parade of contradictory 'I's' parading through the mind is very upsetting but an important part of the process of Self-discovery. The temptation is to restrict deliberately the field of observation by looking for only pretty things to take pictures of. Though this seems to simplify life somewhat it also leads one to entertain certain untruths with respect to his Self, one of which is that a human Self is fairly simple and easily comprehended. It may be a comforting thought but it is dangerously wide of the mark. The truth is that the undiscovered Self is a complex universe without limits. When the ego tries to narrow it down to comfortable limits (for itself) it blocks Self-discovery very effectively.

On the other hand, if a person deliberately opens the way for longer and longer parades of 'I's' through his mind, he gradually wears down the barriers to Self-discovery. Eventually, all the myriad 'I's' will disappear and the only thing left will be

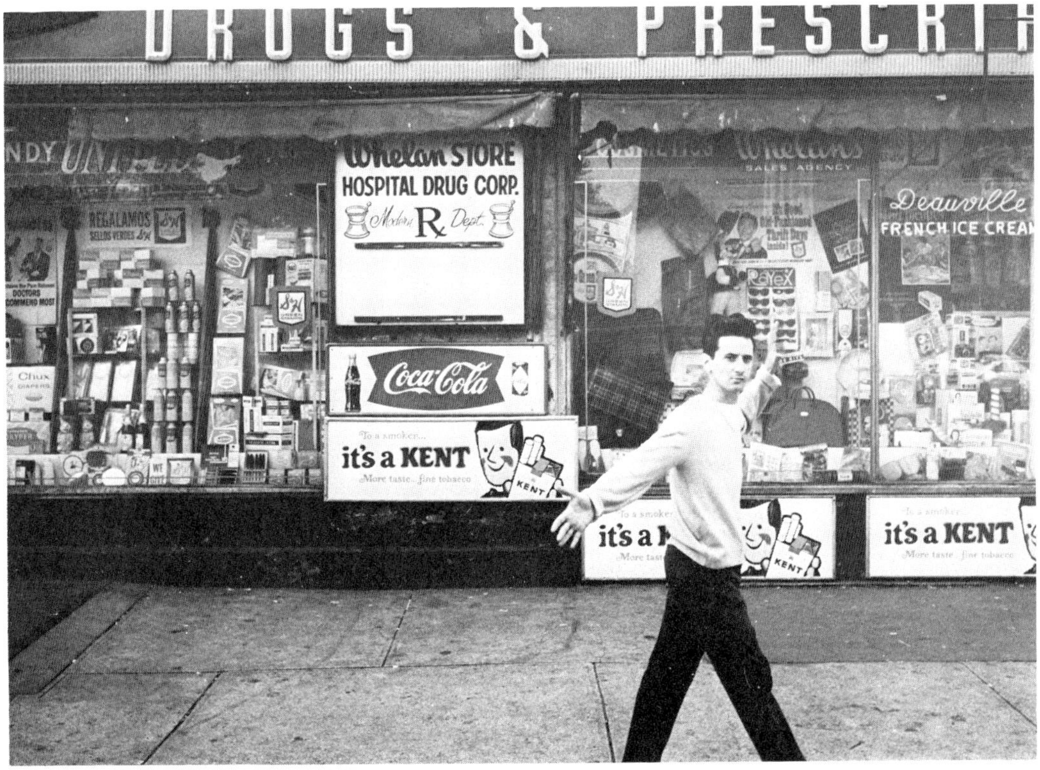

Drugstore windows are a crime against beauty and human sensibilities. Why are they always so extremely ugly? Is there no druggist alive who has any visual taste? Or are we supposed to be made miserable so we'll buy more pills? If so, even the addition of dead fish to the windows couldn't make them more effective. How about a nice display of ruptured appendixes (or is it appendices?) in the window?

Have power over others: Signs like this (right) appeal to a destructive drive in people. Since I've had problems with power hang-ups I'm disturbed. And it's my studied opinion that even in the hands of 'experts' hypnotism is as dangerous as a hydrogen weapon.

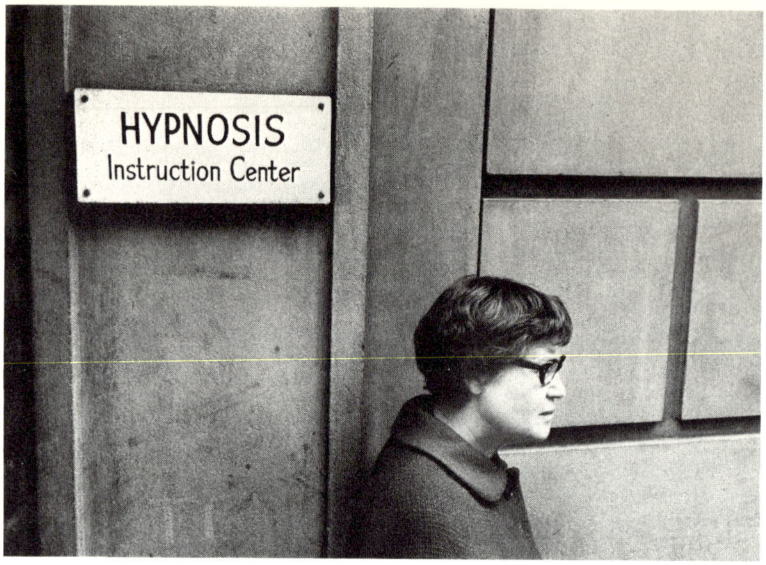

Picasso's "Guernica" (below) is almost alone in a hushed room and we're practically told to prostrate ourselves before this work of genius. I don't buy it, for all I see is the artist's colossal ego.

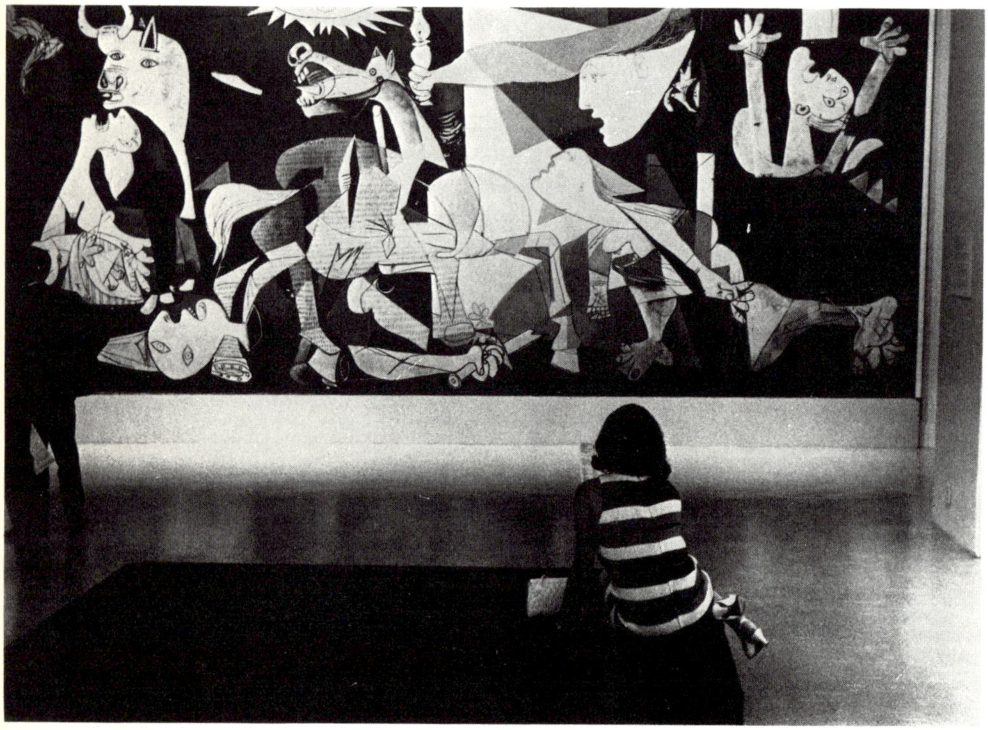

Oh joy, oh joy, it's so nice to be led to think about the pleasant things in life. And this lovely, tender, thoughtful sign (right) is always with us. What would we do without it? But we need more signs: Preparation Z Curdles Gizzards; Solution E Shrinks Eyeballs; Compound F Festers Sinuses; Bankers Ultra-Fidelity Loses Money; Ice Box Q Spoils Meat. How about, "Everyone Rots Sometime: Time Yourself With an Agnew wristwatch." Who needs all this free happiness?

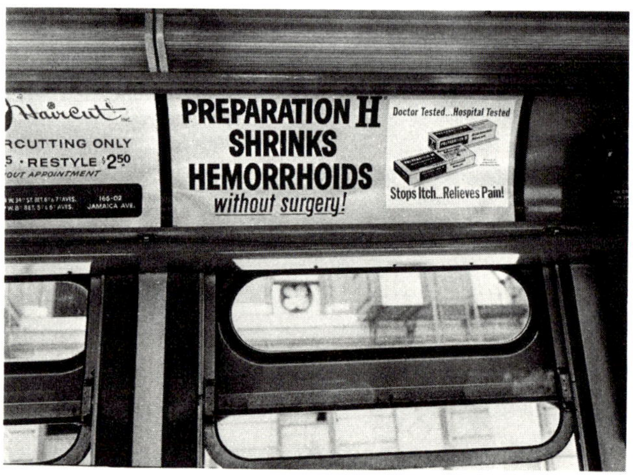

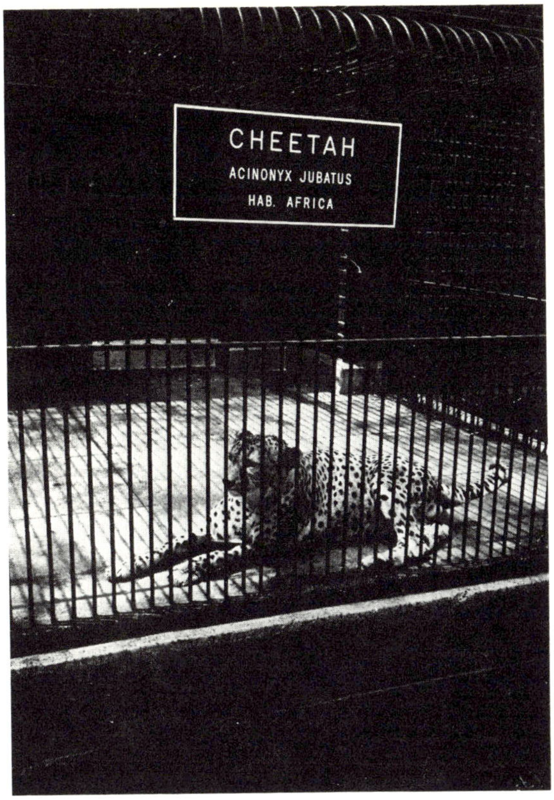

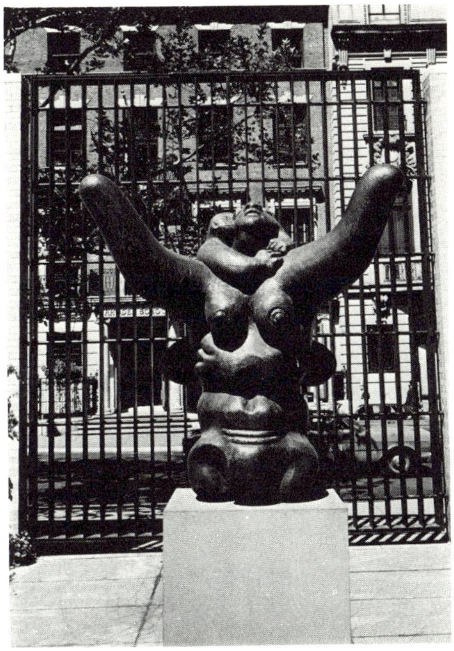

Which is uglier (above), the bars or the sign? This prince of speed deserves better than this. Sculpture (top right) made hideous by its background. A nice tribute to the labors of the sculptor. Dirty dishes (right) still plunge my heart to the depths, though I never have to wash them anymore. Had Einstein had soap-reddened hands he'd have solved the problem of dirty dishes instead of wasting his time.

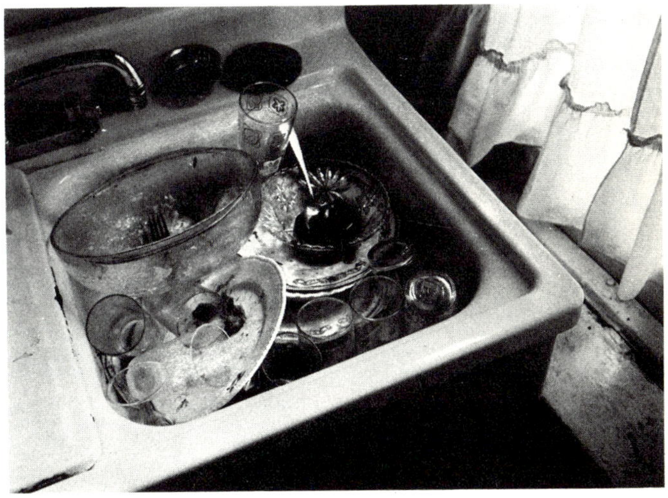

the Self. It's a painful but necessary thing to do.

In this light you can see that the lesson opens the way for more 'I's' to reveal and give expression to themselves. The fools and maniacs for whom I'm writing this chapter will undoubtedly say that this lesson is simplistic in the extreme. Merely opposing like and dislike, or love and hate, when one is looking for pictures doesn't give much range for mind or emotion. True, it may not for people with long histories of introspection. But it is a revolutionary idea for non-introspective types.

On the surface, therefore, the lesson may have little to offer my fools and maniacs. However, they can take the principle which is involved and easily expand the lesson enough to make it complex enough to engage fully the entire attention of their complicated, introspective minds.

The basic principle here is to take two reasons for making pictures of things—because they are likeable or pretty—and add their opposites as additional reasons. My suggestion to these weirdos (my soul-mates) is that they go out on shooting expeditions with written lists, as long they can make them, of opposites: ugly-beautiful, logical-illogical, meaningful-meaningless, personal-impersonal, good-bad, interesting-dull. The list could include both types of pictures and various reasons for making them. Make all contradictory types of pictures for all contradictory kinds of reasons. But the real challenge is to keep track of all the 'I's' which come into your head while you are doing it.

My soul-mates may argue that this is a miserable way to spend the day, that they've been through it all many times before and that it's better to drop acid and leave the ego and all its screwy children (the 'I's') on a sidetrack somewhere. They also know what my answer will be: You can never get rid of this crew permanently

Appetite stimulator (below). This nauseating display was obviously designed to start the gastric juices flowing. Unfortunately, it stirs up the wrong kind of juice. I'm not as disturbed with the display itself as with the kind of mind that created it. How could any human being know so little about what motivates his fellow men?

I get awfully tired of shadow pictures, even mine. Can't we just end it all right here? I'll promise, cross my heart, to stop it if you will.

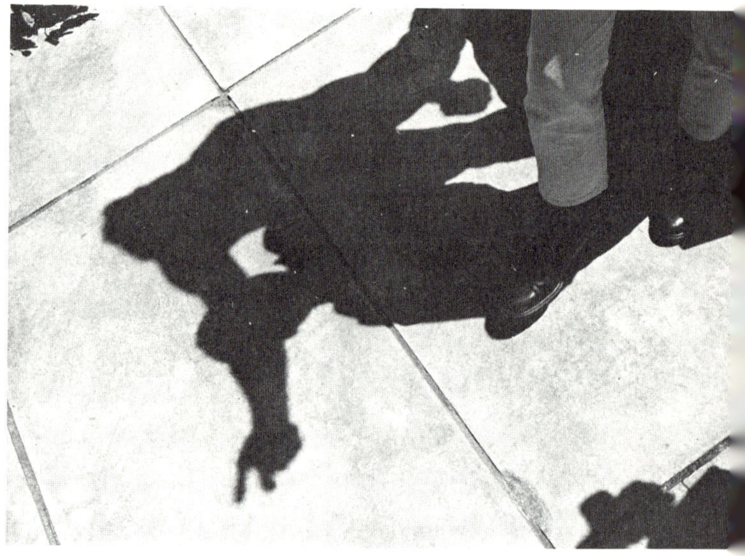

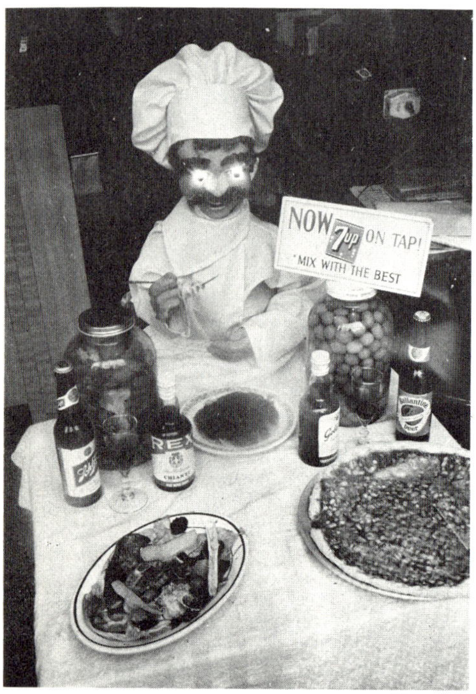

Oblivion (below right). I'm disturbed how thin is the wall between happiness and total despair. Onionskin-paper-thin.

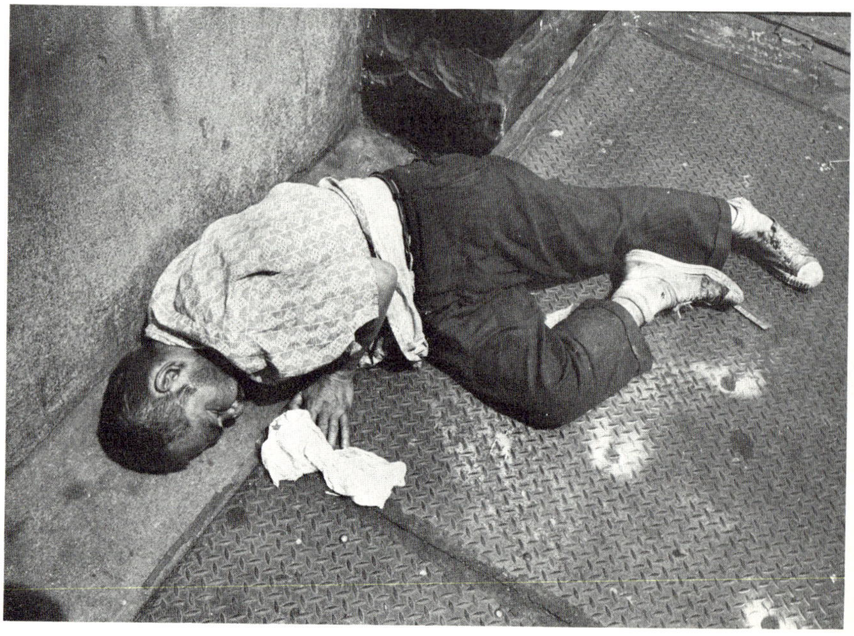

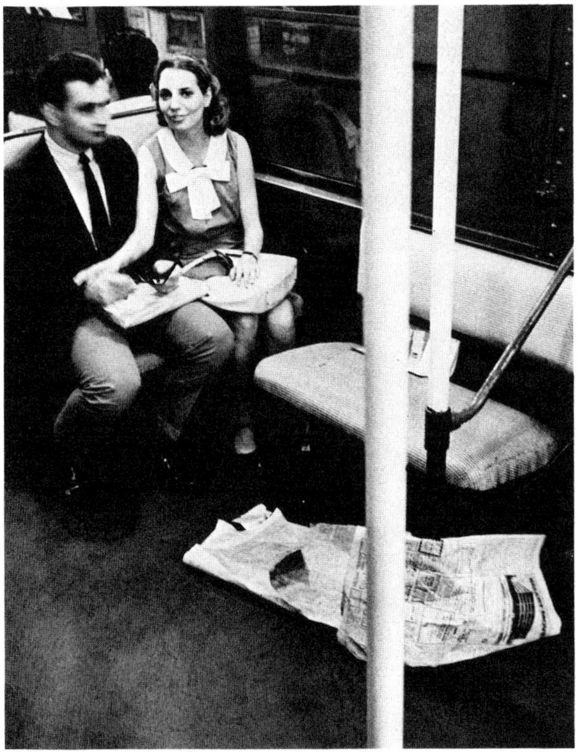

The hostile trash on the floor describes the world awaiting these young lovers on a midnight subway.

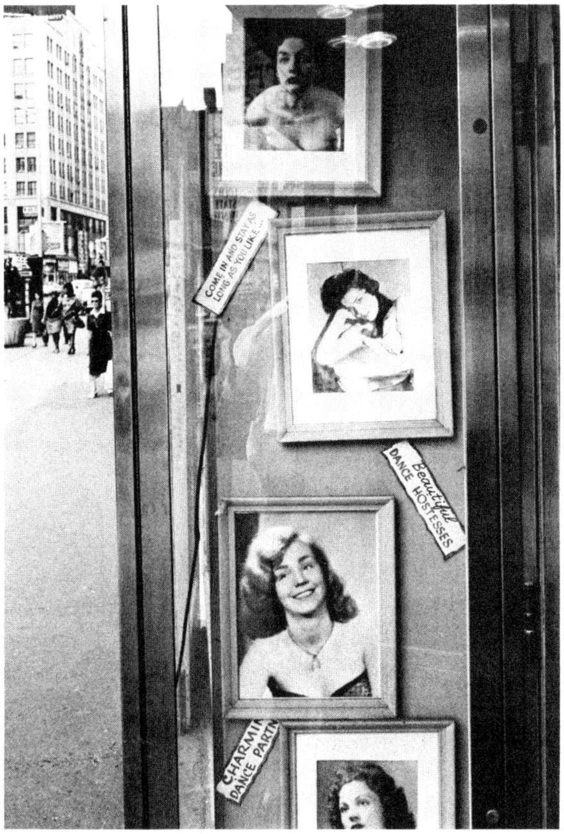

Ancient pictures of dime-a-dance girls (above). They remind me of my youth, when I wandered alone in strange cities, yearning for romance. I sometimes got so desperate that I believed money would buy affection or adventure.

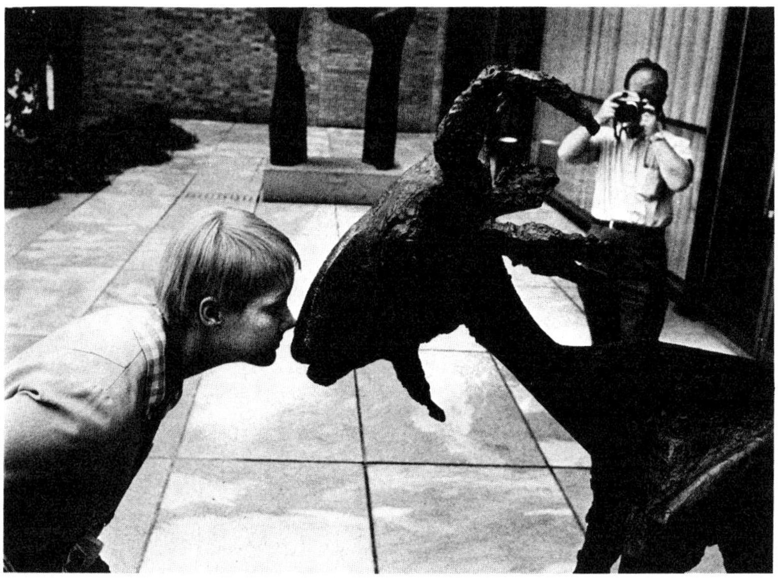

With his telephoto lens a man is stealing my very corny picture idea. I didn't really care, for I get lots of ideas and my career is to give them away. However, I feel a little sorry for a person reduced to stealing an idea as uninteresting as a girl pretending to kiss a bronze goat.

except by intentionally letting them come on stage countless times, do their sorry little self-centered acts, then temporarily slip back into limbo. Eventually they make themselves so miserable by exposing themselves that they go away permanently. Taking drugs doesn't eliminate them. It only adds to their number and their dominion over the psyche. The same thing applies to flipping oneself into a manic or schizophrenic episode.

For relatively uncomplicated people, the lesson "Hate It? Shoot It!" is merely Self-revealing good fun. For wilder heads it is slow, grueling work and the only way to realize permanently the glowing promises of LSD, mushrooms and manic-euphoria flipouts. This is not a moralist speaking here but a middle-aged man who speaks from the experience of screwing up his own head in an almost infinite number of ways.

The Lesson:

The pictures are lousy but don't flip the page until you learn some good reasons for deliberately making rotten pictures now and then, beyond the fact that it is fun.

There is an ancient dictum in the arts: Talk about what you love or what you hate; what's in the middle doesn't matter much. If you follow this dictum you express your whole Self, not merely the part that wishes to see the world as a bowl of cherries. If you express your whole Self through photography, it will mean much more to you. On the other hand, if you force yourself to see only the positive side of things, as so many amateurs do, you can sometimes make yourself miserable, for the bile builds up in you at some of the things you see and it must be released before it does you psychic harm.

In doing this project don't limit yourself strictly to photographing what you hate; you may not be aware of hating anything at all. Photograph anything that distresses you, even if you don't know *why* it does. An interesting part of the project is to look at a photograph and try to figure out as accurately as possible why its subject upsets you. The answer may be in the subject, or it may be in yourself. You may find that your response is actually not hate but sadness, despair, fear, confusion, resignation, etc. Don't settle for the first answer that pops into your mind, but keep on probing. Instead of finding just one emotion involved, you may find many. Or you may discover that what you thought at first was anger is actually fear disguised by anger. If self-analysis distresses you, don't do it. Merely taking the pictures will do something for you.

Things to do with your upsetting pictures:

1. See if other people can figure out precisely why you are upset; this can be an interesting game.

2. Learn to what degree your personal dislikes are shared by others and to what degree they're not.

3. Make big enlargements and give them as presents to friends who like 'campy' things.

4. See what response you get if you tell someone you think one of your ugly pictures is beautiful. Do this with a straight face.

5. See if you can get one published. Some art directors are suckers for anything ugly enough, though they don't know it.

6. Put them away in a box and see if a year later you still feel the same way about them. You may not.

7. Try them out on children to see what they think about them. You'll probably be surprised.

8. Enter one for the monthly camera club critique and watch for the members' evasive responses.

9. Show one to a self-professed critic and ask for his help in improving it. See how close he actually comes to seeing what is really disturbing in it. He may fishtail around all over the place without even coming close.

10. You may find someone who likes them all. If you do, try to figure out what makes him tick.

11. If you have a psychiatrist friend he may like to try them out on his patients to see if they're disturbed by what upsets less neurotic people.

Let the Subject Create

This lesson tells people who are neurotically preoccupied with control one of the ways for getting out of this very bad bag. Though it deals mainly with learning how to surrender control over one's models it also gives clues concerning how to deal with the control hang-up in general. However, it doesn't go far enough in showing that one can have in fact neurotic involvements with control.

Up to a point, control is both necessary and good. A photographer should have complete control over his medium, of course. If he hasn't he just can't make all the kinds of pictures he wants to. He should also be skillful at controlling or directing his models. Thus control as such is certainly not bad. It's just that people can easily get hung up on it.

The last lesson in this chapter ("Games Photographers Play") does a very thorough job of telling how one can get badly hung up on control. It talks about the standard hang-ups of photographers, calling them Self-destructive games. Six of the games named 'Smasher,' 'Possessor,' 'Imitator,'

My son Cleve said, "Photograph me wiggling my fingers." I interpret my enjoyment of him while he was doing it as a sign I may eventually learn the meaning of love.

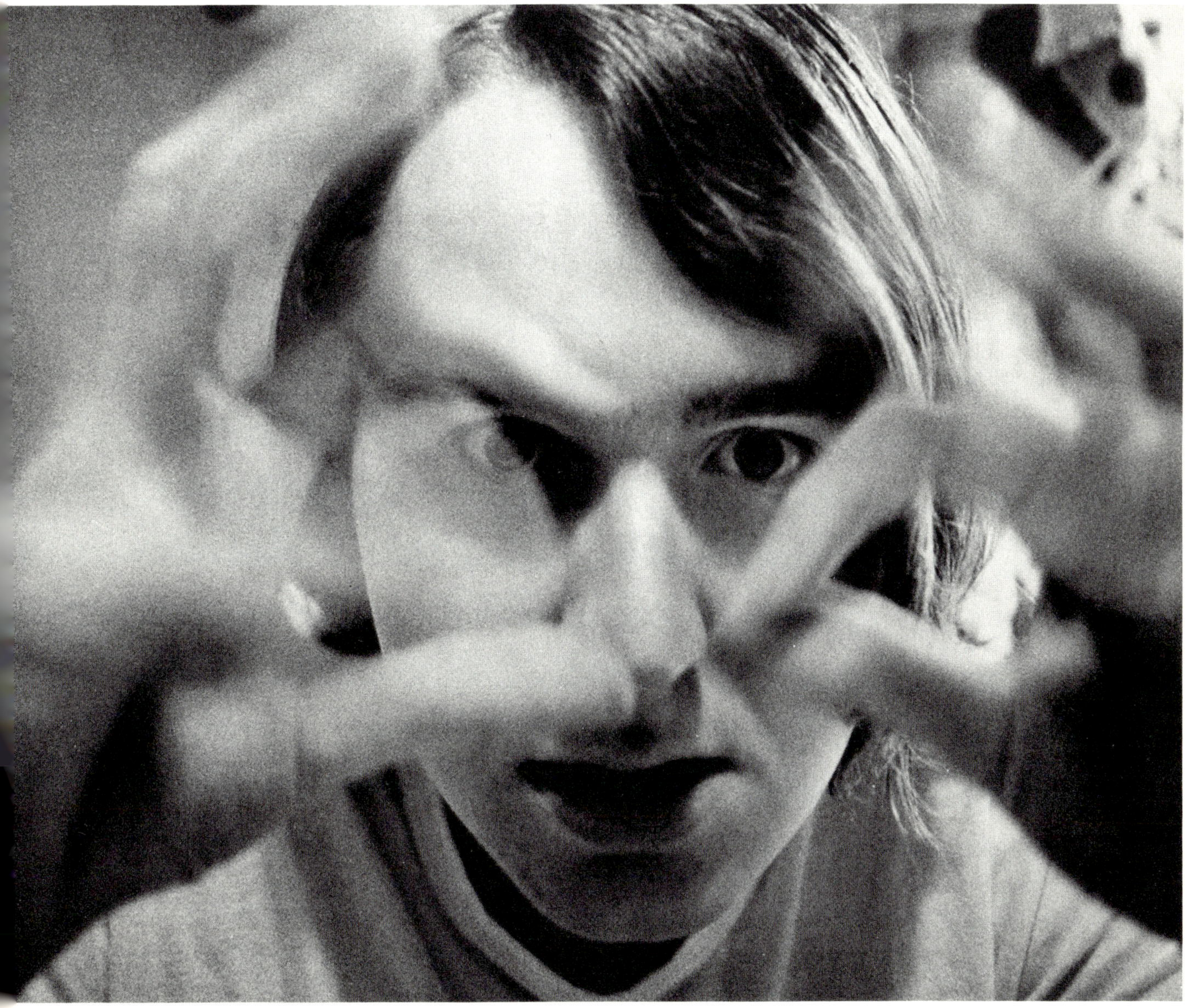

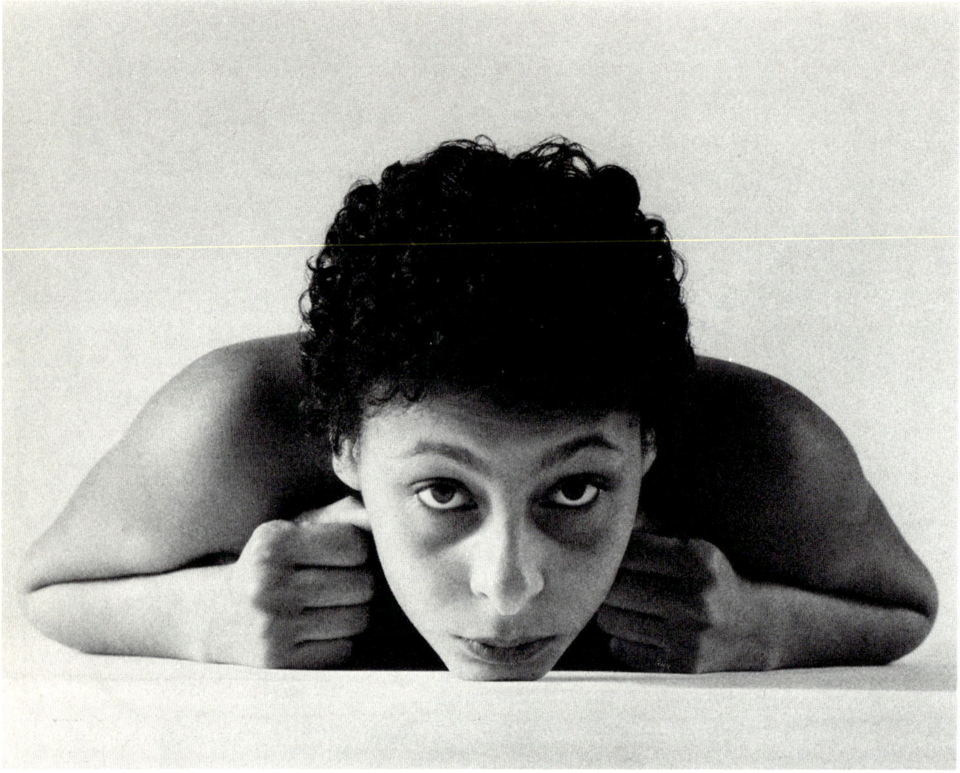

Dorothy made this little pose as an offering to me, then waited hopefully to see if I would photograph her. Going against my egotism, I did click the shutter, yet I didn't print the picture until twelve years later. I couldn't bear the thought of having a subject make my picture for me. Now the picture makes me realize what a nice person Dorothy is and that I've always been very fond of her.

He said, "I'm the mayor of this street (below), do you want to take my picture?" In my youth I would have ridiculed him with my camera or only pretended to click the shutter. Now I feel grateful to him for the gift of himself in a picture that I like very much.

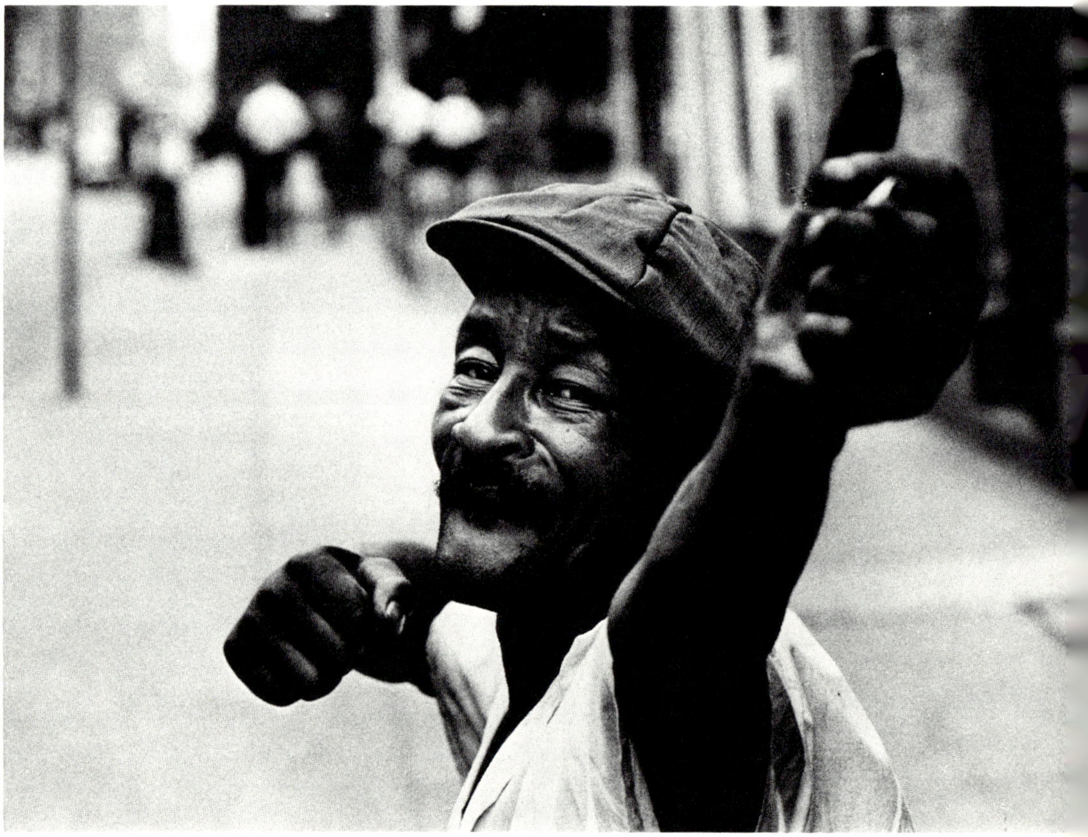

'Printer,' 'Power' and 'Saint' involve various kinds of hang-ups on control. After you've read about them you'll probably agree that the wrong kind of relation to control can be very neurotic indeed.

Another subject which the lesson introduces and deals with too briefly is the relation of my ideas concerning attachment, or identification, to the teachings of certain great religious leaders. I didn't specifically state my reasons for mentioning their names. But it was to let perceptive and informed readers know where my head is, who I regard as my mentors, where I get the philosophical and metaphysical ideas which underlie my writings, and the approach I'm taking to discover what these Great Teachers really said.

My mention of Enoch and Melchizedek is a clue that the approach is through esoteric religion rather than traditional, for there is practically no available information on either man through traditional sources. Those readers who know what esoteric religion is will recognize the names and realize that the lesson, and this book as a whole, is a treatise on esoteric religion as it applies to photography. The teaching itself is ancient. Only the application is new.

The terms attachment and identification should be explained a bit more. They mean the same thing but are encountered in different kinds of literature. For example, identification is a key term in general semantics and shows up frequently in books on psychology. Attachment is more likely to appear in English translations of Indian Vedic literature and its derivatives, e.g. *The Bhagavad-Gita.* For my money, attachment is the better of the two terms, for it is more graphically descriptive.

The Vedic literature, the source of the immensely sophisticated Eastern psychology, says that one of man's greatest problems is that he attaches himself to things.

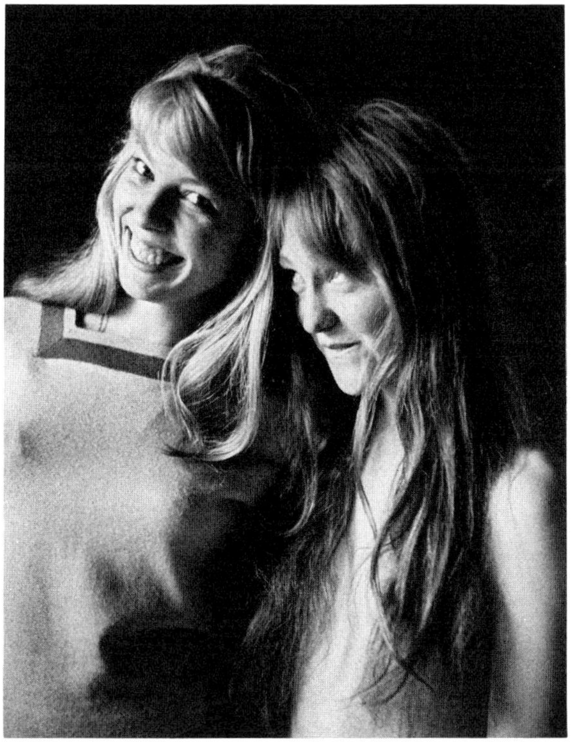

My ego was miffed because Hazel and Anita (left) were expressing themselves with such charm and humor. I felt I should be controlling the situation and telling them what to do. I was proud of my photography and irritated by the fact that they were creating a better picture for me than I could have created for myself.

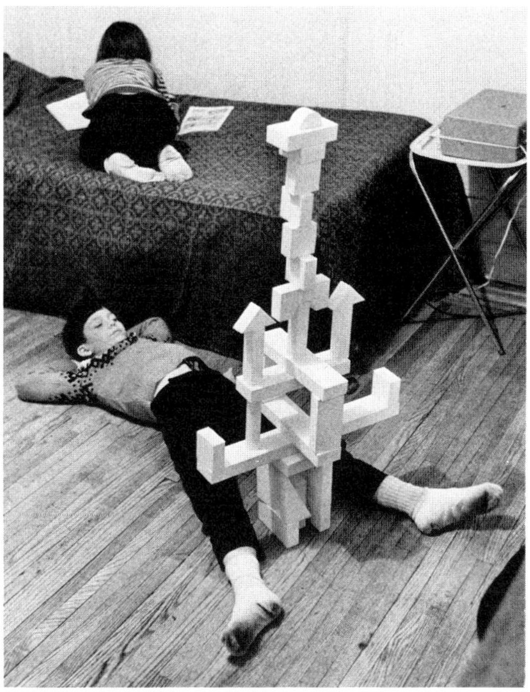

My stepson Bobby Turner poses with his masterpiece, while his sister Kathi is busy turning out one of her own. I felt a twinge of wanting to tell him how a child 'ought' to pose with his creation, but managed to squelch it in time.

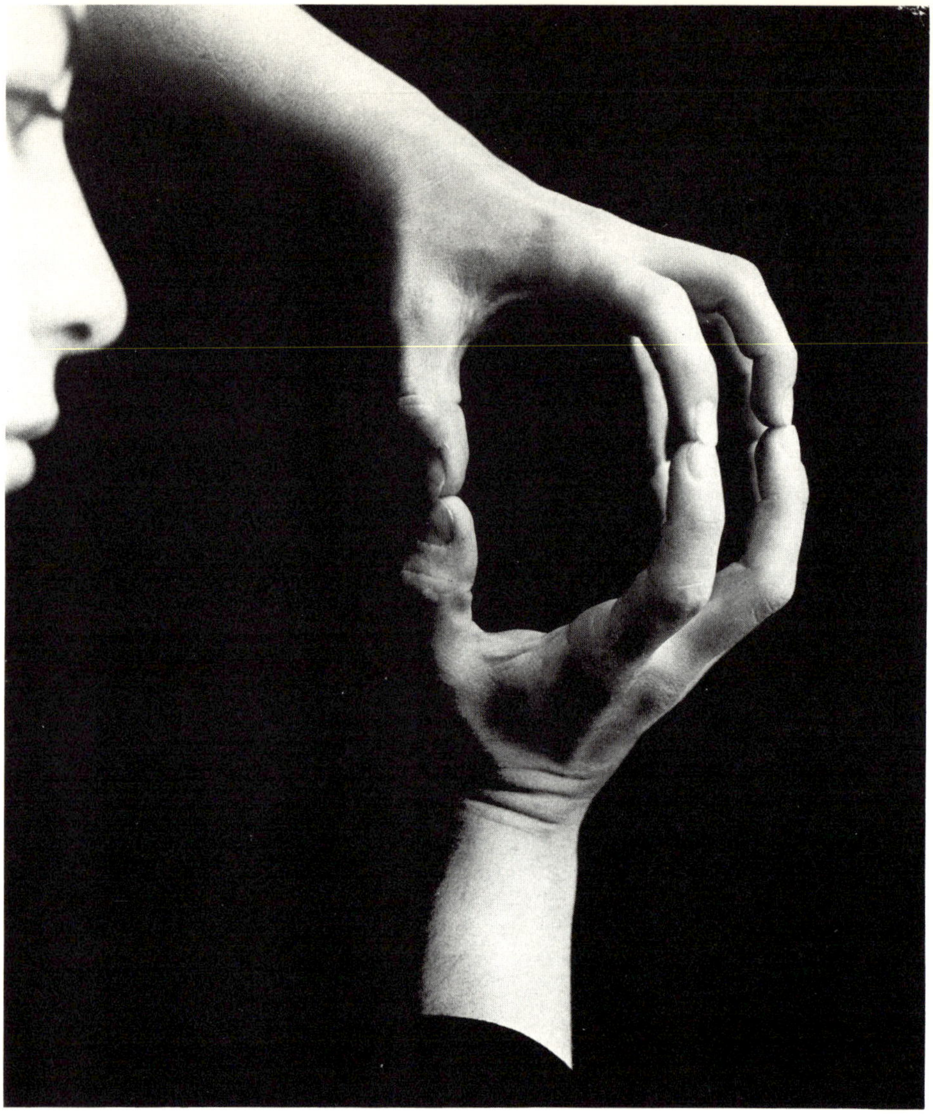

While I was photographing Laura she started creating shapes with her hands, hoping to please me. Against my will I shot pictures of them. My ego wasn't too happy that Laura was creating my pictures for me. However, life has taught me that giving the ego a hard time is the only way to diminish its dominance over the psyche. Thus, in giving in to Laura I was doing my Soul a favor.

Until he learns this is bad, and takes steps to detach himself, there is little chance his psyche will develop properly. In my opinion, no truer thing has ever been said.

Attachment is something the ego does. Figuratively, it projects itself and latches onto things, like a lamprey on a shark. Then it gets hung up on the relationship and resists all attempts to dislodge it. Attachment is a very common phenomenon in photography, though few people have recognized it for what it is or understood it is something which should be overcome. What happens is that the photographer's ego projects itself into his work, so that he perceives his pictures and himself as a unity. In other words, he sees his work as an extension of himself. A lot of photographers have become aware that they do this but haven't realized what a heavy price they pay for letting it continue.

Some of the symptoms of attachment to photography are a great reluctance to have your pictures criticized, an ambivalent love-hate attitude toward them, temporarily being unable to make photographs, a strong reluctance to use your photography for other people, self-hate associated with failure on a photographic project, being precious about your work and being unwilling to part with your pictures. For more symptoms, read the concluding lesson in this chapter. If you play any of the games you are most certainly attached in some way.

To say that a person is neurotically preoccupied with control is the same thing as saying he's attached to it. Or we could say he's hung up on it. A person in this state is concerned with having control for ego-defense or ego-glorification reasons, not primarily because having control is necessary for accomplishing certain things in photography. There is a very large difference between these two things, though they often overlap. One can control the medium and the things he photographs with very great skill and at the same time not be attached to control as such. This is the desirable way to be.

To be attached to control is to be a slave to photography and its subject matter, which is not so good. However, many photographers have become enslaved and think that anyone who isn't has something wrong with him and that he's not a 'real' photographer. They even brag about how hung up they are, not realizing what a pitiful thing it is. A person who is not attached to photography should easily be able to give it up at a moment's notice and not have to take another picture as long as he lives. How many so-called serious photographers can do this? Those who can't have chained themselves to their art.

Though attachment to photography is bad it is also an opportunity—if it is used properly. When a person projects himself into his pictures (becomes identified or attached) he makes certain areas of his unconscious mind more accessible to him than they ordinarily are. His unconscious thoughts and attitudes appear in his pictures in the form of symbols. Thus, if he examines his relation to photography, and digs for his symbols and their meanings, he can learn a good deal about himself. The process is painful, however, for the ego doesn't want this unconscious material brought into the light of day. In a sense, when a person gets attached to photography he turns himself into a battlefield on which the Higher Forces in himself can struggle with the ego. If he surrenders to attachment he moves toward becoming a vegetable. However, if he uses it as a field on which to join battle deliberately against his egotism, or selfishness, it becomes for him a great spiritual opportunity.

One sign that the battle of Self against ego is going well is a feeling of anxiety. Photographers who are preoccupied with 'making their pictures,' with totally controlling their subjects, will find that letting their subjects create their pictures will make them feel very anxious and insecure. If there is no anxiety in such people it usually means that the ego has slyly introduced a warp factor. That is, it has sidetracked the attack against attachment and is still playing control or power games, though the games are cleverly disguised. For some photographers the most useful thing might be to use this lesson to help them learn to detect when they introduced ego-inspired warp factors to de-rail attempts to free themselves from attachment.

The Lesson:

A common hang-up with photographers is the notion that they must invariably and without fail make *their pictures. By this, they mean that they should never shoot something just as it is but should themselves make as many 'contributions' to it as possible. Only then, they say, have they the right to call their pictures their own. They do not, of course, realize that this is a neurotic point of view and that its hidden implications would show them in a very bad light.*

On close examination, these so-called contributions often turn out to be nothing but well-disguised (especially from the photographer himself) expressions of egotism, fear, thirst for power, neurotic attachment, or the urge to meddle with other people. The contrary point of view, that people should *never* manipulate their subject matter, is equally *sick*.

The reasonable thing to do is to both *make* pictures and *find* them and not get yourself hung up on either approach. Such hang-ups only put you in a box that gets smaller and smaller as the years go by.

About this egotism thing, I happen to know a good deal about it, having for many years suffered the bitter consequences of it. By the grace of God, however, I've nearly always realized (if sometimes dimly) that I alone was the sole cause of my misery. And I know very well indeed how egotism expresses itself in photographs, having expressed it myself so many, many times.

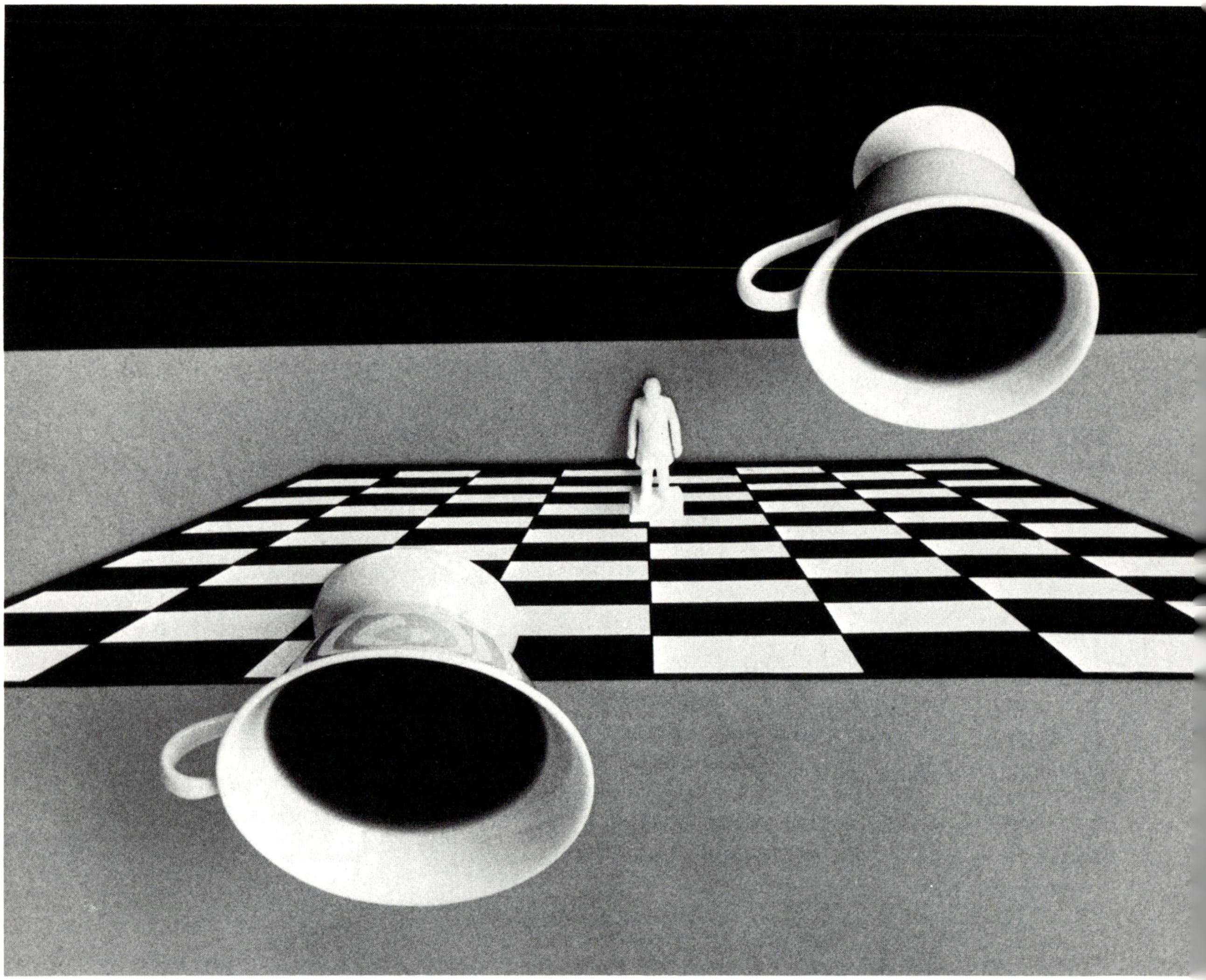

Turn this picture upside down and see if that helps you to figure out how it was made.

One of the ways in which we project egotism into pictures is through using the so-called photographic controls to always change things (mostly people) from what they are into something more acceptable to ourselves. Though this is often nothing less than playing God, it is rationalized as the desire to 'show things in their best light,' 'capture the essence,' and many other types of photographic mumbo-jumbo with which our whole field is well polluted.

Throughout the ages our great teachers—Enoch, Melchizedek, Krishna, Buddha, Jesus Christ, Mohammed—have invariably taught that 'attachment' is a primary cause of human woe. Though the teachings of the great seem very far from photography, they are in fact at the very center of it. Let us, then, see what this attachment means. Its synonyms are identification, partiality, subjectivity, and selfishness. In modern idiom it is expressed as 'my bag' or 'my 'hang-up.'

You can tell if you're in this bag by Self-observation, though Self-observation as a whole is an immensely difficult art. Just observe yourself as you look at your own pictures. If you are either greatly elated or depressed you're most certainly attached or hooked. One of the best times to make such Self-observations is when other people are looking at your work. Fright, anger, the urge to apologize, the urge to brag, a knotting in the solar plexus, leg cramps, and headaches are indications that you're attached or identified. This means very simply you're using photography against yourself, rather than for.

But photography can be used in many ways to fight this vicious, self-initiated plague. In fact, our greatest photographers have always intuitively done it, which is why we call them great. One of the best ways to fight is to force yourself—and I really mean *force*—to let your subjects be what they are with no interference whatsoever from you. Just take what they give you. If you find that it grinds against your personal grain, all the better. This means that the battle has been well joined.

This grinding in the solar plexus burns out the hate in you, so bless the Lord! This is what the great teachers mean by self-purgation or self-mortification. It is also the fundamental means by which one recovers his long-lost, natural creativity. The popular techniques of creativity often have the opposite effect.

I'm very aware, incidentally, that many photographers will be made terribly angry by what I've said so far. Such people have a vested interest in *not* understanding photography because they are using it to maintain and protect their own neuroses. Well, they should rub their own noses in this lesson, for it will help them (now or in the future) cut down their bill for psychiatric counseling. In accusing Ralph Hattersley of colossal egotism, they might also ask themselves if they haven't, perhaps, got it backwards and that their own egotism is provoking their reaction. Why should they get so steamed up about *words?*

Since the same lost souls will accuse *Popular Photography* of allowing me to destroy all the joy in photography, I feel ethically obliged to contradict them. The joy they speak of is a chimera, an illusion. This project, and other human behavior of the same sort, is a fundamental means of finding joy, not destroying it.

Essentially, I'm asking you students to follow a photographic approach that will help you focus your attention on the problem of learning how to put up with other people. It involves the specific kind of suffering we must go through in order to possess our souls and to avoid a much more terrible suffering—isolation. When the price has been paid the reward is genuine joy and true communion with one's fellow men, or so our teachers have told us through the ages. I, for one, believe them.

The pictures in this lesson have one thing in common: I didn't make any of them. I just snapped the shutter at the subject's real but unspoken request: "Please accept this part of me." I didn't want to take most of them, frankly—a measure of my own ego problem, now and in the past. Of all my pictures, at least three-fourths were taken against my grain, but they're the ones I really enjoy now, to my delighted surprise.

Spacemanship

You've probably discovered by now that most of the projects in this book are fun to do. Others, however, may have gotten you very uptight. One of the reasons for this is that they can be inadvertently used as attacks against conditioning. When such an attack is even partly successful it gives rise to great anxiety. It doesn't matter whether it was done on purpose or happened accidentally. What happens is that an assault against conditioning undermines our sense of security, which is largely founded on strong unconscious belief in various illusions. The conditioning systems imprison us but are at the same time the very illusions we desperately cling to in order to have a feeling of security. False though this security is, we are extremely reluctant to permit anything to disturb it and the illusions on which it is based.

Though this lesson on creating visual illusions is also an attack on conditioning, the chances are very remote that it will upset you. On the contrary, you will probably find it great fun. It seems that many people already have, for it has been translated into three other languages and reprinted on two continents. Furthermore, people have been playing with the ideas which it contains for hundreds of years without unduly messing up their heads. Nonetheless, they will help you undermine conditioning, especially if they are pursued for a considerable distance.

Though we usually flee from anxiety as quickly as we can, it is often a sign of something good happening in us, for instance a conditioning system undergoing erosion. In this sense, lack of anxiety is frequently a bad sign, for it can mean that conditioning is so firmly entrenched that nothing can touch it. This may be the case even when it is under deliberate attack. The ego may slyly introduce a warp factor into whatever we're doing to try to de-condition ourselves. It is an expert at such machinations, for its security depends in large degree in maintaining the delusional conditioning systems which are under attack. The warp factor sidetracks the attack, so that it still appears to be an assault but is actually a harmless marshmallow which leaves the conditioning untouched.

Another reason for failure is that the conditioning may be very powerfully intrenched, which is precisely the case with visual conditioning as a whole. Our entire world view depends on it. Moreover, we are terribly dependent on it, despite the fact that it makes us see reality upside down. Though our scientists have been telling us for many years that reality as we perceive it and as it actually is are aeons apart, their information has had no effect whatsoever in lessening our visual conditioning. In fact, the scientists themselves continue to be as tightly trapped as ever in their visual delusions.

All this should give you assurance that there is little chance of your upsetting yourself by doing this project, but it may leave you wondering why you should be be asked to do it as an effort to undermine your conditioning (as a part of the process of freeing the Self).

My answer is that it may give you an intellectual basis for seeing that what I've said about our seeing reality upside down may have some basis in truth. If not that you will at least learn that people cling very strongly to their visual habits, for the success of all visual illusions depends on this fact. When you've come this far other possibilities are open to you. If a proposition holds up intellectually you will permit yourself to investigate it further.

Before this testing by intellect the very idea of investigation might seem absurd. So you prove a point to yourself, then move on. I must warn you that if you want to make a significant dent in your visual conditioning, you'll have to work very hard on the problem for the rest of your life. In the meanwhile, working in this area is very interesting and a way of getting many exciting pictures.

It is one thing to say that we are visually conditioned (this is easy to prove) and another to describe how we would see if we weren't. As a species we've had very little experience with de-conditioned vision and can only speculate on what it might be like. My guess, supported by about ten years of reading on the subject, is that people who are psychic come closest to having it. One could even define a psychic as a person who has escaped his conditioning to an unusual degree.

For an idea of how psychics see, try reading the book *Breakthrough to Creativity,* by Shafica Karagulla, M.D. Dr. Karagulla, an experienced neuropsychiatrist who is well known in her field, talks about people (many of them doctors) with x-ray vision, vision disassociated from time and space, vision which functions free of attachments to the human optical system, vision which magnifies or shrinks objects at will, vision which sees colored energy fields (auras) around human beings and so on. For descriptions of the kind of behavior which leads to the development of these kinds of deconditioned vision, I suggest you turn to the various books and pamphlets which have been written about the work of Edgar Cayce, America's foremost psychic.

There are numerous people who have had experiences showing what deconditioned vision *might* be like, though there is no way of proving that they describe actuality very well. I'm thinking here of those who have tried such things as LSD, mescaline and the hallucinogenic mushrooms. I think we can say with certainty that they cancel (or drug or stupefy or sidetrack) conditioning, including conditioned vision. I think we can safely say that some of these drug experiences represent true unconditioned vision very well indeed, which helps explain why people get hung-up on drugs.

From what I've read on the subject

it appears that people who experience acute schizophrenic episodes may also escape from visual conditioning. Abrupt escape would account for some of the terror involved, for our sense of security depends largely on conditioning. Shatter it at a blow and terror results. With schizophrenia there is another problem, however: True, deconditioned vision is inextricably mixed with outright hallucination.

As I've already said, there is hardly any chance that you will substantially shake your visual conditioning by doing the "Spacemanship" lesson, thus little chance of upsetting yourself. But you can use it to prove to yourself that you are, in fact, heavily conditioned. You will perceive this only on the intellectual level, not the Emotional. Visual illusions will not work without conditioning and our heavy dependence on it. For example, the first picture in the lesson (coffee cups and checkerboard) works because we are thoroughly conditioned by our long experience in seeing checkerboard patterns (like floor tiles) and the horizon. Unconsciously, we use such things to orient ourselves in time and space and thus become powerfully dependent on them, though we're not aware that we are. We are also terribly dependent on the fact that the horizon is always at eye level and that the floor tiles (or things like them) in a given place are always the same size.

When the horizon is put in the wrong place and isn't, in fact, a horizon at all, we insist on seeing it as being in the right place. Powerful evidence to the contrary (the coffee cups full of coffee) doesn't shake our conviction. When a checkerboard is made with squares that aren't actually square at all and which also vary in size, we insist on seeing it in terms of past experience of such patterns, instead of in terms of the present reality. In clinging to past experience we turn reality upside down. This is true not only for the picture but for life in general.

If you will take the picture and turn it upside down you will see that it seems just as normal that way as it does right side up. Whether we look at it right side up or upside down, our perception goes entirely against common sense. However, we willingly go against common sense rather than surrender well-entrenched visual habits (conditioning). In truth, it is impossible for us to give up the habits quickly, no matter how hard we try.

The odd thing is that it is very difficult for us to see that our perception of the picture is ludicrous. It is very much like a person who has thoroughly conditioned himself to believe that elephants are very small. When he tries to put one of them in his pocket, he doesn't see anything peculiar in what he is attempting.

There are quite a few other tricks in the lesson. They all depend on our conditioning and the fact that we are completely stuck in it. Those interested in learning about them should get the Ralph Evans book, which is mentioned in the text.

The Lesson:

Very few people, even professionals, realize the tremendous degree to which space can be manipulated in photography. In this lesson I show you some simple tricks for doing things that have seldom been done before. They are much easier than they may appear to be at first. Any ten-year-old can do them once he knows how.

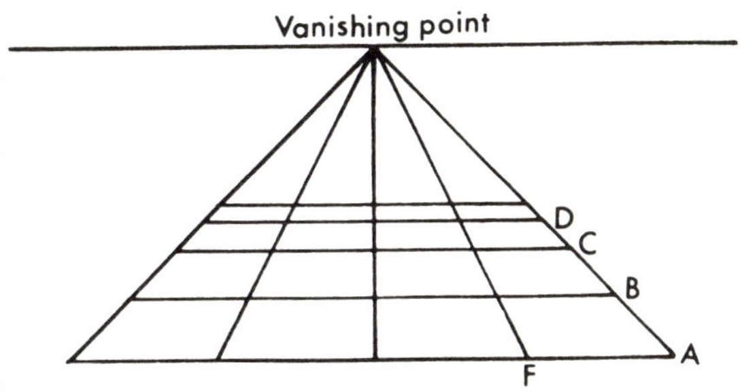

Draw a figure like this (but with more lines) and fill in alternate squares with india ink or tempera. Note that distance AB is greater than BC, and BC is greater than CD. AF is always considerably greater than AB.

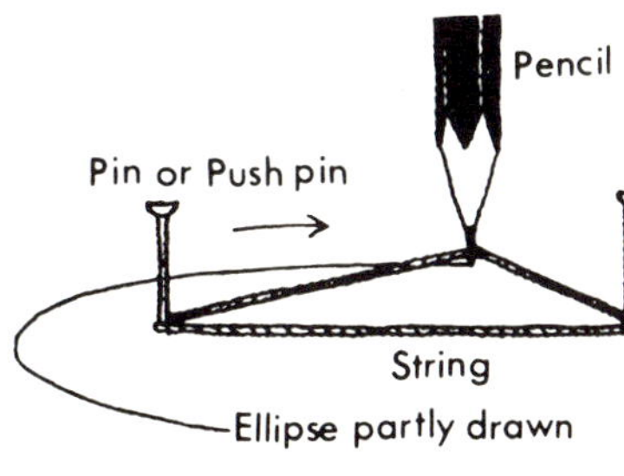

Perfect ellipses are easily made by this method. The width depends on the distance between the pins, and fatness on whether the loop in the string is loose or tight. Draw ellipses, then cut them out with scissors.

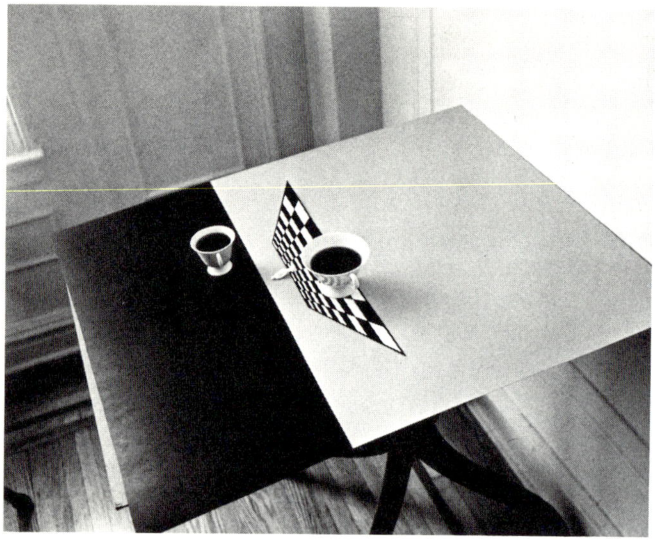

You can now see (left) how the coffee cup and checkerboard picture was made. The drawing on the previous page shows you how to make a skewed checkerboard like this. The camera was outside the setup at the left. The little man was lying on his back, upside down to the camera. Using two colors of cardboard created an artificial horizon, but it was in the wrong place. Such phoney horizons can help create powerful illusions. To some people the picture will seem more natural upside-down than right-side up, despite the coffee in the cups, which would hang upside-down in the air. It is not necessary to use a checkerboard to twist space this way. Any strong repeated pattern drawn in simple perspective would tend to do the same thing. It is the very familiarity of the checkerboard that makes it work so powerfully. An unfamiliar pattern would work, but not as well. Note that one coffee cup is quite a bit larger than the other.

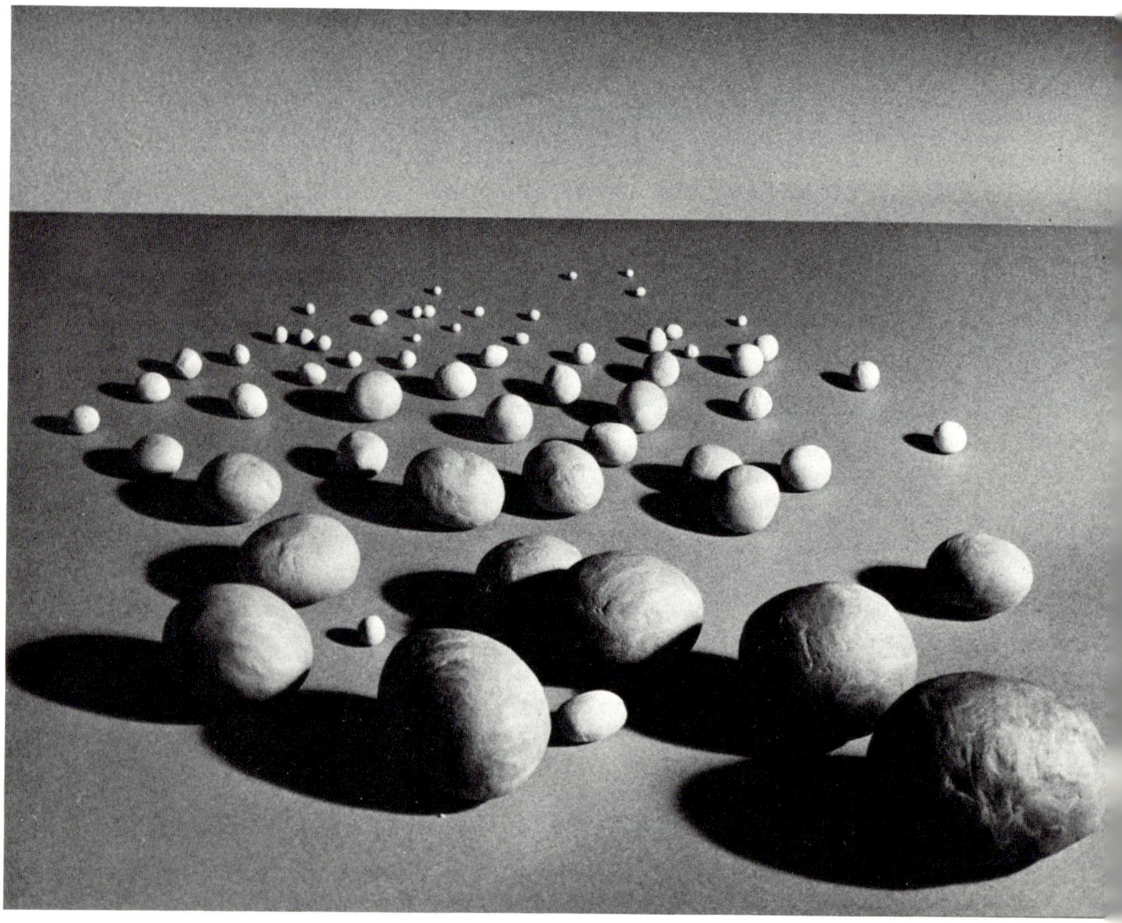

These modeling-clay balls vary from baseball size to half the size of a pea. This is actually the checkerboard principle, used with solid objects. The strong cross-lighting in picture on the opposite page adds greatly to the feeling of space, as does the fake horizon. Note how space is diminished (right) by using soft bouncelight from in front of the balls, nearly eliminating the shadows. In the picture below, the balls were reversed, with the small ones closest to the camera. The horizon was then put in the wrong place. To some, the balls will seem to hang in mid-air. Others may prefer to view the picture upside-down. I used these clay balls only to illustrate a point. Many kinds of objects would have worked just as well. If you're short on ideas, refer to Evan's Eye, Film and Camera *(John Wiley and Sons, 1959). He gives enough ideas to revolutionize your photography. However, the illustrations in the book aren't very imaginative. This is a great pity, for it led most of the people who read it to overlook the power of Evan's ideas.*

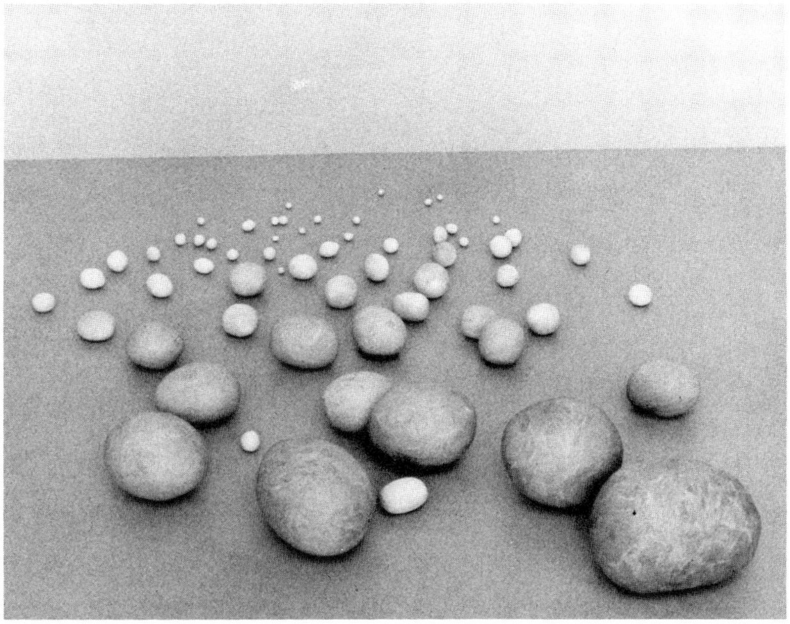

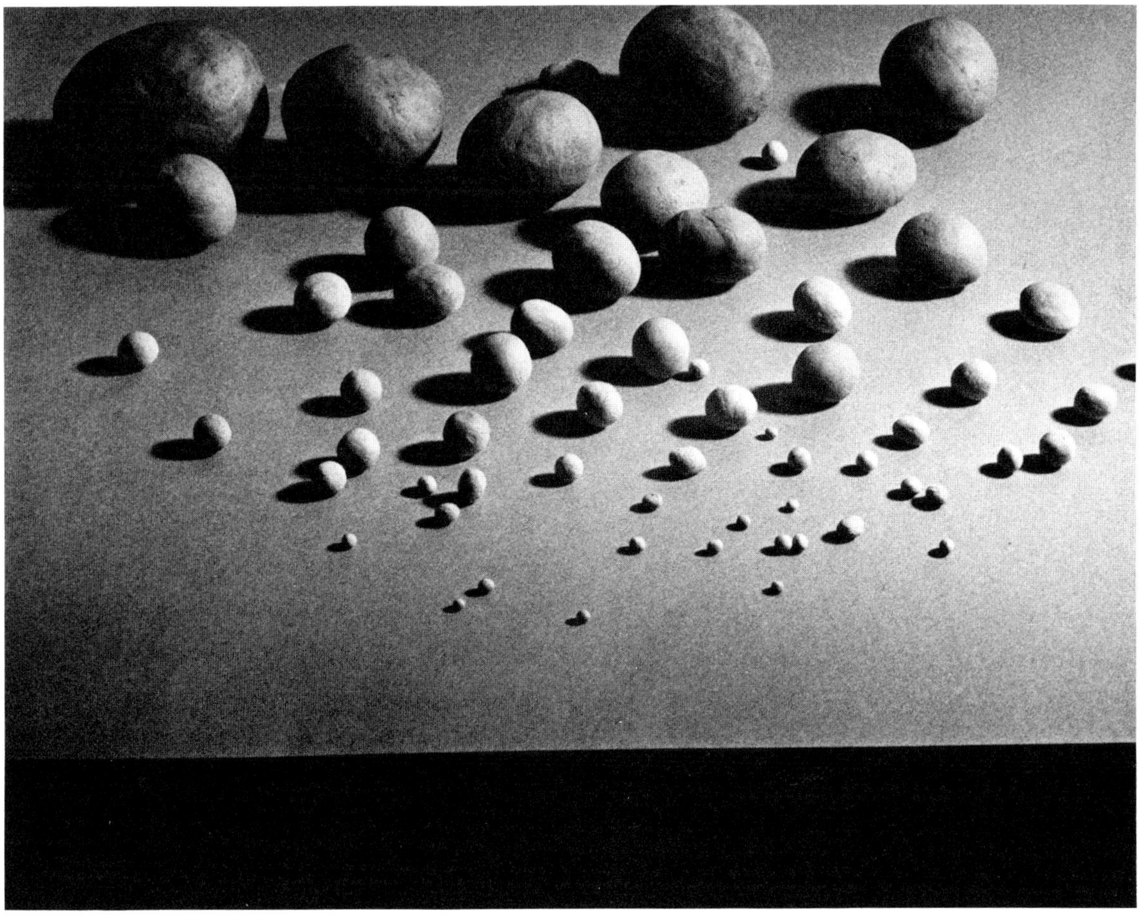

Though the pictures may seem creative, they are actually as uncreative as I could make them. I kept them as simple as possible so that you could figure out what had been done and put the tricks to use for yourself. All the creative possibilities were left for you to play with; and there are a great many of them. For example, instead of using just one checkerboard in a picture you could use two or three and twist space into truly wild contortions. If you do this project with even a little imagination you will absolutely astound yourself.

Though some of the pictures were actually made to be shown upside down, we decided to show them all right side up, just as the camera saw them, to help you figure out what was going on. In your pictures you don't have to restrict yourself this way.

The cups of coffee were put in some of the pictures just to prove that space had been distorted. Had they been left out, space would still have been twisted out of shape, but you would have accepted it as realistic and I would never have been able to persuade you anything had been done. I suggest that you use distortion-provers in your pictures, too. Try to think of something other than cups of coffee, however.

For more information, read *Eye, Film and Camera in Color Photography,* by Ralph Evans. It's a space classic.

It's important for you to realize that space illusions are created by manipulating objects that are observed in everyday life. People have strong—though unconscious—preconceptions about the natural position of objects such as coffee cups. But less familiar objects (such as the seashell shown on page 209) can be seen upside down and the viewer may not be aware of the change.

The objective of this lesson was to help you learn to see space better, not merely to show you how to make gimcrack pictures. However, making such pictures will improve your space vision a great deal. There's a lot more to space management in photography than has been explained here, so perhaps we'll have other lessons on it. Though our illustrations may appear gimmicky and the principles involved may seem to be of limited importance, these principles actually operate in many photographs. Since you have to start somewhere in increasing your sensitivity to space, you might just as well begin with this lesson. You may even wish to try to duplicate some of my pictures exactly. I think you will be surprised if you try such an experiment. It will open your eyes to a new way of observing objects in space and will help to make you a more perceptive photographer.

Breaking the Three-Foot Barrier

Though this lesson contains splendid advice from one of the world's masters at working very close to people with a camera, it was a complete flop. Very few people sent in pictures to *Popular Photography,* and those who did entirely missed the point. They sent in pictures of children and babies. Well, there is no problem here, for children and babies don't frighten us. Ken Heyman's advice concerned working up close to adults, which is an entirely different thing.

What Heyman tells us is how to work close to other people without evoking fear in them. It doesn't tell us how to cope with our own fear. One of the ways is to make ourselves more knowledgeable concerning how people react to being photographed. For this type of information turn to the essay "The Psychology of People Pictures" in Chapter Two. There you will find a detailed account of how people interpret being looked at or photographed. You will also read things which tell you how to make people want to be photographed. When you have these kinds of knowledge well in hand you will find that your fear of photographing other people has been substantially reduced.

Another thing which will help is an understanding of a certain electrical phenomenon in human beings. You may be aware that people are energy emitting and receiving stations. Perhaps you've noticed how a person can mess up a television image by walking too close to it or that other people's vibrations upset you sometimes. These things suggest that we both emit and receive energy. Peope are actu-

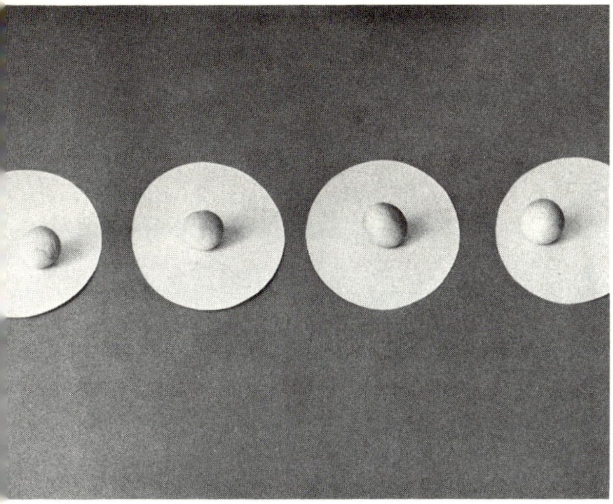

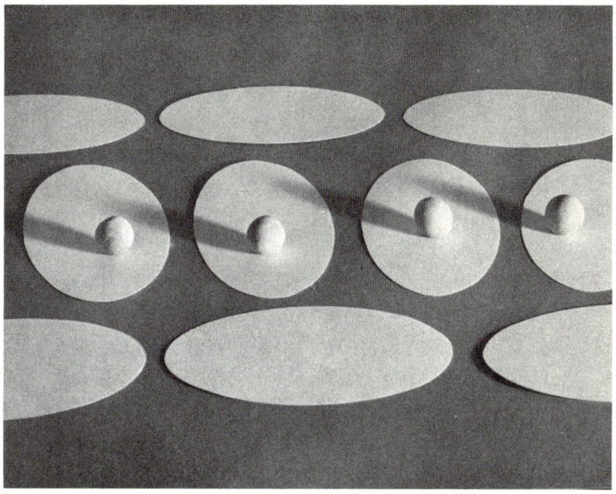

All the cut-out paper shapes in these pictures were ellipses, though some look like circles. I made these pictures to show that an ellipse will make the plane on which it rests seem to tilt. In the top picture, the ellipses were turned endwise to the camera to make them look like circles and to make it seem that they rested on a plane perpendicular to the lens axis. Actually, the picture was shot from a low angle, as proved by the coffee cup resting on one of the very same 'circles' in the bottom picture. The same camera position was used for all three pictures, but ellipses turned sideways to the camera were added to the one at top right. Ellipses will not only tilt planes but increase or decrease the apparent distance across them, which is what the checkerboard did, too. Turn the book sideways now and look at the picture with the extra ellipses in it. Believe it or not, all the paper shapes in the picture are identical ellipses which were made from just one cardboard pattern. Same size. Same shape. If I said it ten more times you still wouldn't believe me, would you? Yet it's the truth.

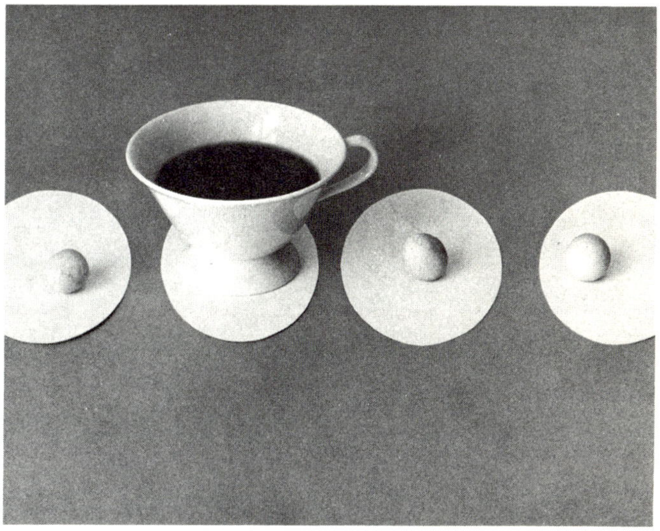

ally very sensitive to energy vibrations of this sort, though few are aware that they are. If you emit the right kind of vibrations you'll never get hassled by other people when you are photographing them. Most people intuitively know this already, so that if they are emitting the wrong vibrations they can't even force themselves to come close to other people with their cameras. If the vibrations are right they find it very easy to do.

People sense their own vibrations on the intuitive level, which means that on the conscious level they may have little idea of what is going on. It would help if we were more conscious of such things. For greater awareness we need information. The key information is that thoughts and attitudes are splendid indicators of the types of energy we emit. That is, for each thought or attitude there is a particular kind of energy (or level of energy vibration). Though people like L. Ron Hubbard have made detailed charts of various attitudes and the rates of energy vibration which accompany them, it is sufficient for

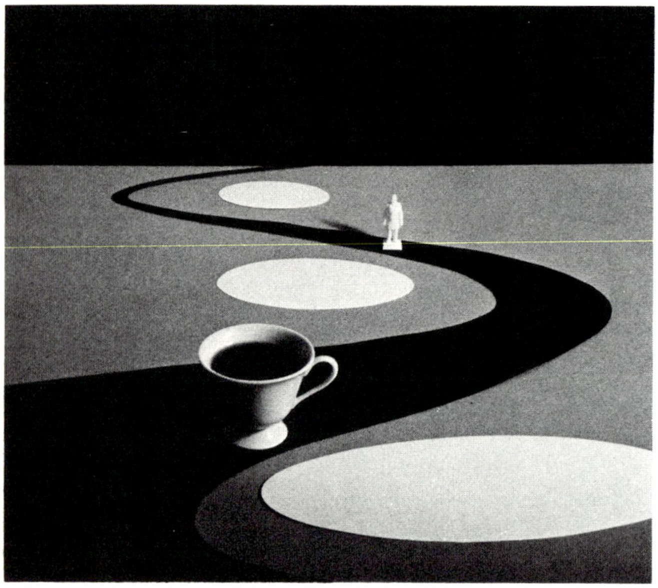

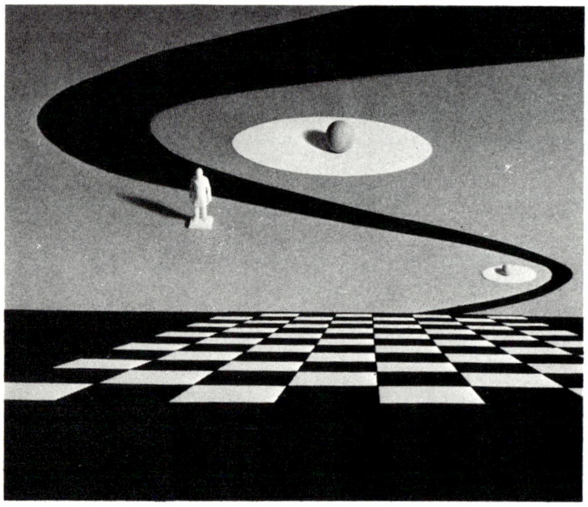

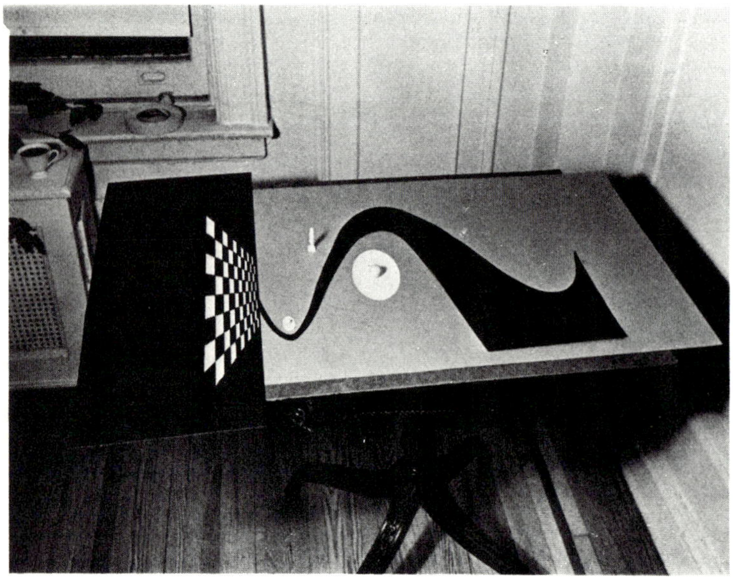

Some kinds of S-shaped curves can increase space or turn it upside-down. The identical S-curve was used for all three shots. Notice that one end of it is thin and that the curved part is flattened. The other end is wide with a fat curve. In the picture with the cup, the fat part of the curve was closest to the camera, which created a lot of depth. It also tilted the plane to a certain degree, though it is almost impossible to detect. I used ellipses of three different sizes and a faked horizon in two different positions. In the center picture, note that I turned the S-curve around so the small end was nearest the camera. I tried to create the illusion of a curve going up in the air above the checkerboard, then contradicted the illusion with ellipses and the figurine. I wanted to see if they created an impression strong enough to overwhelm the space-creating S-curve. The checkerboard serves to turn the edge of the black cardboard into a horizon and supports the illusion of the flying S-curve.

our purposes to merely divide attitudes and vibrations into just two groups: positive and negative. It is accurate to say that positive attitudes are accompanied by high (fast) vibrations, negative attitudes by low (slow) ones.

The next piece of information we need is that people strongly dislike being invaded by negative vibrations emanating from other people. They unconsciously interpret this as a form of attack—which it indeed is—and react accordingly. Their own hostile or negative attitudes are aroused and they give their attackers a rough time. In the case of invading photographers they insult them, threaten violence, snub them, treat them with contempt, walk rapidly out of camera range and so on. This is a special case of "Like begets like" or "As ye sow so shall ye reap," and it never fails to happen.

The next crucial fact is that we have more control over the vibrations we emit than we think we do. The means of control is simply to think deliberately either positive or negative thoughts. Our vibrations will go up or down accordingly. This sounds simplistic, I know, but it works nevertheless. If a photographer wants to photograph people without having them hassle him, all he has to do is prepare himself by putting his thoughts up into the positive range. He doesn't even have to think positive thoughts about people; any kind of positive thought will do very well. He can think positively about turtles, if he likes. When his vibrations are up he can then approach other people and not be intuited by them as a threat.

I know that the fools and maniacs for whom I am expressly writing this chapter will be very sceptical about this, for most of them have trapped themselves deeply in negative thinking. My suggestion to them is that they try to remember back to moments when their attitudes were positive, then try to remember how other people reacted to them. I think they will then agree with what I've just said. However, they'll not agree that it is easy to think positively. They themselves would find it easier to chop off their own toes.

For the fools and maniacs I now have an especially uncomfortable bit of information: The only way out of your fear is to confront it. In photography, this means working up close to people, even when you are terrified. Since terror is a very negative vibration you will certainly evoke corresponding negative responses in your subjects. The only thing you can do is take them on the nose and ask for more. Not a happy prospect, eh? But you know very well that I'm right. You also know that this kind of taking it on the nose will eventually get you where you want to go, whereas your pills, mushrooms and psychotic flights will only increase your burden in the long run.

Your pills and flights may have brought you genuine spiritual insights, this I do not deny. If so you must now learn to accept the fact that such insights have a very heavy price on them. Everything really worthwhile has. You must now strangle your egotism, or selfishness, and pay the price in ego-suffering. Using your camera to help you confront your terror is as good a way of doing this as any. And everyone will admire you for trying.

One more bit of advice for my weird-

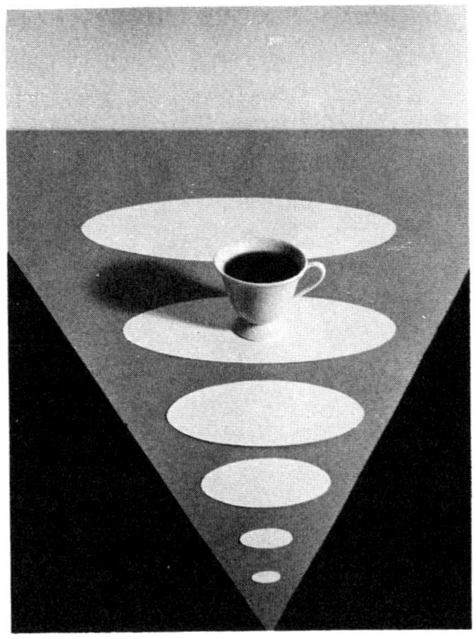

A space battle results when reverse-order ellipses and reverse-order converging lines fight to make you see space in one way while the cup tries to make you see it in another. Which illusion seems to be dominant?

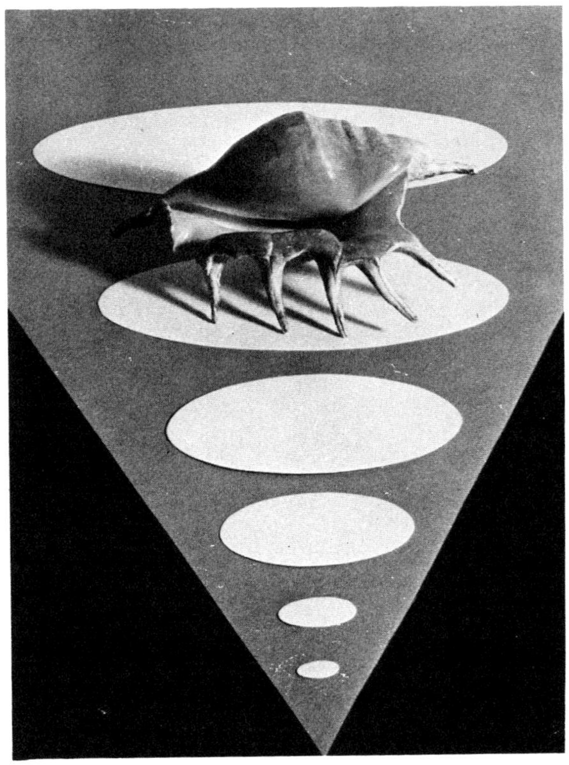

This picture shows how space can be manipulated by placing an unfamiliar object on reverse-order ellipses. Turn the book upside-down to look at the photograph. Then decide if the shell looks natural in this new position.

os: Don't get carried away by vanity and start confronting tough strangers with your camera. All you'll prove is that vanity begets mayhem and that some people are tougher than you are. Work only with your friends, for they need this kind of confrontation just as much as you do; and you'll find yourself loving them more after it's over.

The Lesson:

Photographer Ken Heyman is a huge bore (about 250 pounds). He even likes being a bore. In fact, he's worked for years on the art of being totally boring. This would seem to make him a first-class creep. And what I've just said might even provide grounds for a libel suit.

But there'll be no suit, for being boring is intentional and an important part of Heyman's art. He's such a bore that he can work very close to his subjects—and usually they pay no attention to him at all. So close does he come that he now makes 80 percent of his pictures with a 21-mm lens, which means that he is very close indeed. As his subjects see him he has no more existence than a chair or a piece of wallpaper.

Certainly, getting close to people with a camera, even as close as six feet, is a serious problem for most beginners and a great many pros, too. So Heyman's skillful techniques for unflustered moving in close are of great interest. And they *are* techniques, carefully thought out and deliberately developed.

To be a complete bore is more difficult than one might think, especially since we spend most of our lives trying to be quite the opposite. It requires careful study of all available bores to learn what makes them so lumpish and then constantly working on one's own lumpishness. I suggest that many people will find it a great relief being a lump instead of constantly trying to show the world how smart they are—and there's a good payoff in a very interesting kind of photography. So, start now: Be a bore! But remember it takes practice and intelligence. After you've become an effective bore you'll find greater security in people's presence, knowing they couldn't care less whether you exist and couldn't be bothered having hostile feelings toward you.

Here are some of Ken Heyman's tips:

1. Look like a bore, dress like a bore, move like a bore, stand like a bore, talk like a bore.

2. Never, *never* look your subject in the eye. Eye communication is very primary, very powerful; and eye contact always stirs up emotional issues that are best left unstirred. Do all of your seeing out of the

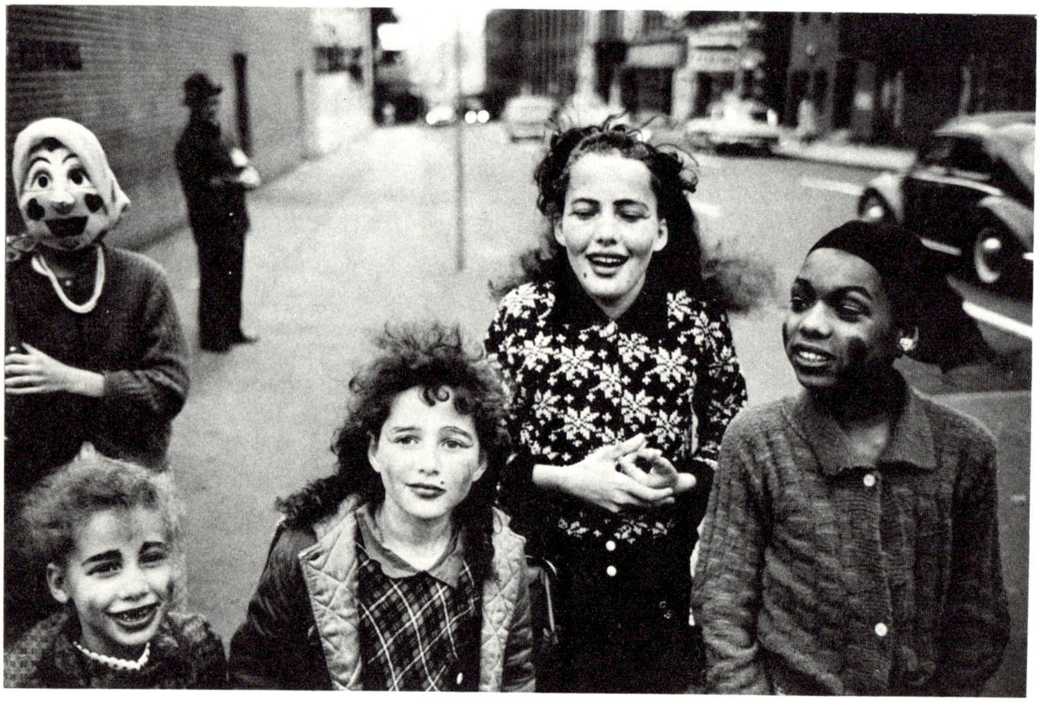

Ken Heyman caught these Manhattan Halloweeners with a 21mm lens. He made himself so boring they didn't even see him.

photo by KEN HEYMAN

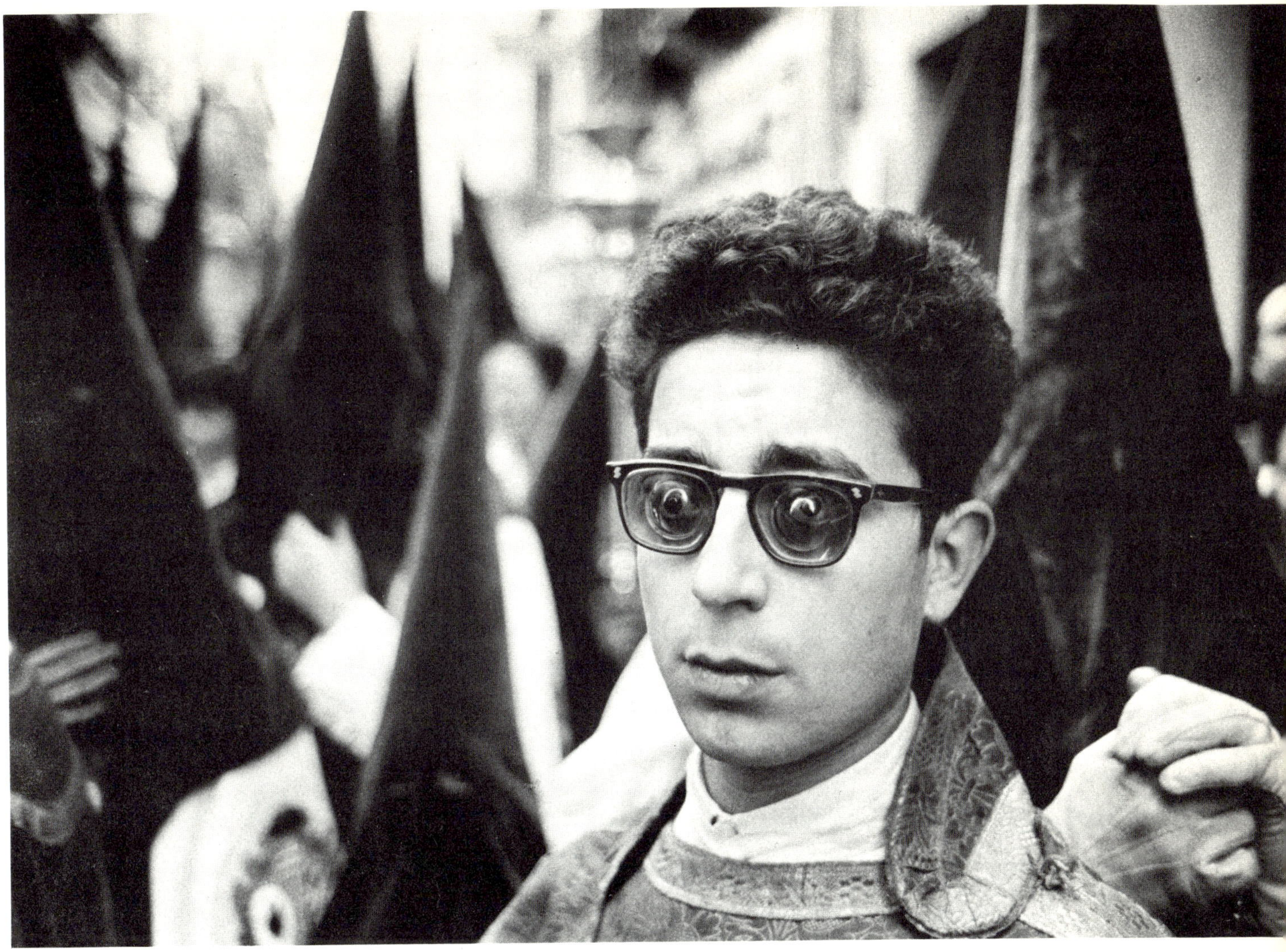

sides of your eyes.

3. When you look toward a subject, keep your eyes 'out-of-focus.' He'll think that like everyone else you're seeing right through him, paying him no attention.

4. Don't focus your camera on the subject; focus on something else at the same distance.

5. Don't read your subject with a meter; read an equivalent object.

6. Dangle your camera casually, its strap around your wrist, not your neck.

7. Fiddle with it so your subject will think you're interested in it, not him.

8. Show interest in a likely subject near the person you want; when he loses interest in you, swing around slightly to take his picture, then back to where you were.

9. Photograph people only when you really like them and are unafraid. Dislike and emotional distress are catching to others.

10. If someone is expecting you to photograph him, leave your camera somewhere until you've established in his mind your interest in him as a person. Now your friend, he will make the photographing easy.

11. People have what might be called defense perimeters. Inside their perimeters you're a threat, outside you're not. Learn to feel these perimeters so you can tell whether you're inside or out.

12. When you see a picture at a distance, pick your spot in advance. Then find a reason your subject would accept your presence there (other than photographing) and amble casually into position, paying no attention to him.

13. If your subject is moving, station yourself on his path of advance, giving him plenty of time to notice and lose interest in you.

Since Heyman never looked him in the eye, this young man thought he was photographing the religious spectacle behind him. Not looking at people keeps them from getting upset.

photo by KEN HEYMAN

14. Keep a bored, expressionless look on your face.

15. Every time you take a picture of a person you are using him. If you don't intend to use him well, he'll know it and react against you. Keep your motives clean.

16. If you're honestly trying to use people to show other people what the world is like, and see this as a very important thing, your subjects will sense something of this and let you approach them.

Use these tips with both strangers and people you know. Though Heyman has many other tips, it is perhaps best that you work yours out for yourself. When he is working, Heyman is probably most often seen by his subjects as a rather dull clod filled with silent good will. The good will is real; the cloddishness, art. This image has worked for him in all parts of the world. It has kept him almost constantly inside the three-foot barrier making fine pictures.

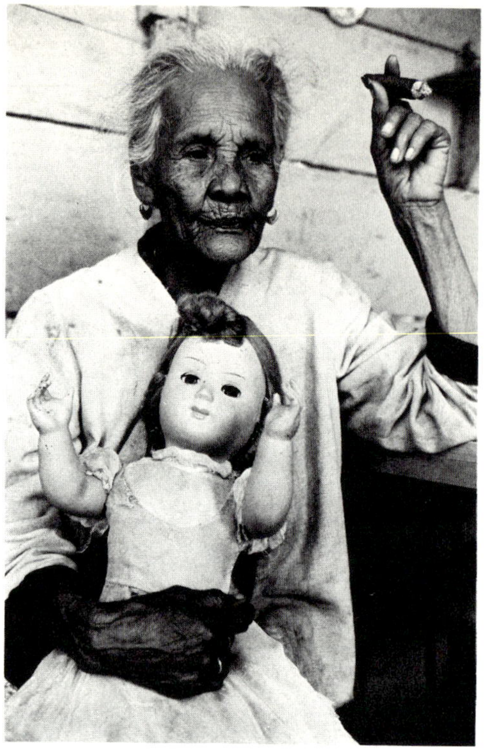

This lady was so pleased with Heyman's low pressure approach to her that she later invited him into her home to take more pictures of her and her granddaughter, who is the proud owner of the doll.

photo by KEN HEYMAN

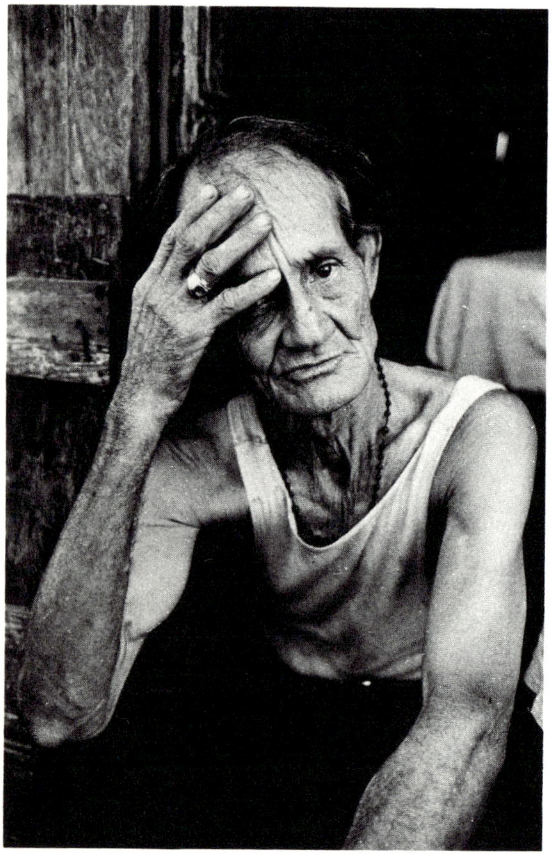

As Heyman was photographing, this man watched him. Ken swung casually around, snapped his picture, then went back to work on his assignment.

photo by KEN HEYMAN

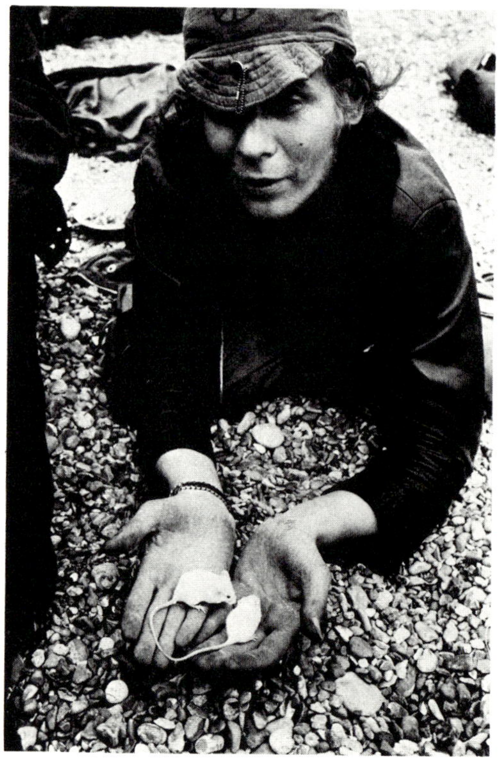

The mice live under this Englishman's hat, making their nest in his hair. Heyman put him at ease by sitting beside him and his chums. He dangled his camera until everyone was at ease with him.

photo by KEN HEYMAN

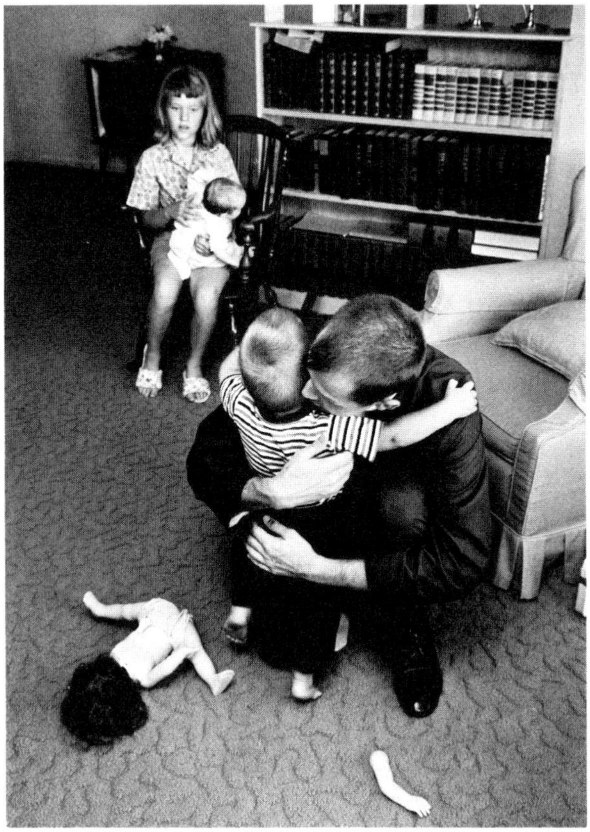

This whole family has forgotten Heyman's presence, though they had looked forward with excitement to his coming to photograph them. He makes so few claims for attention that people forget he's there.

photo by KEN HEYMAN

Games Photographers Play

When this essay appeared in the *1969 Popular Photography Annual,* it caused a controversy. A few people liked it. Others thought it maligned the photographer by setting him out from the rest of humanity as a special kind of buffoon or neurotic. This was by no means my intention, however.

The only thing special about a photographer is that he is a photographer. Otherwise he is like any other human being and has the very same strengths and frailties. Any neurosis or hang-up in photography has counterparts in many other places. My intention was to show what the hang-ups look like when they've been adapted to photography. The reason for pointing them out is that they are bars in the cage in which photographers imprison themselves. Non-photographers imprison themselves by the very same means, but they appear in different guises when not associated with photography.

Having read thus far in my book you certainly know my opinion that the human race is in a very sorry pickle. The culprit in this, as I've said many times before, is human egotism, or selfishness. And I've also pointed out that the way out of the mess is to give egotism a hard time. In this light you can see my reason for writing an essay designed to make photographers squirm. I see it as a friendly act on my part. If an ego suffers enough it will eventually stop playing games and give the Self its freedom.

No one asked me how I happened to know this much about the games photographers indulge in. Anyone with a knowledge of human nature can tell you that photographers certainly didn't divulge the facts to me. One reason is that they don't know they're playing the games. The other is that they wouldn't talk about them even to God if they did. My entire source of basic information was myself. I used my long experience with other photographers only as a check against my personal experience as a photographer. Mainly I drew on my experience as a human being. Photography was just one of the many fields on which I played neurotic, Self-defeating games. The games I wrote about in the essay were merely the ones I had caught myself playing as a photographer.

Some readers may think it requires either great arrogance or total ignorance to learn something about oneself, then ascribe it to the rest of the human race as well. Not so. Anything that is deeply true of one human being applies also to the rest of mankind. The reader should keep this in mind when he attempts to follow my advice, which is: Study this essay until you are certain that you are now playing, or have played, nearly every game which is described in it. Though this will make you very uncomfortable it should

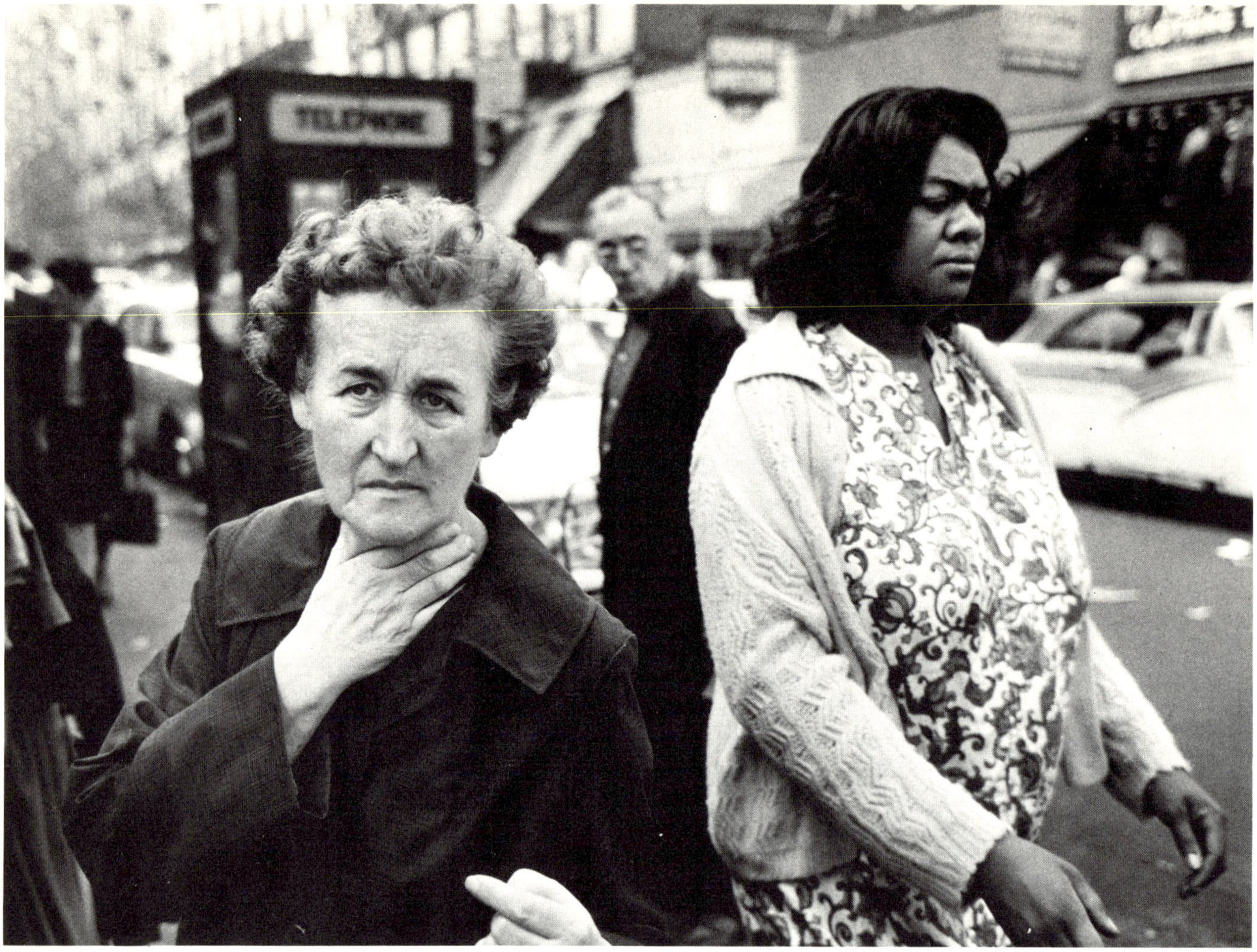

Though Heyman was nearly treading on their toes, the women (above) didn't notice him. He says that the best way to keep from disturbing people is to avoid attracting their attention in the first place.

photo by KEN HEYMAN

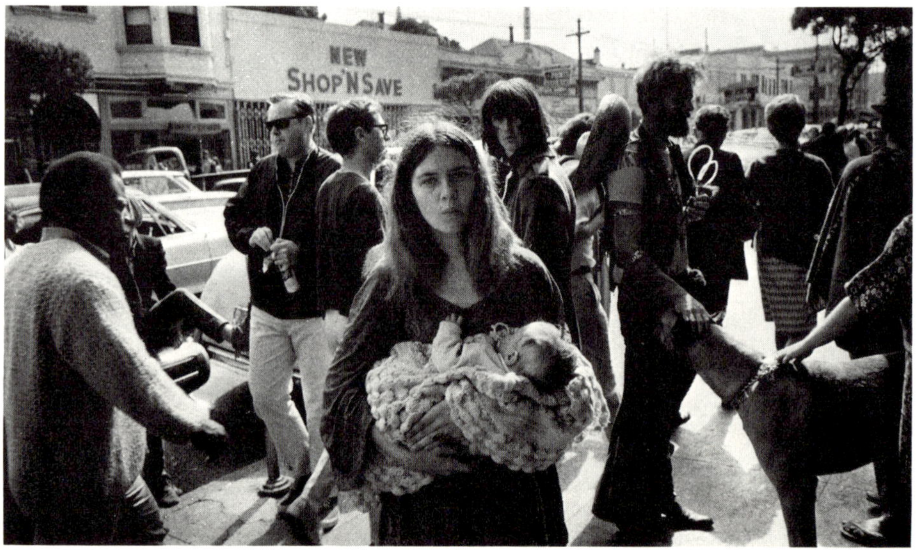

A huge man, Heyman might have frightened this girl. That he did not is a tribute to his ability to efface himself. She seems to find him mildly amusing.

photo by KEN HEYMAN

give you solace to know that your experience is helping you discover the human race. A few more experiences of the sort and you might even find yourself willing to join it. This will make it easier for you to solve your major life problems.

In a way, Chapter Five of this book is a preamble to the essay. It gives a general background for understanding the games and why photographers indulge in them. There wasn't room for this in the essay itself, for the editors gave me very little space to work with. People who write for magazines often have to leave out about 99 percent of what they'd like to say as there is no room for the rest. It even happens in books, as I'm now learning to my rue.

Since the writing in the essay seems to be entirely negative I think I should make a few comments about this. It is more realistic than it is negative. It does, however, talk about Self-destructive games, making little mention of constructive ones. Here again the space restriction was a problem. Another factor is that almost the entire photographic press devotes itself exclusively to talking about the positive side of being a photographer and is not thrown out of balance if one person writes about the other side.

This apparent negativism could be interpreted as an invitation to Self-condemnation. This would be a very sad mistake for any reader to make. I believe that we are given certain rights by the Higher Forces but that Self-condemnation is not one of them. Furthermore, Self-condemnation is nothing more than a vicious form of egotism in disguise. It is Self-destructive and Self-imprisoning. A person studying this essay should avoid Self-condemnation like a plague, therefore. He should do his best to have an affimative attitude toward himself, no matter what embarrassing thoughts pop up with respect to his egotism, or self-centeredness.

In Chapter Five I suggested calling the ego 'the wolf' as a means for developing more objectivity concerning it. Here I suggest something a little more friendly, such as 'Little Joe' or 'Tender Billy.' Such a ploy will help sidestep Self-condemnation and at the same time see the humor of the situation. There is, after all, a good deal to laugh about in the way we keep blindly tangling ourselves up in silly games. When you get to my age you can see life as a comic circus of tempests in teacups. This thought goes down well with the third glass of wine, or even the first.

The illustrations by Jerry Uelsmann deserve your special attention. He is without doubt one of the world's finest photographers. He has a terrific knack for talking about man's inner life with good humor and calm acceptance. What a relief after the terrors of Freudian psychology! His photographs show the unconscious mind as weird but groovy. At least, that's what I think they are all about. If they are actually about traveling in the astral world or the seventh plane, that is also fine with me. I'll write to Jerry and see if he can schedule me for a six-month's tour. I'll bring the sandwiches and he can provide the flying saucer.

The Essay:

Man is always trying to put tags on himself. He has defined himself as a creature with a soul, a logical animal, a creator of cultures, a communicator, a storer of information. Dr. Eric Berne, author of Games People Play, *has shown how man is also an inveterate inventor and player of games. Perhaps the most readily accessible definition of what Dr. Berne means by games can be seen in the movie* Who's Afraid of Virginia Woolf? *Berne's own definition, written for other psychologists, tends to be a bit technical. Even so, his book became a runaway best seller.*

In the book and in the movie we see that "games" are not played for fun but for less acceptable reasons. Players never really win anything—they always manage to lose. Instead of spreading happiness, games create havoc. Like ordinary games, these have rules, although the players are seldom aware of them. With rare exceptions they don't even know they are playing games; and if they do they don't know what kind. The spirit of the play may be desperation or malice. Players relate to one another as enemy soldiers. And the results are chaos.

Dr. Berne described the games that people play together. However, since photography is essentially a lonely art, I shall examine the games that photographers play mainly with themselves—that is, the ways they use photography in self-deception. The information I present is based on long years of observing a very muddy stream, photography, and the surprising creatures who swim in it.

Game Number One: BLEEDER

The first game—Bleeder—is very common in photography, but like all games it is seldom seen for what it actually is. The object of Bleeder is to suffer. I could have called it Suffer (giving it a certain dignity) or Kick Me Jack, but the suffering in the game has an element of phoniness. (Kick Me Jack suggests that the player asks for pain but places the source of it outside himself.) Though the Bleeder often provokes outsiders to punish him he is more likely to do the punishing himself.

A former student of mine—I'll call him Tom—is a good example of how effectively games can be played in photography. In his four years of college training in photography, Tom did little else but bleed. The pain was written in every line in his face, in every gesture, and in every word he spoke. He provoked it simply by failing at everything. He could be relied on for dull prints, silly or meaningless picture ideas, ugly lighting, broken equipment,

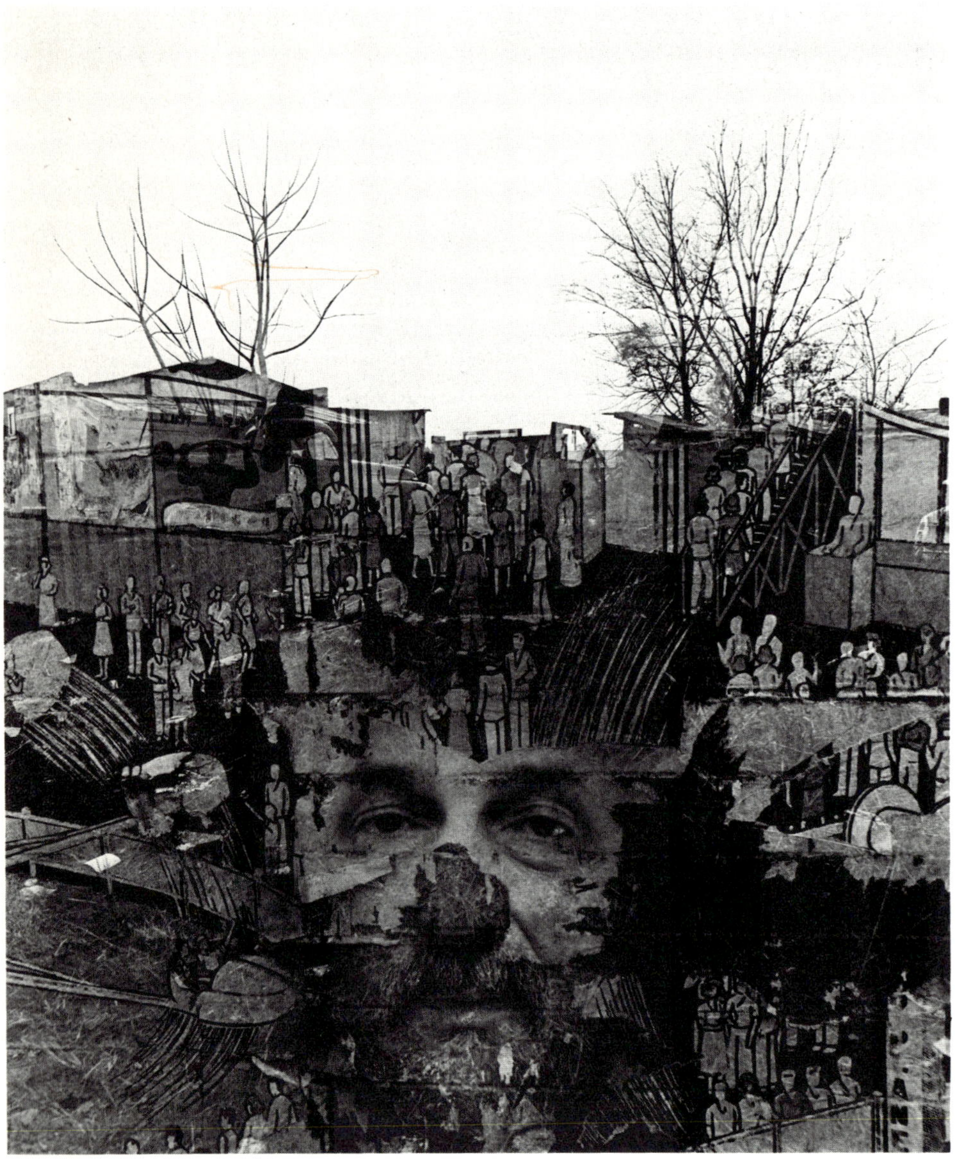

photo by JERRY N. UELSMANN

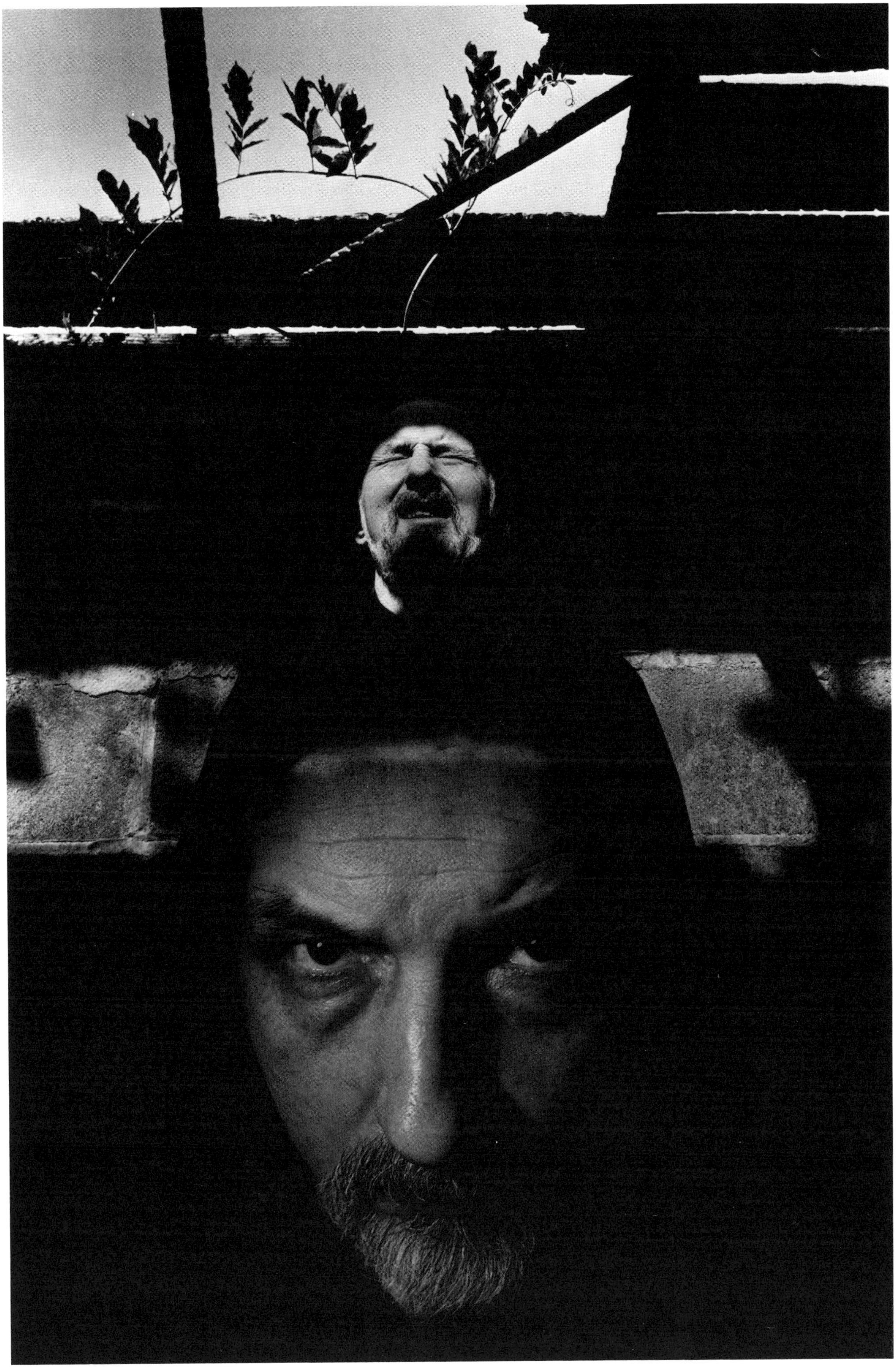

photo by *JERRY N. UELSMANN*

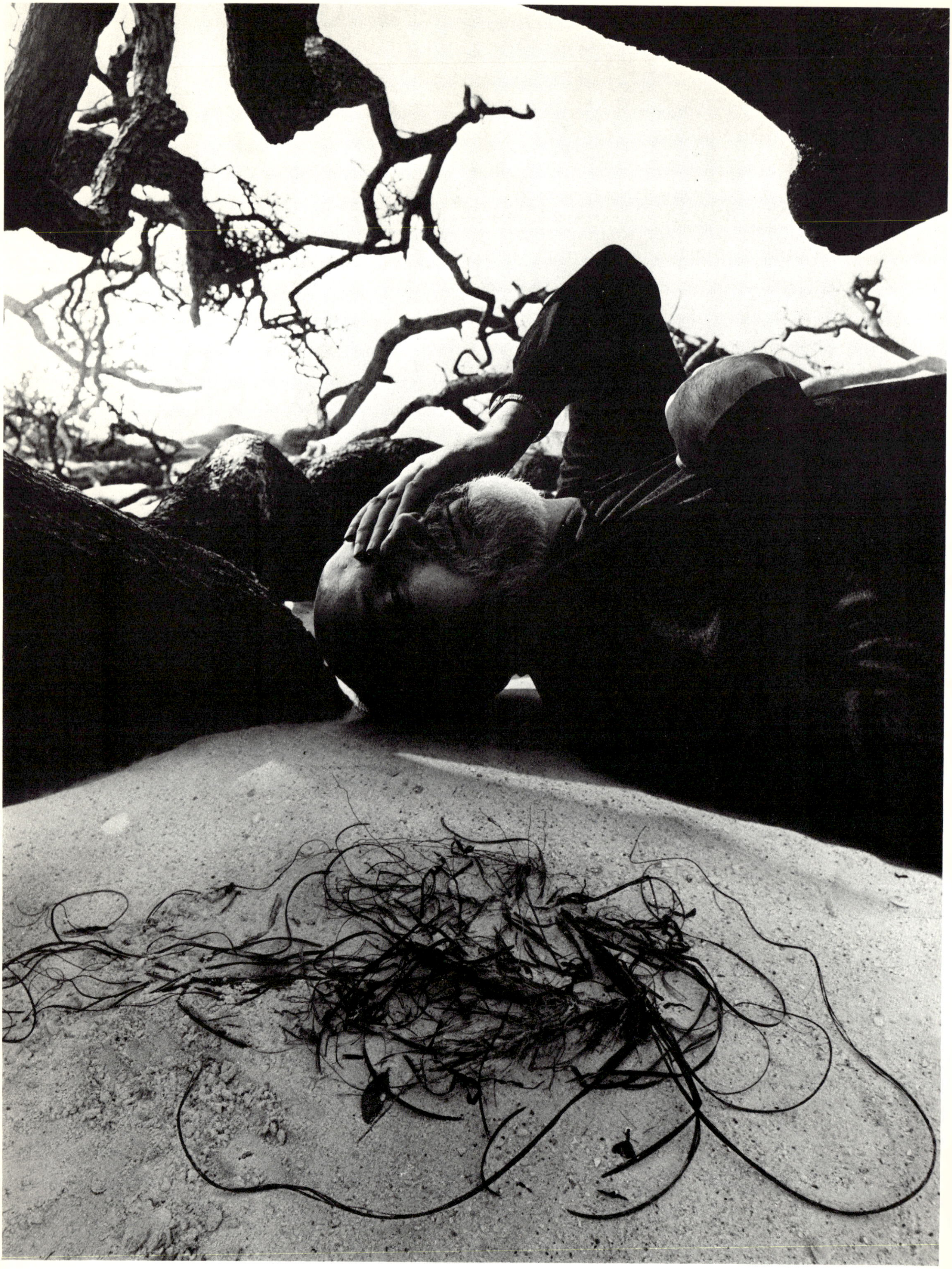

photo by JERRY N. UELSMANN

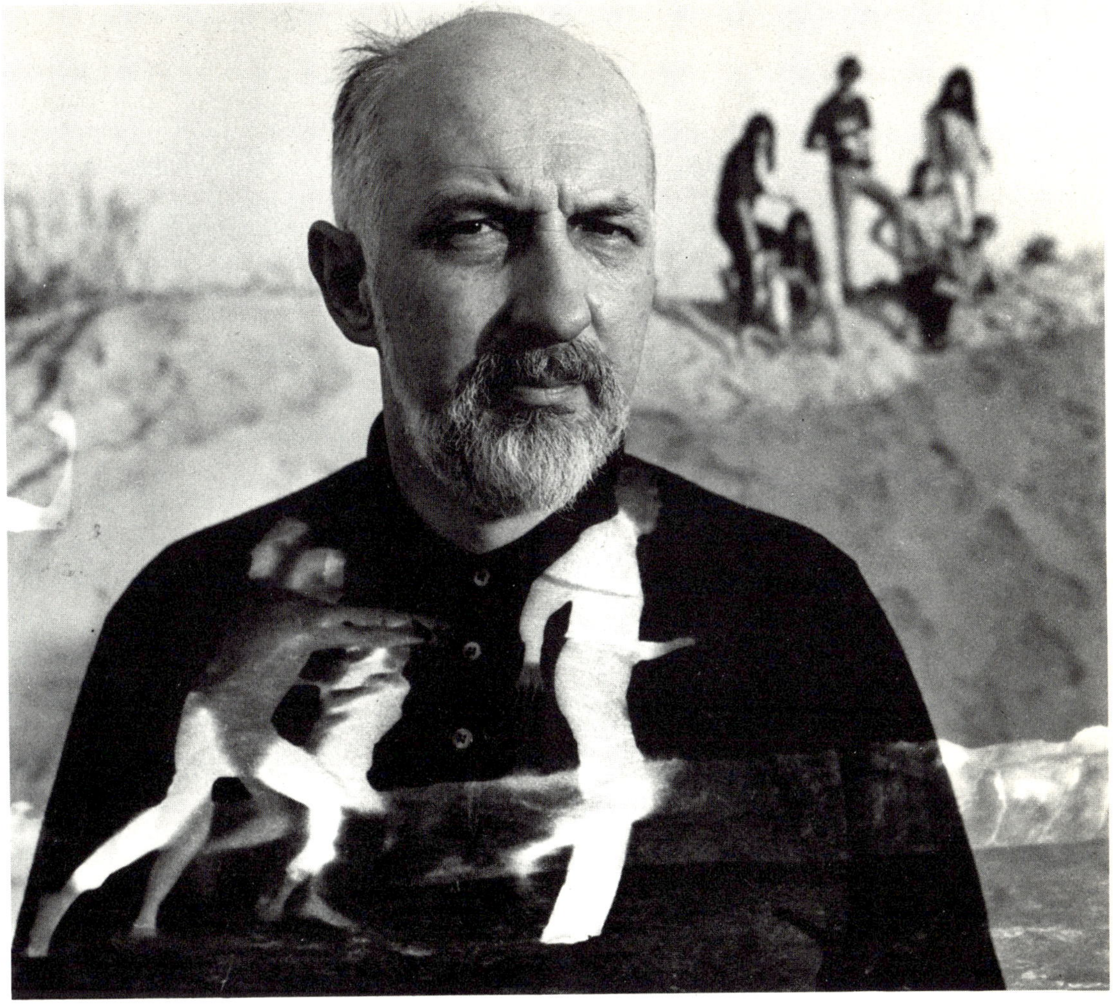

lost film, inane comments in critique sessions, and chaotic compositions. You name it—everything a photographer doesn't want to do he did, again and again and again. His fellow students fell into his trap and gave him all the punishment a heart could desire: unkind comments, withheld praise, intimations that he was a fool. He himself added to his pain by thinking of himself as a total failure, which he wasn't because *he was actually doing what he set out to do.*

Though I've called Tom a Bleeder, could he have been just an ordinary failure? All his teachers thought so, myself included. It wasn't until years later that I figured out what Tom was really up to. First of all, he was really quite intelligent. He did very well in his college board examinations and in all his courses outside the photography department; thus stupidity couldn't account for his total ineptitude in photography.

Then there were clues such as his print quality. In four years he didn't manage to make even one good print. Despite what some photographers say, printing is not *that* difficult. With all the help Tom had, even an intelligent ape would have been making good prints within six months.

Tom's choice of companions was significant: he always chose those whose work would show him up the most and whose contempt for him was the most obvious. The teacher he clung to was the one he could depend on to cause him the greatest suffering. Needing an outlet for repressed hostility, this man latched onto Tom as the ideal sufferee. Almost daily he told him that he was a photographic nincompoop and a personality failure.

Consider the fact that Tom remained

oto by JERRY N. UELSMANN

four years in a field in which he and everyone else knew he was a failure. Tom didn't have to be a photographer. No one does. Anyone not needing to suffer would have left photography long before.

Tom was totally committed to photography, too. Nothing else in the world existed for him. This over-commitment was necessary to produce the greatest amount of suffering, for if he didn't care enough about photography how could he properly suffer by being a failure?

Tom tricked most of his teachers into his game. He used to hang around them for hours, seeking help. A week later he would come back with pictures that proved that his instructors hadn't gotten through to him on a single point—unless one could see it as a game, with Tom as Bleeder and his teachers as both stabbers and victims. At Tom's invitation they stabbed him by criticizing, withholding praise, and not concealing well enough their despair at his lack of improvement. They got stabbed in return by his weekly proof that they couldn't teach.

During this whole experience Tom was unaware he was playing the game or even that he was suffering. People have a remarkable ability to block from consciousness what's going on in themselves. What Tom did to himself is exceptional neither in intensity nor in kind. What makes it seem so improbable is that I've stripped his game to its bare bones. However, one must remember it took years to do this. The game as actually played was obscured by every kind of flim-flam a desperate and intelligent mind could think up.

The General Nature of Games

Now for some questions on games in general. First of all, how can a person play a game for so long without being found out, even by himself? Simple: What the gamesman does is just not something he or anyone else would expect and be on the lookout for; for example, who would think that someone would want to suffer? Furthermore, the cardinal rule in all games is that the protagonist will do everything in his power to prevent anyone, including himself, from learning that a game is being played, what particular game it is, what motives led him to start it, how the moves in the game relate, and what he hopes to accomplish. This rule is motivated by one's unconscious terror of being found out by one's self or by others. As for other players in the game, they're maneuvered into accepting the same rules by being tricked into playing roles they're suckers for; and they have as strong reasons as the protagonist for not wanting to see what is going on.

Another question is: If a person can play games by himself why does he enlist others? One answer is that he's less likely to discover what he's doing; he can blame them for anything that happens instead of having to see that he himself is responsible. For example, the Bleeder picks himself a stabber, gets himself properly chopped up, then says to himself, "This is that man's nature and I am innocent."

Even fine photographers can play Bleeder around the pain-through-failure theme, and many do. But they don't have to do it by such obvious means as making bad prints or using poor picture ideas. They can suffer even while making splendid photographs. All they have to do is set their self-criticism standards so high that no performance, even a great one, can measure up to them.

Though there are many other ways in which the average photographer plays Bleeder I limited myself to only one and described it in considerable detail in order to explain what is meant by a "photographic game." Another very common source of pain for the photographer is in letting himself discover he's playing even one of the games discussed in this article. Though games are heavily disguised and unconsciously played, he can let himself penetrate the disguises if his need to suffer is great enough. After all, he himself invented the disguises, not some stranger. What he invented he can let himself see if something in his unconscious impels him to. The suffering from this particular kind of Self-revelation can be very intense.

Game Number Two: SMASHER

The purpose of playing Smasher is to clobber things—the world in general, people, institutions, customs, and beliefs. Since obvious hostility actually expressed in smashing things ordinarily leads to reprisal, there has to be considerable covering up. In the game of Smasher the destruction is usually symbolic, which is emotionally nearly as satisfying as the real thing. Plausible excuses are found for picking certain targets (they deserve destruction, stand in the way of progress, are actually unharmed by being attacked, etc.). The Smasher disguises the fact that he's tearing things up by saying, "I'm not putting things down but showing them as they really are." Rather than attributing his actions to hostility, he sees them as flowing from his love for God and man, or love of truth and beauty. This kind of cover-up is common to all games.

Playing SMASHER at Home

Since photographers can play Smasher in a great many ways we might as well start with something close to home: what often happens when the average photographer tries to make a carefully done picture of his wife. He really smashes her, as almost any wife who has gone through it can tell. However, the photographer himself usually hasn't even a clue to what he has really done except for a very vague premonition that in the interests of marital peace he shouldn't photograph his wife anymore if he can help it except possibly to make quick, unseeing snapshots.

Marriage, as we're constantly being told nowadays, is a tremendous source of repressed (unconscious) rage. It brutally confronts every intelligent man and woman with the fact that they are complete washouts as lovers in the sexual, ethical, and religious senses. This is extremely hard to bear. In addition, it confronts them with their inability to live up to their own lifelong ideals, which is again very painful. Instead of accepting their failures graciously and learning to live with them, they repress them to the unconscious and project the blame and their own hostility onto their mates. But they must do this in clever, indirect ways or they will become aware of what they're doing and suffer the pangs of guilt. Photography, mainly because it isn't understood very well yet, is a very good outlet for such disguised hostility.

Let us see just one of the ways in which the photographer plays Smasher with his wife. If he's been married awhile he intuitively knows all her most desperately defended illusions for herself, though he hasn't consciously thought about them. If he understood himself and her better he could use his camera to support them or to gently replace them with truths about herself she is ready to accept. Instead of this his pictures brutally strip these badly needed illusions away. What's more, he then confuses his unconscious sadistic delight in her pain with an image of himself as a saintly teacher whose sole reason for causing pain is her spiritual enlightenment.

Just one example of illusion stripping: The wife needs to see herself as a blithe spirit, gay and gentle. Husband catches her with a cold glint in her eye, emphasizes strong jaw muscles, chooses a grim background, fails to rearrange her disordered blouse and polishes her off with a lighting justified only for Satan himself. He doesn't consciously know what he's seeing, of course, but experienced in photography or not he always manages to see just well enough to do a thorough demolition job. Having known a great many photographers who have tried once to get really good photographs of their wives I don't see anything at all unusual in this pathetic little story. Oh, there are some who photographically clobber their wives more than once—those completely insensitive to other people's emotional needs or who have badly frightened and timid wives.

So, we write about marriage, eh? Most people use photography about their families anyway. And unfortunately families are a central place for playing games, too.

SMASHER in Fashion Photography

A somewhat similar version of Smasher is played in American fashion photography. Here a woman's beauty is not necessarily taken away from her, just her soul. She's shown as a zombie. Recently, it has been popular to make her into a lesbian. It is also a common custom to change women into men in the name of making them more feminine, of all things. The list of fashion photography devices for surreptitiously smashing women is very long; the photographers who invented them are immensely clever. Some say this goes on because homosexual male fashion photographers love to clobber women, others that women are just begging to be clobbered. The truth is that as in all games it is a marriage of convenience for everyone concerned, with Smashers and Smashees getting exactly what they want without ever having to find out exactly what it is. Finding out might be very painful. One thing for sure, the facts about the true nature of women are brutally ignored, obscured, or distorted. The psychic damage this does to women on a national scale must be positively tremendous.

We Disguise Our Games From Ourselves

Certain variations of Smasher are remarkably well concealed. A close friend of mine —a world-famous photojournalist—played the game in a neatly camouflaged version. Several years ago he went into a terrible spiritual slump, which invariably provokes inner hostility, either turned against the self or the world in general. In this state of inner rage nothing in his photography changed except his print quality. For nearly two years his prints were a miserable, depressing gray. Symbolically, he was committing the whole world and everyone in it to muddy oblivion. Some photographers might say he'd 'lost his eye'; this is utter nonsense, as is so much that is said about photography. He was condemning the entire world to perdition, which he has since learned to see for himself. When he was doing it, however, he didn't have a clue.

But why did his anger have to come out in bad print quality? The answer is fairly simple: It was here that he was least likely to become aware of it and what it was impelling him to do, smash everything. If he'd gone around making hostile pictures of people he might have suspected his own hostility immediately. In fact, if he'd done anything dramatic at all to change his photography he might have been led to wonder about himself. A change in print quality could gradually sneak up on him and catch him unaware.

The explanation thus far is oversimple, however. Not only was this photographer playing Smasher but several other games as well, one of which was Bleeder. To smash things brings on guilt, even if you're not consciously aware of doing it. Guilt invariably demands expiation through punishment. In this man's case, the same device used in playing Smasher also worked in Bleeder: bad print quality. As a fine craftsman he hated bad prints and could punish himself for being a Smasher by making them. The punishment worked even though he didn't consciously realize his prints were terrible.

One Game Leads To Another

This is still a great oversimplification. There are games within games within games. In a sense, all games are one, and separate definitions arbitrary. Playing one game may provoke another. A game played in everyday life may necessitate a compensatory one in photography, and vice versa. Should a photographer even begin to discover he's playing a certain game he'll automatically quit playing it and unconsciously start searching for another version of it he won't be able to recognize. Roles that the various players take are often switchable. The whole substructure of photographic gamesmanship is heavily disguised by the players. They will not and cannot divulge any information on their own games. Though they've always left clues—unconsciously but deliberately—they are deeply obscured by esoteric symbolism. Should they suddenly discover clearly their own games they would be compelled to stop photographing altogether. These are some of the reasons that the games photographers (or anyone else) play have been written about so seldom, and this is a warning to the reader that he should regard what is written here merely as a starting point, not as a neat summation of all that really goes on.

More About SMASHER

Before going to the next game, I wish to drop just one more clue as to the prevalence of the game Smasher. A very common version of it is 'Garbage Can' photography. Here the player picks a subject that is actually distasteful, thinking that in doing so he is only righteously calling a spade a spade. The fact is that he picks garbage cans and cluttered alleys because he is hostile and wishes to call the whole world rotten. Symbolically, the garbage cans *are* the world. The photographer may even be momentarily in love with them for allowing him to express his rage through them. The garbage can idea could be extended to include anything distasteful or distressing, such as poverty, water pollution, civil strife, or urban decay.

Game Number Three: HIDER

The object of playing Hider is to express yourself without anyone, including yourself, finding out who you are. It's like shouting "Yes I am, no I'm not." Though the contradictory features are to hide oneself and to be revealed, the most salient feature is the hiding, thus the name. Such contradiction is characteristic of all games.

On any level of performance photography is one of the world's great natural hiding places. The beginner trots along comfortably, intuitively aware that no one can look at his pictures and discover the motives behind them. He tends to see in cultural stereotypes, anyway—the right mountain to photograph, the right statue, the standard snapshot of friends or family, and so on. Stereotypes hide the individual very well. Even without them the beginner would be entirely safe from discovery; he can't see well enough as a photographer even to know what he's getting into his pictures, thus he is not really responsible for it, and has little or no conscious expressive control over his medium. Though it is barely possible he might see from his photographs that he has used cultural stereotypes, he would only interpret this as seeing things as they really are, not as a form of unconscious bondage to cultural patterns. As long as he doesn't really learn anything about photography he is entirely safe from discovery.

As he begins to see better and to control the medium he is in danger—he thinks. Things have crept into his pictures without his conscious intention; and he begins to suspect their presence, vaguely sensing that they may represent unconscious motives he wants no one, including himself, to know about. Immediately, he loses himself in one of the many versions of Hider constantly on display in the world of visual communication, especially in the camera magazines. If he doesn't intuitively understand them for what they are, he may give up picture making and go into something less dangerous such as being a camera equipment bug or playing golf. However, most people who actually stick with photography never go through this period of nervousness. Either they continue with their original stereotypes, changing them only by technical refinement, or they slide easily into hidey-holes they had unconsciously selected when first interested in photography.

How To Be a Hider

Perhaps the easiest way for a person to play Hider is to photograph something he isn't really interested in. If his interests would reveal him, he can avoid detection by seeming to be interested in something he's not. It would be impossible to tell how many thousands of photographers use this particular ploy, for the natural human capacity to stir up a fictitious interest in something is enormous.

An interesting thing happens in a class in photography when a teacher suggests, correctly, that all photography embodies a measure of unconscious self-revelation (such teachers often claim to have considerable ability in "reading pictures," though this is usually only self-deception). If the statement is cleverly made and supported by verbal gymnastics in pictorial criticism, about half the class will be taken in and stop photographing altogether. This is the half with some degree of intuitive self-understanding. The other half will completely block from awareness or unconsciously distort what the teacher has said and continue to make the same kinds of pictures as before, types which embody some of the common versions of Hider. Some of the stall-outs will gradually, cautiously creep back into action as they feel out versions of Hider for themselves. The remainder never will, trusting in no game to hide them well enough—from themselves and others. I think this classroom situation is echoed everywhere when people come together to ask themselves seriously what photography is all about. Camera clubbers should take very careful note of this paragraph.

No Need To Be Found Out

Very sensitive photographers will realize that I've just dropped an enormous bombshell into photography. Therefore, some assurances are most obviously necessary, unless my intention is to clobber amateur photography altogether. Be assured, sensitive ones, that with all the versions of Hider that are available there is absolutely no necessity for any photographer whatsoever being found out, if that's what he unconsciously fears. Even the most expert of experts can't penetrate the disguises. He may see that you are hiding—most photographers are—but he hasn't more than the slightest chance of learning what from.

There is a fly in the ointment, however, and that is the side of the Self which is trying to make itself known. It never ceases in this effort, never. It sneaks into even the most determined game of Hider, trying to make it into a game of Revealer (not listed elsewhere among the games because it is essentially healthy, not self-destructive as the rest of them are). If it didn't exist the photographer could easily solve the problem of remaining concealed by simply dropping photography altogether. It's not really *that* important now, is it? But this hidden self may not let him quit. It says, in effect, "Dammit, Jack, you've *got* to keep on making pictures *to let me out!*" It backs its argument with tremendous internal pressure, make no mistake about this.

Another assurance is now required: Even impelled by the powerful urge for self-revelation there is little chance of a hiding photographer to be found out except by people who thoroughly understand what is really going on. Such people are one's natural friends, soulmates as it were. They are usually as safe to be around as plump, pink angels.

An interesting version of Hider was observed at a university conference on photographic communication I attended a few years ago. A well-known artist-photographer displayed a group of abstract nature pictures, which he said were related to one central theme. He said he would leave the room so we could talk freely among ourselves in trying to discover what it was. Though many of those present knew the photographer well and some had extremely sharp critical minds, the discussion went on for about two hours before even a minority had decided what he meant. When he returned our spokesman asked him, "Are you trying to tell us you are a homosexual?" "Yes, that's what I'm talking about," was his only reply, his face white with suffering.

This would seem to show that experienced critical minds can penetrate even the disguises of abstract nature photography. Not quite. Most of us already knew the photographer was a homosexual, that he liked to embody personal secrets in abstract photographs and that he believed in public self-revelation as a good thing. We were also very familiar with this type of use of the medium. Even so, we wouldn't have had a chance but for one picture, the only non-abstract in the bunch. It was a very sensual, romantic male nude. Shown alone it would have revealed his so-called secret immediately. As it was, the other pictures which were supposedly designed for the sole purpose of revealing the secret were functioning as red herring. And the fact of his homosexuality was no secret at all, you will remember. His real secrets—never uncovered—were what made him homosexual, his feeling about it, his private behavior as a homosexual, and what he hoped to gain by bringing public suffering on himself. So here we had a classic example, a man trying with all his

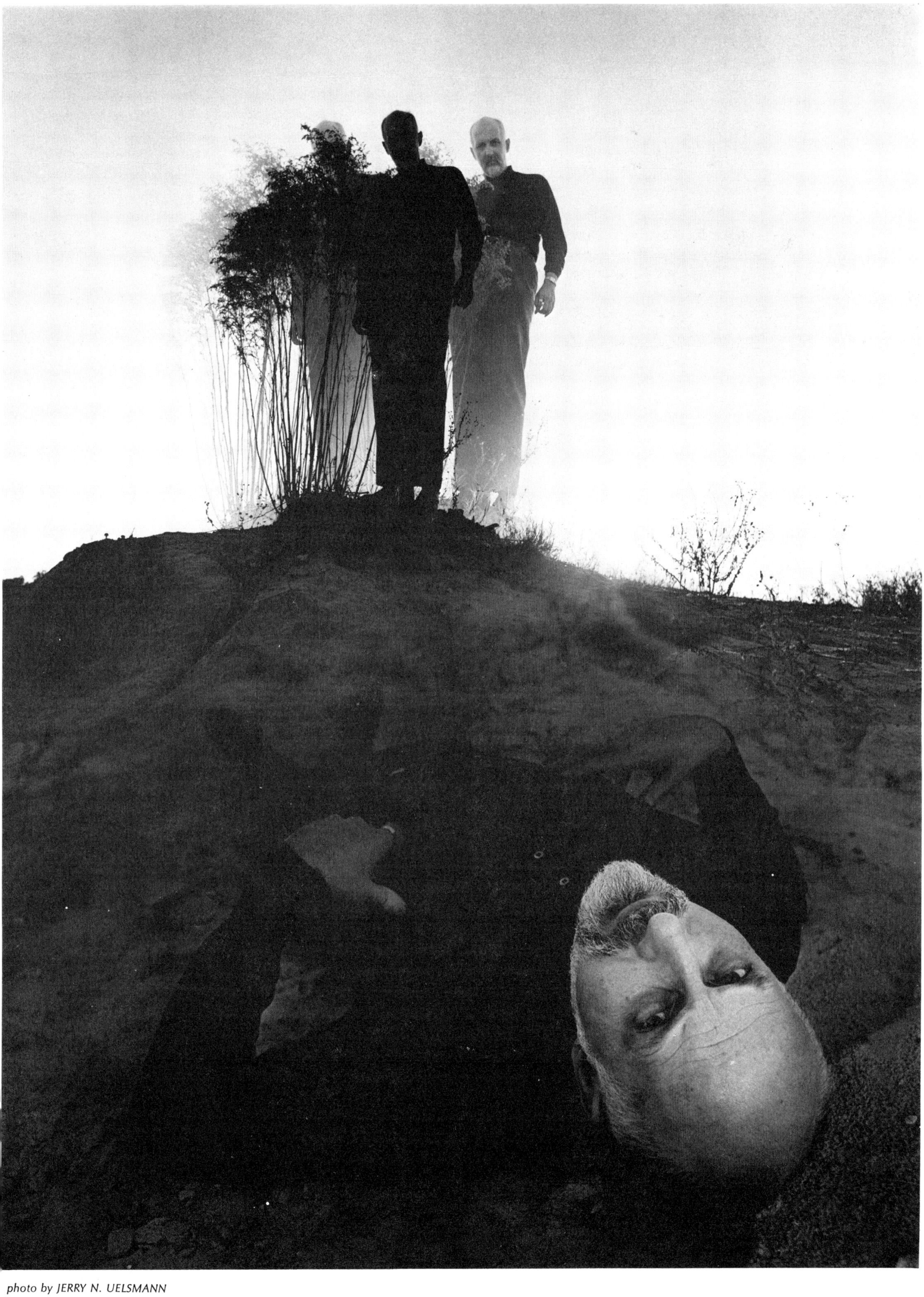

photo by JERRY N. UELSMANN

heart to give himself away and at the same time making sure it wouldn't really happen.

Some Excellent Hiding Places

I've known a great many people who chose abstract nature photography in which to hide, but have never been able to tell from photographs alone what was being hidden. Oh, phallic symbols and such things crop up frequently, yet what do they mean except that a person has the normal human involvements in sexual problems? And an experienced Hider often knows about sex symbols, anyway. Though so-called critics sometimes devote themselves exclusively to trying to unravel Freudian sexual hang-ups, more often than not sex has nothing whatsoever to do with what is being hidden in photographs. Most of what is there is as innocent as pigeon's milk.

Another extremely common hiding place is in imitation. Though it is usually construed to mean only lack of imagination, I've learned to be very suspicious of this idea. People are by nature immensely more imaginative than we think, and when they surrender their God-given creativity for abject imitation there must be reasons for it. So culturally important are the factors underlying this surrender of creativity that I've devoted two whole sections to them (Imitator and Repeater). In relating imitation to the game Hider it is sufficient to say that absolutely no one can tell who a given photographer really is if he makes photographs like everyone else's.

Another excellent hiding place is in 'objective' photojournalism. There the photographer can say—and everyone will believe him—"This is the world revealing itself, not me revealing myself." We're just now beginning to see that this statement isn't true and that so-called objective photojournalism is only a popular myth. But as long as the public doesn't understand this too well, photojournalism will remain a first-rate hiding place.

The whole field of salonism adapts itself admirably to the game of Hider by being powerfully imitative. Were it not for the fact that it offers its followers great psychological safety it wouldn't even exist. Though salon photographers say they're looking for creativity, it is actually the last thing they want, for creativity reveals.

Game Number Four: PROJECTOR

The object of playing Projector is to externalize painful unconscious feelings so that you can relieve yourself of their pressure by attributing them to outside objects or persons rather than to yourself. There is also a strong element of wanting to see yourself and simultaneously being afraid to, so you imagine yourself but refuse to see it.

In painting, the projection can sometimes be fairly direct, as the artist in a sense is responsible for every single brush stroke. Photography is less direct. The photographer projects through selection, finding things in the exterior world that already represent his interior feelings. Then by use of photographic controls he modifies them so that they'll represent the feelings more accurately. Since few people even suspect that this game can be played in photography, they often don't disguise their messages very well.

A photographer of mountains may project his inner pre-occupation with power. A portraitist may use each new face as a blackboard on which to write his illusions for himself; if he's non-commercial, he may image disillusions, perversions, hopes, and anger. A distressed person may find distressed people (or things) to photograph. A person with messianic compulsions will photograph what passes for messiahhood in others. A weakling may gravitate to the strong to project through them his greatest wish for himself. A man with strong but feminine leanings may use women to draw unconscious self-portraits.

Often the projection is in opposites: Inner chaos imaging structure, hostility imaging love, fear imaging boldness, frigidity imaging spontaneous sexuality, fear of complexity imaging simplicity.

Since the photographer doesn't usually realize he's projecting, the projection may be very straightforward, fairly obvious to anyone who knows what to look for. However, there is always a psychological out for the photographer: Things in photographs aren't actually his feelings.

And there is no way to prove this is indeed what they are. The photographer can make a very convincing but spurious argument that his subject is entirely responsible for whatever meaning gets into his pictures, especially to other photographers. They know very well that controls reflect intention, unconscious or otherwise.

Game Number Five: PEEPER

The game called Peeper is motivated by fear of people, immense curiosity about them (sexual or non-sexual) and the desire to find intimacy with them despite the fear. But intimacy itself is feared, to it can only be of a symbolic kind. Photography is a natural for this kind of symbolism, which to the unconscious mind isn't symbolism at all but the real thing.

It doesn't take much imagination to see that a person who favors telephoto lenses, concealed cameras, or sneaky tactics might be playing Peeper. However, photographers who can come right up to people frequently play the game, too. With them the model-photographer relationship becomes a thinly disguised seduction scene, the model eagerly joining in because she (or he) also wants intimacy but is equally afraid of it. Though both may be aware of the sexual play for what it is—it is very unlikely they'd be aware of the great intensity of their unconscious fear, thus that the "love game" actually represents frigidity expressed in opposites.

A less obvious reason than sex for playing Peeper is to discover another person's inner secrets or to create the illusion that you have. A photographer will confront a model and wait for expressions revealing the side of the model's self that she wishes to conceal. Or through lighting, pose, or camera angle, he will create the illusion of this revelation. The model may not be in the least aware of what is actually going on, thus the photographer's unconscious fears are safely hidden from her. In general, however, people who are being photographed are intuitively very astute in such matters, so the photographer has to be a very fancy dancer indeed. Many of them are.

Once the photographer has made his pictures he can more or less roll around in them, unconsciously distorting his memories of what actually happened when they were made or using them as the basis for fantasies that he is loved, desired, accepted, appreciated, understood. He can say to himself, "I am the kind of person to whom others truthfully and willingly reveal themselves." This is the highest form of intimacy.

Game Number Six: POSSESSOR

Possessor is somewhat related to Peeper, but is more motivated by possessiveness, the desire to dominate, and selfishness. The Possessor's object is to own other people without having to give anything of himself in return. He can't do it directly, since people don't generally like to be owned, so he does it symbolically. He unconsciously equates having pictures of people with actually possessing them.

One gain to the Possessor is that he can buy people cheaply and at the same time avoid the face-to-face relationship that might force on him the fact of his selfishness and the necessity of his doing something about it if he wants to have harmonious relations with others.

Like the Peeper, the Possessor may sneak up on his unknowing victims with his camera. However, he may be only selfish, not shy, and thus be able to make pictures of people in all the usual ways.

Game Number Seven: IMITATOR

The object of playing Imitator is to avoid being original and simultaneously to create the illusion that one *is* original. The unconscious motives are to lessen one's fear of insanity (which can be aroused by any truly creative act), escape isolation by finding a place in the herd, build a basis for self-appreciation ("I'm doing exactly what other photographers do; what so many do must be right"), and escape being found out (if everyone does the same thing who can tell one from another?). Another motive is to avoid the frightening discovery that one is merely a creature conditioned by his culture, without any ideas of his own (even attempting originality might show this up dramatically). Thus it can be seen that the motives for imitation are very strong, as they are in all games. They can be reasonably compared to large and vicious devils chewing holes in the human gut; no exaggeration intended here.

The illusion of originality is created by inconsequential manipulation of the same gimmicks used by all other photographers, amateur and pro. In even using them at all the photographer is playing Imitator to a degree, but he practically never sees this. He sees only the 'originality' in his own more or less meaningless diddling with these culturally determined gimmicks. Nor does he ever see the unconscious content underlying the gimmicks themselves. In other words, he in large measure doesn't even know what he is saying with his own photographs, for most of the meaning in pictures is their unconscious content. Since very few photographers understand that 'meaning' and 'unconscious content' are practically synonymous, few of them are disturbed by—or even notice—what is going on.

Some gimmicks used in Imitator as it is played today include: graininess, telephoto suns and moons, black seamless backgrounds, out-of-focus foregrounds, monochrome or semi-monochrome color through use of filters, wide-angle lens distortions, the Renaissance painting type of figure and portrait lighting, blurred movement, and anti-logical croppings. Since a great deal of diddling can be done with each gimmick, and some of it is rather clever, photographers easily convince themselves they're being genuinely creative by doing it.

Game Number Eight: REPEATER

Repeater is actually a special case of the game Imitator—perhaps the most desperate type. All the motives that apply to Imitator also apply here, but there are also special ones applying only to Repeater. In playing it the protagonist imitates only his own work, though it may have originally been an imitation of others. As in Imitator, the photographer convinces himself he is being original by superficial diddling.

Some of the additional motives in Repeater seem unusual, though they're not so to any student of the human psyche. In playing Projector the photographer may have projected such an unconsciously accurate or effectively self-deceptive image of himself in a certain type of photograph that he is literally compelled by unconscious forces to repeat it again and again and again. Made desperate by fear of failure he may be compelled to repeat endlessly earlier successes, deceiving himself that the laurels they won are still green. He may repeat because he's so desperately clinging to his present concept of himself that any change in his photography might make him think it is falling apart. Or on the verge of discovering he doesn't know anything of real importance he may repeat in order to convince himself he does and that it is embodied in his photographs, his unconscious notion being that he obviously wouldn't repeat himself if he weren't saying something important.

The Repeater may play his game because he unconsciously thinks it's easier to stay in the repetitious straitjacket his experience has put him in than to fight his way out toward normal creativity. Or he may repeat himself because he's become so blind to his repetitious pictures that he stands absolutely no chance of getting unwelcome glimpses of his hidden self by looking at them—he just doesn't see them at all. Repetition might also give him a desperately desired feeling of continuity in himself and in the world.

Diddling Is Often Called 'Art'

From all this one would expect Repeater to be a common game, which observation will confirm. However, the observer must learn to differentiate between substantial originality and superficial gimmick-diddling. This is very difficult because diddling has been heavily romanticized and misconstrued as art, almost all editors and photographers have been taken in by it, and there's hardly any other kind of photography around for a person to look at. Furthermore, every amateur or pro playing the game is doing his valiant damnedest to convince the whole world he's not.

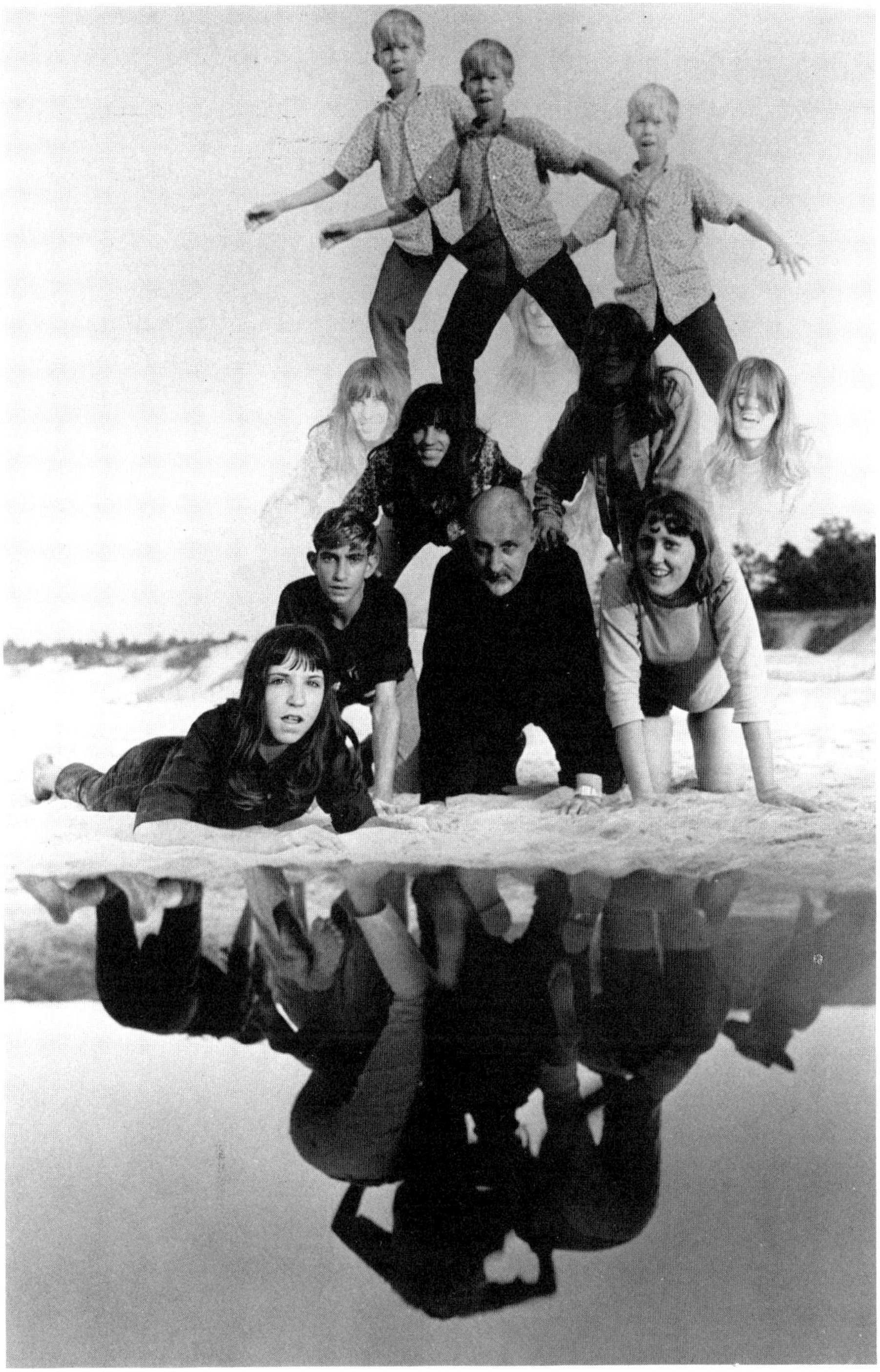

photo by JERRY N. UELSMANN

Since amateurs are so very strongly influenced by what pros do and say, we ought to take a look at them in terms of this particular game. These pros say (to each other), "We have to repeat ourselves more or less in order to sell our work. Otherwise, our clients wouldn't know what to expect from us." Though there is truth in this, one truth can be used to obscure another. What the professional unconsciously conceals from himself is that he may originally have chosen his field because it allows him to repeat himself in the particular way he is unconsciously impelled to. Within his special field there is enough superficial variation allowed to enable him to convince himself he's being creative when he's not. Though beginners

—amazed by everything whatsoever in photography—think a great many ideas are generated in professional photography, wise old pros are surprised if there are as many as five a year in the whole country. If the average pro couldn't constantly play both Repeater and Imitator he would have to quit photography, so important are they to his emotional survival. Fortunately for him his clients insist he keep on playing both games.

Game Number Nine: PRINTER

The object in playing Printer is to con yourself and other photographers (not laymen; this peculiar game won't work on them) into thinking you're saying something important in a picture when you're not. This is done very simply by making a 'great print.' So tremendous is an experienced photographer's respect for great print quality that he unconsciously tends to assume that any picture that has it must be meaningful, even if he himself can't comprehend what the meaning is. Thus he can be conned very easily; but so can the Printer himself, by his own prints.

Part of the satisfaction the Printer gets is that he can make other photographers feel very bad; they assume that they themselves must be really stupid for not getting the message which so obviously must be embodied in such a fantastic print. Perhaps the Printer's main motive is to obscure from himself his alarming lack of coherent ideas about himself and the world. Though a great many people have this bitter problem it is something they desperately hate to face up to; and photographers are no exception.

The person who plays Printer tends to choose his subject matter in terms of whether or not it will lead to a great print, not for other more logical reasons. This fact explains a surprising number of photographs.

There is a substantial number of people, many of whom have had college educations in photography, who have extended the concept of Printer far beyond the print itself. They do such things as mounting their prints on very expensive Strathmore board, framing them in expensive frames developed especially for photography and giving them very precious display in their homes on walls painted specially in colors ideal as backgrounds for photographs. They make a great deal of fuss about the marvelous quality of the small print, saying that "anyone who *really* knows what photography is all about" appreciates only this size. I have known many who would mount contact prints from 4x5-inch negatives on 14x18-inch boards or larger, and one who made 35-mm contacts for display.

The concept is extended further by putting the Great Prints in splendid handmade books, often with quotes from esoteric poets, philosophers, or disciples of Zen—in handset type. Great Prints are kept in specially made boxes, interleaved with expensive vellum sheets. They are stared at in devout silence at special photographic seances. They are given special showings at little galleries devoted to 'fine photography.' It is entirely reasonable, of course, that really great photographs should be given this splendid treatment, and many of them are in galleries, museums, and homes. However, the fact that they are so treated also helps the printer in his unconscious con game, for people assume that if great pictures are often seen in fine frames, every other picture in such a frame is also great. Silly, but that's the way it goes.

The most extreme practitioners of Printer have isolated themselves in 'schools' of photography (West Coast School, Chicago School, Boston School, etc.). Though there are some fine photographers in these groups, they are few and far between.

In its simpler form Printer is played throughout all photography wherever someone can be found who deeply respects a craftsman's print without prying into his reasons for it and their consequences. The game is made even easier by the fact that literally no one in this whole wide world knows how to think or what to say about photographs. But no one seems to be aware of this fact. Consequently, people tend to assume that if they're left wordless or puzzled by a photograph, it must be their own fault and that

photo by JERRY N. UELSMANN

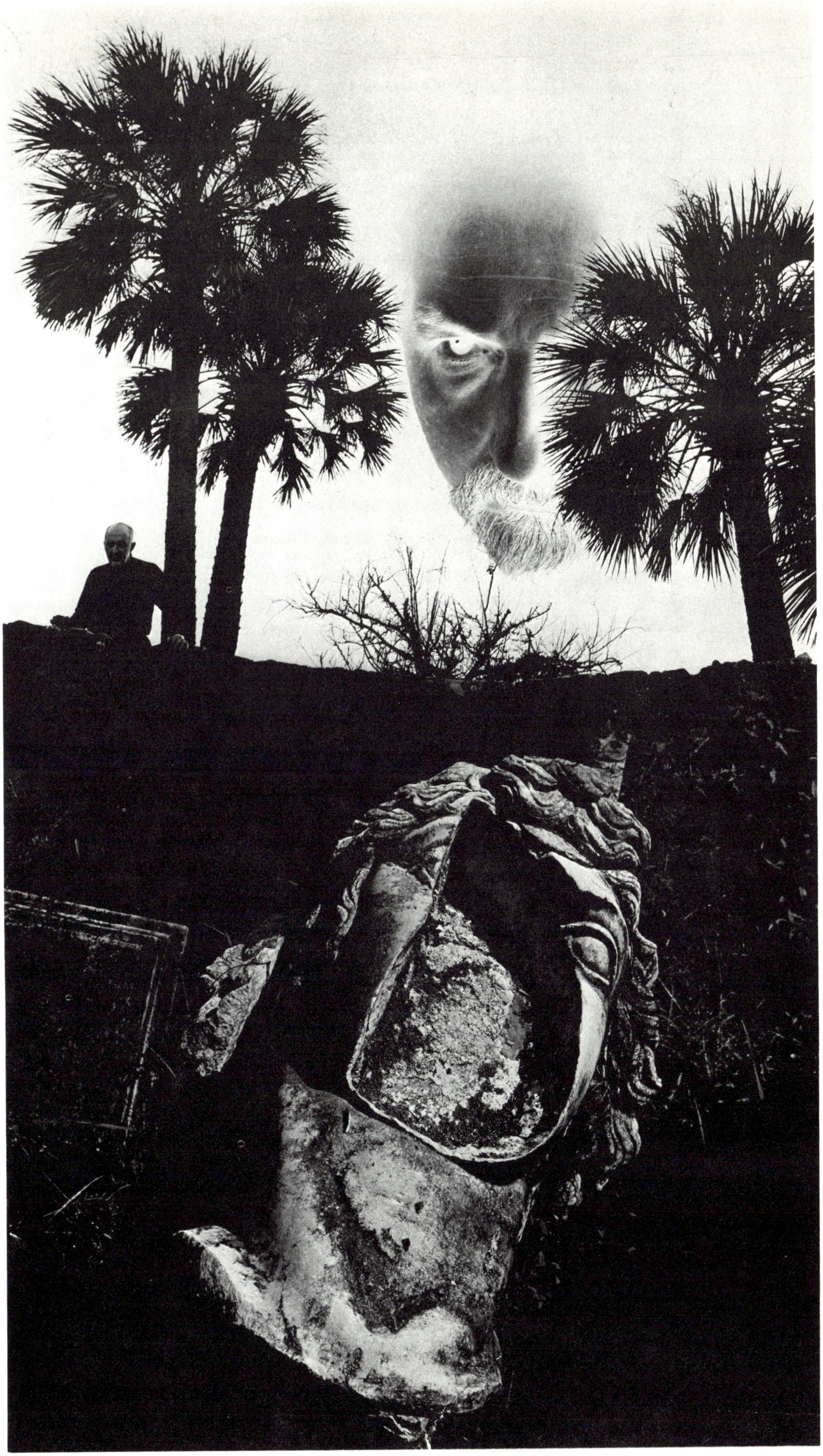

the picture itself must be good if someone says it is. If *all* the gim-crackery of the Printer is used to back up the photograph, such people can find no argument whatsoever against it except, perhaps, that they may not like it. Though this is the best argument of all, many people are ashamed to use it, thinking timidly that it would reveal their ignorance or lack of good taste. They should have more faith in themselves and less in con artists.

Game Number Ten: POWER

Power is the game for people preoccupied with controlling things. For some, the driving force may be the intense unconscious fear that they themselves are losing control or in danger of it; in exerting control over other people and things they create for themselves the illusion they are in control of themselves. For others it may be an aggressive drive to bend and twist things for their own ends. Certainly, there is often a sexual factor, as when control represents masculinity. Repressed anger may be a factor too, with control being a symbolic displacement of destructiveness. As with all games, motives can't be neatly pinpointed, though I may have given the impression they can. As there are games within games within games, so are there also motives within motives within motives.

One of the ways of playing Power is to use the so-called photographic controls to change everything from what it is into something different—darker, lighter, larger, smaller, fatter, thinner, sillier, wiser, happier, unhappier, younger, older, etc., etc. For a person experienced in photography this is easily done. The power-oriented photographer generally convinces himself he is not really changing things for the sake of power but bringing out some hidden essence, emphasizing some accidentally obscured truth, bringing order out of chaos or some such plausible thing. There is always just enough truth in his excuses to help him conceal from himself that he may be unconsciously playing God, that as God he is merely improving an unsatisfactory world.

Another way of playing Power is to use photography to identify oneself with things symbolic of power. In effect, one unconsciously says to himself, "I *am* this powerful thing I am photographing." It is easy to see how this would work in architectural photography (powerful building), industrial photography (powerful machines), or landscape photography (powerful mountains). A photographer might identify with heroes—political, athletic, or warrior. He might identify with powerful social organizations or social movements, unconsciously seeing himself as the source of their power. The things an average person can identify with in the name of power are beyond number. And man's capacity for self-deception through unconscious identification is almost unlimited.

The photographer-model relationship is a great source of psychological power for the photographer, whether the model is amateur or professional. By unspoken covenant the model yields to the photographer in order to make the picture come out well. Nonetheless, the photographer unconsciously feels her (or his) yielding as due to the force of his own personality. Some photographers greatly enjoy the relationship as a battle of wills because they so often win it. However, it is a spurious, lopsided battle, for the model can only win by ruining the picture, which he very strongly does not want to do. When the relationship is a heavily disguised sexual drama—which is frequent—the photographer draws psychological power from his male role. Since the very situation puts great power in his hands, some timid models respond by abject submission or make only a token play of resistance, which the photographer greatly enjoys. Some photographers consistently seek such models, as through them they can enjoy a feeling of God-like power. They are, of course, unaware of their motives.

The photographer-as-communicator also has power. The more this modern world depends on its communications, the more power he receives. Those photographers who work for publication have no difficulty in unconsciously thinking of themselves as warrior kings, especially since the people they work for—art direc-

photo by JERRY N. UELSMANN

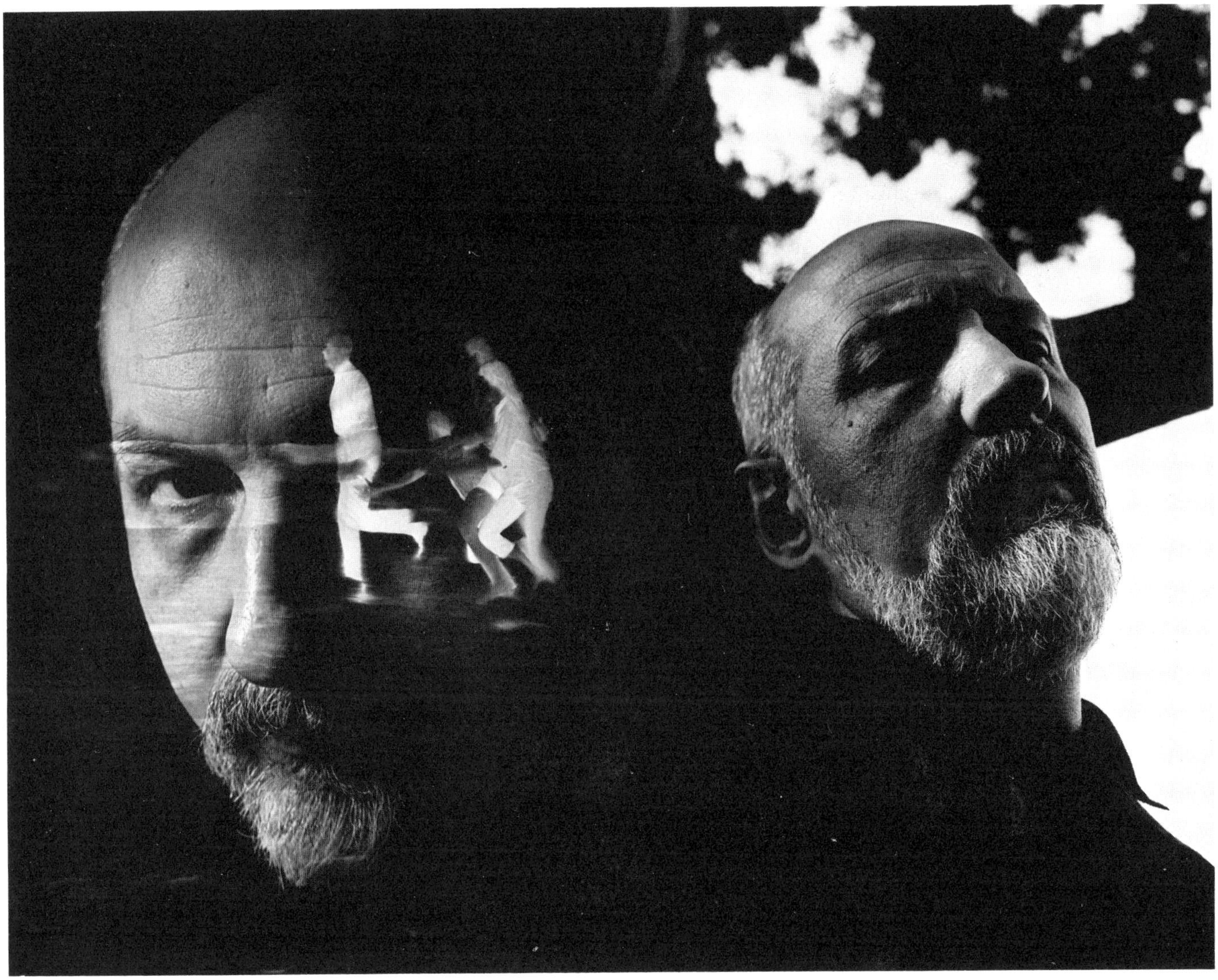

tors, picture editors, and editors—tend to agree with them unconsciously.

The very process of effectively shaping a message, for whatever purpose and in any medium, also gives one a great feeling of power. Though communication per se should certainly not be called a game as the term is used here, the unconscious uses a photographer makes of his power are something else. Such power easily lends itself to unconscious perversion. As Lord Acton so aptly said, "All power corrupts." One shouldn't take this statement lightly if he values his own mental and spiritual health.

The ability to see better than others is a tremendous source of power. Since the photographer erroneously assumes he can do this he feels very powerful. Though a good deal of this power is real, the deeper truth is that he can only see better *as a photographer,* for in learning to see as a photographer he's effectively blinded himself to things other people see quite easily. This might be called negative self-conditioning and it is certainly an important factor to understand in examining any art or communication form. Despite his unconscious self-limitation the photographer thinks he has full creative freedom and power. The game Power involves not only scrambling for real power but for illusions of it, too.

The process of controlling the photographic medium is a source of power. Unconsciously, the photographer sees himself as a sorcerer creating divine magic.

Game Number Eleven: LEECH

The object in playing Leech is to feast from other people's emotions without having to offer them sustenance in return. People ordinarily feed from one another's emotions, ideally a reciprocal process from which everyone gains. But like his animal namesake, the human Leech is unable to engage in reciprocity. He has blocked off his own emotions so far that he can only take, not give. Nonetheless, as a human being he wants terribly to engage in normal emotional interchange. Through photography he can create the illusion of it, which can serve him in lieu of anything better.

The Leech gets his pitiful satisfaction by running around with his camera to places where emotions are normally displayed: boxing matches, plays, night clubs, protest marches, baseball games. His object is to get as much emotion in his pictures as possible. Then he can go home and surround himself with them, unconsciously saying, "These images are really people who are sharing their emotions with me."

The Leech can also work directly with models. The thing he tries to do is provoke emotion in them 'for the sake of the picture.' If the emotion isn't genuine he can often make it seem that it is by use of various photographic controls. Later, he can conveniently forget the model was emoting for the picture or that he himself created the illusion of it.

Game Number Twelve: SAINT

The reason for playing Saint is to try to convince others and yourself you're the exact opposite of what you unconsciously think you are. In the game the Saint always photographs all the Good Things in the Right Way for the Right Reasons. Or he photographs Bad Things in such a way as to show that he, the Saint, can see some saving grace in them. The Saint desperately avoids showing through his photographs what he really thinks, as he would otherwise bitterly condemn himself and expect equal cruelty from others. The Saint only photographs cultural stereotypes for Goodness or the Right Thing, though he may do it so cleverly that no one, including himself, realizes they are stereotypes. People aren't more than dimly aware of cultural stereotypes, anyway; they see in them only representations of 'the way things really are.'

The Saint is trying desperately to have a good opinion of himself. He thinks that if he can get other people to say he's a great guy he will eventually come to believe it himself. But when they say he is, he never believes them.

One danger in playing the game is

that in lying to himself so constantly the Saint can completely lose track of what he really thinks about almost anything, which puts him in a very sorry psychological pickle. He can also, through his own photographs, provide himself with—and be strongly influenced by—a dangerously unrealistic version of reality.

Game Number Thirteen: CONFUSER

The object of Confuser is to make confusing photographs, thus muddying up the water so thoroughly that the player can't see certain painful facts clearly, or perhaps at all. For example, the Confuser may have unconscious feelings about a model he doesn't want to become aware of—homosexual attraction, hostility, jealousy—and he hides them from himself and others by making confusing photographs. If he made straightforward pictures he might be in danger of unconsciously revealing to himself what he actually feels. Confusion is thus a desperate means of escape.

Many who play the game are young people who have reached a point in their lives when they need to understand what is going on in their culture in order to advance themselves in it. Instead of facing the fact that they just don't understand their environment, they play Confuser as an attack against something from which they are essentially alienated. It can also be seen as a desperate attempt to establish a new culture outside the old one. In playing Confuser these young people are not so much standing *for* something new—they haven't a clue as to what their pictures mean—as fighting *against* something old which threatens to overwhelm them. The so-called psychedelic photography fits into this and other categories of Confuser.

Another motive for playing Confuser is the misconception that there are easy shortcuts to the hidden self. The player thinks that if he deliberately gives up conscious control of himself the unconscious will take over and reveal itself. Though there may be some truth in this it is extremely difficult to do in an effective way. What results is not revelation but mere confusion, though the Confuser often thinks that his anarchical and essentially mindless photography embodies great mystical secrets of the self. Though the secrets are actually there—heavily disguised by the ego's defenses against premature, therefore painful, insights—it takes a great deal of insight and long experience in self-exploration to discover them and interpret them accurately. Thus for the psychologically naive the whole effort is essentially wasted. There *ain't* no shortcuts, LSD notwithstanding.

Another motive underlying Confuser is the photographer's powerful desire to see himself, and be seen as, an individual. Looking around in photography, he sees so much that has already been done that the only way he can make himself stand out is through wooing the muses of the ridiculous, the anarchic, and the mindless. However, these muses have already been so thoroughly wooed that all the Confuser gets is photographs similar to what others have gotten. If he keeps at it long enough he's eventually led to see that there is no shortcut to individuation, though this is a very hard to see truth.

Blasting the World

One of the main reasons for playing Confuser is to release repressed hostility. Making confusing photographs can be seen as a way of blasting the world. They can also be used to upset the so-called squares—conservative people who accept and defend the status quo. Confusers can get a great deal of sadistic satisfaction from turning them up-end-to, and masochistic satisfaction from being attacked in return.

Of course, confusion is also a great hiding place. Since the Confusers are often the so-called artistic types, a person can hide in confusion and still respect himself for it. He thinks that instead of hiding he is actually following a great artistic tradition developed by the great creative minds.

My object has been to describe the games ordinary people—not psychotics—play in photography. If the reader has seen himself in some of these games he has probably found this essay rather uncomfortable reading. My purpose has been to show him a way of using photography for Self-discovery rather than self-deception.

Many people believe—rightly I think—that unless we come to understand ourselves better our chances of survival are precarious. Though the average photographer would prefer to remain unmolested in his hiding place, this is a dispensation which the rest of the human race can't afford to grant him. The tremendous power of photography in today's world makes this unmasking all the more necessary. This great modern force, photography, *must* be understood.

As for my clarity of vision in discovering the games, decoding and writing about them, I make no special claims. As a photographer myself I was probing into things I unconsciously least wanted to know about. So like any other photographer I must have made very powerful unconscious efforts to muddy up the stream. I hope that I have, at least, given the reader some kind of mirror, small or cracked though it may be, in which he can see photography and himself from a new angle.

RELATE to your family better

Using your camera to help you understand your family better and to relate to them on a more effective level.

When I was a young teacher in photography I used to give all of my students a certain jim-dandy homework assignment. Just before the Christmas recess, I used to tell them: "While you're home, I want you to photograph your parents. However, you must look at them as human beings with feelings, not just as objects to point your cameras at."

Thinking this was a very good project, I felt very self-satisfied. It took me several years to learn that it was the verbal equivalent of a hand grenade. In effect, I was asking each student to pick up a grenade, pull the firing pin, then clutch it to his breast.

7

I eventually discovered the disastrous results of my jim-dandy assignment. Nearly half of my students were so shaken up that they entirely gave up in photography. So painful had been their experience that they couldn't stand to use a camera again. Most were immobilized for a month or two, some for years. A few even left photography altogether. I didn't really understand the why of this until I did the assignment myself. I photographed my own parents as people instead of objects. Well, I can tell you a few things. Photographing one's parents is an excellent idea, and millions of people do it every year without suffering a bit. One reason they can do it is that they don't know enough about photography to project their own symbols into their pictures or to use other people as mirrors of themselves. Furthermore, they neither see what they're photographing nor think about it. If they do think, their egos are so strongly in power that no self-doubt can creep into their minds.

But my assignment for my students had dropped a large fly into the ointment. It was: "*Think* about your parents while you are photographing. *Think* about them as finite human beings, who have the same kinds of needs and emotions as you do." This is a large and muscular fly, indeed. But more: He's also a mirror.

The mirror works in several ways. And there are different things which function as mirrors. For example, people are mirrors. If we do something to them they reflect it to us. Say I neglect someone, then really look at him. Automatically, he reflects my neglect to me. Naturally, many of my students had this happen to them, for there are few children who aren't guilty of neglecting their parents. To discover this in oneself really makes the wolf (ego) suffer, especially if you have no intention of doing anything about it. Young people feel that they can barely cope with their own problems, so they don't plan to add to them by giving proper attention and respect to their parents.

Parents are mirrors in other ways equally painful to the wolf. They reflect our dependence on them at a time when we're naively priding ourselves on having overcome it entirely. Feeling dependence rise up in oneself provides a painful shock to the ego. The truth of the matter is that psychological dependence on parents often continues through a person's entire lifetime.

Parents reflect our illusions, too. To understand how this happens we must investigate how children see their parents. To a very large degree they don't see them at all. They invent them. That is, they take these adults who are rearing them and cloak them with childish illusions. They think these illusions are their parents.

Our motives for inventing parents are easily explained. They can be expressed in terms of what we project into our creations. As we see them, our parents embody all the conceivable virtues and strengths. We want and need that they should. We make them strong, virtuous, predictable and immortal. This is not only how we need them but how we think they ought to be.

In each life we are given a little time in the Garden, so that we can grow strong minds and bodies and prepare the Soul for the long struggle ahead. Our parents help us stay in it by not insisting that we destroy the illusions we've created about them. However, the time comes when we eject ourselves from the Garden, as we did in the beginning and many times since. By childhood's end the wolf is fully energized again and has taken over dominion of the psyche. The struggle to unseat him must begin once more.

One of our ways of defeating the wolf is to let ourselves see through the puppet parents we've created, to the real ones underneath. By acting as mirrors of our illusions, our parents help us in this. The wolf suffers greatly, of course; but he must if we're ever to be free of him.

In terms of the struggle to end selfishness, the most fruitful battlefield is family life. There the wolf suffers most. Beyond the suffering stand the highest possible human goals. For this reason alone the family would rank as one of God's finest creations for the possible perfection of his children.

Obviously, it's no fun at the age of sixteen or eighteen to find yourself standing almost entirely outside the Garden. The wolf in you (the selfishness) tries with all his strength not to let himself see that it has actually happened. Despite his efforts to prevent it, evidence of the truth rapidly piles up. One of the very best ways to give His Ignorance a hard punch in the jaw is to point your camera at one of your parents and ask yourself, "Who and what is this person I'm photographing?"

Young readers, I already told you that you bought a bag of chili peppers when you paid for this book. You've already eaten many; take one more mouthful. Since the world began, one stiff punch has never been enough to unseat a wolf. If you want to displace this rascal you've got to let your jaw be a punching bag all the remaining years of your life. On the side of optimism: If you'd like to possess the universe, this is the way to do it.

Unfortunately, none of the following lessons is specifically for teenagers or those just into their twenties. They apply more to people who are married and starting their own families.

Seeing the Family

As it is written, this lesson will help you

see your family as an unending and interesting picture story. It tells you things to look for and point your camera at. It says nothing concerning the thoughts which might go through your mind while you're doing it. I can tell you what went through the mind of the photographer who made the pictures, for I am he. For this purpose, I'll talk about two of them. I'll have to give you a little background in order to make my comments intelligible.

As long as I can remember, I've been an extremely self-centered person, a true slave of the wolf, Ralph. I was this way when still very young, which is one of my reasons for believing in reincarnation. I find it difficult to believe that the Lord would afflict this world with such a self-centered creature. If reincarnation theory is correct, however, it means that such beings create themselves that way. Thus egotism could be something I had created in former lives and brought along with me when I came into this one. I've added greatly to it since, you may be sure. But I got off to a flying start.

Whatever be the reason, I've always been an egotist. An egotist in early childhood, I grew ever more egotistical as the years went by. I had a fat wolf and I fed him well. By the time I had reached marriage age I was really in a desperate pickle. Fortunately, I had no idea how desperate, or I might not have permitted myself to survive. Then I would have had to take my egotism with me to still another life and start all over again.

Though they are the lowest of God's creatures, egotists nonetheless have ideals. Sometimes, in fact, their ideals reach the height of the sublime. I was, and still am, this kind of egotist. But do not think that ideals are food for the wolf. On the contrary, they bring him only suffering. He has these high ideals and never manages to measure up to them. Thus his misery is almost constant. Of course, it's very good for him, but most of us wolves don't discover this until much later in life, if we ever do.

Now you have an image of the husband and father who made these photographs. I didn't like myself in either role. In fact, I disliked myself on almost any grounds you could think of in a day's intense cogitation. In this sense I was just like all other egotists, only a litle more so. As for insight into the cause of my condition, I had practically none. All I knew was that I could have pole vaulted under a worm's belly and not come within three feet of touching it.

One time I photographed my first wife, Mitzi, and our daughter Lissa Ann—now a comely young lady of nineteen. At the time I took it, I never thought that a photograph would give me hope; but this one did. For years I had lived almost without hope, so I didn't expect it to come knocking on my door.

What I had hoped for was an improvement in my attitudes toward Mitzi and the children and a lifting of the black fog of selfishness and Self-condemnation. For months I hadn't had a single positive thought for the young woman on whose unfailing optimism I had depended since the beginning of our marriage. In my Self-crippling selfishness, I had nourished myself on it and at the same time persistently done my best to undermine it. My rationale was that such ebullient optimism wasn't logical. Inwardly, I wanted to destroy the thing on which I so greatly depended. At the same time, I deeply condemned myself for what I was doing to Mitzi. My egotistical reasoning could sometimes accept what I was doing, but my heart could not.

On this bright Sunday morning in Spring, however, hope fluttered against the window pane. For the first night in months I'd gotten enough sleep. When my elder son, Cleve, pulled at my arm and said, "Fix some breakfast, Dad," I stumbled out of bed as usual. To my surprise, the blanket of anxiety didn't immediately descend on me. The sunshine caught me up and affably escorted me to the kitchen, where I fed the three children.

I took a breakfast tray to Mitzi in the bedroom. I had done this every morning for years because my father had always done it for my mother. I thought it was a very good thing for a husband to do for his wife. However, every time I did it the angry thought would slice through my

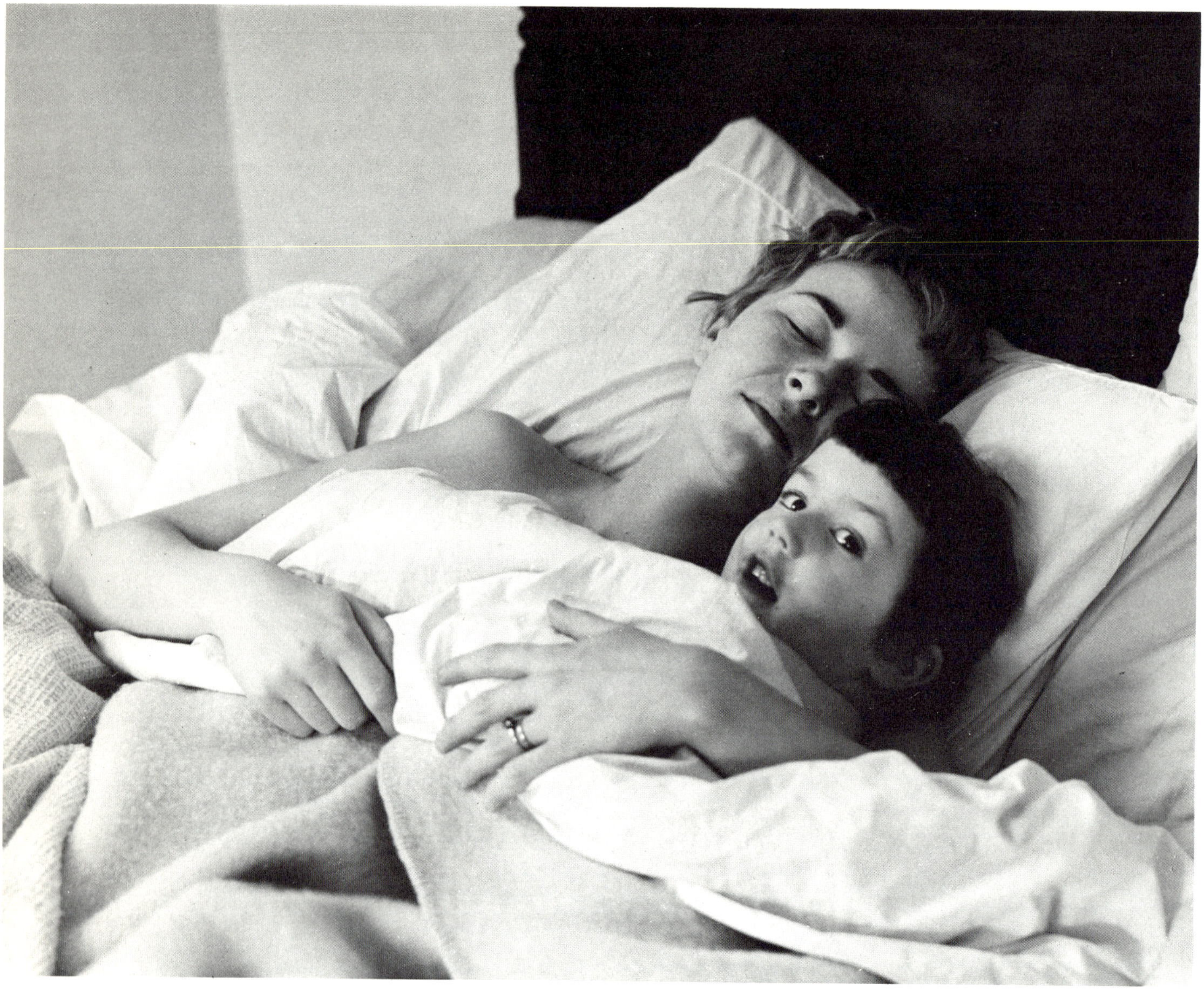

My first wife, Mitzi, and daughter, Lissa Ann. It is a warm, bright morning in Spring. The young mother is beautiful in sleep, the daughter coltish and squirming. So lovely is this vista that it penetrates my fog of self-centeredness, giving me hope that I may learn to be loving.

mind, "Why isn't she doing this for me, instead?" I would then have to suffer the pangs of remorse for feeling this way. On this bright morning, however, the thought stayed away. For the first time in literally ages I enjoyed Mitzi's enjoyment. The breakfast was a good one, for within certain limits I was an excellent cook.

Breakfast finished, the two boys ran outside to join their friends in the clubhouse they had built in the vacant lot across the street. Lissa Ann complained for a moment at being abandoned, then forgot her grief and climbed into bed with her mother, who had gone back to sleep. I looked in on the two of them: Mitzi at peace with herself in sleep, Lissa Ann wiggling around like a frisky puppy. I thought, "This is lovely." Thinking this thought filled me with an unfamiliar warmth.

I got out my camera, put it on a tripod and made two exposures. The rest of the morning went well, but the most magical part had already happened. Later, the photographs helped sustain me many times. I could look at them and remember a moment of genuine compassion for my wife and a wholehearted, uncritical acceptance of my daughter. In this memory was hope for better things to come. Perhaps some day I would learn to love someone. There is nothing more lovely to hope for. And the thought that it might even develop in me sustained me through many dark hours.

When I tried to make an arty picture of my son Craig, he pulled his mouth wide open with his fingers. Now a young stalwart of twenty-one years, he hasn't changed much. In a way, this kid always had his father's number, even when he was only four or five years old. In this picture he's probably eight or nine. He's doing something he had done many times before, teasing his Old Man.

When I got out my camera he knew very well that this wasn't the kind of picture of him that I wanted. Though he certainly couldn't have known precisely what I did want, he took very careful steps to make sure that, whatever it was, I wouldn't get it. That he would behave this way was one of the most predictable things about him. I found his wily dodging aggravating. But at the same time he was such an agreeable cuss that I couldn't get really angry at him. Every time he saw even the smallest bit of frustrated self-pity in my face, he would carefully step on it with a quip or a joke. With a kid like this in the house, parents are bound to get an education.

I hate to see a child pass into manhood and have to get into the struggle with the wolf. When he was nine he didn't have enough ego to fill a thimble. At the same time, he intuitively knew a lot about the wolf and his vanity. He also knew that wit was the most gracious tool for ego-deflation.

Craig Robert Hattersley defeating his father's attempt to make a 'good picture.' I had told him, "Be serious now, Craig, I want to get a really nice picture of you." So, he was very serious—until I was ready to click the camera shutter. Then this, the only pose I could get from him for months on end. A dedicated rascal, Craig.

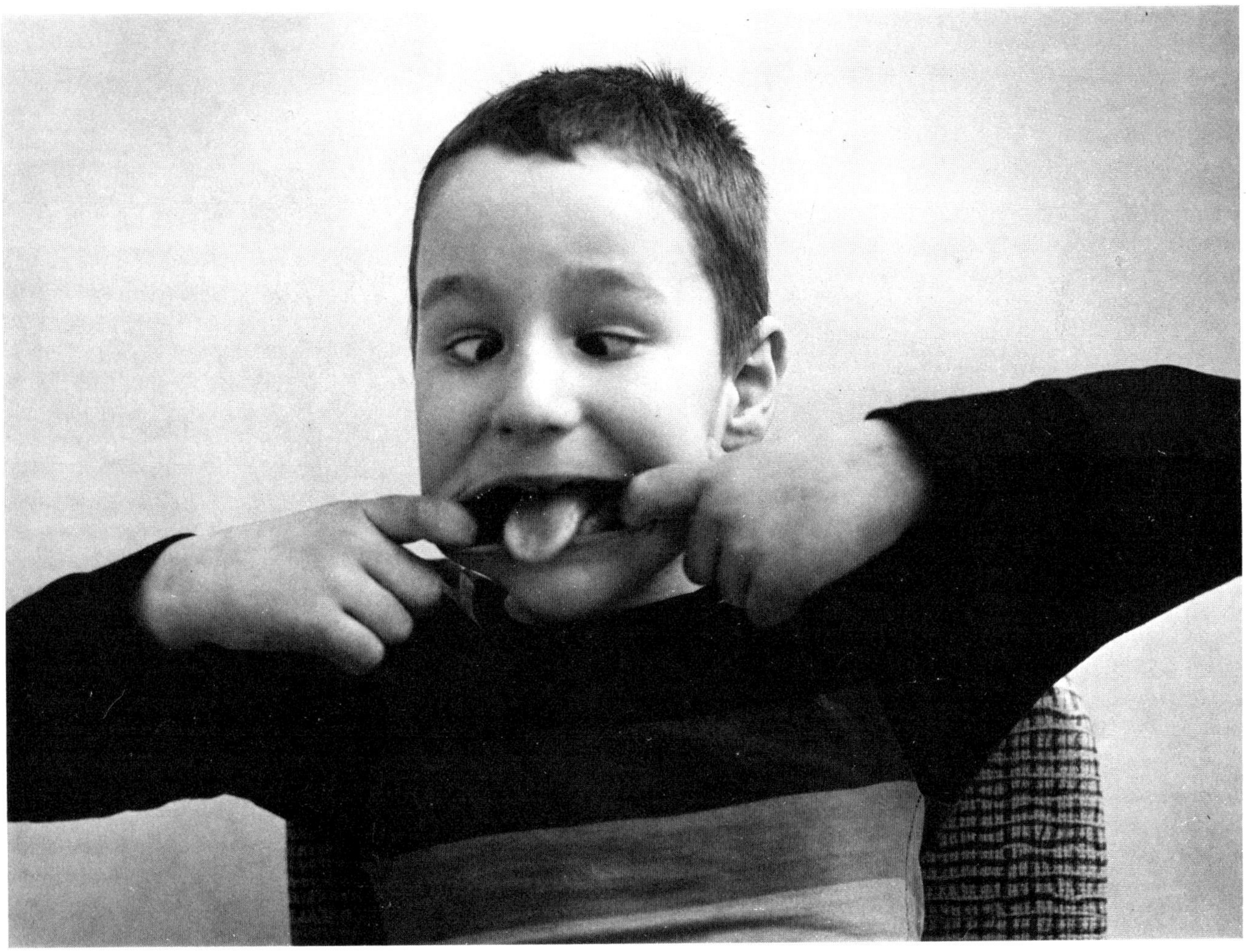

So, the young rascal gave my ego a hard time and I loved every minute of it. His unending skill in defeating my purposes as a photographer gave me much pause for thought. He had deliberately provoked a contest between the two of us and chosen the field on which the battles were to be fought. After thinking for a long time about what he was up to, I finally saw the central issue in our duel. It can be neatly expressed as a question from Craig: "Are you going to permit me to be myself? Or are you going to persist in trying to make me into something I'm not?"

When I finally understand this I was really appalled at myself. The point is that I was a power-happy meddler in other people's lives. Teaching, writing and photography give one ample opportunity for this, and rational excuses for it, by the carload. There is nothing the wolf likes better than meddling or likes less than really trying to understand the people he's trying to change. When people are in their late teens or early twenties it's altogether too easy to rationalize one's meddling with them, especially as a teacher. After all, one's job is to change people, isn't it? It's all the easier because it has never been demanded of teachers that they really understand what they're trying to change their students into. Or what they really are to start with.

Furthermore, when students reach this age it's easy enough to see they're well on the way to being thoroughly screwed up. What better excuse can the arrogant wolf ask for to set out to unscrew them? Add that the people one manipulates aren't around most of the time so that if a teacher feeds a student the wrong medicine, he doesn't have to stand by and watch him suffer stomach cramps. While the student is wondering what hit him, his teacher is at home casually losing himself in a dry martini and complaining to his wife about the barricades students set up to prevent his 'wisdom' from getting through to them.

It's quite a different proposition with one's own children. It doesn't take much insight for a parent to see that he doesn't really have a clue as to how he should rear his children. Most of his educational ideas either work backwards or not at all. His children clearly represent a perfection which he himself has long ago lost. Thus it isn't too awfully hard for him to comprehend that when a child says "Accept

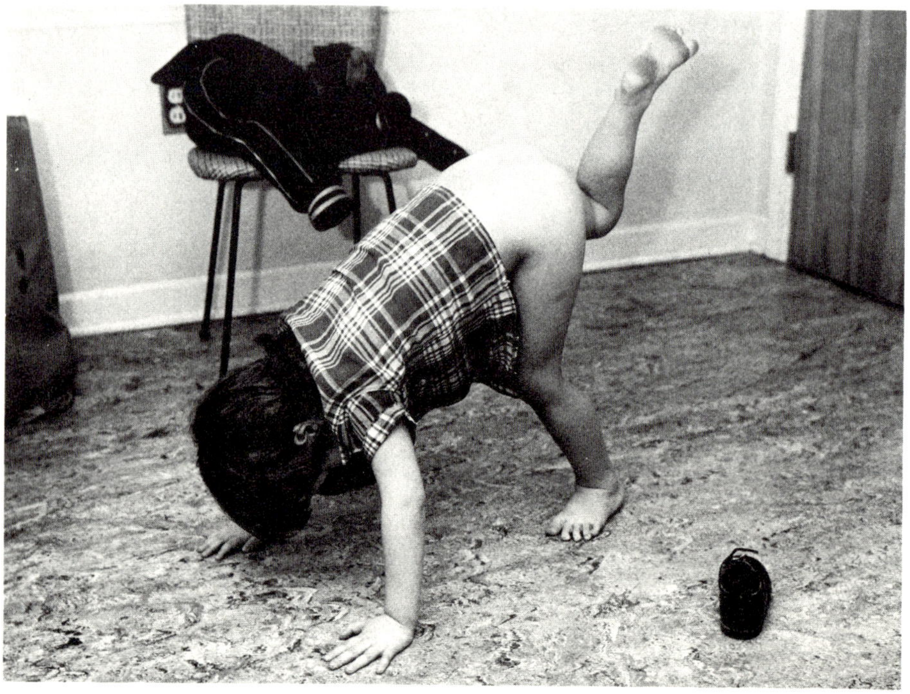

Lissa Ann proving to her father that she can stand on her head. This is the closest she ever came to it, except for the time she went over too far and landed, howling, on her back. That time I didn't photograph her, for children deeply resent parents' photographing their tears.

me as I am," he may have a good point.

So young Craig, abetted by brother Cleve and sister Lissa, made this point to me. Working much against my professional pride, I turned myself into a family snapshooter. This means that I forced myself to take only what they offered my camera. I could not bring myself to use them only as material for good pictures. Though I thought of it all the time, my Conscience (still dimly in the background somewhere) just wouldn't let me do it. I must tell you, however, that my artistic pride was offended again and again, for in those days art meant changing things. Now I see that it also means recognizing things for what they actually are.

The first lesson in learning to leave

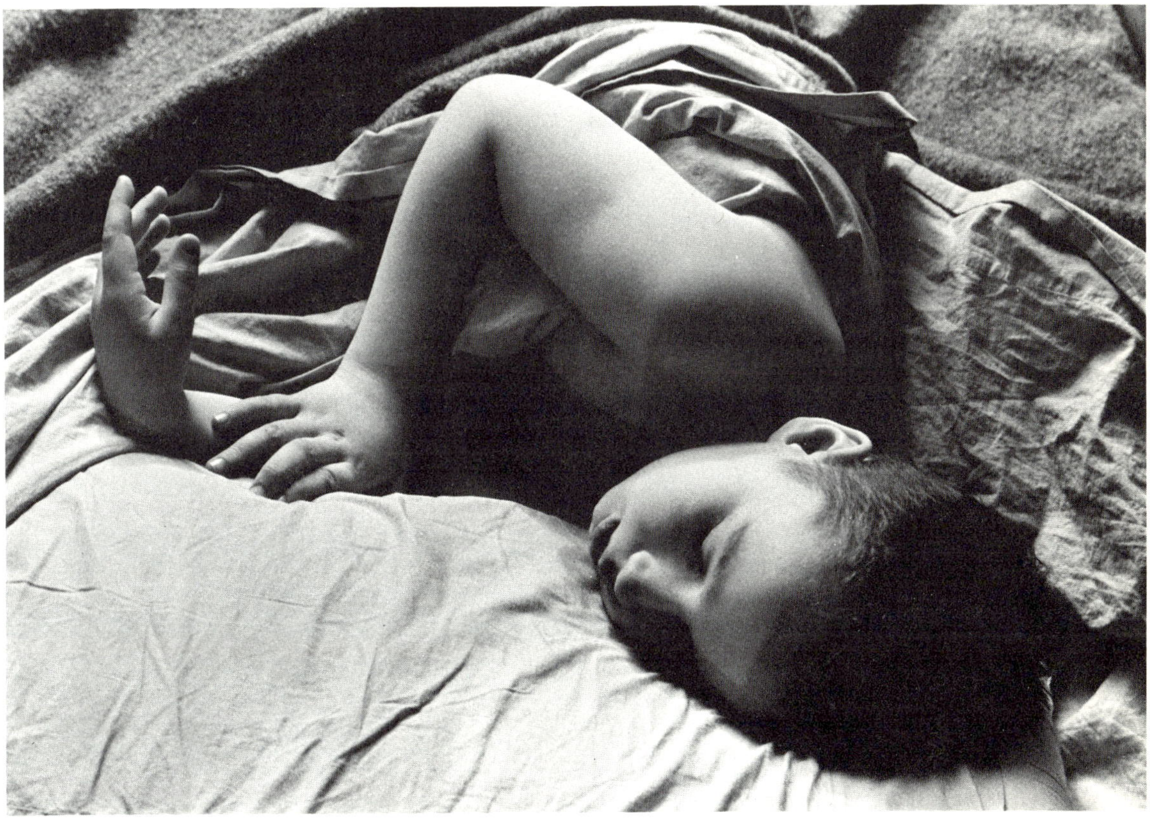

Craig Robert (above), a study in beauty and grace. Is there a father so blind he can't warm to such loveliness as this?

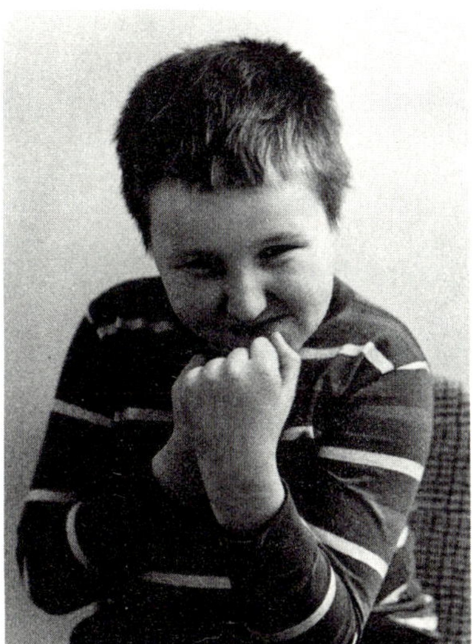

Cleve Marshall Hattersley (left). The blood of the wolf runs in our family, as Cleve's terrifying ferocity clearly indicates.

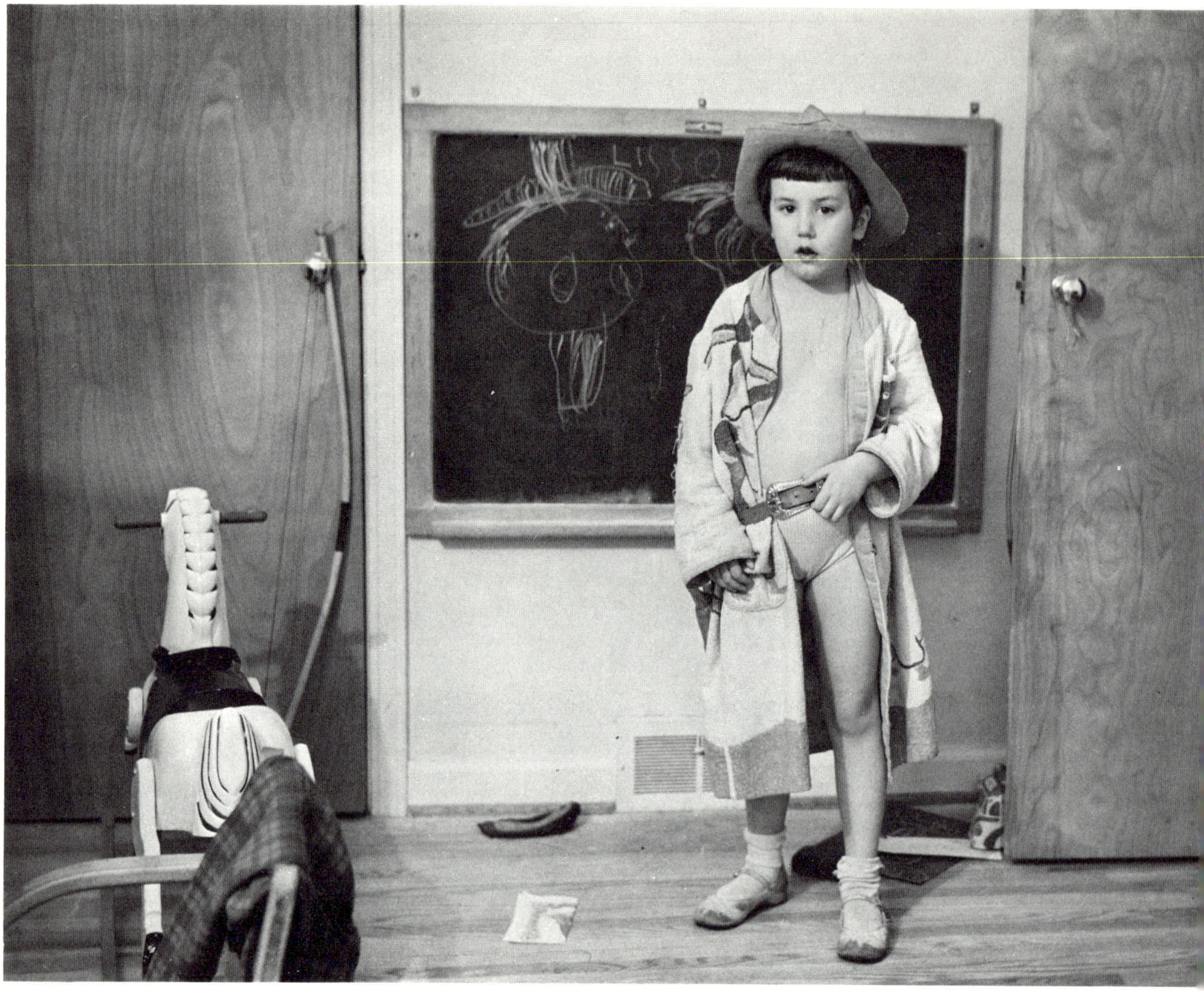

Lissa Ann Hattersley, the fastest gun in the West. Her favorite tune is "I know what I want when I want it." In her lighter moments she's called Lissy Poo.

people alone is learned best in the family. Do not interfere with the central being, the Essence, of your wife and children. The next lesson is to extend this idea to everyone else. Since I'm still in the process of learning this one I can't give you any final answers on what you feel like after you've done it. However, I've seen that meddling is an aspect of judging. If a person didn't judge people insufficient, why would he bother to try to change them? As we judge others, so do we judge ourselves. It's a very nice way for building a cage around the Self.

I'm not going to say much about the other lessons in this chapter. You know now that your author has run into very serious ego problems in his own photography of his family. They are not expressed in these lessons which are very optimistic. However, it is every writer's prerogative to express only the best in himself if he wishes.

The Lesson:

The family is the most photographed part of American life but visualized the poorest. Of the millions of family pictures made each year very few penetrate the surface. They show in a superficial way what family members look like but not what they are, how they feel, how they relate, or what they mean to one another.

To help you see some of the thousands of possibilities I'll toss you several dozen ideas. Think up more for yourself. To simplify things somewhat, I'm confining myself to the home, where most family pictures are taken.

Scale: Family relationships involve largeness and smallness: Baby's hands in Mother's, little feet trying on big shoes, a tiny tot trying to climb a huge chair, trying to reach the faucet to get a drink, or wearing adult clothes.

Conflict: The contested toy, refusal to eat vegetables, parents' argument, striking a parent, reaction to discipline, refusing caresses, pestering, taunting, parents losing tempers.

Teaching and learning: Homework, the problem of shoelaces, fundamentals of dishwashing, parents studying children, how not to make a bed, experiments in getting babies to eat, learning games with string, training a young carpenter, experiments in getting dressed, training the dog.

Loving: Mother and baby, loving gestures, toddlers swarming over Dad, loving eyes, quiet love, playful love, love and strength, demonstrative love.

Drama: Baby's first step, bumps and bruises, illness, fear of the dark, the frightening uncle, roughhouse games with Dad, hair-pulling and fist fights, ghost stories, tricycle racing.

Soap and water: Soap in the eyes, how not to wash the kitchen floor, washing the dog, games with soap suds, blowing bubbles, soap tastes bad, avoidance of soap.

Composition: Tiny baby on huge bedspread, pictures on the wall and people, Suzy at the window, silhouetted people-shapes in front of lighted wall, eccentric positioning on the sofa, young head and interesting chair contour, composition with young hands, children as interesting shapes on the rug, offbeat framing of Dad in doorway, whole family in long horizontal composition.

Laughter: Getting tickled, fake laughter is fun, uncontrollable laughter, puppies bring laughter, jeering laughter at Dad the photographer, teasing laughter, Bobby trying to get Mary to laugh, Grandma laughs really hard, laughter through tears.

Tears: Life is just too tough for children, phony tears to impress Mother, play-acting at crying, tears of joy, angry tears, tear tracks on dirty face.

Confusion: Chaos at the supper table, children's "help" in sorting the laundry, the neighborhood children plus yours, wrapping paper on Christmas morning, packing for a trip, the playroom, tangled bedclothes and children, parties get out of hand, Mother in despair at confusion.

Safety: Mother's protective grip on Baby,

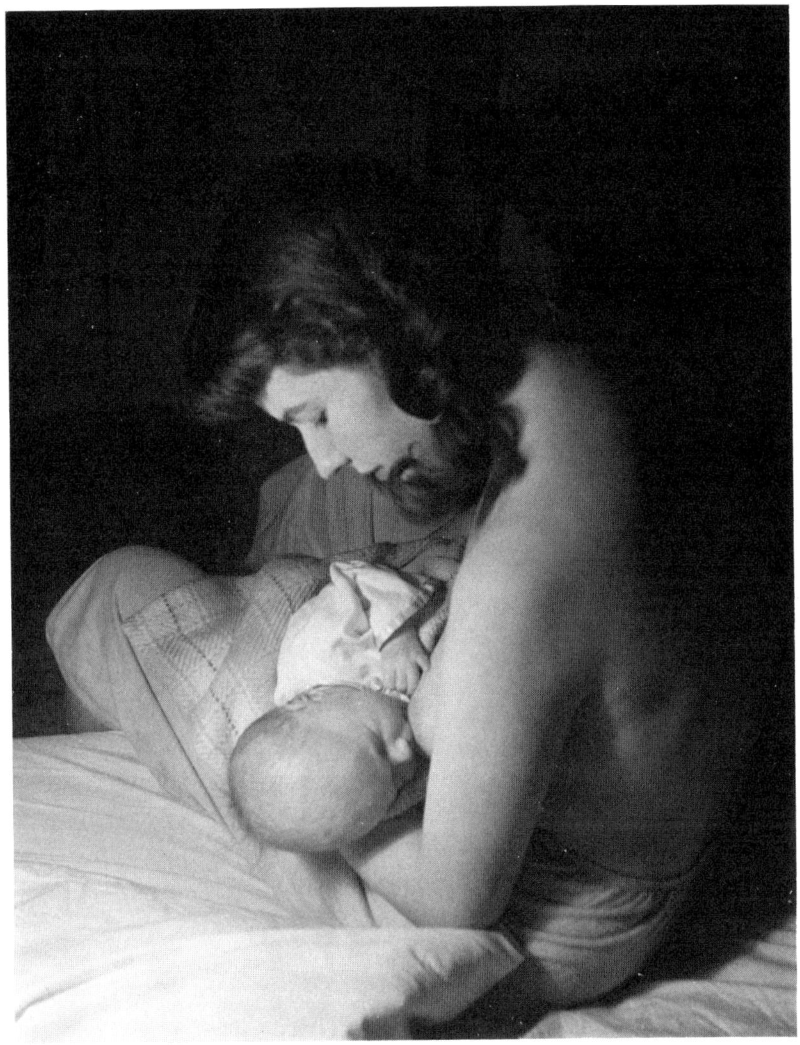

Mitzi Hattersley and her first baby, Cleve. This picture really used to bother me, for it confronted me with the fact I loved neither mother nor child as much as I should. Later I learned that loving is mankind's very highest art and that a person shouldn't condemn himself if he's trying but still hasn't mastered it.

Lissy Poo at her loveliest. She is looking at her father, who holds the camera. I couldn't see myself as lovable because I wasn't loving. Pictures like this gradually convinced me that my children loved me anyway. I think this is my favorite picture of Lissa Ann.

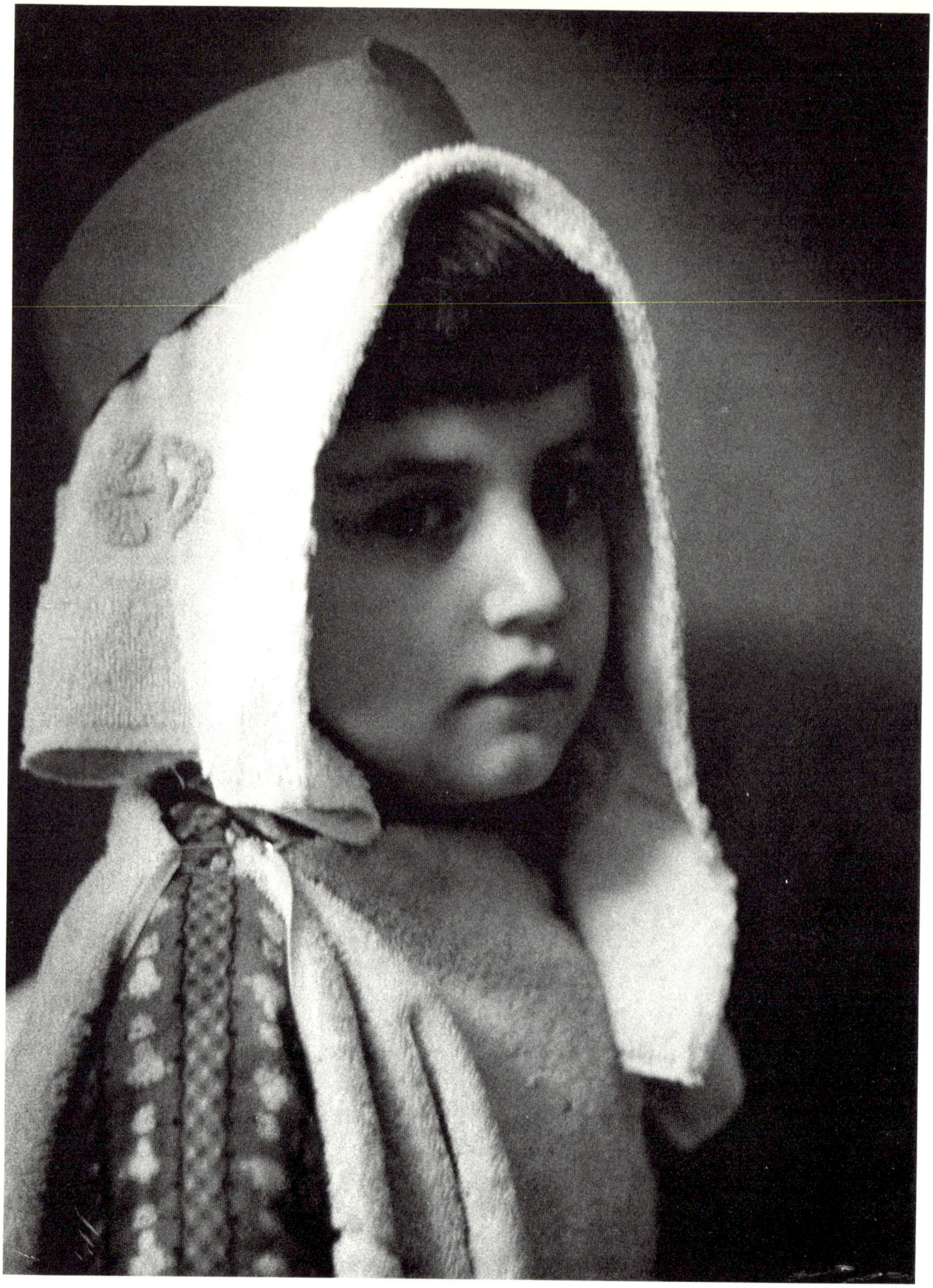

pulling children back from trouble, safe but unwilling custody in the playpen, rescuing Tommy from atop the bookcase, children's efforts to escape from the house, safety rigs for toddler walking, lifting Baby out of bathtub.

Success: Family triumph over beautiful cake, Molly with her great work of art, Joe's successful imitation of Dad, triumph over completed model plane, the winner at Indian wrestling, successful eavesdropping, getting away with stealing Kathy's toy.

Defeat: Father frustrated in disciplining, toy puzzle defeats child, angry Jimmy helpless in Mom's grip, the tragedy of the stuck zipper, toppling toy-block structure frustrates Larry, Billy can't get shoe tied, monthly bills defeat Dad, children's screams defeat Mom.

Inclusion: Small boy included in adult conversation, Amy hears secret from Mother, daughter's fingers allowed in mixing bowl with her mother's, Millie lets baby brother help her play with dolls, Craig admitted to family council.

Exclusion: Big kids exclude little ones, Sonny excluded from adult party, Mother doesn't want help cooking supper, children ignore Dad's efforts to join in their game, Mom is giving all her attention to the baby, girls don't want Freddy to play house with them, making funny faces doesn't distract Dad from his reading, everyone's having fun but me.

Dignity: The solemnity of children's prayers, the sweet dignity of a little girl in a new party dress, Dad presides over the supper table with dignity, Lisa's conversation with Grandma, dignity and hurt feelings, playing house is dignified.

Animals: Dogs leap into beds with boys, getting licked by a dog is pleasant, pet fur feels good on faces, bare toes go well with puppies, it's fun to be walked on by a kitten, touching noses with a turtle, teaching the dog to walk on his hind feet, child's face framed by hamster cage, dogs like to tussle with kids.

Touching: A child's neck is sweet to kiss, Baby explores Mother's face with tiny hands, holding Dad's hand is security, children hugging each other, tickling Mother's nose, Bobby likes to have his back scratched, a mother's bosom quiets tears, bare feet on bare back.

I hope these suggestions will help you see beyond the posed snapshot. They are all very photographable. With a little effort and some observation of what happens in your own home you should be able to double or quadruple this list. I suggest you do it.

Following are some shooting tips:

1. Through your camera viewfinder make a careful survey of your home, looking for simple, orderly backgrounds for family action.

2. Shoot lots of pictures. Shooting only a picture a week will never get you a good one.

3. It's better to shoot ten pictures of one small bit of family action than ten of ten different actions.

4. Try copying the style of professional family pictures so you can learn to see what can be done and how.

5. Carry your camera around your home so much that your family forgets it. Then the shooting will get good.

6. Arrange deliberate distractions for your subjects. The less attention they pay you the better.

7. Keep your camera on the shelf ready to shoot.

8. Work out your technical problems in advance for each kind of action that interests you. Make plentiful notes for quick reference.

9. Practice shooting by natural light, bounce flash, and bounce flood. They gave a much better feeling of reality than direct flash on the camera.

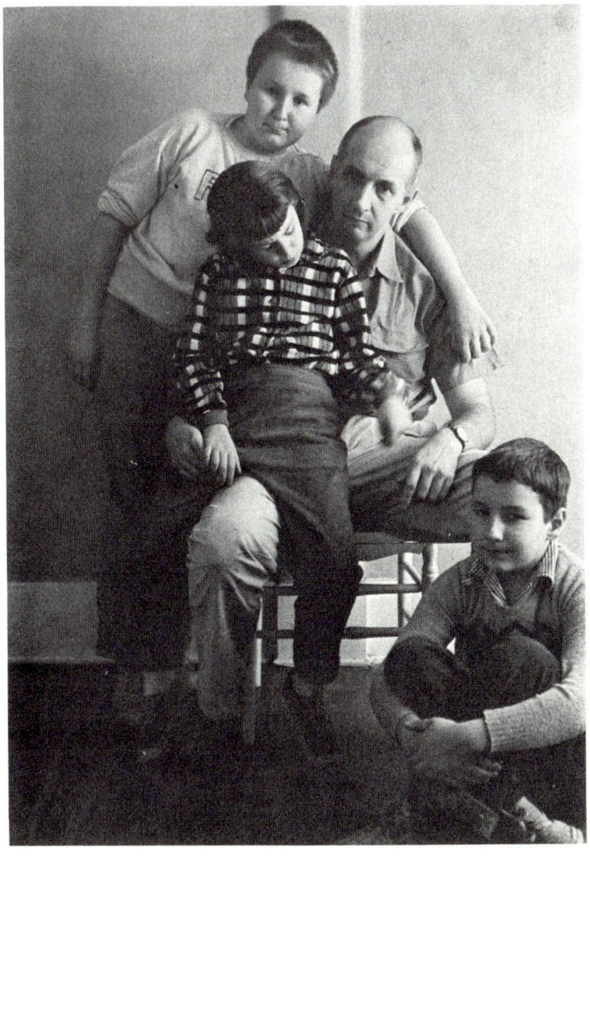

Family group a month after Mitzi and I were divorced. The children's liveliness and love each weekend helped me mend my badly shattered ego.

photo by DENNIS MARTIN

10. When in doubt, come up as close as possible to your subject.
11. See how few things you can manage to get in your viewfinder.
12. Look beyond your subject in the viewfinder to make sure you've included nothing that doesn't help the picture explain itself.
13. Try different camera angles. Shoot from the floor and from atop a step stool.
14. Don't get trigger happy. If you miss something good wait until something else happens. Be patient.
15. Don't try everything at once. The family at dinner is enough for one shooting session, playing with toys in the bathtub for another.
16. Don't expect great shots each time and remember that the others are fine for the family album.
17. Make your shooting sessions casual, friendly affairs that people enjoy.
18. Let your shooting follow family mood. You can't get gay pictures of tired people, nor tender ones of angry people.

Kids in the Tub

This is a lesson dedicated to the irrepres-

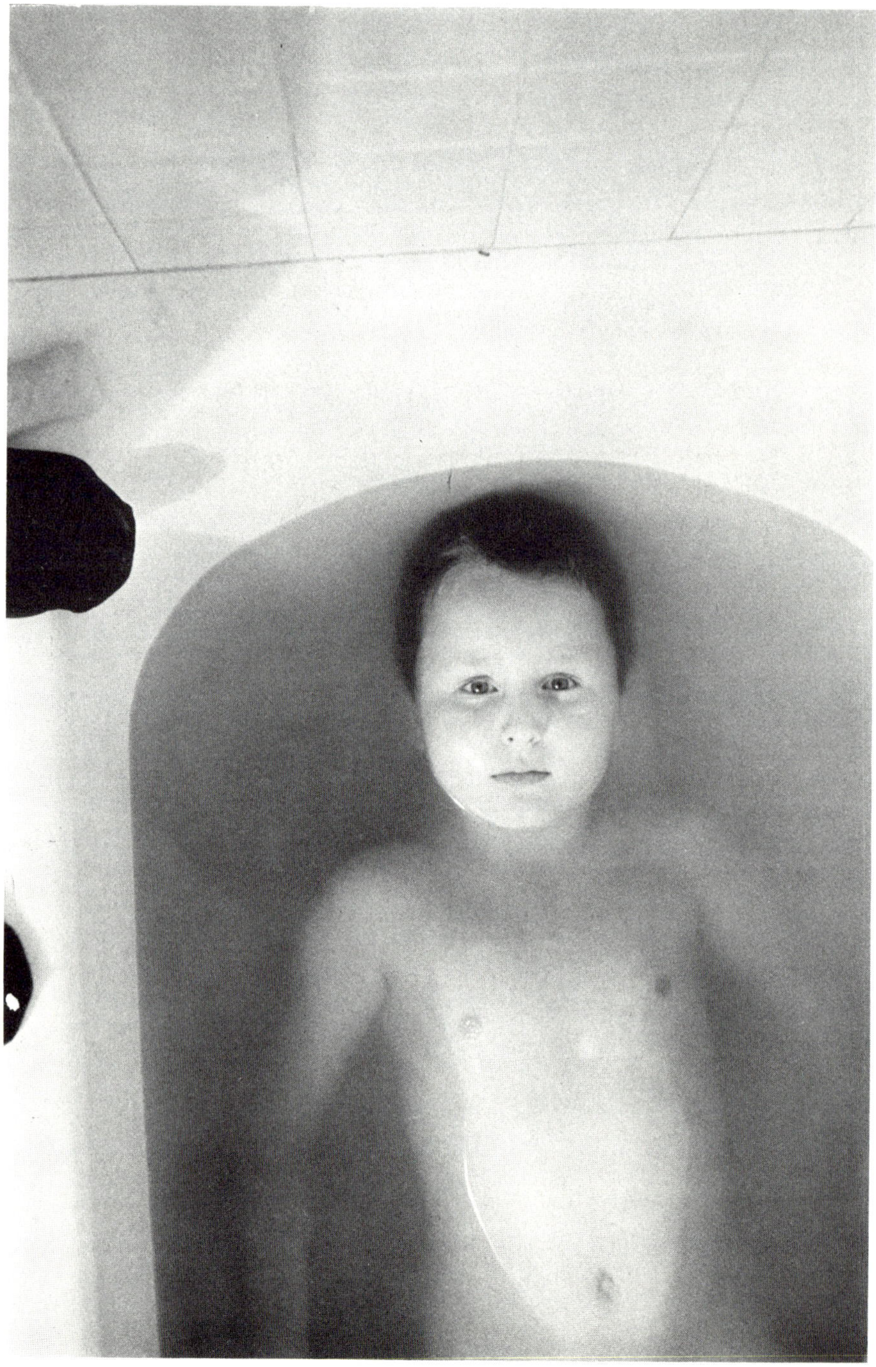

sible liveliness of children. It suggests that one way of getting it on film is to limit oneself to photographing children on just one of the many stages on which they play their lively games. They do so many, many things it's hard to keep track of them otherwise.

The Lesson:
One of the best ways to photograph is to search for natural theaters of action. Having found one, all the photographer has to do is sit patiently in front of it with his camera, waiting for whatever will happen. In some cases, these natural theaters are so good that one can keep a vigil for months, even years, and never run out of good pictures. In a family with small children, the bathtub is such a place.

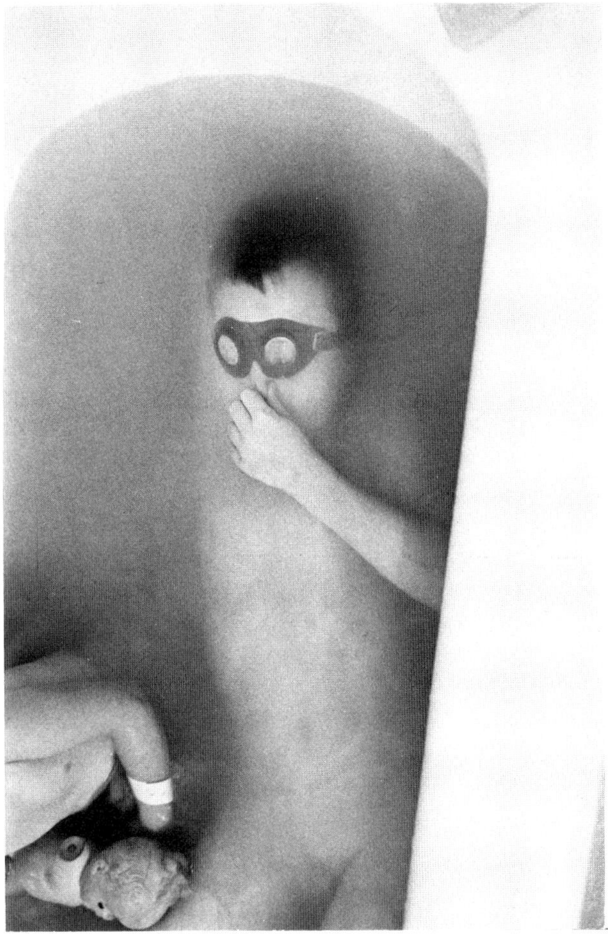

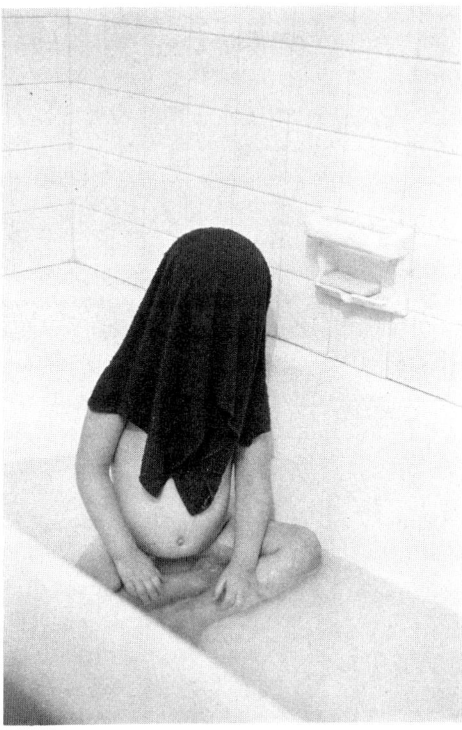

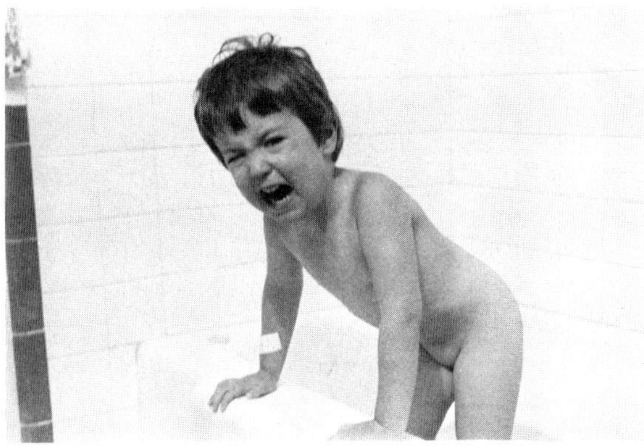

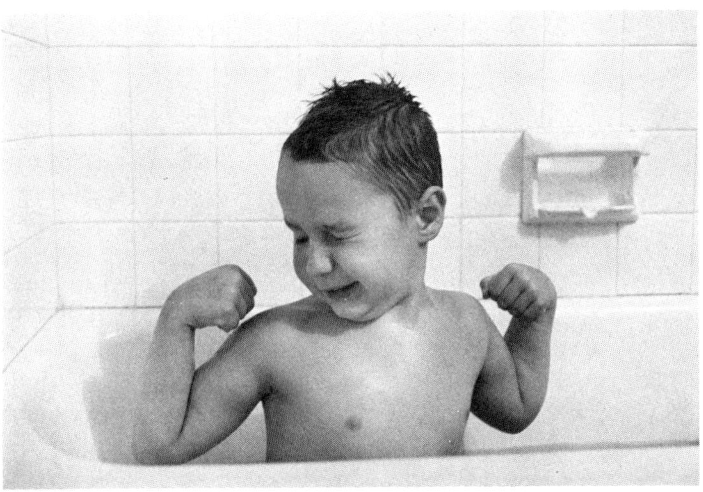

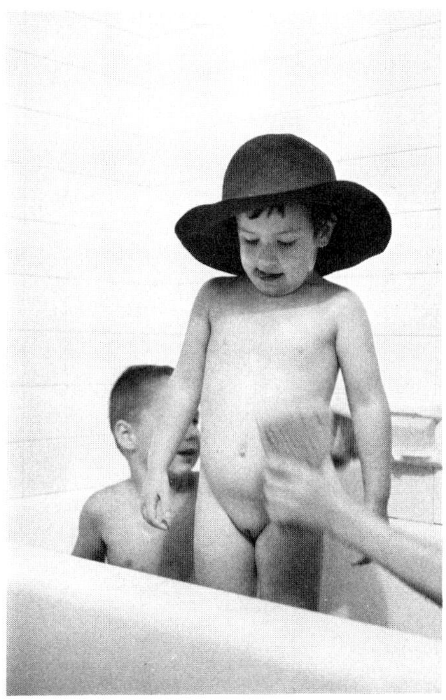

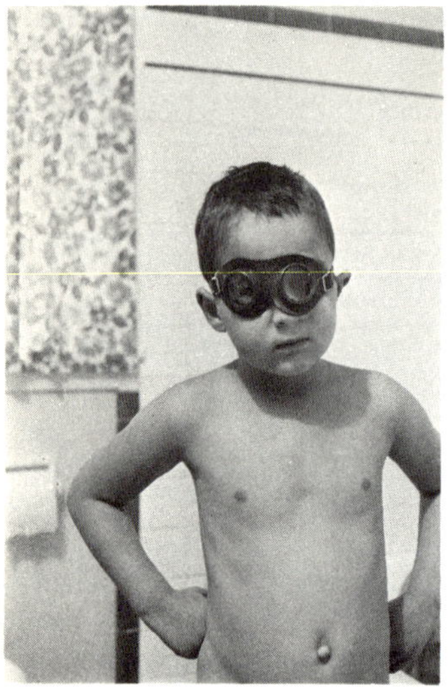

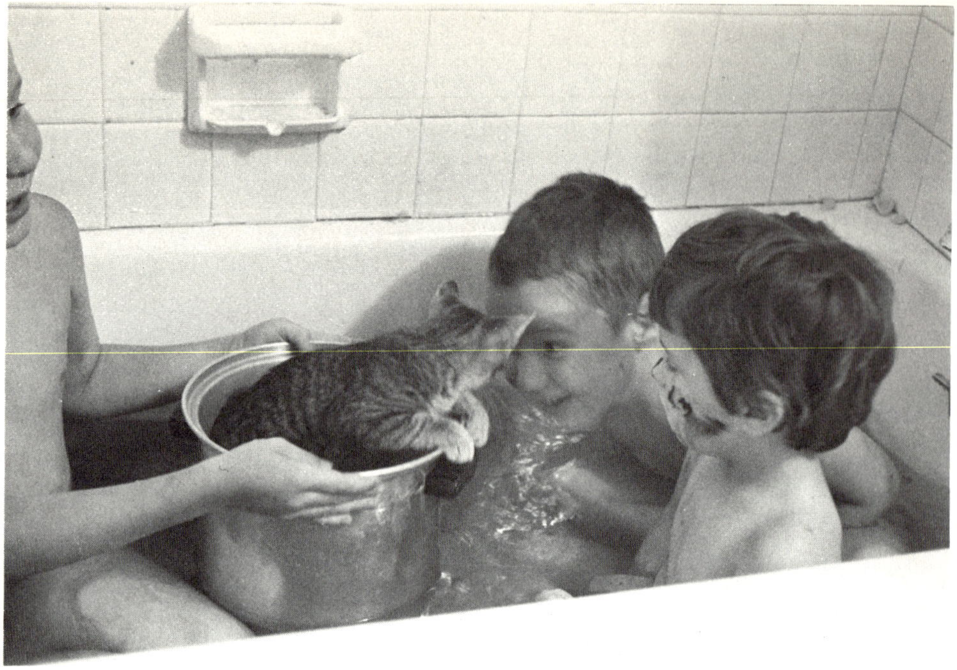

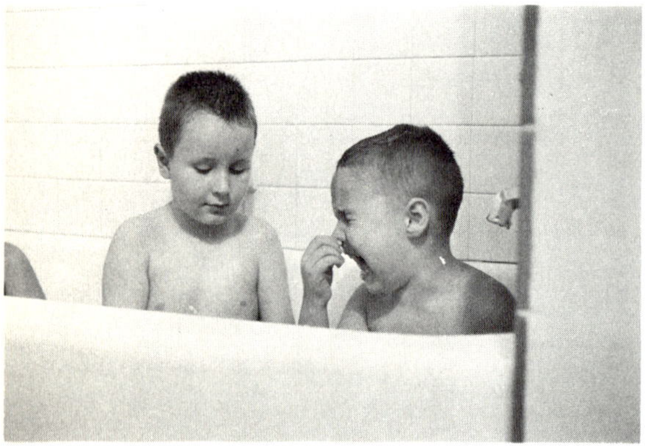

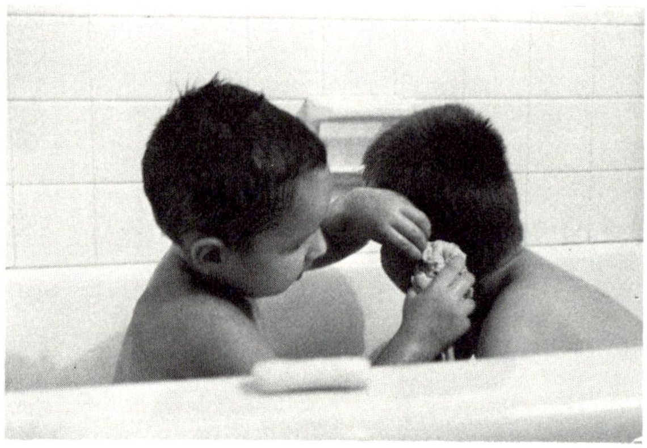

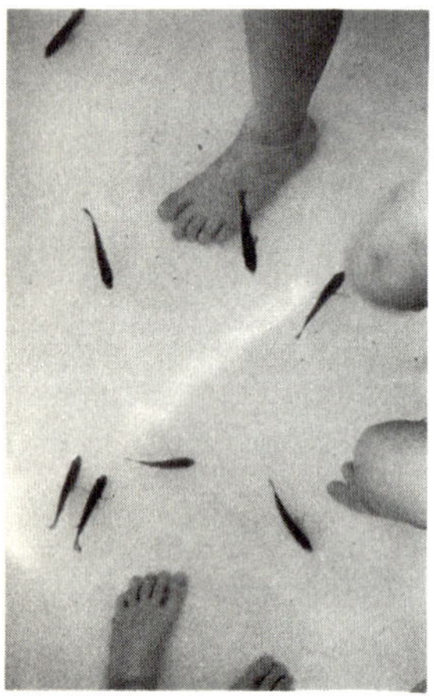

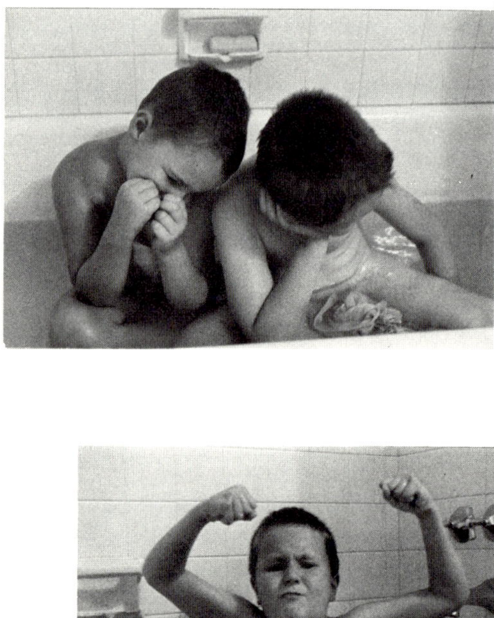

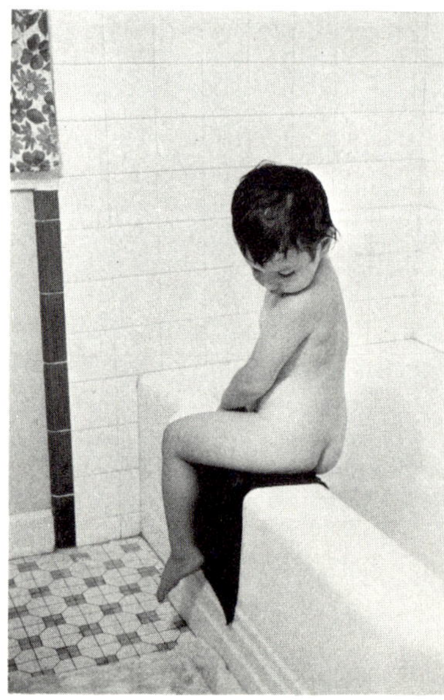

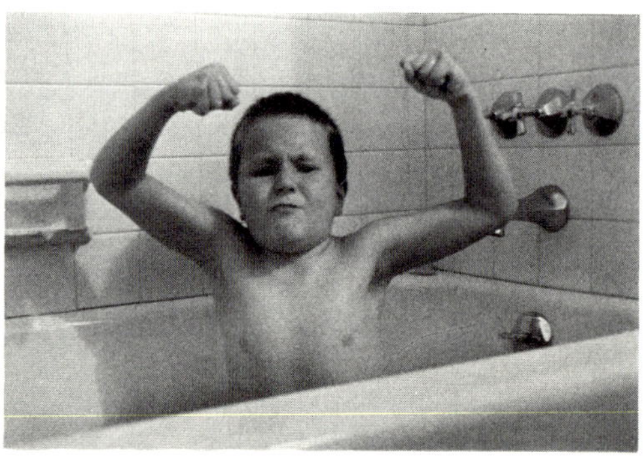

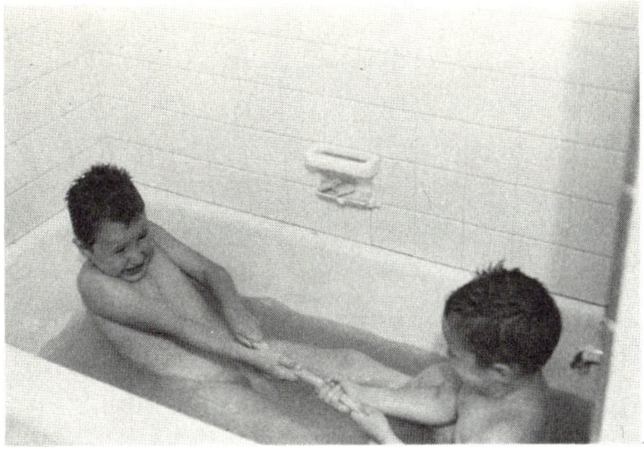

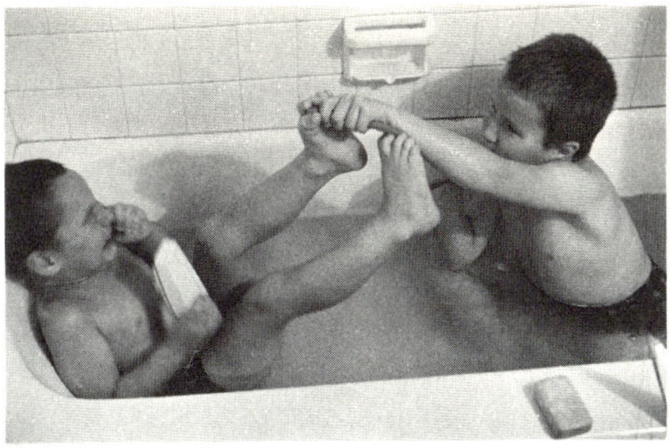

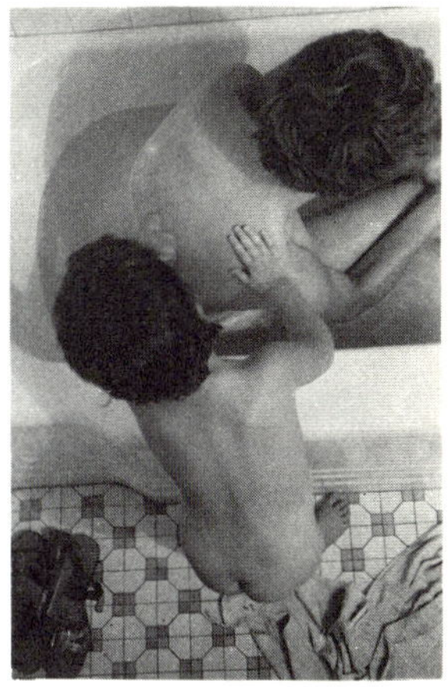

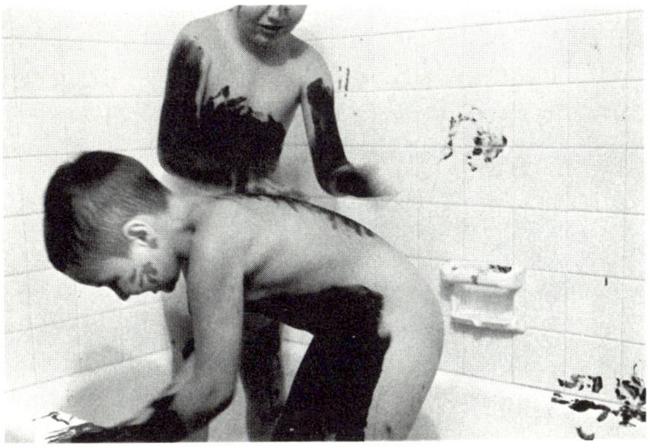

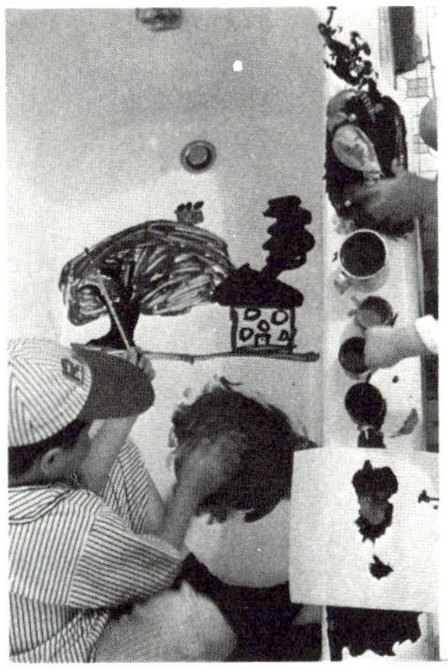

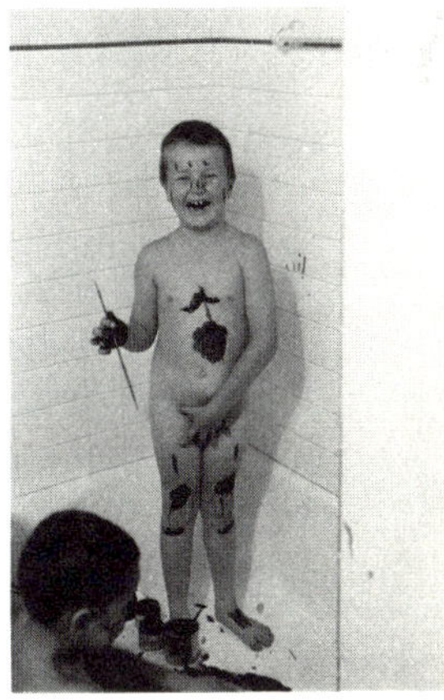

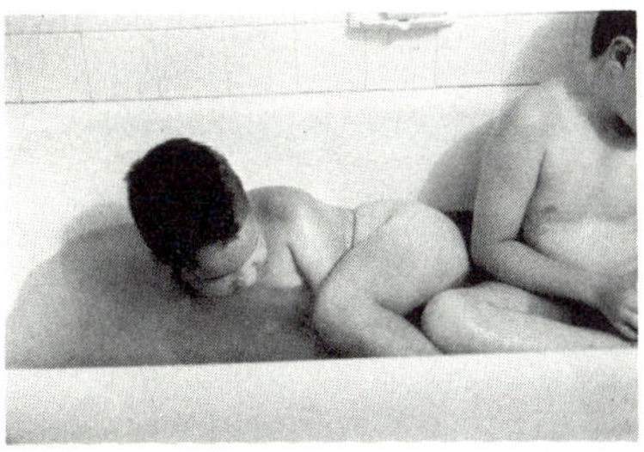

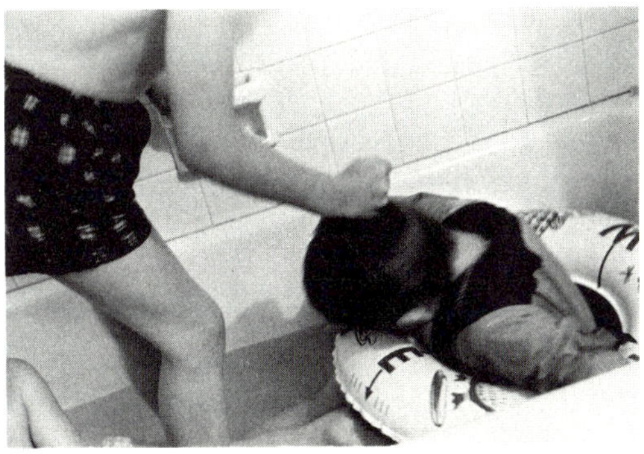

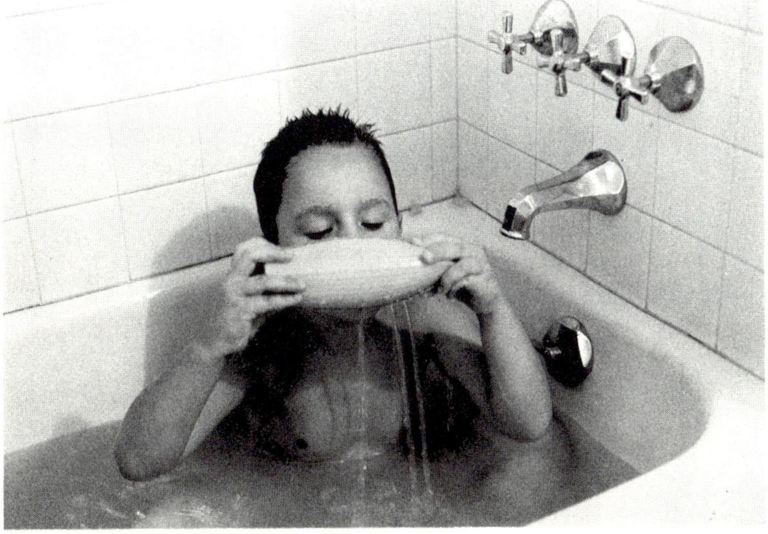

As every parent knows, the only thing a child hates more than getting into a bathtub is getting out. Every time he gets inveigled into it, he finds he has at least four hours of things to do before he will happily consider getting out. The only thing he *doesn't* want to do is to get clean. But what he does want to do invariably makes memorable pictures, especially for a parent.

The pictures this month were selected from a group of 800 I made over a period of two months when my own children were small. As a parent looking back almost fifteen years, I hereby affirm that every single one of them is precious to me. You young parents, take an older man's word for it: If you do such a project with your own kids you'll be thankful the rest of your lives. Not only will you have a record of what they looked like but you will have captured the very essence of childhood. It's something that memory alone cannot retain.

Now we come to a subject about which the editors and I argued at great length. They argued that Hattersley's pictures weren't much as photographs go, that they lacked all the zap and bang that photographs should have. You know—no camera angles, lens selectmanship, soft-focus fiddoodling, etc. I argued that in a situation like this, one should pay attention only to what his children are doing and say goodbye to all photographic razzledazzle. So what if you get snapshots? You'll love them as long as you live.

Don't try for great pictures

That's what I say to you. Forget photography as such for awhile and pay attention only to your children and the marvels of whatever they choose to do. Don't waste your time trying to make great pictures, trying to turn your children into art. Young parents take note: Your children already *are* art. Just record what already is. Find expression for your photographic ego elsewhere.

In light of the above, I suggest that you keep everything very, very simple. Use one light, one lens, one kind of film, one camera, and a minimum of camera angles. The minute you start to expand on this, you'll forget to see who and what your children really are, which is, after all, the entire point of a project like this. If you can really see your own children, you will have done quite well enough.

For lighting, I suggest a clamp-on floodlight bounced off the ceiling. If you have electronic flash, bounce it. String your cords carefully around the top of the bathroom and tie them in place with stout cords. Make sure that everything is out of splashing or touching range of children.

Now we come to a very important point—Momma and/or Poppa. If you're going to capture the essence of your own children, you've got to change your ways. You've got to get loose. No more of this getting uptight about the drinking of bathwater, hauling toys into the tub, flooding the floor, inviting all the neighborhood kids into the tub, giving free baths to willing dogs, and water polo. Your rule should be: Anything goes that's safe. In other words, adopt the attitude that will persuade your children that when you're present they can safely do what they automatically do when you leave the bathroom.

How to raise mayhem

Building your children's trust will take quite a while, especially if you've hitherto been a nag or a screamer. In some homes, the only way genuine kid pictures can be made is for hubby to send his wife out to get lost in traffic while he raises mayhem with the children. As long as he cleans up the mess before she gets home, she won't even know the difference. Don't worry, Dad, the kids won't tattle on you, especially if you've formed a secret society with them to keep her in the dark.

I suspect that mostly this is a weekend-type project for fathers who are looking for an excuse not to mow the lawn or patch up the driveway. By this time of the week, most mothers will be ready to commit hara-kiri or burn down the house. They should be chased off to the hairdresser or the neighborhood coffee klatch down the street. If the kids object to leaving their little friends in order to bathe, let them make it a communal project. You might fill the bathtub with Kool-Aid and bet them a quarter that all twelve of them can't drink it in an hour, from inside the tub, of course. But remember, Dad, for your own safety you must without fail remove all traces of the raspberry flavor before your wife gets home, including running a fast load of towels through the wash if necessary.

Do not expect to work your kids up to the Kool-Aid level of trust in your affability right away. This takes time, maybe even a month or two. And for heaven's sake don't be miserly with film. You know very well that if you do this project, it will be for one time only. Any more you couldn't take. So set yourself a film budget of 25 rolls or so. Buy it all at once so that in a week or so you will have forgotten how dearly it cost you, and feel free to use it gaily. A lot of dough, yes. But unlike investing in a new transmission for your car, which will fall apart in another year anyway, this is an investment in memories that grow sweeter by the year. This you can count on.

Edgar Gelabert's Family Photography

Several years ago, *Popular Photography* printed a lesson I wrote on Ed Gelabert's photography of his family. We called it "In the Name of Love." It was a pretty good lesson, I think, but it just didn't say enough. Ed and I thought that it ought to be expanded considerably for this book. So now you'll find it completely rewritten and stretched out to more sensible bounds.

I first met Ed Gelabert six years ago when he registered in my Saturday class in photography at Columbia University. He was a quiet, affable person then in his late twenties. He was already a fine photographer, but unable to express any of his thoughts concerning his pictures. More accurately, he hadn't as yet discovered what his thoughts were. His very face showed that there were thoughts inside bursting to get out; but what they were he just didn't know.

The class he entered was a seminar devoted to photographic criticism. The students would bring in pictures each week. Together, they and I would criticize them. Criticism, to us, meant trying to figure out what a picture had to say. We thought every picture said something, but weren't at all sure what it might be. Our approach to finding its meaning was to express any thought which seemed in any way germane to what was in it. This led to a good deal of jumping around.

For example, one student might be struck with the picture's design. We would then try to analyze the design and see what it implied. Another would notice something about its tonality. We would take this up. Next we might jump to subject matter, the photographer's conscious or unconscious intentions, technique, probable or possible audience responses to the picture, aesthetics, psychology, philosophy, history or what have you. We all enjoyed the class and found our group efforts rewarding.

I remember one of Ed's early pictures, though I'm not sure we examined it in this particular class. No matter; what Ed and I learned from it typifies what the class was reaching for. It was a very handsomely printed 11x14-inch photograph showing a section of the back of one of Ed's hands. It didn't look like a hand at all, more like sand dunes at dusk or gently billowing waves. It was a very fine looking picture, reminiscent of the best efforts of salon photographers.

When Ed first saw this image appear in the print tray he found that he was quite disturbed by it. Later in the week when he presented it to his classmates, he was still disturbed. The question was: Why? On the surface, it wouldn't seem to make much sense to be upset by a picture of the back of one's own hand, even if it looked more like dunes at dusk than flesh. Nonetheless, Ed was quite distressed and didn't have the vaguest notion why he was. And none of the rest of us did either.

I don't remember what I told him at the time, but I can tell you what I think about the picture now. Ed was distressed because the picture symbolized possibilities for his Self that he hadn't even suspected before. The ego likes to see the Self as small, for it can thus dominate it better.

Something in the picture was saying to Ed: "Look, Friend, this Self you're calmly squeezing into a small box is actually an immensity."

How was this immensity symbolized? Well, Ed started out with four square inches of skin on a very ignominious part of the body, the back of his hand. Had he taken an eye or a mouth or a penis it would have been another matter, for we can readily recognize them as standing for important things. But no, he started out with some skin so unimportant he hadn't even bothered to think about it for the previous twenty-five years. Then he photographically turned it into a Sahara or a Pacific. That he was actually talking about an immensity of some sort was fairly obvious. The fact that the immensity was Ed's Self is hard to understand unless one is familiar with symbolism and the actual scope of the Self.

Do not think, however, that Ed's ego was happy in receiving this message from somewhere inside himself. The message was actually very blunt: "You ignorant fool, in your fear and thirst for self-gratification you are strangling an immensity in yourself. This immensity is the real Master of the house you've stolen. Not only have you stolen His domain, you don't even know He exists."

It's easy to hear of this happening to someone else and to say, "Well, he mustn't be very bright. Were it to happen to me, I would both recognize what it meant and be properly grateful to hear the good word." How little you know of your ego! Rather than to admit such a thing, your ego would gladly chop off your toes to distract his attention from it!

The picture, its meaning and Ed's reaction to it describe very well his way of using photography. You might say that he's a specialist in giving his ego a rough time in order to free his Self. He seems to have accepted the fact that it's a long, long row to hoe and that in order to stick to it he will have to develop infinite patience with himself.

After taking my course once, then going through it once again, Ed kept track of his teacher. Every six months or so he would bring me pictures, usually ones which had him very uptight. Each time, we would sit down together and try to figure out what they meant. During all this time, Ed could speak well on other matters, but when it came to verbalizing about his pictures he was almost speechless.

Ed photographed the back of his hand, then found that the picture disturbed him profoundly.

photo by EDGAR GELABERT

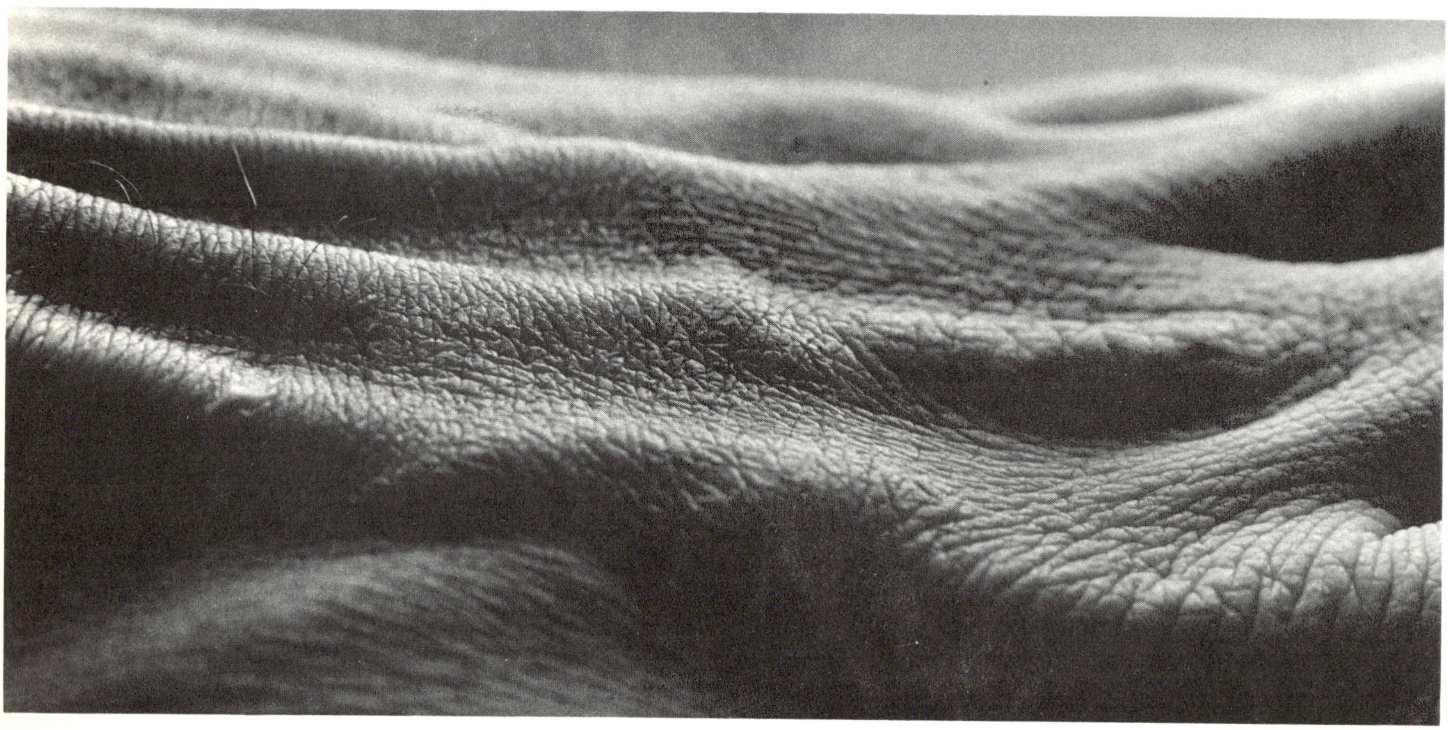

A few weeks ago I had occasion to be delighted for him. I went to his home to talk over the pictures for this book. To my surprise, I discovered that he'd finally learned to verbalize very well. By this, I don't mean that he could just chatter about his pictures. I mean that he was doing a very good job of finding out what his deeper Self wanted him to know, then translating it into words. This clearly implies that he'd actually begun to discover that hidden Self. We must not suppose that photography was his only tool for this. But it certainly was one of the more important ones.

When I first knew Ed, getting him to say something about his pictures was like pulling teeth. He was willing enough to try, but the words just wouldn't come. He had thoughts, no doubt, but they were on the unconscious level and still out of his reach. In those days, he would always talk when asked to but what he told his classmates and me was only a playback of what we had already told him concerning what we had seen in his work. I'm sure this embarrassed Ed, but he was not one to back out of an obligation, to share his understanding with his classmates.

Things are very different now. He can talk coherently and at length about almost all of his pictures. In fact, he told me so much about the ones I'm printing in this book that I only have room for a very small part of what he said. It is important for you to know what kinds of things he says, what good it does him to say them, and the things he prefers not totalk about. He prefers not to talk about techniques, though he's a remarkable photographic craftsman. It isn't so much that he minds doing it; it's that his deeper interest lies elsewhere. As far as Ed is concerned, technique is only a means to an end. I've run across nothing else which he steers away from in criticism of his own work. No matter what you ask him, however personal it may be, he's willing to try giving an answer. He is committed to the notion that photography is a fine means for developing Self-understanding; with this commitment has grown a willingness to share with others the things he's discovered about himself.

The Payoff

Edgar Gelabert is a specialist in giving himself a hard time through photography. Despite all I've said about making the ego suffer in order to get growing room and energy for the real Self, you probably wonder what the payoff is. Well, there is a payoff, a very large one. There are also small payoffs all along the way.

First, you must understand that nearly all of Ed's photographs have dealt with his family—his wife Carmen, his son Edgar Junior, his parents, his brothers and their families. You must also know that he has intuitively taken the hard way. That is, when he takes a picture, or later when he's printing it, he always asks himself, "Who and what am I really seeing? Why am I seeing it in the particular way I am?" When you look this closely at members of your own family, you frequently don't like what you discover about yourself (your ego) while you're doing it. In fact, the pain is often so great that you have to give up photography for awhile. Some of Ed's pictures have caused him to drop out for as long as six or eight months. In one year, he shot only five rolls of film altogether.

What pains the ego most is uncovering the lies it has told itself, then pushed into the unconscious and held imprisoned there with psychic energy. These lies also imprison the real Self, making his growth, freedom and expression an impossibility. These same lies also cause the ego suffering, for they are constantly sneaking out of the unconscious. When the ego sees them he suffers. The more lies are there, the greater his suffering. The more lies one represses, the smaller and more finite one conceives the Self to be. With the concept of such a limited Self, the ego sees nothing but death, and the fear of death, ahead. He just can't make himself believe that the Self cannot die. Even he can't die, though he can surrender the energy he's stolen from the psyche in order to keep his lies repressed in the unconscious. In his fear, the ego thinks he must steal more and more energy. He doesn't understand that the only way out of fear (and into happiness) is to make himself suffer deliberately by seeing his lies, so that the energy used to repress them can be released and used for the needs of the real Self.

The kind of family photography that Edgar Gelabert does makes ego-suffering a certainty. Mild and gentle though he appears to be, he's actually pretty tough. No one can be a real family photographer without psychic toughness. His ego suffers when he shoots his pictures, when he prints them, when he shows them to other people and admits to the unpleasant things he discovered about himself in the whole process. The latter thing is psychologically the equivalent of walking nude down Main Street at mid-day. Yet it also serves to make it unnecessary for the ego to defend the lies thus revealed, which gives him more freedom and releases psychic energy for better uses in the future.

Defending lie and conditioning systems consumes well over ninety-nine percent of our energy. This is why a perfectly healthy eighteen-year-old can feel exhausted all the time. Since we're used to having very little of our energy available to us, we've come to think of it as the normal way to be. Furthermore, we can't even conceive of the amount that's really there. It's no exaggeration to say that the energy potentially available to a human being exceeds that of a megaton hydrogen bomb by a large order of magnitude. When Christ said that a grain of faith the size of a mustard seed would move a mountain, he was telling a literal fact.

The immediate payoff for Gelabert's kind of family photography is a growing pool of available energy. Every ego-lie discovered is energy no longer in bondage. Though it is released by psychological means, it is the same kind of energy the body uses. It's just at a higher level of vibration. Right now, Gelabert may have a good deal more available energy than he had, say, ten years ago, even though his body isn't in quite as good shape as it was. Looking ahead, if he persists in crucifying his egotism he may end up as an eighty-year-old with an immensely greater energy output than he had at the age of twenty. Don't laugh; it happens fairly often. So you see that there is a very real payoff.

There is a long-term payoff, however, which goes far beyond merely feeling better and having more energy. When one struggles against egotism and selfishness, he promotes the growth of Love in himself. We might say that Lovingness feeds on ego-suffering. What actually happens here is that lower energies are changed into higher ones. All energy is One, but it has different levels of vibration. And we have more potential control over our vibration levels than we ordinarily suppose. The highest vibration of all is Love.

Though we don't usually speak of Love as a form of energy, it is one, the highest energy man can experience. We think of energies in terms of blowing up things with them. Love may not be good for this. On the other hand, Love holds a universe together. We must admit to ourselves that that implies a very high energy indeed. I'm not speaking metaphorically here. I mean that there is actually an energy which makes the universe work. The name which comes closest to describing what it is is Love. Since 'love' has been used to describe a good many things which have nothing to do with real Love, it is used here only in the sense that our Great Teachers have used it—beings like Jesus Christ, Buddha, Mohammed.

In giving us a chance to recognize the depth of our selfishness and the motivation to struggle against it, marriage is the ideal growing field for Love. It's a fortunate thing that photography can help us focus our efforts in this struggle. This is why the original *Popular Photography* lesson on Edgar Gelabert's photography was entitled "In the Name of Love." Though he doesn't use these terms to describe what he's striving for, Lovingness in himself is precisely what he's trying to create. As long as you do the right things it doesn't really matter what name you give your goal. Ed may think that his goal is merely to understand himself and his family better. That's fine; no one would argue with it. At the same time, nonetheless, he's promoting the growth of Lovingness in himself. Understanding is only an aspect of Love.

I've been speaking here of Love as something which is created in a marriage, not as something we bring with us to the altar. To change ordinary energies into the highest requires a very fiery crucible indeed. Marriage, with its opportunities for struggling against selfishness, provides us with it.

Of course, young folk think they're in love when they marry. What they mean by love has nothing to do with the real thing. Even by the farthest stretch of the imagination the two things can't be connected. For young folk, 'being in love' is a delusional state, delicious of course, but entirely a product of young, yearning selfishness. As a delusion, it's not good for people and must be overcome.

Being 'In Love' is Not the Same as Loving Someone

Bad as they are for us, even our delusions have certain value. For example, if we couldn't delude ourselves about Love, the sacrament of marriage would very soon disappear. In a more Puritanical age, we could expect the sex urge to drive people into marriage in order for them to satisfy it. But our sexual taboos are rapidly going out the window and we must depend on the 'love delusion' to bring young people together in matrimony.

It happens that it is impossible to be egotistical and Loving at the same time. The two states are entirely antithetical. To Love one's fellow men truly (or even one of them) is to exist in a very high spiritual state. It is immensely better than being the Lord of Xanadu or of all Alexander's conquests. To be a true Lover is man's highest art and, like any other art, it must be learned and earned. Being 'in love' is no more like true Loving than a flea is like the sun.

But being 'in love' does get people into matrimony, and that is at least something to say for it. Once they're there they have a golden opportunity to learn what marriage is really all about. As much as anything, marriage is about selfishness being revealed in no uncertain terms. If a youngster has arrived at the marriage age without discovering his (or her) own selfishness he or she is in for a rude awakening. Let us say he is very selfish but has very high ideals for himself. Unless his ego is self-deluded to the very last extremity, he very soon begins to suspect he may be very selfish indeed. When countless time after time he finds himself putting his own interests before his helpmeet's, it's no wonder that such a suspicion gets itself fostered. For it not to be, a person has to be very self-deluded indeed.

So, marriage is an institution in which one learns he is thoroughly selfish and that his ideals are frayed paper angels. There is also a good chance that he will rediscover his Conscience, for no matter how long it has been safely plowed under, it will still rise to the surface now and then when it finds the ideals being constantly violated.

Again, marriage is a contract in which anger is finally discovered, not the anger which arises when a sneering stranger jabs you in the ribs but the everyday, self-strangling anger we manage to hide from ourselves most of the time. Always irrational (unless it is that extremely rare thing called 'Righteous Anger'), this anger is even more irrational in the context of marriage. Because it is so irrational, there's a good chance we'll discover that it is and try to do something about it in ourselves.

It is irrational because it is the anger of the ego being forced by innocent circumstance to see through some of his most cherished illusions. High on the list of cherished illusions is that one is a true lover, or easily could be with just a little bit of time, thought and effort. As illusions go, this is about as naive a one as you'll find. The anger springs to life when the ego finds its ideals are only paper. It's a shocking thing to discover about oneself, as bad as a ferocious lion's discovering in his fifth year that he's actually a one-legged duck. He is terrified, and out of his terror grows anger.

Since Love is man's only salvation, it's not surprising we're unconsciously terrified when we discover how far we are from it. The terror turns into a slow, grinding anger, which is also unconscious most of the time. But bits of it keep popping up in the most juvenile way in the little things we do to our helpmeets. The anger is really there and we can easily do only two things with it: take it out on ourselves or on our mates. To eliminate the anger is an immensely more difficult thing. By merely existing, our mates constantly confront us with our inability to Love. It is only to be expected (people being what they are) that we should turn our anger toward them.

It is a very interesting fact that a man's unconscious anger toward his wife will often show up in his photographs of her, if he happens to be a pretty good photographer. One reason competent photographers stop photographing their wives soon after marriage is that the anger is expressed so clearly there's a very good chance they'll see it themselves. Rather than let their egos suffer intensely at the sight of husbandly ideals being so flagrantly violated in a photograph, the husband gives up photographing his wife altogether. I haven't seen this in wives' pictures of their husbands, so I assume their anger must express itself more naturally in other ways.

This is one of the reasons I've called Ed Gelabert psychically tough. He's seen his anger get into his pictures of his wife, Carmen, been shaken badly by seeing it and somehow managed to go on taking pictures of her. Of course, it helps that she takes his hang-ups and his photography philosophically.

So marriage is a college in which we can discover our selfishness and all the ego hang-ups which stem from it, including anger. However, it is not even a kindergarten unless we deliberately foster the discovery. It is only a sacrament if two people join together to fight their selfishness in the name of Love.

Young married folk know nothing of marriage as a sacrament. All that holds them together is the illusion of being 'in love' and sex. Sex serves the dual function of creating children and holding two people together long enough for them to creep slowly up on the responsibility that marriage as a sacrament entails.

In the beginning sex is merely masturbation de deux, for it lacks entirely humility and lovingness. At the same time, it softens the otherwise unendurable shocks that two young egos experience when they come together in matrimony. Sex has this ameliorating function, for its purpose is to protect life as well as create it. If young people were suddenly confronted with marriage as a sacrament and could plainly see the selfishness it must overcome, the shock would be much too great for them.

Sex converts ego-suffering into erotic pleasure and stretches out the discovery period long enough for the couple to begin to adjust to the realities of marriage. The realities are this: Two egotists are brought together in a union, the pain of it disguised temporarily by sex. They have three choices: Struggle together against the selfishness which is the cause of the pain; through anger destroy one another and themselves; terminate the union and the opportunity.

Young folk may think that this is a very black picture of marriage, but it's not. Marriage as such is a great opportunity for crucifying selfishness and learning to Love. The blackness resides only in the selfishness which young folk bring into marriage with them. Whether they get married or not, they've still got to come to terms with it.

The young may say, "We've seen lots of married people and not seen these things you've talked about." That is right, they're not generally on the surface where they can be easily seen. But underneath the surface selfishness is a slow, corrosive stream. It can be left untreated so that it destroys both husband and wife. Or it can be fought against with patience and humility. In either case it may not be visible to the youthful eye.

Though I haven't used Ed Gelabert's name much in this section, I've been talking about him all along, also about you and me and our parents, grandparents and remote ancestors. Even the Queen of Sheba and all her court. We're all in the same leaky boat: selfishness. And we all have the chance to either do something about it or to refuse to try. Most of us try, for we intuitively feel, rightly, that we'll never be free if we don't. But we don't always use our marriages as well as we might in behalf of our mates and ourselves. Marriage is an uncommonly difficult thing.

We have the tendency to fight against our selfishness in a passive way. We let our

Consciences nag at us for our sins of commission and omission, but don't actively do much on our own to overcome them. Oh, we try in fits and starts, then run like hell in the opposite direction whenever we get half a chance. It's harder to run when you have a camera in your hand, which is one reason many people pick up cameras no oftener than they have to.

The camera tends to turn passive suffering into active. By deliberately making suffering active, it works faster to diminish selfishness. Photography provokes a hassle within oneself, a very productive and therapeutic one. It is a brawl where a higher part of the Self works through the mind to attack egotism, or the ego. It is good for one to invite this inner conflict.

The ancients had a very useful name for the ego: the wolf. We should all borrow the idea, for giving ego a name helps us cope with him. It also helps us differentiate between ego and Self, for they are not the same at all. Ego thinks he is the Self, but he isn't. Compared with SELF, ego is a walnut shell lost in the Pacific Ocean. So we should call His Selfishness 'the wolf', then set out to educate him so that he can stop lying to himself. For educational purposes we've got to hassle him, for that is the only kind of teaching he'll listen to.

For awhile I'm not going to talk about Ed Gelabert. When one is talking about *all* men it isn't necessary to single just *one* of them out. Furthermore, you should clearly understand that this essay on Gelabert is about everybody, including yourself.

Hassling Brother Wolf

We've got to have someone to conduct the hassling sessions, so we'll choose Mind for the job. Basically, Mind is very critical of the wolf and doesn't hesitate to give him a well-earned rough time. We'll say that Mind knows how to operate a camera and understands that photography is as good a way as any for hassling brother wolf. Now we'll see how Mind leans on him.

Mind says, "Brother wolf, you're wife would like you to take a picture of the baby in that little blue sleeping bag before he outgrows it. Your mother-in-law made it by hand and put a lot of loving care into it. Since you happen to be at wit's end for something to do this Saturday, right now would be just the time to do it."

Suddenly, brother wolf grimaces with pain. He gets hot flashes, feels smothered, gets shooting pains in the solar plexus. Then hope dawns, for he sees an out. He says to himself he hasn't got any film, but Mind inexorably reminds him of the four brand-new rolls in his overcoat pocket. But dawn breaks once again as he says to himself, "Now I remember what I've been trying to think of all morning: cigarettes. If I don't get another carton within the hour I'll certainly die of nicotine deprivation by tomorrow night. I wouldn't want people mourning me."

He tucks his tail in his pocket and strolls toward the front door. His Selfishness is greatly pleased with himself for having gotten the afternoon's importances so well balanced, for he's also thought of getting himself a hot fudge sundae.

As he's enjoying his sundae a while later, Mind cuts into his chocolate revery: "Not going to tell your wife about this sundae, are you? Don't want her to know you'd gorge yourself and not bring her any. Or if you told her and she said, 'That's swell, Honey', you'd have to admire her for her understanding sympathy. Can't have any of that, can we? Can't have her coming off as more compassionate than you, can we?"

"Never forgiven her mother for sewing for a month on that cuddly sleeping bag, have you? She should have spent all the time on you, of course. That little pouch is really yours, isn't it? A womb for brother wolf. It's your hidey-hole womb, so you're darned if you're going to take a picture of the kid sleeping in it. Of course, if you took the picture it would be for your wife, wouldn't it? And you don't want to share your photography with anyone, because it's your toy. Can't have someone else enjoying it too, can we?

"Think you're being funny when you refer to the baby as 'The Monster,' don't you? If he really were one you'd know you hadn't sired him. Then you'd have a good excuse for not wanting to take responsibility for him. You'd also feel better about being sore at him for stealing your wife's affection from you. She should be nursing you, not him. Those are your nipples by right, ain't they Buddy Boy? So you're not going to take a picture of a bosom thief sleeping in your womb, not if you can help it. Think this is all a joke, don't you, and that you're mighty suave for having thought of it. Well, Sonny, you didn't think of it, I did."

You may think that this kind of a hassle on top of a hot fudge sundae isn't really so bad, after all. But when it happens to you, and every bit of it is true, it won't be so much fun. We'll now see how Mind hassles His Selfishness on account of a portrait he recently made of his wife and which pleases him inordinately.

"Really accented the scar on her chin, didn't you? You're paying her back for demanding some of the attention you'd rather spend entirely on yourself! You say to yourself you're going to help her by curing her vanity. Well, sweet little guru you. You're a real rotten-to-the-core guru, Your Saintliness. You don't really give a hoot about whether her illusions and her vanity are good for her. All you want to do is pay her back for loading a little responsibility on your shoulders."

"Aha! I see you're now changing the rules of the ball game. You're feeling proud in being so noble as to marry a woman whose scar makes her a little less beautiful than Helen of Troy. That's the kind of a beauty you really deserve, and how compassionate of you to marry a lesser being. Well, you beneficent Casanova, Helen of Troy wouldn't have touched you with a ten-foot pole."

"Another rule change, eh? Now the pity is welling up in you. You're feeling sorry for her because she looks scarred and skinny in the picture. Feeling real concern that she's so worried about her looks. Well, cheap thrill for you, Mahatma Gandhi. You're rolling in your pity as if it were a mud wallow; and that's about all your so-called pity is good for. You couldn't tell real compassion from a hole in your underwear."

For one last sally, we'll turn to a picture which His Selfishness made of the baby when it was two weeks old. His wife disliked it strongly; and he was rather put out with her for it. In this dialogue, Mind will make clear the reasons for her dislike.

"Oho, Dear Boy, you've made the baby look like a greasy little toad, haven't you? And here you are admiring yourself for your command of photographic technique. Well, you should. Anyone who can use photography to turn a fine baby into a dirty white grub sure has technique, alright. You'd like to hit The Monster with a hammer, wouldn't you? You know you can't, so you turn your picture into a hammer, instead.

"You're paying him back for stealing your wife's affections and your home. You don't like the thought you're working for him now, do you? Well, you damned well are, and that's the way it should be. Your greasy toad is the hope of the world. You're just a pot-bellied egotist afraid of his shadow. Aha! I see a tear in your eye. Poor, old you! My, my, ain't we pathetic!"

For all its seeming flippancy, this is exactly the kind of interior dialogue that goes on in the head of serious family photographer. His wolf finds it very hard to take, which explains why so few people go in for this type of Self-exploration. Among literally dozens of types of photographers, the serious family photographer is the rarest breed of all.

Of course, I have no way of knowing if thoughts such as these actually went through Edgar Gelabert's head. If I did know, it wouldn't be my right to reveal them in public. However, I believe I'm an expert on such matters, for I've so frequently observed the very same thoughts going through my own head. There is one think we can know for a certainty: What we see to be true of ourselves is also true of others. If you or I think thoughts of this kind, other people do, too. They may not be consciously aware of them, but they're there, nonetheless. Of course, they don't go around admitting to other people that they have them. They wouldn't admit it even to God.

Fortunately, there are also thoughts of a more positive nature which come to mind while one is making family photographs. These have more to do with informing us concerning the nature of the real Self than with egotism. However, they are quite a bit harder to get to than egotistical thoughts. When we start talking about Gelabert's photographs I'll tell you what some of them are. The two of us have managed to identify and understand quite a few of them.

Some Advice From Ed Gelabert

Ed is one of the best serious family photographers in the country. Therefore, you can rely completely on what he has to say about it. He wants everyone to know that family photography is not a bowl of cherries. If you go into it seriously you're really going to be putting yourself through the miseries.

It is his experience that you can't expect anyone to understand what you're trying to do. Ed has two brothers, both of whom are interested in photography. They think that what he's doing is rather odd and they don't really understand it at all. He received no guidance or encouragement in what he was doing until he discovered the class at Columbia University. There was nothing in camera magazines or books to help him. He says the whole subject of serious family photography is a great vacuum. The professionals won't understand what you're trying to do. The amateurs will think you're crazy. One big problem, Ed found, is that you may constantly lose faith in your methods and purposes yourself. After all, it seems very strange that in a country devoted to the pursuit of happiness a person would use his art in order to make himself suffer. Very few people understand suffering and that if it's done properly it's a high religious art.

Ed says that you're going to have to force yourself to make pictures. There is nothing your ego desires less than to have to suffer. It will manufacture all kinds of dodges to keep you from picking up your camera. Frequently, it will stall you altogether—for months or even years at a time. Your ego doesn't want to know the lies it's been telling itself, for it depends on them for its comfort. So, you're going to have to force yourself to go against its wishes.

You're also going to have to outwit ego. Your mind can learn to do this if you give it plenty of practice. Thus, when your ego is dragging its heels and making you refuse to pick up the camera, you can feed it a fancy con man's line and make it want to make pictures. Such a line could be, "Show everyone what a hotshot you are in photography." Or what a good husband, father, son, daughter and so on. Since your mind has already had a good deal of experience in outwitting the ego, you can expand on this idea for yourself.

Ed says that one thing which will help you carry on such a difficult task is to know there is a payoff. He has experienced it hundreds of times. Nearly every week he takes out his pictures and looks at them. Every time he is rewarded with new insights into himself and his family. He finds that many thoughts which used to really get him uptight no longer bother him at all. This is indicative of a wider self-acceptance, a more humane and reasonable attitude toward one's self.

I've already mentioned that in confronting your ego with things it would rather avoid, you release energy it has tied up in protecting itself. I'm sure that Ed has experienced this, too. In fact I know he has, though he hasn't told me. One indication of this is his ever-expanding sense of humor. Humor grows from Self-knowledge and uses energies formerly employed in defending illusions.

I'm sure that Ed feels his struggle against selfishness has made him a much better husband and father. Certainly, it has given him much greater ease in family relationships. His grace of behavior with outsiders is also developing steadily. He has discovered that Self-exploration through serious family photography is well worth any effort you put into it.

Carmen and Ed went together for two years before they were married. When the picture of Carmen behind a leaf was taken they had been engaged for about six months. On this day they had spent a good deal of time wandering around in the Bronx Botanical Gardens. In one of the greenhouses, Ed excused himself and went off to make a picture he had in mind. When he came back, he saw Carmen before she saw him and took a picture of her.

I asked him why he took it. He answered, "Well, she was angry at me. I think I just wanted a picture of her being angry. We had been there quite awhile and she was tired. She didn't really like the idea of my wandering off to make more pictures." I asked him what he thought he'd gotten out of her being angry at him. He said he'd gotten a big kick out of it. I asked why. "Probably because it meant that I was still independent, that I could still do what I wanted to do. Even if she got angry at me, I could still do whatever I pleased. Of course, her being angry at me also meant she felt something for me, otherwise she wouldn't care."

Ed agreed that making her angry had made him feel very much of a big, tough, independent guy, very much in control of things, including Carmen. Men are prone to go to considerable lengths to stir up emotions in their sweethearts, and they don't really care too much which kind they stir up; any emotion at all will do. This ability they interpret as control. Attempting to control women is, of course, one of the classical preoccupations of men. It's only fair to say that women get a big ego-kick out of trying to control men, too.

Having a picture of someone we've made angry is raspberry sherbert for the ego. This old wolf can tell himself more lies while looking at it than there are fish in the ocean. Just a few of his favorites are: "I have the power to manipulate her emotions as I please. She finds me very frustrating, but I'm so attractive she can't stay away from me. I just snap my fingers and beautiful women come running up to me. What bothers women is my strength; they get angry when they can't overwhelm it." And so on. Count the number of fish and fill in the rest of the fanciful stories for yourself.

You will notice that Ed's picture makes Carmen look very imperious, very regal. There is no doubt that his wolf enjoys the thought of dominating such a queenly creature. Maybe something beside ego got into his picture. Perhaps his Self is giving him fair warning, saying, "Look Buster, you're inclined to think that marriage will be a playground for your egotism. Look at this woman you're about to marry. Does she look like a person who will put up with it? You'd like to dominate her, but do you think you really can? You'd like to be the stronger of the two of you, but do you think you really will be?"

It is strange that Self so often gets into pictures which seem to be purely egotistical. It may be that Self hooks the wolf by giving him small pleasures. Underneath them, Self has hidden very heavy punches in the jaw for His Selfishness.

Since the picture was made about eight years ago, I asked Ed what he thinks about it now and if he recognizes its subject as Carmen. He said, "No, it's not really Carmen. I sort of recognize her, but that's all. It never really was Carmen. She liked the picture, however, and still does. She likes the way her eyes came out. When she gets angry her eyes really light up."

Before Ed and Carmen were married he took hundreds of pictures of her. He says that like most young men he used his photography mainly to indulge in his fantasies. Since he didn't know her so well, he could give them free play. He could make her into anything he wanted her to be and not upset himself by doing it. There was nothing in his experience to tell him how far he was off the track in seeing Carmen as she truly was. In those days, photographing her was pure fun.

After marriage, a man finds it harder and harder to photograph his wife seriously. That is, hard to photograph her and really think about her while he's doing it. On the national scale, most men give up serious photography of their wives within a year after being married to them. The problem is that they project things into their photographs which they just don't want to see, namely things indicative of the depth of their selfishness. These really give the ego a rough time.

Six years ago, Ed photographed his aunt, Mrs. Julia Court, and her twenty-one-year-old daughter Antoinette. Ed's recollection is that he wanted to show, or verify, a relationship between the two. He made the

The beautiful Carmen before she and Ed were married.

photo by EDGAR GELABERT

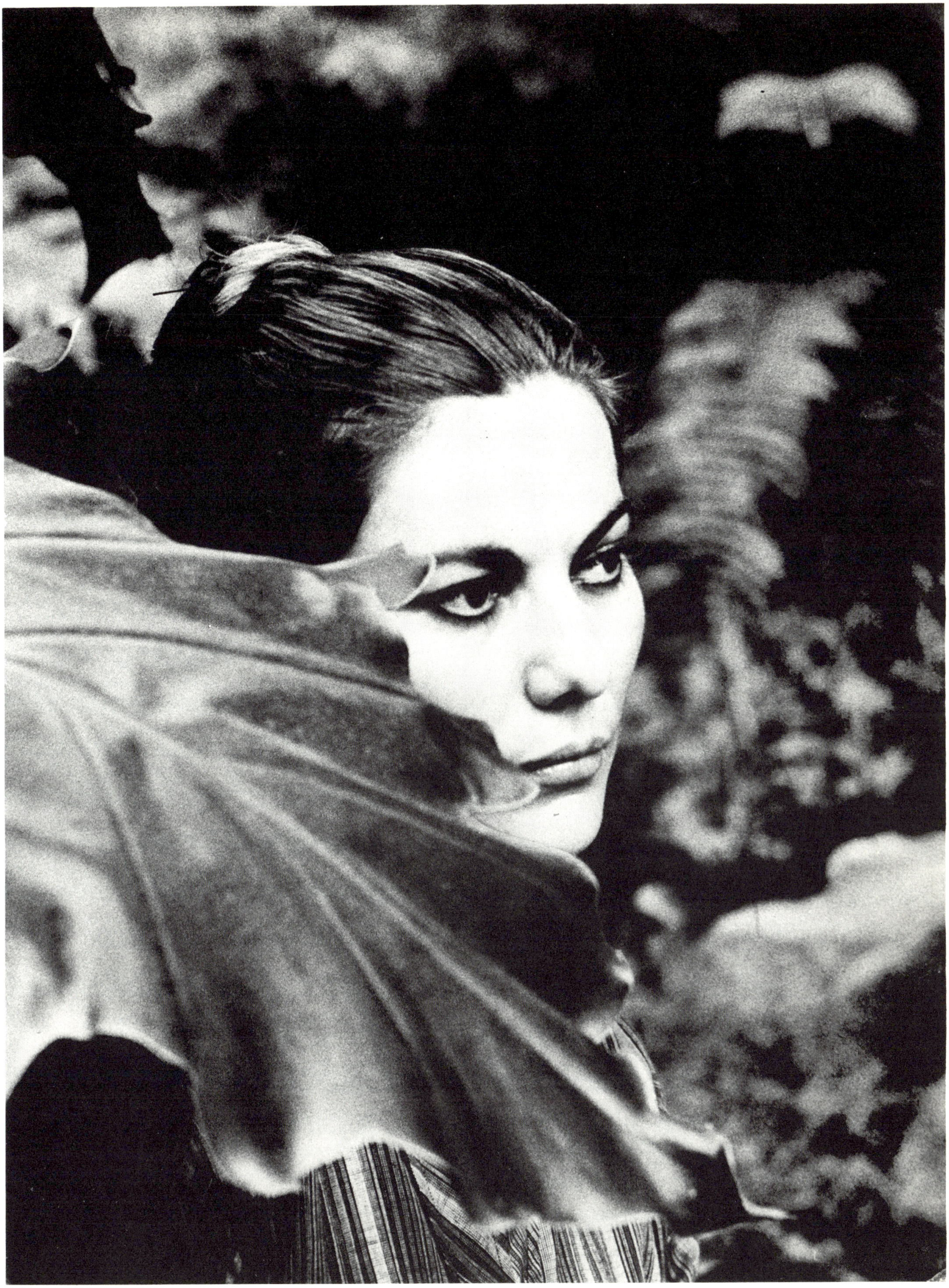

picture entirely for himself in order to help himself see how they related. He thought he knew, but he wasn't sure.

Their life situation at that time was such as to burden them both heavily. After losing her husband when Antoinette was barely into her teens, Mrs. Court had taken charge of the household and earned the living for the two of them. However, by the time her daughter was about seventeen, Mrs. Court was almost entirely crippled by arthritis and bedridden most of the time. So Antoinette had to earn the living, as she has ever since. Under the very best of circumstances, it may often be difficult for two women to live together, even if they're mother and daughter. With the trials and tribulations his aunt and cousin were facing, Ed thought the strain must be very great for them indeed as they were tightly bound together by Mrs. Court's illness.

Ed shot a roll of pictures of the two of them together. As you see, his Aunt Julia was able to get about a little bit on this particular day. This picture is the only one like it on the roll. In fact, it's the last one he shot and the only one he printed. Always fond of his aunt and cousin, Ed tried to use his photography to see their life together as having more sunlight in it. Ed wanted to see them happy and lighthearted; and he would use his photography to make them look that way, if he could. He says he's frequently found himself trying to do this with his camera. So he posed them in various ways so as to suggest the relationship he wanted them to have. In the final picture, however, he asked his Aunt Julia to look at him and his cousin to stand profile and look out the window. And this is the only one he could bring himself to print of the two of them together.

Ed says that he's more than once tried to use his camera to change things around but that somehow they always manage to defeat him by looking the way they really are. It's probably not the medium itself which causes this, but something in Ed himself. When he's intent on changing the world into a bowl of cherries, this something—his Self, perhaps—won't let him do it. Often he's thought he's managed to do it. When he makes his prints, he finds that he hasn't. In the case of his aunt and cousin he may very well have made several pictures which suggest their lives are sunny; Ed is a good enough photographer to do this, if he tries. For his last picture, he himself broke off the illusion by the way he asked them to pose. He asked his aunt to look in one direction, his cousin in another. This is hardly what he'd do if he were trying to get across the idea of unity.

When Ed printed his picture of his mother and father he was so distressed by it that he couldn't take any more pictures for the next eight months. What upset him in the picture no longer does. Discovering it in himself, and learning to accept it have made a substantial contribution to his life.

On the surface, there was nothing unusual in the way the picture was made. The elder Gelaberts were visiting Ed and his wife. Ed recalled that he didn't have a picture of them in his album, so he decided to shoot one. He had them stand side by side near the window, but found he couldn't get back far enough to get them both in the viewfinder. So he had his father stand behind his mother. This didn't look quite right, so he asked him to put his hand on his wife's shoulder.

Since Ed had the lens wide open, he knew his father would be out-of-focus, but he didn't consciously think about it. After Ed had shot his roll of pictures, his father said, "Did you know I would be out-of-focus?" Since he had worked with cameras quite a bit himself, he knew this had to be the case. Ed was a bit disturbed at his 'error,' but didn't think much about it until later.

As he was shooting, he was mainly aware of his mother and that he was rather angry at something. He can't to this day make up his mind whether he was angry at her or himself. He was aware that for the first time in his thirty-one years he was beginning to see her as a human being. This was not what he wanted. What he really desired was the mother stereotype to which he had accustomed himself. His mother was 'supposed to be' only understanding, angelic, loving and so on. As he shot the roll of film he saw that she also had the capability of being angry, one-way, selfish, jealous, prideful, and all the other things which human beings are ordinarily capable of. At the time, this displeased him. Now he is very glad that it happened and that he can see her as a human being and still love and respect her as much as he ever did. In truth, this means he loves her a good deal more. We cannot love illusions of people; we can love only those who are real to us.

When Ed decided to make prints, he looked at his contact sheet and picked out just this one image. He has never printed any of the others. When he saw the 11x14-inch print, he disliked it greatly, saying to himself, "This is the worst picture I ever made." It was only much later that he began to see that there was much more behind his choice than he had originally supposed. Something in him wanted Ed to confront a truth or verify a suspicion.

The confrontation comes to this: His mother was looking at him in a very pos-

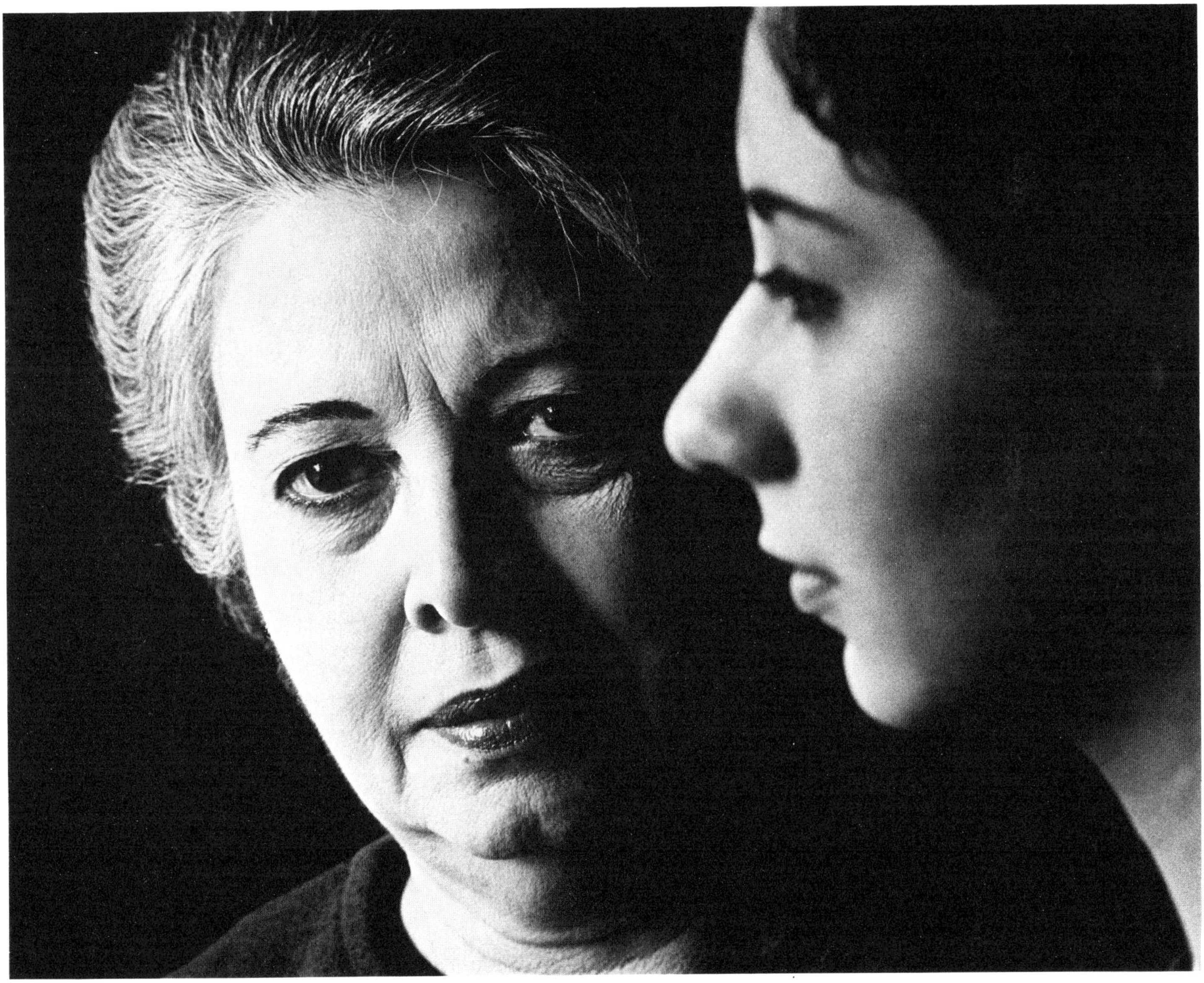

Edgar's aunt Mrs. Julia Court and her daughter Atoinette.

photo by
EDGAR GELABERT

sessive way. The expression in her face was clearly saying, "Edgar, you and I are the real team. Your father is here, but he's not really a part of it." Though mothers have felt this way about their sons since time began, sons have never liked to see it written in their faces. It makes them angry because they feel exactly the same way; and it makes them feel very guilty for excluding their fathers. Of course, Ed will now have to see such expressions flitting between his own wife and his own son. Discovering it happening between his mother and himself has, thus, prepared him for it. It is a call of the blood, whose strength cannot be denied if one respects the truth.

This discovery more than anything else forced Ed to accept his mother's humanity. Since he's accepted it he's closer to her than ever. His picture also helped him move closer to his father. As he puts it, it acted as a catalyst producing a long chain of thought concerning his father and his own relationship to him. He said it was the first time in thirty-one years he'd really thought about him at all.

As soon as he got off on this track he knew why he had made his father out-of-focus in his picture. It was a way of excluding him, of putting him into a position of unimportance. Out-of-focus, his father was only a wraith, not a real human being. This you can clearly see when you look at the picture. It then struck Ed that he'd been doing this to his father all his life. He felt guilt, but at the same time a new warmth for his father. He thought, "Though it's late, I can give my father affection. And I will. Perhaps he needs it now even more than he did when I was a little boy." His son's changed behavior startled Mr. Gelabert at first, but now their relationship has grown very warm and friendly. This is a major indication that serious family photography has its payoffs. It can help lead a son back to his father.

When Ed took the picture of Carmen lookthing through a curtain, she was very pleased with it. One reason is that she has beautiful hair, and every time Ed takes notice of something she's done with it she's happy. This time, he took notice by photographing her. There's more than this, however, in her interest in his photographs of her. Ed thinks she's very remarkable in what she'll put up with. I agree, for Ed uses his photography to change her around a lot. Sometimes he photographs her as beautiful, other times as homely as a mud fence. I can even remember one photograph in which she resembled a praying mantis slightly. This, you will agree, is going pretty far.

When this picture was taken they had been married about three years. By this time, Carmen had come to see her husband's pictures of her as a little game. Ed says, "She's very rare in the way she'll let me photograph her as I want to. She's come out so many different ways, and she is always intrigued by seeing herself from these new viewpoints. It doesn't upset her. Or if it does upset her, she's so intrigued by the idea of looking at herself in a specific way that she really studies closely the picture which shows it.

"She keeps staring at the picture, probably thinking to herself, 'Is this me, or not?' She's in the game. At this point it's a game we play with each other. She doesn't always know what to think of the pictures, but they don't upset her. This amazed me in the beginning, for some wives get very upset by their husbands' pictures of them. When I understood she was permitting me to play this game, and had become a partner to it, I just kept on pushing it. After many years of it, I've finally realized how unusual she is in this respect. I still don't know quite what to make of it."

What to make of it is indeed a very large question, though some of the more superficial answers come readily to mind. Carmen may have concluded, quite reasonably, that her husband may see possibilities for herself which she is unable to see. Though most wives wouldn't credit their husbands with this much perception, they may err in this. Certainly, the average wife could broaden herself by trying to learn what her husband has learned about her, even if he hasn't seen her correctly.

On the other hand, Carmen may be

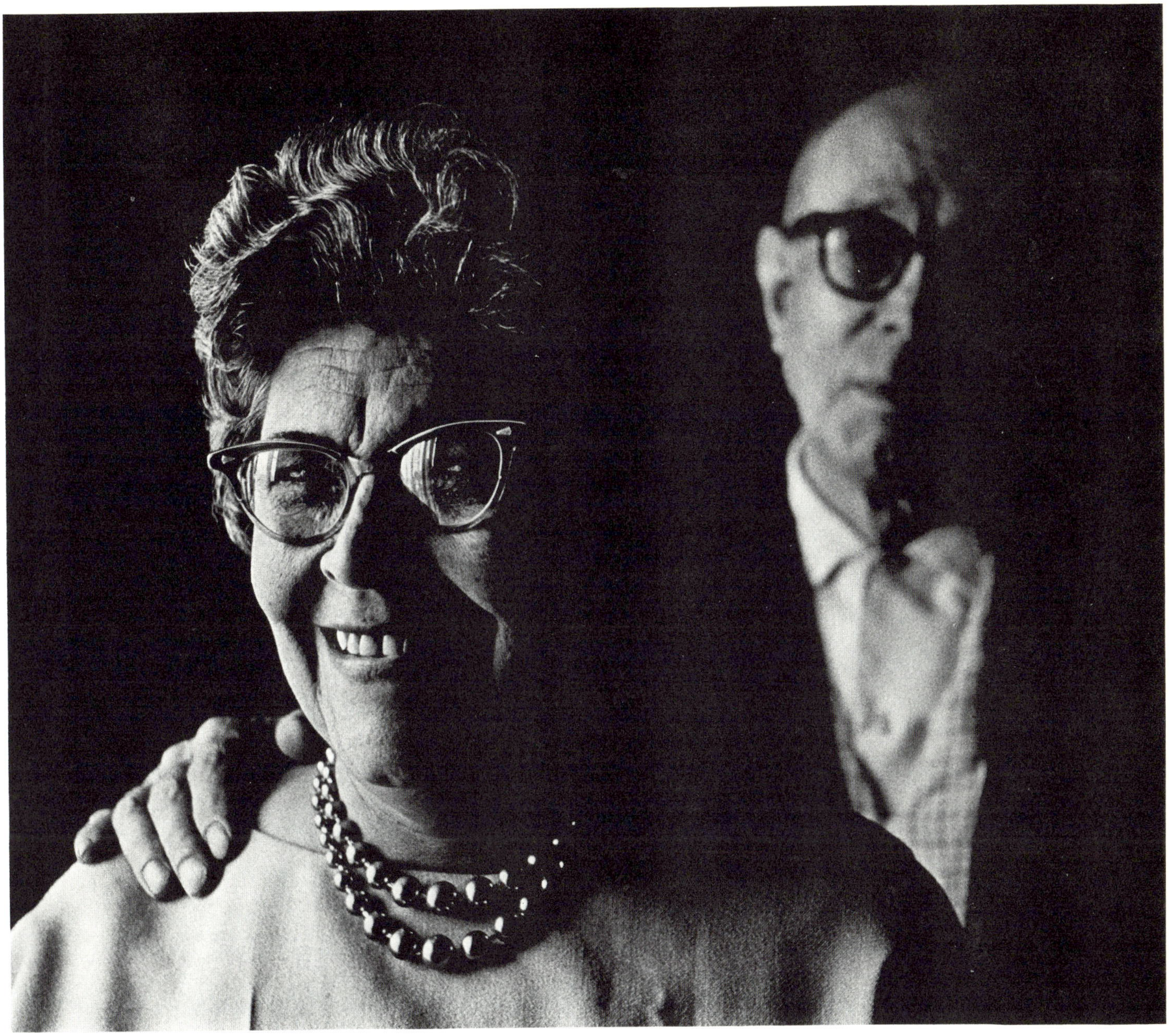

Edgar Gelabert's mother and father.

photo by EDGAR GELABERT

making an entirely different use of Ed's pictures of her. She may be keeping track of the various ways in which he thinks about her. She could use her observations as an index to his psychic growth, to the state of their marital relationship and so on.

I don't think Carmen is as comfortable with his pictures as Ed thinks. She's undoubtedly taken pains to cover up any distress she might feel. We can safely guess that her ego has taken a rather thorough drubbing. It may be that she welcomes it on the correct theory that anything which pains the wolf is good for her. It is, of course, very unusual for a person to think this way.

When Ed made this print of Carmen behind the curtain he was surprised at what came out, primarily at the look in her eyes. "This look says she's really got me under her thumb and she knows it. When I took the picture, I couldn't see her eyes, and she must have known that, too. The way the light struck the curtain really put a barrier between us, as if she were behind dark glasses. She knew she could look at me in any way she wanted to without my seeing her. I doubt if she was aware of the fact that in the print it would come out so clearly. I think the curtain in front of her face just opened her up."

I asked Ed if Carmen liked the picture. "She was delighted with it," he said. "Oh, yeah, she got a tremendous charge out of it. She didn't tell my why, however." Ed chuckled at this thought, clearly tickled at the idea he had revealed his wife so well, even though she hadn't admitted to him what the picture said about her. He continued, "I've noticed that every time I take a picture in which she has this imperious look, she's overjoyed by it. I remember her telling me once, a long time ago, that she thinks that in some past life she must have been a queen. And I think she's always had this in her mind, for Carmen believes in reincarnation." In this context, it's worth pointing out that her mother is a very highly developed psychic and that Carmen is psychic herself. Thus the picture may bring back memories she was unable to hold onto. Ed said, "Sometimes I wonder: Why must she feel that way when she's looking at *me*?" He chuckled again. It's a punch in the ego to realize that your wife may be a real somebody.

Ed thinks this is one of her two favorites of all the pictures he's taken of her. The other is of her holding her belly when she was pregnant.

When I first saw the picture of Carmen with a towel, I thought that Gelabert had finally stepped over the line of her cheerful acceptance of what he says about her with his camera. As you see, he has made her appear a good deal older than she actually is and turned a very handsome woman into a homely one. However, Carmen accepted the picture in good grace and even found it interesting. I was very pleased that she did, for it shows a surprising lack of vanity in her. Few women would feel this way toward such an unflattering picture. Though women's vanity is no greater than men's, it is sufficiently different for us to wish they would get rid of it. Here was a woman paying vanity no attention whatsoever. Good for her, I say.

Ed says that when he took this picture Carmen had just taken a shower and come into the living room wrapped in a towel. Ed said, "Hey, this is great! Let me take a picture of you." Carmen was a bit taken aback, until she understood she could hold the towel in front of herself. Then he told her, "Just stand near the window. We'll take a few pictures and see how they come out." When she saw the resulting picture, she liked it. When I asked Ed why, he chuckled, "When I take a picture of her and she likes it I don't ask why. I just leave it alone." Since we don't actually know why, we'll just have to speculate on her reasons.

Carmen's Self may have been pleased to see her not decked out in the trappings which female insecurity generally demands. Here, she is stripped down to the human essentials. A face, a body and hair —no more. Perhaps her Self thought it would be a good thing if she thought of herself this way more often. Or maybe she's already inclined to see herself this way and needs encouragment in order to

Hidden behind a curtain, Carmen's face becom[es] very queenly and strong.

photo by EDGAR GELABERT

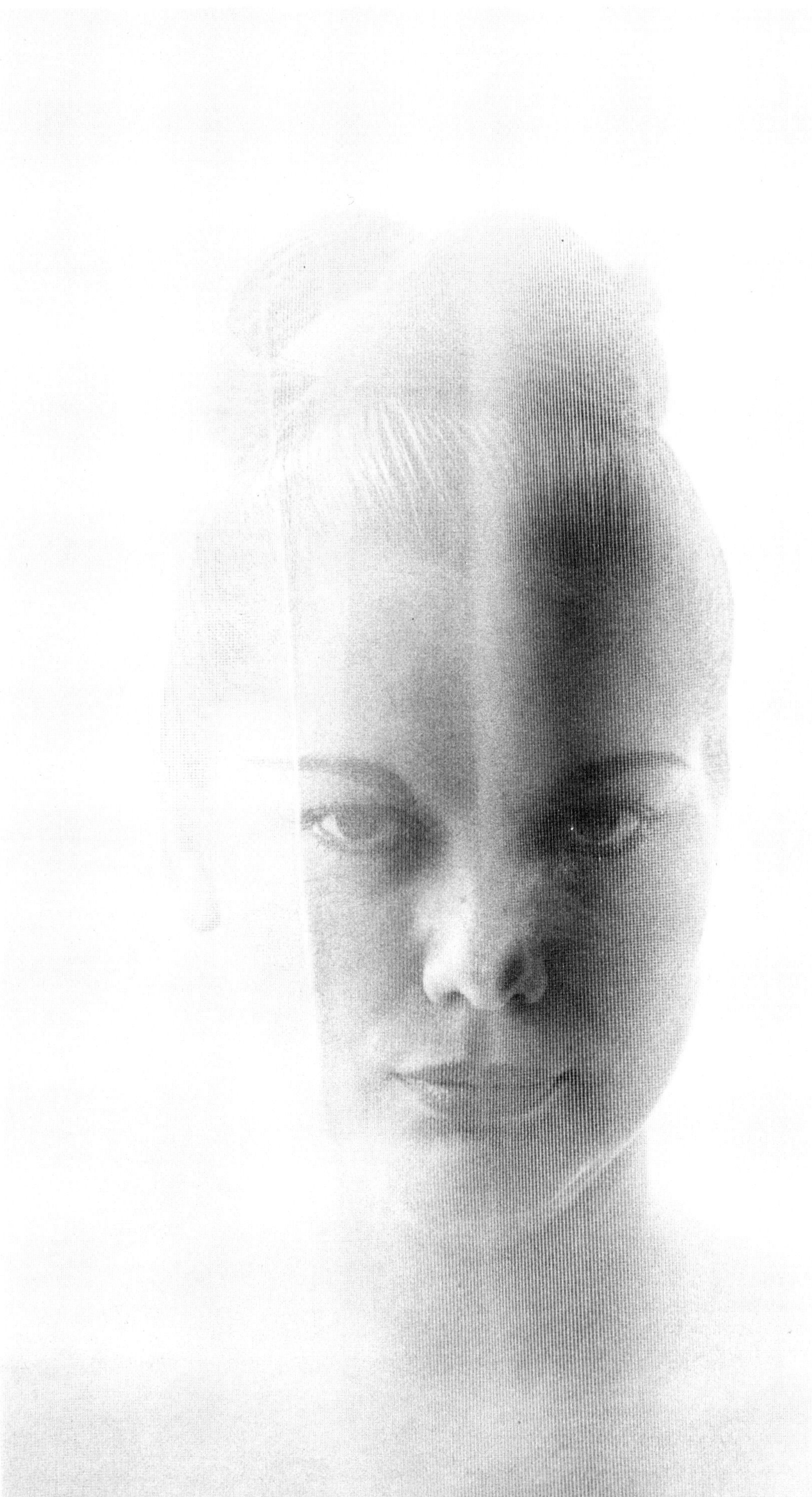

do it more of the time.

To Carmen's Self, Ed's desire to photograph her in the bare essentials may have been an indication that he, too, might be growing more willing to see her as she really is, rather than as a semi-illusion partly created through the cosmetic art. Men shouldn't be too critical of women's supposed vanity, for much of which we take for vanity is merely a response to our ego-need to see them as more glamorous than they really are. We force them into certain types of behavior, then criticise them for what they do. Perhaps Carmen's Self saw that Ed's picture went against such a thing in him.

When we come to what Ed was actually up to, we should see it both in terms of his ego and his Self. His ego is naturally pleased to catch Carmen without her clothing and to hold her immobile in front of the camera. This is one of the ego-factors lying behind so-called art photography of the female nude: Men gain power over women by stripping them of their defenses (clothing).

The wolf plays still other games, one of which is to tell himself "She has removed her clothing in order to give herself to me." It doesn't matter how far from the truth this is, for the wolf is an inveterate liar. Another common attitude of His Selfishness is: "Her nudity symbolizes her surrender to the strength of my masculine will." We don't know which ego games Edgar was playing, but we can be certain he was indulging in some of them. After all, he's human.

Whenever a photographer who is as skilled as Ed is takes a picture, his Self manages to have its say, too. In fact, Ed's Self is probably the motivating force behind most (or even all) of his pictures. One of its central objectives is to delineate for Ed the strange peccadilloes of his ego, some of which we've just described. But the Self also wants to inform Ed concerning matters of the Soul and Spirit.

Ed's Self may be saying to him, "Now that you've made Carmen seem a good deal older than her chronological age in this life, give some thought to how old she may actually be. Then give some thought to what this implies about the human Soul and its relation to the universe. In catching Carmen just out of the shower you've symbolically stripped her down to something. You should do more of this, but in a different way. You're inclined to see her through her ego and the camouflages it throws up in order to protect its illusions. In your mind, strip away that ego and let yourself see the Self which lies behind it. This is the only way to treat both Carmen and your Self fairly."

Carmen and Ed both like the picture of her in a rocking chair. Ed says, "It really turns Carmen on, but she's not sure why. She likes the way the cloth folds across her body and legs. I think she gets a feeling, again, of being a queen. I think she sees herself in this picture as sitting on a throne."

Together, Ed and I explored this in some depth. One day he and Carmen had figured out that when the picture was made she'd been one week pregnant. This seems to fit in with the quietness, the waiting, the strength she shows in the picture. Sometimes a woman knows almost the very instant that conception has taken place. A very earthy woman, Carmen has always felt that childbearing was a part of her nature and destiny. This tremendous earthiness of hers comes through strongly in the picture.

I asked Ed if this picture seemed like a dream to him. He said that it did. More often than they suppose, photographers take pictures which relate strongly to their dream life. And, like dreams, photographs are frequently a communication from the Self to one's conscious being. If they're seen in this light they can be useful to us, for the Self knows a good deal more about us than we're conscious of.

The plant behind Carmen was grown from her wedding bouquet. Ed said that about three months after they were married his father brought Carmen a flower pot with a healthy sprig of ivy growing in it. Unbeknownst to her, he'd gone to the girl who had caught her bouquet at the wedding and gotten a slip from her to plant. Carmen was delighted. Ed said he

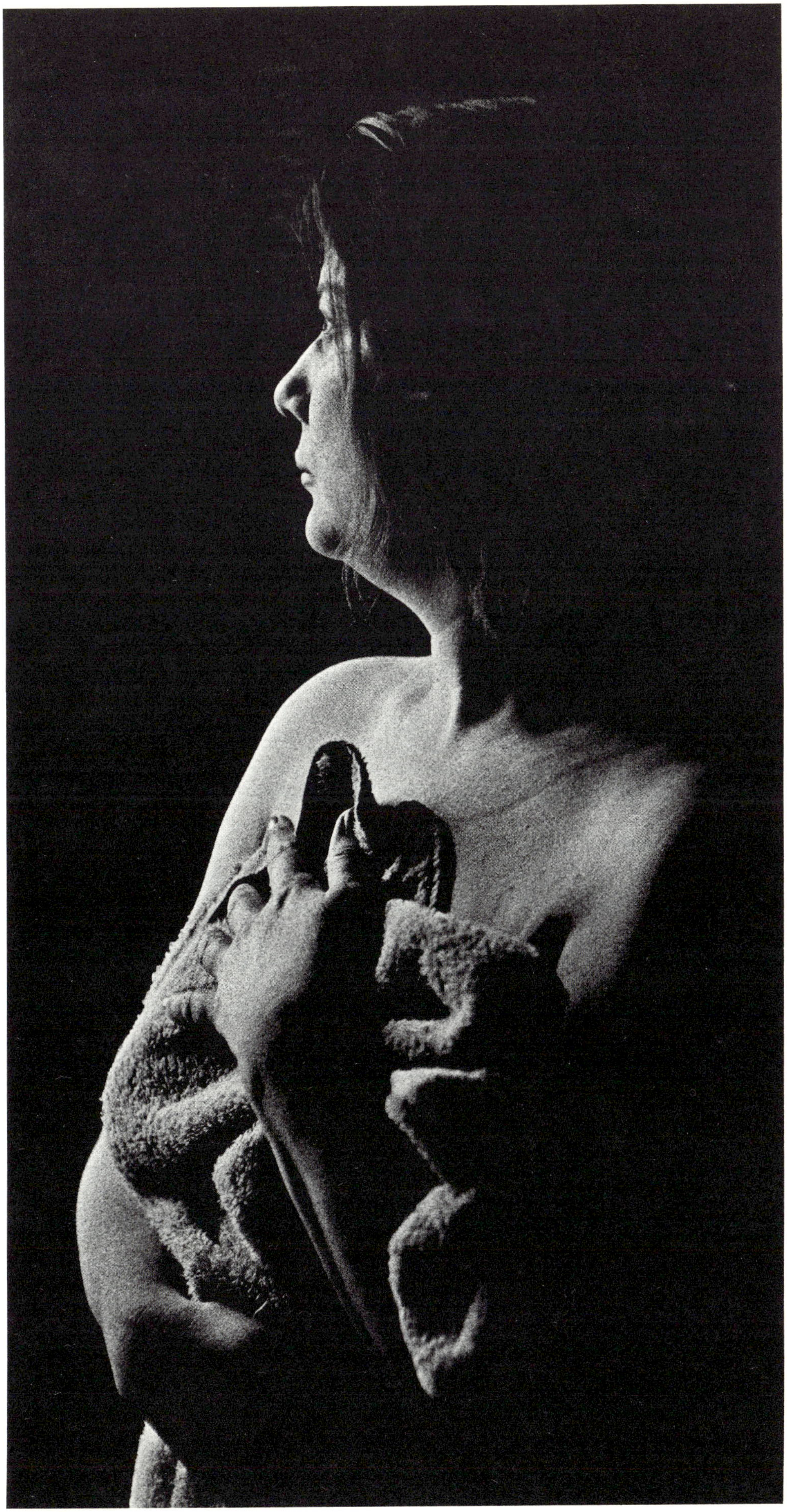

Just out of the shower, Carmen let Ed photograph her. He said she could hold the towel.

photo by
EDGAR GELABERT

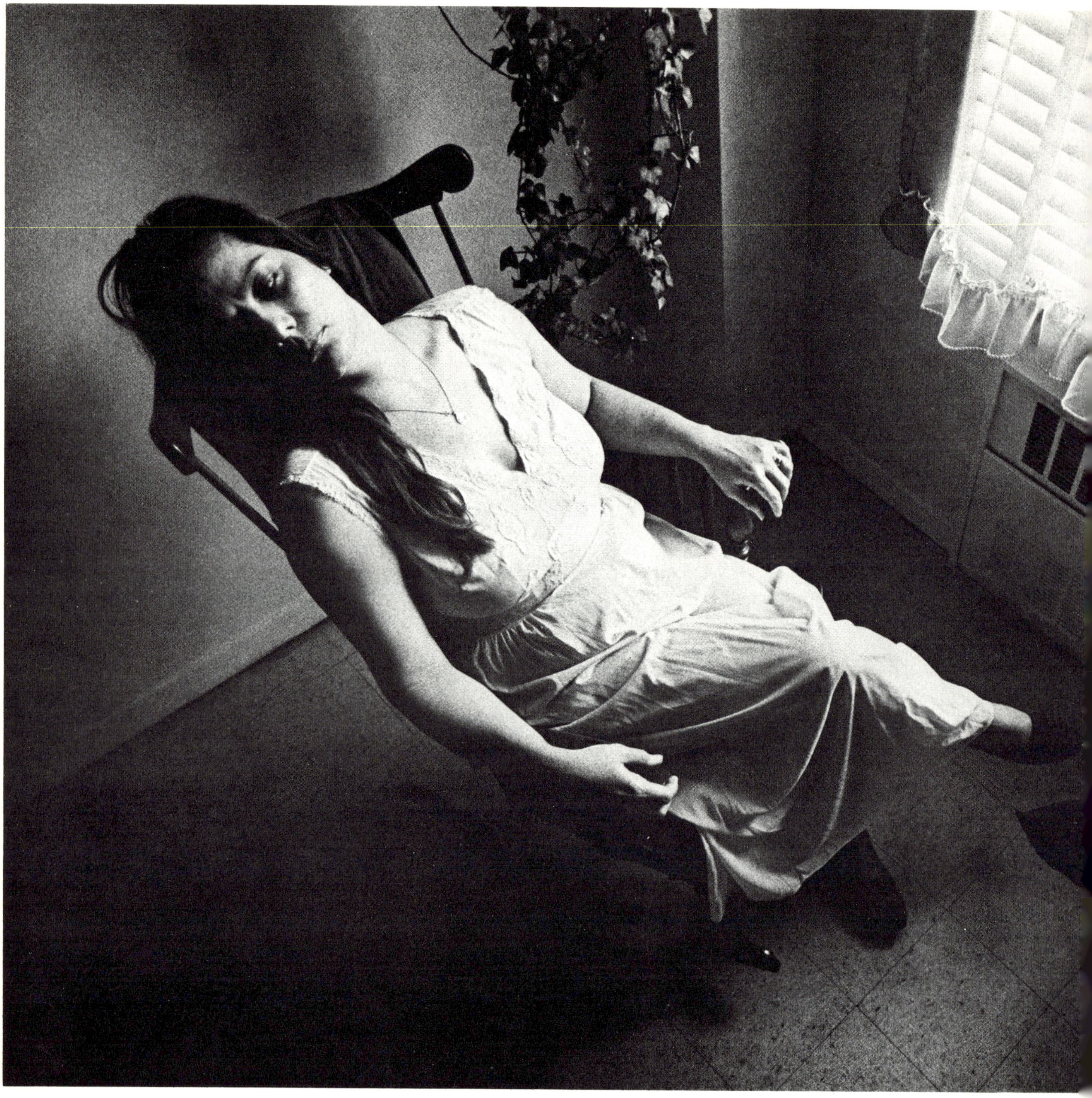

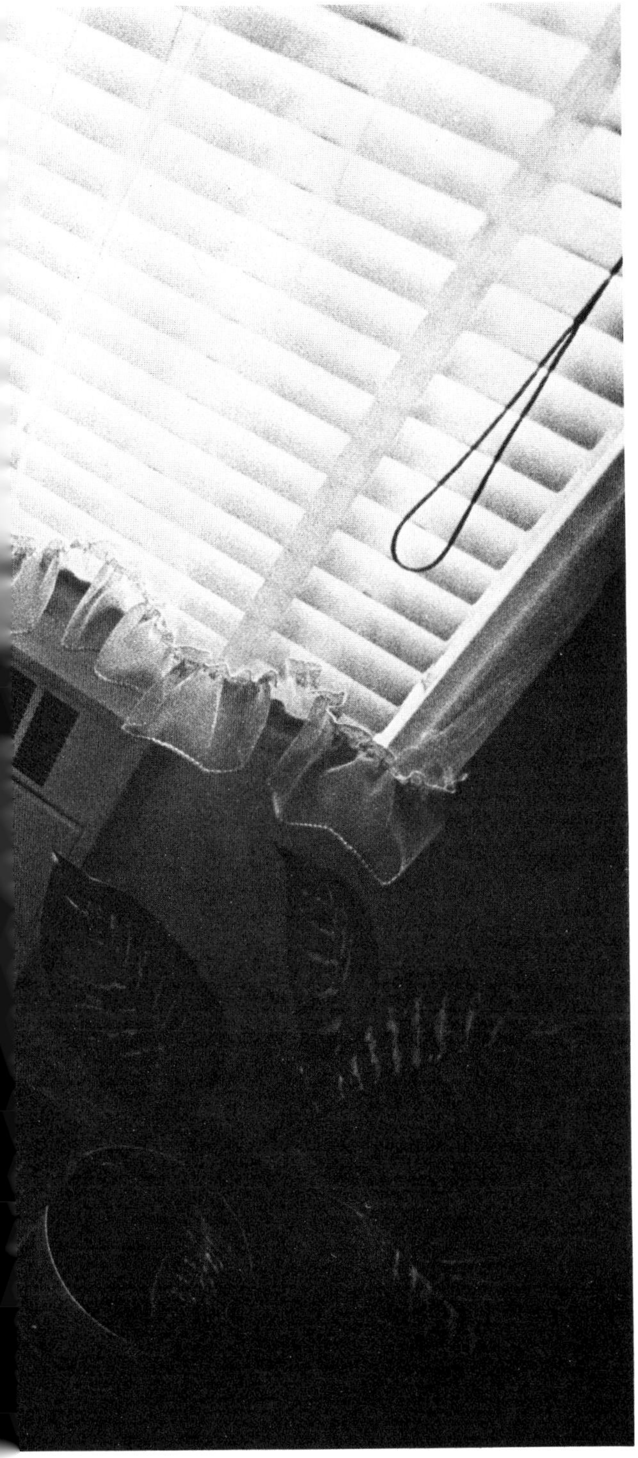

Ed says this picture reminds him of a dream, that he sees Carmen, one week pregnant, as floating into space. Both he and Carmen like it.

photo by
EDGAR GELABERT

wasn't so happy, for Carmen said to him, "If you don't take care of this plant—if it dies—you go right out the door." It did die eventually, but Carmen didn't give him the boot. At the time the picture was taken it was about fifteen feet long. Ed felt he had to have it in his picture. It's fairly obvious that it stands for his union with Carmen.

Ed says that he just sort of kicked the other plant into the picture, nudged it in with his toe. Later, he got to thinking about it and decided that it is one of his private symbols for himself. He thinks of is as *his* plant and takes very good care of it. It is interesting that in a picture of a women so regal, Edgar would appear in such a muted role off in a dark corner. Undoubtedly his ego-wolf was thinking, "Since I am paying so much attention to my wife, I've got to pay a little attention to myself, too. Since this picture is going to be a good one, I've just got to get myself into it."

That the Edgar-plant is in such a subordinate role may also indicate that it is a message from his Self: "It is alright for you to get yourself in the picture, but it's important that you give Carmen your primary consideration. In putting her above your egotistical self you serve me (your real Self) well."

Ed says that the excuse he gave himself (his ego) for making this picture was to try out a new 21mm lens. He said, "When I saw the space relationships through the viewfinder I was really excited. Everything was shooting off into space, and I wanted it to happen to Carmen, too. I wanted to think of her as being more than what was just visible to my eyes." He has,

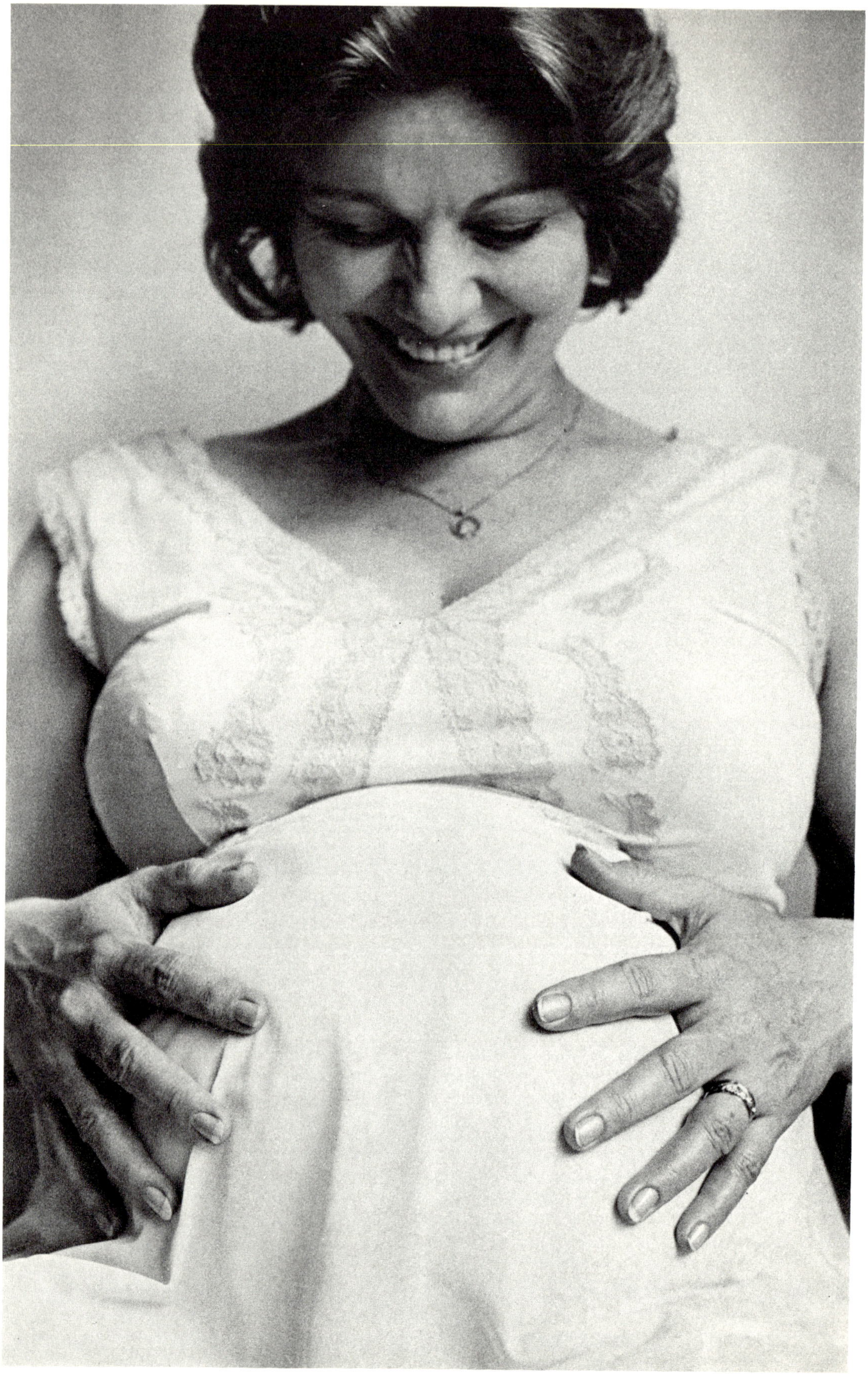

Unborn Edgar Junior kicks Carmen until she laughs with delight.

photo by
EDGAR GELABERT

you see, created a 'cosmic' effect somehow related to Dali's "Leda Atomica." Seeing a woman as floating in space is to admit to oneself her larger possibilities. Conversely, seeing her as always the same and anchored to a familiar context is to deny them.

Though I haven't mentioned it before, Edgar Gelabert is turned on by light in a way which can only be described as spiritual. He uses it to turn all his photographic environments into cathedrals. That is to say that he turns his home into one, for he shoots nearly all of his pictures there. In this one he was thinking both of light and of Carmen as shooting off into space and seeing both as an infinity. It seems reasonable, therefore, to see it as a message from his Self: "This is a good way to think of your wife, as something infinite and spiritual, not merely as the finite being who burns your toast in the morning and distracts your attention while you're trying to read the newspaper. She has an ego, to be sure, but she also has a Self. As often as you can, try to see this Self."

When I recently talked to Ed about his pregnancy pictures of Carmen he said he mainly remembered being all excited about the coming event. In terms of his photography, it would give him an opportunity to make really intimate pictures of Carmen going through something very important to her and to him. I remember that when it was actually happening, when Carmen's womb was really beginning to fill out, his feelings were more mixed.

He took a picture one day when Carmen delightedly told him, "He's kicking again!" He wanted to get the kicking, but knew it wouldn't show up in a photograph. Even more, he wanted to catch the delighted anticipation on his wife's face as she waited for each kick. He knew he could record this photographically.

He asked her to go into the bedroom and sit down on a chair near the window, where the light was good. He sat down in front of her on a little stool. He focused his camera on her hands and belly and began taking pictures. "The look on her face was really terrific to see. First the anticipation, then the delight when the baby began to kick. Her eyes lit up, her face started shining, she got a big smile. Every time she thought he was about ready to move I would take a picture. But when I got *this* picture I knew I'd gotten something really worth waiting for."

This is how Ed recalled the circumstances a few days ago. When he first showed me all his pregnancy pictures a couple of years ago it was a different story. Though he was delighted, he was also scared stiff—as fathers-to-be usually are at the sight of a stomach swollen with their first child. When we were talking about the pictures, Ed was still very uptight. He thought he knew why, but he also wanted another person's opinion on what might be happening inside himself.

As I've said, Edgar Gelabert is a psychically tough cookie, for all his kindly smile and gentle demeanor. He'd have to be in order to do what he did. Taking pregnancy pictures of their firstborns is the last thing in the world that most husbands would be willing to do. The whole pregnancy situation literally scares them cross-eyed, so much, indeed, that they even know they're scared. When fear overcomes a man's ego to the point it makes its pressence known, you can be sure there's a lot of it present. Well, Ed was scared to death, too, but he decided he was going to confront his fear, come Hell or high water.

One of the ways of coping with fear in oneself is to admit its presence to other people. Ed did this by showing his pictures to his friends. We could admire them as pictures. But even better, we could admit that we, too, had been uptight when our firstborn were well on the way. Since taking pregnancy pictures is psychologically very good for a husband, the fear he will experience should be talked about a bit.

First, there is the husband's fear that his wife may have a hard labor, or even that she might not survive. He's concerned for her, of course, but his ego is more concerned for itself. The wolf is deeply distressed at the notion that it probably wouldn't behave nobly and unselfishly should a real crisis arise. The truth of the matter is that he wouldn't, though other people may not be able to see this. This thought awakens Conscience, which provokes a deep sense of guilt. The fear is mixed with guilt, which makes it all the worse. There is nothing more apt to give rise to fear than to be confronted with the depth of one's own selfishness, for selfishness and fear are a very closely knit team. It's hard to tell where one leaves off and the other begins; they may even be the same thing.

There is something inescapable in seeing your wife's belly grow huge. There is no doubt whatsoever that something has radically changed in her and that you had something to do with it. Most of the things we do we can escape by conveniently tucking them into the backs of our minds. The pregnant belly isn't one of them. Not only is it huge but it's as hard as a rock, something we hadn't anticipated.

Add to this the fact that this lump has an independent life of its own. A mother is just a host in whom a baby grows himself. It's a frightening thought that after conception the matter of growth is out of the parents' hands. This gives rise to the notion that Higher Forces may be involved somehow and that the ego's little hangups aren't going to get the deferential treatment they'd like. A more important thing, the baby, is relentlessly pushing them aside.

We must also mention the fear of responsibility. As the lump grows ever larger and begins to kick, responsibility becomes more and more inescapable.

Considering the anxieties it evokes, it's no wonder that more men don't photograph their wives during pregnancy. It would be good for them to try, but that doesn't mean they can find the strength to do it. If they do they can be sure their wolves are going to take a very severe battering about head and shoulders.

Carmen Gelabert likes the nude of Edgar Junior very much, though she's not that fond of all her husband's photographs. She chides him for being very selfish with his photography. Tacitly agreeing with her, he bought her a Polariod Land camera, so that she could get the kind of pictures *she* wanted. Ed says he knows well enough what kinds of pictures she wants but that he often can't force himself to make them for her. He realizes that there is egotism, jealousy of the baby and resentment involved in this inability. To this we might add that there is also pride in being a fine photographer, not a snapshooter.

Part of the problem is that he identifies so strongly with his son. If you identify with someone, you're somewhat like a computer which has been programmed in a certain way. You can only do what your program permits you to. Identification is an ego thing; and Edgar Junior is an ego-symbol for his father. There is also a relatedness on a higher level, which is not identification. On the level of Self, people actually are a unity. Sometimes the baby is Ed's ego-symbol, sometimes his Self-symbol. In this one, an ego-symbol. Ed says he finds himself looking at it and thinking, "Hey, I'm really a *man,* aren't I?" or "Boy! Was I a cute baby!"

He thinks Carmen resents it when he points out how much Edgar Junior looks like him. If she does, it's only to be expected. After all, the baby is also an ego-symbol and a Self-symbol for her, much more strongly so than for her husband. The resentment comes from the fact that people have a great dislike for sharing their personal symbols with others. Ed thinks that another reason for Carmen's reluctance to associate Edgar Junior with Edgar Senior is that it forces her to see she can't possess her son for long. Soon he'll be a man (like his father) and, therefore, not possessable. He thinks that the fact the baby's genitals are showing drives this point home even more strongly, for in a sense they make him look like a man right now. Carmen might not agree with this, but that doesn't necessarily mean it isn't the truth.

Ed finds that he can use his pictures to study other people, as well as himself. With this one, for example, he wanted to learn how many people would be uptight because the baby's penis shows. He started with his wife: "How would you like it if

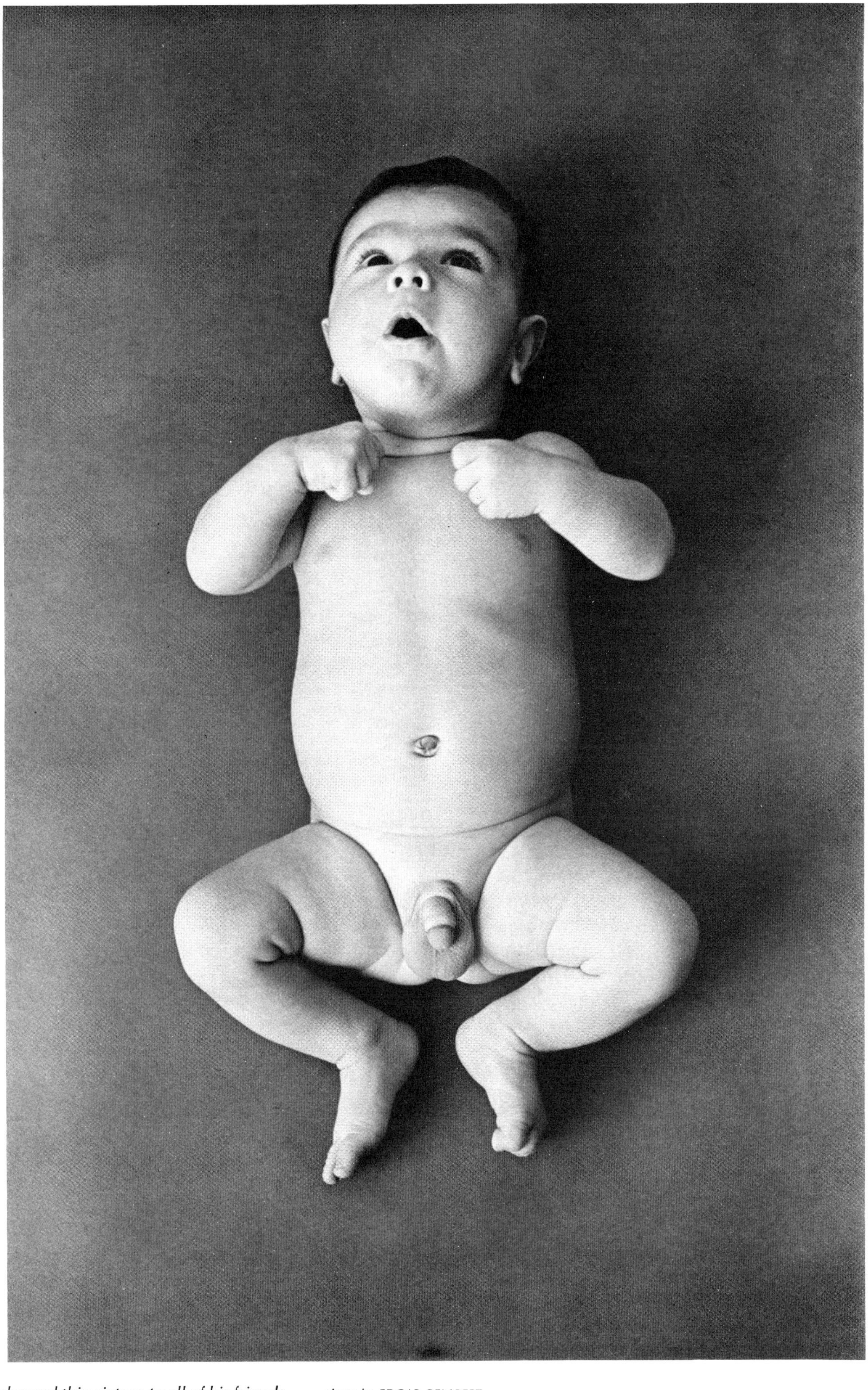

Ed proudly showed this picture to all of his friends. *photo by* EDGAR GELABERT this picture were published in a national magazine?" Carmen said she wouldn't mind at all. Some people, however, are greatly shocked at the idea, especially among the older generation. They often try to cover the cause of their concern by saying, "Think of your son! How will he feel when he grows up and sees this picture?" Considering the way numerous young folk have reacted to it (they were delighted) he'll probably think nothing at all.

Ed's notion was that if people get uptight at seeing a picture of a nude baby there is something definitely wrong with the way they look at sex. He also thinks that if a parent reacts adversely to the nudity of his baby it's a very bad thing. He is quite correct in this, for it's the sign of a serious hang-up in the parent. It can easily drive a wedge between parent and child.

Since both Ed and I have always tried to use photography in the pursuit of the truth, I think it is appropriate that I now give him a hard punch in the ego. There is more to his showing the picture around than getting information on other people's sex hang-ups. Remember that he identifies strongly with his son. This means that, psychologically, he was showing a nude picture of himself and indirectly bragging about his sexual endowments, which are plain to see in the photograph. He is also bragging about having fathered such a fine child. I'm certain that on some level, probably unconscious, he was greatly titillated with his 'research project.' Is it any wonder? I know him well enough to think he wouldn't be surprised by this revelation and suspect that he's probably already figured it out for himself.

With some people, I would be greatly reluctant to suggest such a thing, for it would upset them terribly. That it wouldn't upset Ed is a sign that his kind of serious family photography really pays off. He's now able to accept things in himself—innocent and naive things—that would shock many people speechless.

When Ed decided to grab his son's hands and take a picture, he knew he was going to have trouble holding him still, for infants strongly dislike being held tightly. Probably a part of Ed also knew he was asking for trouble with his wife. Ed said, "As I was struggling to hold his hands, Carmen came into the room. She saw what I was doing and exclaimed, 'What are you doing to my baby!' "

Ed tried to pass it off, saying, "Look, he's enjoying it. He's smiling," (which, of course, he wasn't). Carmen didn't believe him then and thoroughly disliked the picture later. As he and I were looking at it, Ed said, "I knew he really didn't like it. He was getting mad and I just didn't care. I remember saying to myself, 'Ed, you Little Bastard, I'm going to take this picture if it kills both of us!' " He laughed, obviously enjoying the memory.

It was good that Ed took the picture in exactly the way he did. You see, he knew very well that his ego deeply resented the baby stealing Carmen's affection from him and turning him into a servant in his own home. But his knowing was largely an intellectual proposition. The harmless tableau with his son, and the token struggle, gave him the opportunity to feel the resentment and to see that there was a good deal more of it than he really wanted to admit to himself. It also helped him see how thinly covered over is something primitive and deeply cruel in himself. To reach maturity, all men must see this in themselves.

Of course, when Carmen came into the room she intuitively knew what was being symbolized: The two men in her home were engaged in a battle to the death. Naturally, she didn't like what she saw, nor could she like the picture later.

When Ed looks at his picture, a part of him remembers its anger and still feels self-righteous about provoking the struggle. His laughter indicates that he enjoyed his revenge. Ed understands that he should know such things about himself, so that he can take steps to counteract them.

So far, we've talked about this only as an ego picture: Ed's ego pitted against his son's. In Ed's strong hand we see the winner, which gives him great ego-satis-

Though Edgar Junior didn't like being held immobile, his dad didn't give a damn at the moment. He said to his son, "It's you against me, Buddy, I'm going to rule this house."

photo by EDGAR GELABERT

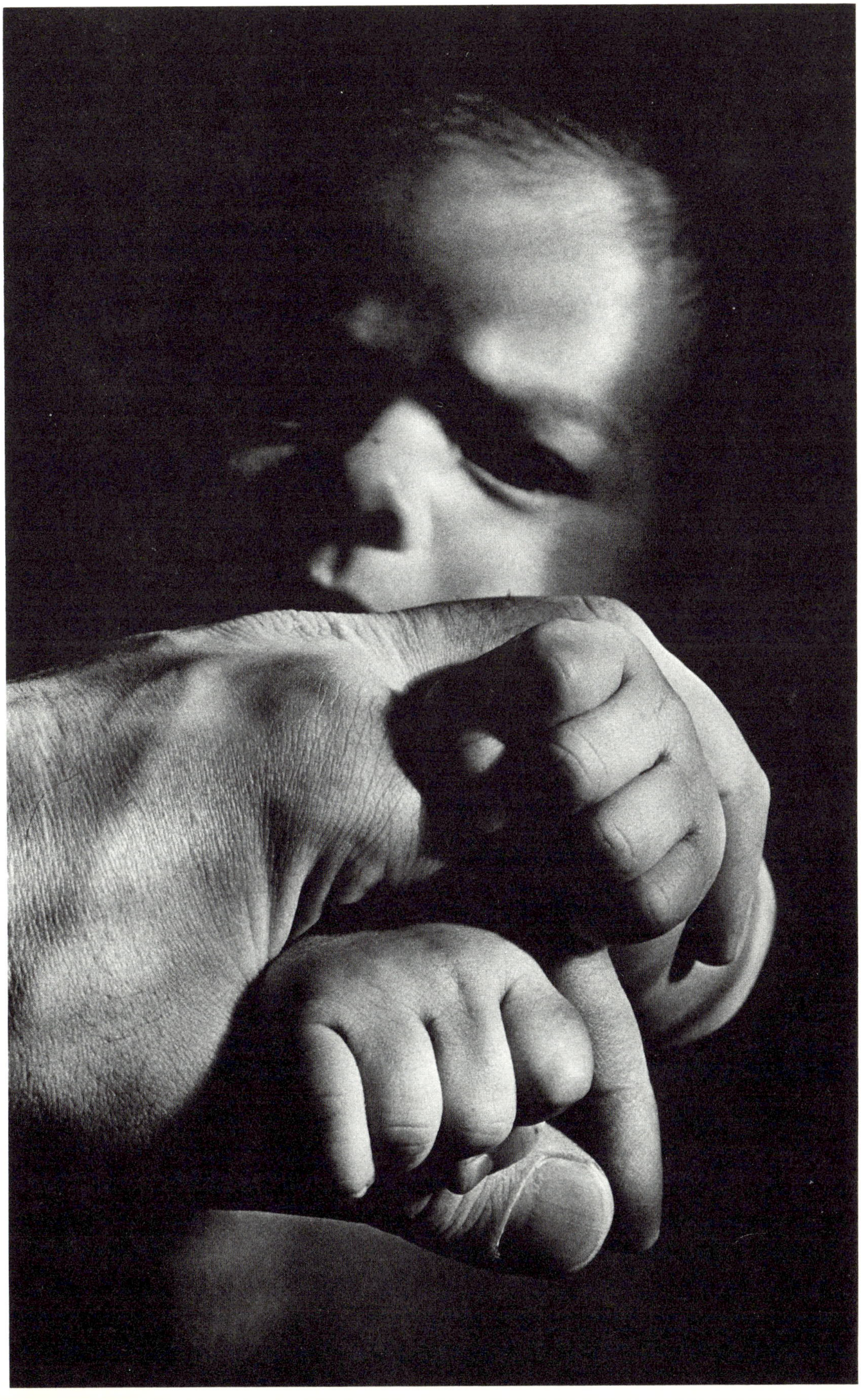

faction. At the same time, he knows he isn't the winner and that it's his ego which is prompting his pleased reaction. He doesn't respect ego, yet he enjoys it. That's the way people are. Though this picture is sweet sauce for Ed's ego, it is other things, too.

In expressing anger and resentment so clearly, the photograph is a constant warning to him that he should always keep a close watch on himself, even in 'harmless' little tableaux. Ed's Self is telling him, "There are things in you which should neither be trusted nor respected; they are stronger than you're prone to think." Though Ed's ego is delighted by the photograph, it also stands warned by Self, which tells him, "It is much better that you be aware of these negative forces in yourself than not." The most dangerous people in the world are those not aware of their own negative forces.

On a higher level of the unconscious, the picture is also a game of 'I see you.' Ed's Self is saying to his son's Self, "Knock it off, Fellow—don't try to tell me you're really a baby. I know an Old Soul when I see one." Parents often get the feeling that their babies aren't as young as they seem, though they find it difficult to put into words. The truth is that they're not, for they were born when Time began, before the earth was formed from the void. Stirring up the baby's anger helps to clarify this thought, for anger is an adult, or ego, thing. Without his anger, it's altogether too easy to see him as a cute, animated lump or as only an extension of oneself.

Stirring up anger also helps break up identification, which is a form of Self-bondage. Until the baby shows signs of ego, it's very easy to incorporate him mentally in oneself: "He is only an aspect of me." Being a sign of an independent ego, anger goes against this thought, which is a good thing. Though father and son are actually one, it is only at the level of Self, where *all* Souls are one. Identification, however, is an ego thing and never good for a person. Ego identifies with things in order to gratify itself or to defend its illusions. As a subtle form of lying, identification is a means for holding the Self in bondage.

We can also look at this picture as a message from Ed to his wife. Ed's Self is saying, "Carmen, you know that I love the baby, but Ed's ego doesn't know what love is yet. His ego suffers, for he sees how much you've turned toward the baby and left him out in the cold. This makes his ego angry. As Ed's real Self, I want you to know that the anger is there and that it's your responsibility to help him defeat and eliminate it. By making you more aware of it through this picture, I put you in the position where you can help me defeat it."

One day Ed said to me. "I got hung up in wanting to take a picture of the baby in a rocking chair. You had your rocking chair picture of your baby son on the beach. So, I just had to have my picture with a chair." One weekend the urge was so strong that he put himself to a great deal of trouble in order to do it. He helped excuse to himself the time and effort he spent on it by remembering that he'd never taken the picture Carmen wanted of Edgar Junior in his bassinet. By now he was too large to fit in it, but Ed figured he could ease his guilt somewhat by putting it in the same room as his son for a picture. In the course of making the picture, and looking at it thereafter, he learned a good deal more about himself than he expected to.

The work involved clearing out entirely a utility room, in which the picture was taken. It was filled to the brim with things which had to be temporarily deposited elsewhere around the Gelabert apartment. Ed had looked with considerable reluctance at all the work which had to be done, so when the urge was strongly with him he said to himself, "Now is the day!" When Carmen saw his frenetic activity she was amazed. She said, "Now what are you going to do to my son?" Ed says that's the way she always puts it—"*to* my son." So, he told her what he had in mind and she helped him with his work. When the picture was actually made she was standing over to the right to watch Edgar Junior, in case he should have difficulty staying in the chair.

Ed decided he would have to use a wide-angle lens, not only to get the whole room in but to introduce a distortion. He says he now sees the picture as surreal: "Real but unreal, a dream type of thing; it's as if you walk past a room and suddenly see a little baby sitting in a rocking chair. You can't believe what you see, for *he's not supposed to be there*. Sometimes the picture seems real to me, sometimes very unreal—it's as if that's me in the rocking chair, not the baby. The fact I'm a father also seems unreal to me, especially when Carmen and the baby are visiting her parents."

Sometimes Ed looks at the picture and gets the feeling he's vaguely remembering one of his own dreams. Everything in it seems to be symbolizing something to him. One of his many interpretations echoes the strangeness of the picture: "It appears to me that the baby had waited until everyone had gone out of the apartment and then let himself be what he really is. Not helpless at all, though he seems to be, he waited until no one was looking, then jumped out of the bassinet and sat in the rocking chair. That's where he *really* belongs, not in a silly old bassinet. He's master of the house, but he can't play the role when anyone is looking.

"Of course, he really is the master, and here he's proved it by taking over *my* rocking chair. Then when he heard the key in the door as we were coming back he jumped back in the bassinet and made believe he was a baby again. Here this little rascal is making himself out to be so helpless, when it's actually Carmen and I who are in trouble. But he's going to play the helpless role for all it's worth."

The meaning of Ed's reverie is very clear. As you might have surmised, Ed has figured it all out for himself. After all, *he* made the picture; and he's obviously trying to tell himself something by means of it. For him, this picture is almost pure symbolism. By thinking about it he's uncovered many of his most personal and hidden symbols. Carmen loves the picture, but Ed doesn't think she sees it in terms of symbolism. She sees the baby—his pudgy little legs, his interest in what he's doing, and so on.

Since everything in the picture is there only because Ed put it there, Ed was certain that it had meaning in his personal symbology. The bassinet, for example, represents security and dependence to him; it's some kind of a womb. Whose, he's not sure. It could be Carmen's or his mother's. Now we can see why he was unable to bring himself to take a picture of Edgar Junior lying in it. The wolf in Ed was darned if he was going to take a picture of someone occupying Ed's rightful place. Such juvenile ego-notions have more to do with our adult behavior than we might suppose.

Ed thinks that the bassinet may even represent his own womb, and so might the rocking chair. In this case, his picture might be saying, "*I*, not my wife, gave birth to this baby." Since Ed is aware he identifies strongly with his son, it could also mean, "*I* was the one who was born two years ago. All this fuss, bother, and anxiety in the Gelabert household was for *me*. *I'm* still cock-of-the-walk here; and that's *me* sitting as master in the rocking chair to prove it."

When Ed made the picture he felt he had to have the plant in it, though he didn't know why at the time. Later, he figured out that it symbolized his father, who gave it to Ed and Carmen ten years ago. It's the only thing of his father's that they have in the house, and Ed has cared for it tenderly all these years. You see that it stands in the background. Ed put his father there for many years. All the same, his father was a constant presence for him. The plant, which is very hardy, is called a cast-iron plant. It represents what Ed, as both an adult and a child, wanted for his father—a strength and hardiness which could be leaned on. It also symbolizes Ed's wish for his parent's immortality. But more, it tells us that Ed feels his father as an immortal part of himself and his child.

I asked Ed if he'd noticed that the plant was very dark in the picture. He said that he had but that he hadn't delved into its symbolism in that context. Of course, it was a very dark plant to start with, so its obscure blackness may have no special

To his surprise, Ed Gelabert found he had used his son, a bassinette, a chair, and a plant to create an allegory.

photo by
EDGAR GELABERT

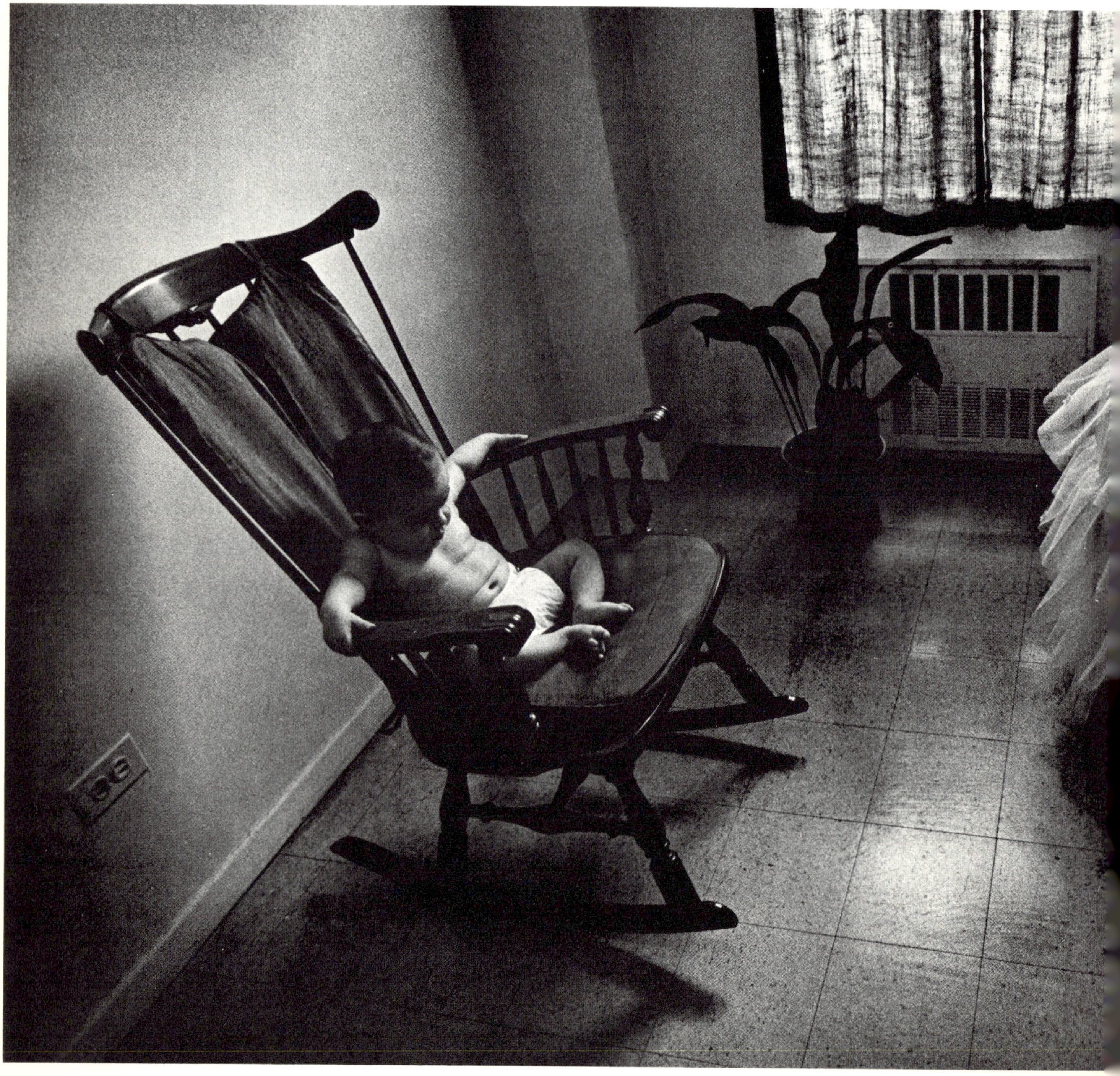

meaning. Remember that Ed felt he had to have it in his picture, even if it threw the whole design out of kilter. Only later did he see that it symbolized his father.

What I've written here is only a small sampling of Ed's exploration into his own symbology through the study of just this one picture. The important thing for the reader is to understand that it can be done and that it's very Self-illuminating.

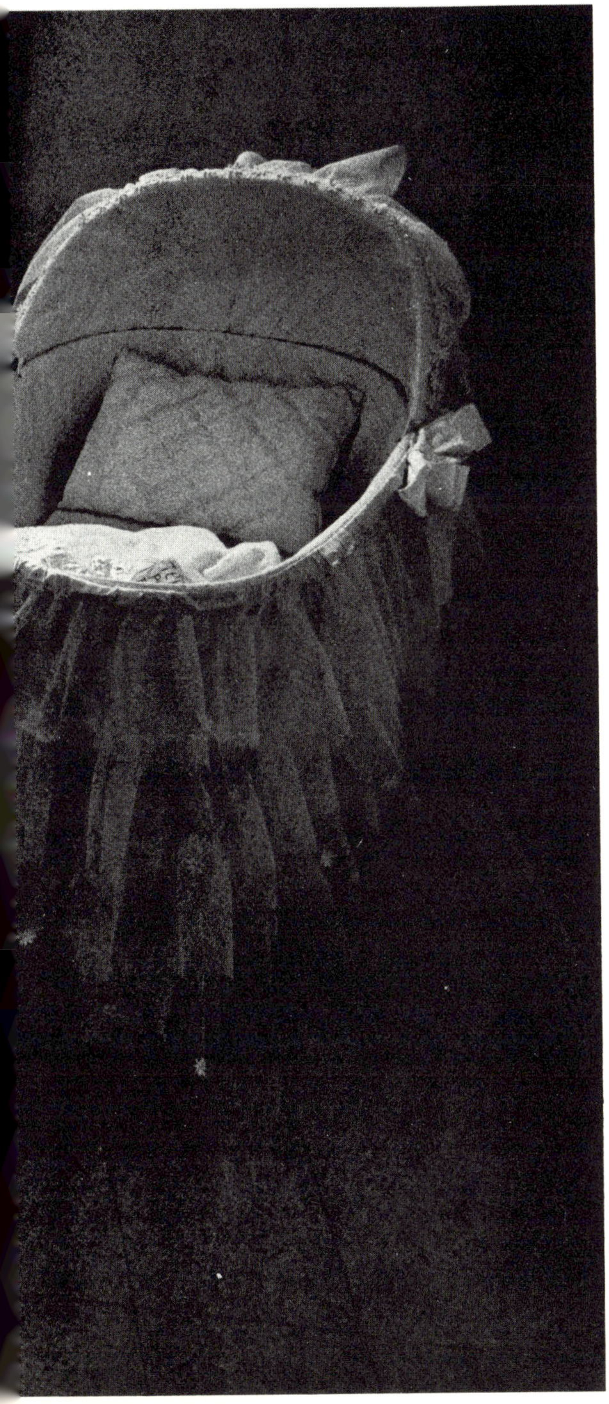

When Edgar Junior was about two weeks old his father took him close to a brightly lighted window. Immediately, he smiled. Ed Senior was delighted. He shouted, "Carmen, come see! He smiles when he feels the light on his face!" Carmen said, "I don't believe it. Babies don't really smile." She came, she saw, and was convinced. While she held the baby in her arms, Ed took the picture. The smile is real, not just a squeezing up of the face to cut down on the light's intensity.

Babies actually do smile and frown and get angry and grow speculative and figure things out. In fact, they do a good deal more than we generally give them credit for. Some of them remember that they've lived before and know that they're starting on a new life, with parents they may or may not have had in previous lives. It is not so remarkable, therefore, that Edgar Junior has reveled in the feel of the sun on his face. He's known the sun for literally aeons and understood its symbolic meaning for man. It has always stood for Higher Spiritual Forces. Is it any wonder he greeted it with a smile?

Ed's real Self may have been trying to communicate these facts to him when it prompted him to notice the baby's reaction and to regard it as remarkable. Ed has been relatively open to the idea that he may have lived before. Perhaps his own picture is trying to add to his certainty.

I asked Ed what he sees in the picture now. He said, "I see life." I then asked him if the baby looked young or old. "Old," he replied. "This is one of the things that got me to thinking when I made the print. Carmen saw that he looked old before I saw it. She didn't really like the picture until lately, until she realized what she'd seen."

The problem is that in a sense some babies are a good deal older than their parents. They've held onto flashes of memory from the distant past, while parents have forgotten it. The person who remembers farthest back is the eldest. It is encouraging that Carmen and Ed saw the great age of their infant son. It attests to their expanding capacity to accept reality.

A mother doesn't particularly like to see the great antiquity of the Soul who has come into her care. It means that her feeling of ownership, which comes very strong with her first baby, is undermined. After all, she cannot own the universe. She can only be its custodian for awhile.

Ed says that one of the reasons for his delight in the picture is that he probably looks on the baby as a reflection of himself. He has also begun to probe his reasons for wanting to print it as a circle, though he has yet to discover the meaning of a circle in his own personal symbology. He has never made a circular print before.

We cannot, of course, tell the circle's inner meaning to Ed. However, the races of mankind have formed and kept many symbols in common over the ages in some kind of a group unconscious in which dwell all the memories of the species. This being the case, the chances are good that the inner meaning for Ed is the same as the unconscious meaning for everyone else.

To explain the universal meaning of the circle I'll quote from *Symbols and the Self,* by Violet Shelley, published by the Association for Research and Enlightenment Press:

> The zero, the circle, represents the superconscious mind, entire before creation. It is a symbol of the all embracing principle of Divine manifestation, perfect and complete, including everything and wanting nothing, without beginning or end, neither first nor last, timeless, sexless, absolute. The circle always denotes the higher planes. From the viewpoint of man in existence, it symbolizes death as the state in which the life forces are transformed. Because of its form it signifies eternity.

Does it seem possible that Edgar Gelabert's Self was trying to get this information through to him? I think it very likely, for what he himself said about the picture is strongly indicative of this. His Self is saying, "The symbolism of the circle tells us the Truth concerning both you and your son."

As I warned you in the introduction to this book, it has been very difficult for me to communicate clearly my conception of what a human Self really is, though we are all looking for it. The notions which we do have are usually far wide of the mark. Though esoteric books like the "Bhagavad-Gita" can give us some guidance, they are so abstract that their concept of Self is nearly meaningless to us. The basic problem is that conceiving the true nature of a Self is a task of the same magnitude as discovering one's Self.

What I've written here about Edgar Gelabert expresses my concept of the human Self. Though I may be wrong in some particulars, I think that I am at least going in the right direction. I hope that my explanations are clear enough to serve as spring boards for those who want to go further in their searches for their Selves. If they have a basis for further understanding, there are many other writers to whom they can turn for further illumination.

I've carefully avoided in this discussion of Gelabert using rigidly Freudian explanations of what is happening to Edgar through his photography. In terms of the symbolism of the circle, the interpretation by Violet Shelley suits me to a T but would probably start poor Freud spinning in his grave. To one of the more unimaginative Freudians a circle practically has to stand for a vagina, a womb, the desire to have intercourse with someone, the desire to be back in the womb again or something of the like. I will admit that these sexual desires are standard equipment for nearly everyone. A good many even more important desires find expression for themselves through the symbolism of the circle. It has symbolized the sun for many nations and peoples. In the West it has stood for the Son, Jesus, the Christ. In fact, the circle has stood for thousands of things of central importance to man. Dismissing it offhand as a symbol only for womb or vagina is, a simplistic and ignorant way to interpret it.

Jungian psychologists might interpret the circle as the archetypal mandala. Mandalas, in turn, are symbols of the Self. This is quite an improvement on the Freudians, for it suggests that there actually is such a thing as a Self. Jungians don't go far enough, however, for they are self-consciously determined to limit themselves to the realm of things which are scientifically provable. I doubt if contemporary scientific methods can be stretched far enough to prove that there is such a thing as a Self, or Soul. The best evidence we have on such matters is the testimony of saints and such beings as Jesus, the Buddha and Mohammed. At the cost of appearing ridiculous to certain contemporary psychologists I have accepted this testimony and have used it for the concept of Self which is the basis of this book on discovering the Self. It appears to me that most books with this objective have limited themselves to outlining the dimensions of the ego. Following the lead of Higher Teachers, I insist that an ego is not a Self.

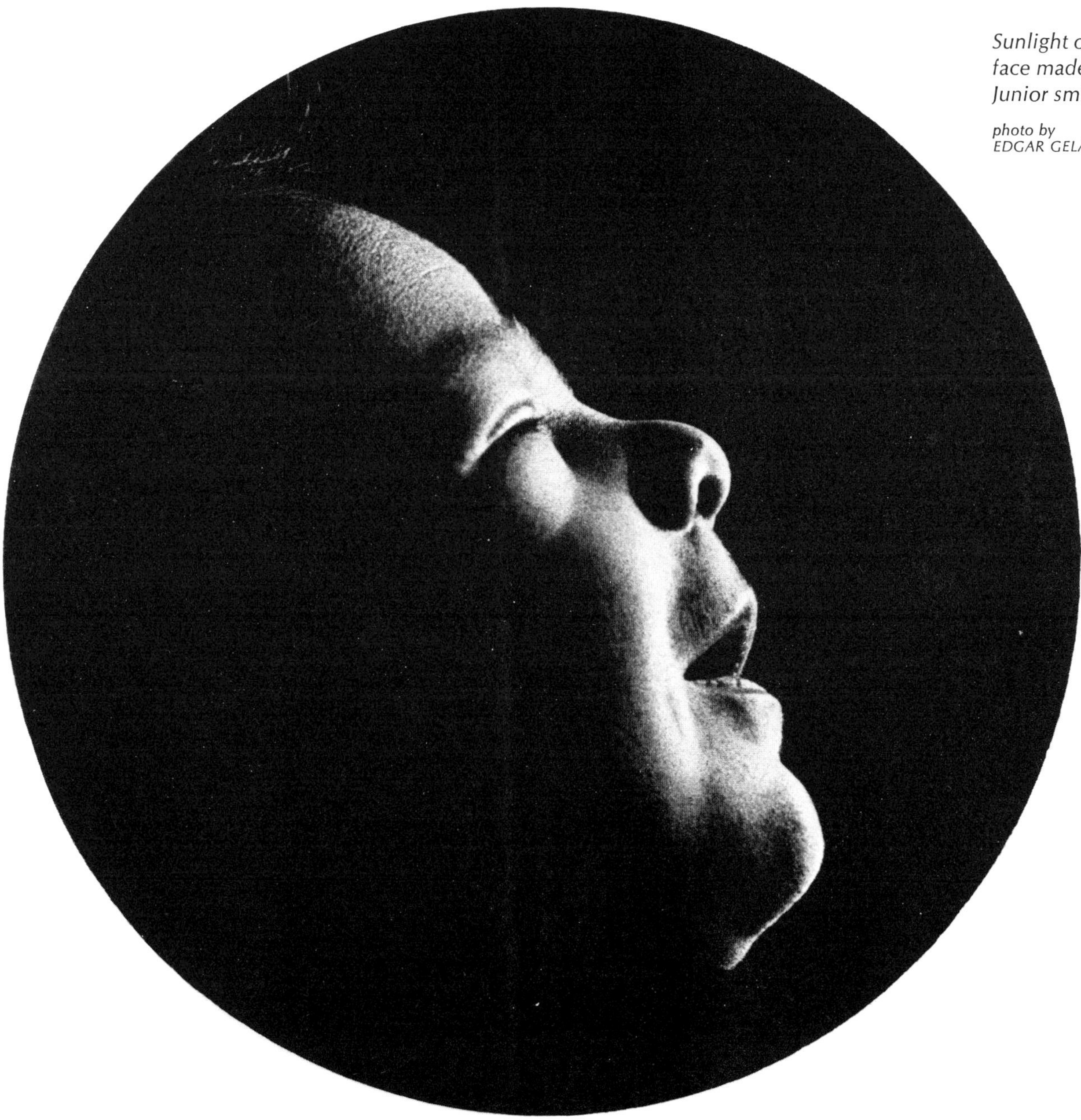

Sunlight on his face made Eddy Junior smile.

photo by EDGAR GELABERT

Returning to Edgar Gelabert, I doubt that he could have carried on his extremely difficult work in family photgraphy if he had limited himself to Freudian notions of what he was trying to do. Strong as he is, this narrow materialism would have been too much for his ego when added to the suffering it was already being forced to endure. His suspicion that his self-induced suffering might have some higher purpose is what made it possible to keep going. He has found that the purpose of making the ego suffer is to free the Self. Without even a suspicion that there is a Self, where can one find the strength to go on?

In concluding this essay I wish to thank Carmen and Edgar Gelabert most sincerely for permitting themselves to be publicly revealed in such depth. They show remarkable courage and good will toward their fellow men. I think that each of my readers should appreciate them for offering themselves as evidence concerning the nature of marriage as a sacrament and a trial by fire. This kind of public self-revelation is uncomfortable for people with such shy, retiring natures. That they have permitted it to happen is a testimony to their willingness to help other people understand themselves.

PHOTOGRAPHY may be a practice of religion for you

The Self-discovery and Self-liberation techniques given in this book relate to various esoteric teachings in Eastern and Western religions. Use photography to help you in Self-perfection.

A great many people are aware that in some mysterious way photography is a kind of religion for them. They wouldn't express it this way, of course, nor would they equate photography with, say, Christianity, Buddhism or Vedanta. Nonetheless, it has come closer to being a religion than anything else they've ever had.

That this has happened to so many people wouldn't surprise students of religion very much, especially those who have delved into its esoteric side. Religion has been many things in the long history of mankind. More accurately, many things have proved to be useful tools for communicating religious knowledge and encouraging deeply ethical behavior. Some of the arts which have proved useful in this respect are archery, carpet weaving, humor, love poetry, music, flower growing, architecture, painting, calligraphy and alchemy. Through all of them religious concepts have been demonstrated.

8

You can prove this to yourself for a certainty, if you are willing to take the time. There is an enormous literature on the subject. However, it is mixed up with a lot of other things. Much of the salient literature which deals with man's religious problems doesn't seem to be about religion at all, so it takes a good deal of time to sort through it and figure out where everything fits.

It doesn't matter whether or not you think you're religious. You can be an avowed atheist or agnostic. Nonetheless, if you use photography (or any other art) in certain ways, it becomes a true practice of religion. At certain times in their lives, many people are much better off to think that they're atheists or agnostics than to suppose, without really thinking about it, that they are religious. There are a good many self-professed believers whose belief is actually an impenetrable barrier between them and true faith. They believe devoutly in the wrong things. The people in this pathetic bind number in the hundreds of millions; often they are high up in the hierarchy of the established religions.

This entire book is about photography as a religious practice. Though I've tested all the ideas in it to the best of my ability, there is not a single one which is my own. With a little thought you should be able to use me, my humanity as you see it, as a measuring rod.

I have made, or am still making, every one of the mistakes I've told you about. These are all spiritual mistakes. At the same time, I've learned through bitter experience some of the consequences of such mistakes. Through experience and observation of thousands of photography students I've learned a few ways in which the medium can be used in overcoming spiritual errors. As you've probably discovered, this book is more a mouthful of chili peppers than a dish of chocolate ice cream. I hope you enjoy the peppers and that the heat in your belly gives you a promise that you can make more sense out of your life. Don't be impatient, however. There are no shortcuts to Self-discovery, or to God. With reference to religious thinking found herein, I've limited myself to explanations, truths which the reader can easily recognize once he has thought about them or delved into his own life experiences. He can use my ideas as they stand, turn them upside-down, or throw them in the trash barrel. Every statement in this book has been worked out from my understanding of esoteric religions, Eastern and Western. If ideas are found wanting, it is because my understanding is not all that it should be.

The Christ in All Things

This lesson, now revised somewhat, was originally printed in the June 1968 issue of *Popular Photography*. I had shot the pictures about five years before for *Esquire* on an assignment given me by Mr. Harold Hayes, who was then the Managing Editor. They were for the Christmas issue of the magazine. Mr. Hayes told me: "Shoot some really controversial Christmas pictures. Really shake people up." When I returned with the pictures, he said they were the best I had ever done. He paid me for them but *Esquire* never printed them.

At the time I photographed the assignment, I was studying under Mr. Eli Siegel, a poet-philosopher who had developed the system of thought he calls Aesthetic Realism. Mr. Siegel's teaching had a profound influence on me, which continues to this day. One of the things he told me at the time was that I wasn't doing a good job of seeing my wife accurately. He said that I wasn't relating her to enough things. Instead, I was encapsulating my perception of her, seeing her as less than she actually is. He insisted that human beings have large dimension and that a way of seeing this largeness is to relate it to many, many things. Refusing to make these relations is a way of lessening a person. The reasons for this diminishing are less than respectable. We compress our notions of others in order to feel superior to them or to stuff them into convenient mental cubbyholes so that we don't have to think about them anymore.

When Mr. Hayes gave me the assignment, I struck on the idea of applying Mr. Siegel's teaching to our thinking about Jesus. I formulated what I wanted to do, then boiled down my concept to a single phrase: the Christ in all things. The idea here is that if Christ is as great as Christians claim He is, we should then be able to see Him or His influence in all things. This is another way of expressing Siegel's notion that the larger a thing is the more it should relate to everything else.

As a drop-out Christian myself I was fully aware that practicing Christians carefully limit Christ's relatedness to things. They let Him relate to churches, Christmas, charity boxes, Sunday morning and statues of Himself being crucified, but to very little else. They are smug about this too, thinking that they are doing exactly what He would like them to do. Having thoroughly lessened Him into something small enough to keep safely jailed in churches they then fly in fury at anyone

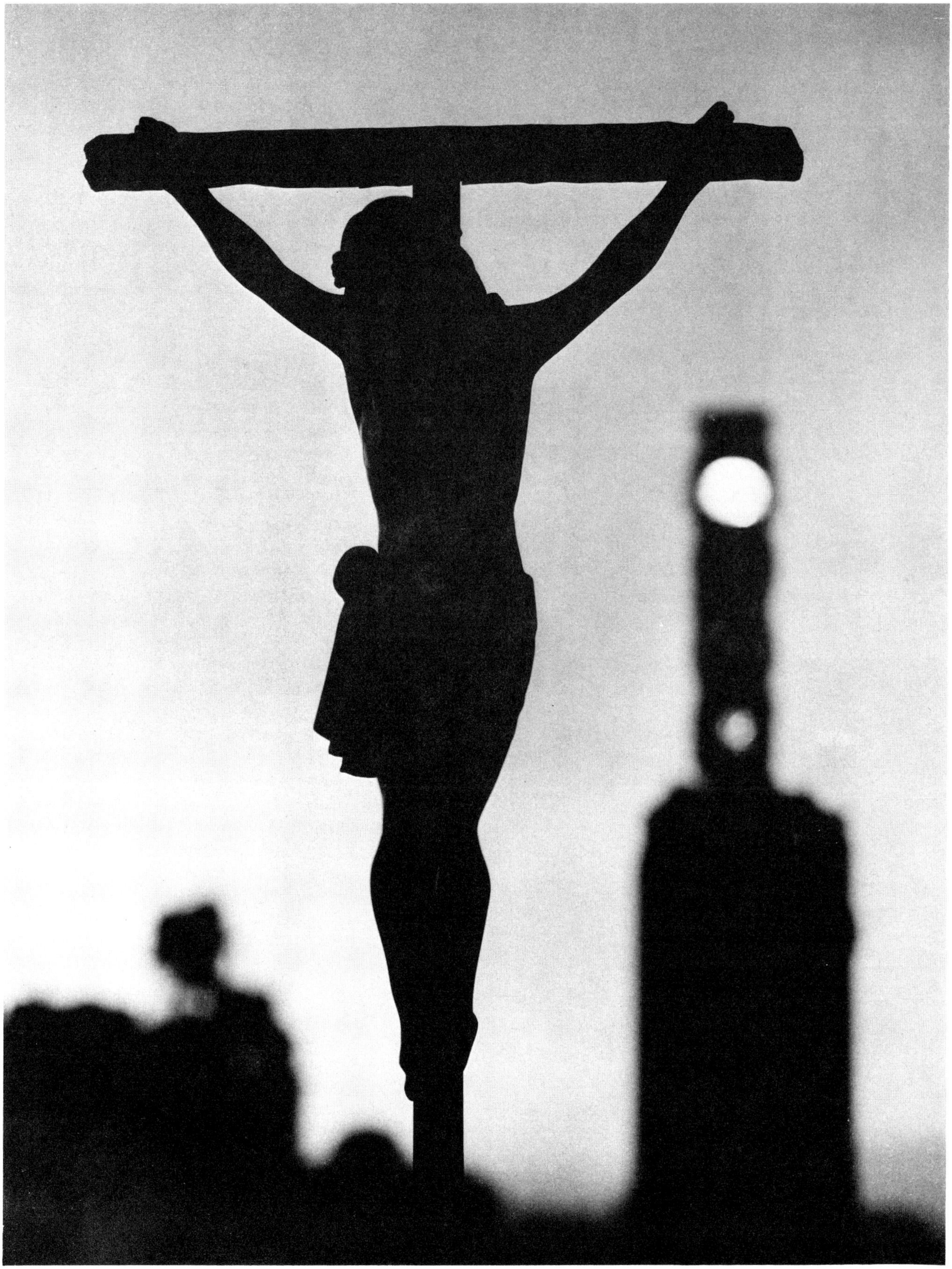

Christ said: "I am the light," and his life was a lesson full of stop and go signals for all mankind. The colors of the signal mean: red—energy, green—healing.

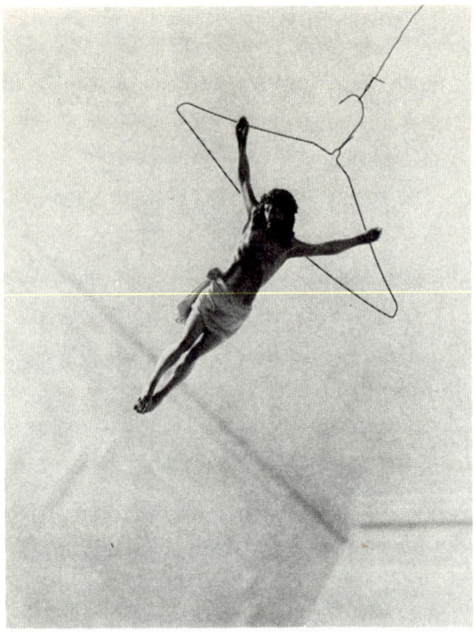

Christ on a coat hanger, is this blasphemy? I think not. It helps us see Him as a spirit of the air, the wind and the stars. The plaster figure of Christ, as humble as Christ Himself, transcends everyday reality with the help of a humble coat hanger.

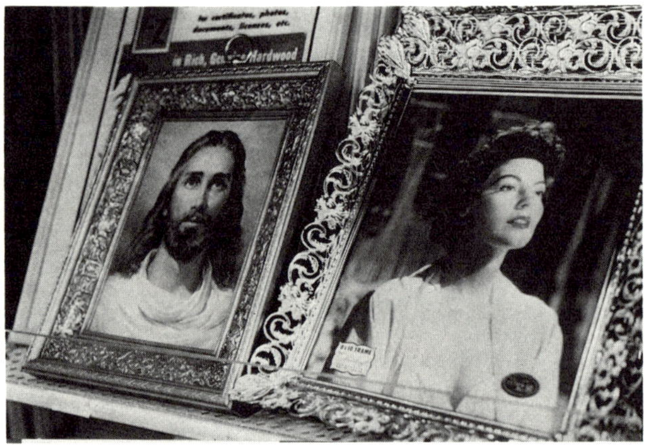

Christ and a movie queen: Both sought the meaning of life, one of them found it. The one who found it wants all movie stars to be so great that through their art they spiritualize all men in all nations.

who tries to show Him in His true dimensions.

Here was a simple answer to the problem of shake-up and controversy. All I had to do was to begin to restore Christ to His real size. Assuming that such a figure relates to everything else, all I had to do was show Him in a visual relationship to a few things with which He is not normally associated. I figured that devout "Christians" would then rise up in the thousands, claiming that His memory had been desecrated and that my pictures were an abomination before the face of the Lord. I reasoned further that the only thing which would actually be desecrated would be the unreasoned narrowness of contemporary Christian vision. It doesn't want Christ in full dimension, as He is much easier to cope with in miniature.

The Romans hanged Christ on a cross. This is industrial barbed wire (below), military barbed wire's first cousin.

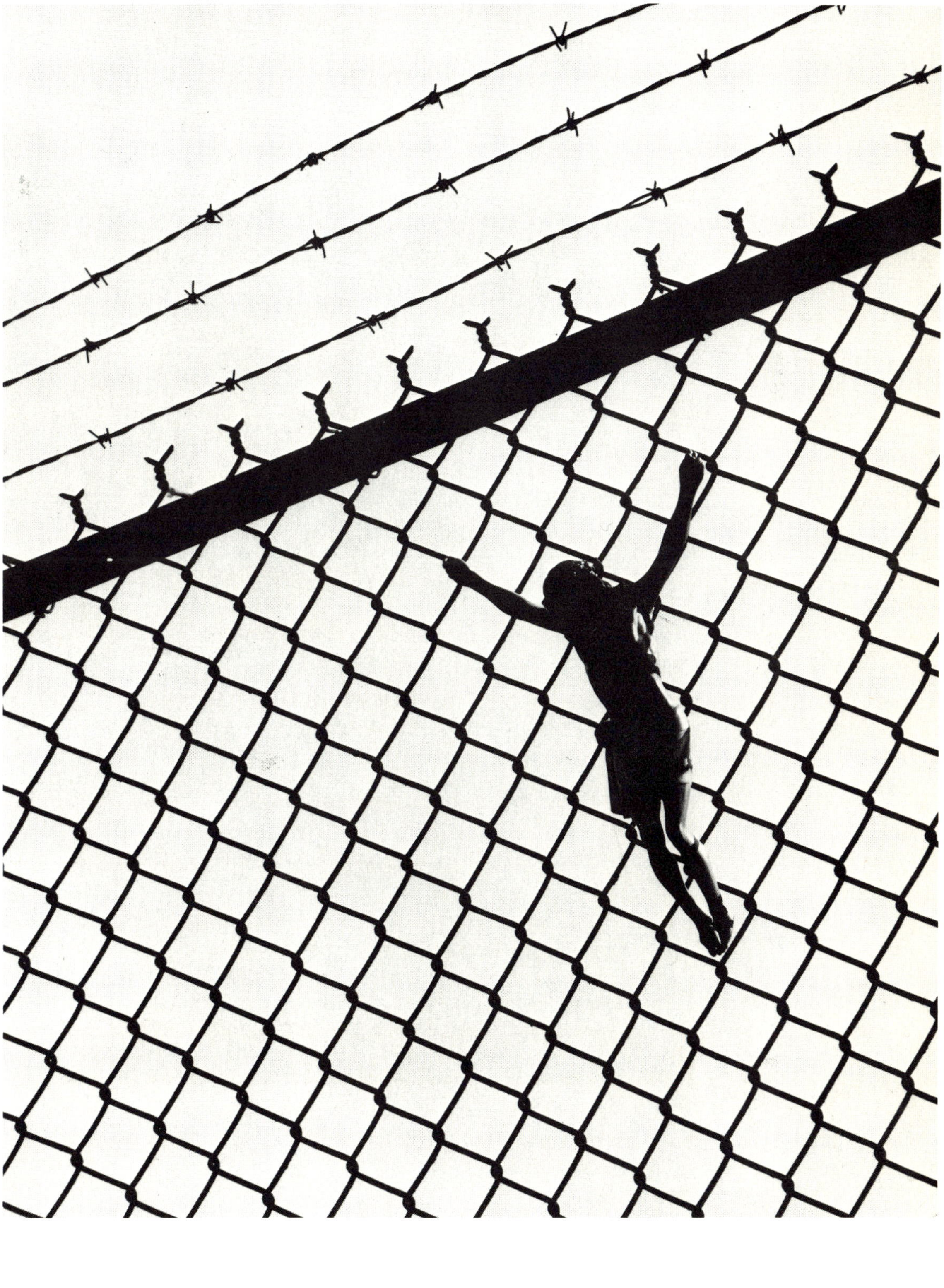

There is but one Way and Christ has shown it: to crucify personal will and desire, to bend oneself to the will of God. Whoever would take a shortcut is a thief and a robber.

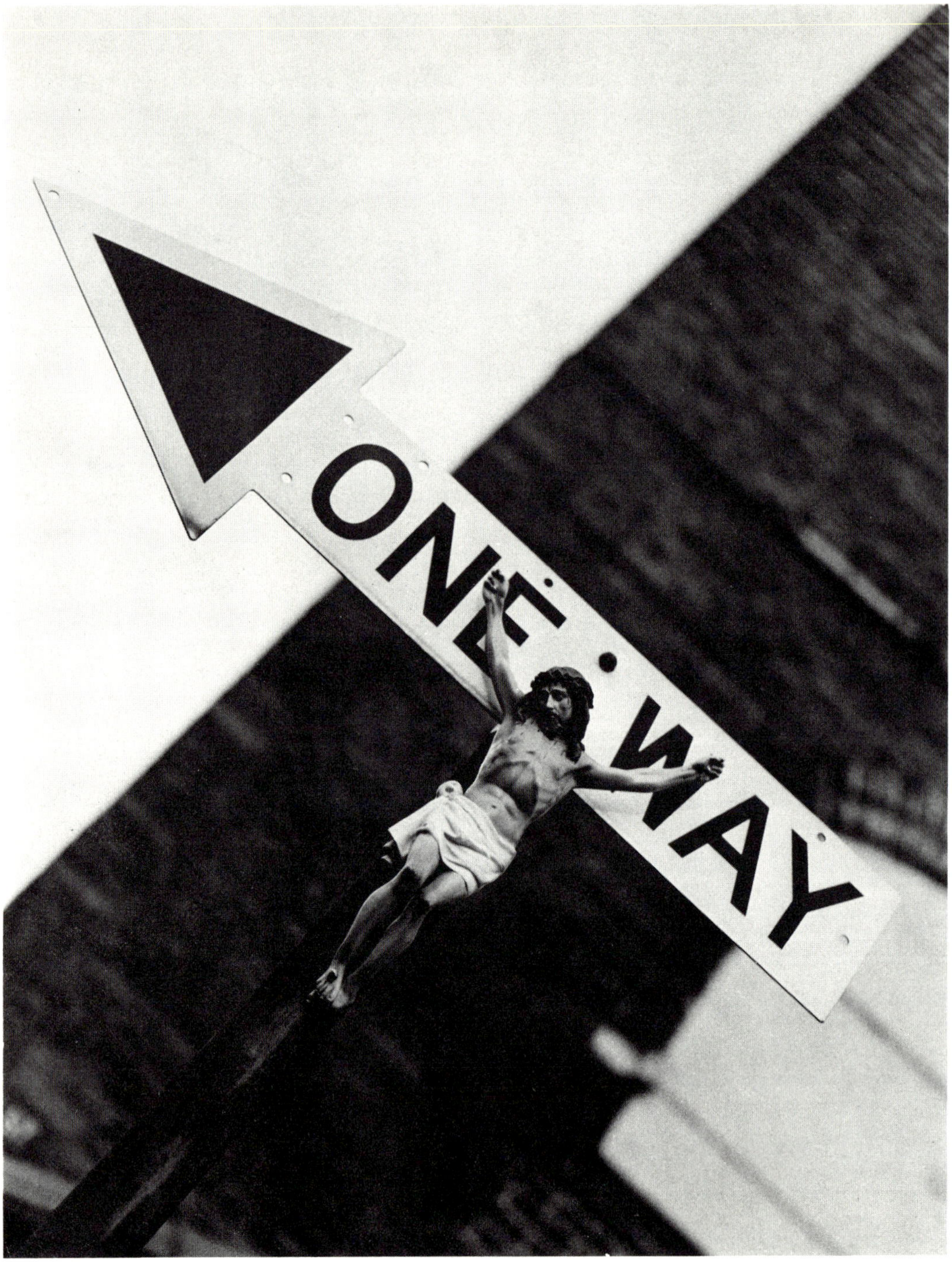

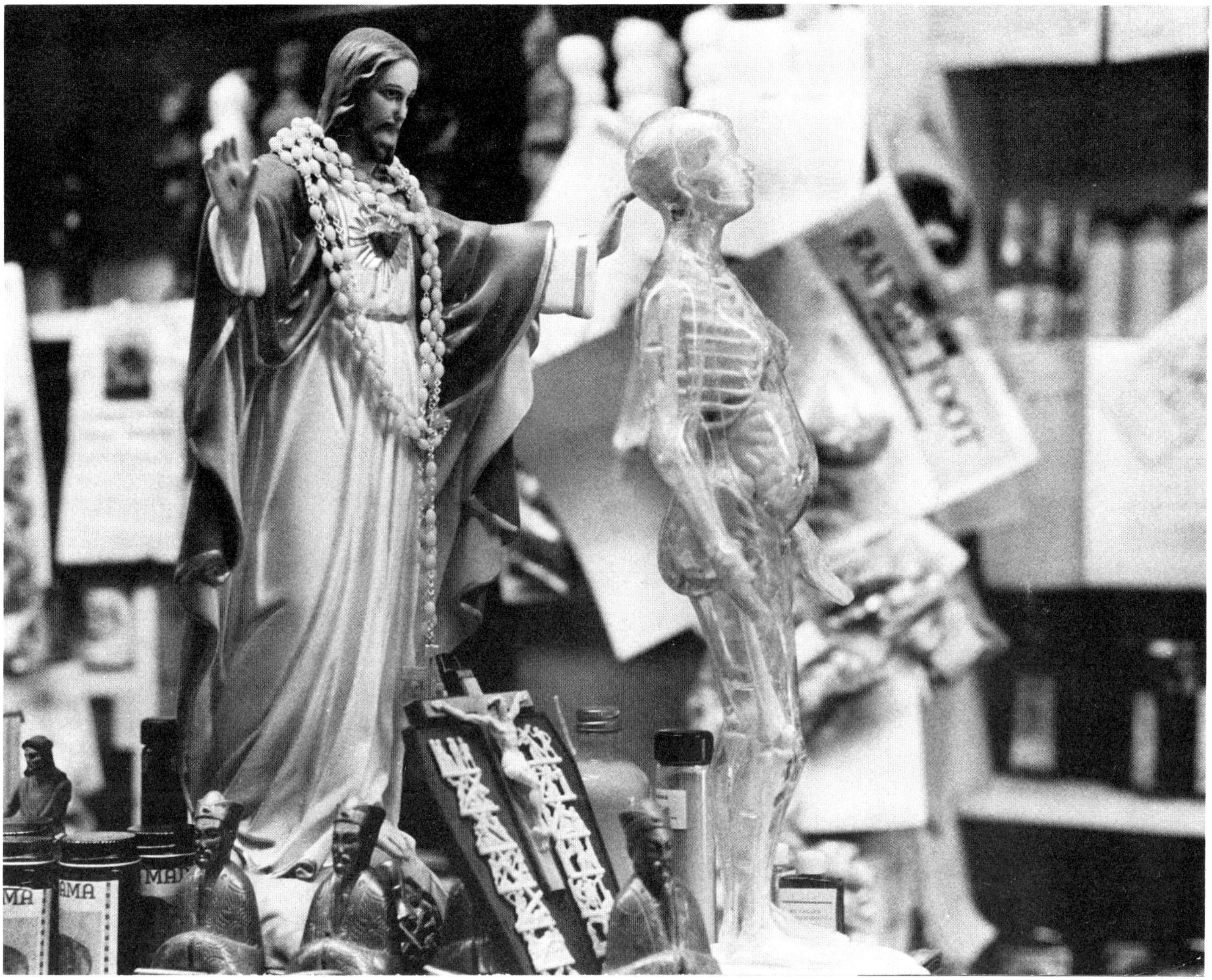

The Christian unwillingness to relate the Christ to all things is at the root of the crisis in the churches. Young folk look at Christianity and see it as irrelevant to their central concerns in life. The same factor is also at work undermining adherence to other faiths. Indeed, it has always been at work in all religions. When the founder of a great new faith passes on, his work is invariably taken over by lesser beings who narrow its scope to fit their comprehension and comfort. As time passes, the once vital faith relates to fewer and fewer of the things people are really interested in.

Our task in life is to spiritualize our guts, to surrender our innards to the service of God. We can't do this unless we learn something about our gizzards, livers, and spinal cords. If we would master them we must learn what they're for.

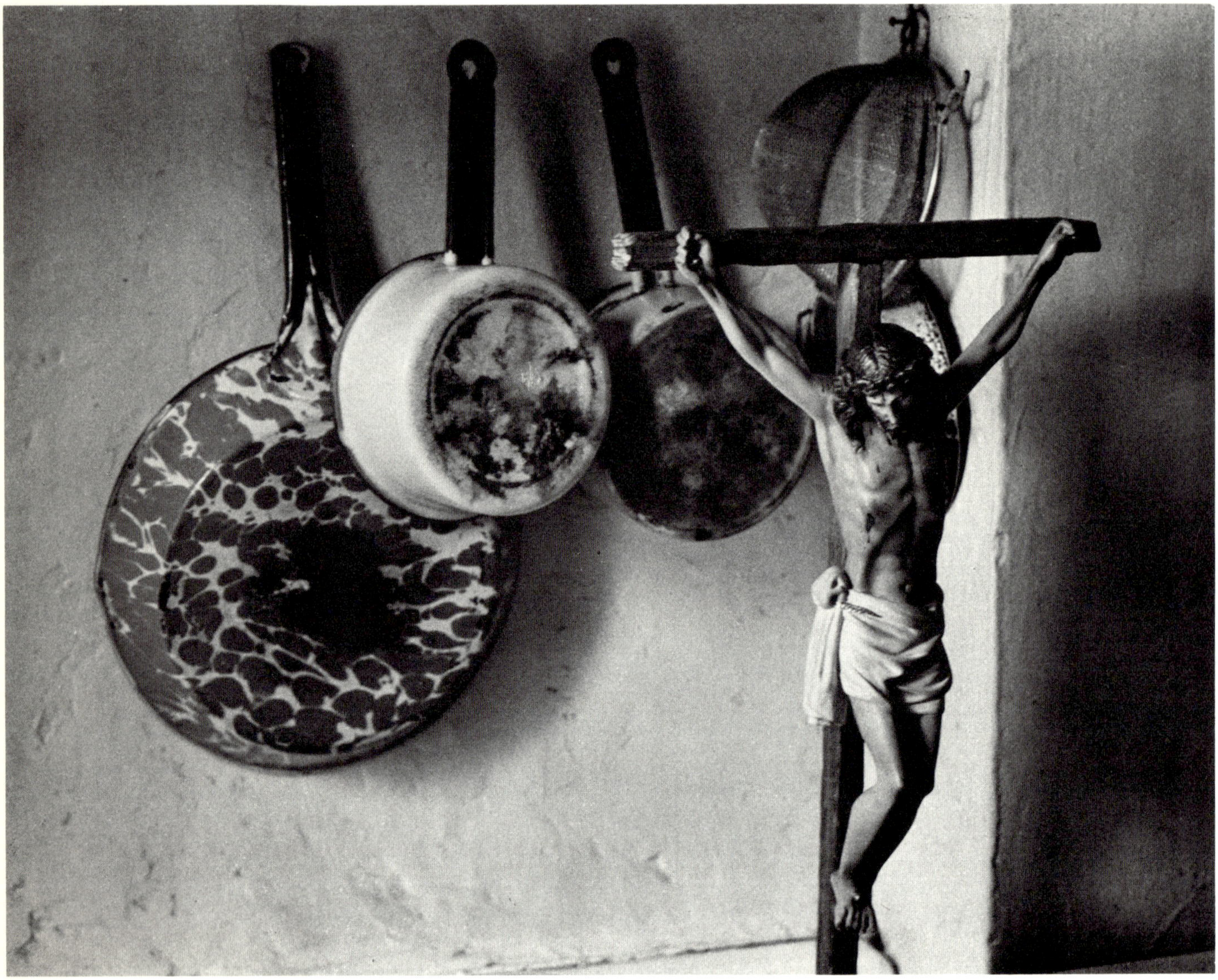

Christ in the kitchen. St. Teresa of Avila found Christ among the pots and pans when she deliberately crucified her Spanish pride by endlessly performing the most menial services for others.

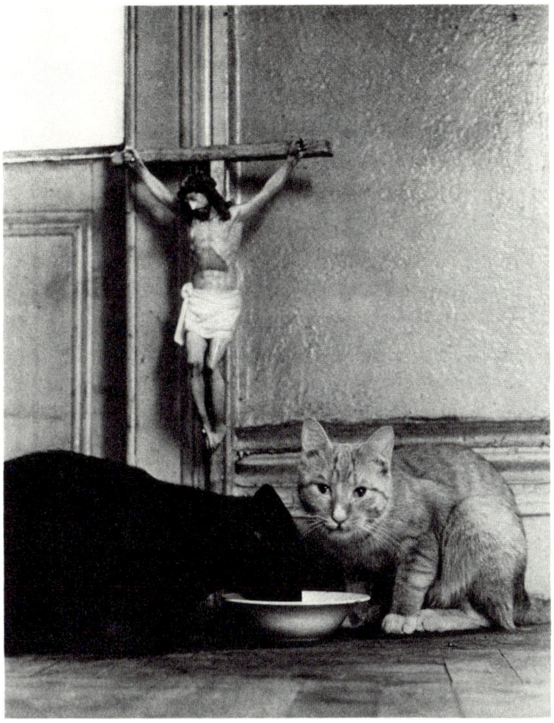

Cats and Christ. If you can't love a cat you won't find Christ. Though true, this isn't a welcome thought to cat haters.

I think that the Siegel formula is an excellent one: If you want to see the largeness of something, see it as related to everything else. Not only will this help you see fully, but it will also help you discover if you have a deeply ingrained reluctance to see large. For example, a Christian should be willing to relate Jesus to everyday things, like a half-eaten lampchop or a worn out shoe. If he rebels, he has a hang-up somewhere which has made him lessen Jesus. Of course, he interprets his reaction as opposite from what it actually is; he thinks that by clinging to the habit of relating Jesus to practically nothing at all, he is serving Him well. Broadening His relatedness he sees as sacrilege. He doesn't see that the motive behind his narrowness of view may be that it enables him to escape trying to lead the kind of life Jesus asked him to lead.

Another nice thing about the formula is that one can apply it almost mechanically and still get meaningful results. For example, I try to broaden my concept of my wife by photographing her holding a piece of wood. Offhand, one might say that the two don't relate at all. With a few minutes thought, I can relate them in at least twenty-five ways. I thereby permit my wife to be larger in my mind than before. Edgar Gelabert (Chapter Seven) is doing this kind of thing with his wife in that he is trying to see her in as many ways as he can. Each time he finds a new way there is a breakthrough in his awareness of her.

The reverse of this is to make up your mind about a person and never permit yourself to change it. This is a way of consigning him to oblivion. It is also a form of judging, which we have been told is very bad for us. In truth, the only really

Perhaps the shopkeeper remembered Jesus and arranged the hanger to let His face show. And perhaps a lonely maiden will remember Him as she turns softly in her sleep and touches the flowers on her new nightgown, for Christ is near to all His children when they sleep.

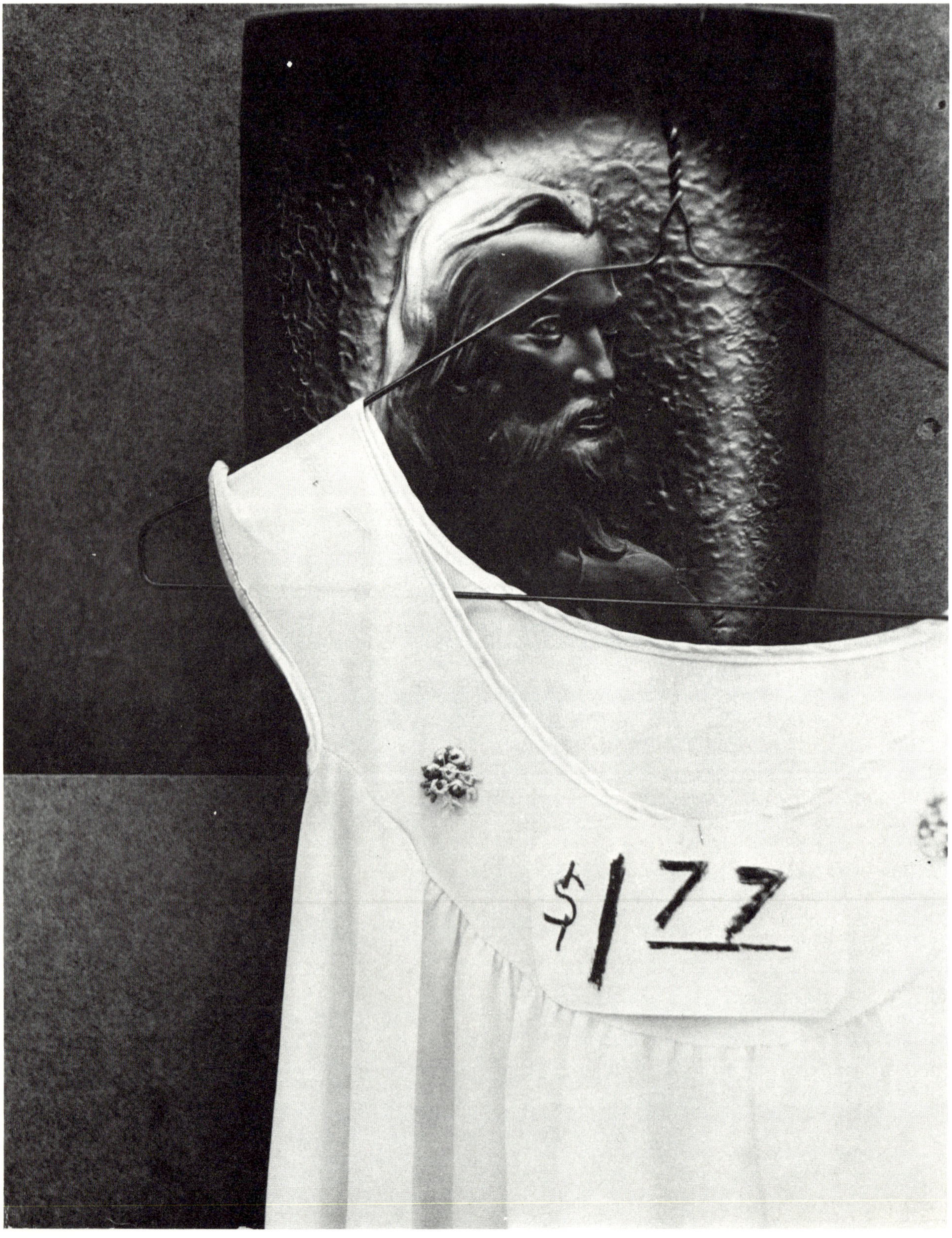

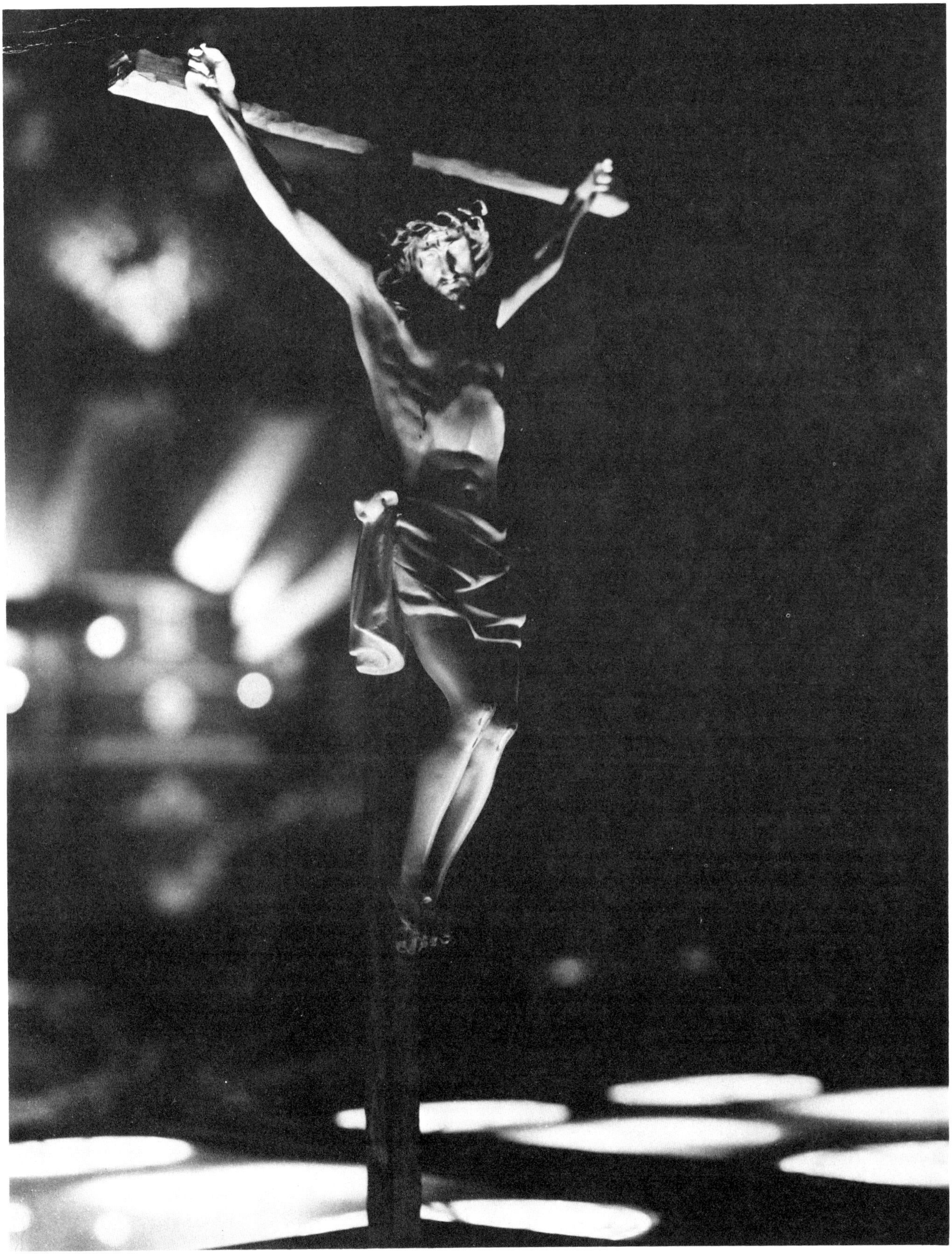

Christ at Rockefeller Center on a warm summer evening. People sit here—Christ with them—enjoying one another and the lights. Perhaps they dimly remember that Christ is light.

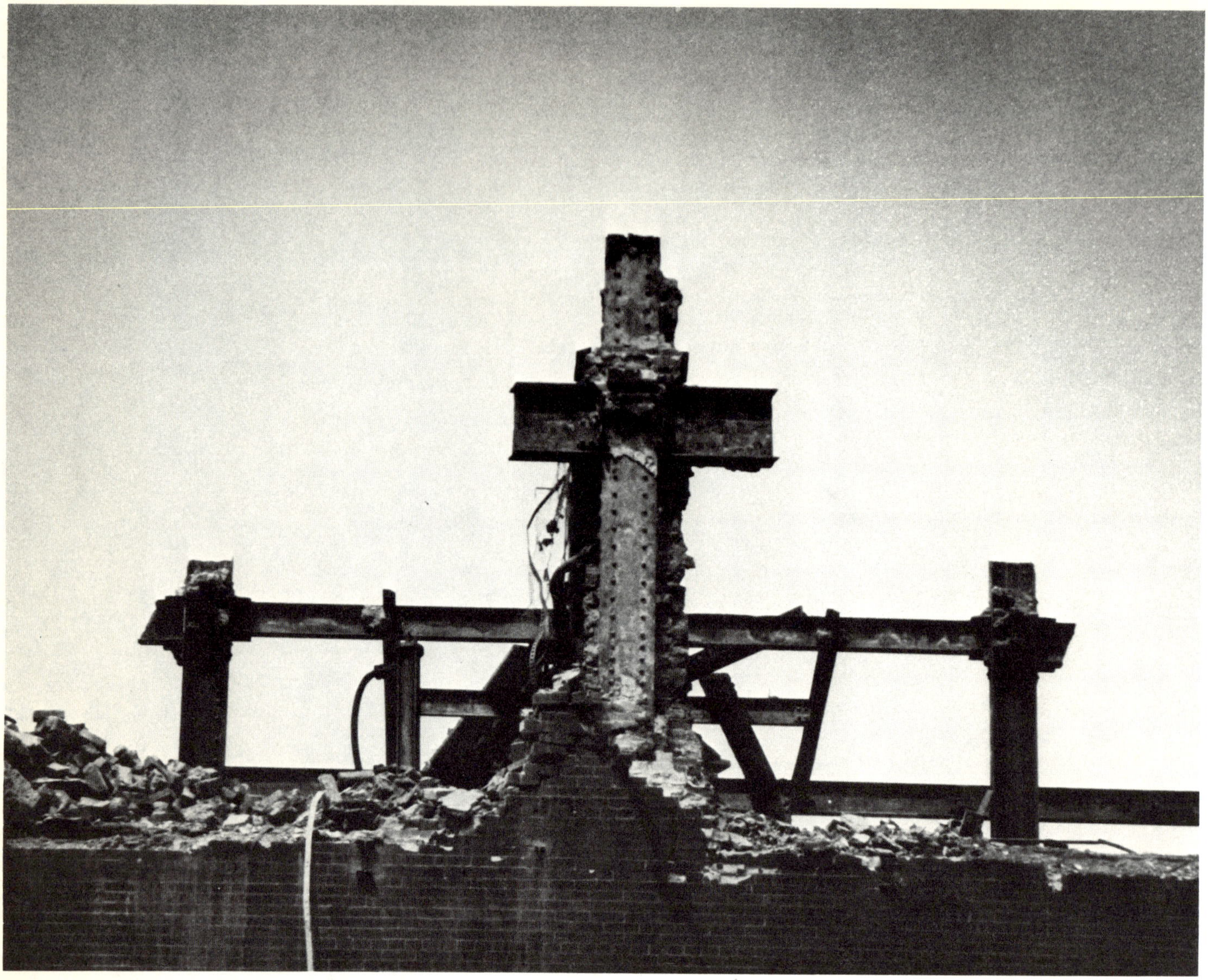

The cross in the ruins symbolizes Man's ruin in opposing the Will of God. With right mind and effort we can rebuild ourselves.

photo by FRED LOMBARDI

healthy way to see another being is as a universe unto himself. Seeing him as less than this is blighting and frustrating your own mind and understanding.

By this light, it is easier to understand photographers who are always trying to photograph things in new combinations and to see that there may be more than just gimmickry involved. In finding new relationships they are broadening themselves as well as creating interesting pictures. It is significant that many people are deeply resentful of this. They become angry every time they see a picture showing a new combination of things. Little do they realize that their anger stems from feeling an attack against the narrowness of their vision and that the attack is the best thing that could happen to them.

The Christian Religion Today

This lesson was originally published in *Popular Photography* under the title "Religion 1968," though it actually speaks only of Christianity. The pictures were sent in by readers in response to the challenge to describe religion today as they see it. In writing the text I chose to ignore the deep pessimism which most of the photographs communicate. I will talk about it here, however.

There is a saying among Zen Bud-

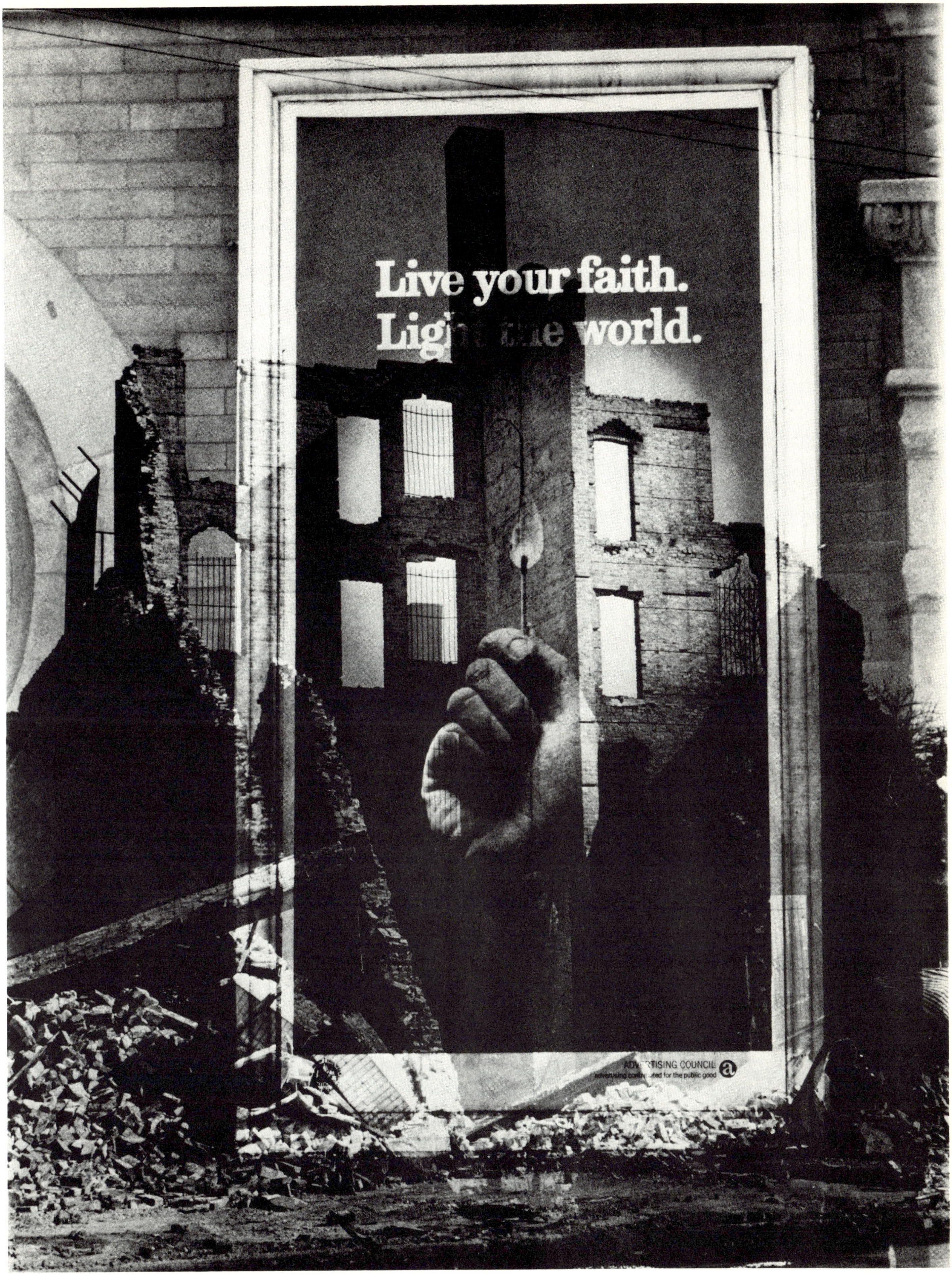

Man is a destroyer, no doubt of that, but the light burns on amidst all the devastation, for God is endlessly forgiving.

photo by DAVID HOFFMAN

dhists to the effect that whoever wishes to attain enlightenment should spit on the Buddha, and a related saying in esoteric Christianity that whoever wishes to realize the Christ within himself must turn away from Him. It seems to me that the photographers who sent in the pictures are unconsciously following this advice in exactly the way it was intended.

Since this is on the unconscious level, they are not really aware of what they're up to. People who deal cynically with religion are often of a strongly religious bent. What they are actually attacking, therefore, is not religion itself but their own misconceptions of it. This is true even though they think they are primarily attacking other people's misconceptions. In this light we can see that the above sayings translate to: "Spit on your concept of the Buddha and turn away from your concept of Christ. As they stand they are too inaccurate and limited to describe the reality of Saintly Beings and the true meanings of their teachings."

It must make you feel odd to be told that when you are attacking things in others you are almost invariably attacking the very same things in yourself, though the latter attack is indirect. Psychologists call this extremely common phenomenon projection. We all make spiritual mistakes and repress from consciousness the fact we're making them. On one level of being we know very well we're doing it, but we lie to ourselves. Then we push (repress) our awareness of the mistakes and our naive lies concerning them into the unconsciousness, where we hold them in bondage with psychic energy. In another context I've pointed out that most of our available energy is used up this way.

Working through the unconscious, Spiritual Forces try to make us aware of our errors. This awareness can be extremely painful, however, an acute form of ego-suffering. One way of lessening the pain of discovery is to attribute personal errors to others. This is projection. When an inner cause brings us suffering we project it onto others in order to escape the guilt feelings it gives rise to.

The Lesson:

By his very nature, man is a God-seeking animal. He has no more choice in this than a dog chasing a bitch in heat or the sun relentlessly pursuing the moon across the sky. God-seeking is coded into his cells, just as light-seeking is in the genes of a plant. When a man holds a bloody enemy head aloft or blows out his own brains on Christmas Eve, he is still a seeker, though far off the Path. Man as photographer is God-seeker too. As such he can stick to the middle of the way and push himself far along it. Or he can use his craft to make as many hells for himself as spiritual ignorance demands.

Once we've projected our own errors onto others we feel relatively comfortable in attacking them. The strength of our attacks, in word, deed, or thought, is a measure of the magnitude of our own errors and the depth of our concern with them. A person who violently condemns something in another person is simultaneously trying very hard to escape a heavy burden of guilt in himself. It is easy to see that if condemnation of others were the whole of it, projection would be a very evil thing. In some people it does stop there, and leads to mob action, unreasoned rebellion, cruelty and paranoid murders.

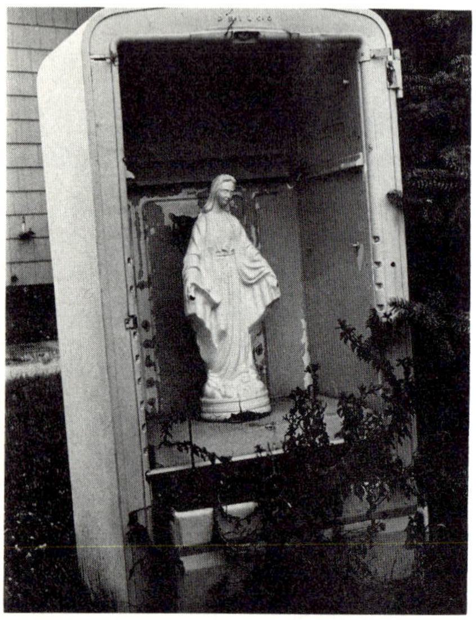

The Blessed Virgin (left) safe from storm and sleet in the most indestructible shrine in town.

photo by KEITH LAUMB

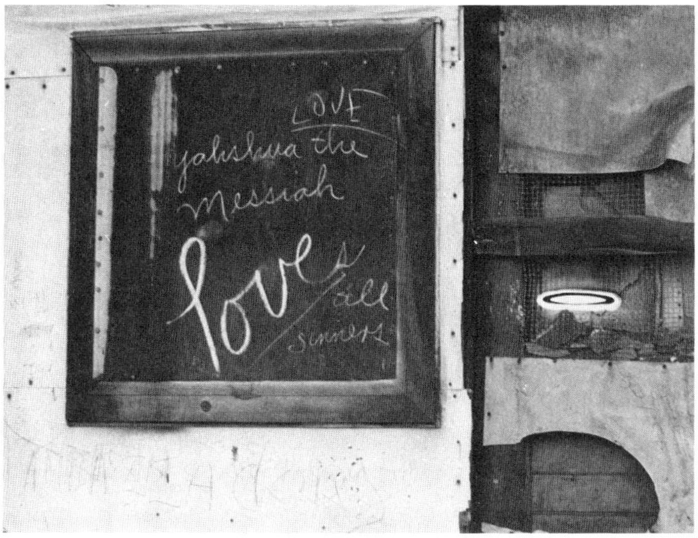

Food for thought for the pietist, and not so blasphemous as it sounds to him.

photo by RUTH KRAMER ZIONY

Christ's main teaching, written by a person who dug His pitch. With a gratuitous halo (above).

photo by HALBERT SPEER

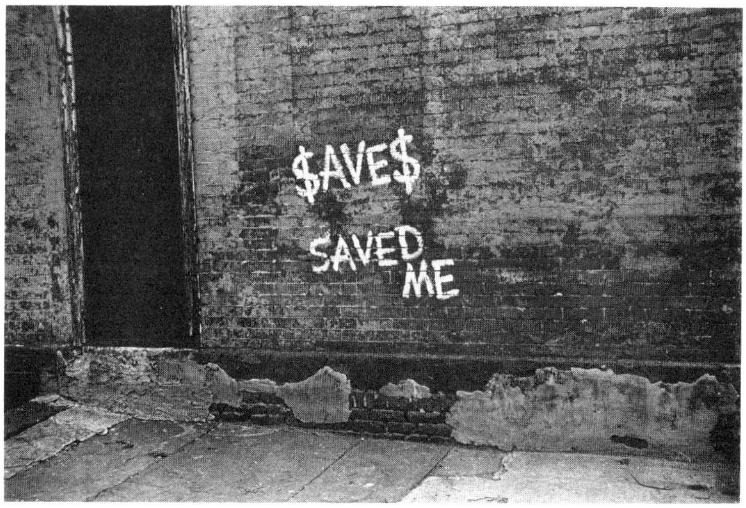

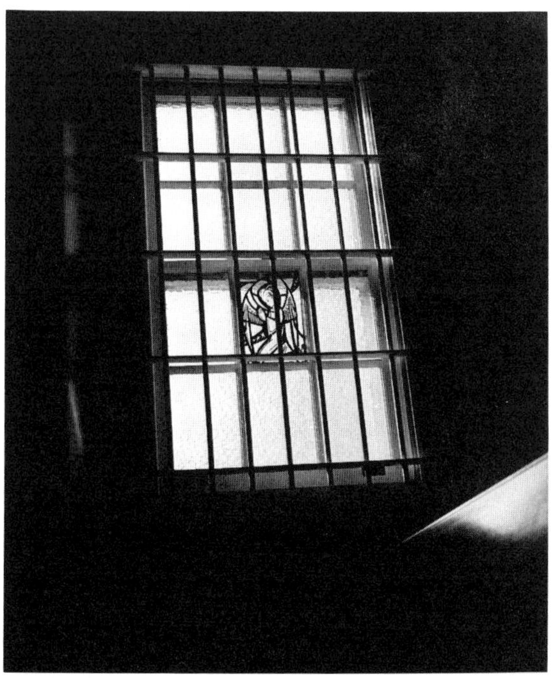

Stained-glass image of the Christ Child at prayer, in a window at the Bordentown Reformatory.

photo by WILLIAM HOUSSELL

Fortunately, the majority of people slowly come to realize that they themselves have been making the mistakes they've been attacking others for. For them, projection helps them to an awareness of errors they might never permit themselves to see otherwise. Sudden discovery would be too painful to bear. Thus, we can describe projection as a way of stretching out the pain of Self-knowledge to make it bearable.

Though projection leads us to treat others unfairly much of the time, it can also be useful to them. Should they examine what we say or think about them, they would discover that there is a certain amount of truth in what they've heard about themselves. Having accepted this, they can begin correcting their errors. Full of self-righteousness, most of us do our best to point out accurately the errors other people make. For this reason our judgments about them have some validity. Though judging others had a bad effect on us, it may be of use to them because of the degree of truth in our accusations.

If the entire projection process is speeded up it can be most useful for the person who does the projecting. He can speed it up by constantly analyzing his own thoughts while he is projecting. The speed-up comes when we realize we're actually looking at our own mistakes. From here we stop projecting and start looking into ourselves.

If we systematically attack our own tendency to project we enable ourselves to escape isolation and join the human race. This comes about when we learn to accept the fact that the basic errors are shared by all of us. When we see that other people are only making the same mistakes we're making, or are fully capable of making, we begin to forgive them. In time, the forgiveness is total. It includes self-forgiveness, a great step forward in spiritual development.

In my opinion, the pictures printed in this lesson represent the phenomenon of projection rather clearly. Consciously, the photographers are telling us the terrible things that other people have done to the Christian religion. Unconsciously, they are telling us (and themselves) that they too have committed the same errors.

I'm all in favor of photographers who approach religion in such a cynical way, for there is a very good chance they'll learn that underneath their cynicism is a yearning to know and believe in great religious truths. They may also discover that much of their cynicism is directed at their own spiritual shallowness and motivated by the desire to break down narrow conceptual barriers and develop greater breadth of vision.

I look with great suspicion at pictures which appear to be wholehearted affirmations of religious faith. They seldom represent more than the superficial religiosity and sentimentality of a self-deluded photographer. Such a person may think he's wearing the armor of a Christ or a Buddha, when he's armored only in self-righteousness and egotism.

The pictures this month are all from students. All are seekers, of course, though some might laugh hysterically at the very thought. Without exception, the photographs can be seen as both religious and as a wholesome leaven for meditation and spiritual discussion. Those who feel compelled to see some of them as blasphemous are perhaps narrow in an unexamined piety. They came to us as part of the overwhelming student response to the lesson entitled "Christ, 1968."

Before discussing the student work, let's consider the general subject of photography and religion. A surprising number of people have arrived independently at the idea that photography is to them an essentially religious pursuit. This doesn't mean only the kind of photography that uses easily recognized religious symbols as subject matter, but *all* of their photography. How can this be? And is the reason valid?

It comes to this: that anyone trying to see better is on the Way. It doesn't matter if he calls himself an atheist or an agnostic. The law is that the closer one is to good seeing, the closer he is to God. Disbelieving in this law makes it no less a law of the universe and no less real. If a man is pigheadedly committed to atheism, he'd

A graphic comment on Christ in a psychedelic coffee house operated by the Columbian Presbyterian Church in La Fayette, New York.

photo by
ROBERT SYLVESTER

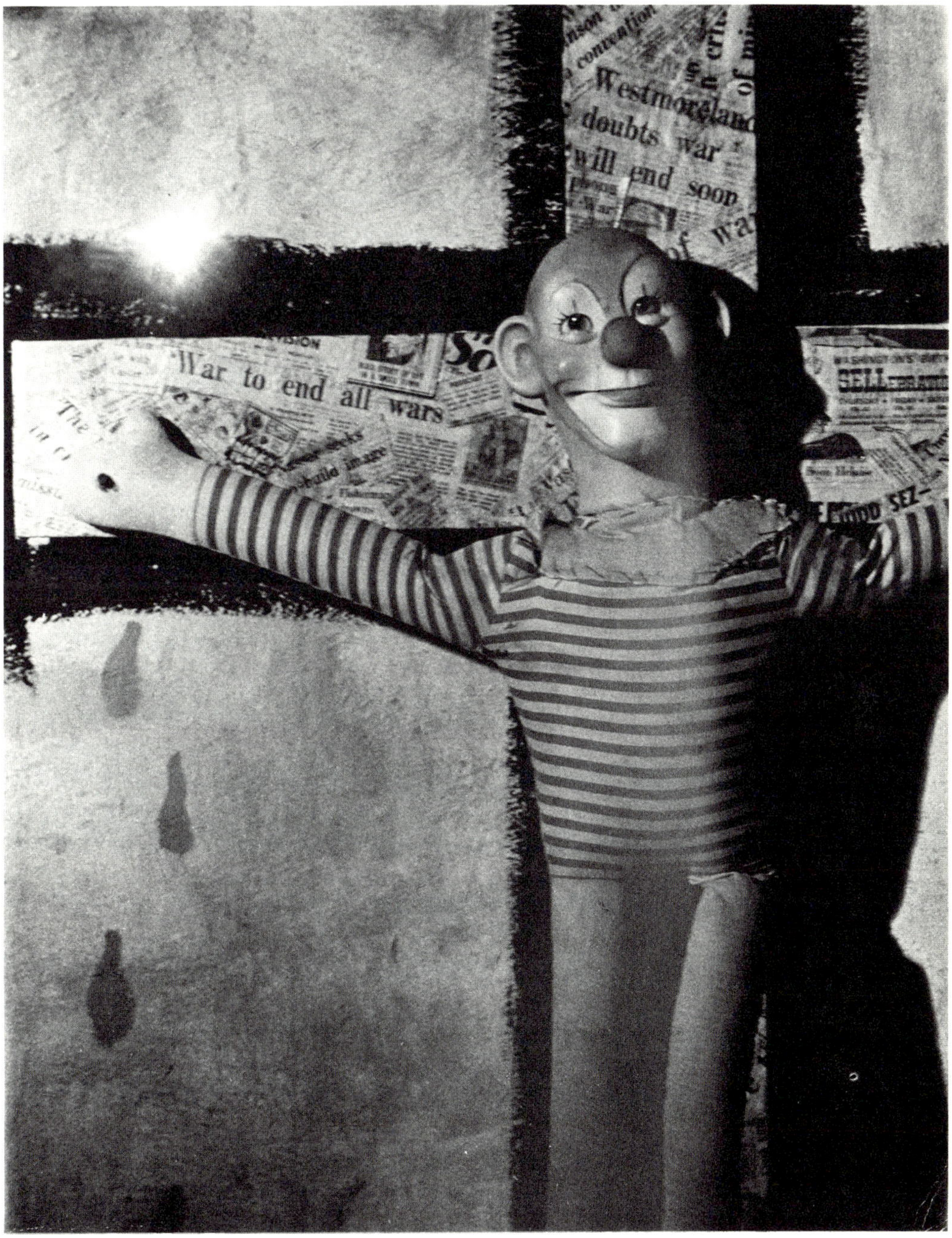

better blind himself, for with any sight at all he is more likely to move toward the Light than away from it. Such a person should certainly steer away from photography.

Most of us are much more religious than we realize. Somehow we manage to disguise from ourselves many of our most fundamental concerns; we are ashamed of admitting them, perhaps. There is our overwhelming concern with light, for example. Of course, photography has to have light or it just won't work. But how many of us have discovered that we entered photography because we, also, need light? This time let's call it Light or Enlightenment. For deeper reasons than we know, we may have sought the art that centers itself around light.

How about our passion in recent years for photographing the sun? Is it possible that we are responding to a species memory coded into our genes, and beginning to understand again that "Sun" and "Son" are symbolically interchangeable terms? In following the sun, are we in reality seeking the Son? History shows that we've hidden our basic drives from ourselves in stranger ways than this.

To photograph is to create with light or to witness such a creation. In our creating with light, are we groping to reflect the Will of the Creator of Light? Certainly, our concern to make our photographic creations beautiful and meaningful and ethical is very suggestive of this. Why is it so important to us that we do our work well if we're not in some dimly felt way attempting to bring our lives in tune with the Higher Forces? Is egotism the basic factor in this striving? I think not, for all our success derives from battles *against* the ego, against the limitations of self.

Consider the struggle one goes through in making a fine print. Many photographers have come to see this as a form of meditation; some have called it a sacrament. What is it we do that makes this process holy to atheist and believer alike? First of all, we try with all our might to tune in to a faintly heard vibration in ourselves. In modern terms, this could be called the wave length of aesthetics. A sophisticated physicist-metaphysician would say that the higher we move on this band, the closer we come to God. More naive types would call it breaking your back to get a really good print. Whatever one calls it, the process is one of attunement to something in oneself and the universe. And the result yields great satisfaction.

Consider next our inner struggles to surrender our power over things outside ourselves. With a knowledge of the photographic controls, we can make something or someone into almost anything we want it to be. We don't have to be concerned with what it really is, nor even care for it a whit. We can see things and people merely as raw material, useful only for letting us express ourselves, something to twist and warp and meddle with. As we meddle, however, we hear a whispered plea from our subjects: "Please see us as we are. Please like us as we are, not merely for what you can make us into. Let us touch your life and be meaningful."

The Lesson:

The battle cry of the young photographer is "I must be involved!*" Fine. A lot of famous photographers have felt the same way. But there are good and bad ways of doing it. When involvement means being hung up on something or someone, it leads only to bad photography. When it means being* attuned *to something, the results, personal and photographic, can be very satisfying. Of course, it makes some difference what you attune yourself to; if you try to vibrate on the same plane as a tiger shark, you probably won't amount to much as a human being.*

Once we hear the whisper, the inner battle begins—egotism against everything else that exists. Insofar as we push egotism down, we let the universe flood into us, bringing warmth and light. We find ourselves using photography as a celebration of all that exists, not just as a record of personal despair and unenlightened selfishness. As we learn to care for things outside ourselves, we find happiness and draw closer to God. We begin to understand what "love thy neighbor" can mean to us and the terrible price of not loving him.

Though there is much more to be said on the subject of photography and religion, I think we should now turn to the pictures from the readers. Some of them plainly say we're not doing a very good job of living up to the religions we publicly profess. Fine. Such things always need saying. But let us also hope that photographers who say this understand that it applies to themselves, too. To be a condemning photographer is easy; to be a forgiving one is extremely difficult for most of us.

Some of the pictures suggest the Death of God controversy. Again, this is fine. The real point of such an approach to photography is not to prove that God is dead but that our own thought concerning him is as lifeless as a mackerel ten days in the sun. We force ourselves to overthrow our personal rituals and religious jargon in search of what is really essential to religion. Oddly enough, as we photograph we think we're only putting down other people's dependence on empty ritual and the assorted lies they tell themselves. In time, we may discover that the whole process was self-purgative, making spiritual growth possible.

I don't think I err in suspecting that the pictures as a whole reflect a great deal of yearning, soul-searching and agony. Even the clown doll nailed to the cross shows this. I think that whoever nailed it there was thinking of the doll as himself, crucified by an uncaring world. Truth is, he's crucified by his own selfishness.

I wouldn't be surprised if our photographer did a considerable amount of reflecting on such things after he spotted this unknown person's wail of self-pity nailed to the wall. Well, whoever he is he's still a seeker. If he should some day find himself reflecting on the true meaning of the cross, he will see that sticking up a clown and calling it Silly Joe Jesus had more meaning to it than he thought. At least it fixed his attention on an idea that could help him if given half a chance.

I suggest that the reader meditate on what I've said and include in his meditations whatever reactions he may have had to the pictures and the text. Those who are cynical might reexamine their cynicism to see if it's honest or just a slick cover-up for a stifled wail of anguish and need. Photographers and editors might ponder the notion that photography is basically a religious pursuit.

Must You Be Involved?

Though it doesn't seem to be, this lesson is a short essay on esoteric Christianity. On the esoteric level all religions are one. The religion that we encounter in churches, mosques and temples is not the same as esoteric religion. Established religion tells us of the virtues we should have, but doesn't tell us how to develop them. Esoteric religion centers largely around method. It tells us how to develop the virtues in ourselves. "Must You Be Involved" is a discussion on method.

One of the peculiar qualities of a teaching in esoteric religion is that it may not appear to be about religion at all, but it invariably involves methods for working on oneself. The goal for such work has been given various names: Self-discovery, Self-realization, Self-deconditioning, Self-liberation, Enlightenment, Cosmic Consciousness and so on. The names don't matter, for the final end is always the same —union with God.

All of these pictures are by a young woman named Bonnie Freer, who is consciously trying to get herself more and more involved with people. Since her pictures are splendid, I think we can safely assume that her involvement is the right kind. Furthermore, she is moving surely and intelligently into a promising professional career in photography. How she defines the word 'involvement' undoubtedly has much to do with this. Though my definition probably won't be the same as hers, I'll bet they're at least first cousins.

At its best, involvement means spiritual unity with the rest of mankind. I sense quite a bit of this in some of Miss Freer's pictures and am proud of her for it. And

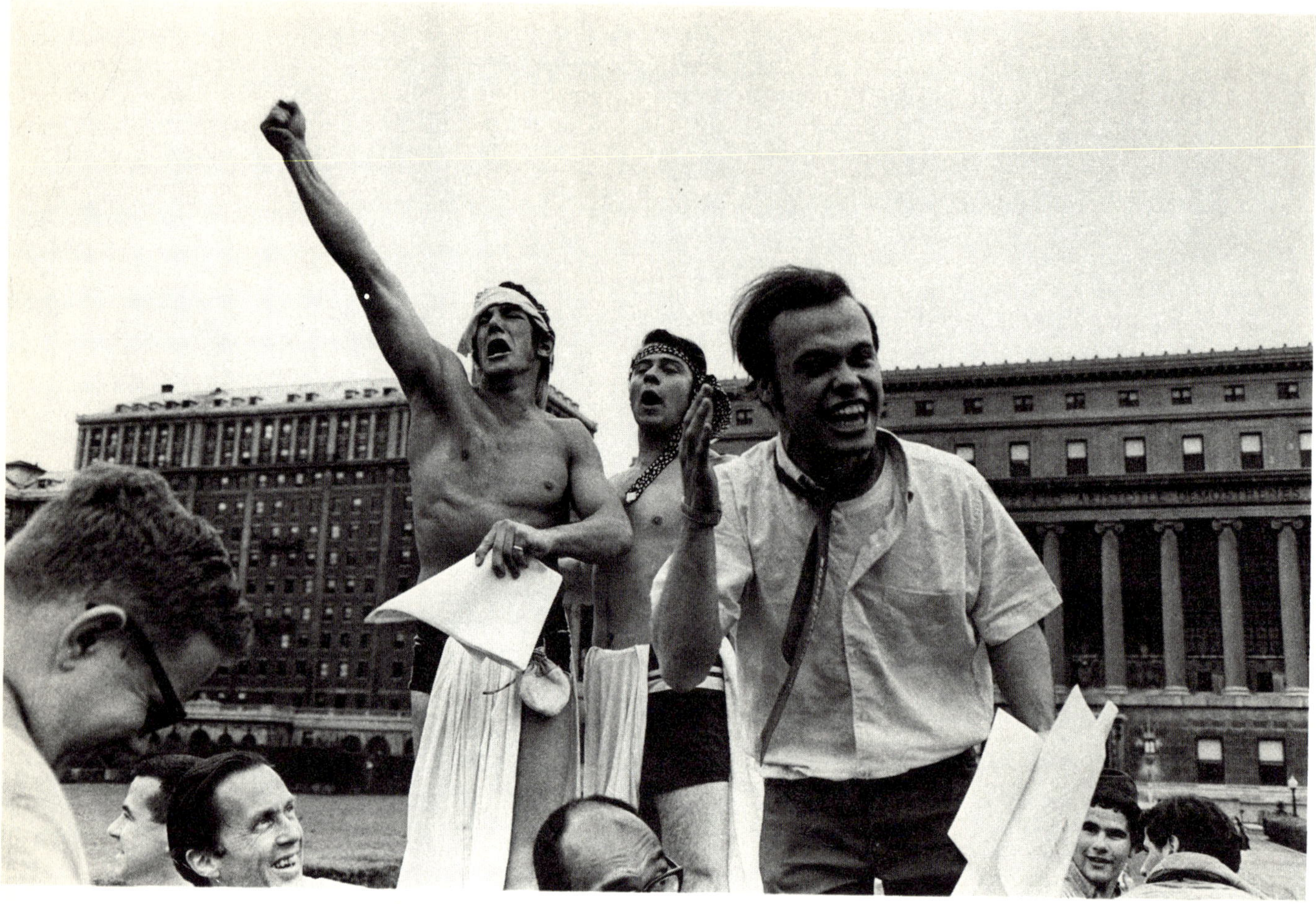

Columbia University: spoofing a student rebellion that later turned out to be serious (1968). If enough students had thus questioned their involvement it might not have happened.

photo by BONNIE FREER

I suspect she's beginning to perceive the price one must pay for this unity, for none of the higher gifts come free. One must pay the price, and pay and pay. There's no coasting or turning back once you've begun the difficult journey.

Part of the payment is in suspending judgment of others, terribly difficult though this may be. We have such *strong* urges to put them down in our words or in our thoughts. It's so easy and pleasurable to bolster our own egotism at the expense of others. But if we do, it lessens our pictures and turns them into visual sneers. Heaven knows, there are a lot of such pictures around, but who can like them and respect himself for it? In photography as anywhere else, ours is not to judge. Our job is to struggle with the temptation to stand in judgment. Out of this struggle comes unity of Self.

Another part of the payment is suffering the pain of forcing ourselves to remain open to others. The pain of listening to them as if through their own ears, while secretly we'd prefer to hold them in contempt and stuff our ears with plaster. This pain we feel tears down the walls of selfishness eventually, adding vast dimensions to our eyes and cameras.

We can pay, too, by tearing down the barriers we've built so that others can't see us. If we leave them up, we get punched in the nose, sneered at, and shut out. Our range for photography is the heartless street through a telephoto lens.

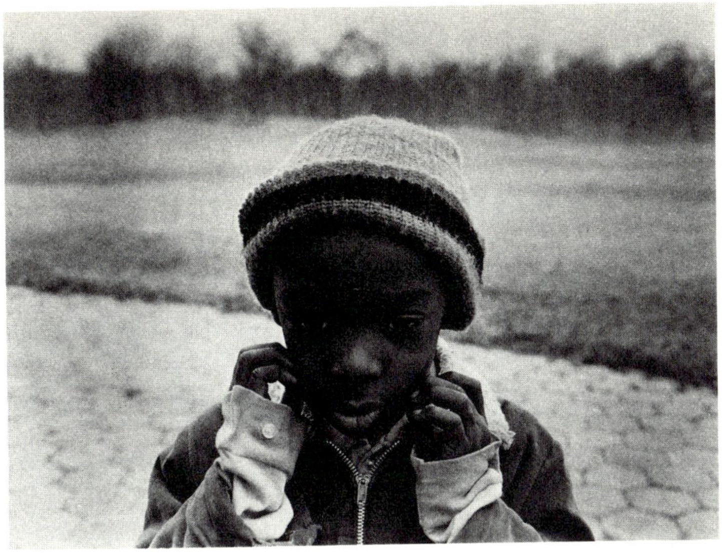

To involve oneself with a child's needs and hopes is a worthy thing to do.

photo by BONNIE FREER

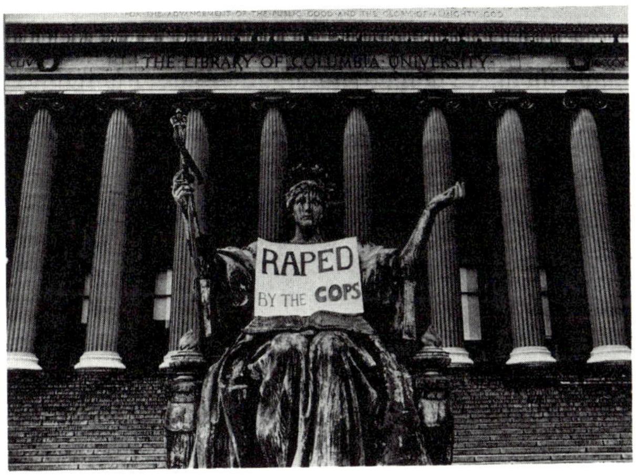

It's certain someone got raped during campus warfare, but who? Is involvement in it worthwhile?

photo by BONNIE FREER

To get off the street and into people's hearts, we've got to walk naked through the world, our selves transparent.

I've had quite a few students who were always getting punched, chased, or sworn at by the people they wanted to photograph. Invariably these students were surrounded by barriers made of the lies they'd told themselves and were contemptuous of their fellow men. They were quick to stand in judgment of others. When they came to me for help, they were certain I wasn't bright enough to help them. I could do little for them.

But now this is turning into another sermon. I think I've made the point that if you're going to get involved with people in the right way, you'll have to fight it out through your own gut. Let's talk about the photographer's gut for awhile. This is his solar plexus—his emotional eye, you might say.

If you strive to be constantly aware of your solar plexus, you can learn a lot about yourself as a photographer and greatly increase your understanding of others. This gut of yours, sometimes called the solar brain, is the window through which you can look at your emotional self. But usually when it's trying to tell us something about ourselves, we quiet it with tobacco, whiskey, pot, between-meals snacks, or sentimental movies.

Most of us would rather not be aware of our solar brain, for it is a psychic regulating mechanism that operates by causing pain. Correctly seen, this pain is a psychic indicator, which by its very existence tells us we've made certain mistakes. If we stop making them, the solar plexus remains as calm and cool as a mountain lake. But, fools that we are, when the pain hits and the gut knots up, we just don't want to know anything about what is really going on. It's a case of down with introspection and up with dry martinis.

Now, every photographer who is worth his salt has had plenty of uncomfortable action in his solar plexus. But very few have had any notion of what it was all about. Though it's a very complex subject, I'll see if I can at least draw a couple of guidelines for you.

In one sense, the solar plexus is a kind of furnace for burning up psychic impurities in yourself. These come from various sources, mostly in your past. Say you're trying to photograph somebody and your gut knots up. One of the reasons for this is a psychic interaction between the two of you which either brings old impurities into your furnace for burning or creates fresh ones. Oddly, this happens only between two people who have the

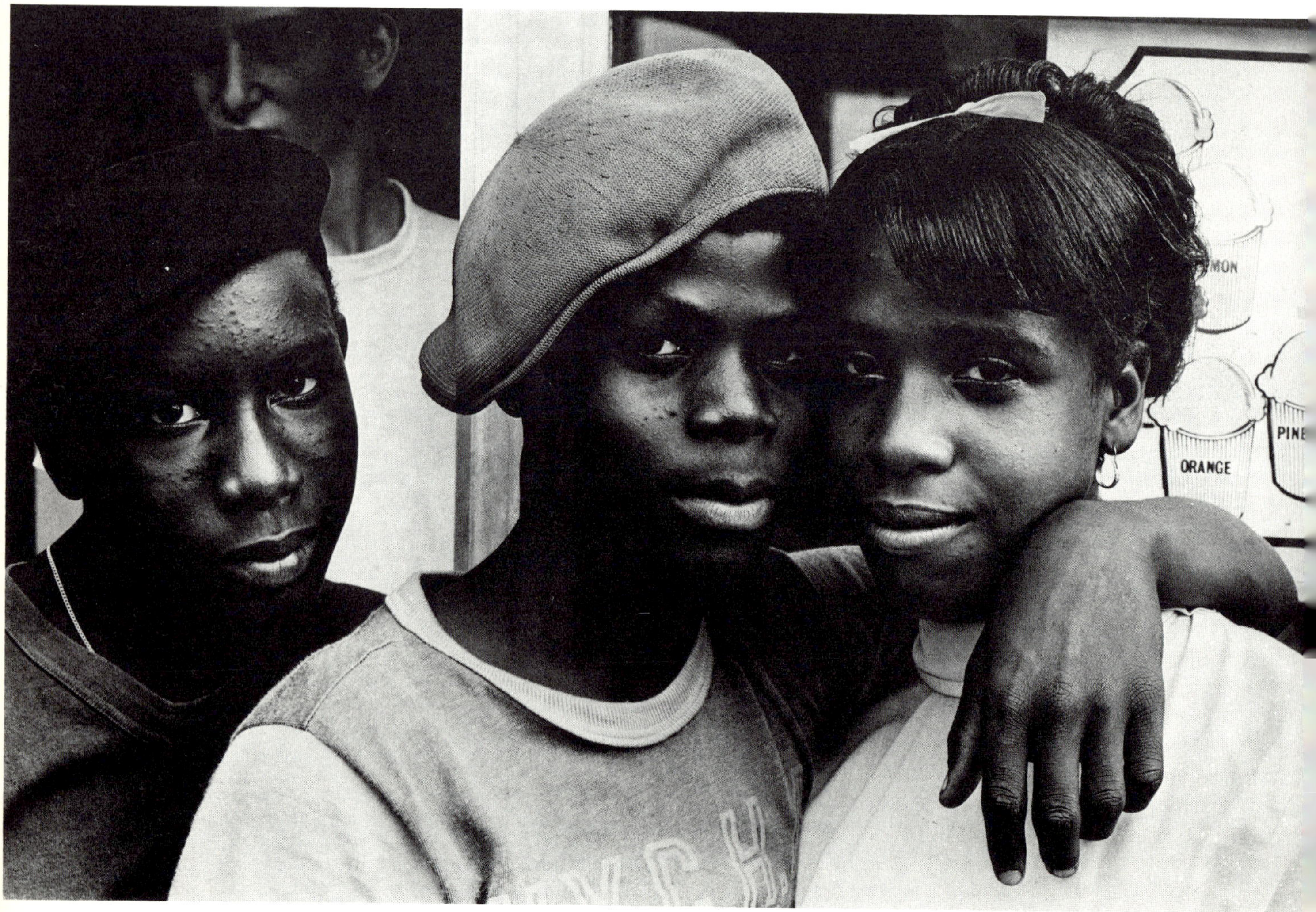

Though these youngsters enjoyed being photographed, Bonnie Freer needed courage to come into their lives with her camera.

photo by BONNIE FREER

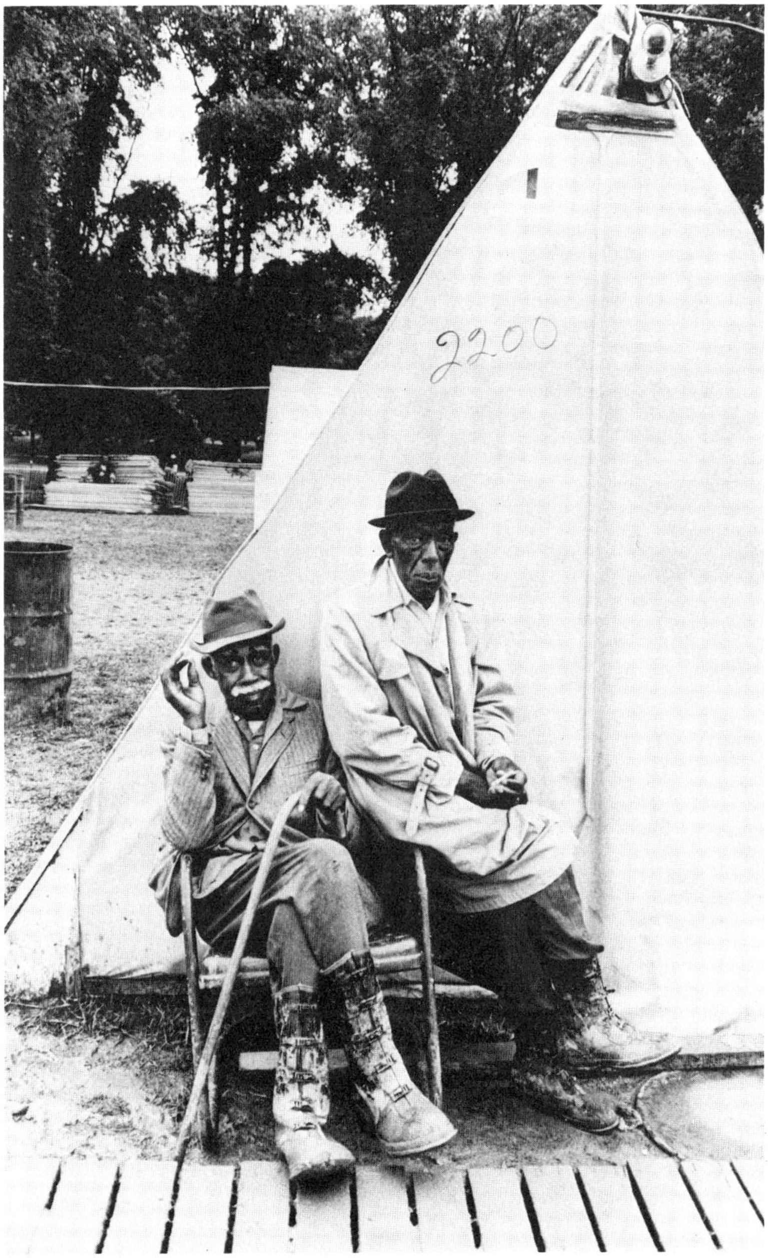

same psychological defect.

Even more odd is that if you associate with this person for a long time, the particular poisons may burn out and never come back. Then you can associate with other people with the same defects as yours as much as you like and never feel a twitter in your solar plexus from that particular cause. This phenomenon accounts in part for the fact that many people have as best friends those who used to drive them up the wall. And it also accounts for friendship's power to in-

(Resurrection City) Men who marched to Washington, D.C. to bring the plight of the Blacks before the nation. Involvement with causes like theirs can be good—if it's done in the right way for the right reasons.

photo by BONNIE FREER

crease human spirituality. In building a friendship, we burn up our psychic poisons.

These shared psychic factors between two people which must be burned up are an invisible but very powerful barrier between two people. They make mutual, high-quality involvement very difficult to achieve, perhaps impossible. Our great photographers have always understood intuitively this barrier between themselves and the rest of humanity and the necessity of solar plexus suffering with which to tear it down. That is why so many of them look so beat up when they're young. They're deliberately taking it in the gut to join the human race. As I said, the price must be paid.

Let us return to Bonnie Freer for awhile. Though I haven't seen much of her in the past few years, I have a strong impression that she's been taking it a lot in the gut. One indication is that she often works in situations in which great psychic stress is almost bound to occur. Another is the increasing warmth that seeps through her pictures. Without the solar plexus cleansing, this warmth has very little chance to grow and flourish.

But the lead picture doesn't look so warm, does it? Nonetheless, I wouldn't jump to any conclusions about Bonnie's reason for taking it. First of all, it's out of context, one picture from a fine set taken at Columbia University during the revolution of 1968. It was shot two days before the police moved in with their clubs. These young fellows, seeing a certain black humor in the total situation, have formed a group called the Pupils For An Indian Society, P.I.S. for short. Here they're arguing eloquently that the best answer to the problem is to give Columbia to the Indians if any can be found who are silly enough to accept it. I think it's a very nice idea.

It is odd that we've related the title "Must You Be Involved?" to some pictures of people who obviously take the idea with tongue in cheek. And they're so very, very right. The formula I've given for building involvement is correct, I believe, but with one thing left out. These boys have put their finger on it: when you start thinking of involvement, yours or anyone else's, always do it with tongue in cheek. Be very careful that in the name of truth you don't start selling yourself wooden nutmegs.

In a Little Spanish Town

This lesson is another discourse on method in esoteric religion. Charles Moore, the photographer, wasn't informed of this, but it doesn't matter a whit. Nor are his views on religion particularly germane to what the lesson is all about. I didn't even ask him about them. I made certain unstated assumptions about him, however.

I assumed that as a human being his genes are programmed to thrust him ever forward in his search for Self-perfection, that his central life problems are ethical in nature and that he almost always does his best to be fair and loving toward his fellow creatures. I don't mean to say that he has reached his goals, few people have, but that he is consistently pushing himself toward them. In examining his striving I found much to say about method.

Whether one is an atheist, agnostic, or believer, using religious methods correctly will lead toward God. This is true even if he thinks he's going in the opposite direction. I don't know what direction Charles Moore thinks he's moving in, for I didn't ask him. I didn't have to. He's trying to do certain things in a profoundly ethical way. On this basis, I already know the direction in which he's moving, whether he knows it or not.

The Lesson:

One of the things most admired by some devoted photographers is an eloquent commitment to very pessimistic ideas. When the so-called serious photographers assemble, the sonorous complainer or prophet of doom is made the center of attention and praised for his intuitive wisdom and artistic sensitivity. Close behind him in prestige is the superb photographic craftsman who runs away from life into one form of abstraction or another. The more his work approaches oblivion, the more he is respected.

It is only natural that this should happen in some circles of photography. For people ruled by a fundamental dissatisfaction with life, the eloquent whiners are natural heroes. To assume leadership among them, all a photographer has to do is develop a powerful command of his medium, then use it ever after to proclaim that the world is entirely rotten, sad, neurotic, confused, meaningless, and so on.

This view is much too limited. There is an important place in the world for a serious photography of hope and good will. And a man who dedicates himself to beauty and joy has as much right to be respected for the seriousness of his intent as any doom-shouter. It is true that many things in life could be greatly improved. But it is equally true that many things are wonderful as they are. These fine things—these evidences of Grace—should be praised to the skies.

Let's look at some work by a man with a conscious and deliberate optimistic commitment—Charles Moore. Though his work consistently affirms life, he is by no means blind to its depressing side. As he sees it, the world is both beautiful and

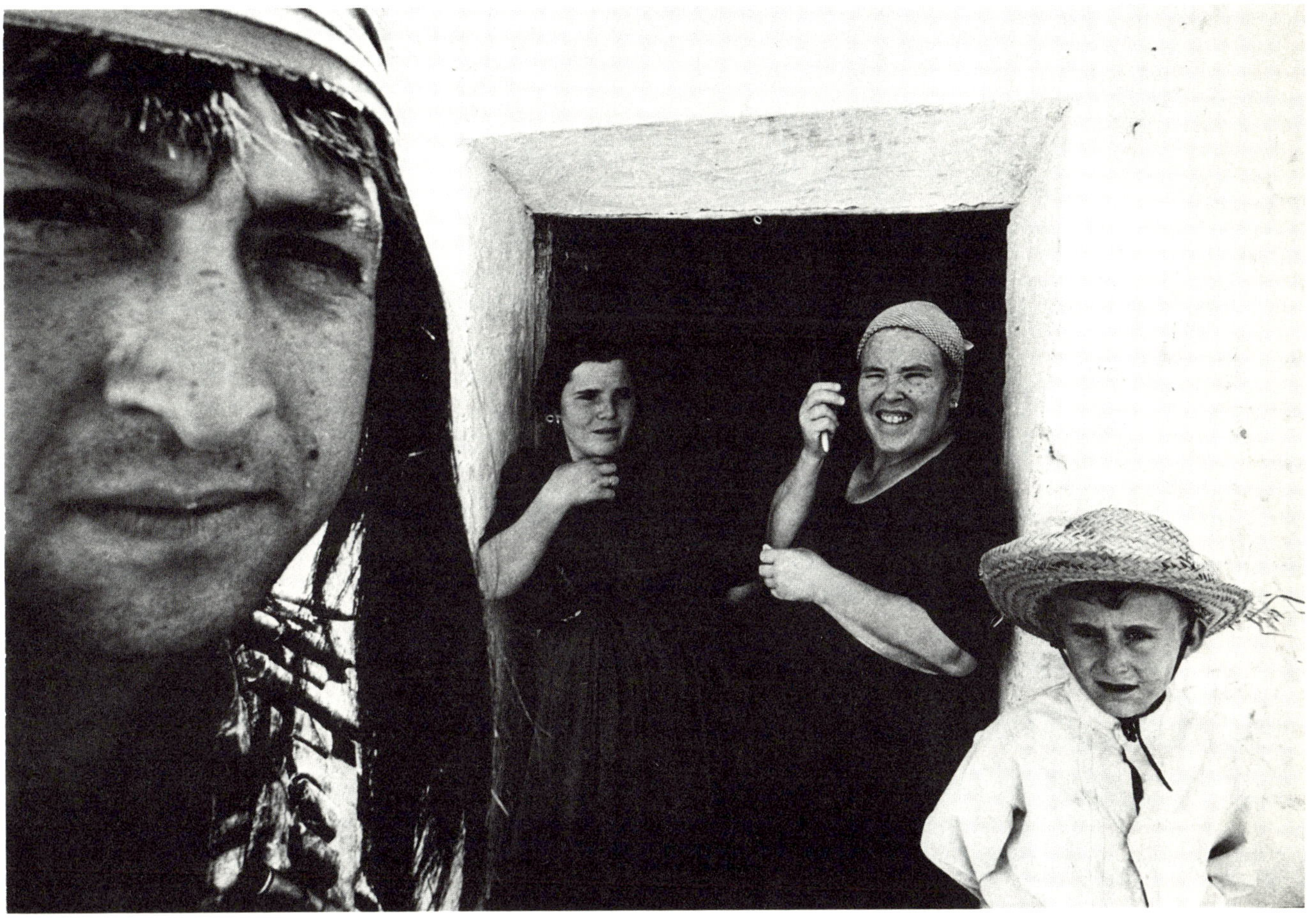

photo by CHARLES MOORE

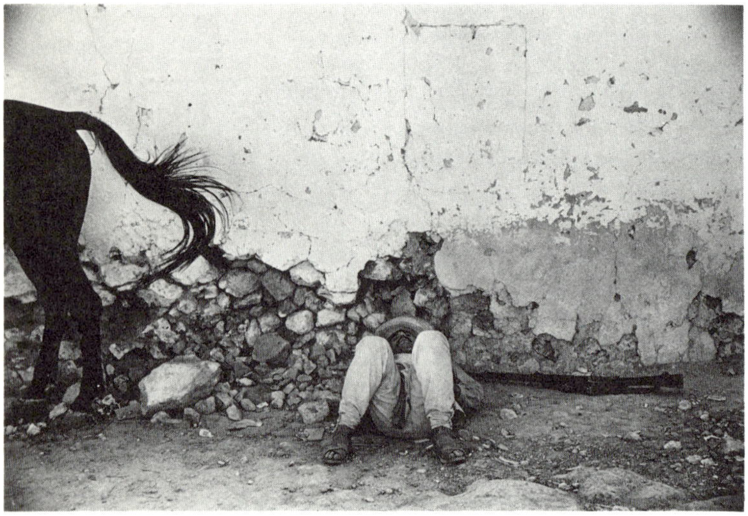

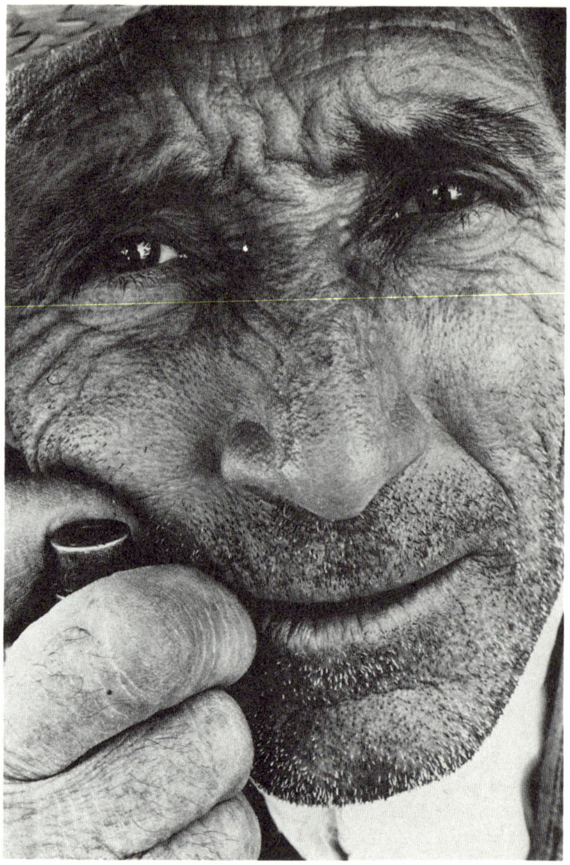

ugly. He believes that it is his ethical right to lay ugliness aside and concentrate his photography on hope, beauty, humor, and the tender aspects of human behavior. To lay ugliness aside is not necessarily to blind oneself to it. Moore doesn't permit himself this indulgence: "As long as I live I intend to keep myself fully informed on all the strife and distress around me. I will continue to feel it and be hurt by it. But I'm *not* going to indulge my own negative emotions by letting ugliness become the subject of my pictures."

Charles Moore rightly feels that humanity has a great need for graciousness and beauty. He sincerely believes he'll be using his life well if he does his best to help fulfill it.

Moore's position is carefully reasoned and deeply felt. He certainly didn't arrive at it by refusing to confront life's bitter side. On the contrary, he's one of our best at photographing the mob scene, man's inhumanity to man, and terror raging through the streets. He's been beaten, had his cameras smashed and his car turned over. He has personally experienced the horror of being chased down alleys by bloodthirsty mobs.

He doesn't desire to do this kind of photography anymore, though he's tough enough to survive long years of it if he still believed in it for himself. As he puts it, he's had his say on the mindless fury and cruelty in the world. Now he intends to talk about the beauty around him.

Although this text is so serious, the pictures are lighthearted and casual. I tried several times to begin on a note of levity, but always felt I was selling Charles Moore short.

To know Moore is to experience a

photos by CHARLES MOORE

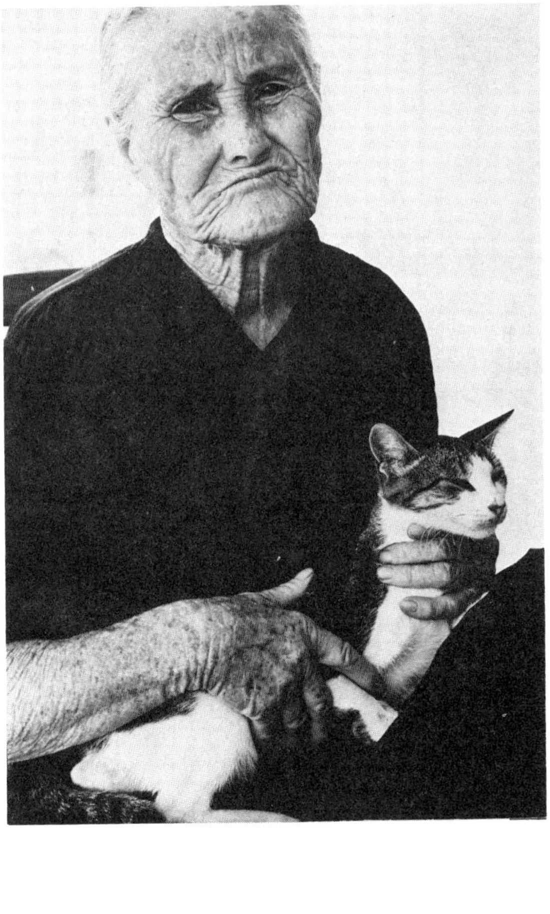

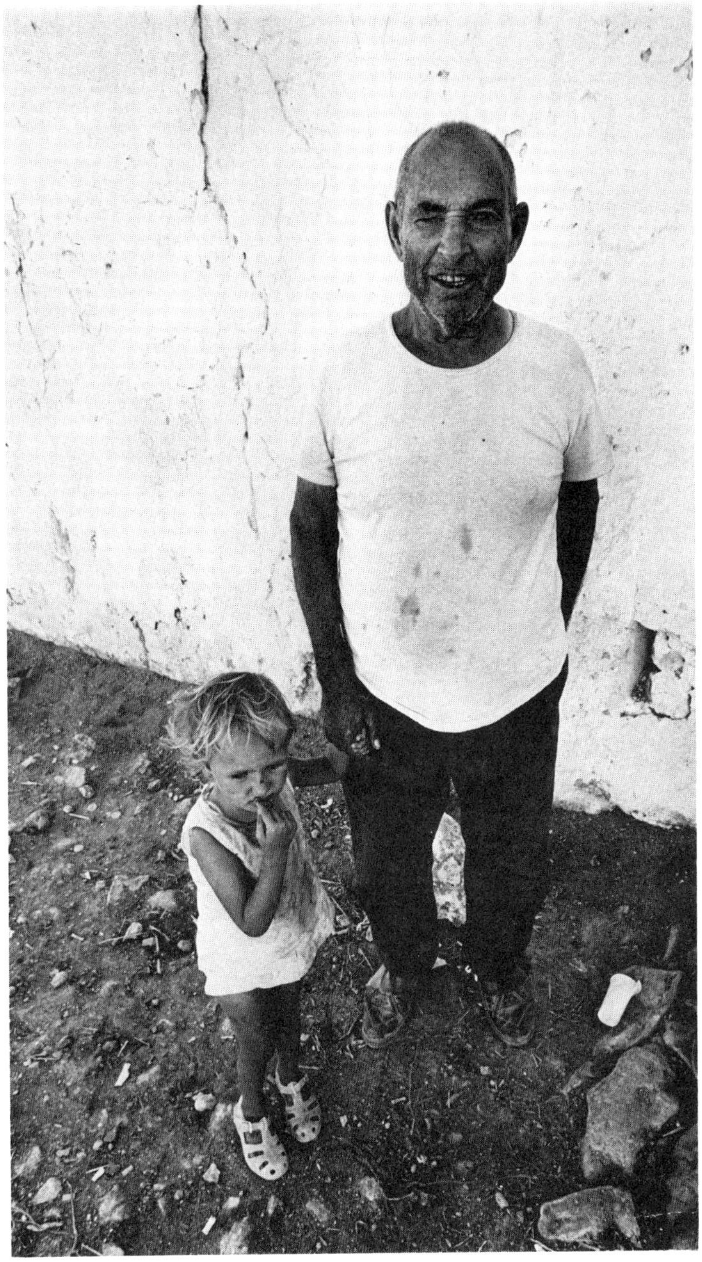

photo by CHARLES MOORE

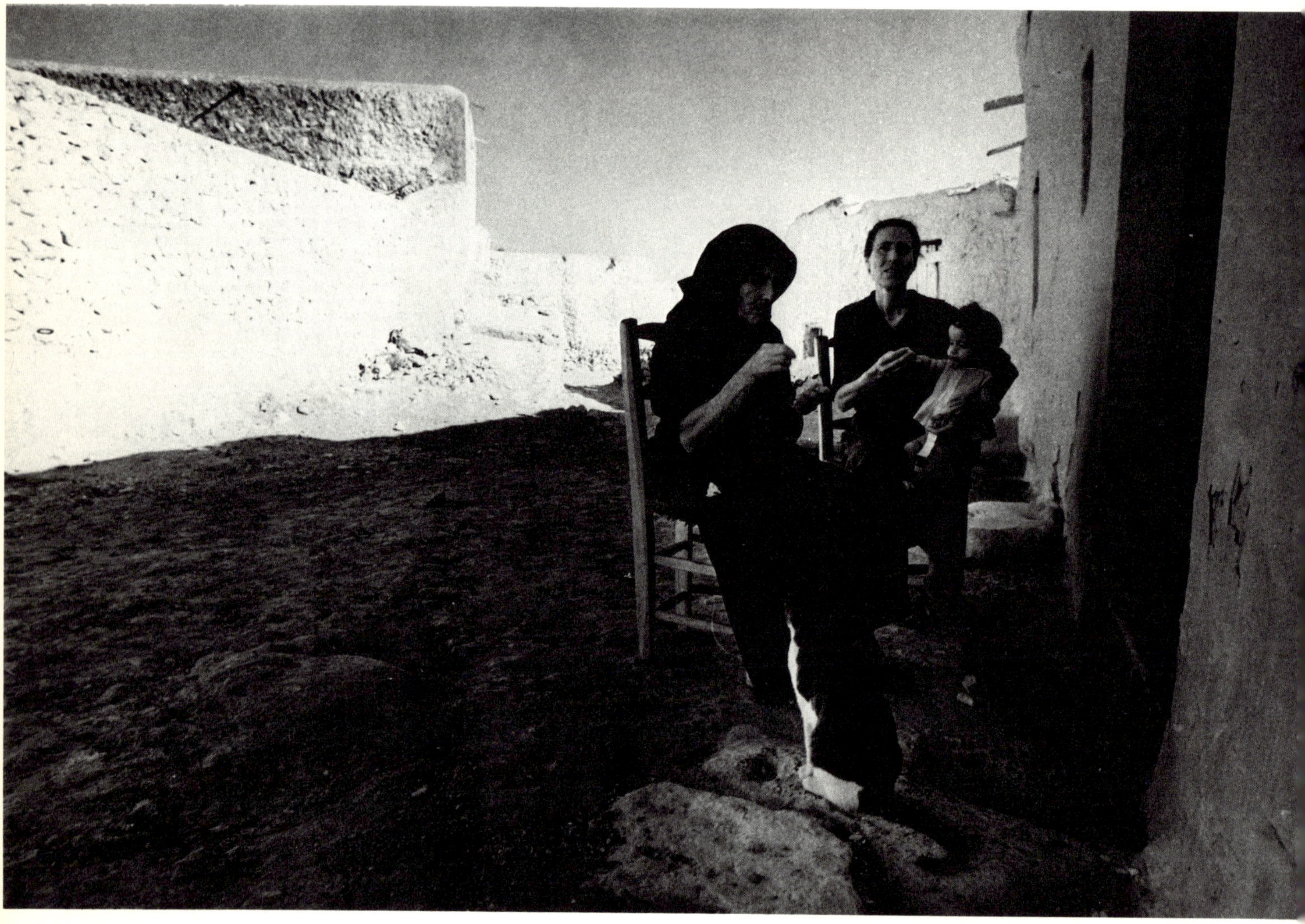

man who is very serious about his work, though he doesn't impose his gravity on people. Out of his dedication is rapidly growing a body of work that is light, humorous, affirmative, tender, and beautiful.

We ordinarily just don't think of such things growing out of a conscious commitment to ideals. But it is surely this that makes Moore's pictures more than just pretty and flip. Their good humor and delicacy are something real that he has discovered in his fellow men, seen side by side with more negative things.

I'm talking now about all his recent pictures, not just the few printed here. In my own mind I call Charles "the young man with the sweet camera." Not poetic, I know, but accurate. In finding inner strength, he's been able to let his natural sweetness come out.

It should be mentioned that, except for feeling and viewpoint, the pictures here don't particularly represent Moore's current work. Nowadays, he works almost exclusively in color; his forte is the lyrical realm. He does a good deal of travel photography and work on location for advertising, editorial illustration, and photojournalism.

He gets a kick out of studio work, which he does very well, and has even become enchanted with fashion photography and rather far-out experimentals—all in color. He says, "I just *love* to photograph beautiful women."

Last summer, Moore was shooting a job in color in the tiny village of Polopos in southern Spain. In the first two days he found he couldn't get the pictures he'd come for, so he diverted some of his time to shooting the pictures here. Though they were a spare-time effort, we felt they really embodied a useful lesson.

The first part of the lesson, as you've seen, is Charles Moore himself. In the second we will examine how a photographer's attitudes influence the pictures he makes.

Moore says that the people of Polopos are very poor but dignified and proud. It is a village of the very young and the very old. Those who are in their working years must go elsewhere to earn their living. In their travels, American amateur photographers often run across the same combination: pride and poverty. And what do they get in their pictures?

'Quaint bugs on slides'

It's mainly anger and dull suspicion, people reacting strongly against being looked at by affluent Americans as though they were quaint bugs on microscope slides. In the pictures, the people look foreign, which is to say they really don't quite look

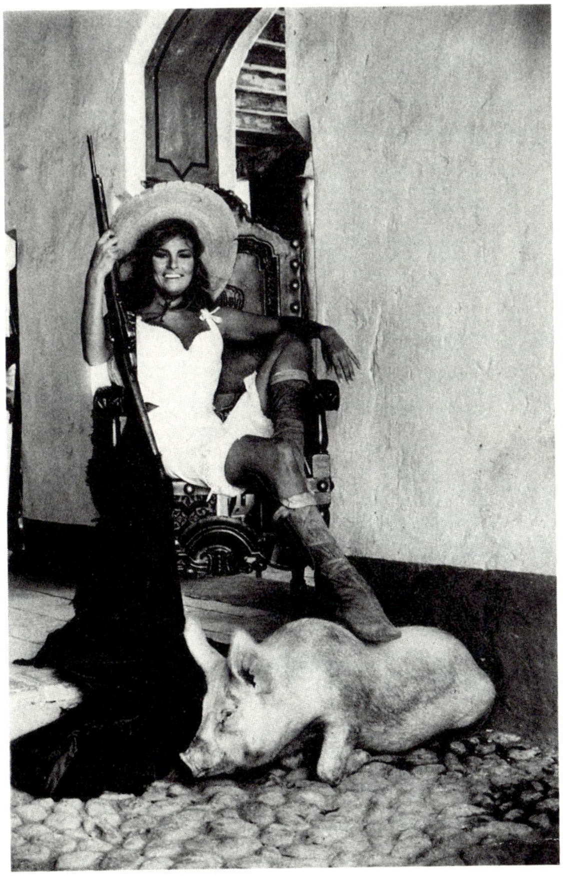

photo by CHARLES MOORE

like people at all. This is what we usually see in the slide sessions after the travelers return. But it's not what Moore brought home with him.

In examining what Moore found, we can have a little lesson on travel photography, but its implications also extend to work done at home. Let us start with Moore's people. They don't look especially foreign, do they? Can't you see them as being like the people in your own neighborhood, even members of your family? The clothes and locale are different, of course, but that's not important.

This could be put in the form of a rule for traveling photographers: Your pictures of people from distant places should look like the people at home. If they don't, you've missed the boat somewhere. Everywhere in the world people are essentially the same. To see them otherwise is not to see them at all.

There is no evidence of hostility or dull suspicion in the pictures. Instead we find a fleeting indication of many kinds of emotions, which is as it should be.

In more than one picture, there are indications that Moore himself was the one being sized up. I would say the Polopons have seen him as a rather odd and interesting duck, not to be openly laughed at, but to be accepted as another everyday oddity in the human family. A threat to them he definitely is not.

These things imply certain rather specific things about the photographer's attitudes toward his subjects and himself. Had he come across as ego-centered, aggressive, and afraid of being looked at critically, his pictures would have shown it.

And what is Moore trying to say about the Polopons in his pictures? It seems he's merely trying to say that Polopons are Polopons, which suggests he isn't trying to

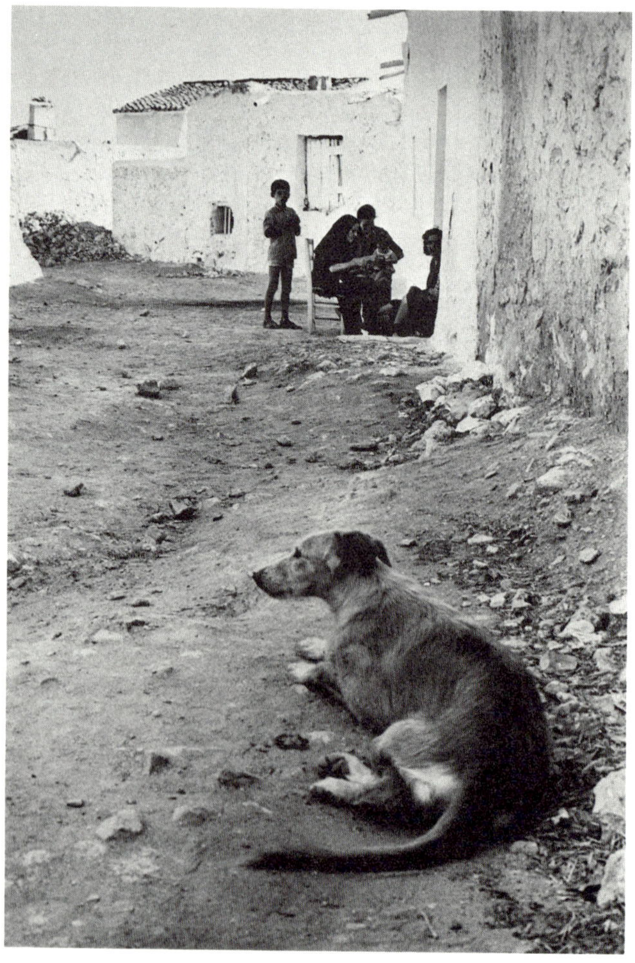

photo by CHARLES MOORE

force them into a preconceived mold. If anyone is communicating it is the people themselves, not the photographer.

No bag is a good bag

This is not the usual in travel photography. Through long experience, we've come to expect either romanticizing or editorializing. In other words, the typical photographer goes abroad and stuffs everyone he meets into the same conceptual bag that all othe other photographers have used.

It usually comes to this: Poverty is romantic, or, all foreigners are hostile and suspicious. Moore's people look singularly unstuffed into any particular bag. The photographer's attitude is that people are all right as they are and don't need to be refabricated.

If more photographers felt this way, we'd have a much better idea of what the peoples of the world are really like. As it is, our notions are distorted by having been strained through the neuroses of various uptight travel photographers.

What are the Polopons doing? Pretty much what anyone would do who lived in a place like Polopos—in Spain, America, Italy, France, or Japan. It doesn't matter much where Polopos is or the national or ethnic derivation of its people. They're just doing the things people do, given a certain environment.

Of course, New Yorkers don't casually lie down in the street and go to sleep, as some Polopons do. But they would if they moved to Polopos—as soon as they got rid of their hang-ups and fear of being robbed.

I think we've answered *what* Moore got in his pictures. Now for a few more words on the difficult *how?* It has been emphasized that his pictures are a result of certain attitudes concerning his fellow men. The person unable to take pictures full of optimism and good will is a prisoner of other types of attitudes that make this impossible.

The question really comes to this: How can a photographer change his own attitudes? It means changing the entire man, a difficult thing to do. Obviously, the method can't be spelled out here, for it's the work of a lifetime. However, I can suggest some starting points.

Examine the contention that a photographer's basic attitudes determine the kinds of pictures he can make. This needs amplification: A person who has a sweet nature will make sweet pictures. One who is depressed will express negativeness. People hung up on power will show it in their choice of subject matter, its treatment and, in their efforts, exalt power through manipulation of the photographic medium.

So it is with all strongly held attitudes, whether or not the photographer is conscious of them. They not only show up in his work but determine its very nature. Don't accept this concept on faith; try to determine its degree of truth for yourself.

Start by trying to analyze your own attitudes and learn how they are expressed in your pictures. It will take time and a great deal of effort. A friend of mine made a set of pictures once at a party. He was in a distressed and angry frame of mind, though he wasn't aware of it.

He shot six rolls of film, and every frame was an act of hostility against his subjects, all of whom were friends of his. You've never seen such mean and angry put-downs. Despite his intelligent, introspective nature and a long-standing interest in psychology, it took him more than five years to see what he'd done.

The important thing for him is that he eventually did see. Now he has no doubt of the relation of attitude to performance and is quite expert in assessing his inner states as they occur. Furthermore, he's had considerable success in replacing negative attitudes with positive ones.

It is this replacement that perhaps is even more difficult than discovering what your basic attitudes really are. Attitudes are largely unconscious; one can be unaware of their nature for years. To change them, a conscious, ethical commitment to the world and oneself is of the greatest importance.

With this ideal in mind, you can gradually chip away at this negative self and through time and sheer persistence, win the game. The mind is the builder. With our minds we choose our ideals; through

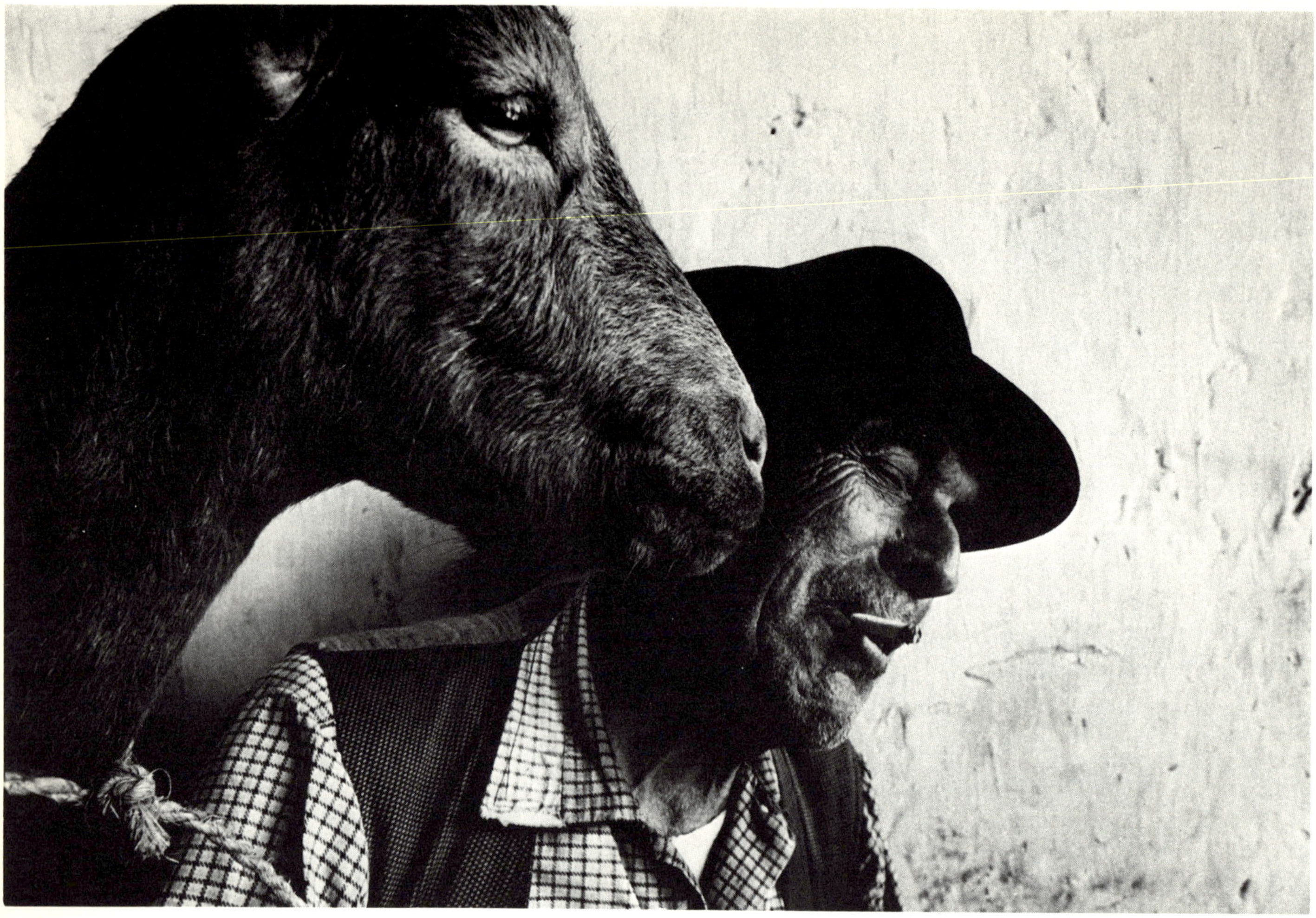

patience, good will, and effort, we slowly rebuild ourselves.

(In re-reading what I've just said, I can understand the gratuitous insult dealt me recently by a young clerk at Willoughby's. Though I'd never laid eyes on him before, he said, "Your writing is awful. It really bores me." He's undoubtedly not alone in this. A young fellow reads this, sees some pictures by Charles Moore, and says to himself, "Terrific! I'll learn his secrets and go right out and use them." Instead of neat litle secrets smothered in succulent sauces, he gets a lecture on ethics.)

If you're going to talk about a man's art, you have to talk about the man himself; to deal with what's central in man, one has to get into the realm of ethics. Writing on any other level about the photographer's secrets is saccharined, rubber strawberry jam.

Charles Moore, I hope I've come at least a little way in explaining how come you make one kind of picture instead of another. It's too bad that such a thing comes out to be very tough chewing for those who haven't yet learned the lesson the hard way. I'm sure you dig me.

We tried to play a litle joke here. It seemed in keeping with the good humor of the pictures, if not with the cold concrete of the text. The fine-looking girl with the pig doesn't actually live in Polopos, though the pig does. She is Raquel Welch, an American movie star. She's also indirectly responsible for the rest of the pictures.

Moore was supposed to photograph her, but couldn't get her to mesh creative gears with him. He figured that if he ignored her for a few days, she would try to see his point of view. Meanwhile, he did the villagers.

The ploy worked; thereafter, he and Miss Welch got along famously. Which brings us to another side of Moore's character: This young man with the sweet eye also functions well as the iron hand in the velvet glove.

Moore was shooting on assignment to Twentieth Century-Fox, doing editorial coverage for *100 Rifles,* starring Raquel and Jim Brown. Charles is represented by Black Star.

Discover Your SELF Through Photography leans heavily on verbal teaching. Equally important is the non-verbal, especially in the visual arts. Not much is known about it except that it actually happens. An artist creates images which somehow communicate on many levels, most of them mysterious.

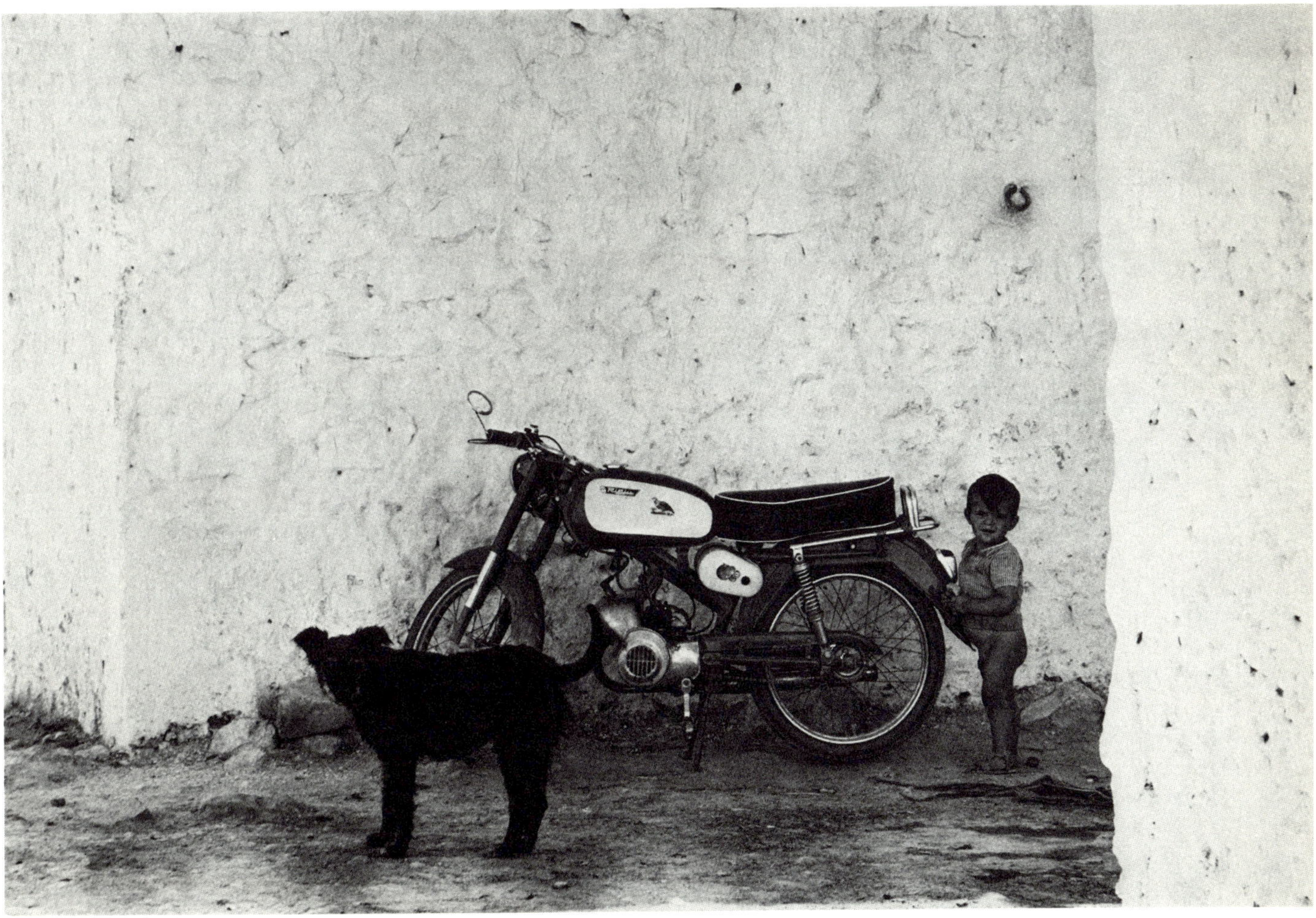

photos by CHARLES MOORE

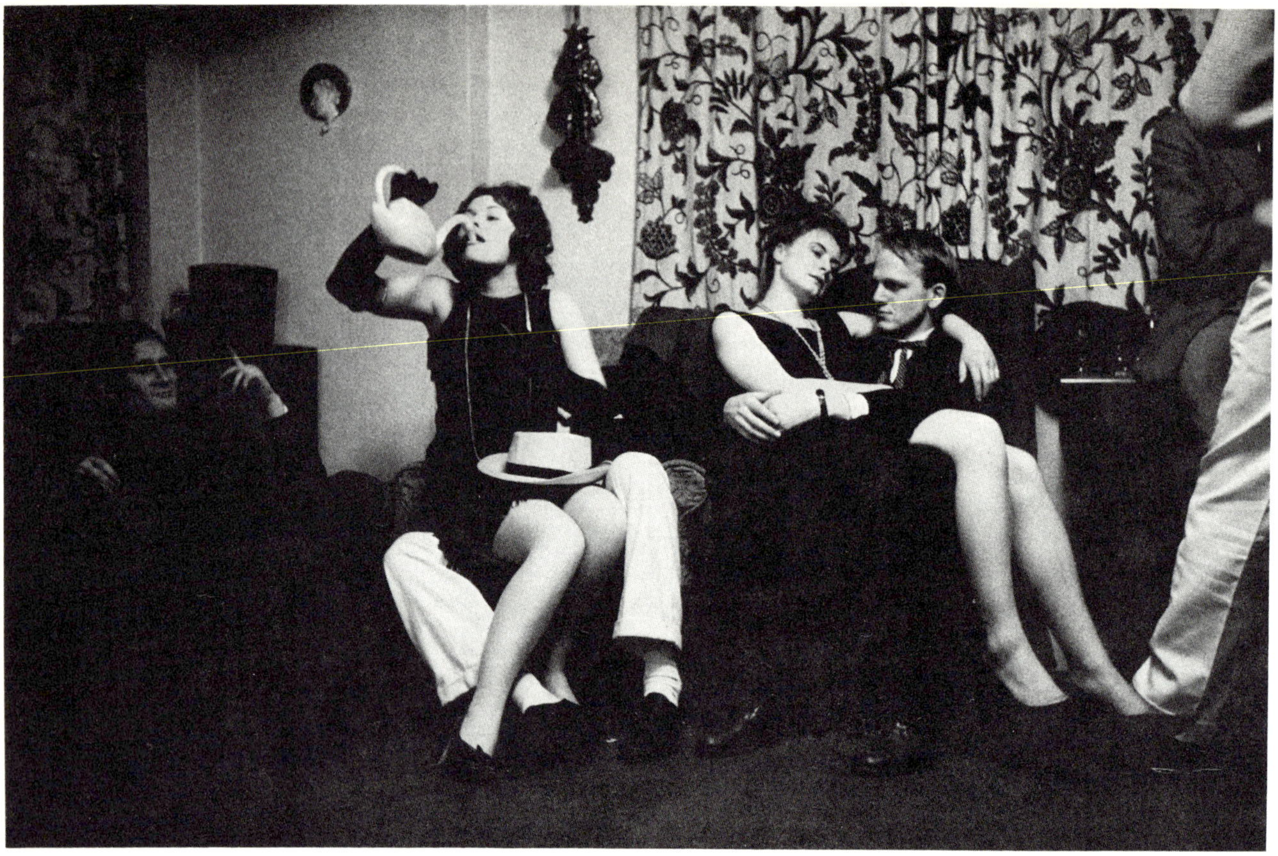

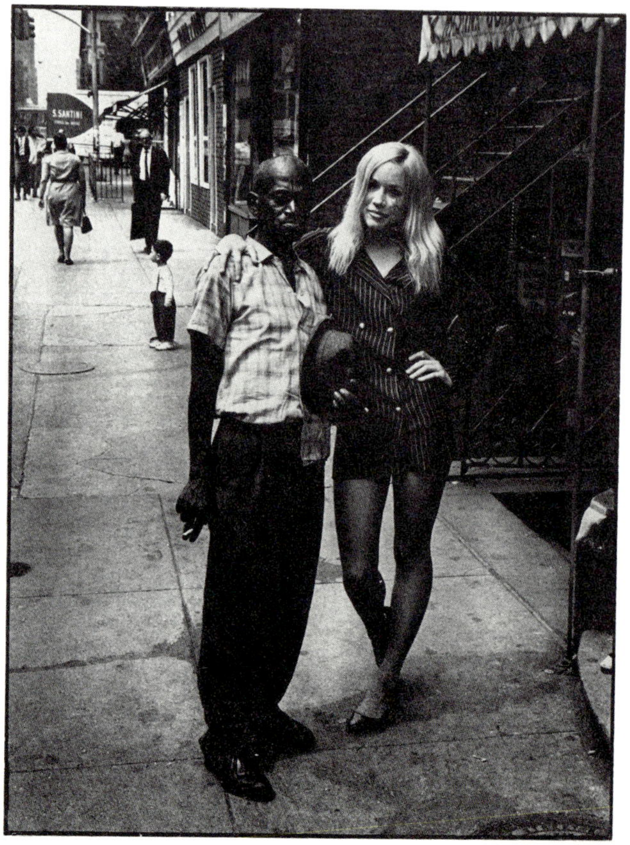

I have enjoyed writing for you and hope you have confidence you can discover your Self. There is no greater challenge, in life, nor any more rewarding. Struggle we must to reach the end of the road, yet struggling itself has its fascinations.

My greatest wish is that we should all travel the Way and some time meet one another among the saints.

Ralph Hattersley